Oh My Goddess!

ああっ女神さまっ   SORA UNCHAINED

Oh My Goddess!
ああっ女神さお **SORA UNCHAINED**

STORY AND ART BY

Kosuke Fujishima

TRANSLATION BY

Dana Lewis & Toren Smith

LETTERING AND TOUCH-UP BY

Susie Lee & Betty Dong

with Tom2K

DARK HORSE MANGA™

PUBLISHER
Mike Richardson

SERIES EDITOR
Philip Simon

COLLECTION EDITOR
Chris Warner

COLLECTION DESIGNERS
Amy Arendts and Debra Bailey

ART DIRECTOR
Lia Ribacchi

**English-language version produced by Studio Proteus
for Dark Horse Comics, Inc.**

OH MY GODDESS Vol. XIX/XX: Sora Unchained

© 2004, 2005 by Kosuke Fujishima. All rights reserved. First published in Japan by Kodansha, Ltd., Tokyo. English translation rights arranged through Kodansha Ltd. This English-language edition © 2004, 2005 by Studio Proteus and Dark Horse Comics, Inc. All other material © 2005 by Dark Horse Comics, Inc. All rights reserved. No portion of this publication may be reproduced, in any form or by any means, without the express written permission of the copyright holders. Names, characters, places, and incidents featured in this publication are either the product of the author's imagination or are used fictitiously. Any resemblance to actual persons (living or dead), events, institutions, or locales, without satiric intent, is coincidental. Dark Horse Manga™ is a trademark of Dark Horse Comics, Inc. Dark Horse Comics® is a trademark of Dark Horse Comics, Inc., registered in various categories and countries. All rights reserved.

This volume collects issues one-hundred five through one-hundred twelve of the Dark Horse comic book series *Oh My Goddess!* and "The Endless Battle" parts one and two, previously unpublished in an English-language edition.

Published by
Dark Horse Manga
A division of Dark Horse Comics, Inc.
10956 SE Main Street
Milwaukie, OR 97222

www.darkhorse.com

To find a comics shop in your area, call the Comic Shop
Locator Service toll-free at 1-888-266-4226

First edition: January 2005
ISBN: 1-59307-316-X

1 3 5 7 9 10 8 6 4 2
Printed in Canada

I CHOOSE YOU, SORA!

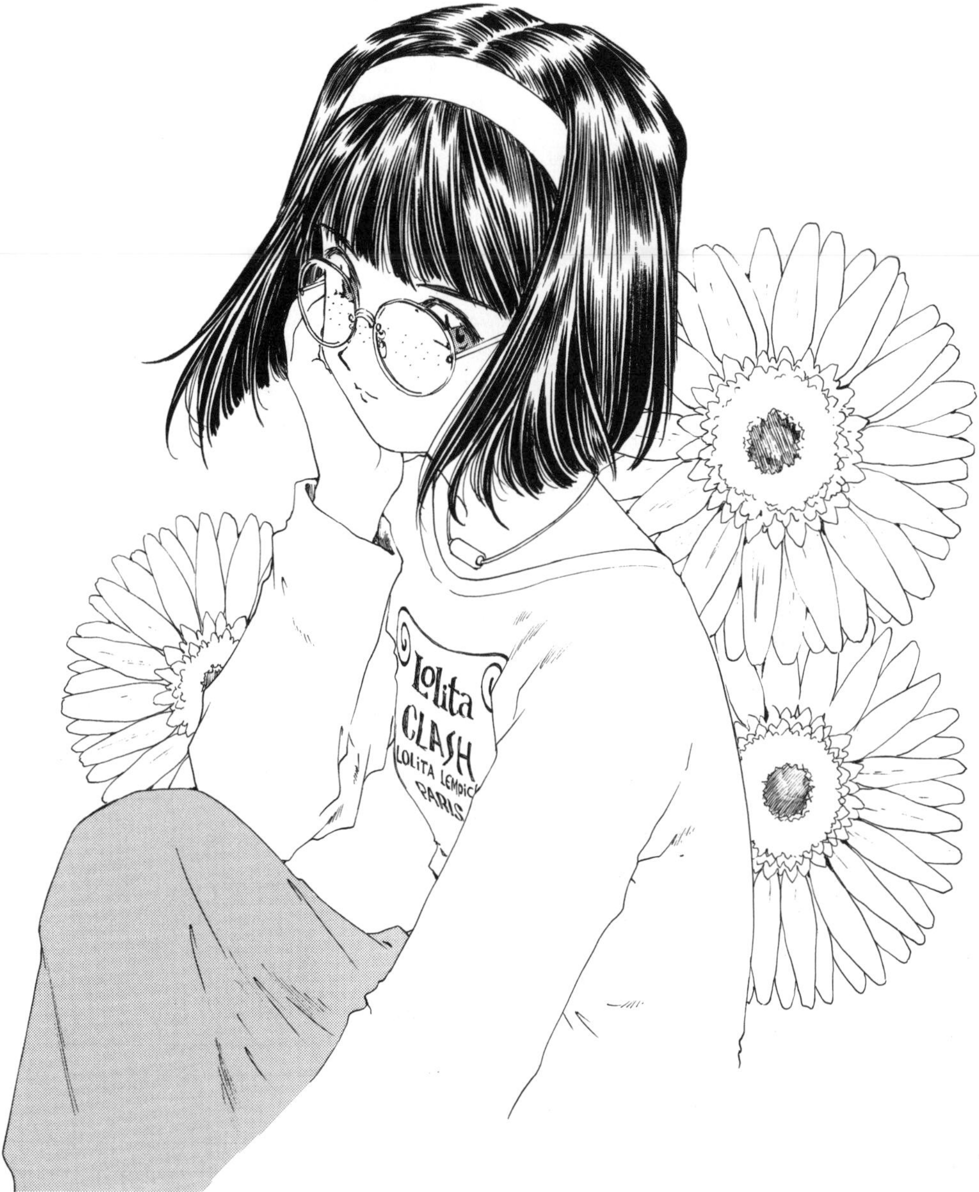
Lolita
CLASH
LOLITA LEMPIC
PARIS

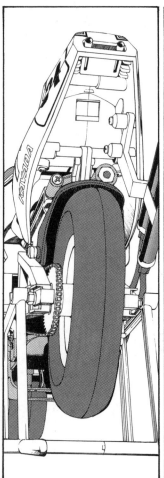

UHH...
BOSS?

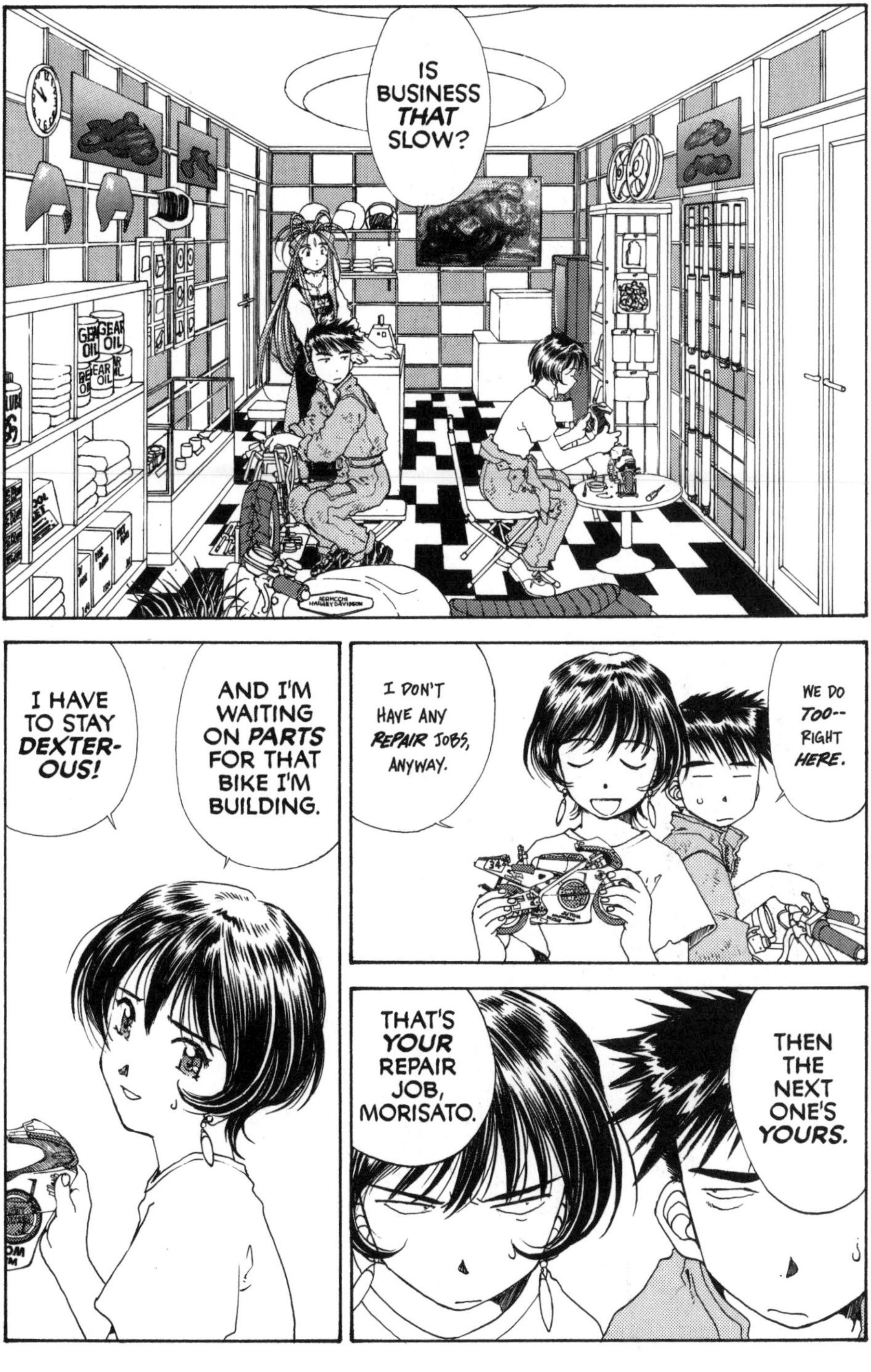
IS BUSINESS THAT SLOW?
I HAVE TO STAY DEXTER-OUS!
AND I'M WAITING ON PARTS FOR THAT BIKE I'M BUILDING.
I DON'T HAVE ANY REPAIR JOBS, ANYWAY.
WE DO TOO-- RIGHT HERE.
THAT'S YOUR REPAIR JOB, MORISATO.
THEN THE NEXT ONE'S YOURS.

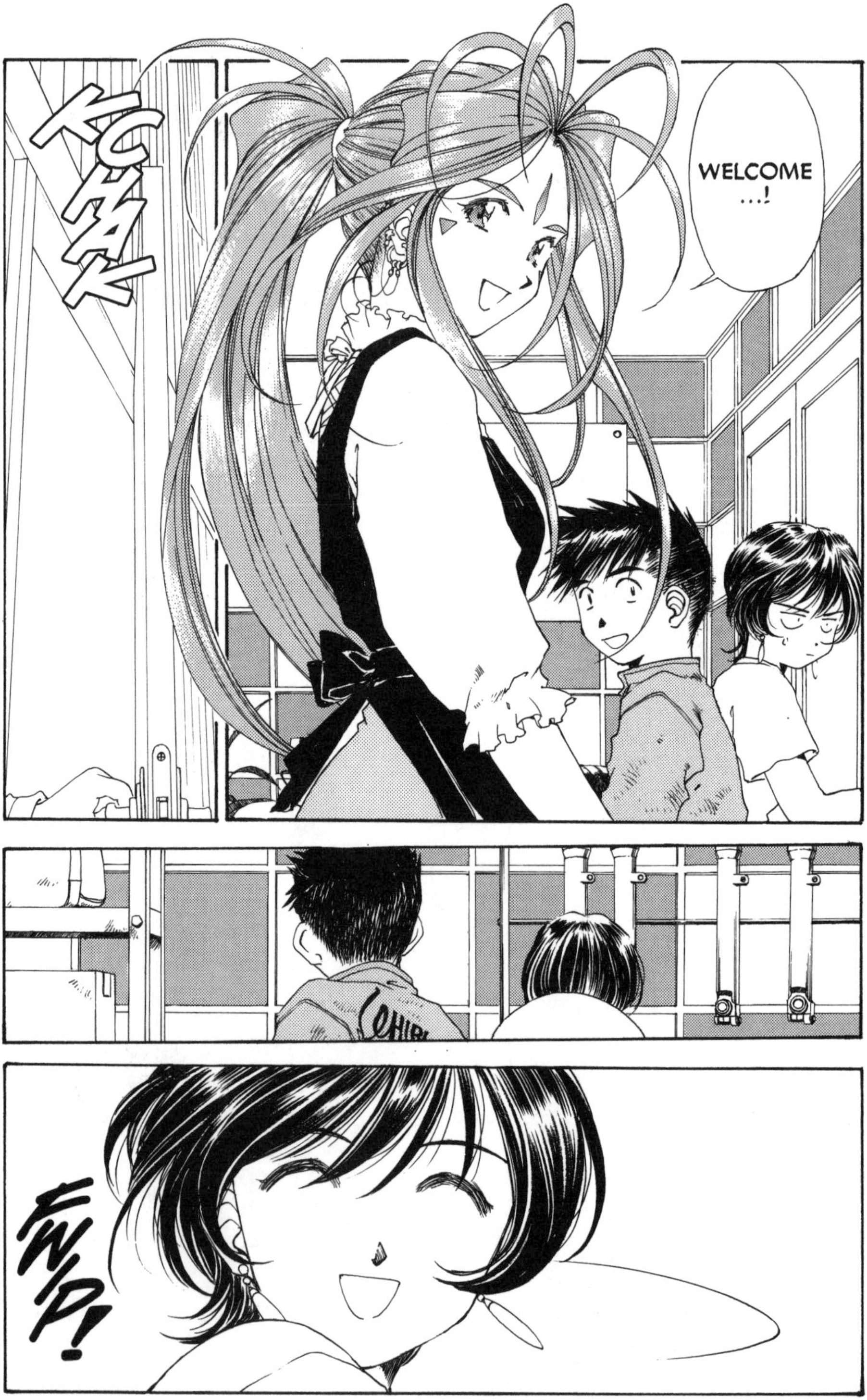
WELCOME ...!
KCHAK
FWIP!

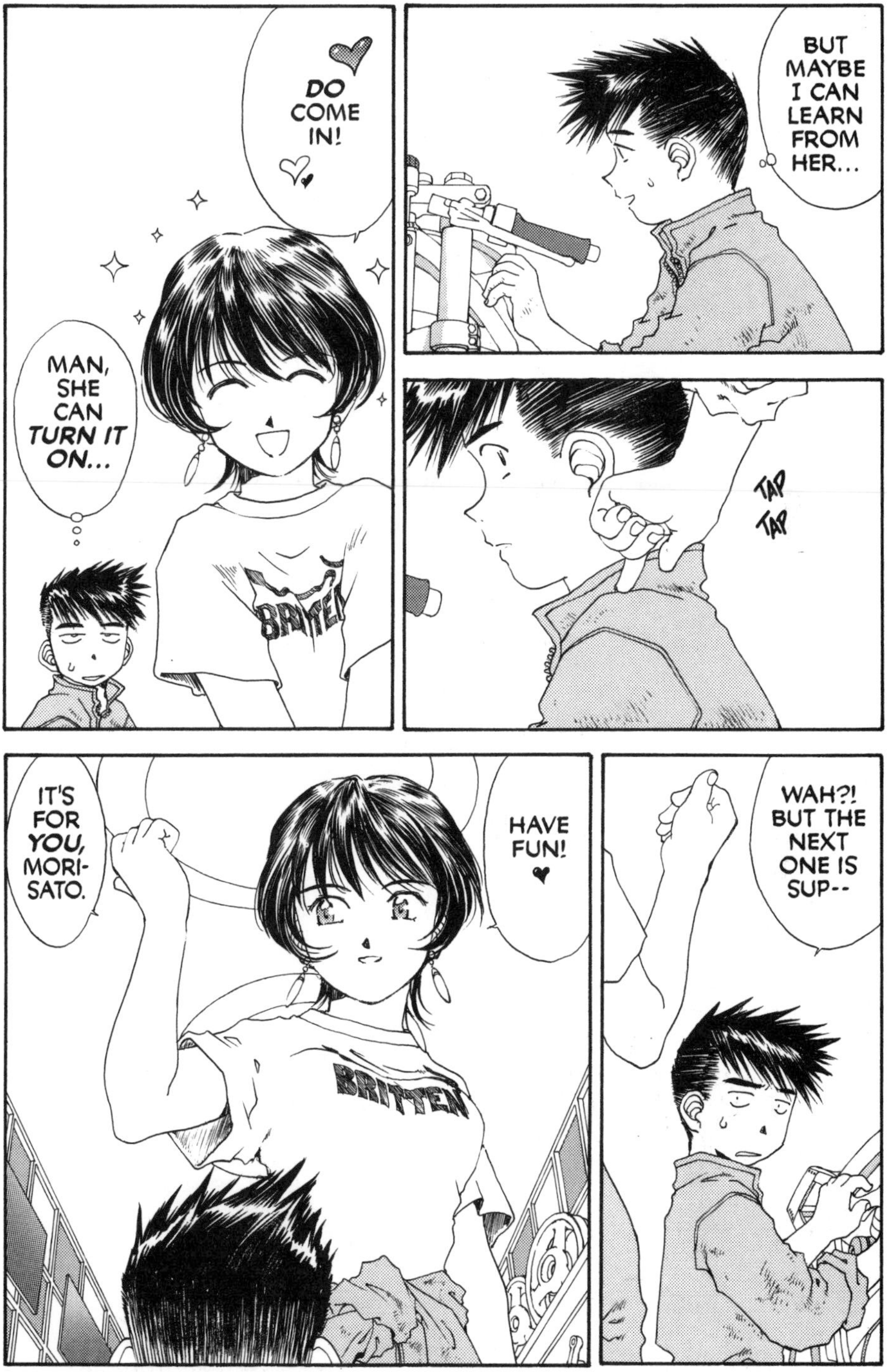
BUT MAYBE I CAN LEARN FROM HER...
TAP TAP
DO COME IN!
MAN, SHE CAN TURN IT ON...
WAH?! BUT THE NEXT ONE IS SUP--
IT'S FOR YOU, MORI-SATO.
HAVE FUN!
BRITTEN

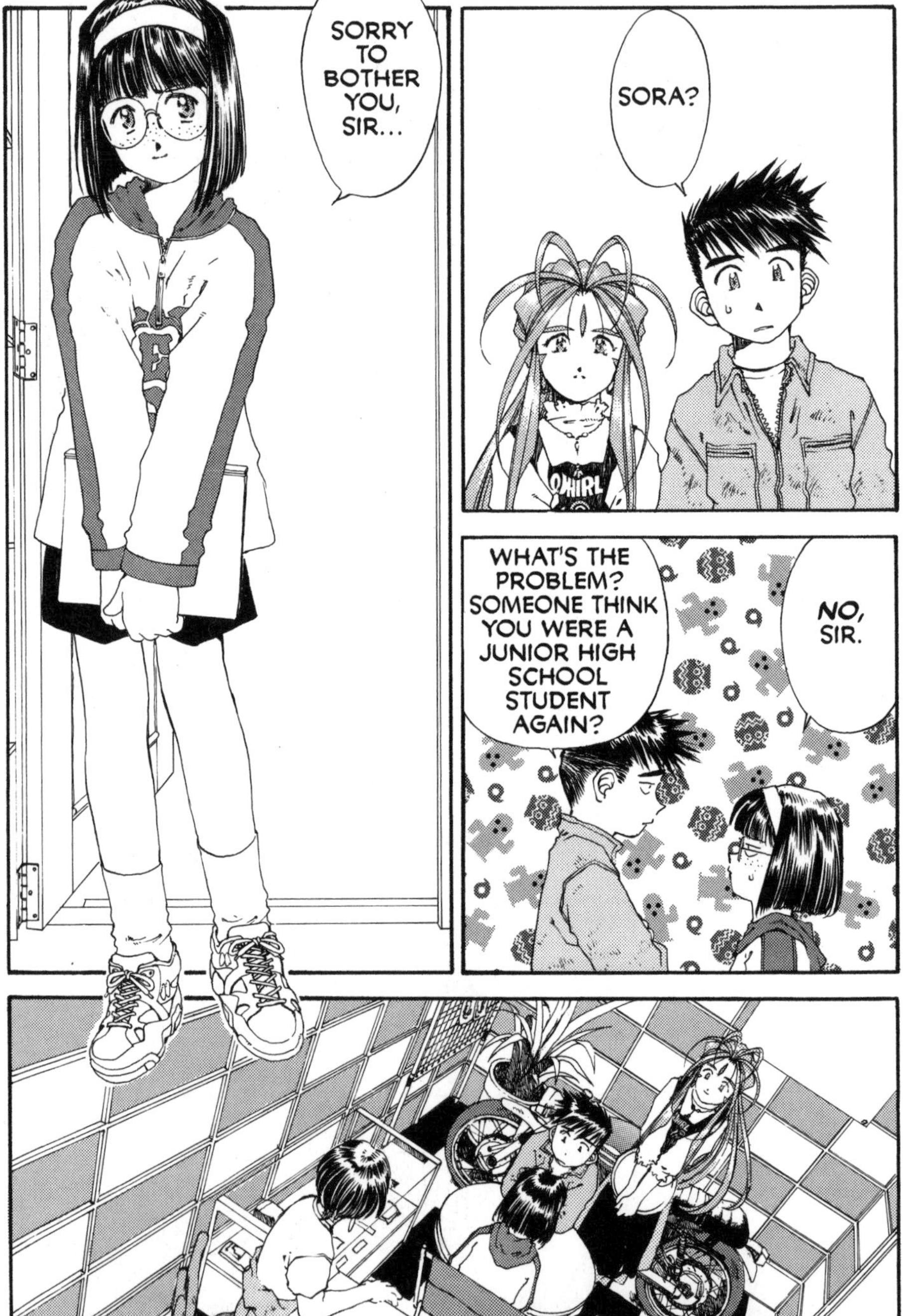
SORRY TO BOTHER YOU, SIR...
SORA?
WHAT'S THE PROBLEM? SOMEONE THINK YOU WERE A JUNIOR HIGH SCHOOL STUDENT AGAIN?
NO, SIR.

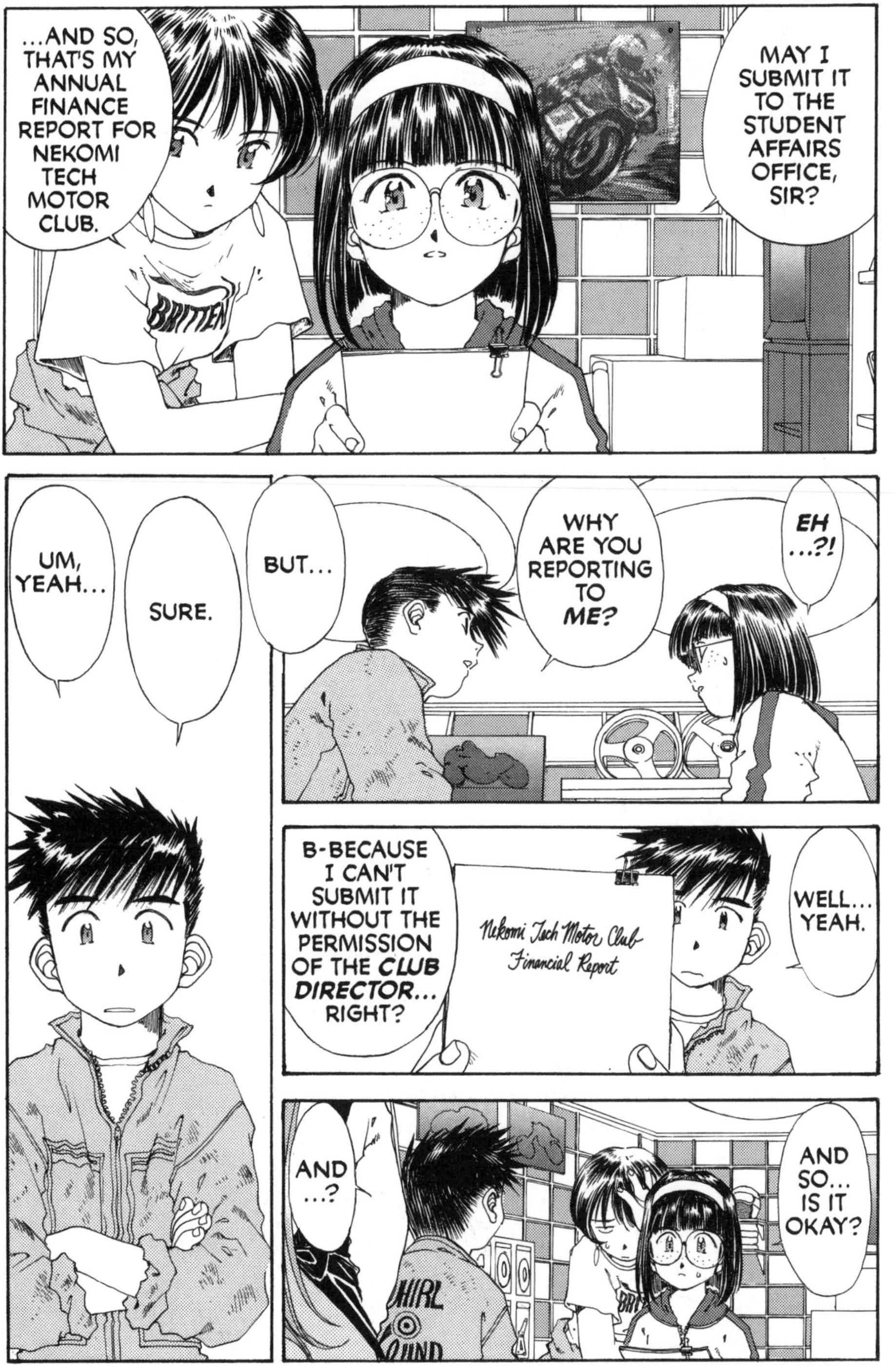
...AND SO, THAT'S MY ANNUAL FINANCE REPORT FOR NEKOMI TECH MOTOR CLUB.
MAY I SUBMIT IT TO THE STUDENT AFFAIRS OFFICE, SIR?
BRITTEN
UM, YEAH...
SURE.
BUT...
WHY ARE YOU REPORTING TO *ME?*
EH ...?!
B-BECAUSE I CAN'T SUBMIT IT WITHOUT THE PERMISSION OF THE *CLUB DIRECTOR...* RIGHT?
Nekomi Tech Motor Club Financial Report
WELL... YEAH.
AND ...?
AND SO... IS IT OKAY?

HASEGAWA, HON... DID YOU GUYS EVER APPOINT A **NEW** CLUB DIRECTOR?

NUH-UH!

SO...

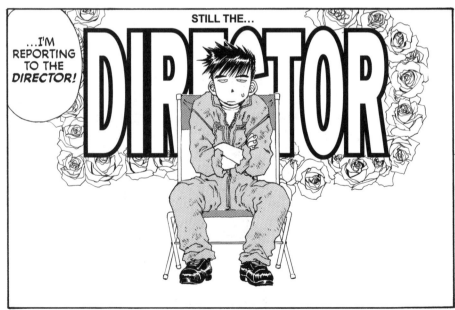

STILL THE...

...I'M REPORTING TO THE *DIRECTOR!*

DIRECTOR

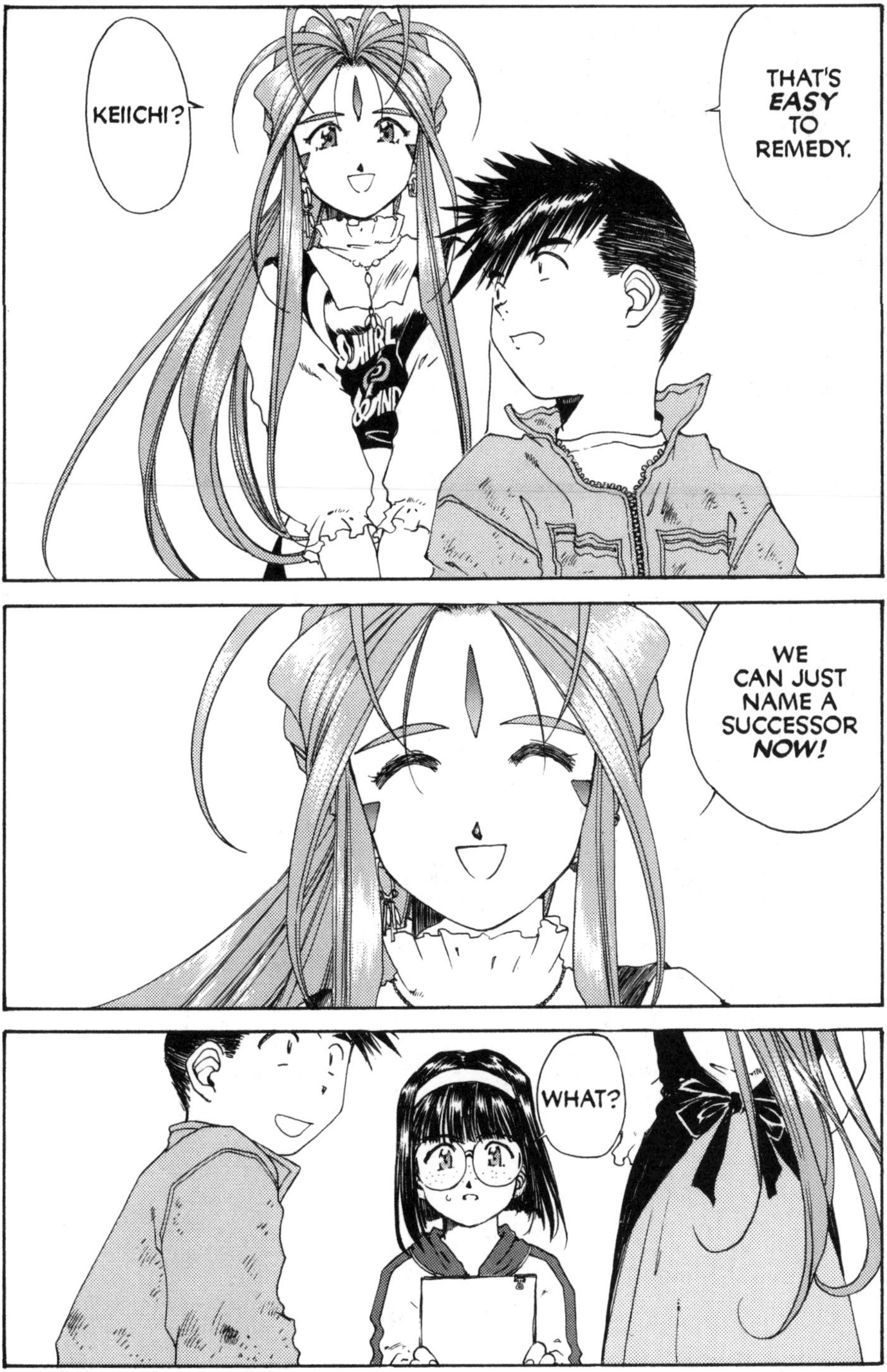
THAT'S *EASY* TO REMEDY.
KEIICHI?
WE CAN JUST NAME A SUCCESSOR *NOW!*
WHAT?

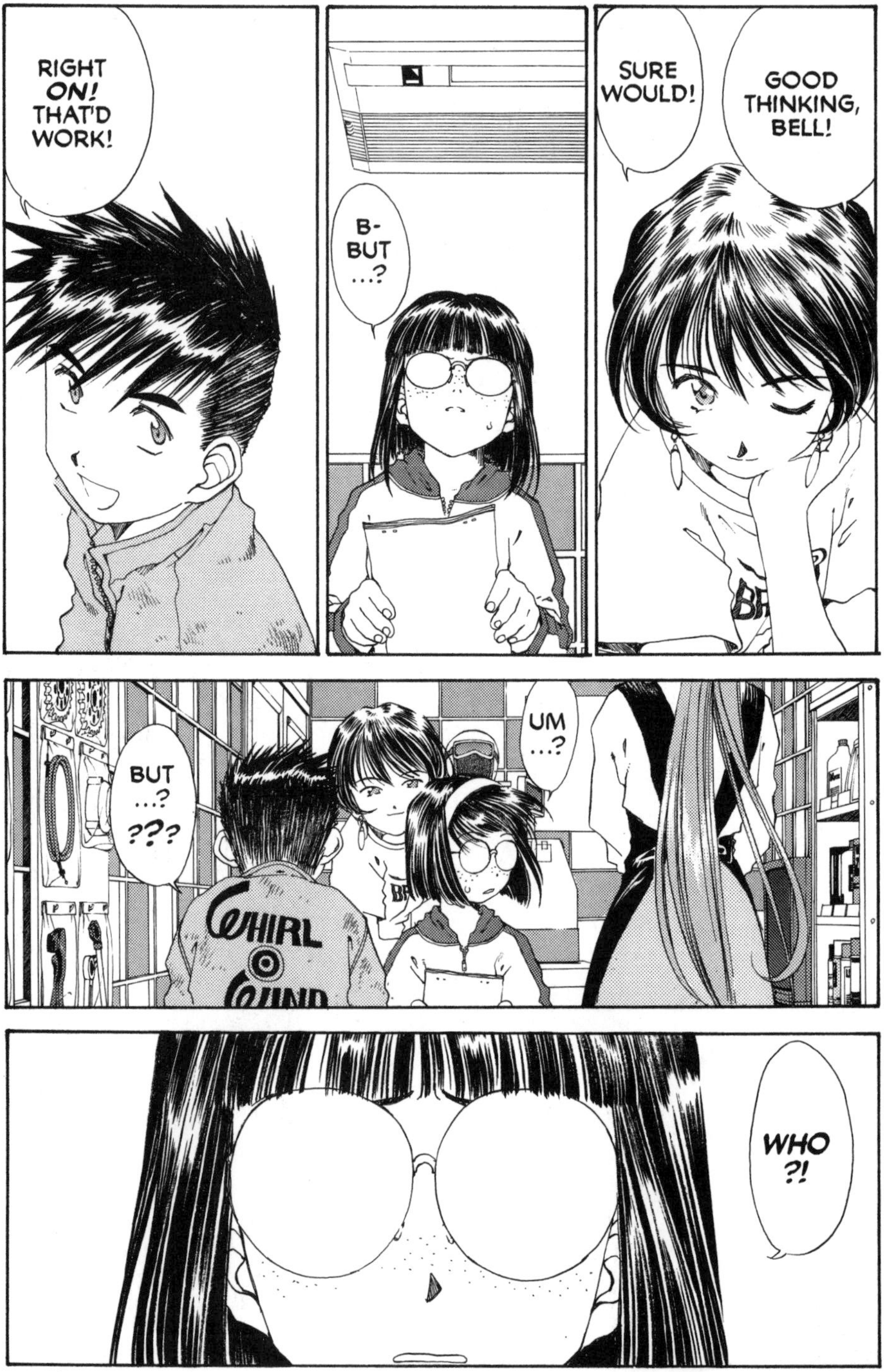
RIGHT ON! THAT'D WORK!
B-BUT ...?
SURE WOULD!
GOOD THINKING, BELL!
BUT ...? ???
UM ...?
WHO ?!

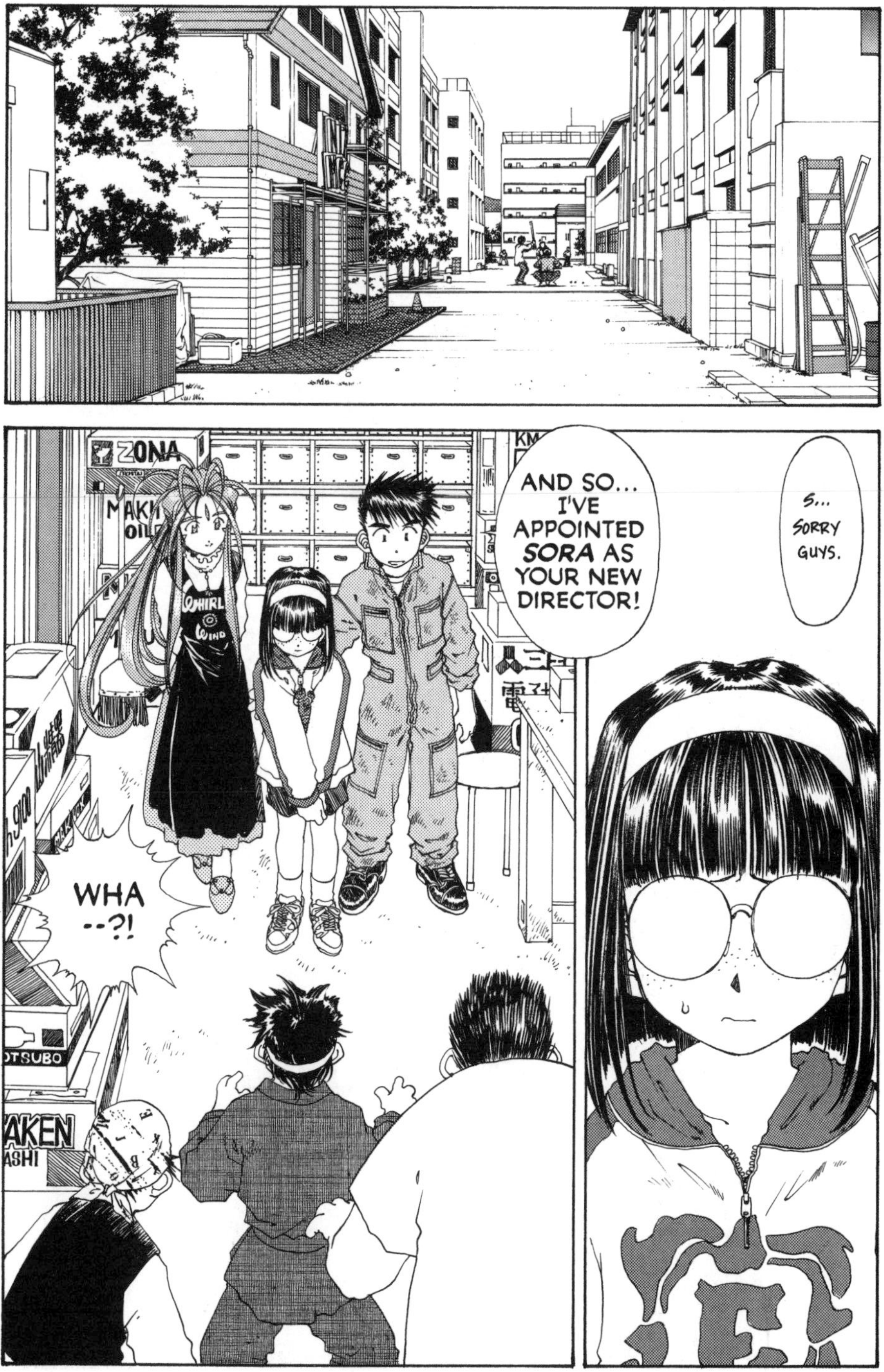
AND SO... I'VE APPOINTED SORA AS YOUR NEW DIRECTOR!
WHA --?!
S... SORRY GUYS.

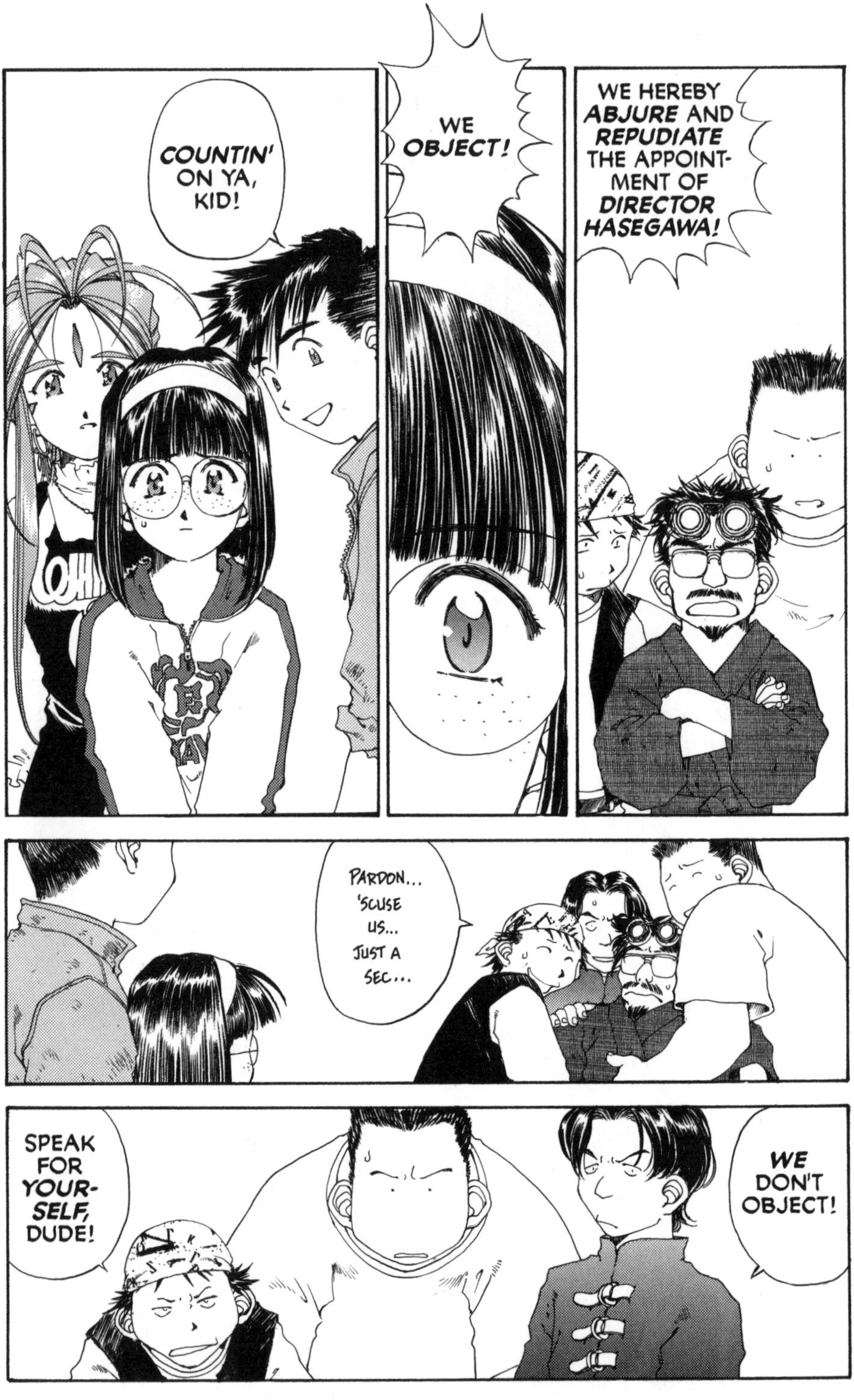
COUNTIN' ON YA, KID!
WE OBJECT!
WE HEREBY ABJURE AND REPUDIATE THE APPOINTMENT OF DIRECTOR HASEGAWA!
PARDON... 'SCUSE US... JUST A SEC...
SPEAK FOR YOURSELF, DUDE!
WE DON'T OBJECT!

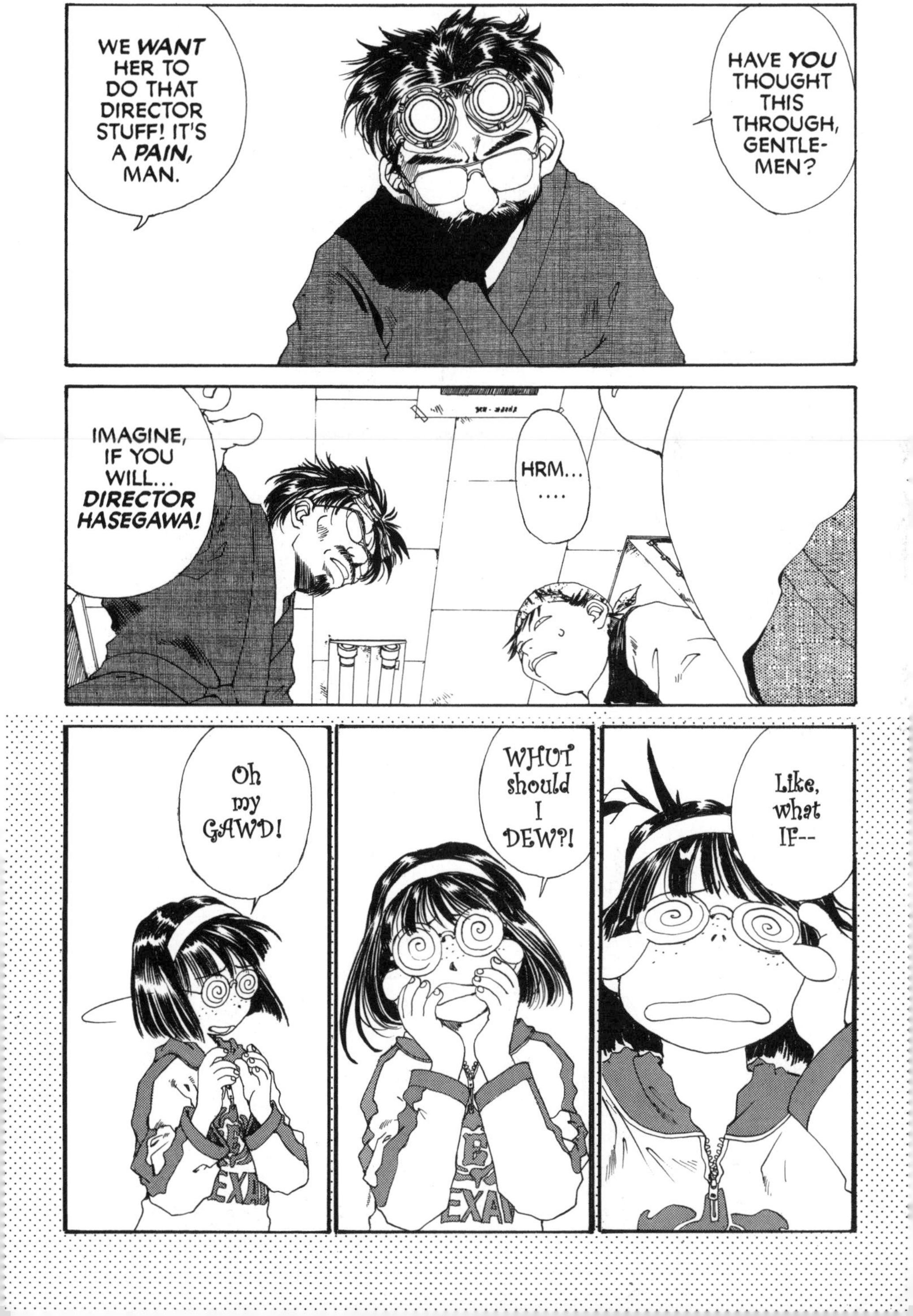
WE *WANT* HER TO DO THAT DIRECTOR STUFF! IT'S A *PAIN,* MAN.
HAVE *YOU* THOUGHT THIS THROUGH, GENTLE-MEN?
IMAGINE, IF YOU WILL... *DIRECTOR HASEGAWA!*
HRM... ....
Oh my GAWD!
WHUT should I DEW?!
Like, what IF--

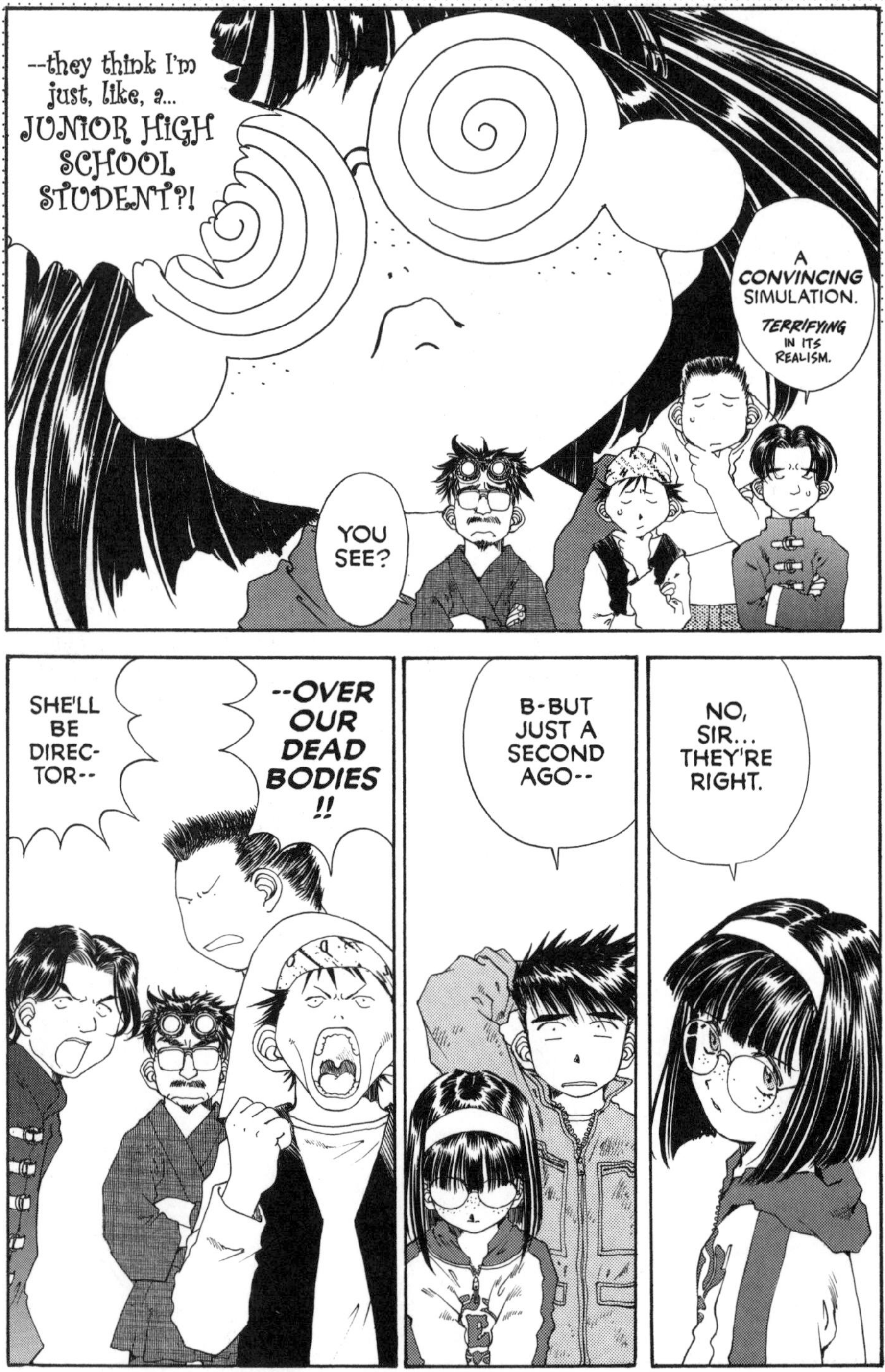
--they think I'm just, like, a... JUNIOR HIGH SCHOOL STUDENT?!
YOU SEE?
A CONVINCING SIMULATION.
TERRIFYING IN ITS REALISM.
SHE'LL BE DIREC-TOR--
--OVER OUR DEAD BODIES!!
B-BUT JUST A SECOND AGO--
NO, SIR... THEY'RE RIGHT.

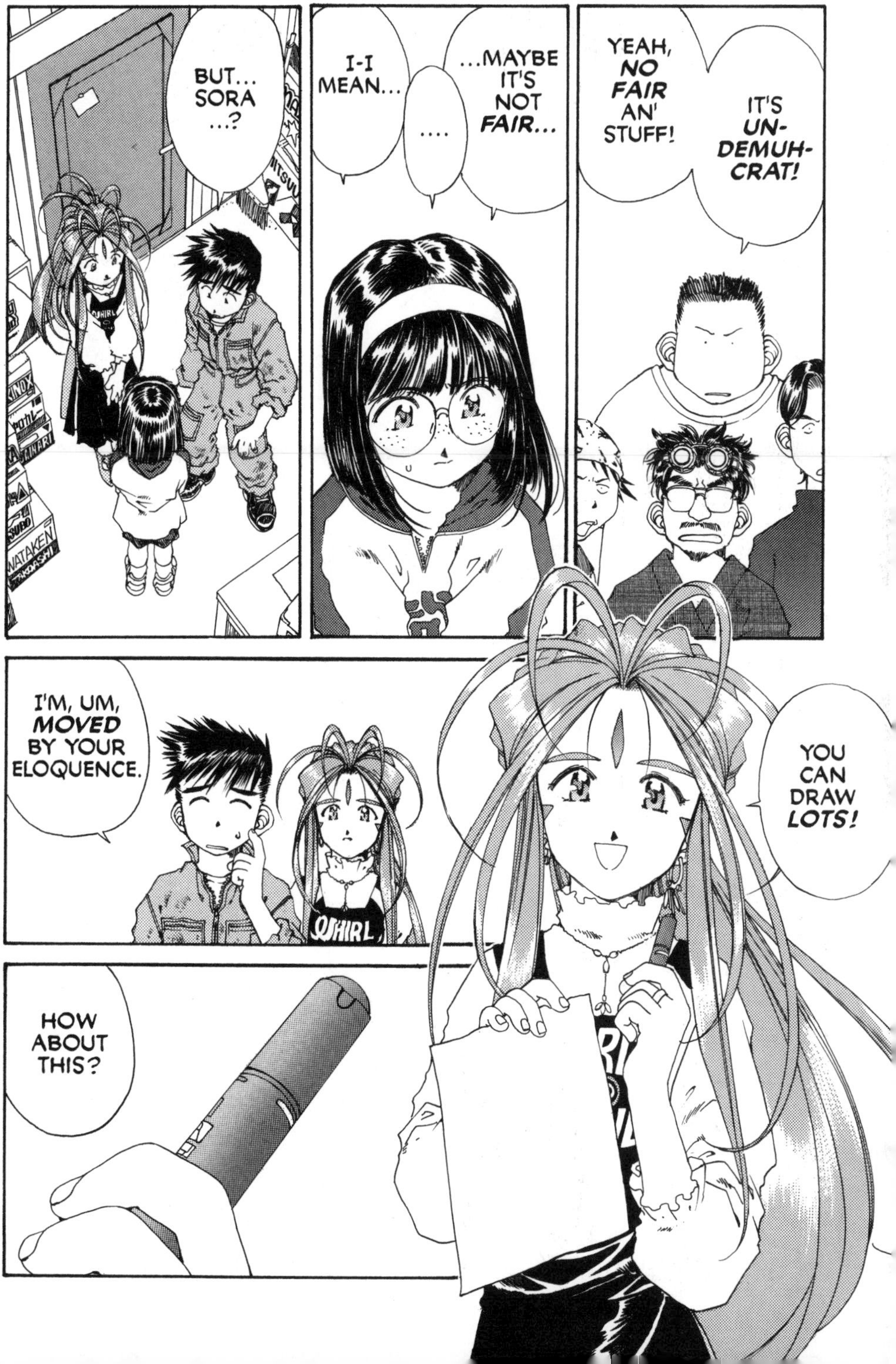
BUT... SORA ...?
I-I MEAN...
....
...MAYBE IT'S NOT FAIR...
YEAH, NO FAIR AN' STUFF!
IT'S UN-DEMUH-CRAT!
I'M, UM, MOVED BY YOUR ELOQUENCE.
HOW ABOUT THIS?
YOU CAN DRAW LOTS!

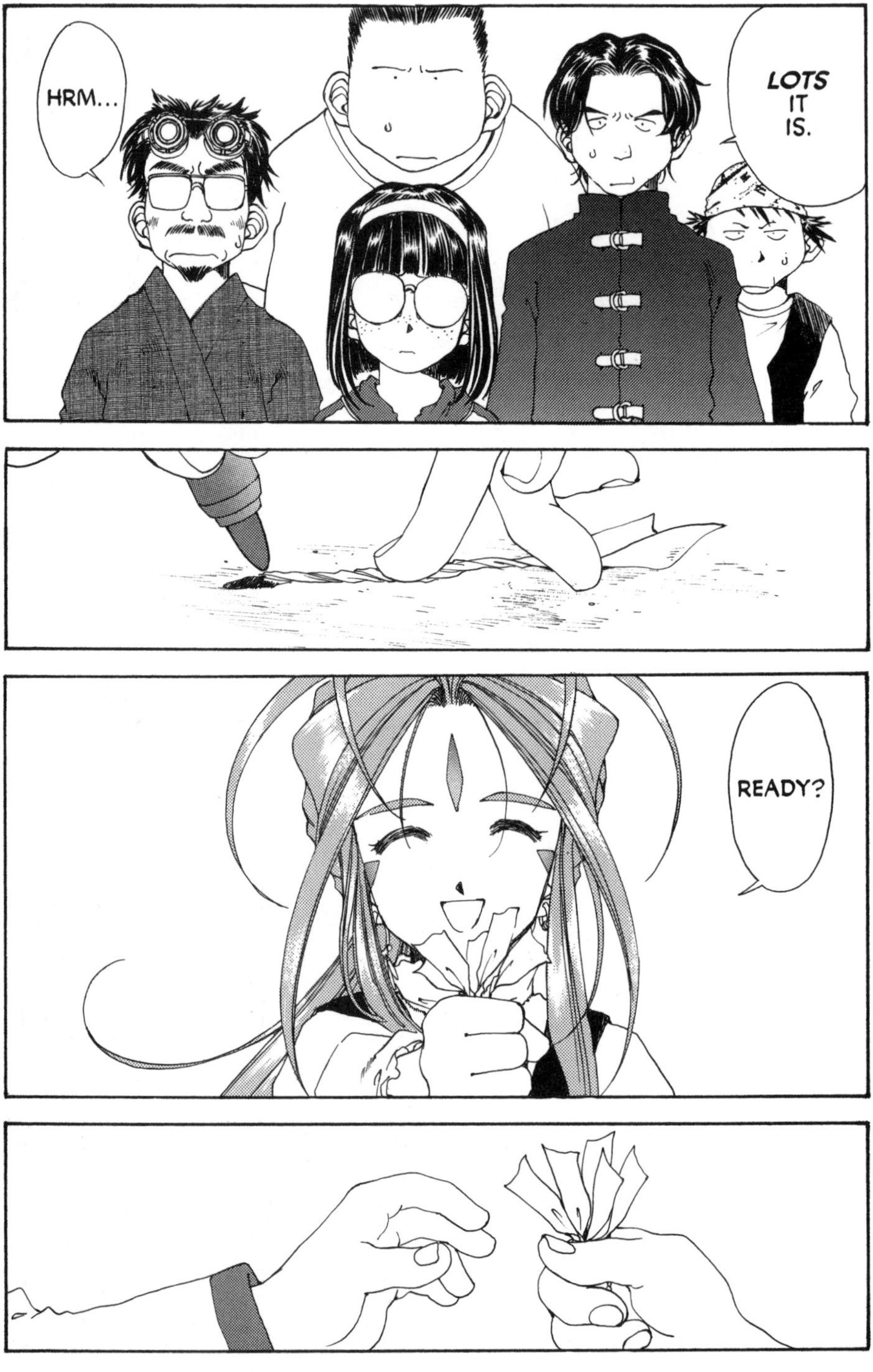
LOTS IT IS.
HRM...
READY?

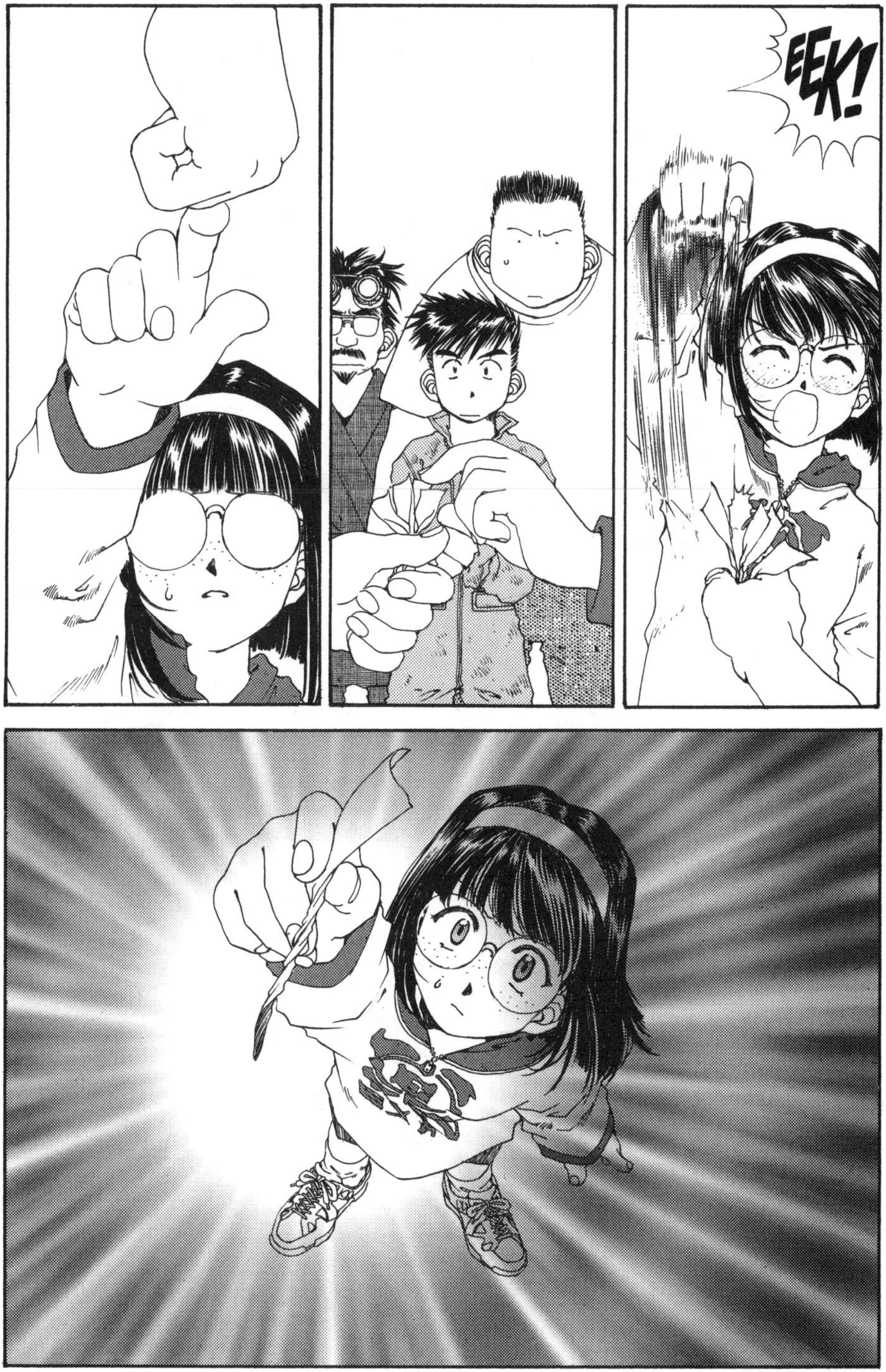
EEK!

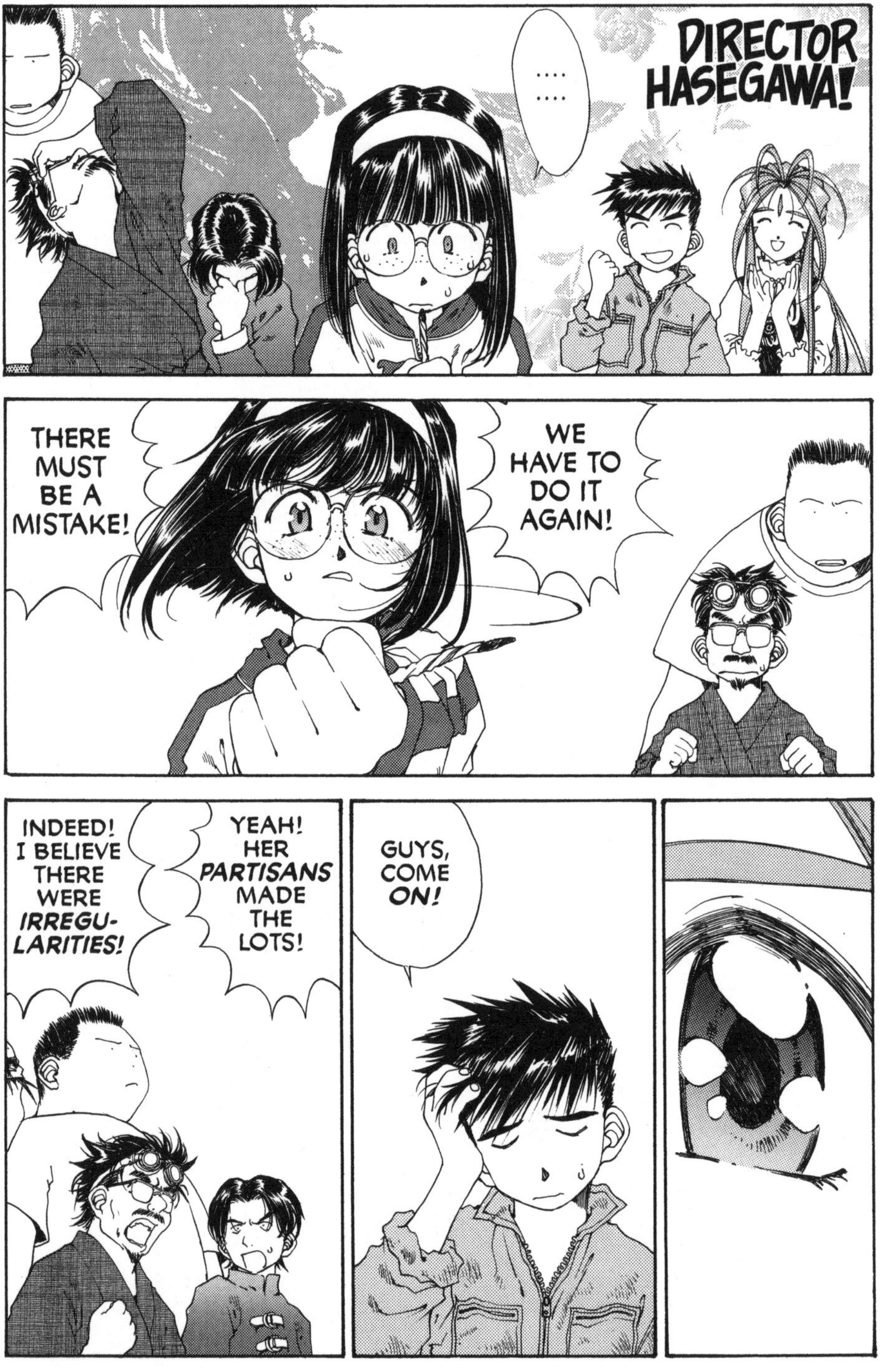
....
....
DIRECTOR HASEGAWA!
THERE MUST BE A MISTAKE!
WE HAVE TO DO IT AGAIN!
INDEED! I BELIEVE THERE WERE *IRREGU-LARITIES!*
YEAH! HER *PARTISANS* MADE THE LOTS!
GUYS, COME *ON!*

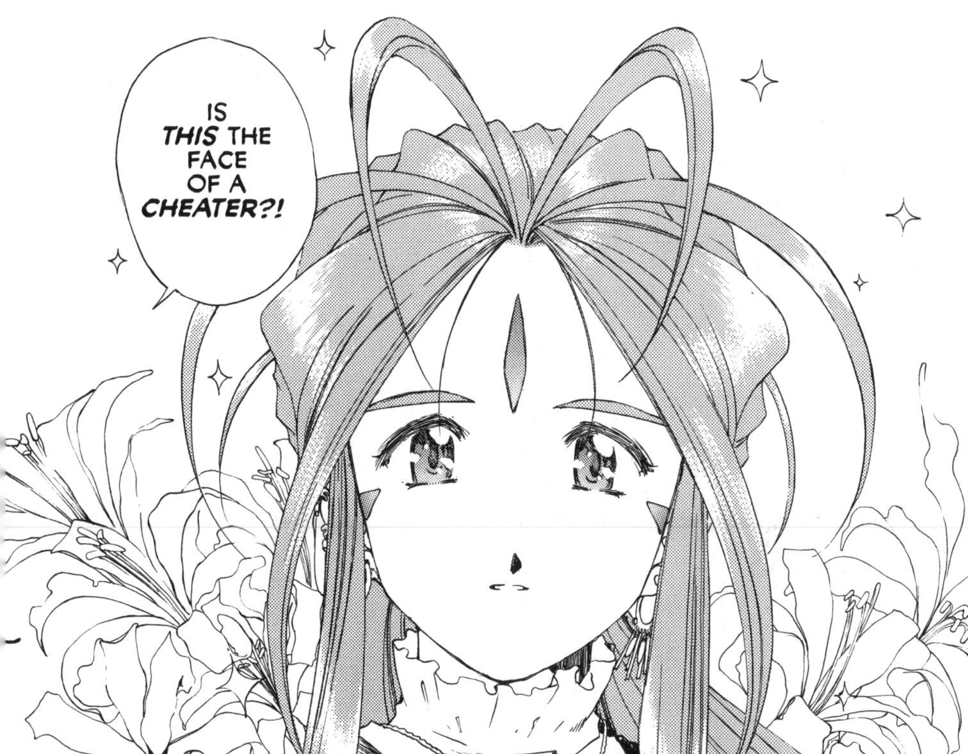
IS *THIS* THE FACE OF A *CHEATER?!*

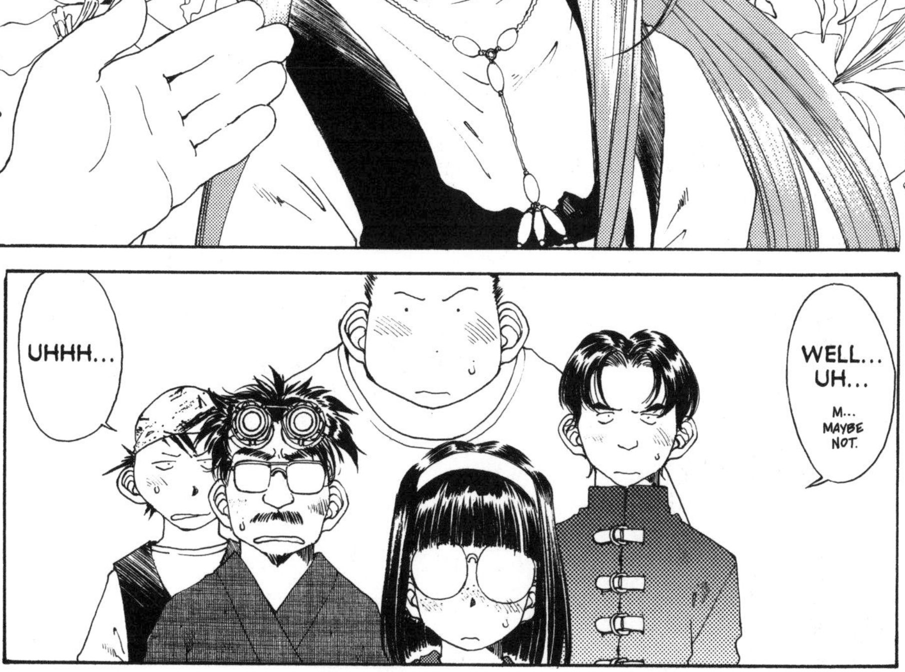
WELL... UH...
M... MAYBE NOT.
UHHH...

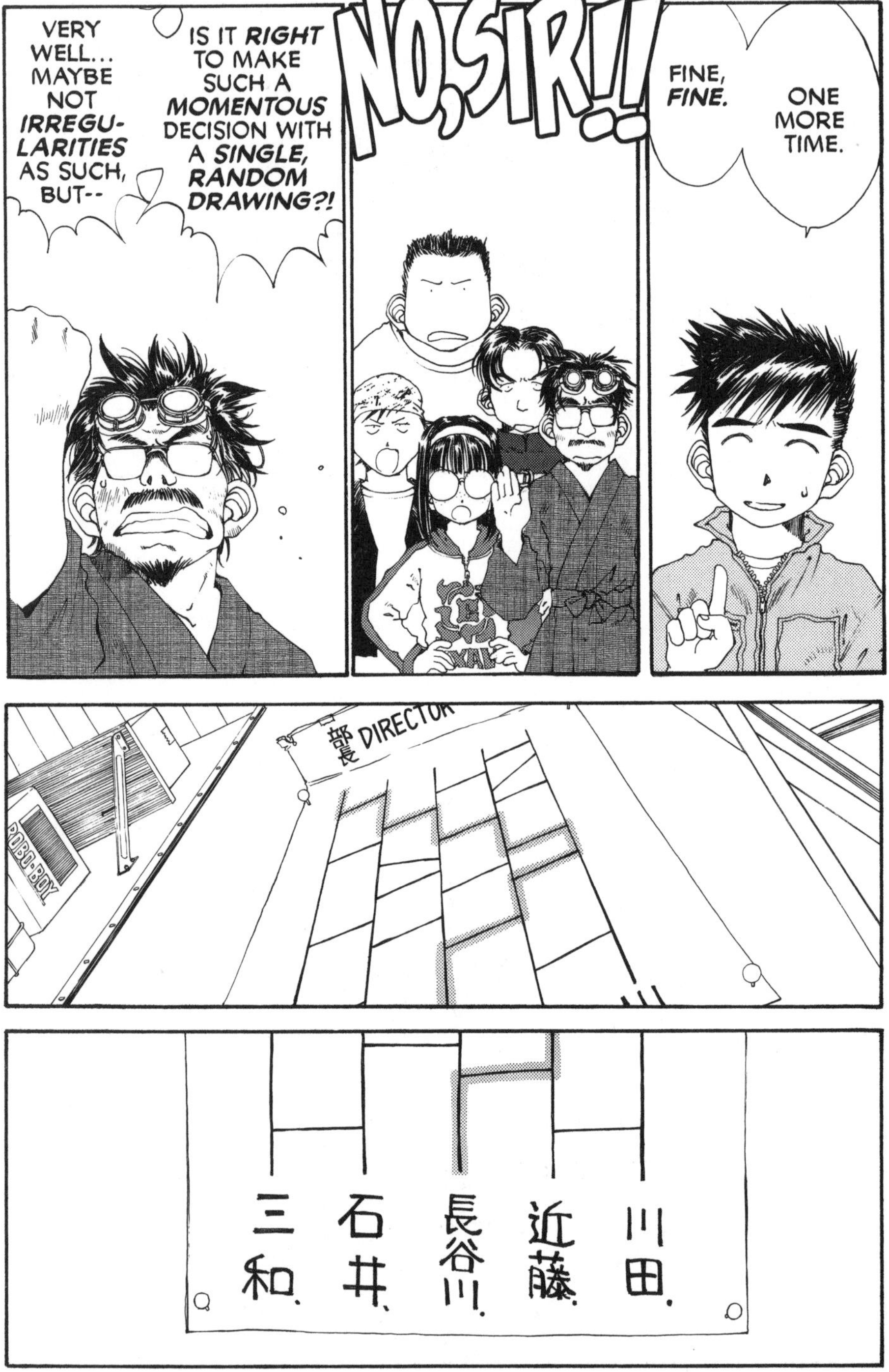
VERY WELL... MAYBE NOT IRREGULARITIES AS SUCH, BUT--
IS IT RIGHT TO MAKE SUCH A MOMENTOUS DECISION WITH A SINGLE, RANDOM DRAWING?!
NO, SIR!!
FINE, FINE.
ONE MORE TIME.
部長 DIRECTOR
ROBO-BOY
三和
石井
長谷川
近藤
川田

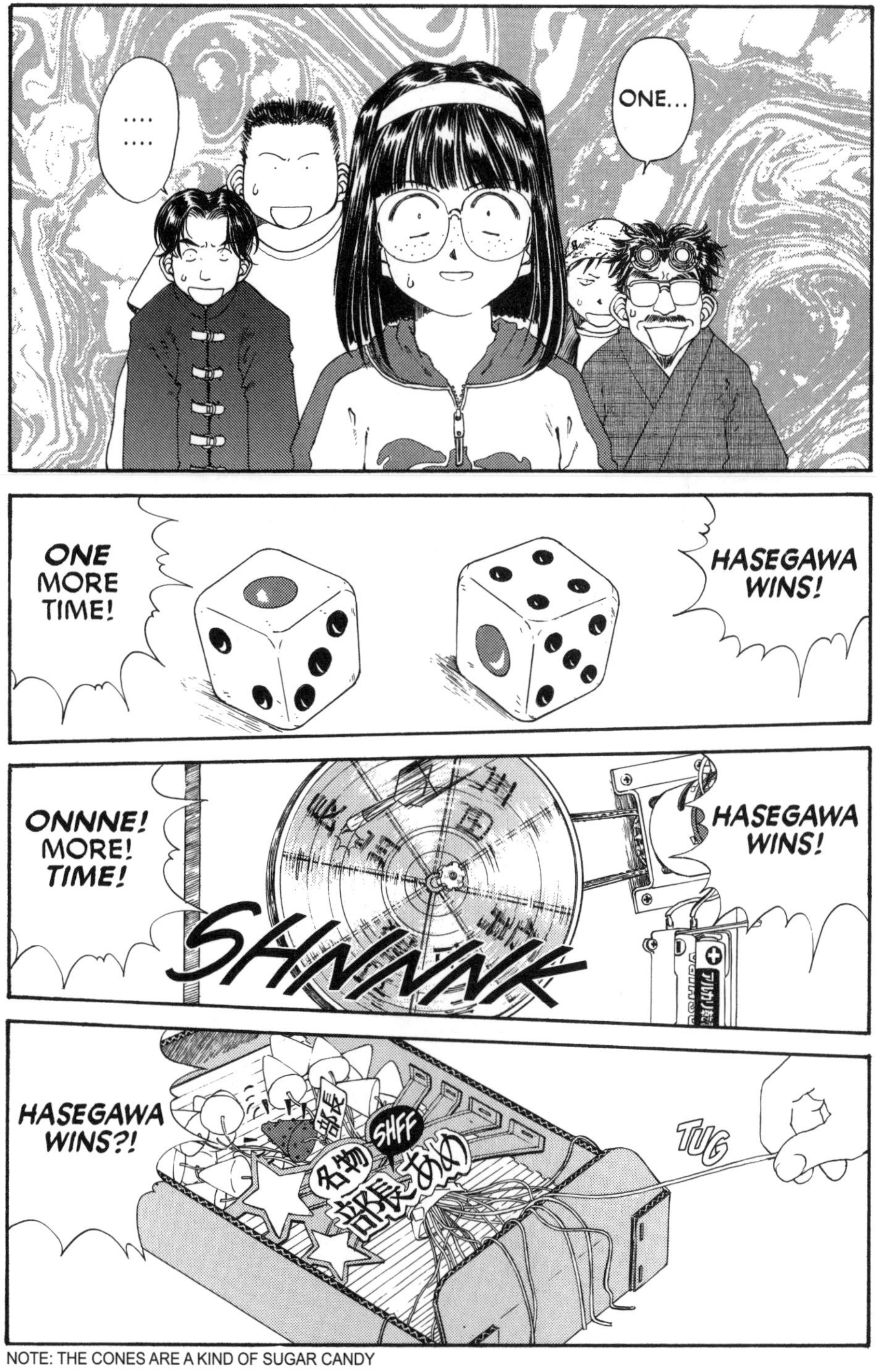
ONE...
....
....
HASEGAWA WINS!
ONE MORE TIME!
HASEGAWA WINS!
ONNNE! MORE! TIME!
SHNNNK
TUG
SHFF
名物
部長あめ
HASEGAWA WINS?!

NOTE: THE CONES ARE A KIND OF SUGAR CANDY

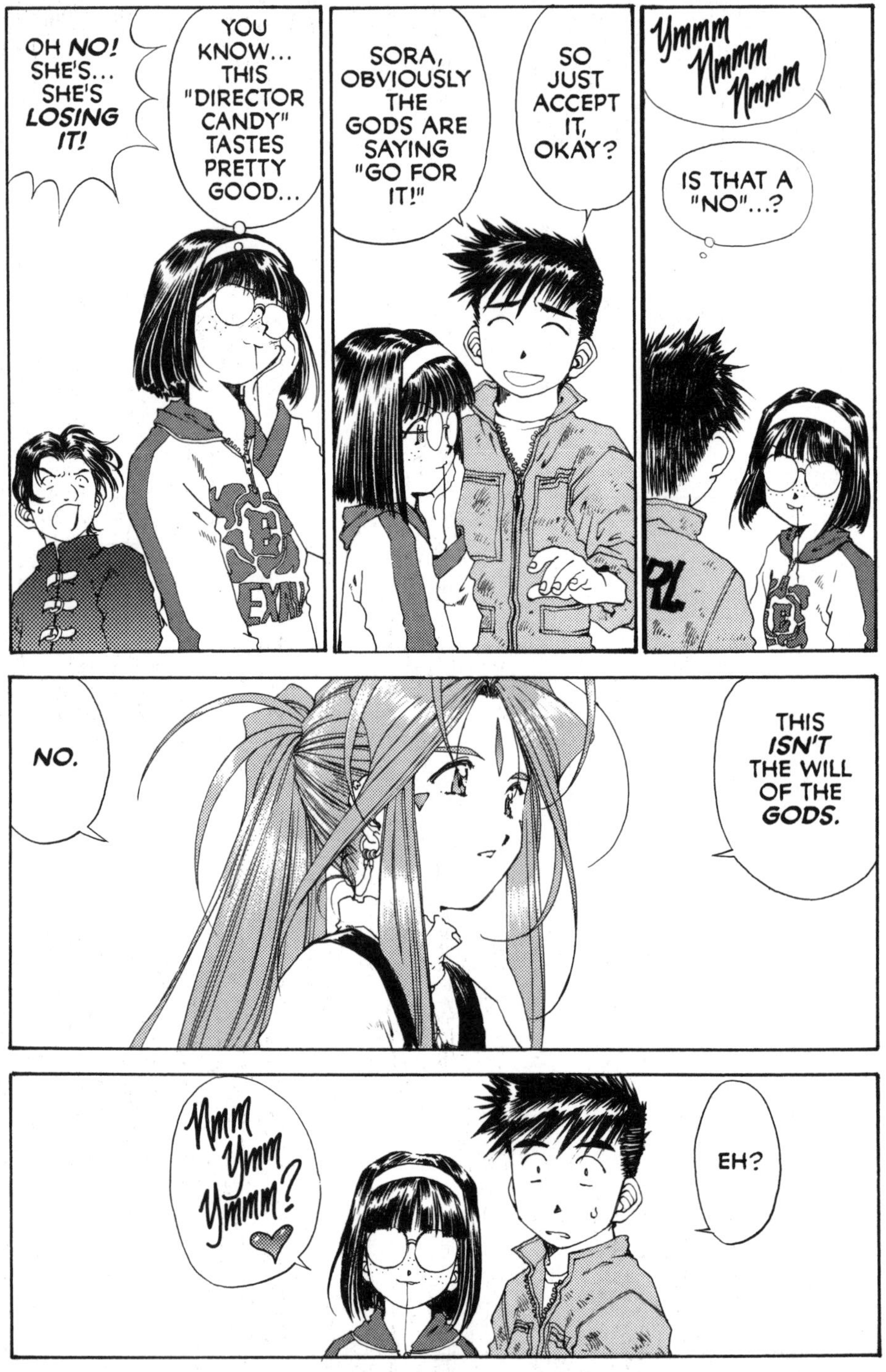
YOU KNOW... THIS "DIRECTOR CANDY" TASTES PRETTY GOOD...
OH NO! SHE'S... SHE'S LOSING IT!
SORA, OBVIOUSLY THE GODS ARE SAYING "GO FOR IT!"
SO JUST ACCEPT IT, OKAY?
Ymmm Nmmm Nmmm
IS THAT A "NO"...?
NO.
THIS ISN'T THE WILL OF THE GODS.
Nmm Ymm Ymmm?
EH?

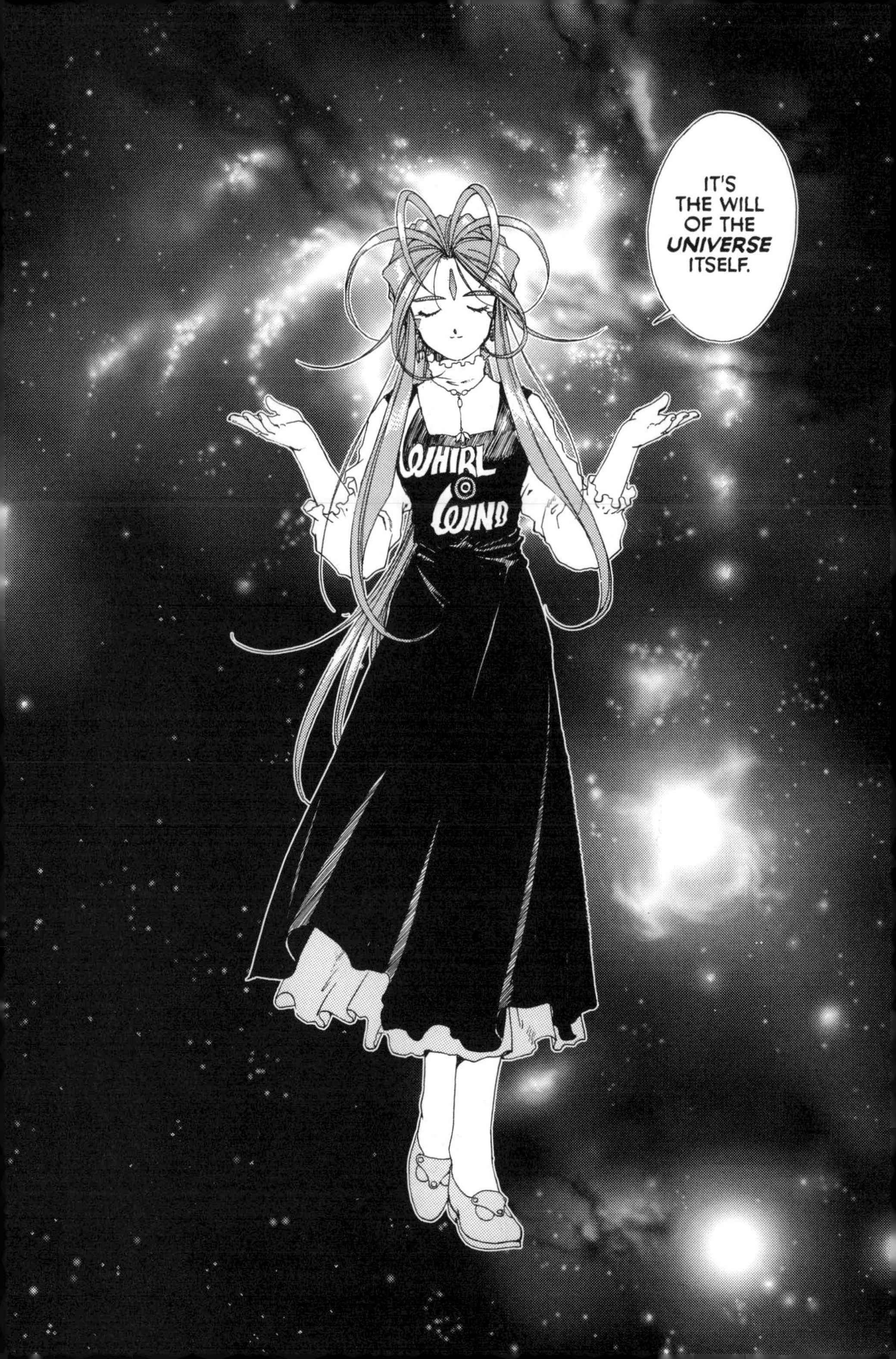
IT'S THE WILL OF THE ***UNIVERSE*** ITSELF.
WHIRL WIND

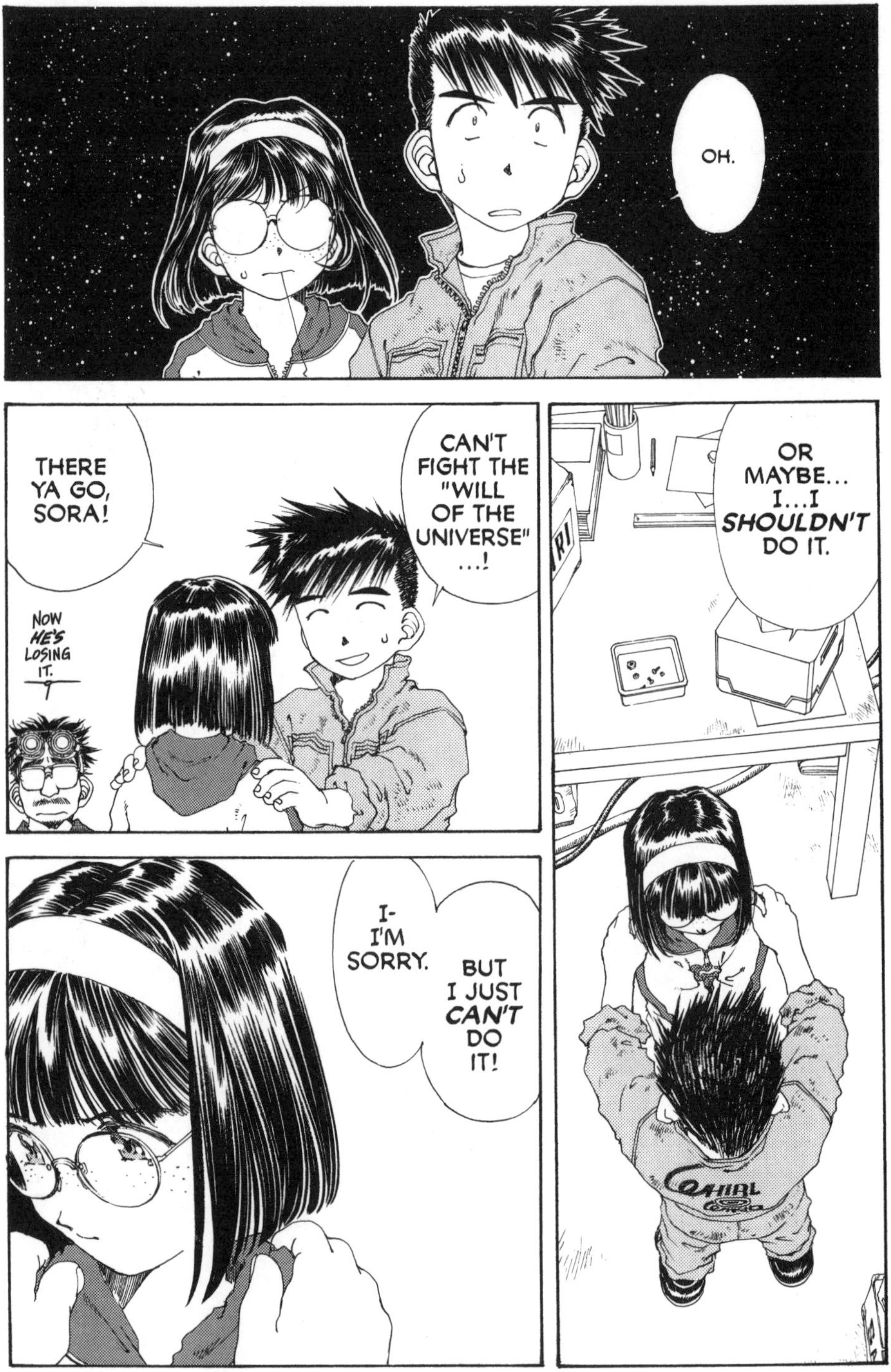
OH.
CAN'T FIGHT THE "WILL OF THE UNIVERSE" ...!
THERE YA GO, SORA!
NOW *HE'S* LOSING IT.
OR MAYBE... I...I *SHOULDN'T* DO IT.
I- I'M SORRY.
BUT I JUST *CAN'T* DO IT!

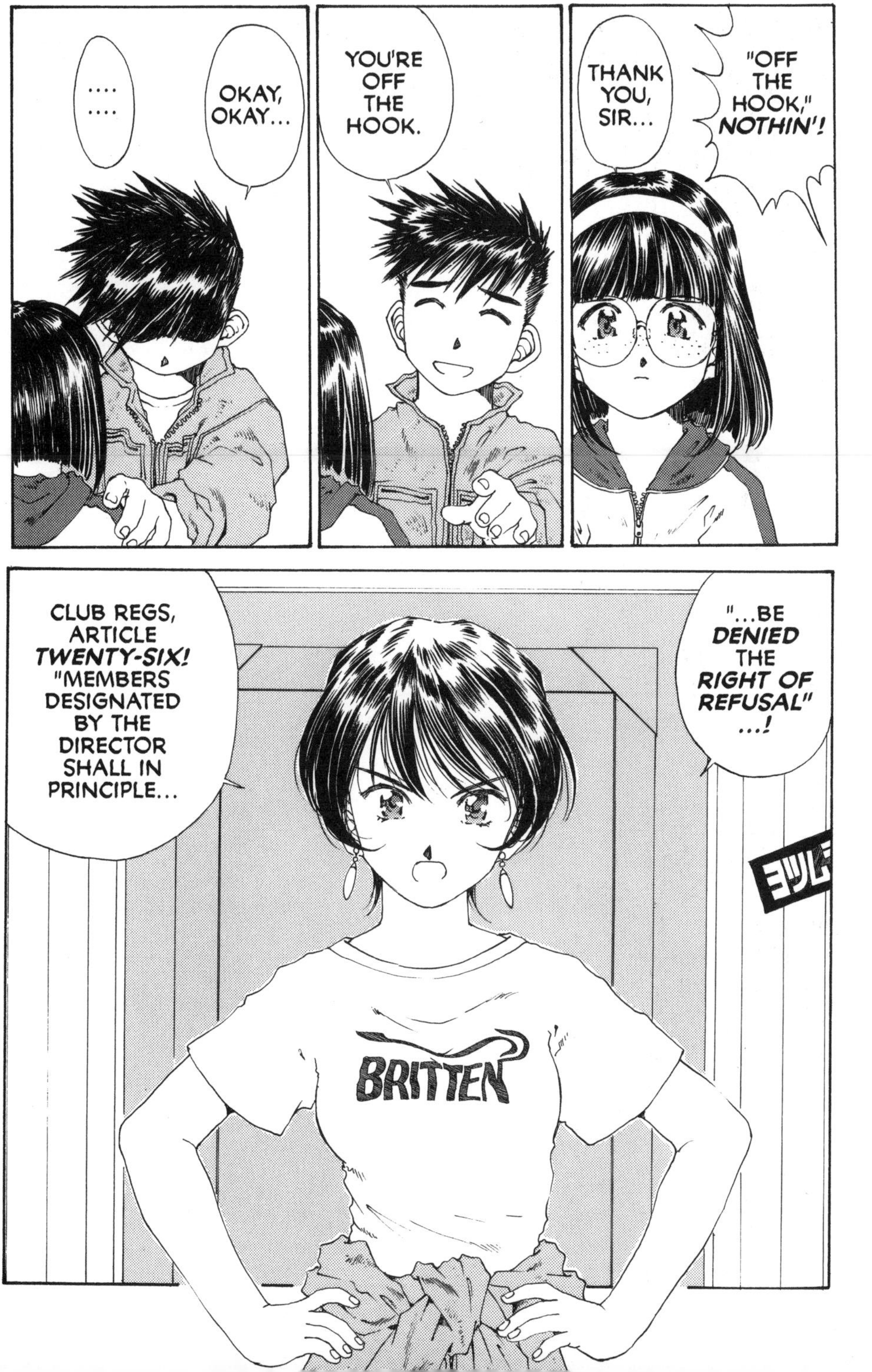
....
....
OKAY, OKAY...
YOU'RE OFF THE HOOK.
THANK YOU, SIR...
"OFF THE HOOK," *NOTHIN'!*
CLUB REGS, ARTICLE *TWENTY-SIX!* "MEMBERS DESIGNATED BY THE DIRECTOR SHALL IN PRINCIPLE...
"...BE *DENIED* THE *RIGHT OF REFUSAL*" ...!
BRITTEN

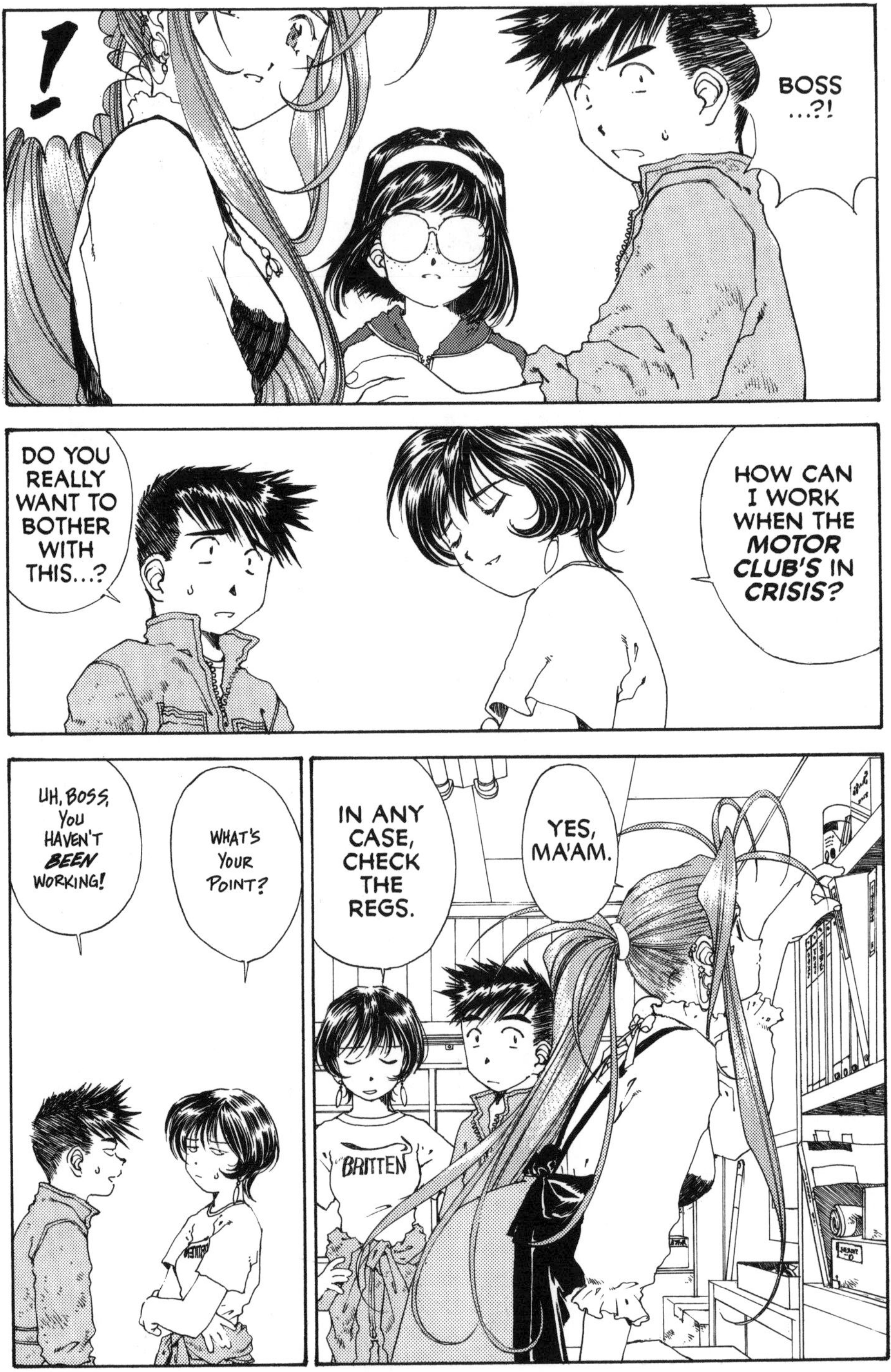
!
BOSS ...?!
DO YOU REALLY WANT TO BOTHER WITH THIS...?
HOW CAN I WORK WHEN THE MOTOR CLUB'S IN CRISIS?
UH, BOSS, YOU HAVEN'T BEEN WORKING!
WHAT'S YOUR POINT?
IN ANY CASE, CHECK THE REGS.
YES, MA'AM.
BRITTEN

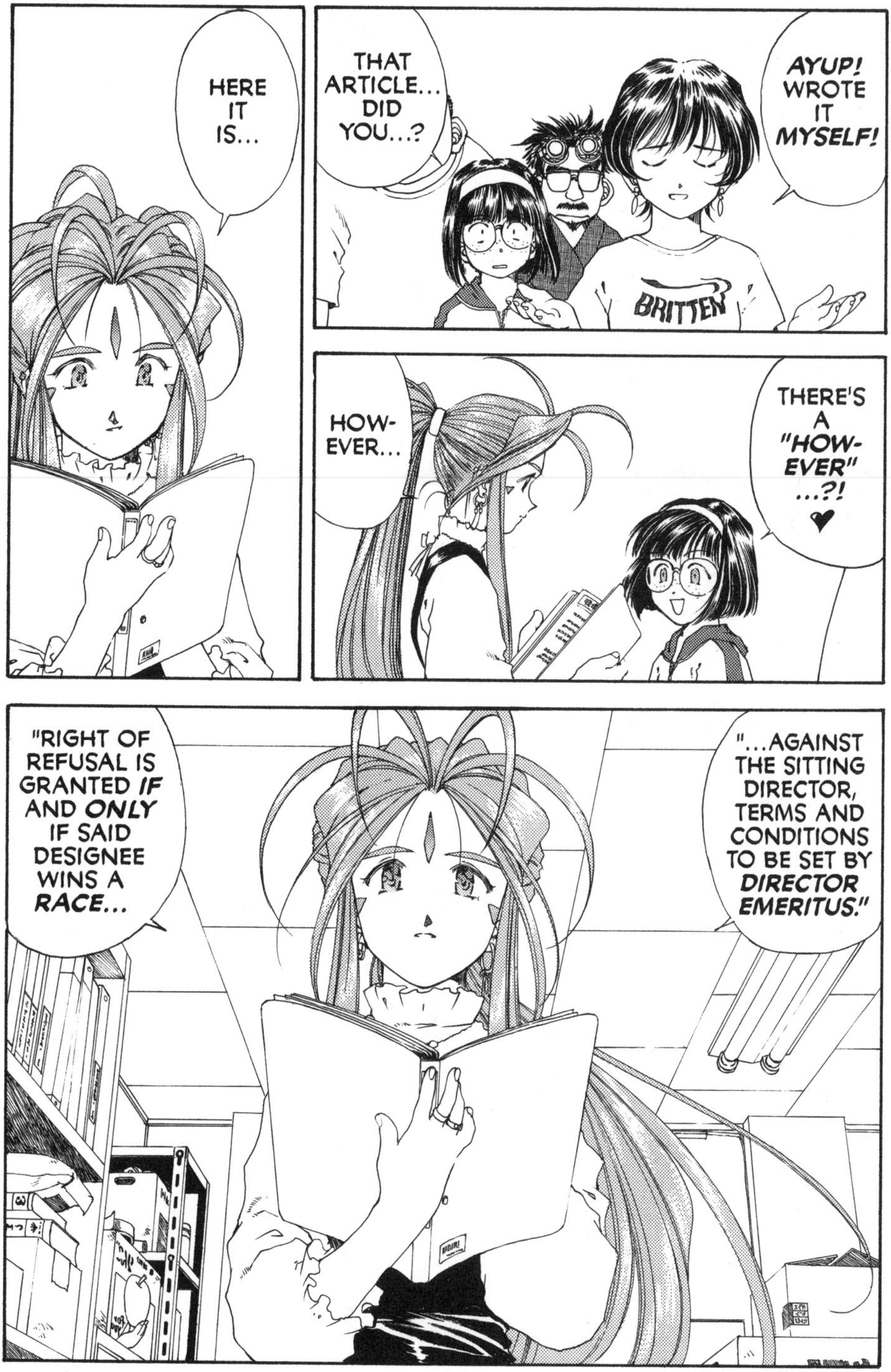
HERE IT IS...
THAT ARTICLE... DID YOU...?
AYUP! WROTE IT MYSELF!
BRITTEN
HOW-EVER...
THERE'S A "HOW-EVER" ...?! ❤
"RIGHT OF REFUSAL IS GRANTED IF AND ONLY IF SAID DESIGNEE WINS A RACE...
"...AGAINST THE SITTING DIRECTOR, TERMS AND CONDITIONS TO BE SET BY DIRECTOR EMERITUS."

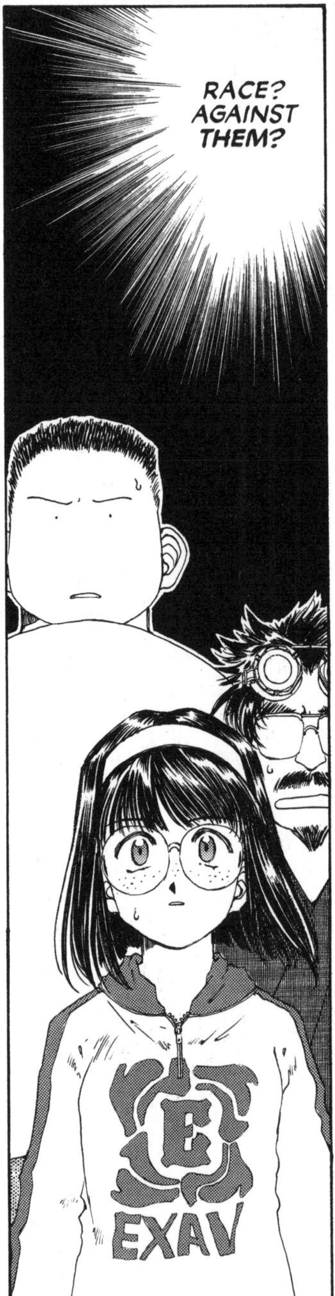
RACE? AGAINST THEM?
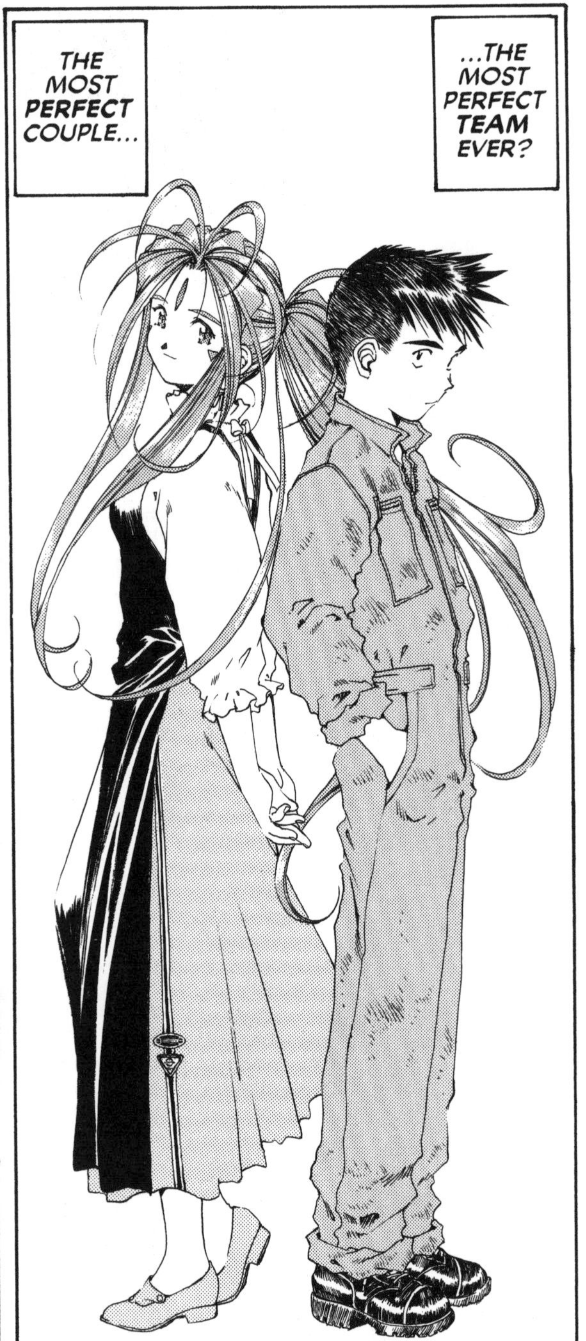
THE MOST PERFECT COUPLE...
...THE MOST PERFECT TEAM EVER?

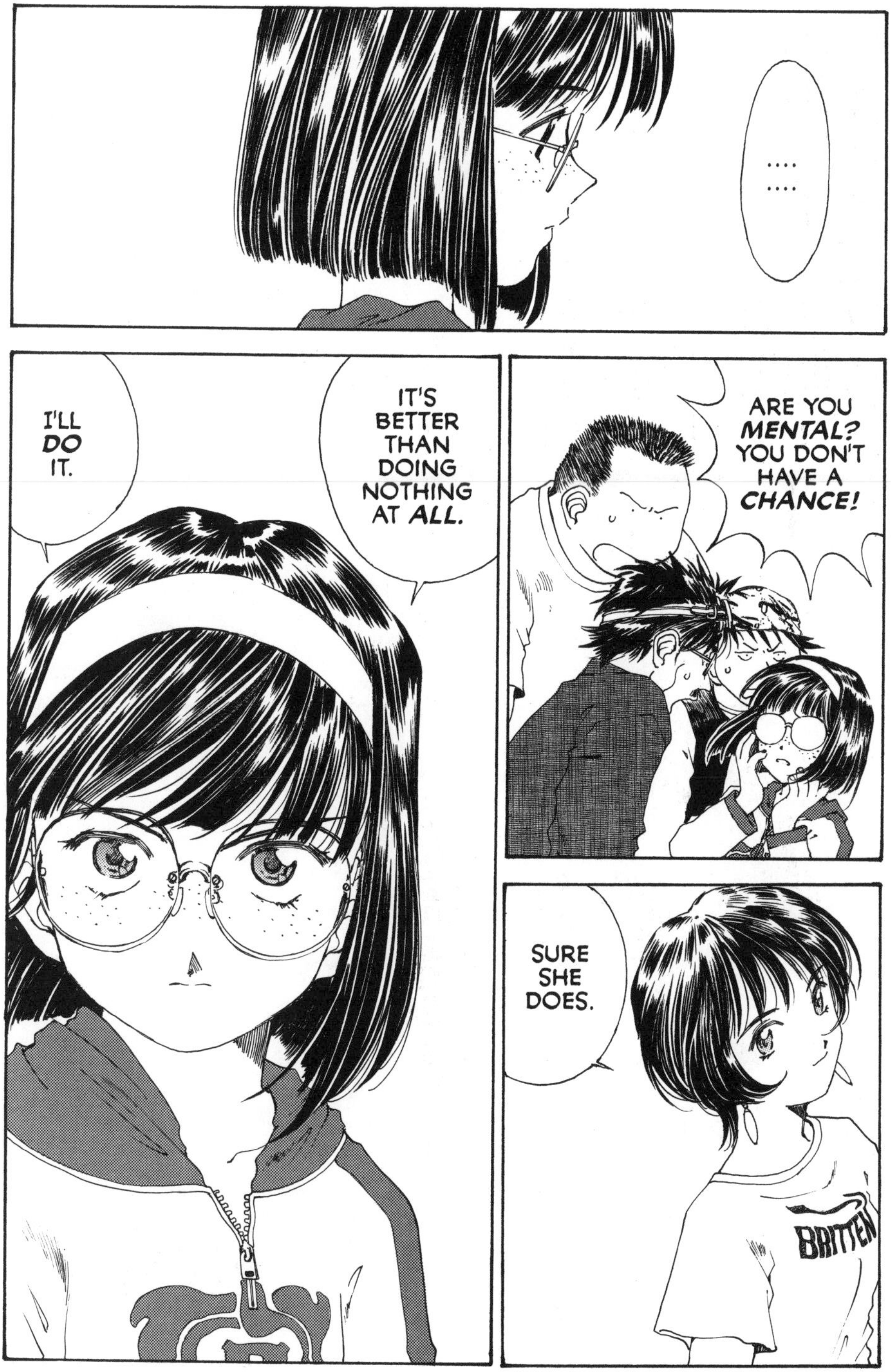
....
....
I'LL DO IT.
IT'S BETTER THAN DOING NOTHING AT ALL.
ARE YOU MENTAL? YOU DON'T HAVE A CHANCE!
SURE SHE DOES.
BRITTEN

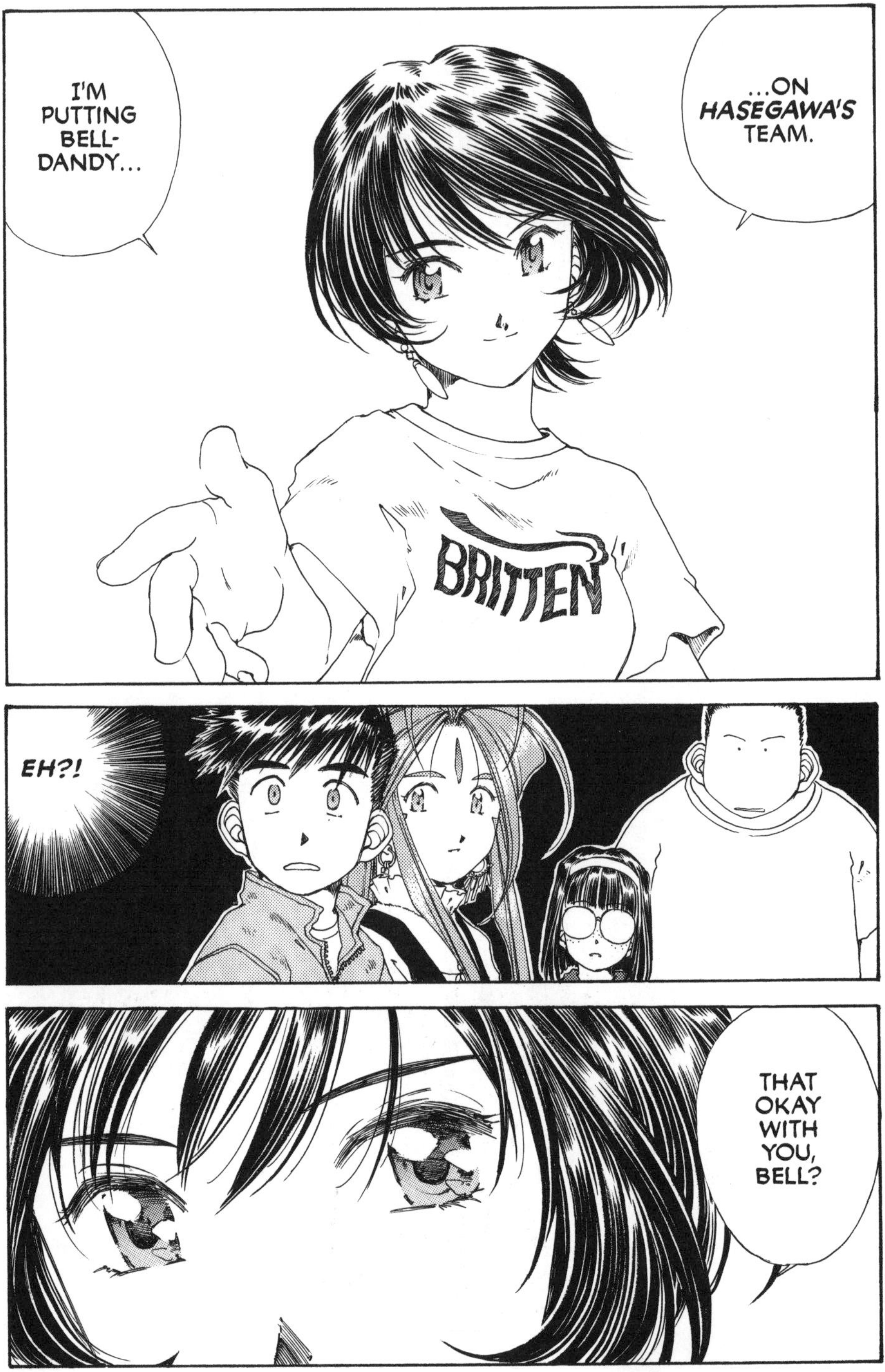
I'M PUTTING BELL-DANDY...
...ON *HASEGAWA'S* TEAM.
BRITTEN
EH?!
THAT OKAY WITH YOU, BELL?

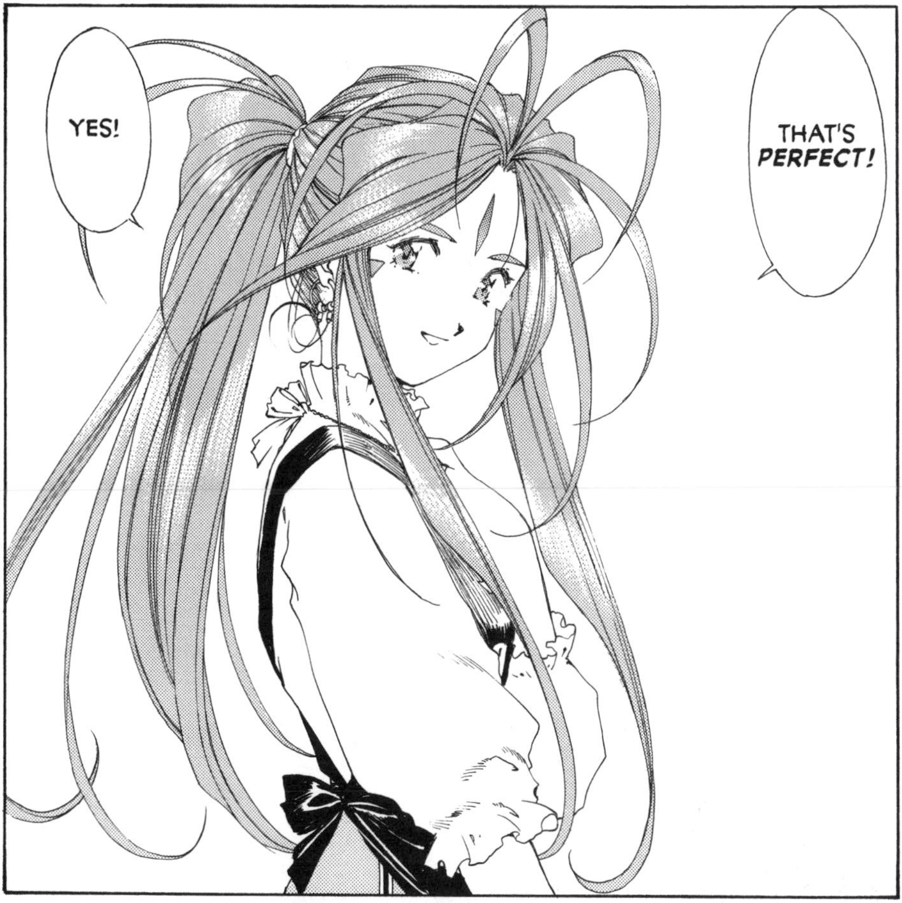
THAT'S *PERFECT!*
YES!

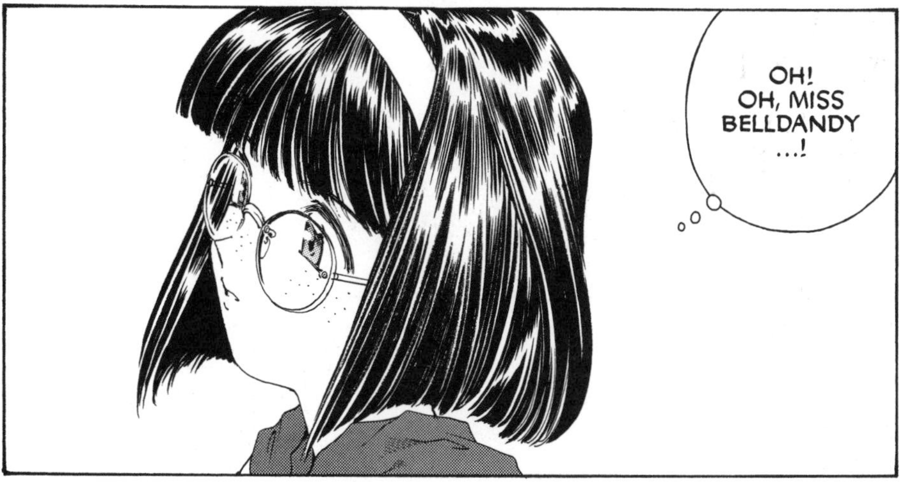
OH! OH, MISS BELLDANDY ...!

THE SHORTCUT TO WINNING

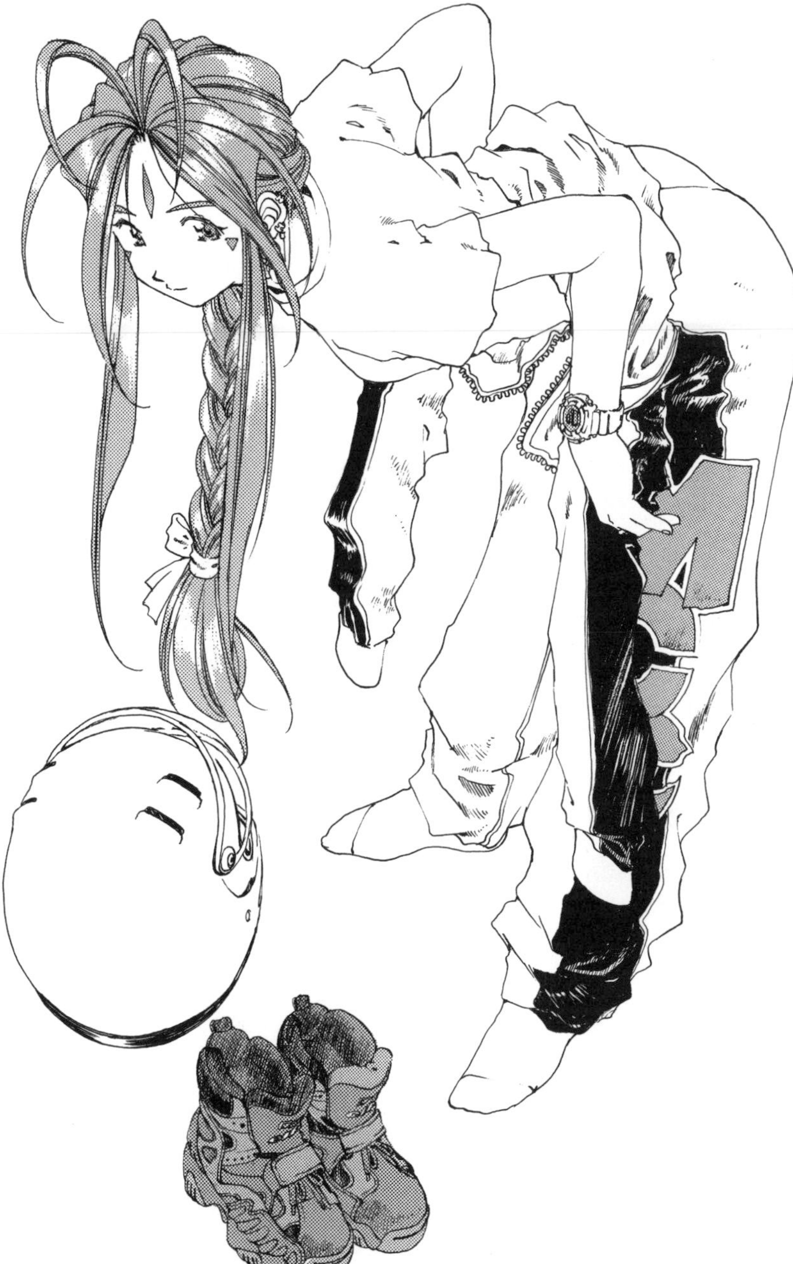

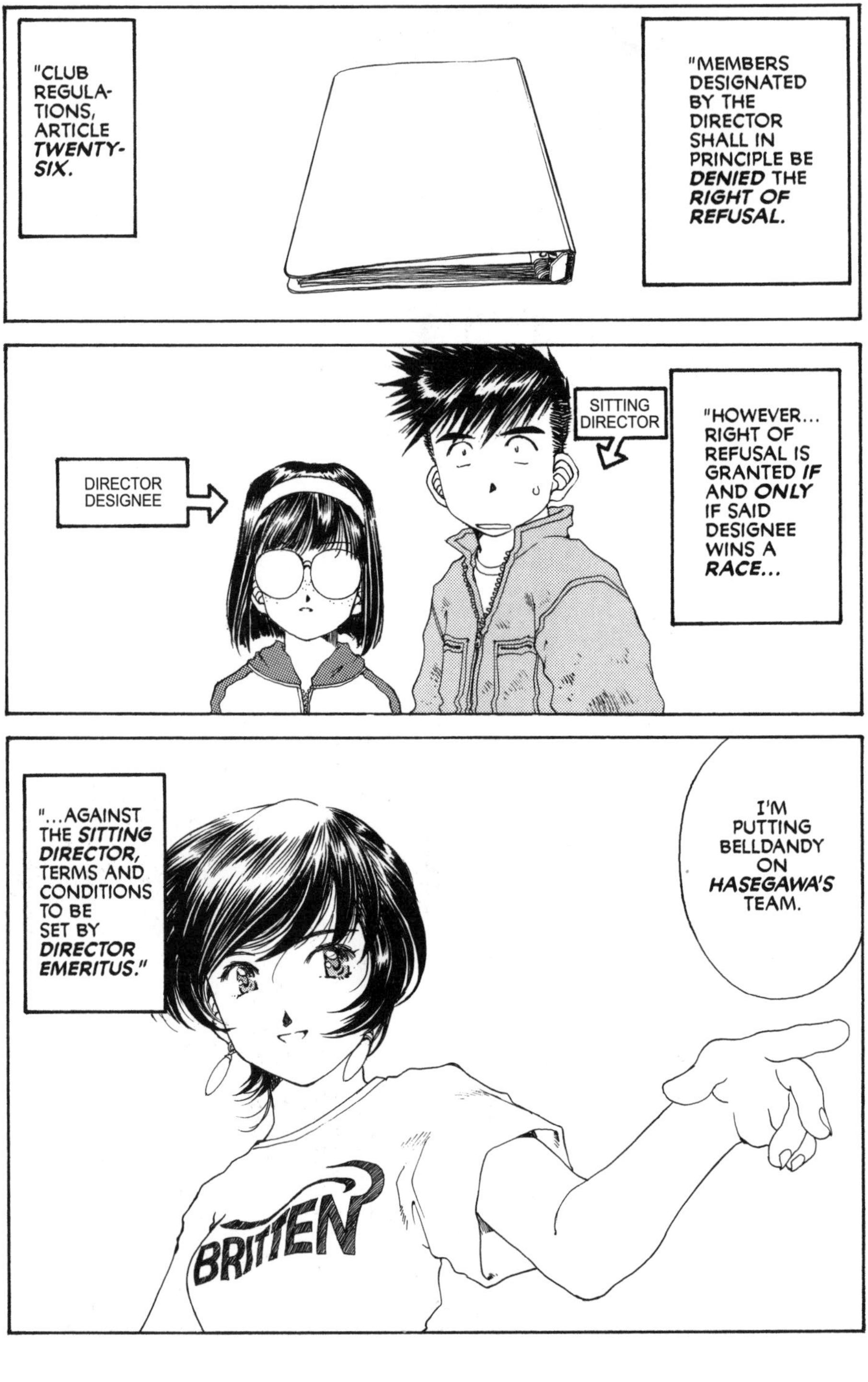
"CLUB REGULATIONS, ARTICLE *TWENTY-SIX.*
"MEMBERS DESIGNATED BY THE DIRECTOR SHALL IN PRINCIPLE BE ***DENIED*** THE ***RIGHT OF REFUSAL.***
DIRECTOR DESIGNEE
SITTING DIRECTOR
"HOWEVER... RIGHT OF REFUSAL IS GRANTED ***IF*** AND ***ONLY*** IF SAID DESIGNEE WINS A ***RACE...***
"...AGAINST THE ***SITTING DIRECTOR,*** TERMS AND CONDITIONS TO BE SET BY ***DIRECTOR EMERITUS."***
I'M PUTTING BELLDANDY ON ***HASEGAWA'S*** TEAM.
BRITTEN

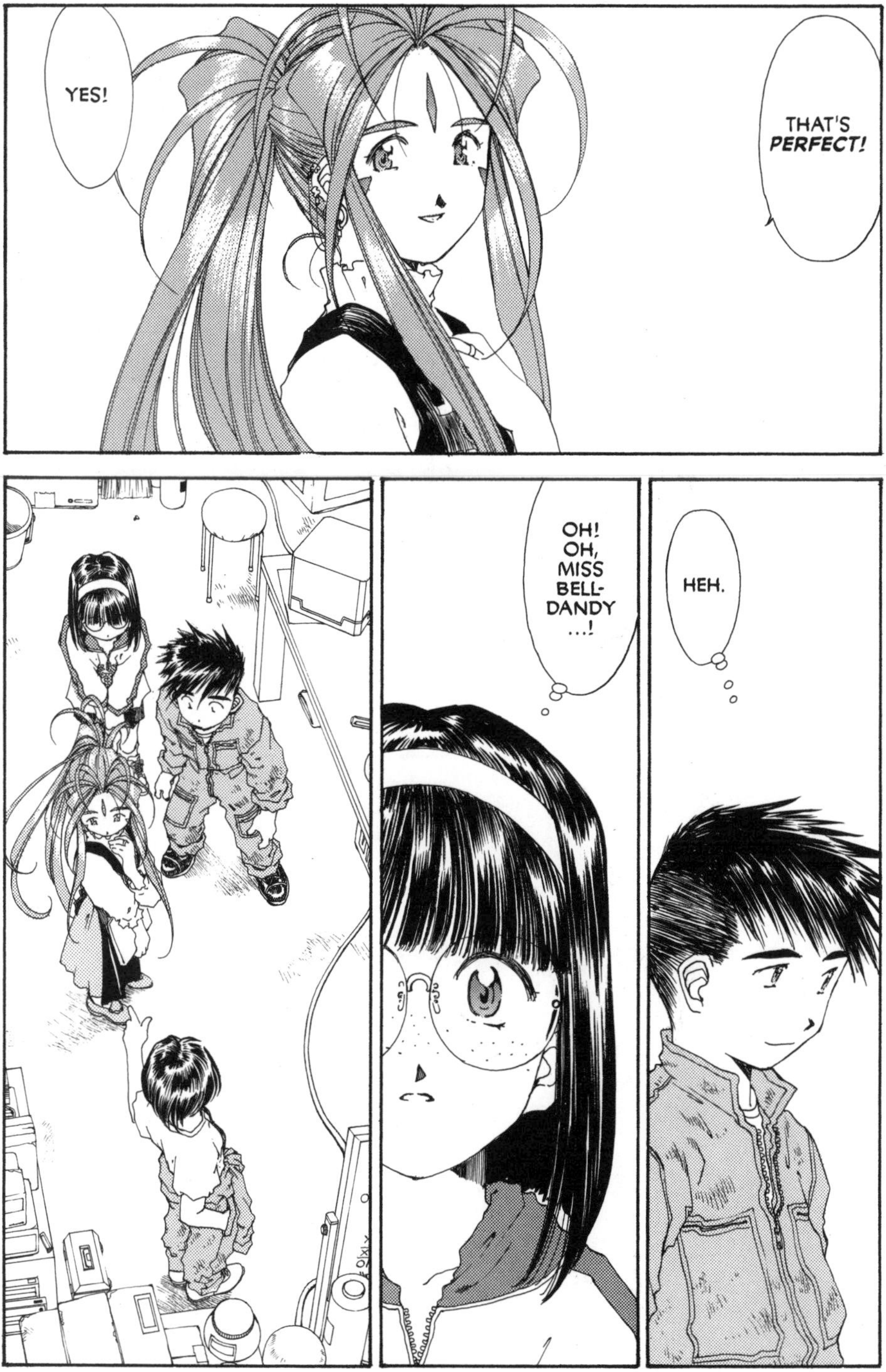
THAT'S *PERFECT!*
YES!
HEH.
OH! OH, MISS BELL-DANDY ...!

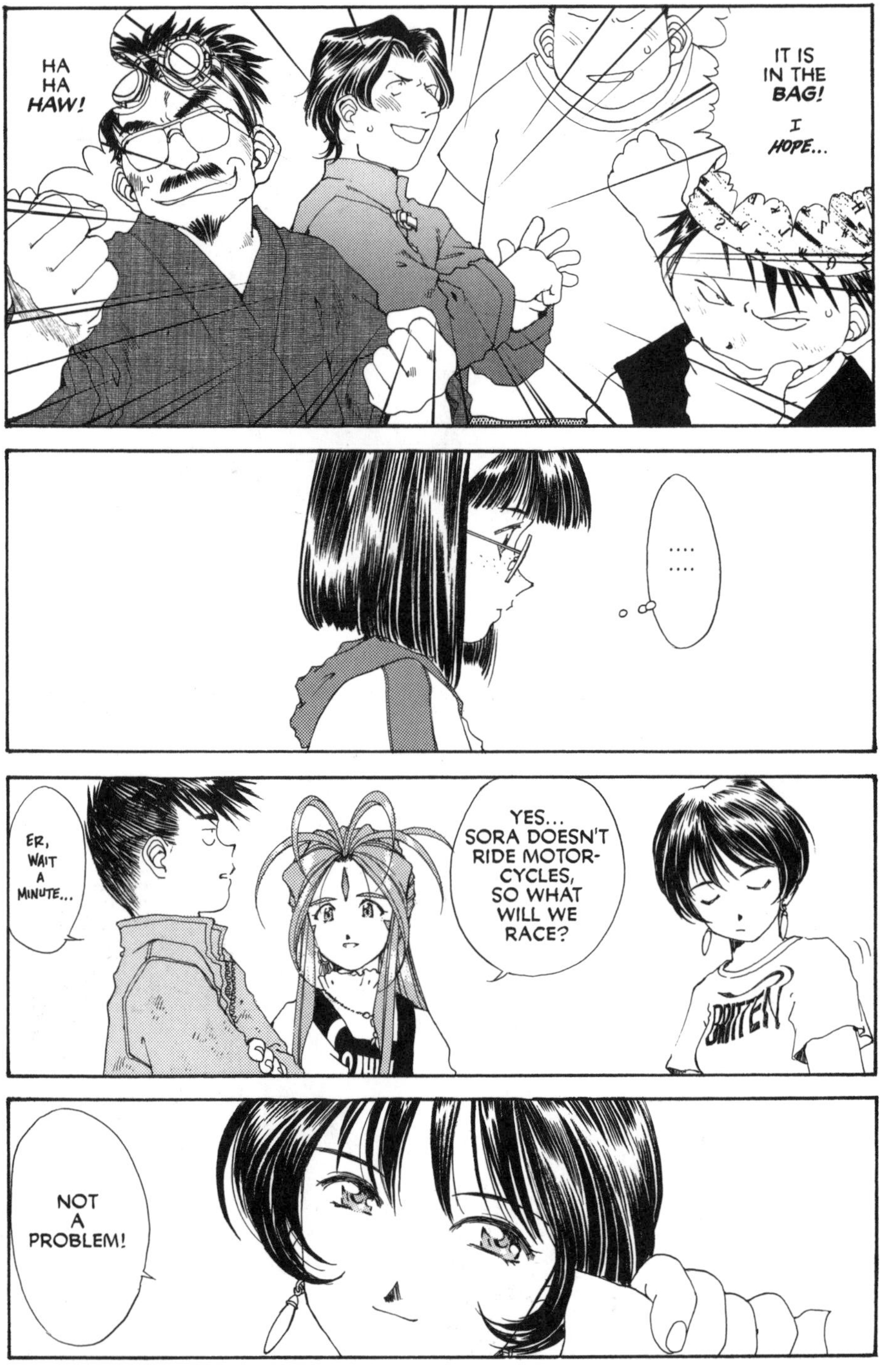
HA HA HAW!
IT IS IN THE BAG! I HOPE...
....
....
ER, WAIT A MINUTE...
YES... SORA DOESN'T RIDE MOTOR-CYCLES, SO WHAT WILL WE RACE?
NOT A PROBLEM!

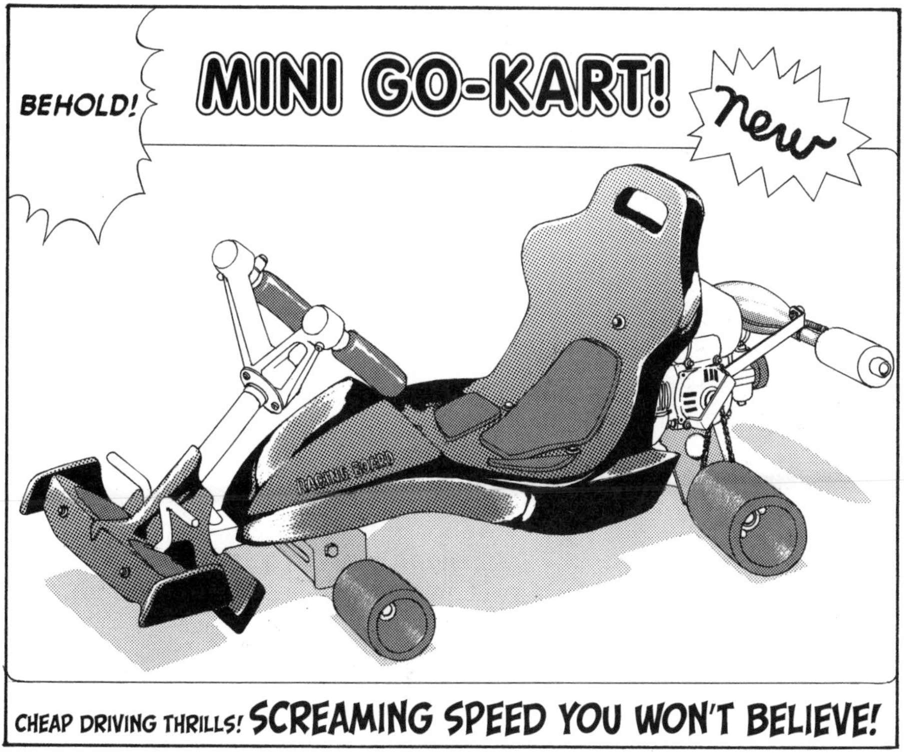
BEHOLD!
MINI GO-KART!
new
CHEAP DRIVING THRILLS! SCREAMING SPEED YOU WON'T BELIEVE!

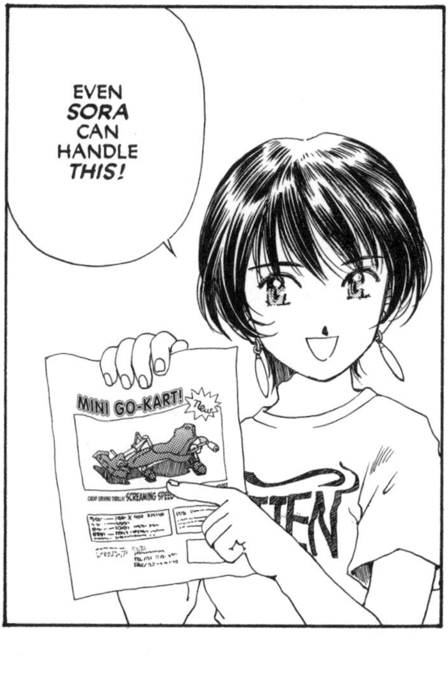
EVEN SORA CAN HANDLE THIS!
MINI GO-KART!

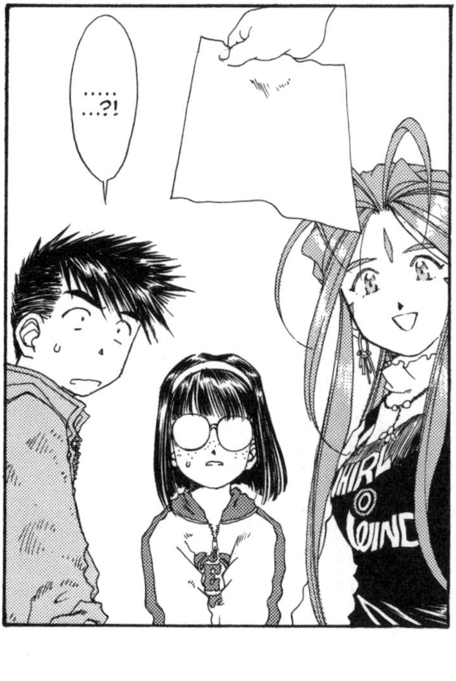
....?!

ANOTHER TOY, BOSS?

...IT *STOLE MY HEART!*

WELL, IT...

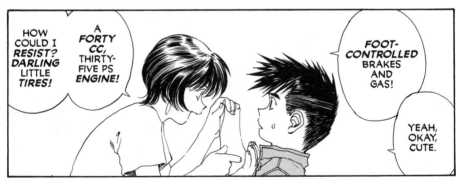

HOW COULD I *RESIST? DARLING* LITTLE *TIRES!*

A *FORTY CC,* THIRTY-FIVE PS *ENGINE!*

FOOT-CONTROLLED BRAKES AND GAS!

YEAH, OKAY, CUTE.

BUT WHY ARE *YOU* DECIDING EVERYTHING, BOSS?

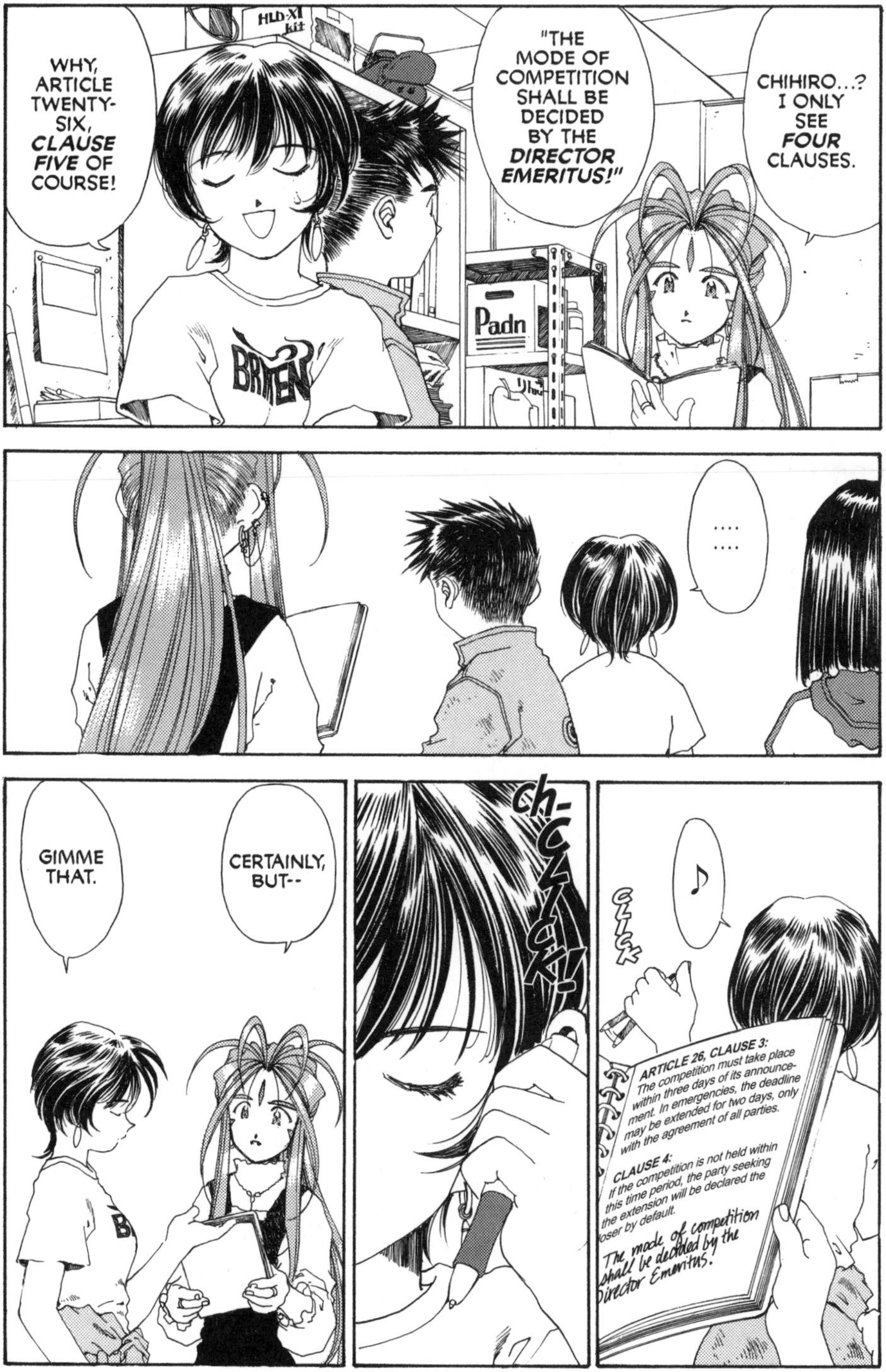

HLD-XI kit
WHY, ARTICLE TWENTY-SIX, ***CLAUSE FIVE*** OF COURSE!
"THE MODE OF COMPETITION SHALL BE DECIDED BY THE ***DIRECTOR EMERITUS!***"
CHIHIRO...? I ONLY SEE ***FOUR*** CLAUSES.
Padn
BRITEN
....
....
GIMME THAT.
CERTAINLY, BUT--
CH-CLICK!
CLICK
♪
ARTICLE 26, CLAUSE 3:
The competition must take place within three days of its announcement. In emergencies, the deadline may be extended for two days, only with the agreement of all parties.
CLAUSE 4:
If the competition is not held within this time period, the party seeking the extension will be declared the loser by default.
The mode of competition shall be decided by the Director Emeritus.

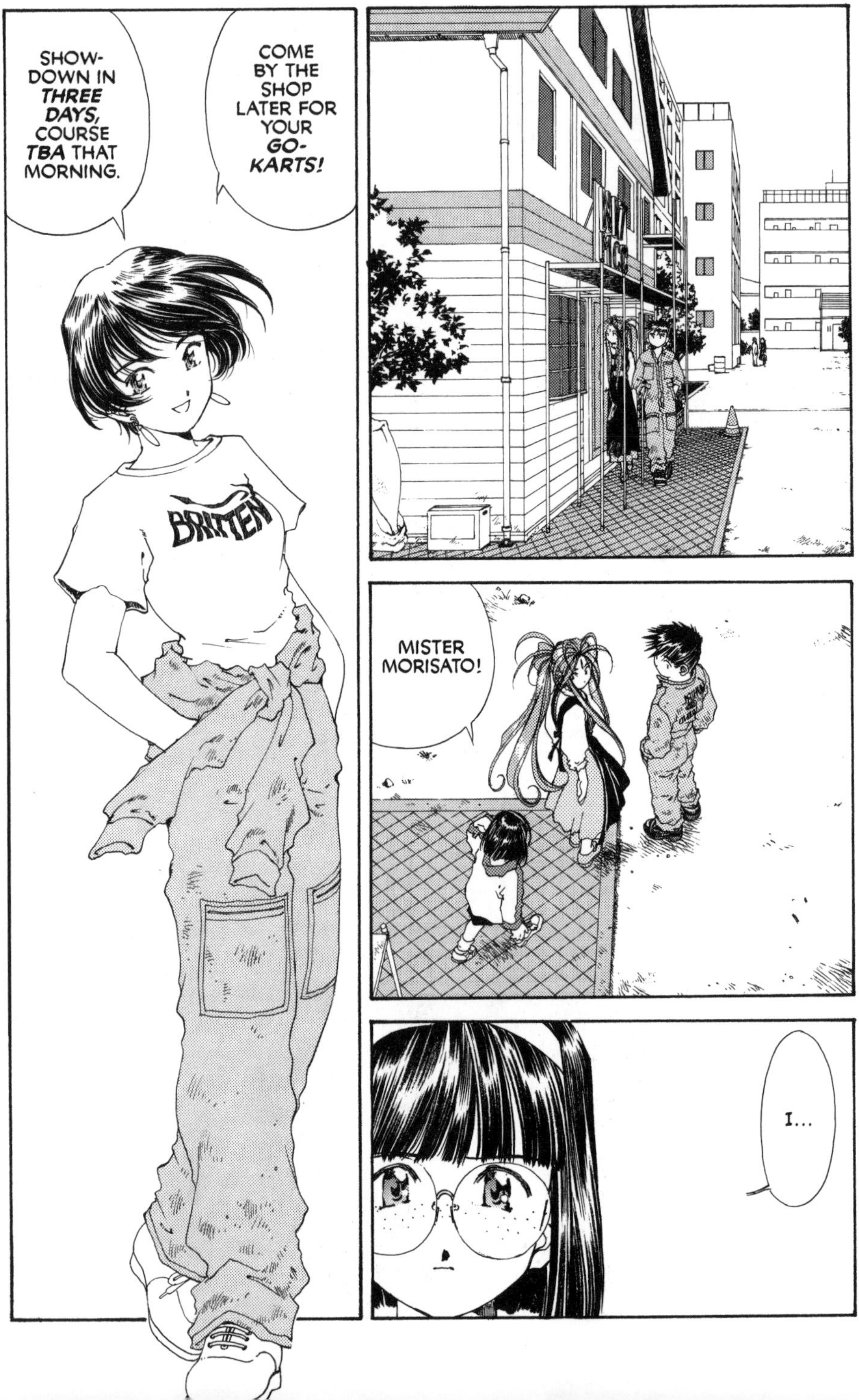
COME BY THE SHOP LATER FOR YOUR *GO-KARTS!*
SHOW-DOWN IN *THREE DAYS,* COURSE *TBA* THAT MORNING.
MISTER MORISATO!
I...

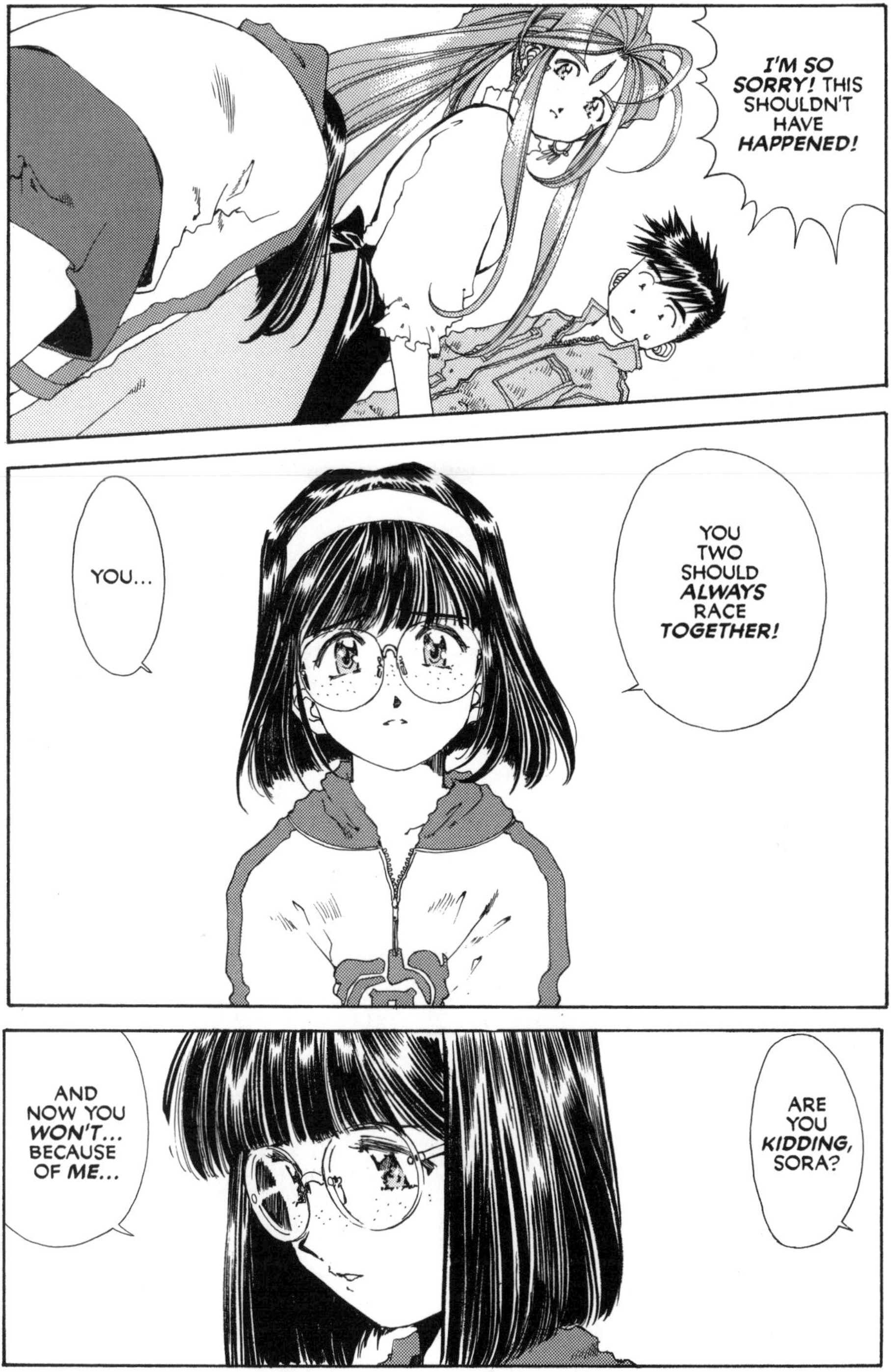
I'M SO SORRY! THIS SHOULDN'T HAVE HAPPENED!
YOU...
YOU TWO SHOULD ALWAYS RACE TOGETHER!
AND NOW YOU WON'T... BECAUSE OF ME...
ARE YOU KIDDING, SORA?

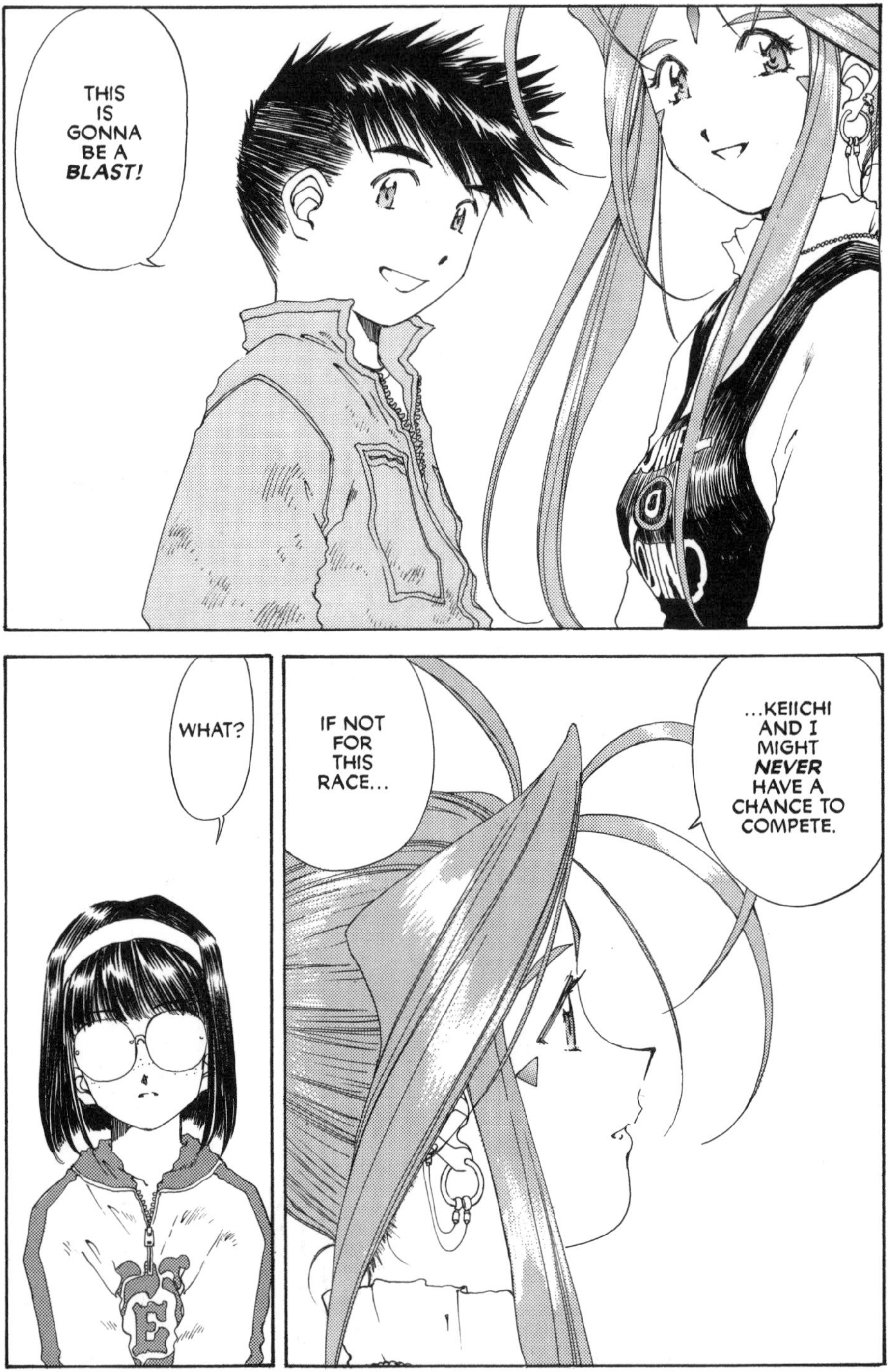
THIS IS GONNA BE A *BLAST!*
WHAT?
IF NOT FOR THIS RACE...
...KEIICHI AND I MIGHT *NEVER* HAVE A CHANCE TO COMPETE.

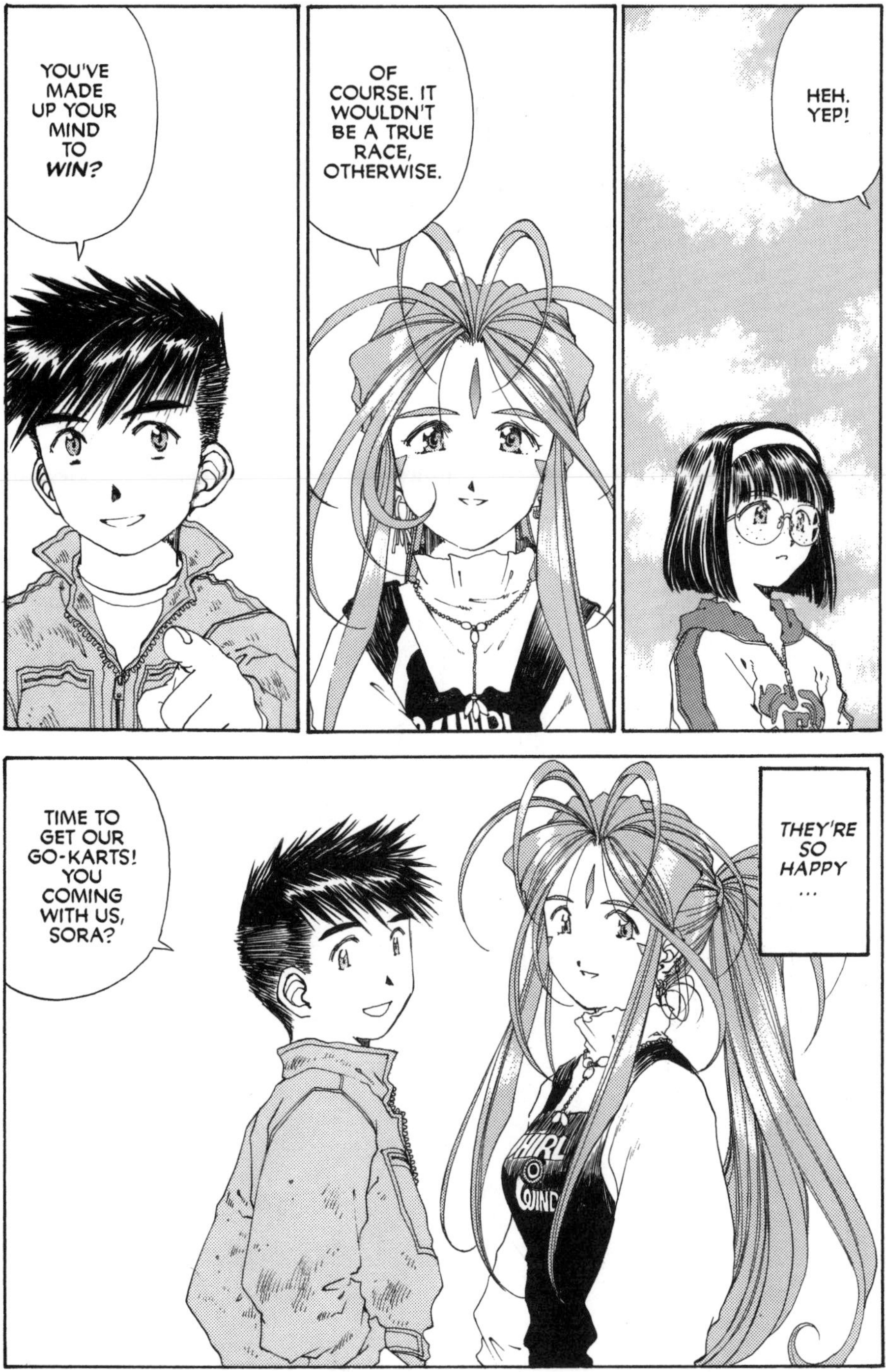
YOU'VE MADE UP YOUR MIND TO *WIN*?
OF COURSE. IT WOULDN'T BE A TRUE RACE, OTHERWISE.
HEH. YEP!
TIME TO GET OUR GO-KARTS! YOU COMING WITH US, SORA?
THEY'RE SO HAPPY ...

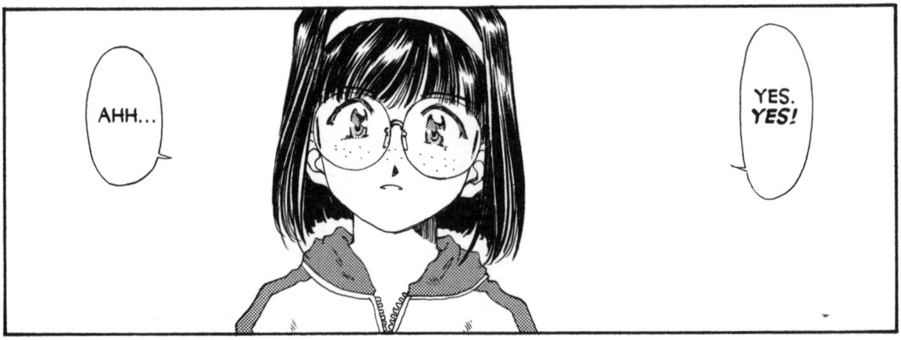
YES. YES!
AHH...

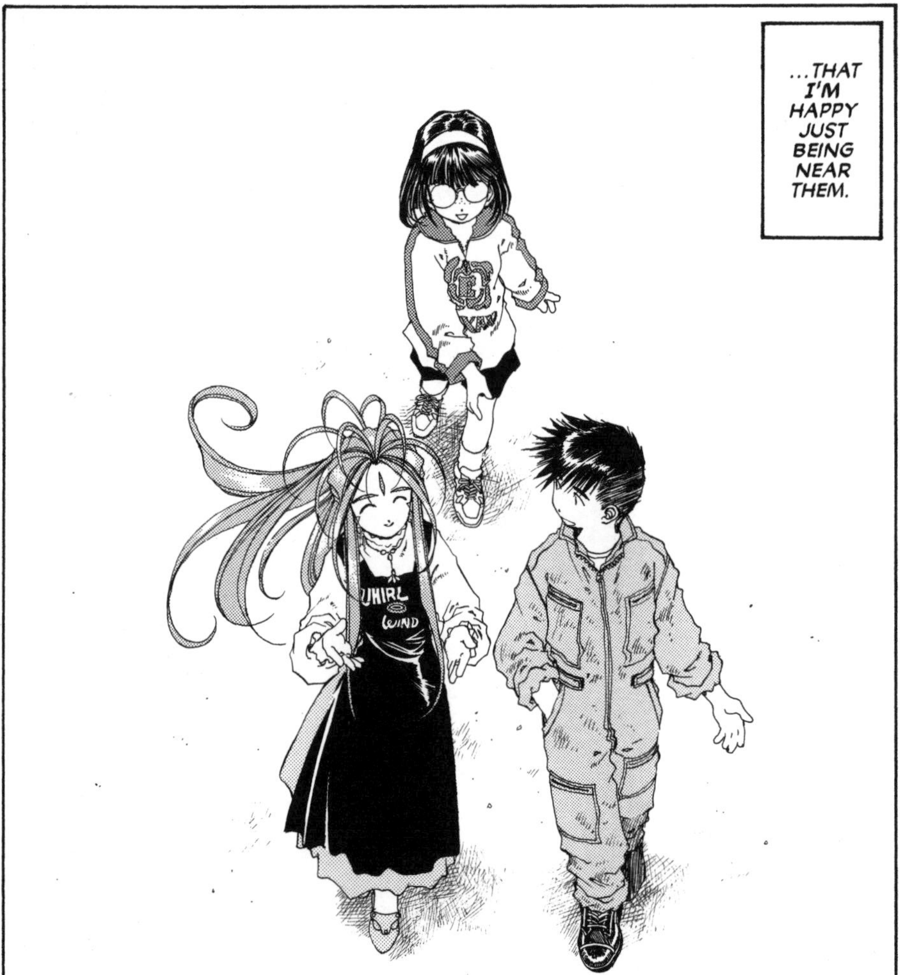
...THAT I'M HAPPY JUST BEING NEAR THEM.
WHIRL WIND

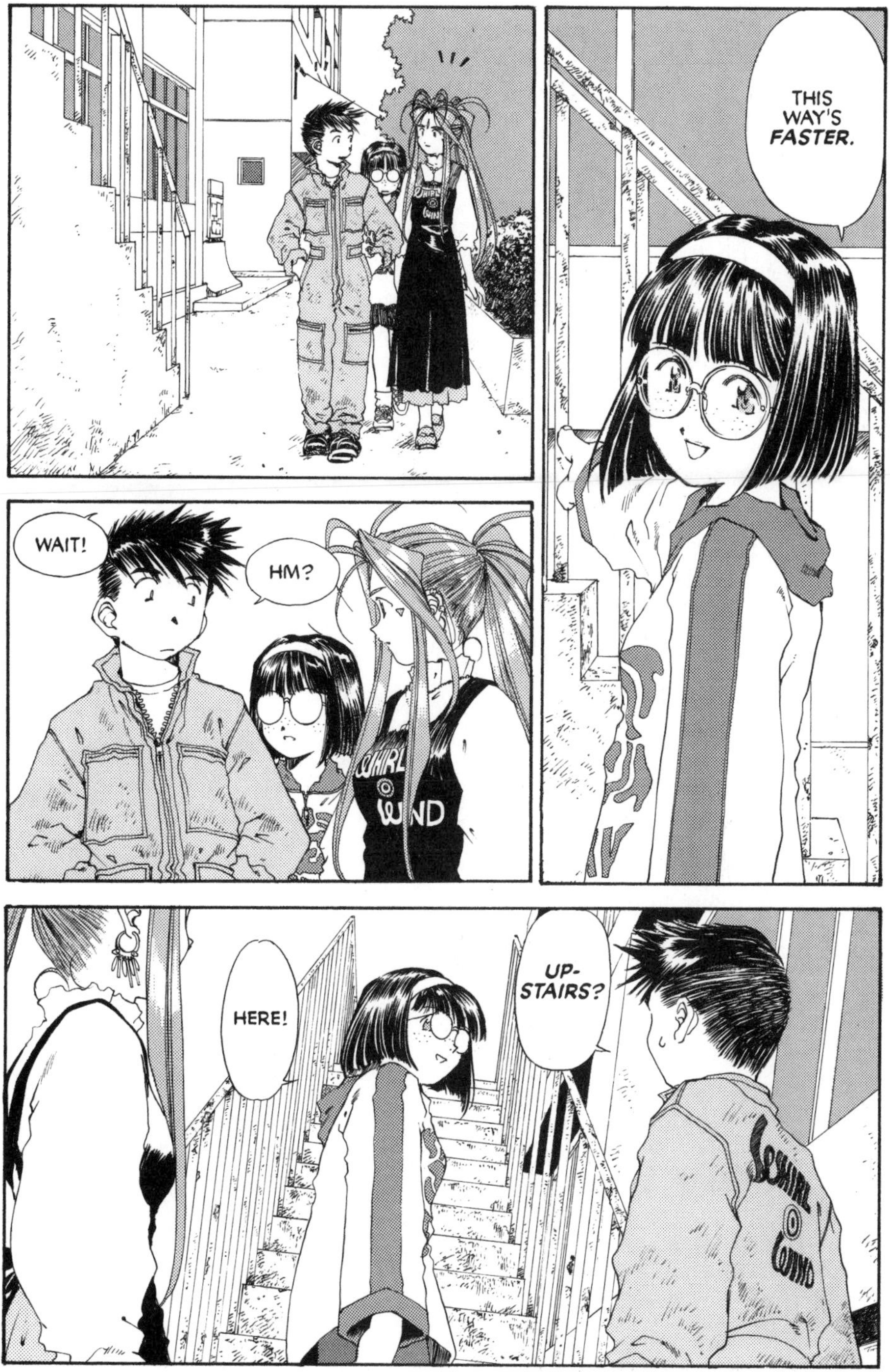
THIS WAY'S FASTER.
WAIT!
HM?
UP-STAIRS?
HERE!

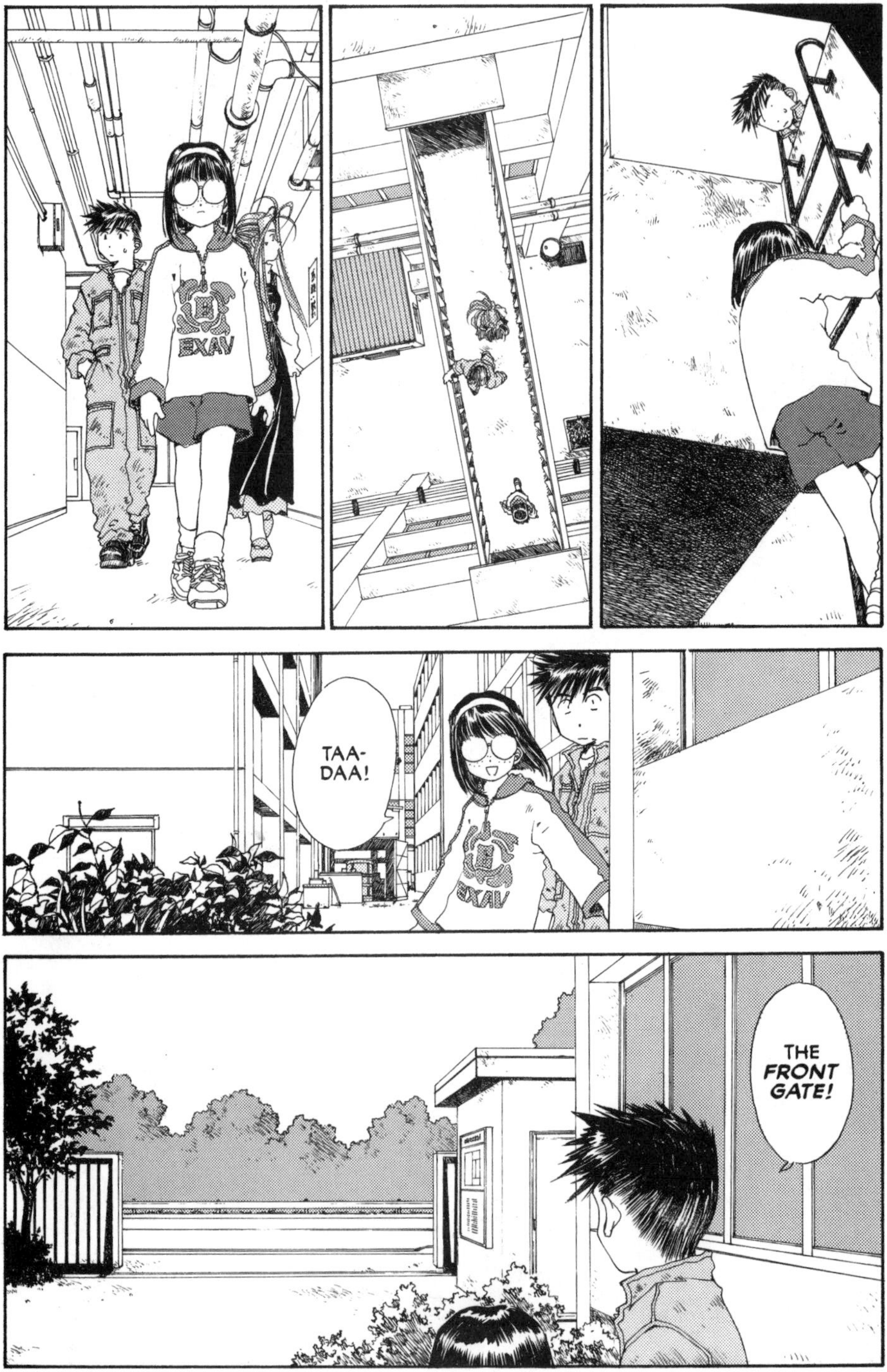

EXAV
TAA-DAA!
EXAV
THE FRONT GATE!

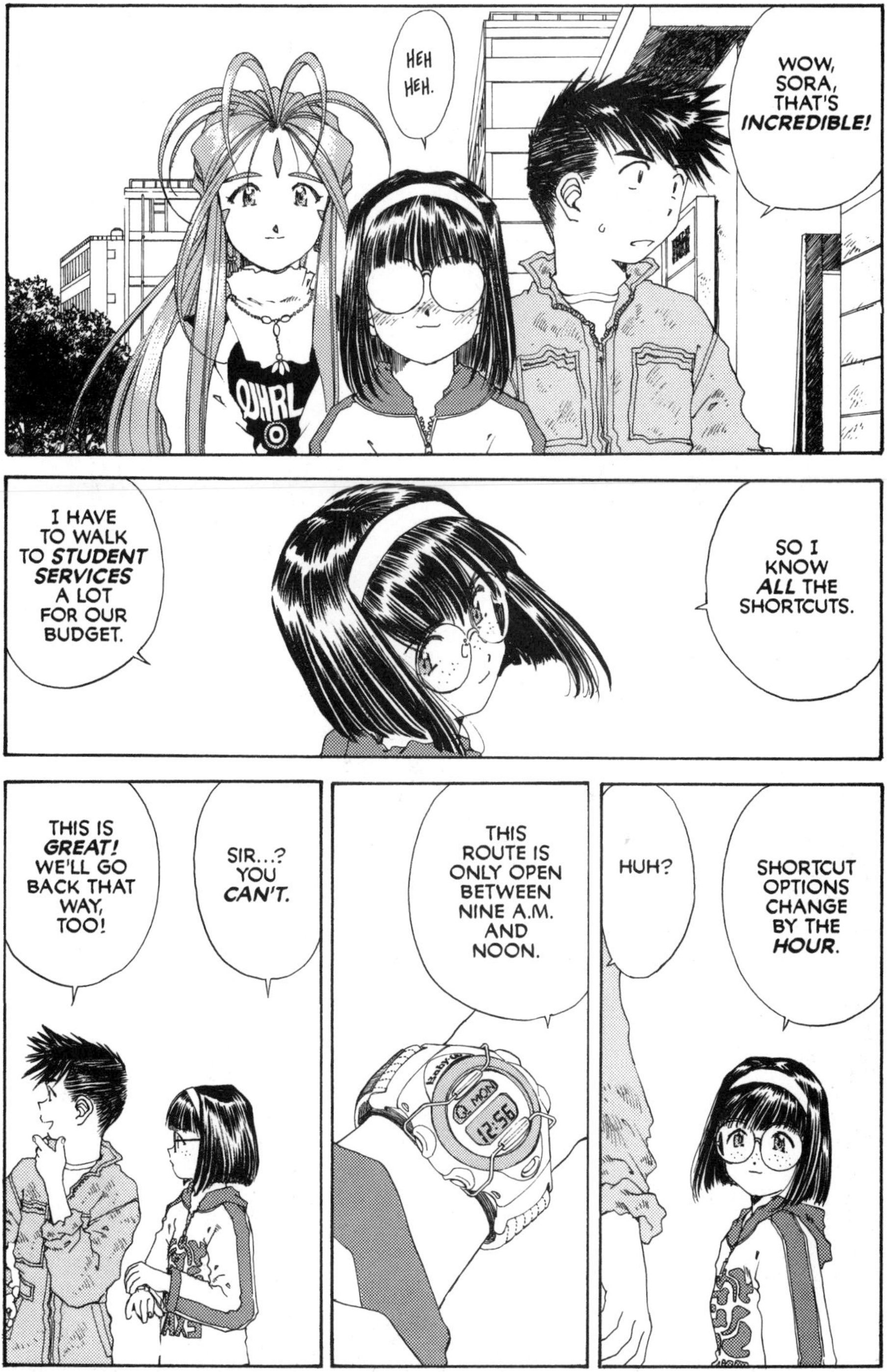
HEH HEH.
WOW, SORA, THAT'S *INCREDIBLE!*
I HAVE TO WALK TO *STUDENT SERVICES* A LOT FOR OUR BUDGET.
SO I KNOW *ALL* THE SHORTCUTS.
THIS IS *GREAT!* WE'LL GO BACK THAT WAY, TOO!
SIR...? YOU *CAN'T.*
THIS ROUTE IS ONLY OPEN BETWEEN NINE A.M. AND NOON.
HUH?
SHORTCUT OPTIONS CHANGE BY THE *HOUR*.

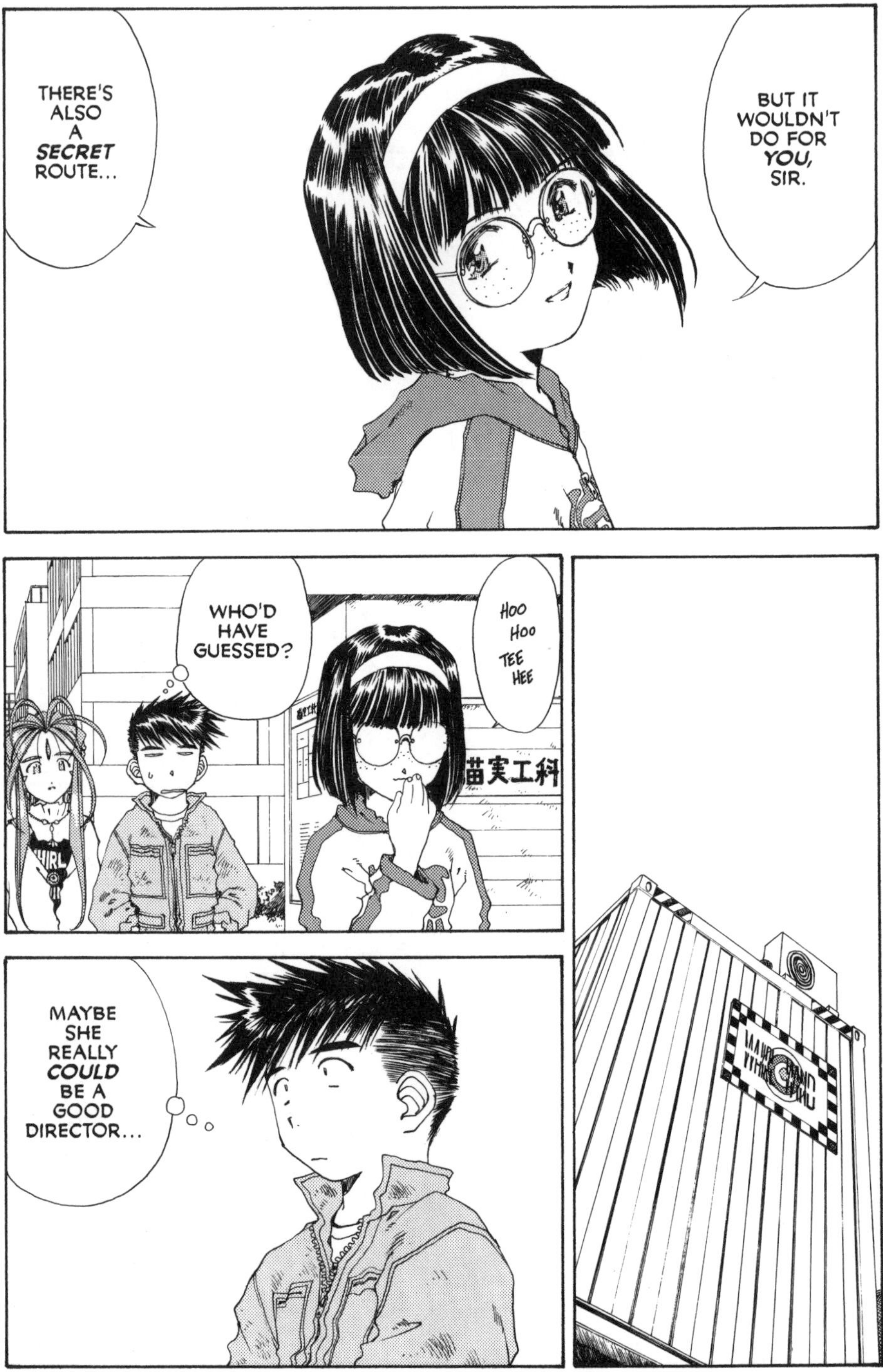
THERE'S ALSO A *SECRET* ROUTE...
BUT IT WOULDN'T DO FOR *YOU,* SIR.
WHO'D HAVE GUESSED?
HOO HOO TEE HEE
MAYBE SHE REALLY *COULD* BE A GOOD DIRECTOR...

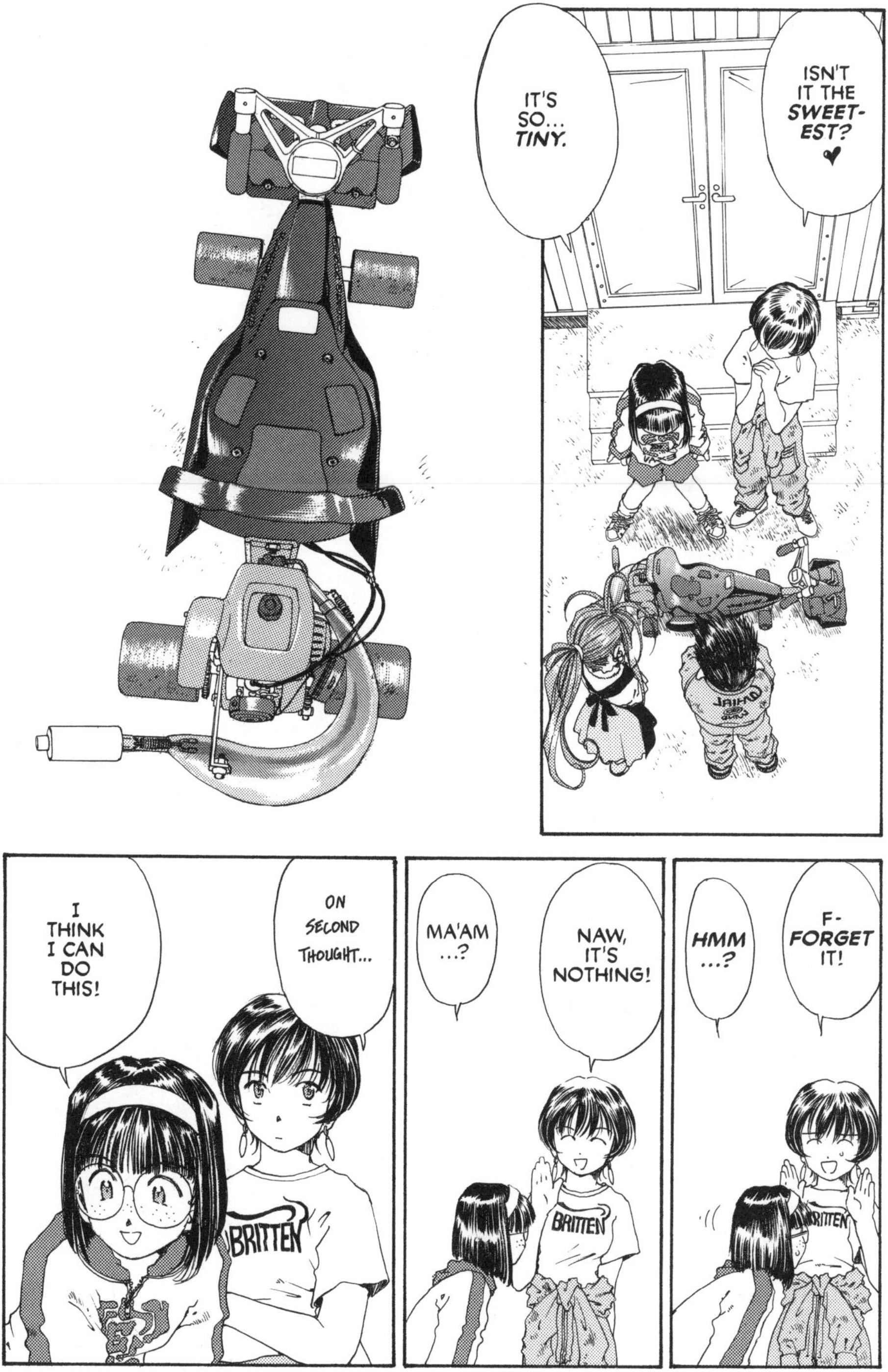
ISN'T IT THE SWEETEST? ♥
IT'S SO... TINY.
F-FORGET IT!
HMM...?
NAW, IT'S NOTHING!
MA'AM...?
ON SECOND THOUGHT...
I THINK I CAN DO THIS!

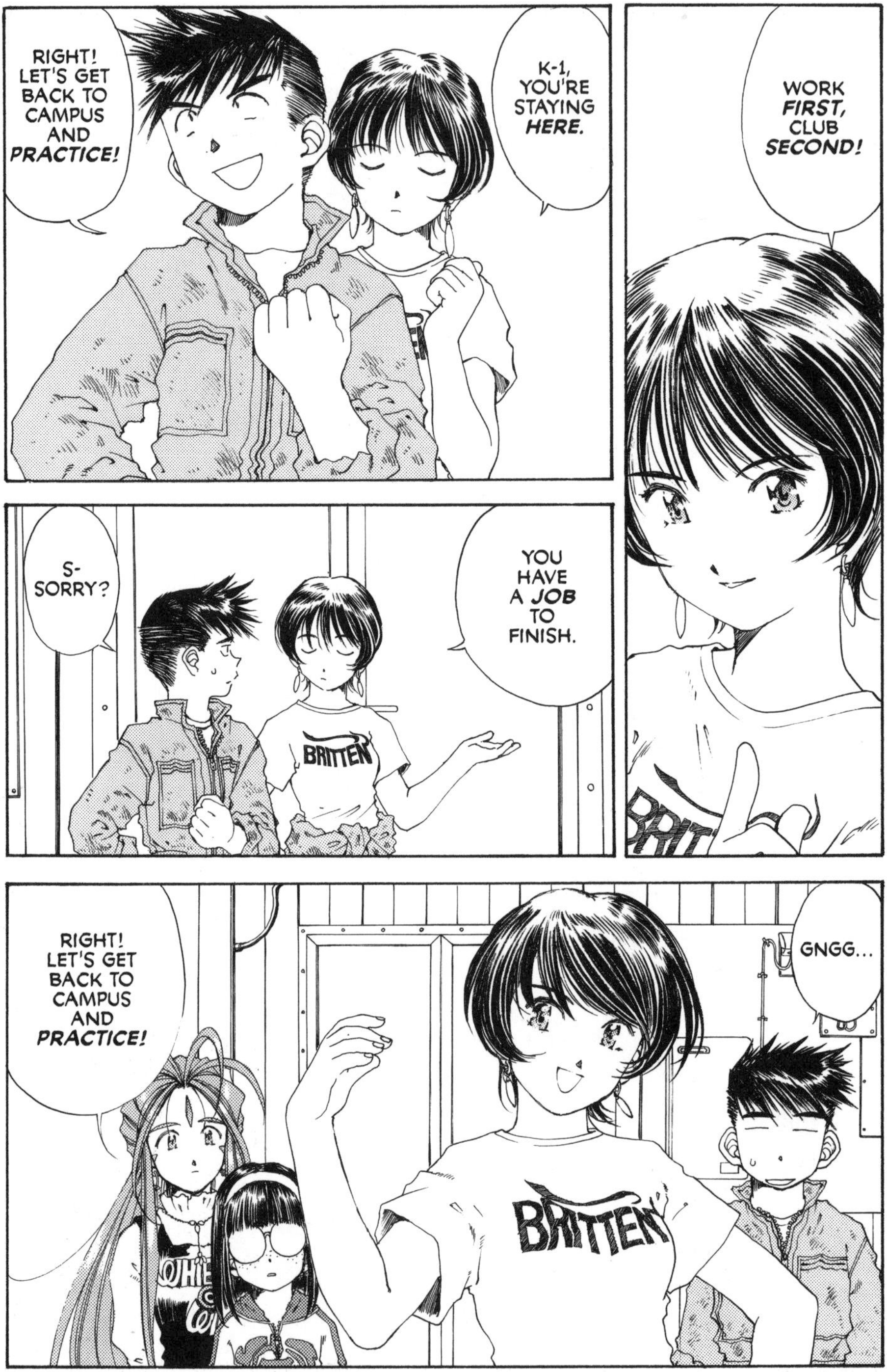
RIGHT! LET'S GET BACK TO CAMPUS AND PRACTICE!
K-1, YOU'RE STAYING HERE.
S-SORRY?
YOU HAVE A JOB TO FINISH.
WORK FIRST, CLUB SECOND!
RIGHT! LET'S GET BACK TO CAMPUS AND PRACTICE!
GNGG...
BRITTEN

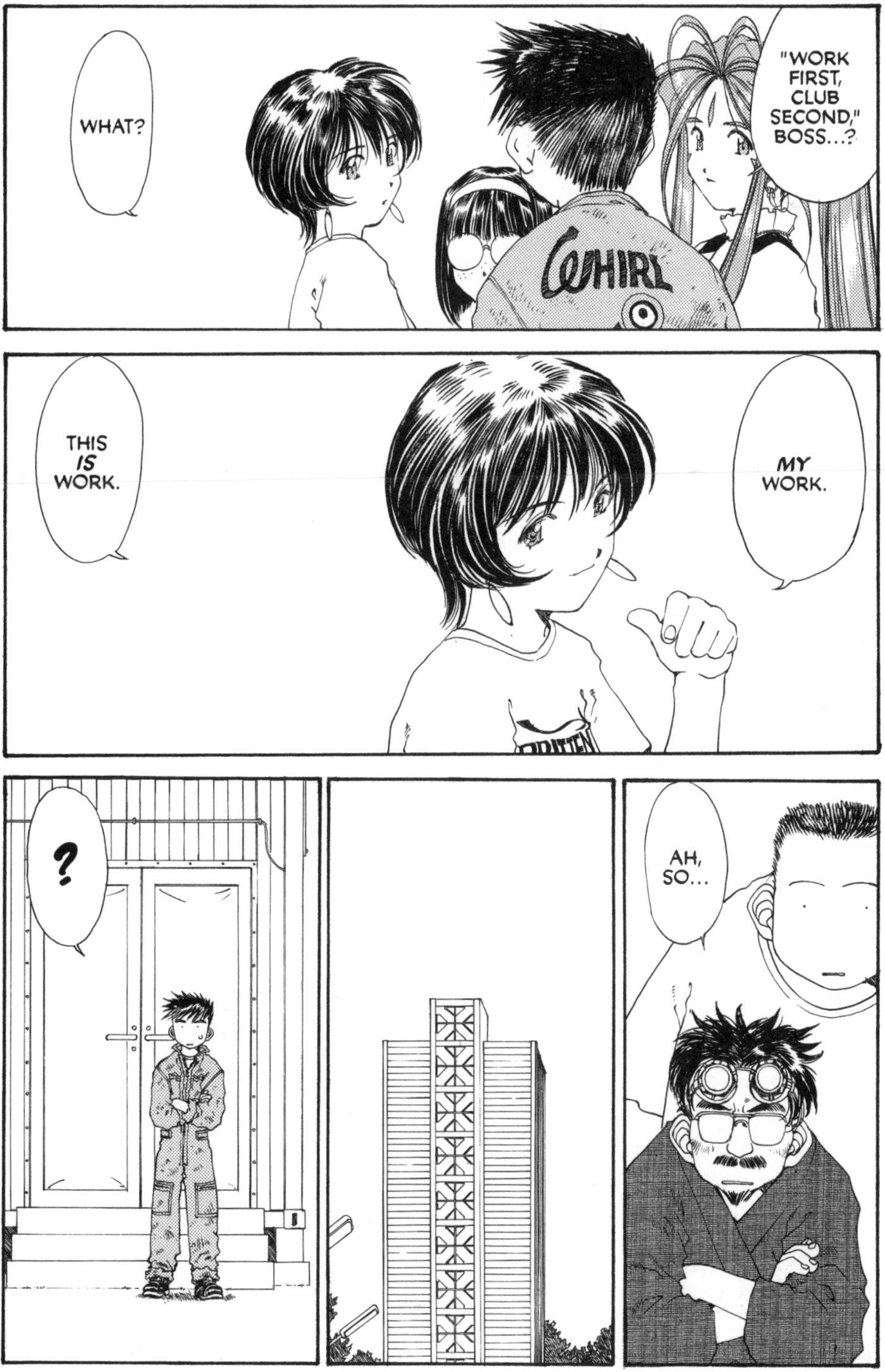
"WORK FIRST, CLUB SECOND," BOSS...?
WHAT?
MY WORK.
THIS IS WORK.
AH, SO...
?

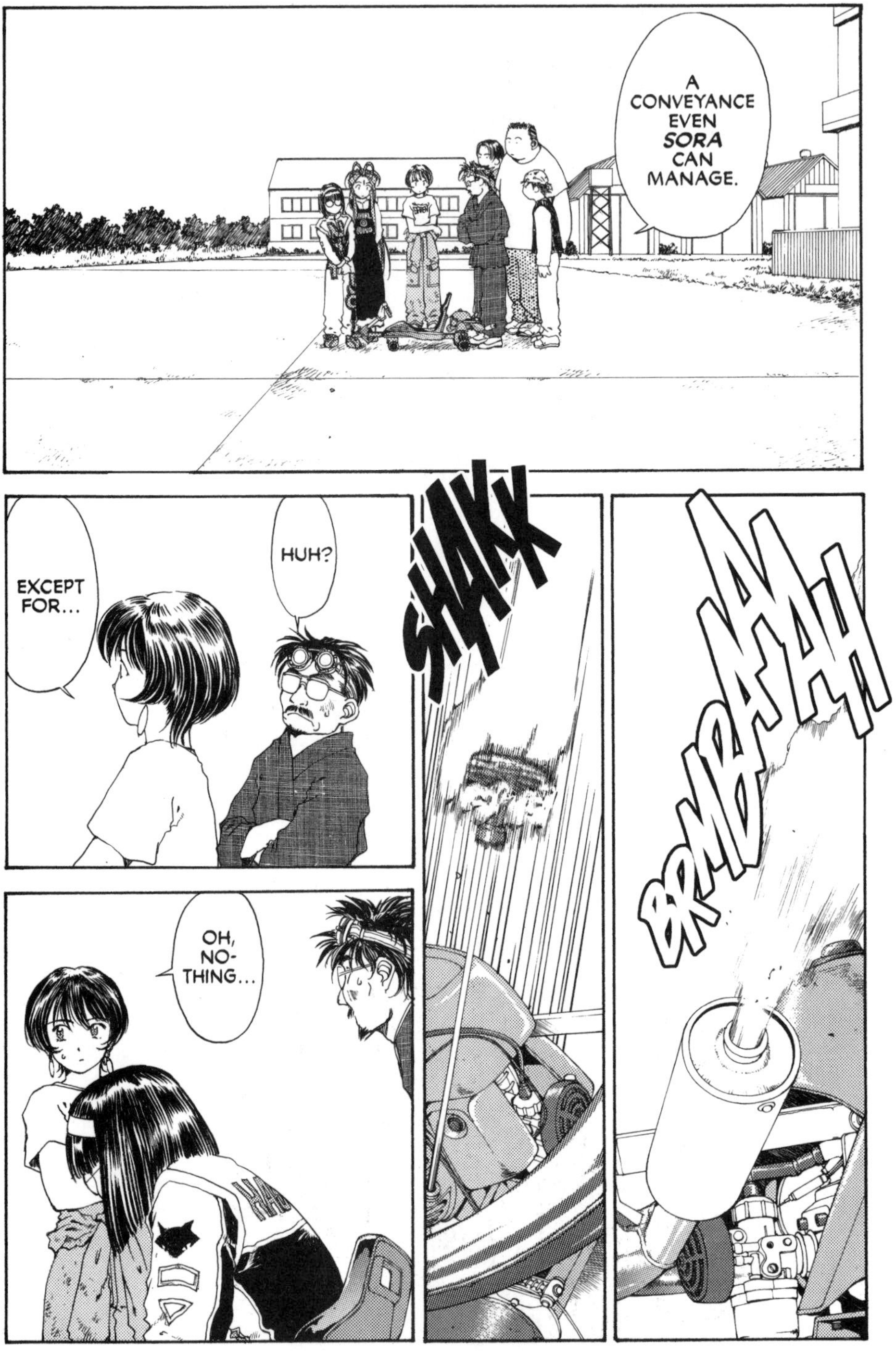
A CONVEYANCE EVEN *SORA* CAN MANAGE.
EXCEPT FOR...
HUH?
OH, NO-THING...
SHAKK
BRMBAAAH

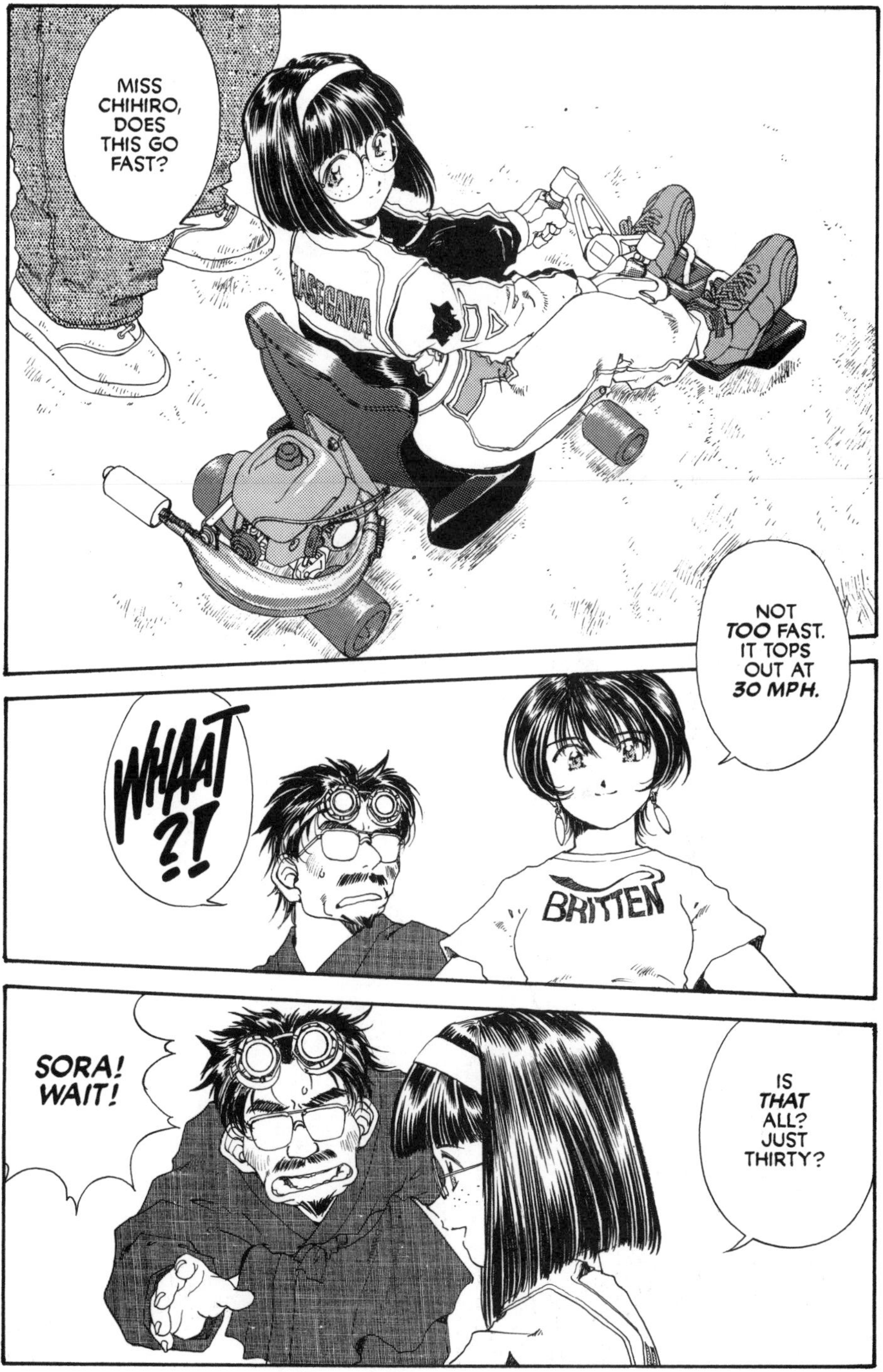
MISS CHIHIRO, DOES THIS GO FAST?
HASEGAWA
NOT *TOO* FAST. IT TOPS OUT AT ***30 MPH.***
WHAAT ?!
BRITTEN
IS *THAT* ALL? JUST THIRTY?
SORA! WAIT!

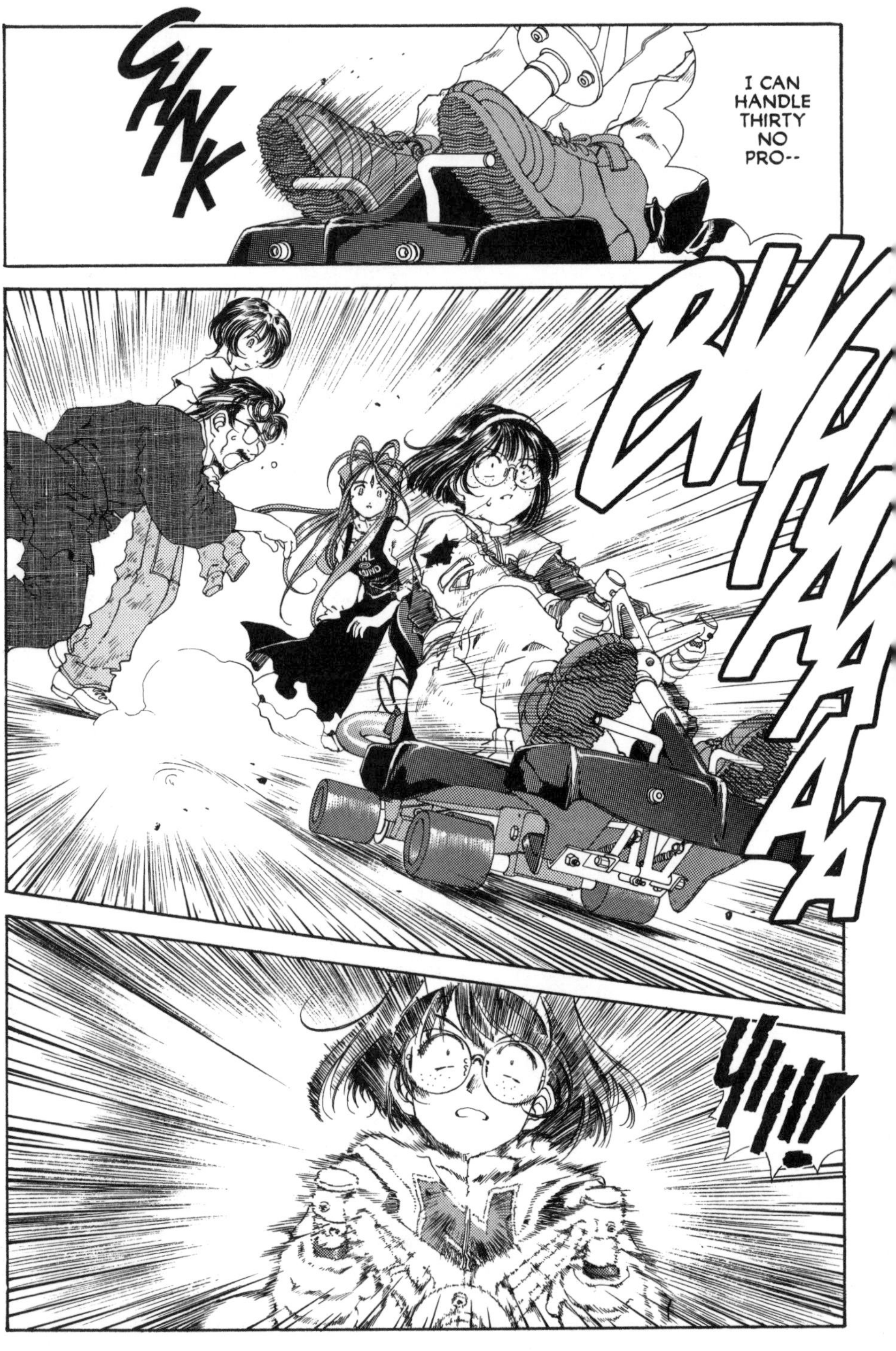
I CAN HANDLE THIRTY NO PRO--
CHINK
BWAAAAAA
YIII!!

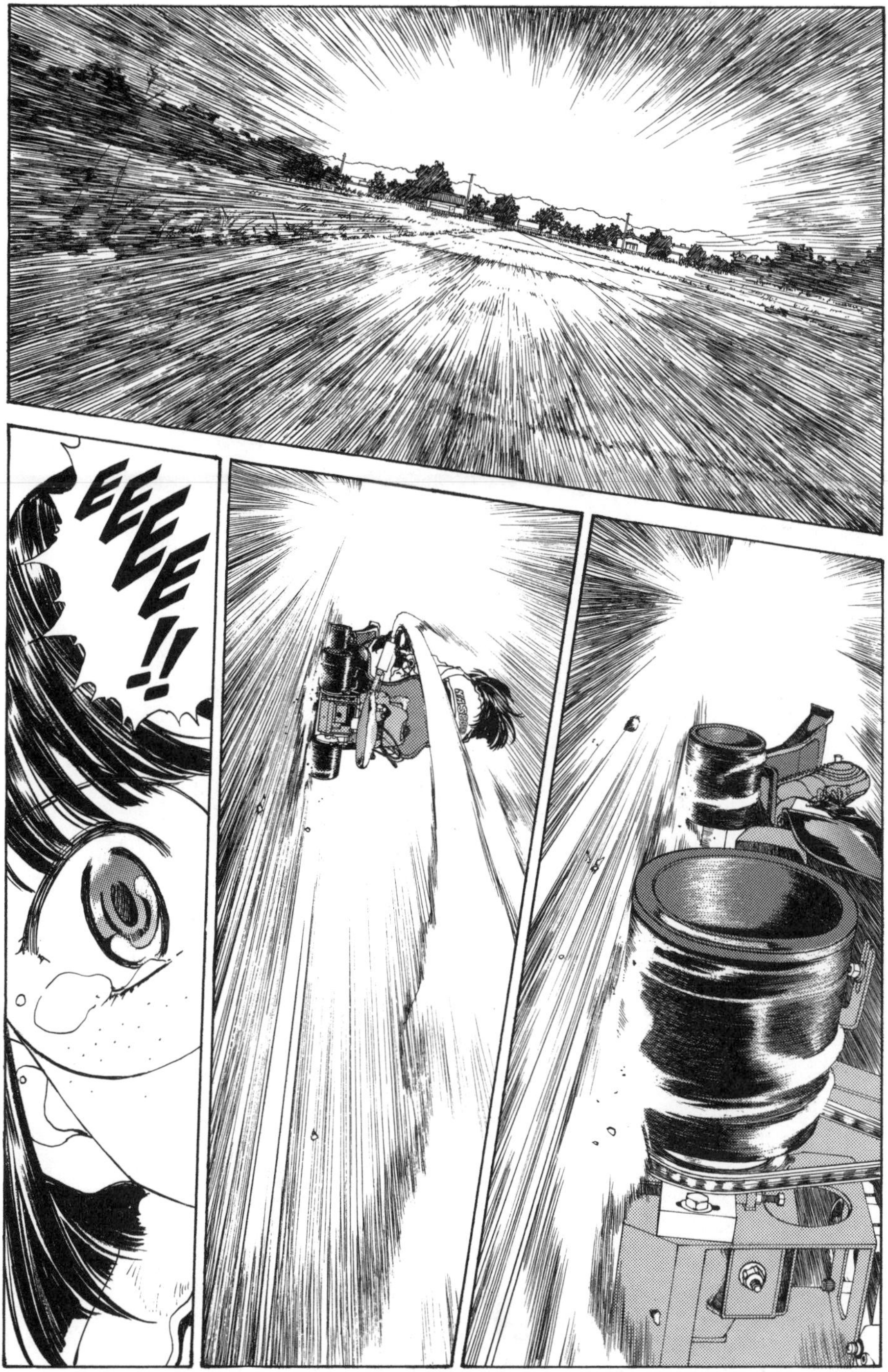
EEEE!!

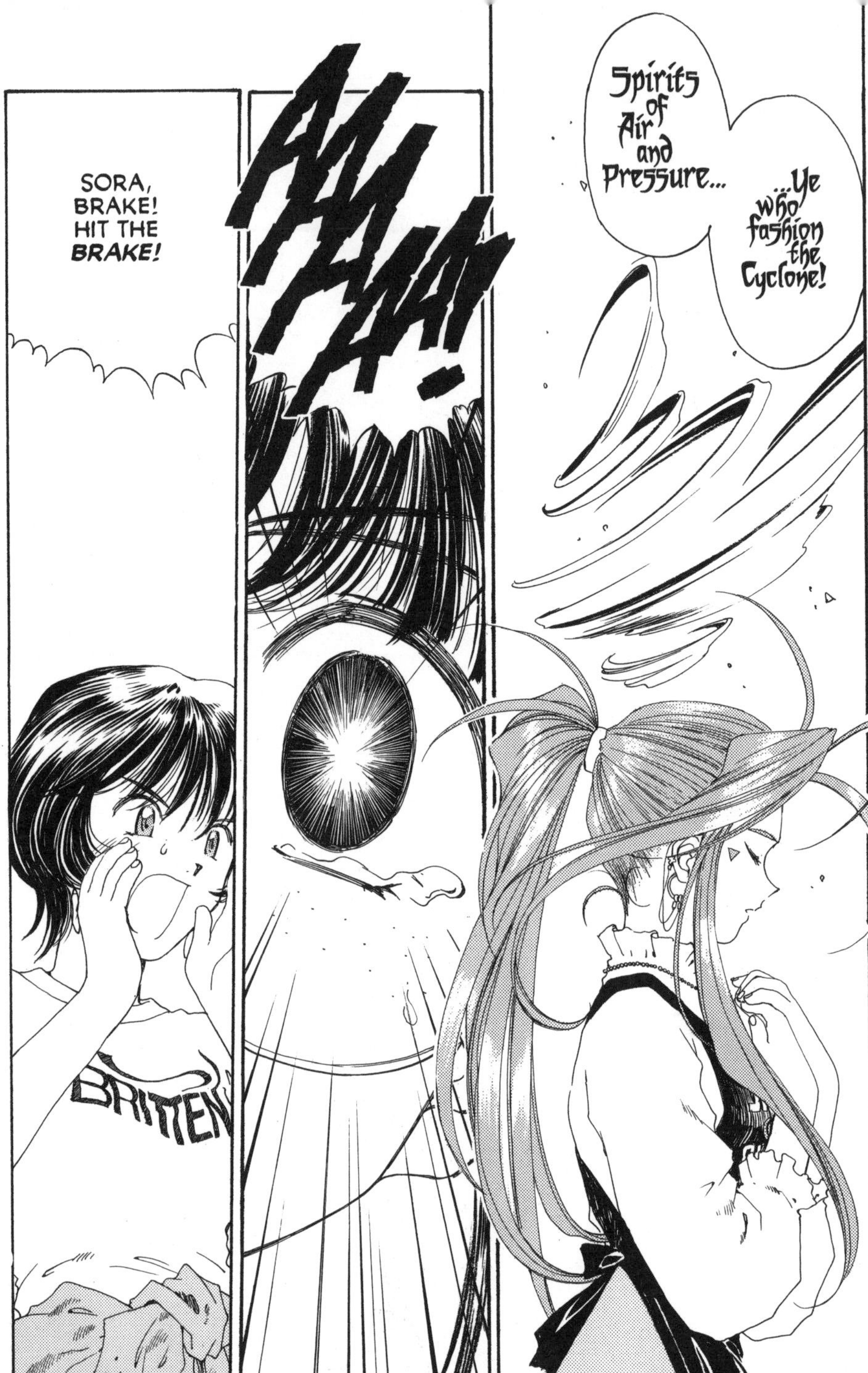
Spirits of Air and Pressure...
...Ye who fashion the Cyclone!
SORA, BRAKE! HIT THE *BRAKE!*

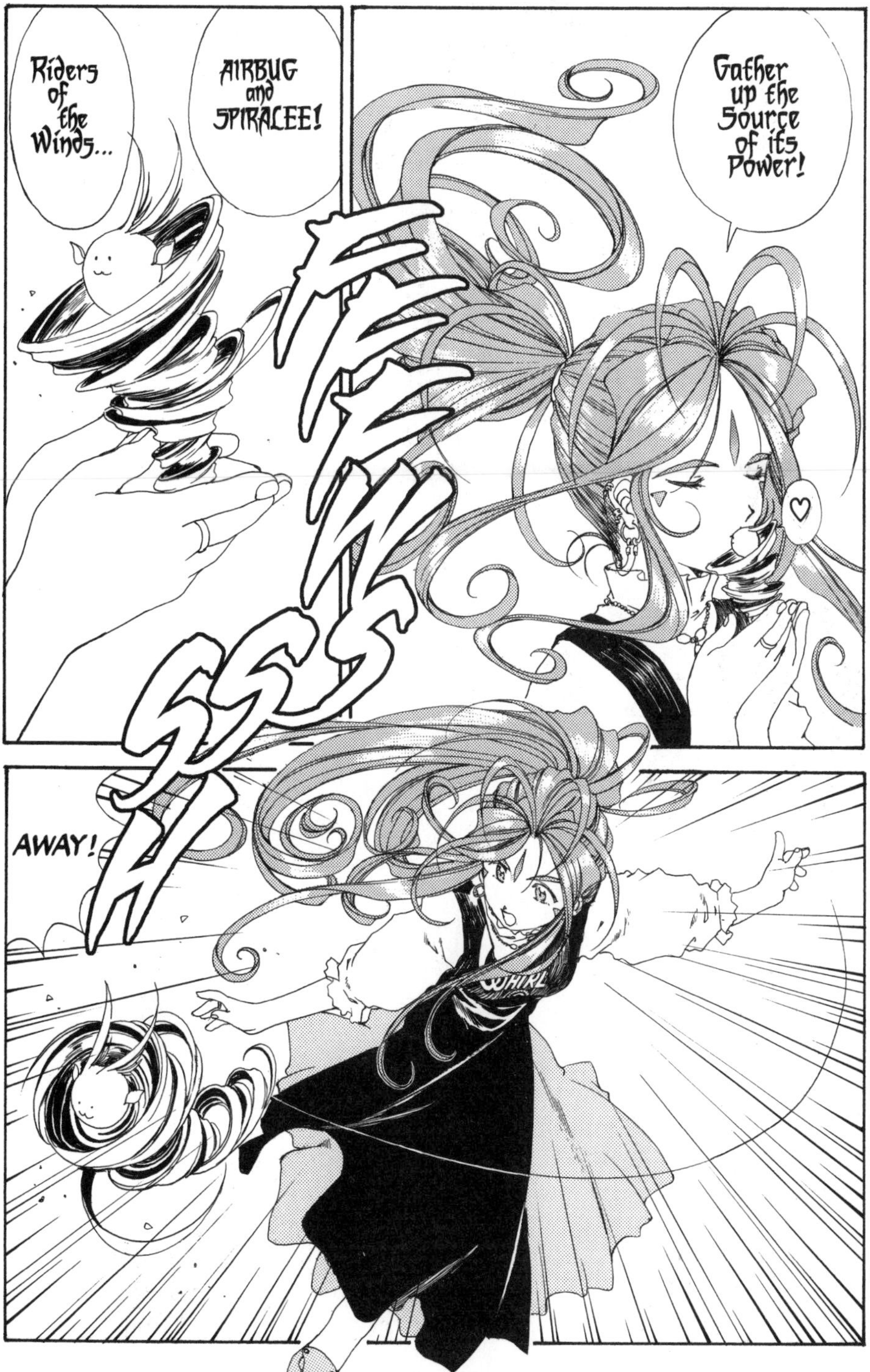
Riders of the Winds...
AIRBUG and SPIRALEE!
Gather up the Source of its Power!
FWSSSH
AWAY!

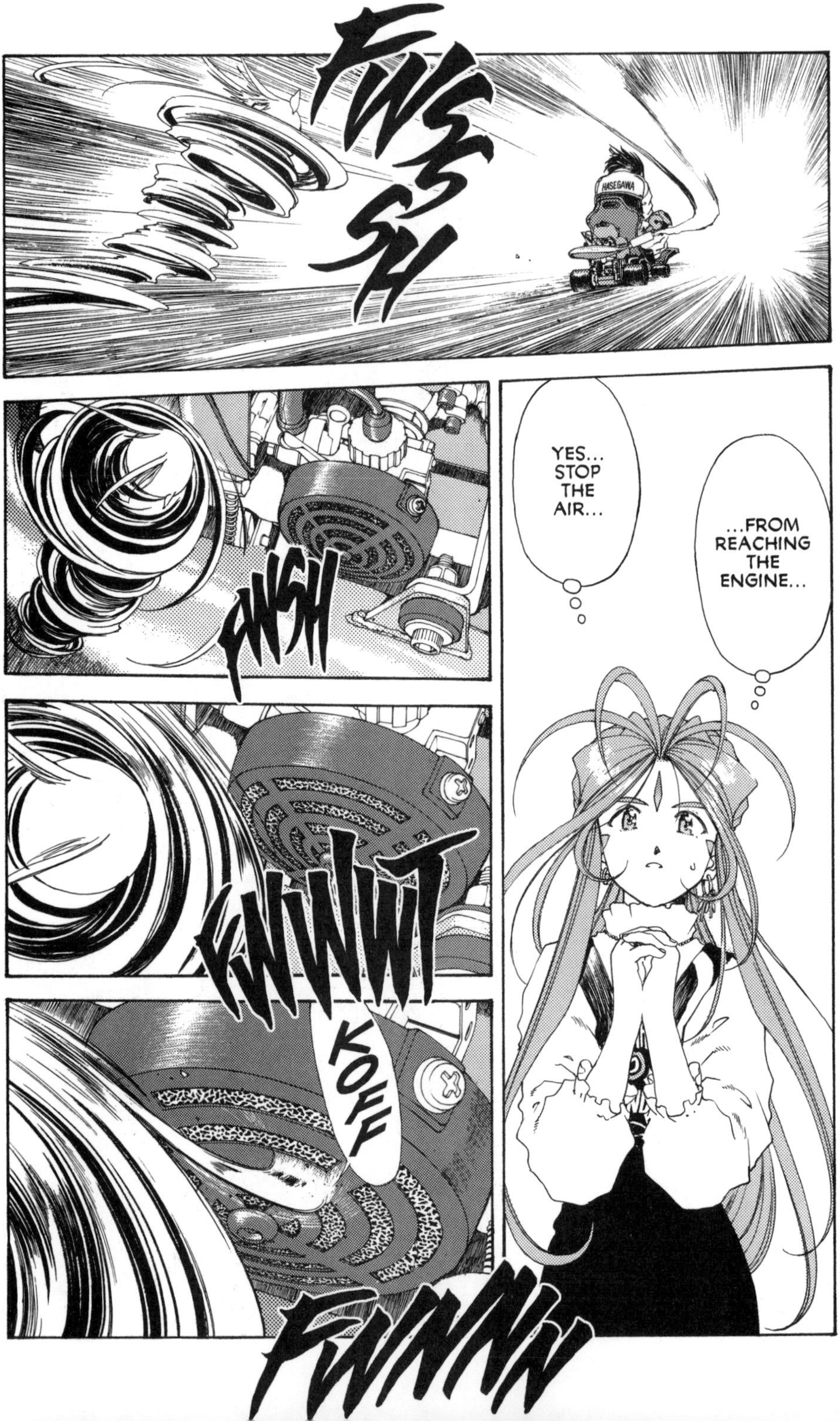
FWSSSH
HASEGAWA
YES... STOP THE AIR...
...FROM REACHING THE ENGINE...
FWSH
FWWWT
KOFF
FWWWW

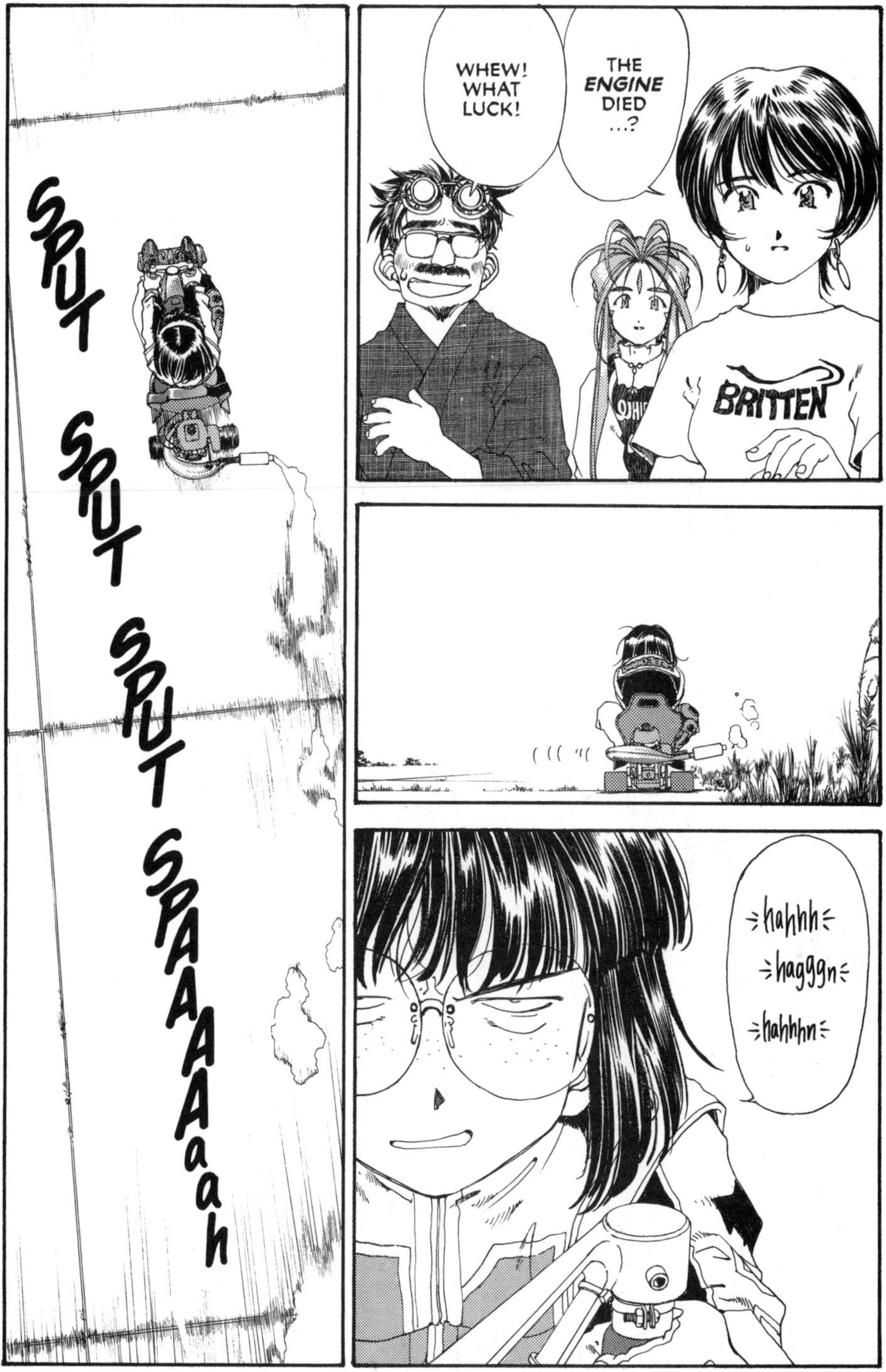
THE ENGINE DIED ...?
WHEW! WHAT LUCK!
BRITTEN
hahhh
hagggn
hahhhn
SPUT SPUT SPUT SPAAAAaaah

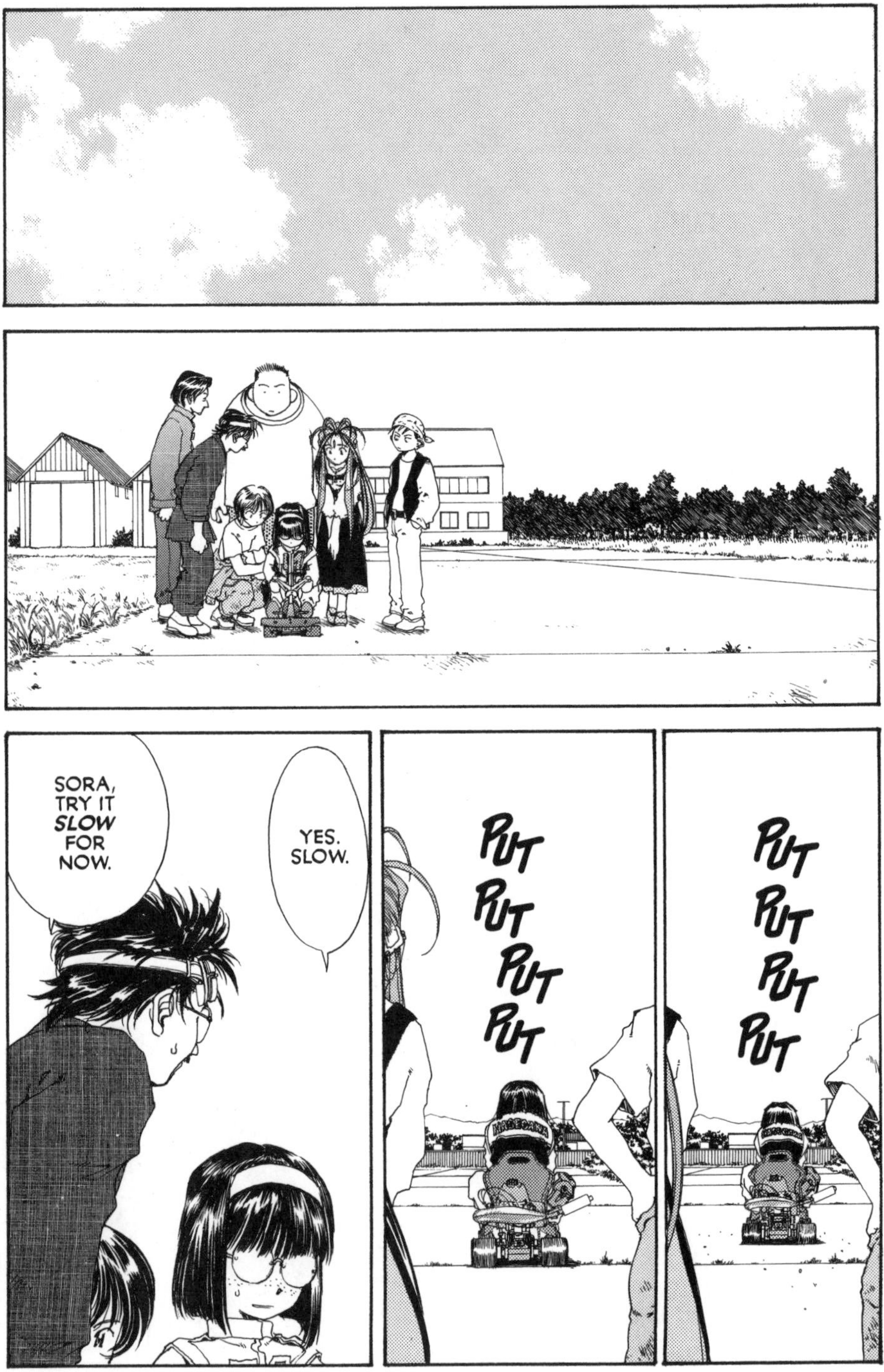
SORA, TRY IT *SLOW* FOR NOW.
YES. SLOW.
PUT PUT PUT PUT
PUT PUT PUT PUT

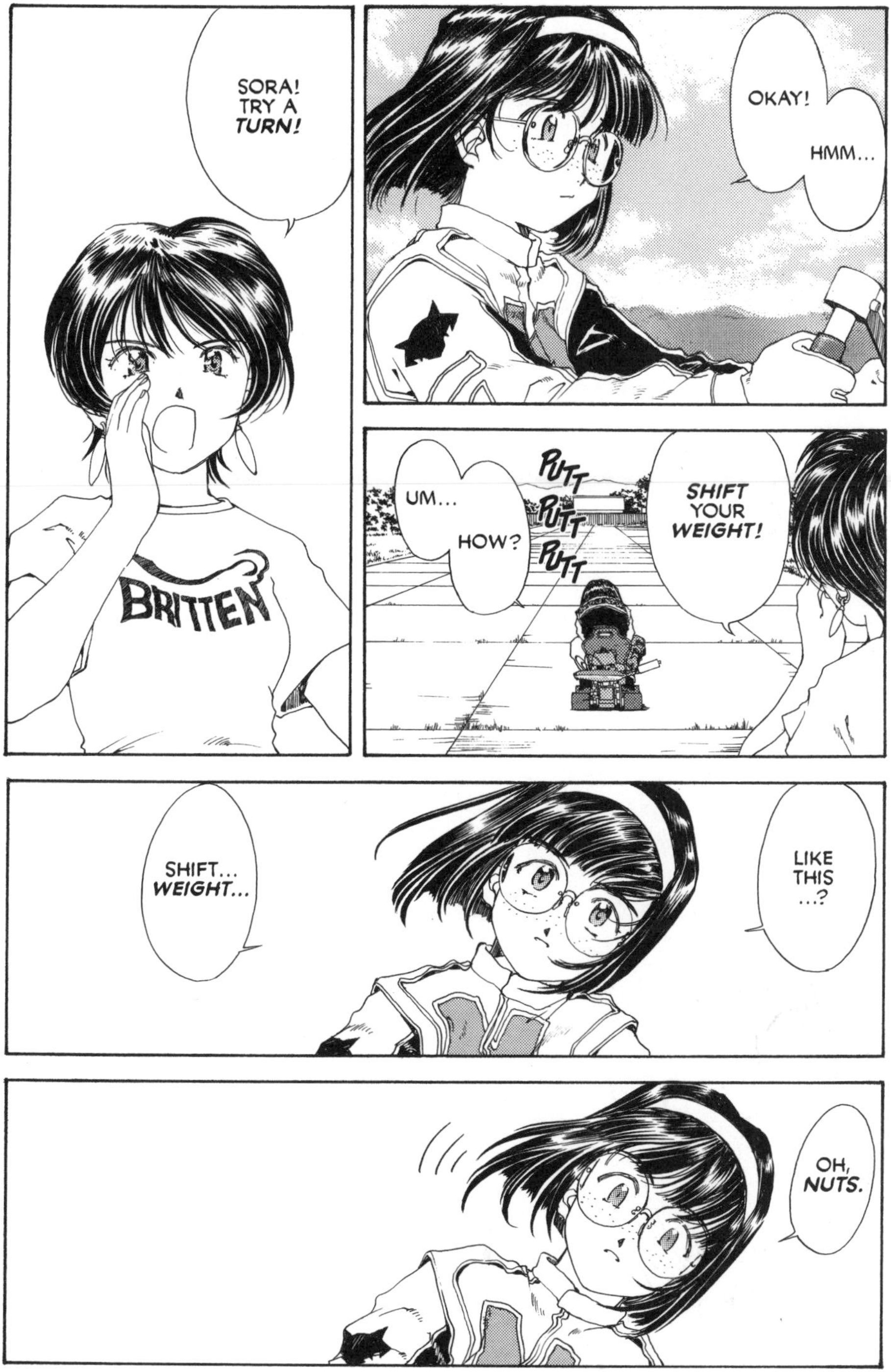
SORA! TRY A *TURN!*
OKAY!
HMM...
UM...
HOW?
PUTT PUTT PUTT
SHIFT YOUR *WEIGHT!*
SHIFT... *WEIGHT...*
LIKE THIS ...?
OH, *NUTS.*

RRR...
SKRASH
SORA, DEAR?
....

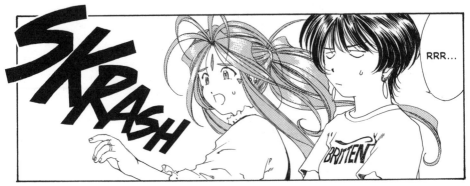

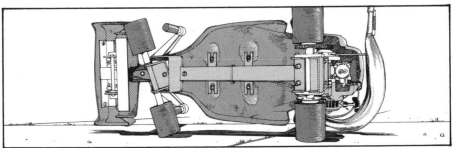

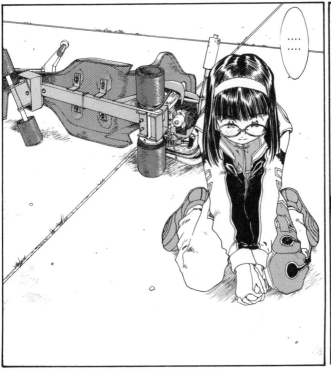

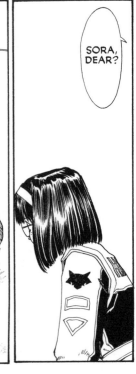

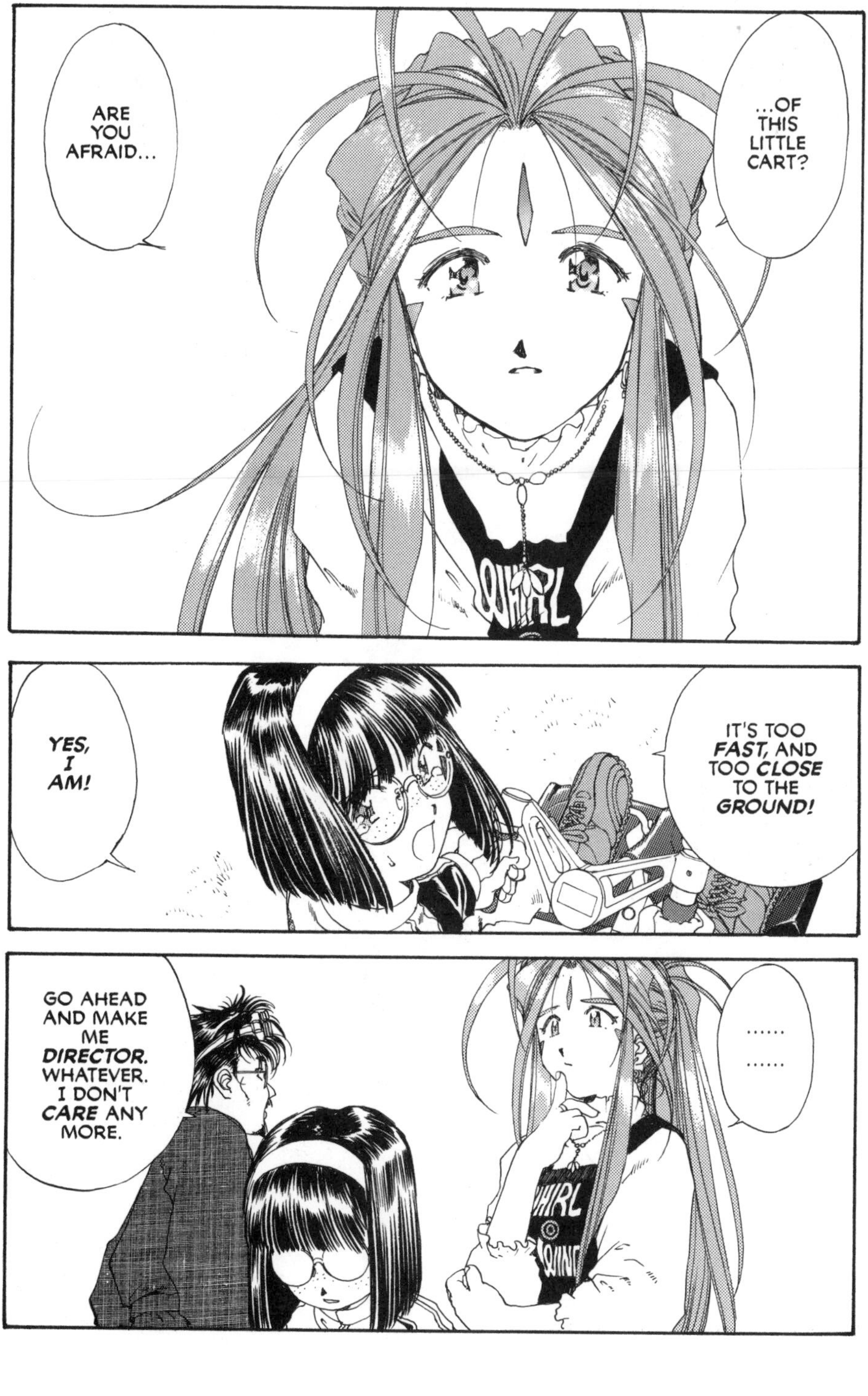
ARE YOU AFRAID...
...OF THIS LITTLE CART?
WHIRL
YES, I AM!
IT'S TOO FAST, AND TOO CLOSE TO THE GROUND!
GO AHEAD AND MAKE ME DIRECTOR. WHATEVER. I DON'T CARE ANY MORE.
......
......
WHIRL
WIND

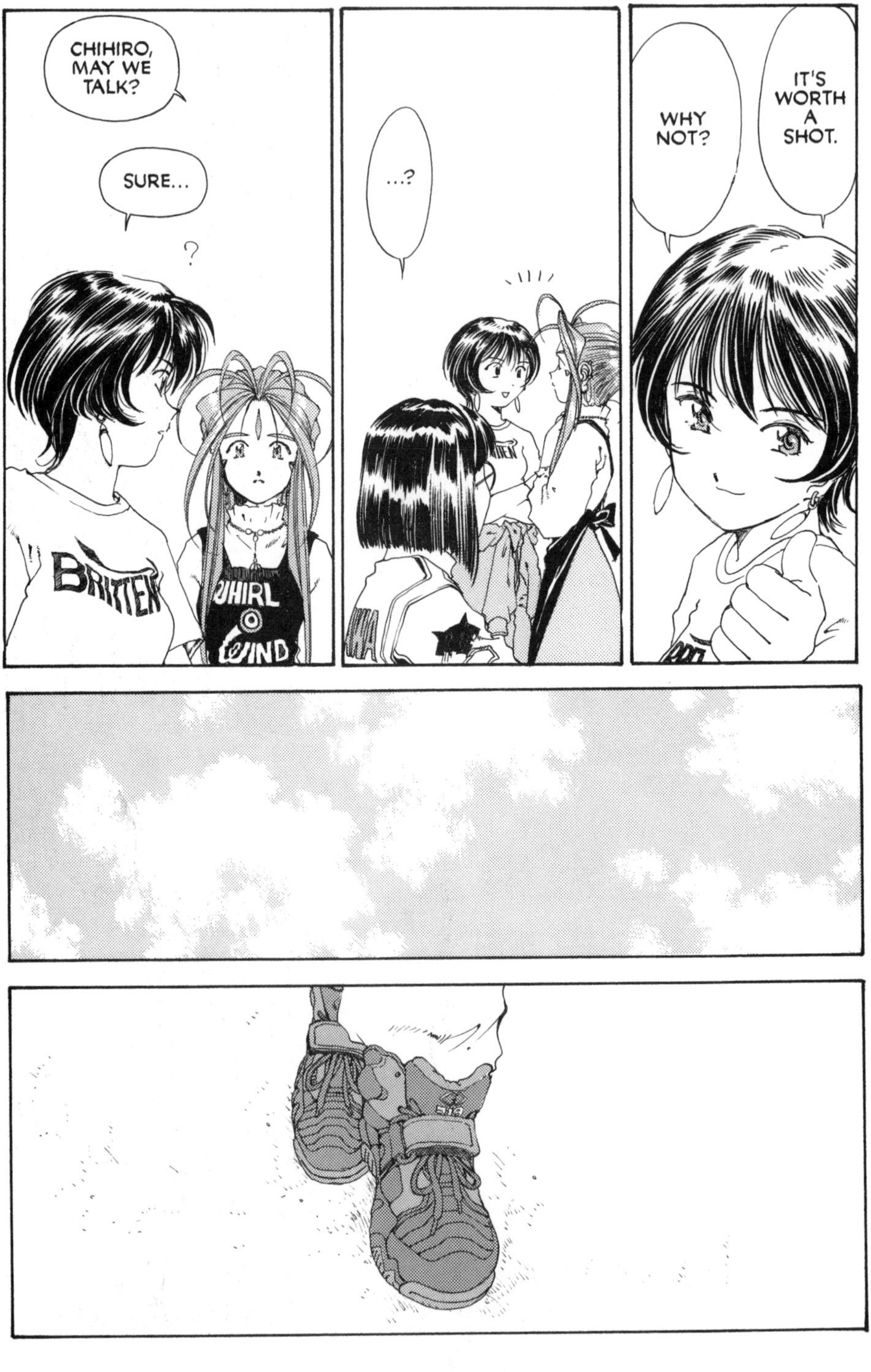
CHIHIRO, MAY WE TALK?
SURE...
?
...?
WHY NOT?
IT'S WORTH A SHOT.

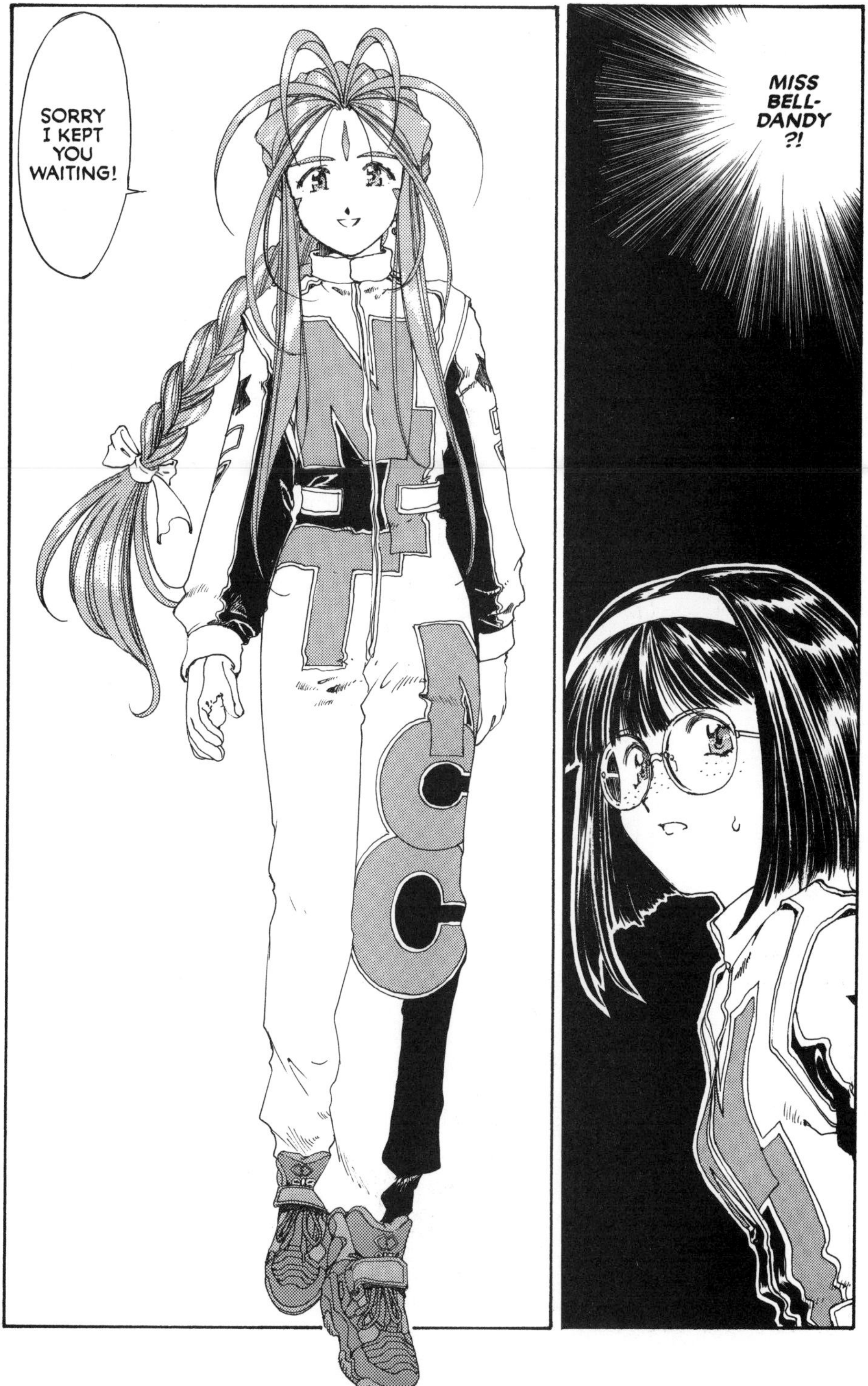
SORRY I KEPT YOU WAITING!
MISS BELL-DANDY?!

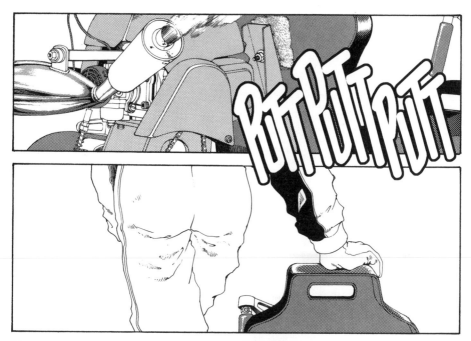

PUTT PUTT PUTT

NOW,
DEAR,
HOP
ON.

UH...

ON
...?

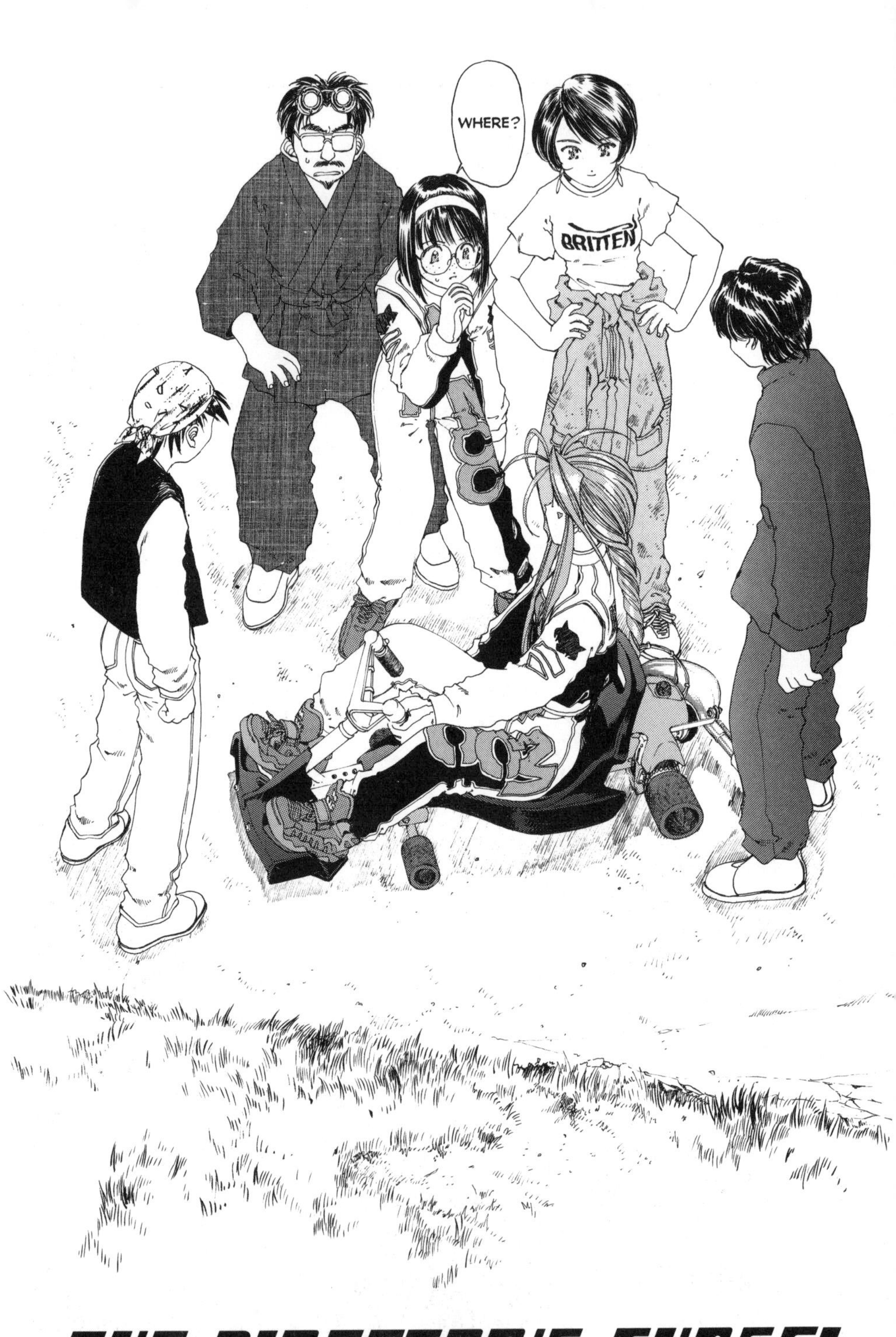
WHERE?
BRITTEN

THE DIRECTOR'S CURSE!

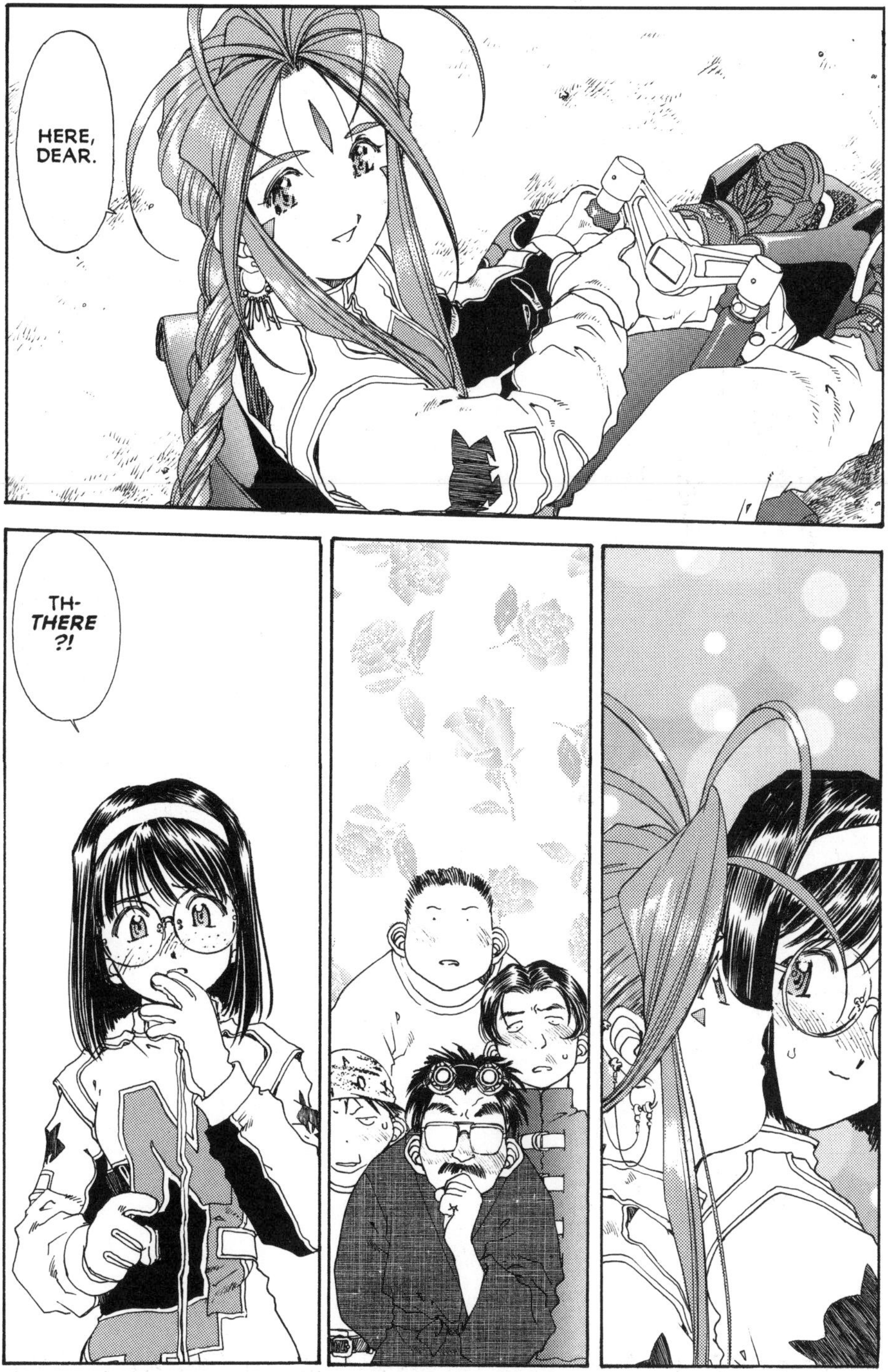
HERE, DEAR.
TH- THERE ?!

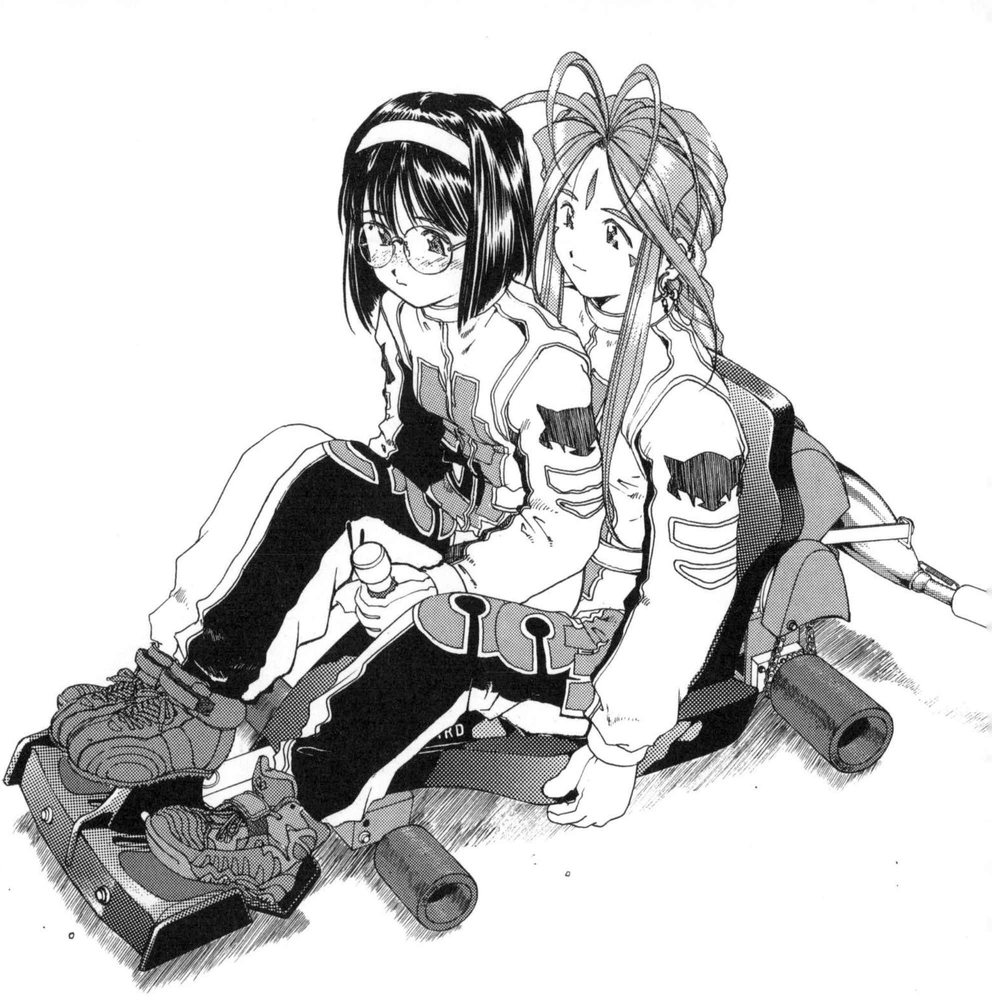

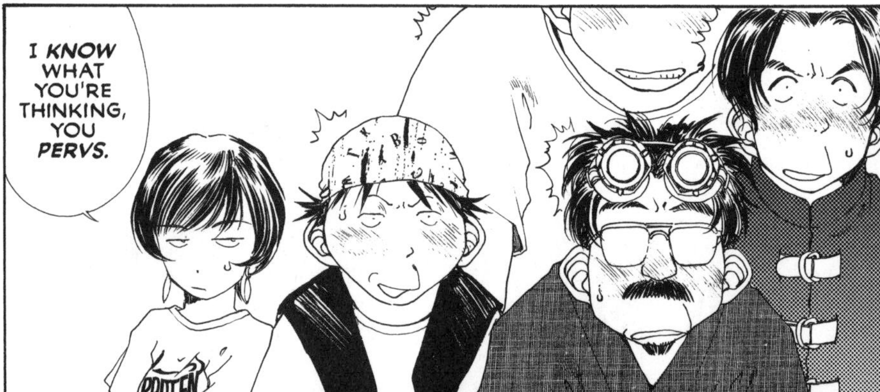
I KNOW WHAT YOU'RE THINKING, YOU PERVS.
BRITTEN

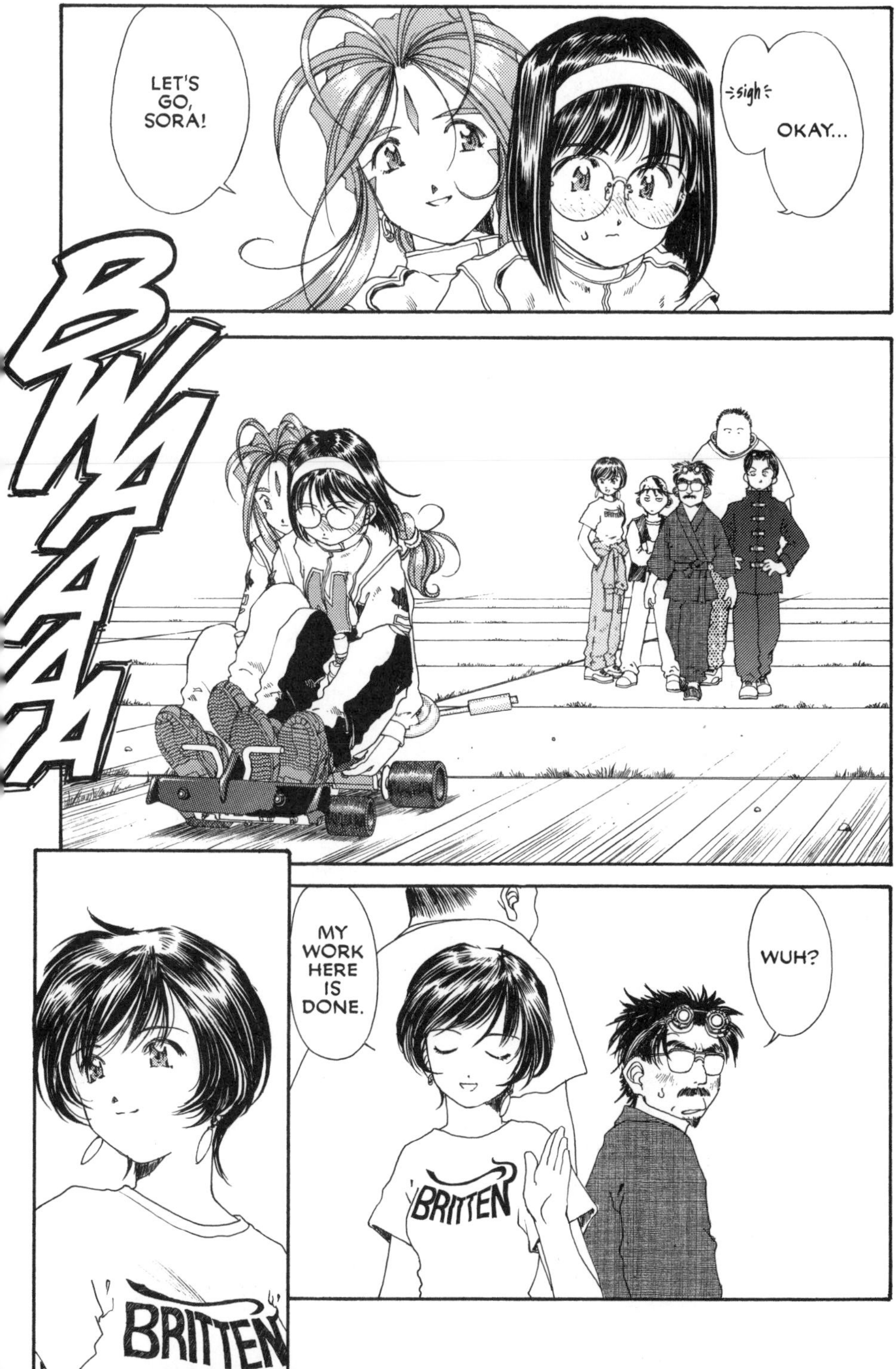
LET'S GO, SORA!
sigh
OKAY...
BWAAAA
MY WORK HERE IS DONE.
WUH?

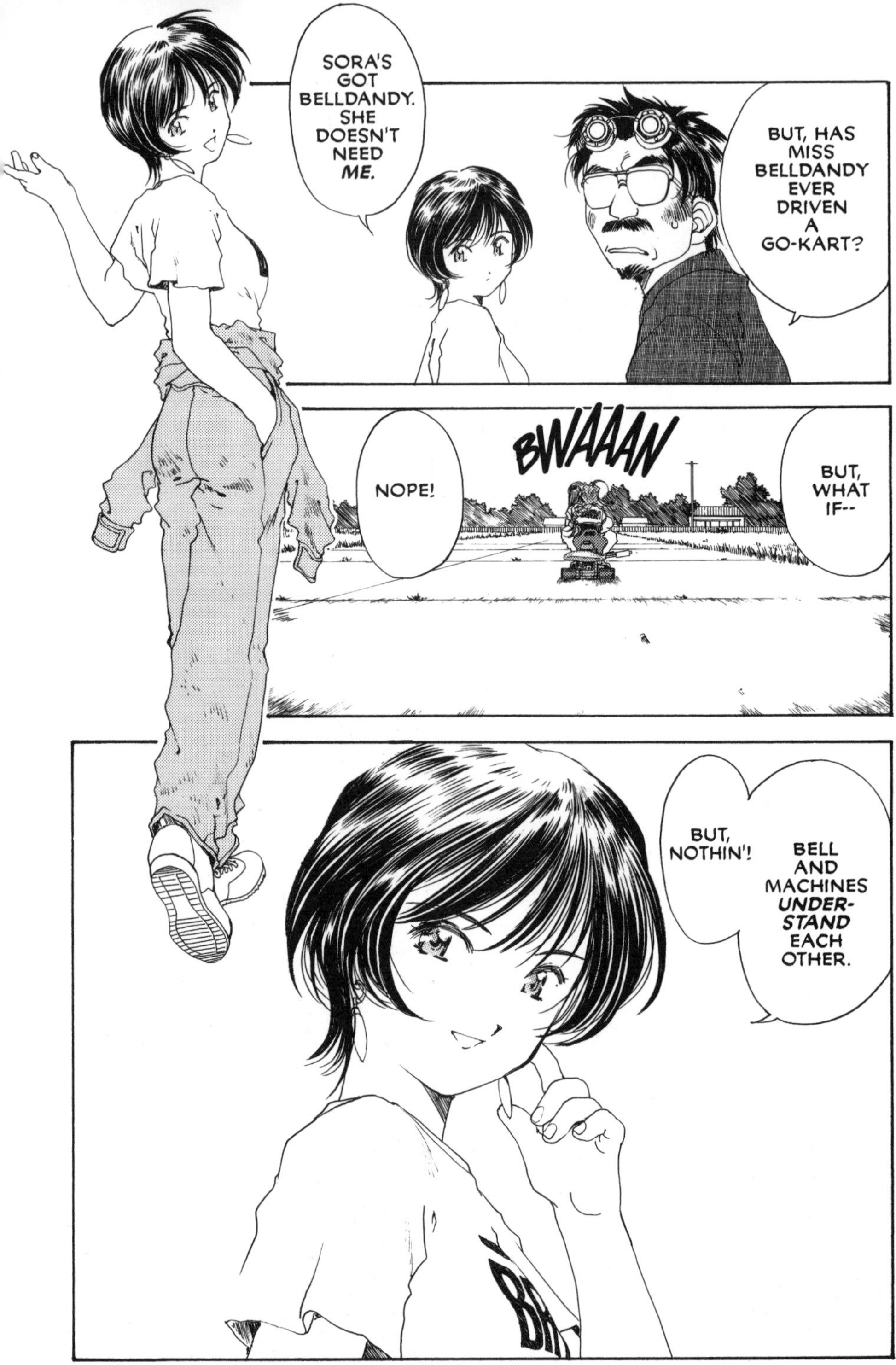
BUT, HAS MISS BELLDANDY EVER DRIVEN A GO-KART?
SORA'S GOT BELLDANDY. SHE DOESN'T NEED *ME.*
BUT, WHAT IF--
BWAAAN
NOPE!
BUT, NOTHIN'! BELL AND MACHINES *UNDERSTAND* EACH OTHER.

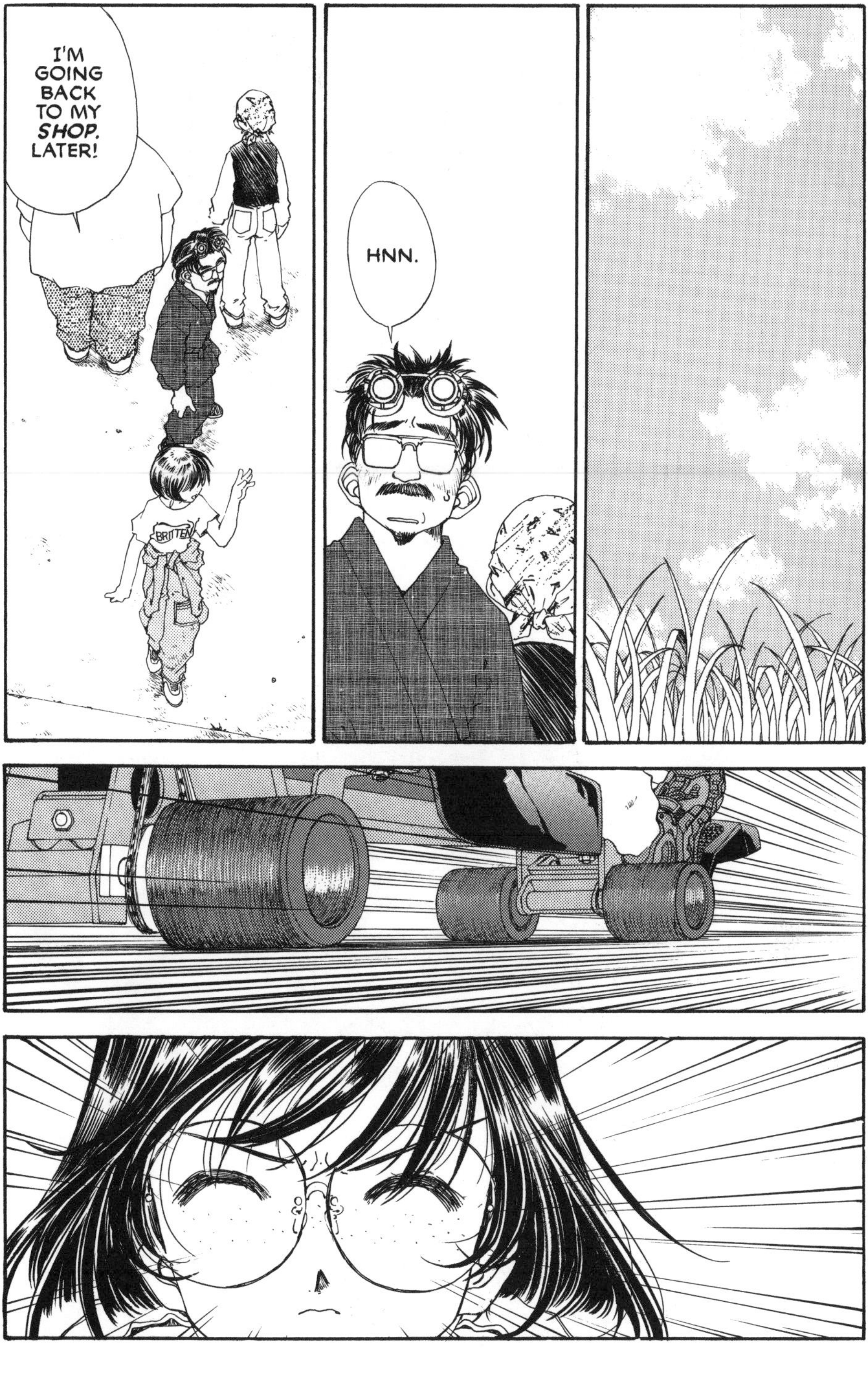
I'M GOING BACK TO MY *SHOP*. LATER!
BRITTEN
HNN.

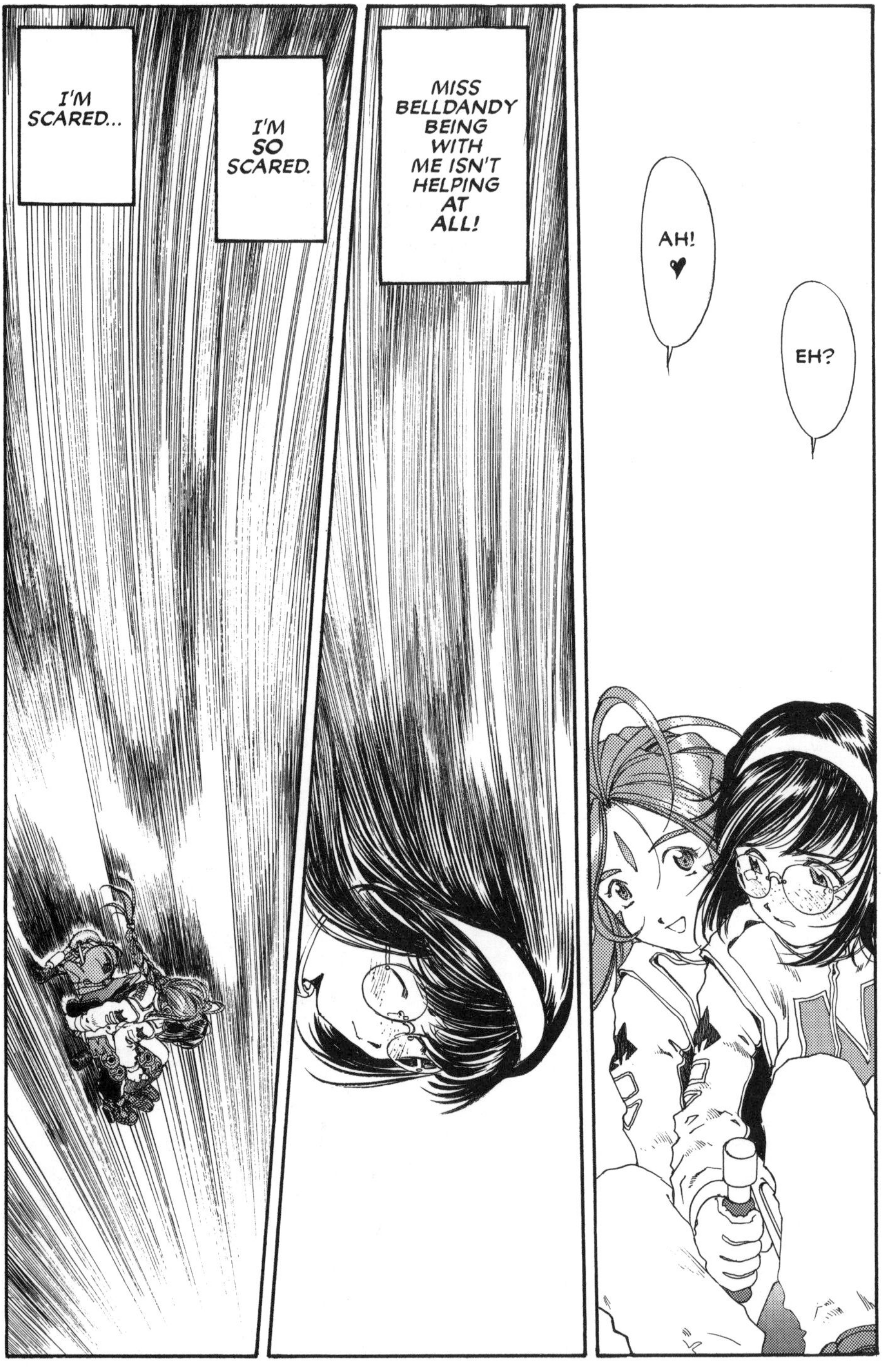
I'M SCARED...
I'M SO SCARED.
MISS BELLDANDY BEING WITH ME ISN'T HELPING AT ALL!
AH! ♥
EH?

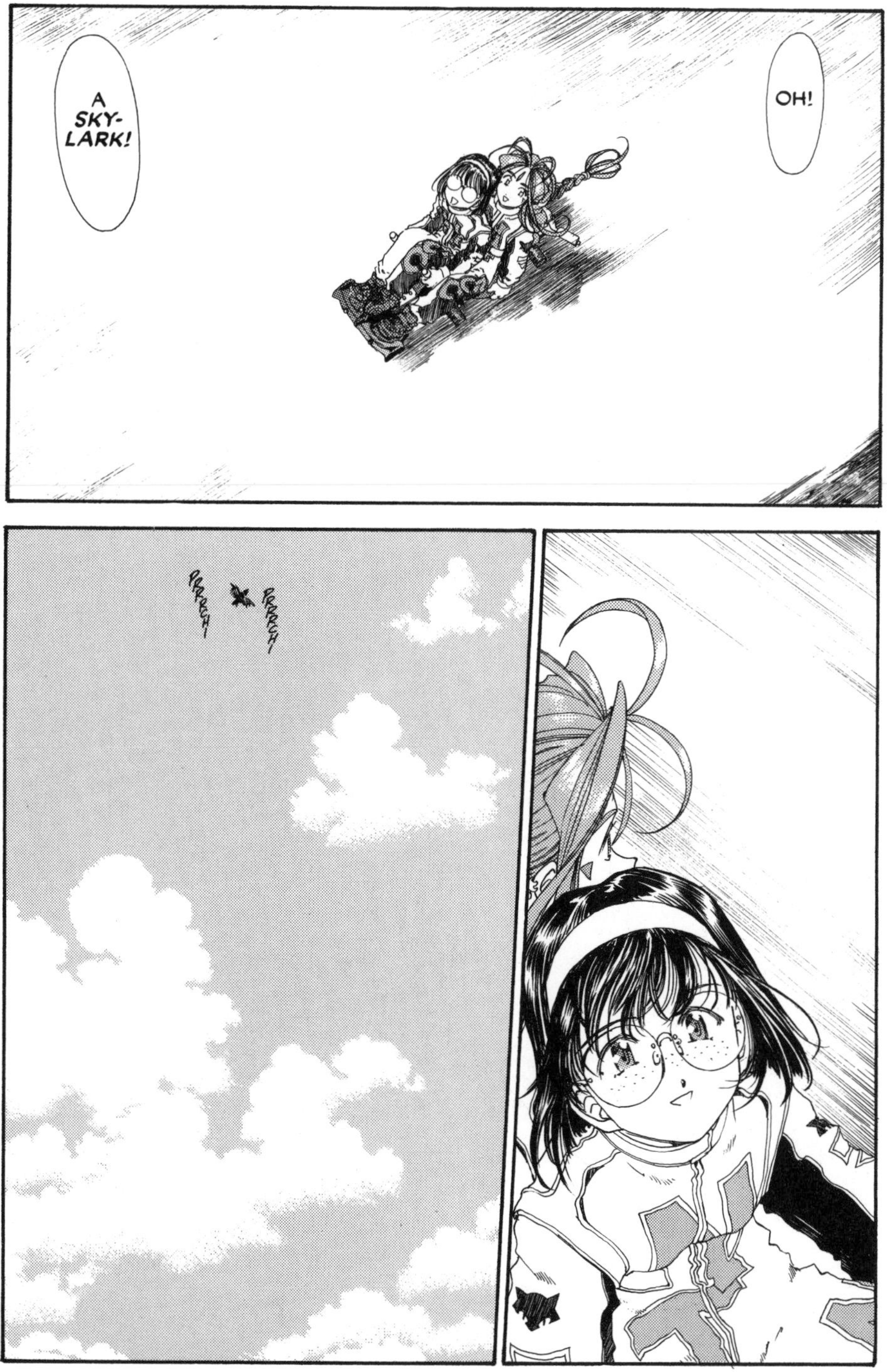
OH!
A SKY-LARK!
PRRRCH!
PRRRCH!

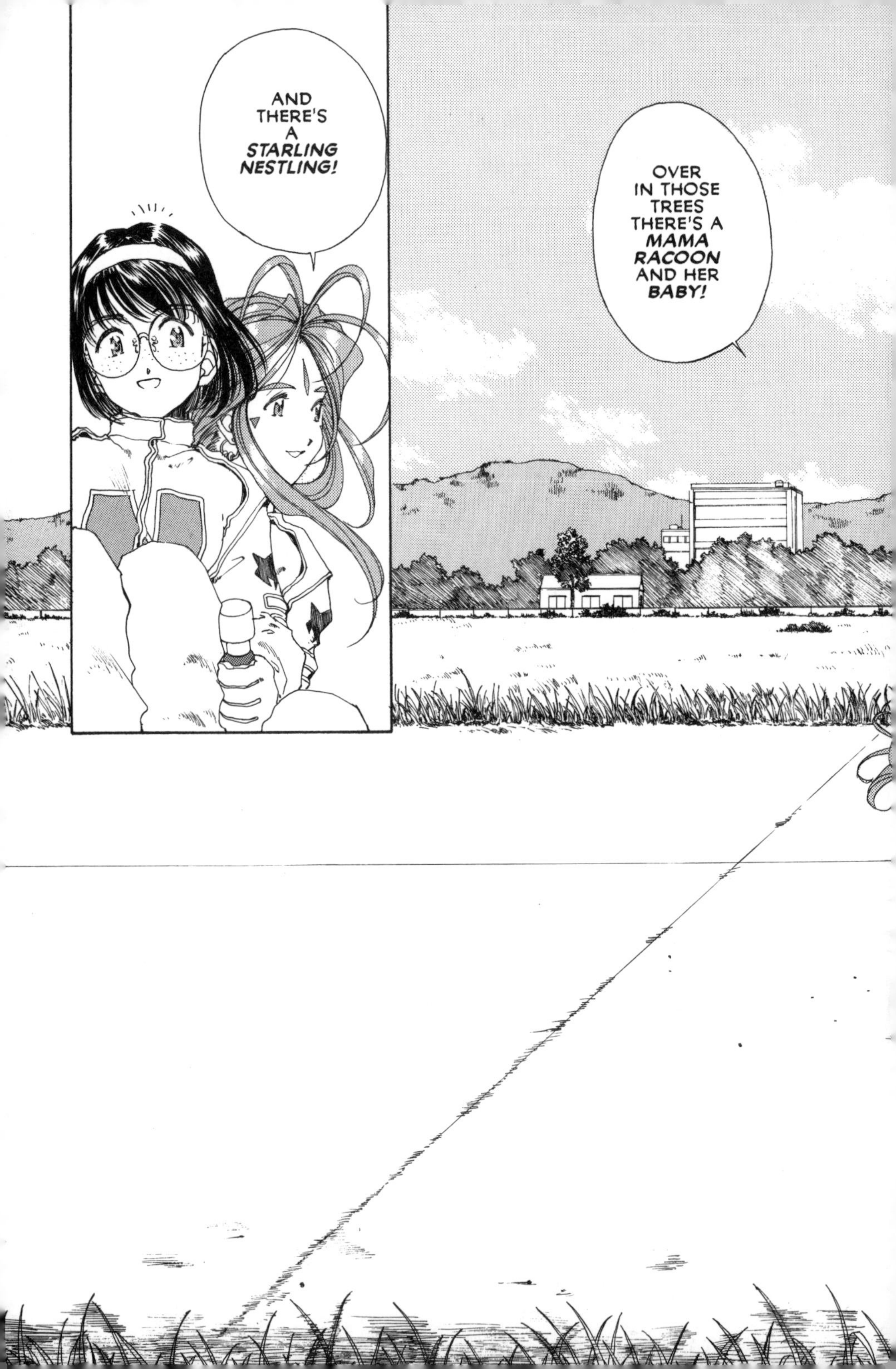
OVER IN THOSE TREES THERE'S A *MAMA RACOON* AND HER *BABY!*
AND THERE'S A *STARLING NESTLING!*

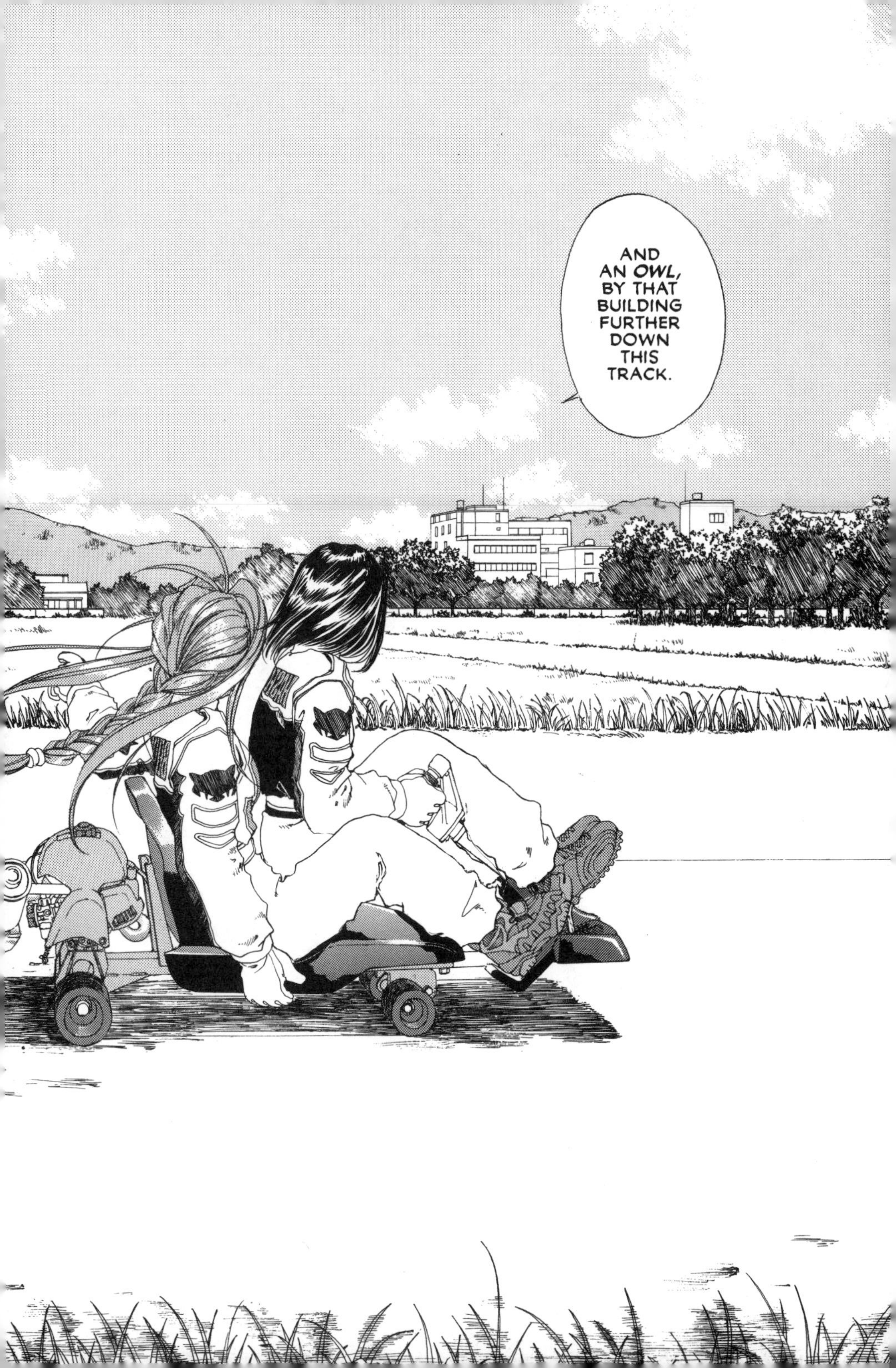
AND AN *OWL*, BY THAT BUILDING FURTHER DOWN THIS TRACK.

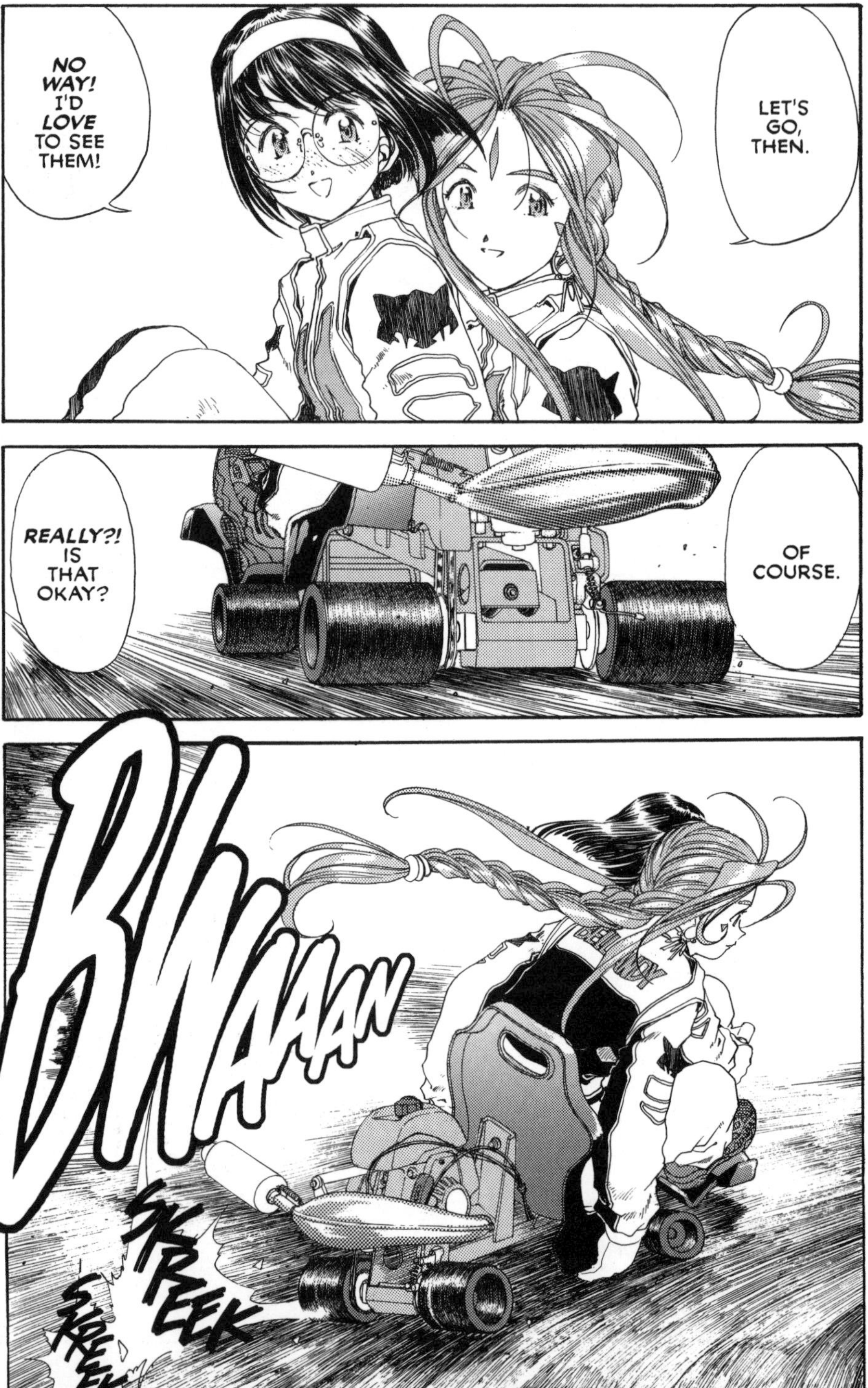

NO WAY! I'D LOVE TO SEE THEM!
LET'S GO, THEN.
REALLY?! IS THAT OKAY?
OF COURSE.
BWAAAAN
SKREEK
SKREEK

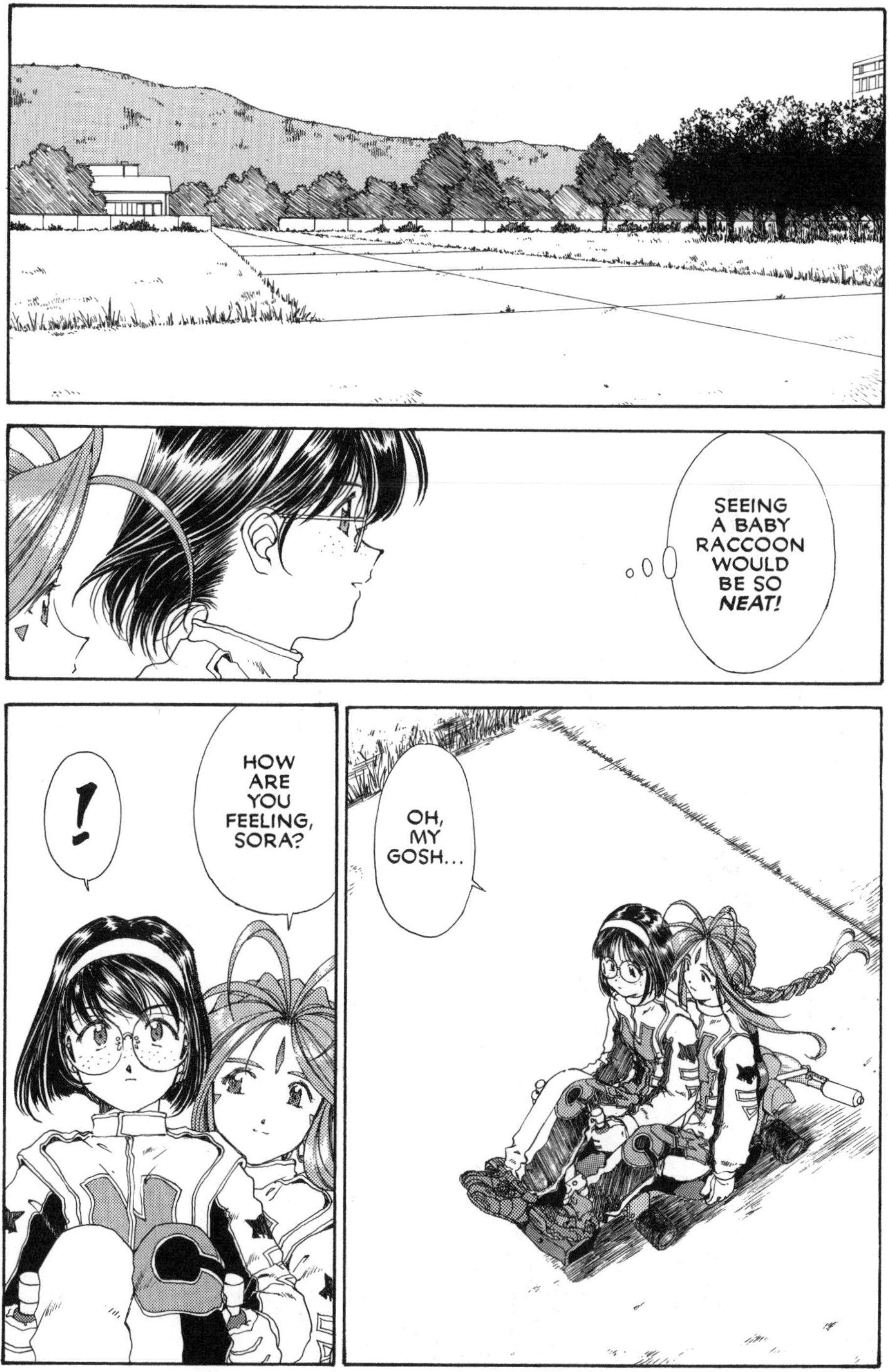
SEEING A BABY RACCOON WOULD BE SO *NEAT!*
OH, MY GOSH...
HOW ARE YOU FEELING, SORA?
!

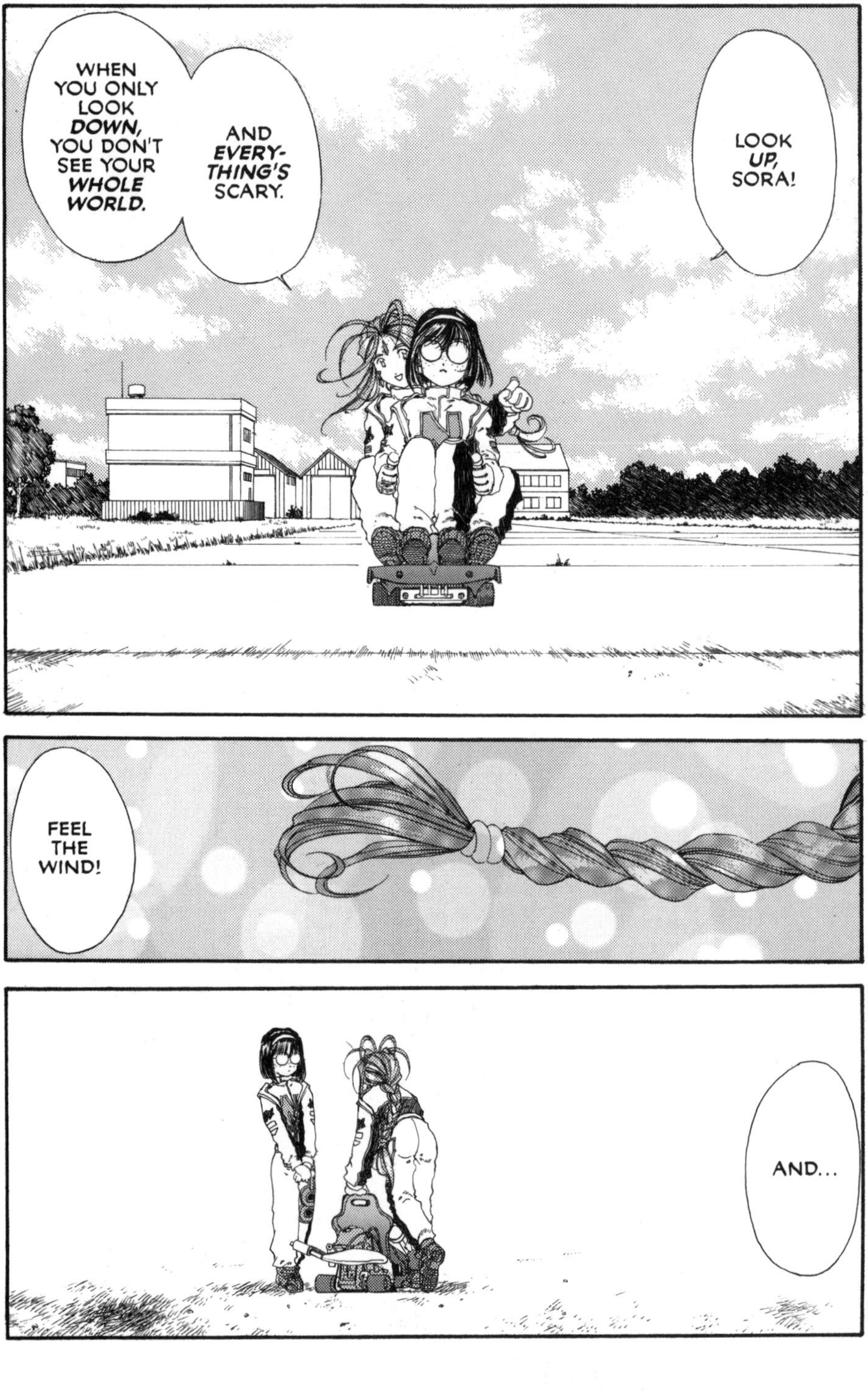
LOOK UP, SORA!
WHEN YOU ONLY LOOK DOWN, YOU DON'T SEE YOUR WHOLE WORLD.
AND EVERY-THING'S SCARY.
FEEL THE WIND!
AND...

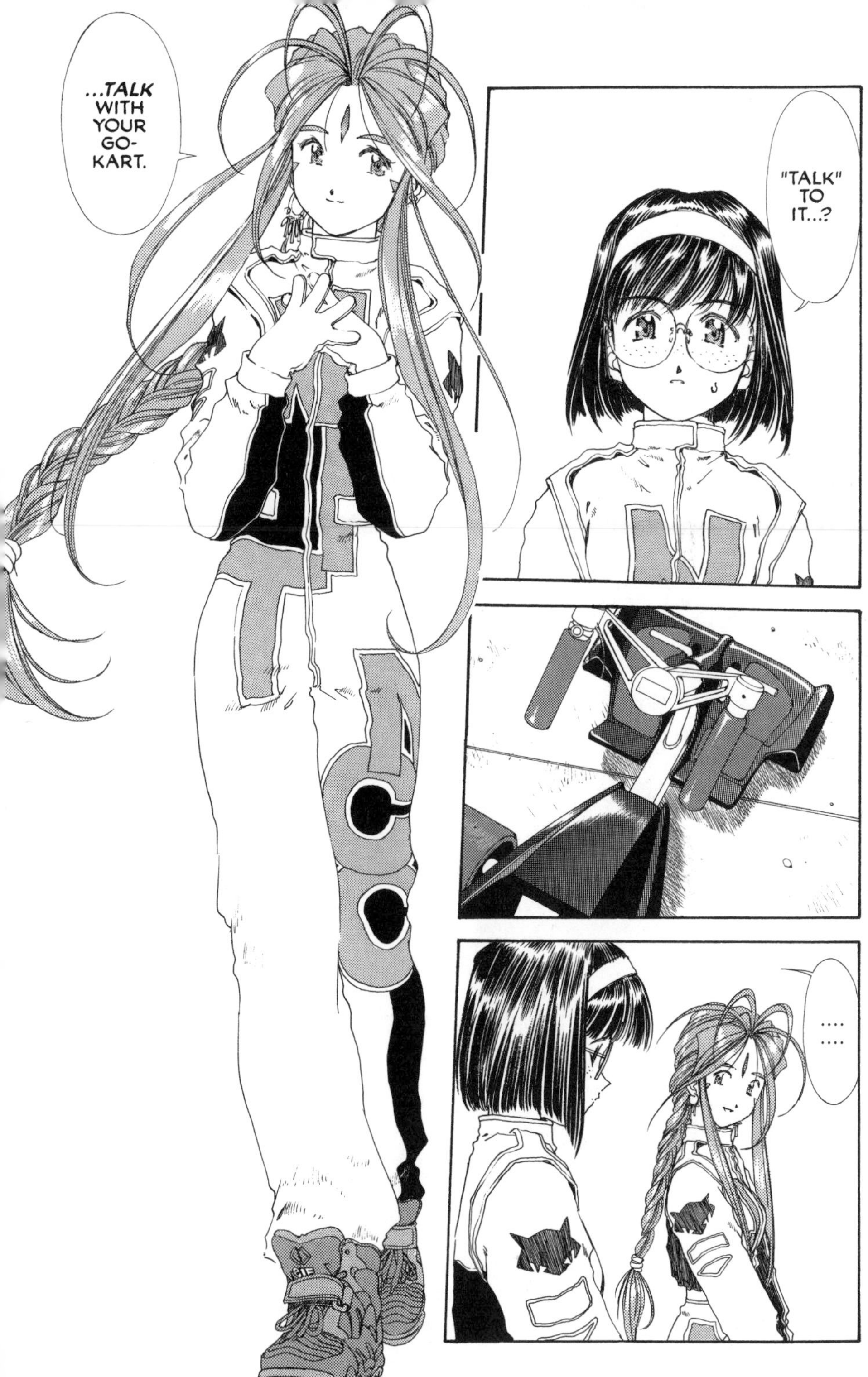
...TALK WITH YOUR GO-KART.
"TALK" TO IT...?
....
....

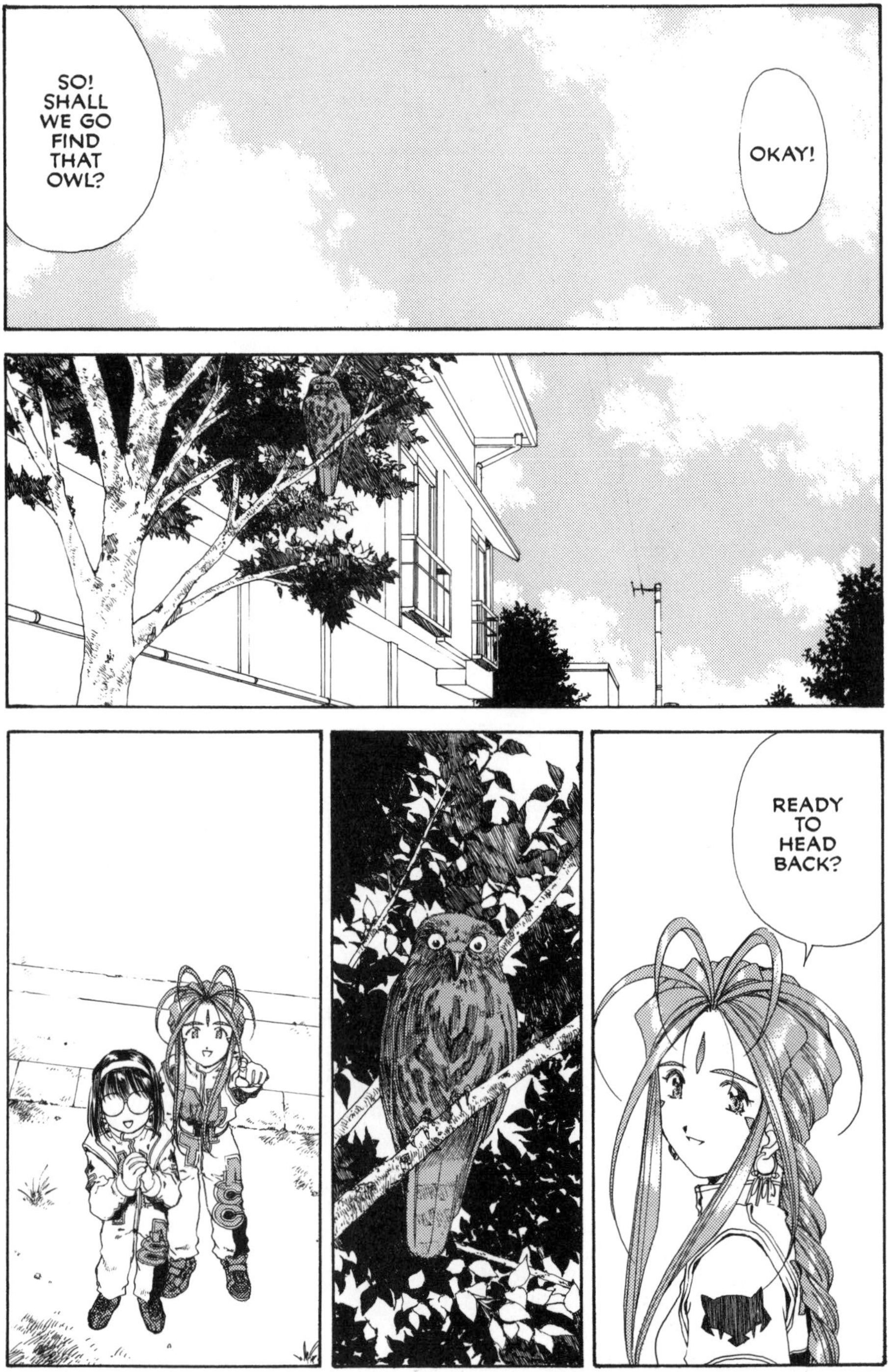
SO! SHALL WE GO FIND THAT OWL?
OKAY!
READY TO HEAD BACK?

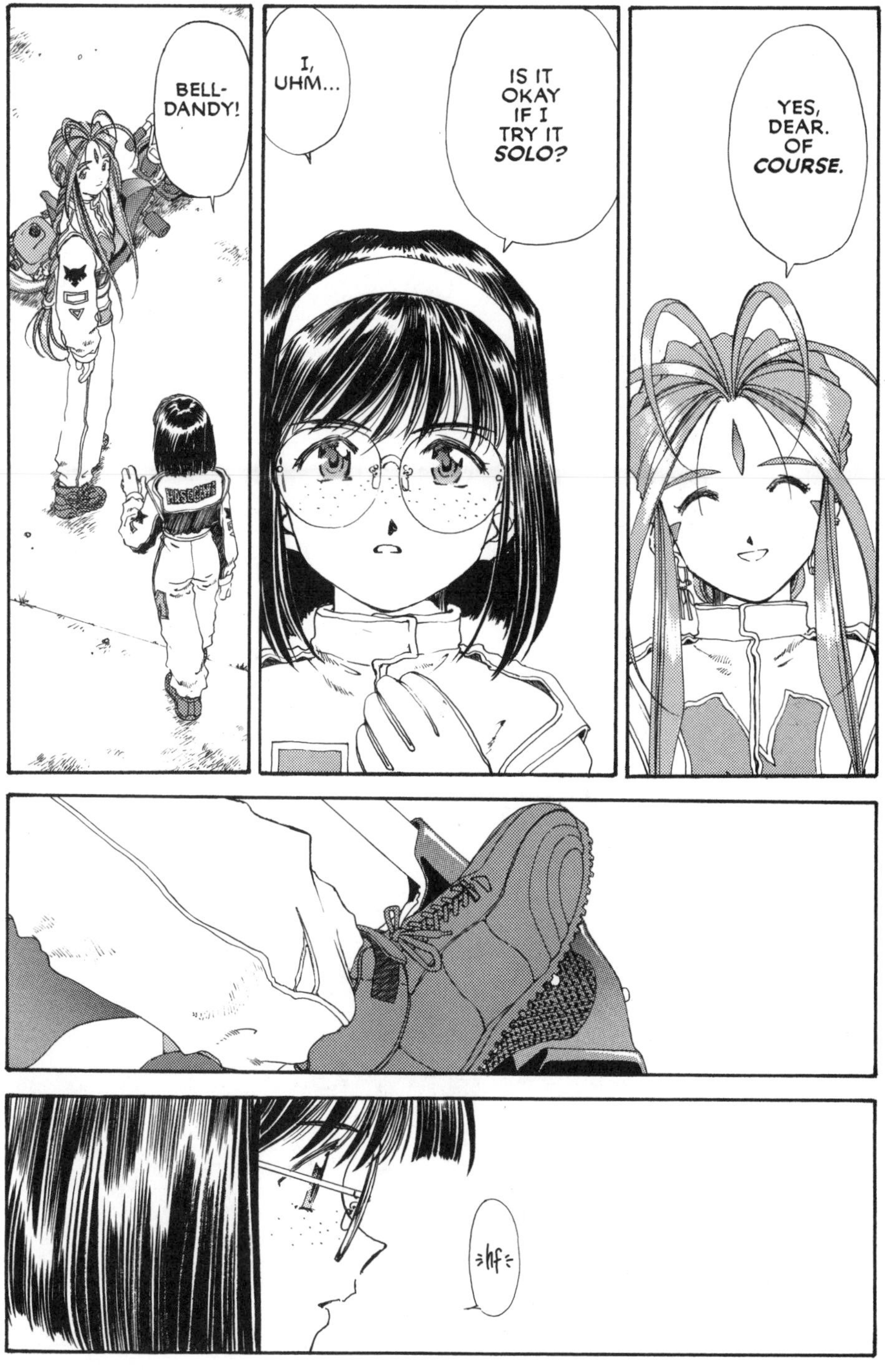
BELL-DANDY!
I, UHM...
IS IT OKAY IF I TRY IT *SOLO?*
YES, DEAR. OF *COURSE.*
hf

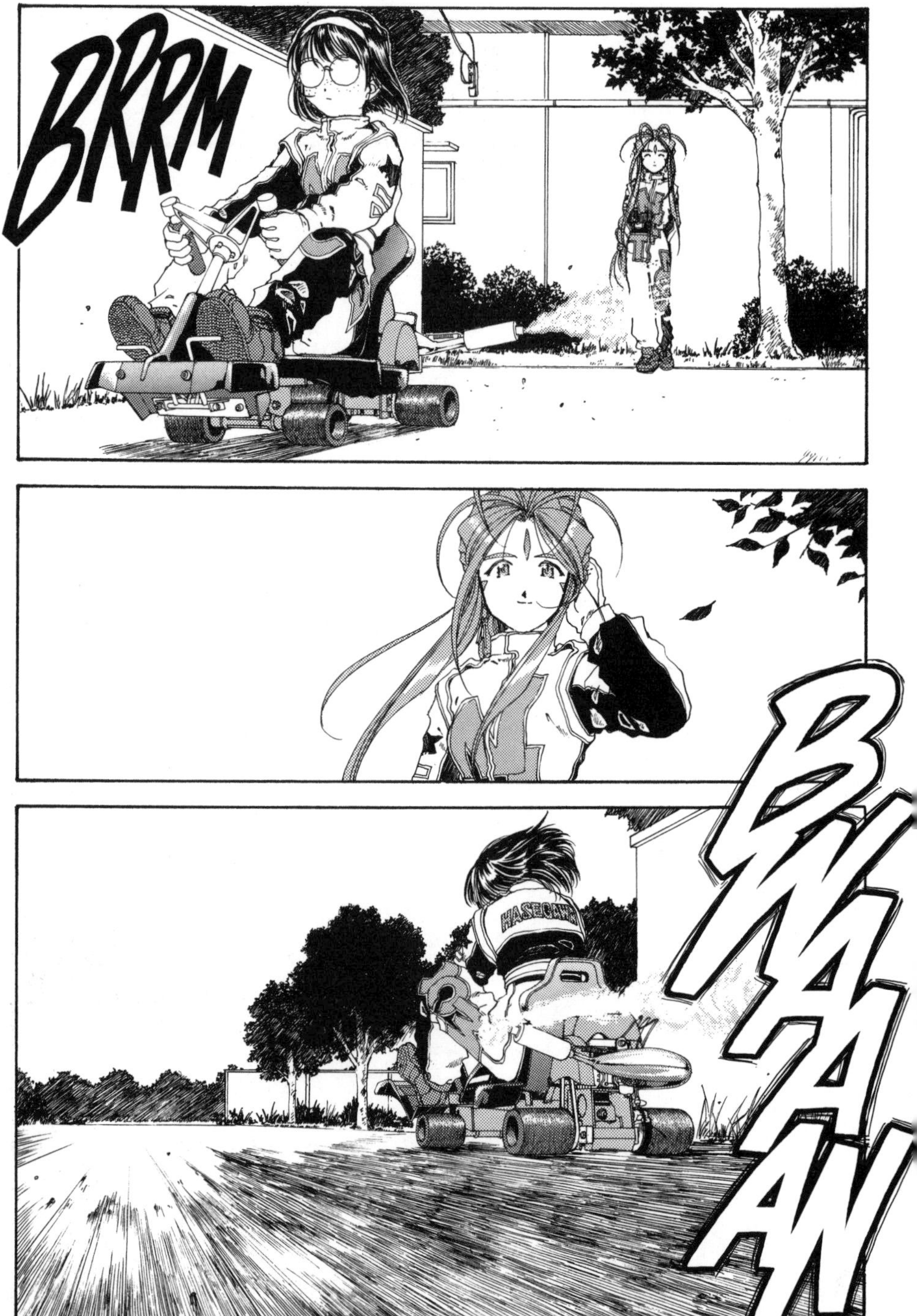
BRRM
HASEGAWA
BWAAAN

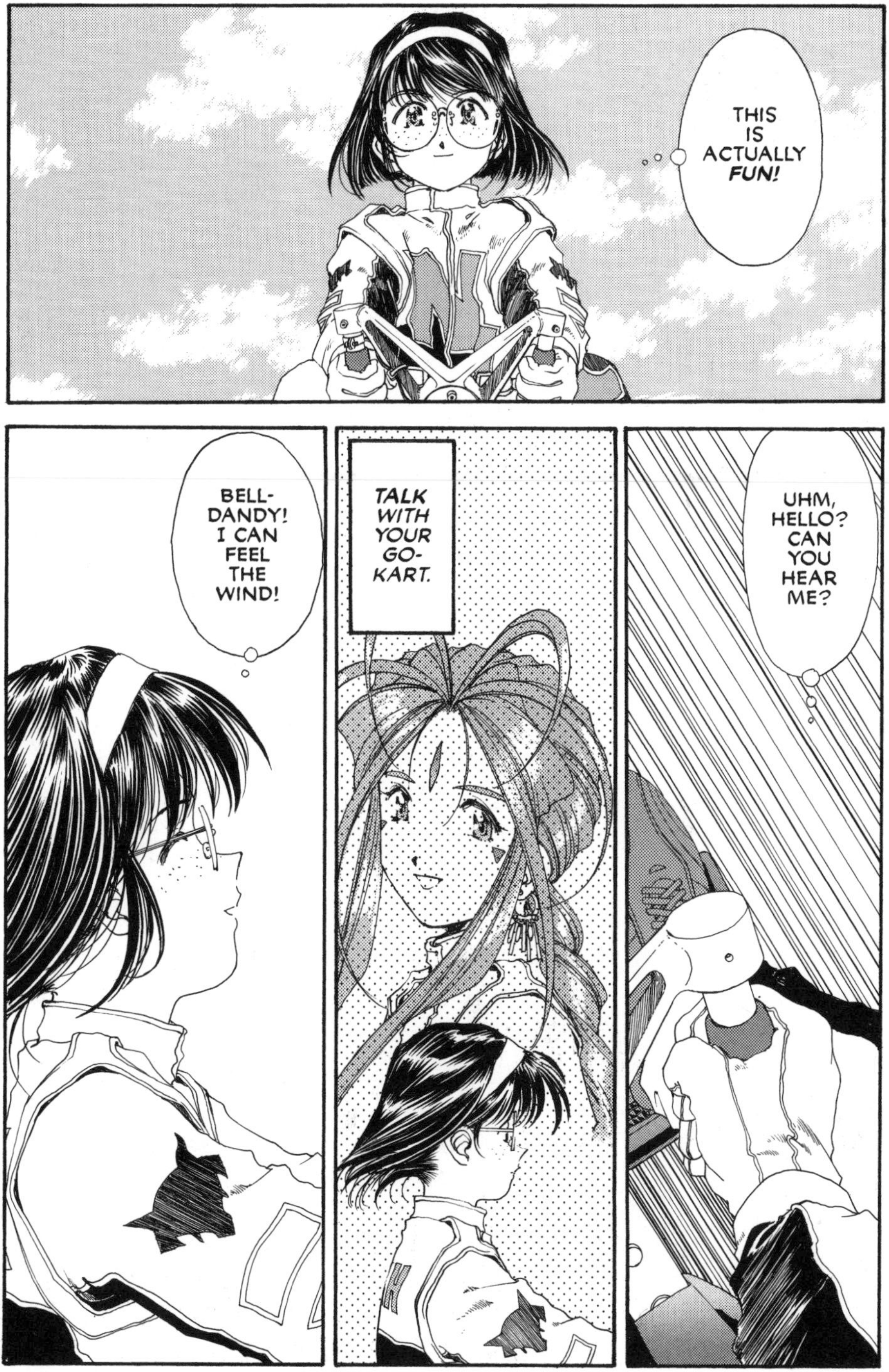
THIS IS ACTUALLY *FUN!*
UHM, HELLO? CAN YOU HEAR ME?
TALK WITH YOUR GO-KART.
BELL-DANDY! I CAN FEEL THE WIND!

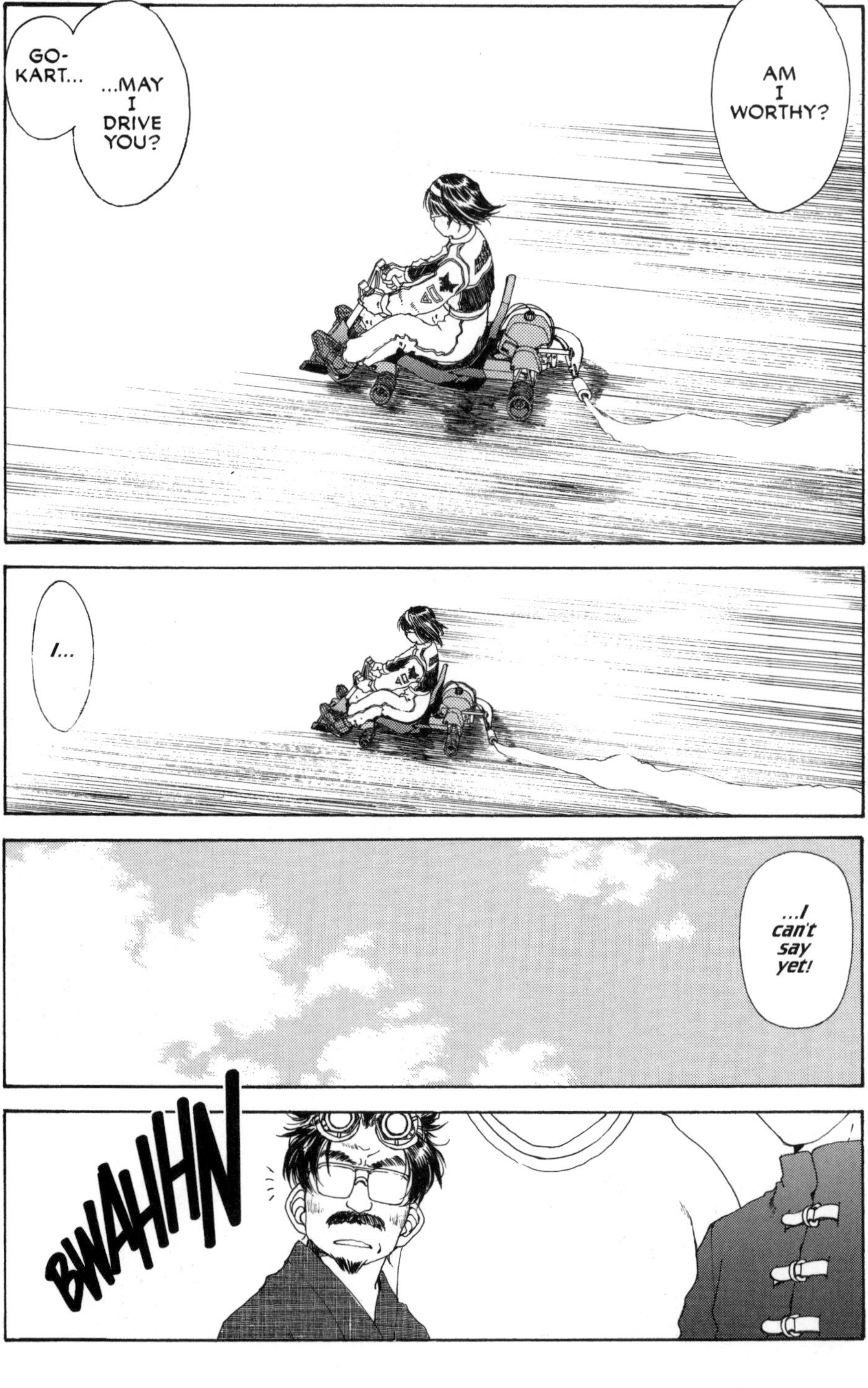
GO-KART...
...MAY I DRIVE YOU?
AM I WORTHY?
I...
...I can't say yet!
BWAHHN

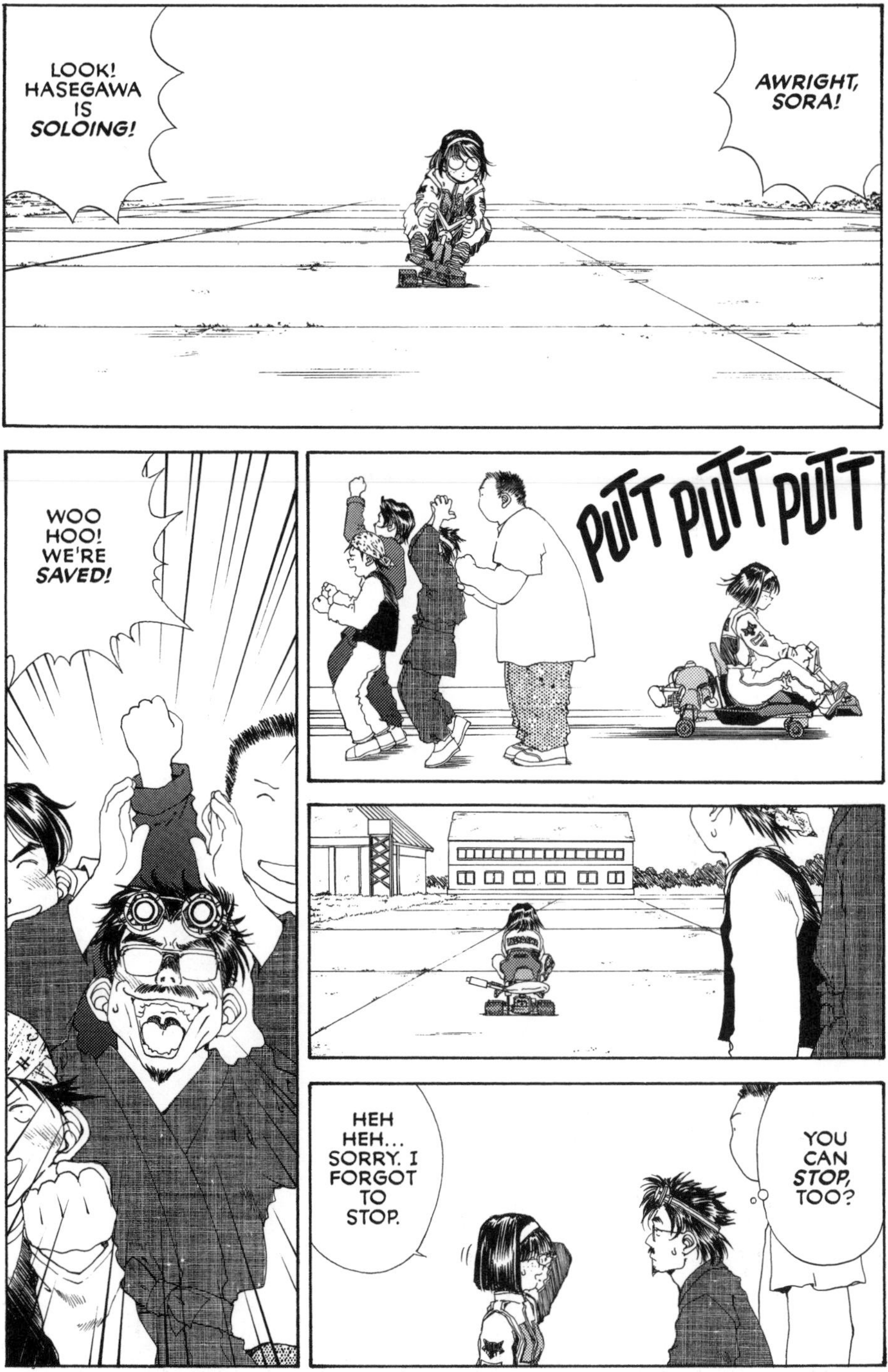
LOOK! HASEGAWA IS SOLOING!
AWRIGHT, SORA!
WOO HOO! WE'RE SAVED!
PUTT PUTT PUTT
HEH HEH... SORRY. I FORGOT TO STOP.
YOU CAN STOP, TOO?

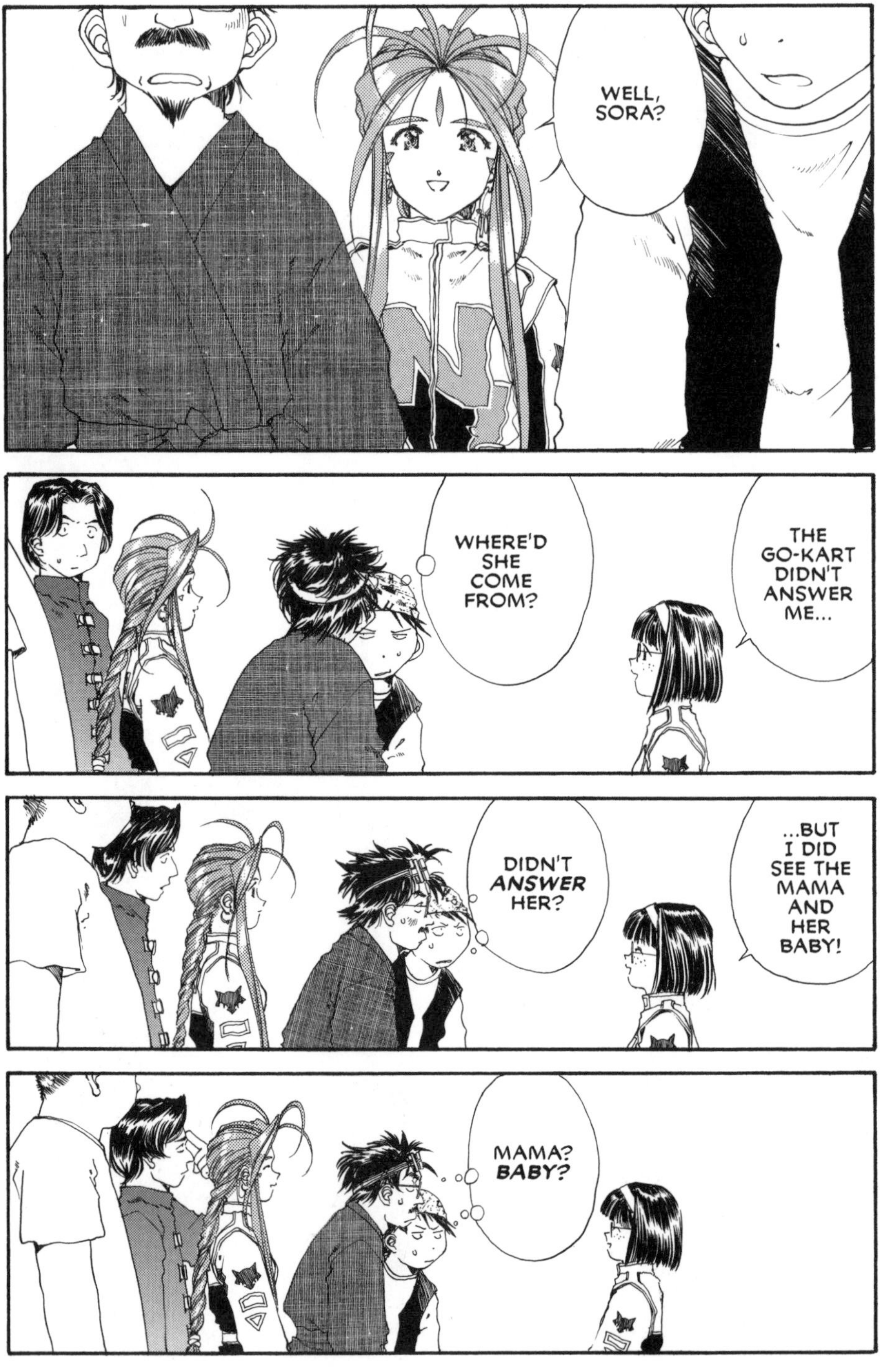
WELL, SORA?
THE GO-KART DIDN'T ANSWER ME...
WHERE'D SHE COME FROM?
...BUT I DID SEE THE MAMA AND HER BABY!
DIDN'T *ANSWER* HER?
MAMA? *BABY?*

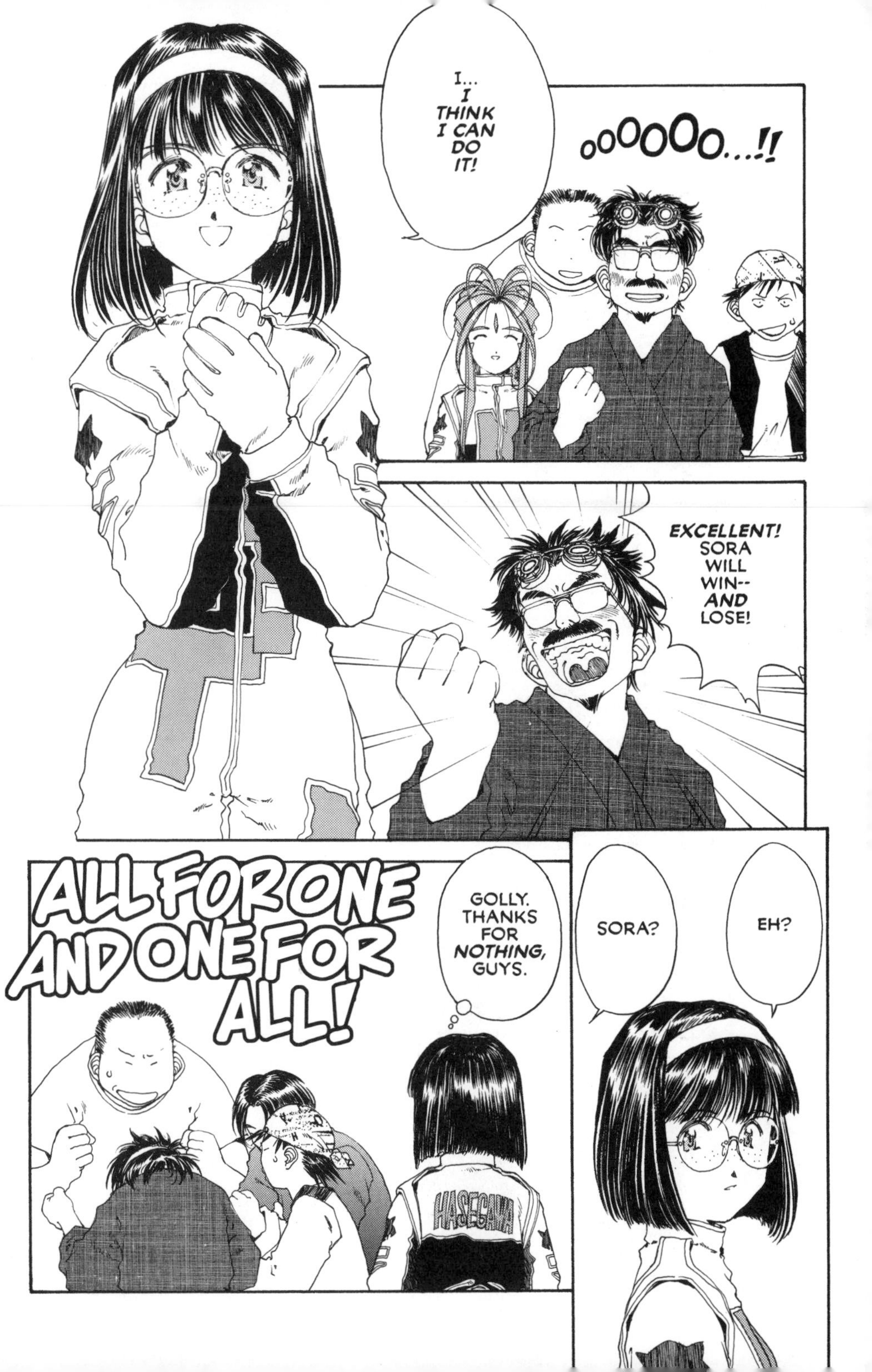
I... I THINK I CAN DO IT!
oooOOo...!!
EXCELLENT! SORA WILL WIN-- AND LOSE!
ALL FOR ONE AND ONE FOR ALL!
GOLLY. THANKS FOR NOTHING, GUYS.
HASEGAWA
SORA?
EH?

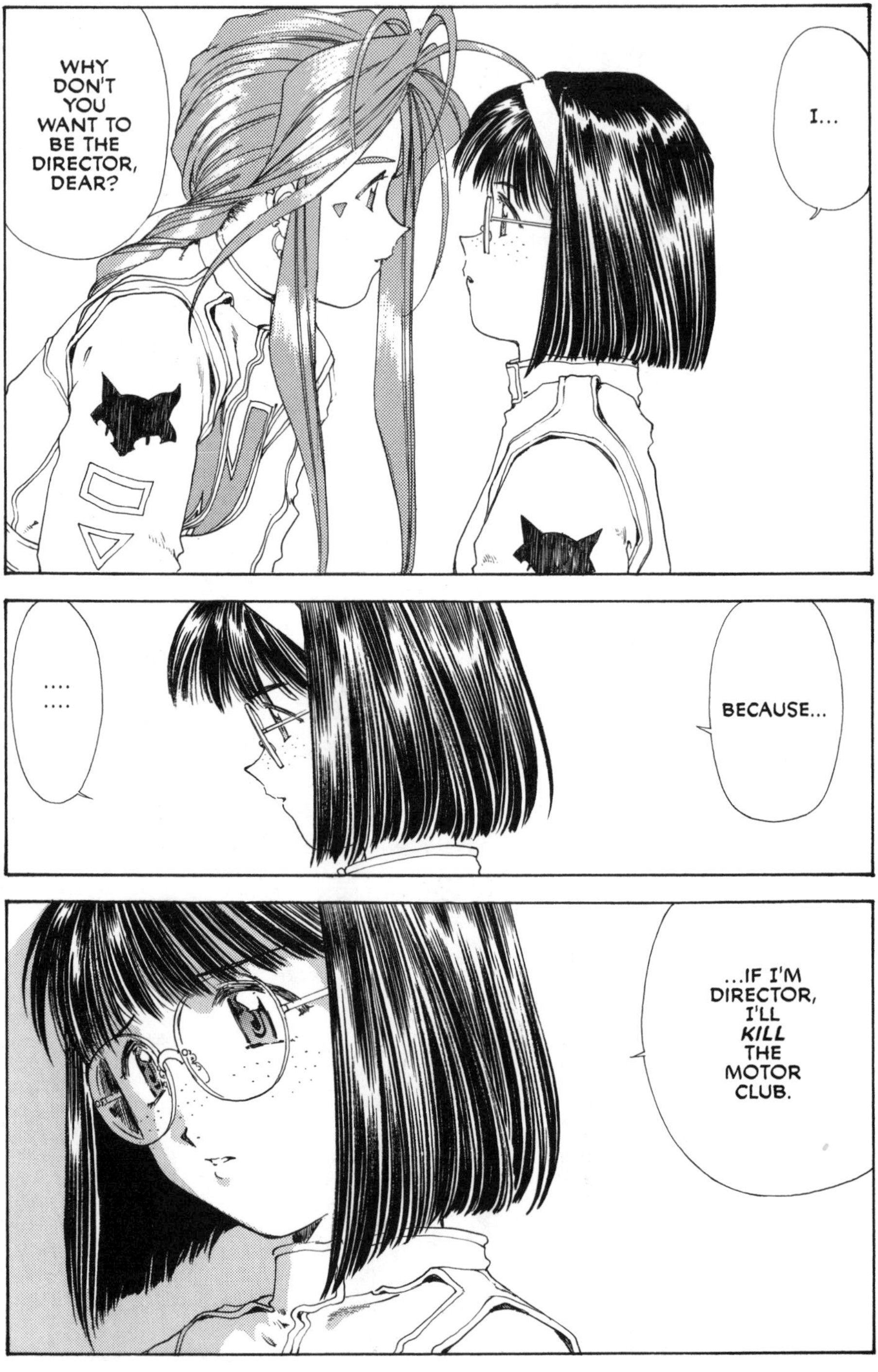
WHY DON'T YOU WANT TO BE THE DIRECTOR, DEAR?
I...
....
....
BECAUSE...
...IF I'M DIRECTOR, I'LL *KILL* THE MOTOR CLUB.

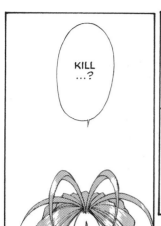

KILL
...?

MISS BELLDANDY. DO YOU REMEMBER MY NICK-NAME?

YES...

"HASEGAWA, THE *CHEF ASSASSIN*."

RIGHT.

AND I HAVE *ANOTHER* NICK-NAME...

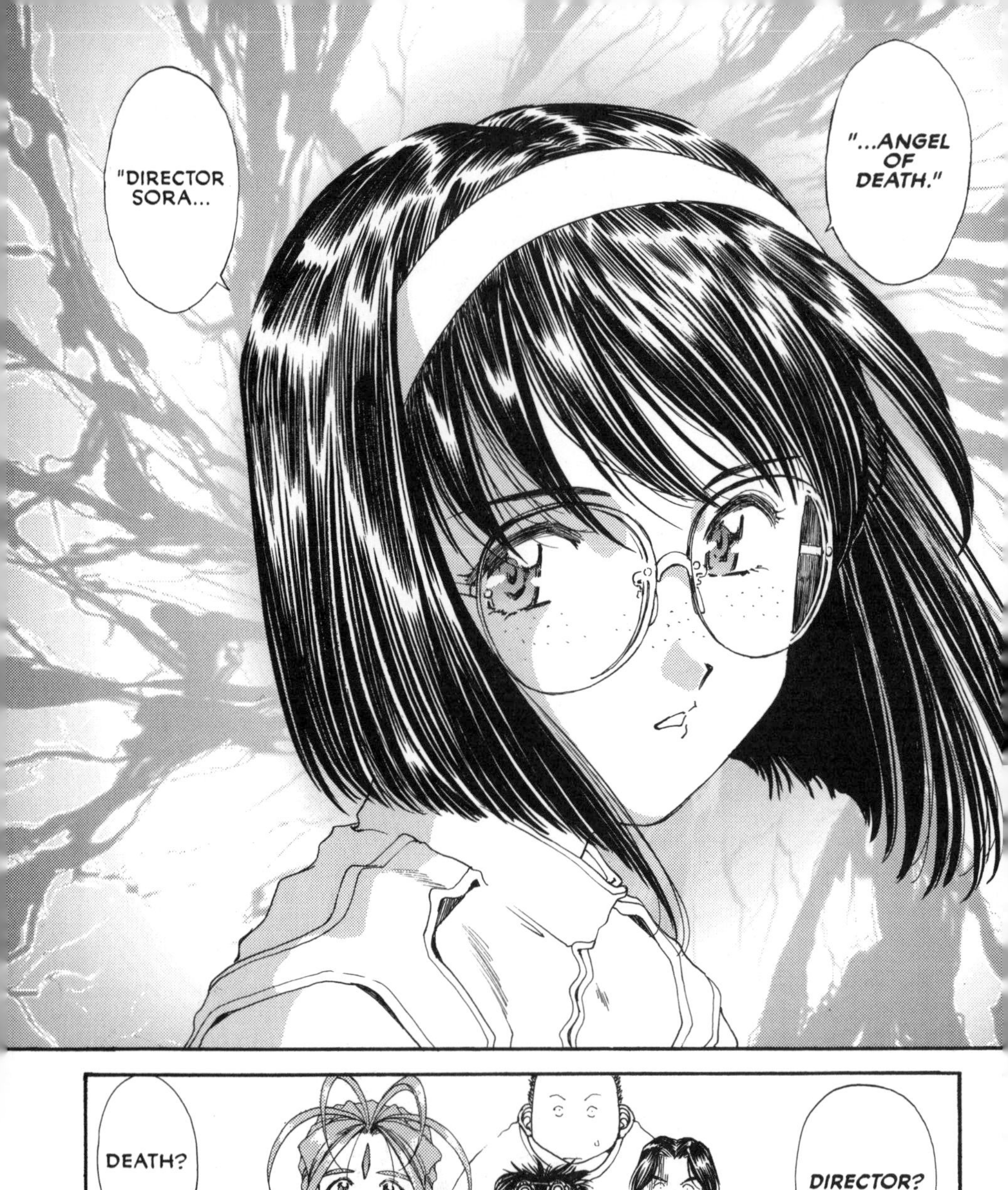
"DIRECTOR SORA...
"...ANGEL OF DEATH."
DEATH?
DIRECTOR?

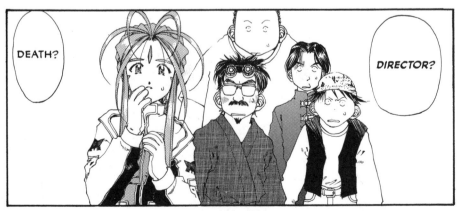

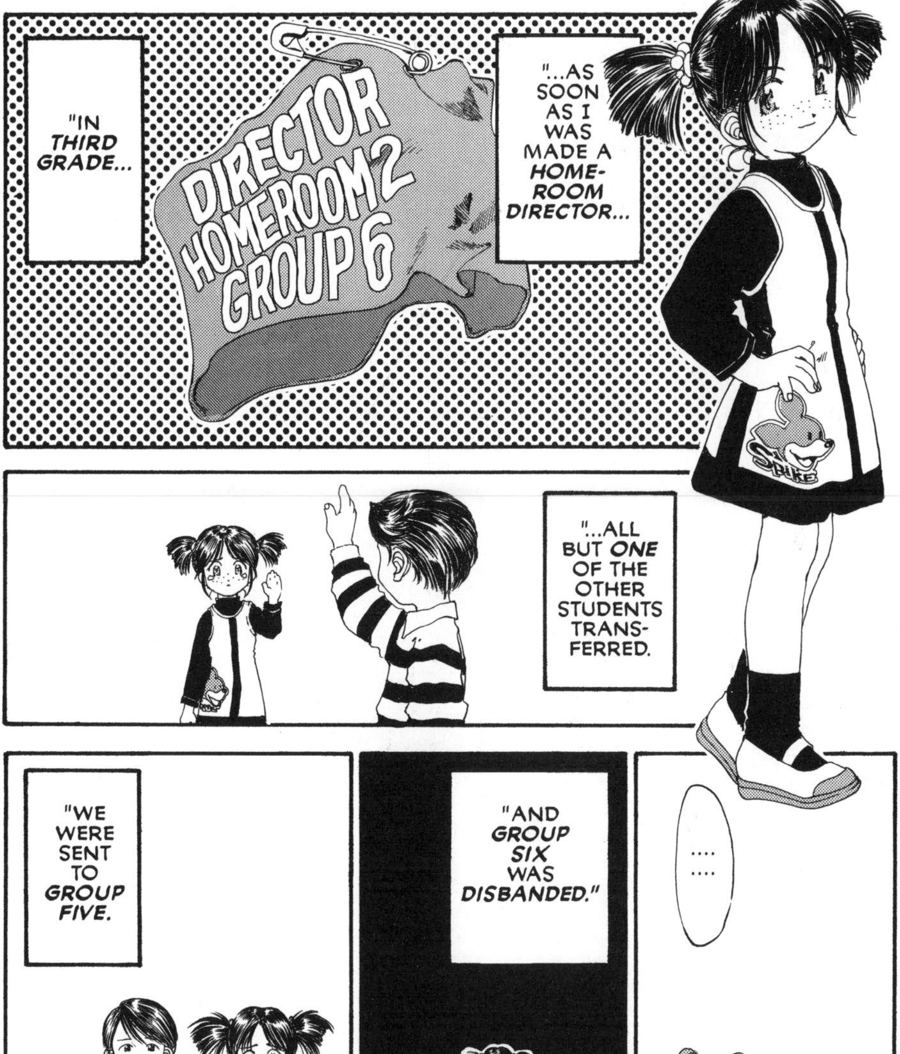
"IN THIRD GRADE...
DIRECTOR HOMEROOM 2 GROUP 6
"...AS SOON AS I WAS MADE A HOMEROOM DIRECTOR...
Spike
"...ALL BUT ONE OF THE OTHER STUDENTS TRANSFERRED.
"WE WERE SENT TO GROUP FIVE.
"AND GROUP SIX WAS DISBANDED."
....

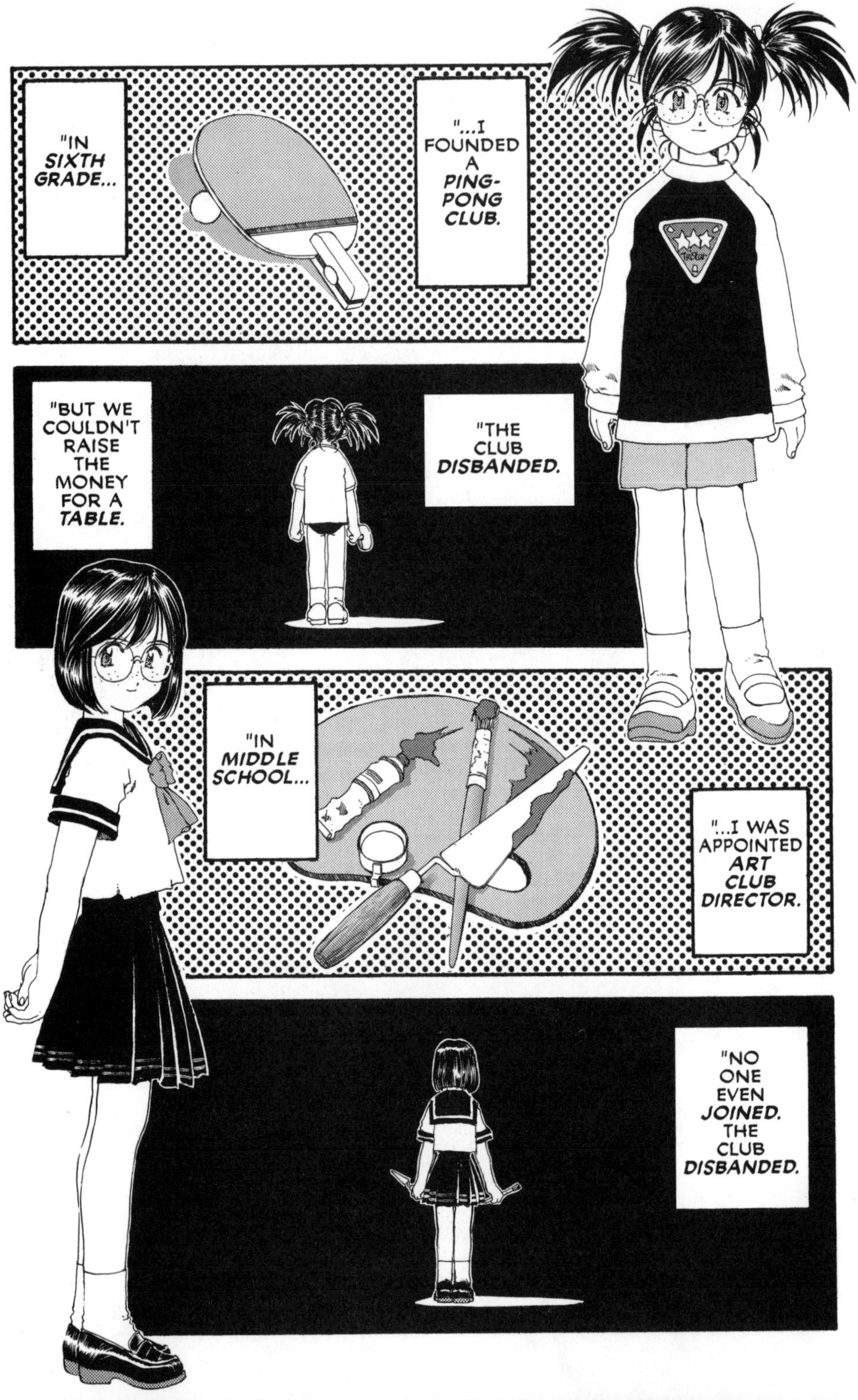
"IN SIXTH GRADE...
"...I FOUNDED A PING-PONG CLUB.
"BUT WE COULDN'T RAISE THE MONEY FOR A TABLE.
"THE CLUB DISBANDED.
"IN MIDDLE SCHOOL...
"...I WAS APPOINTED ART CLUB DIRECTOR.
"NO ONE EVEN JOINED. THE CLUB DISBANDED.

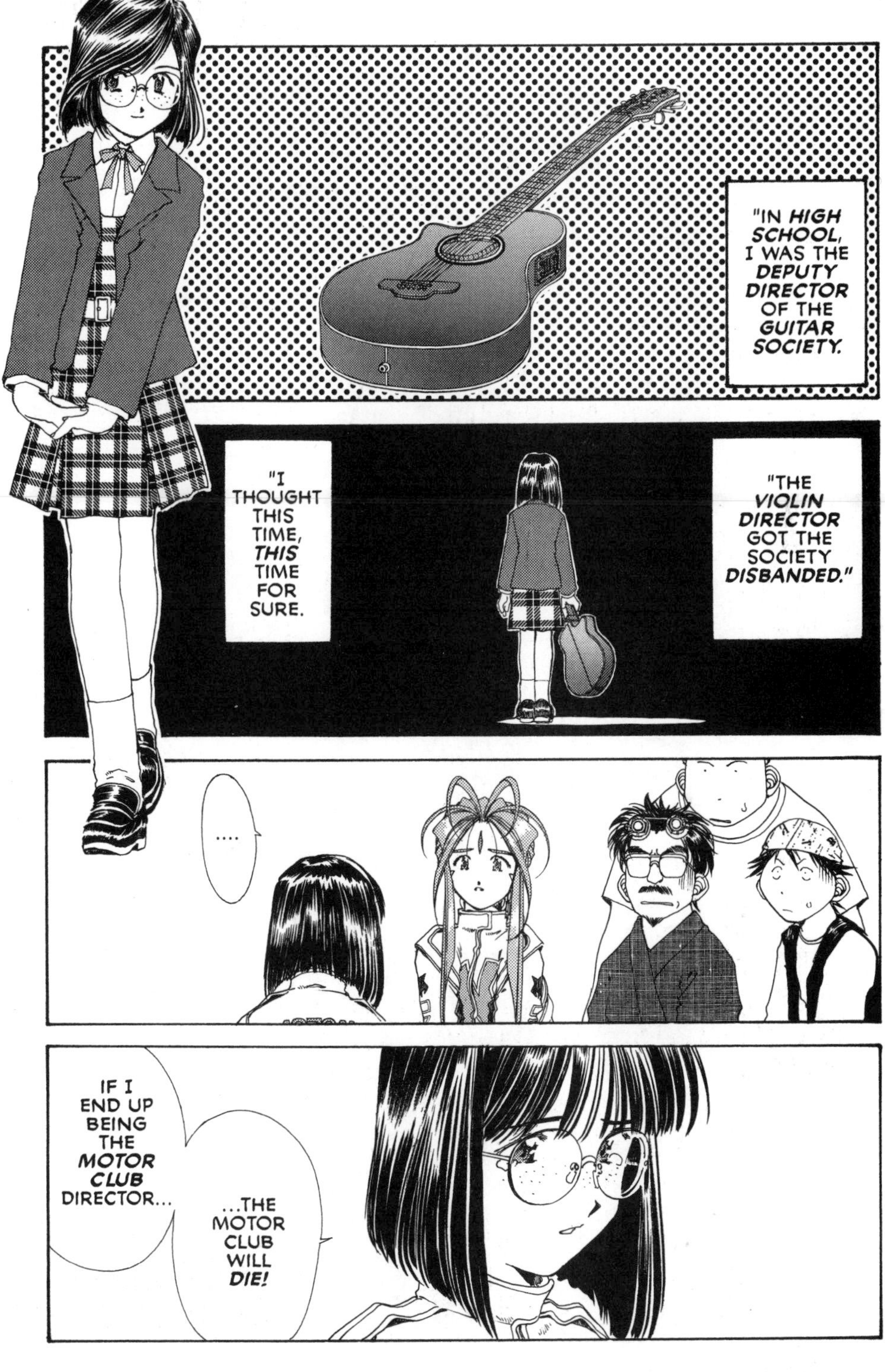
"IN HIGH SCHOOL, I WAS THE DEPUTY DIRECTOR OF THE GUITAR SOCIETY.
"I THOUGHT THIS TIME, THIS TIME FOR SURE.
"THE VIOLIN DIRECTOR GOT THE SOCIETY DISBANDED."
....
IF I END UP BEING THE MOTOR CLUB DIRECTOR...
...THE MOTOR CLUB WILL DIE!

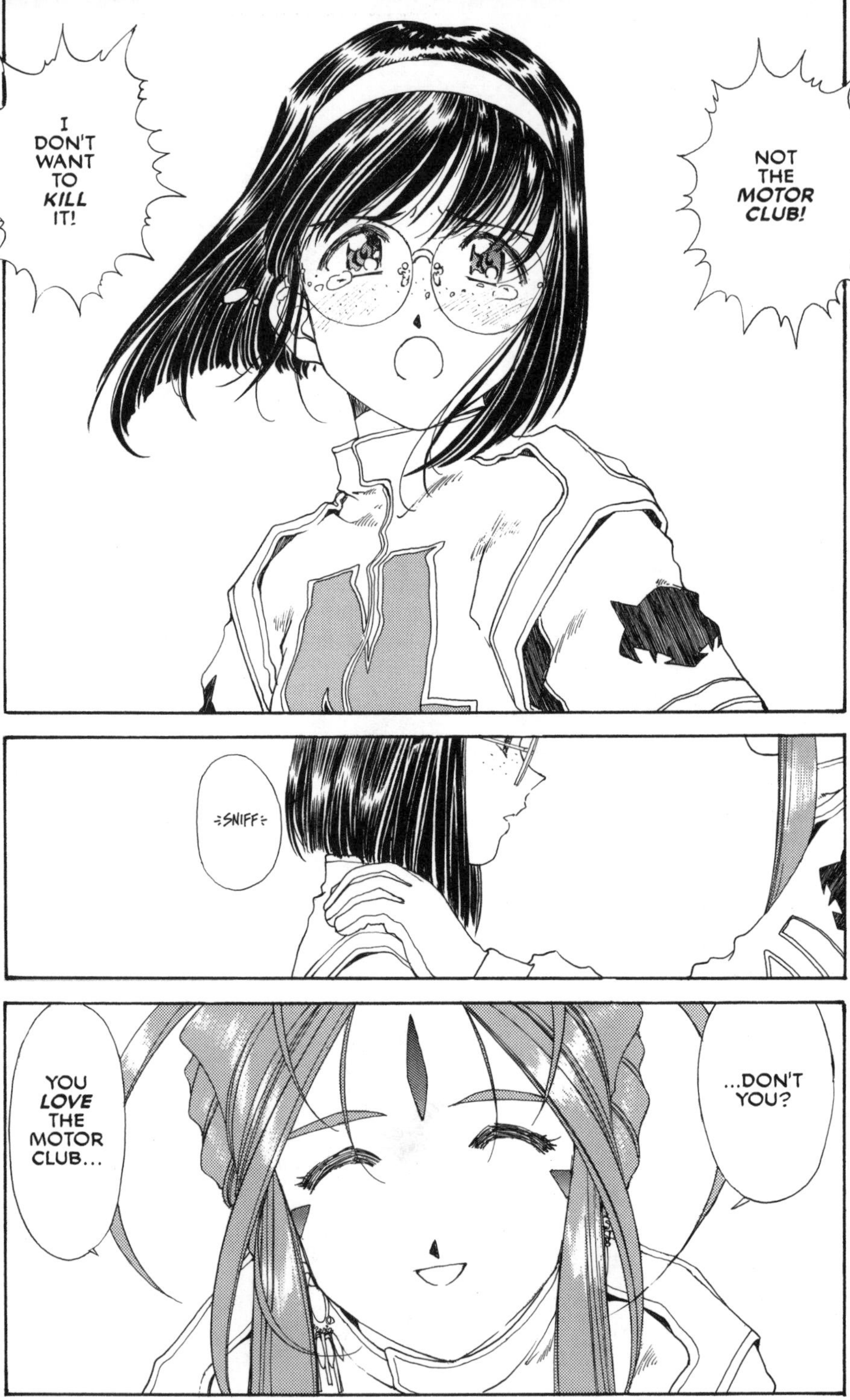

I DON'T WANT TO *KILL* IT!
NOT THE *MOTOR CLUB!*
SNIFF
YOU *LOVE* THE MOTOR CLUB...
...DON'T YOU?

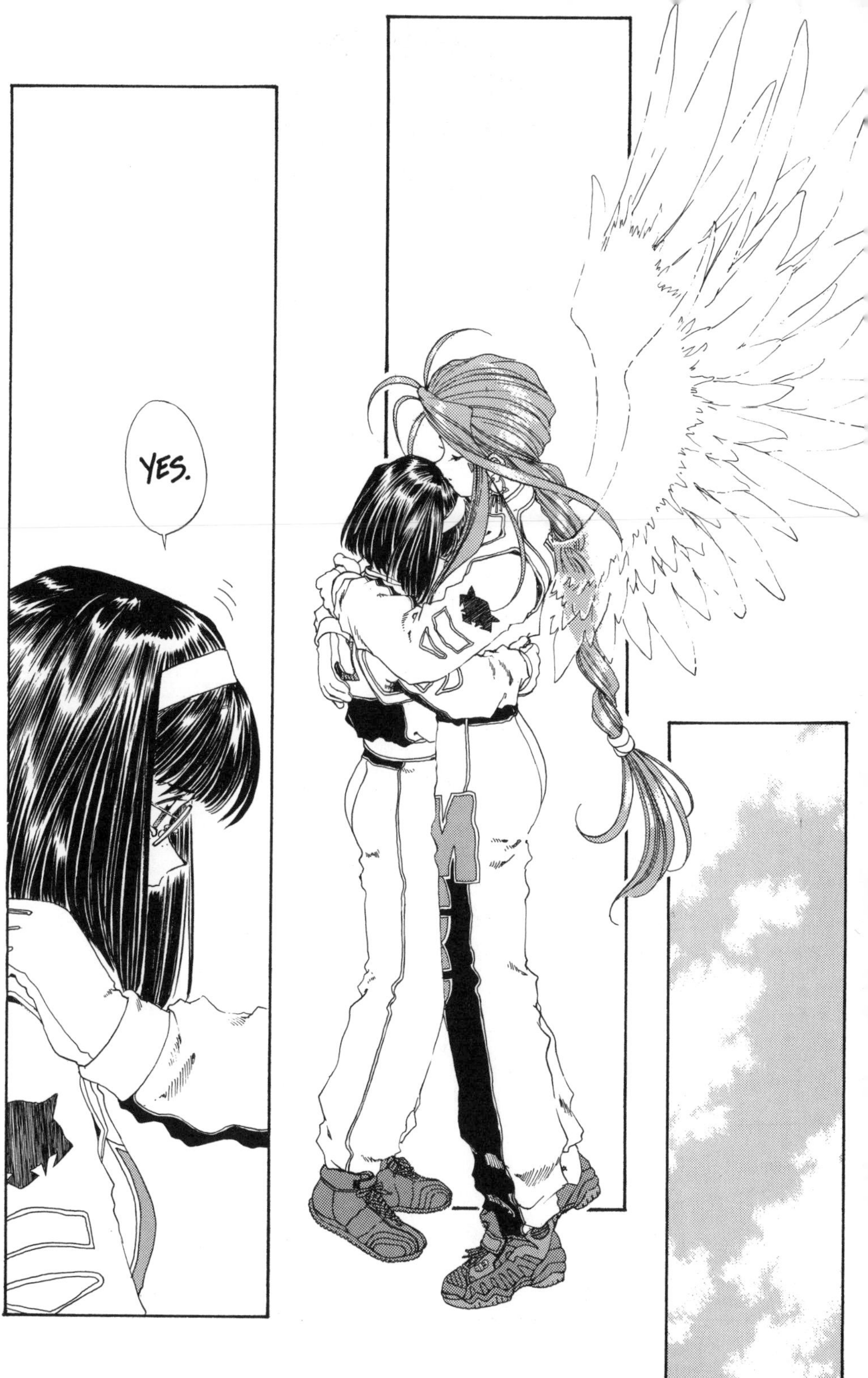
YES.

SPECIAL TRAINING

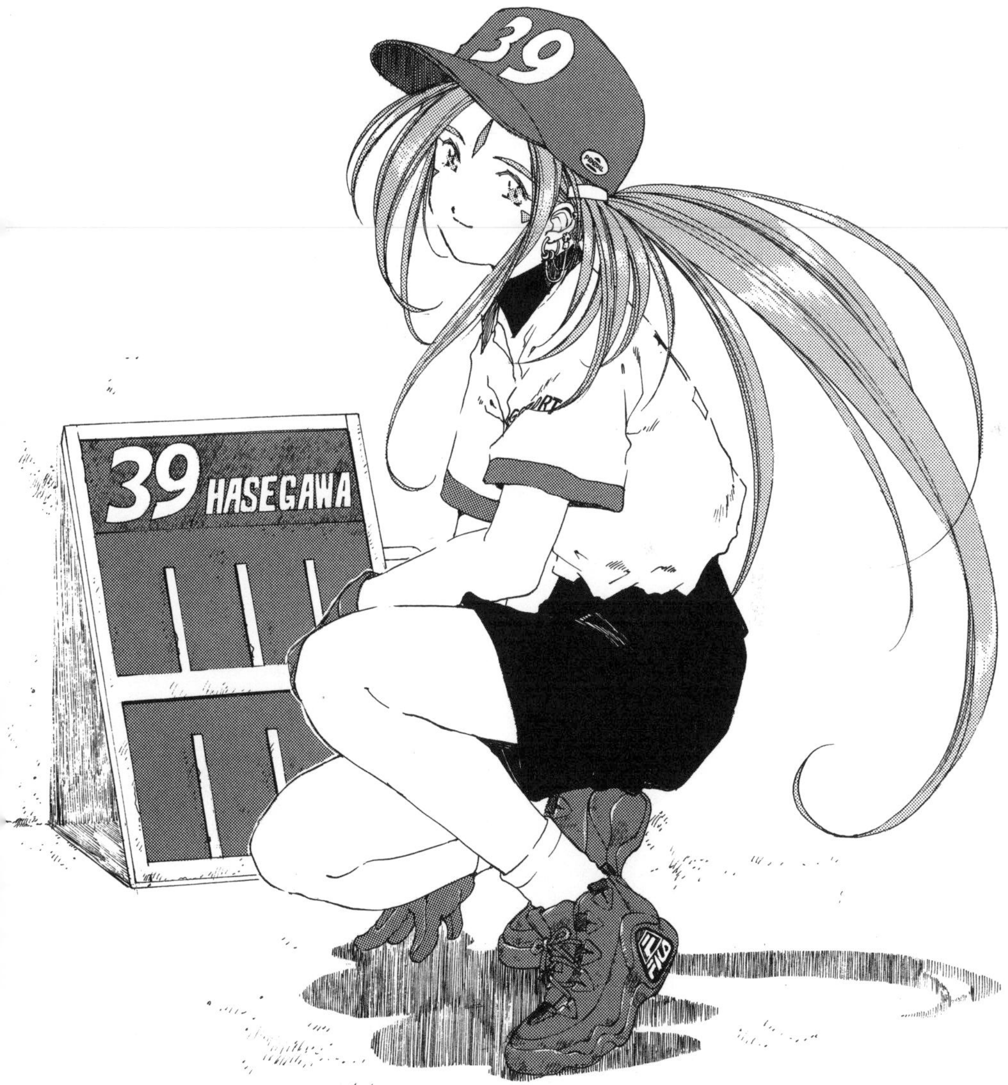
39
39
HASEGAWA

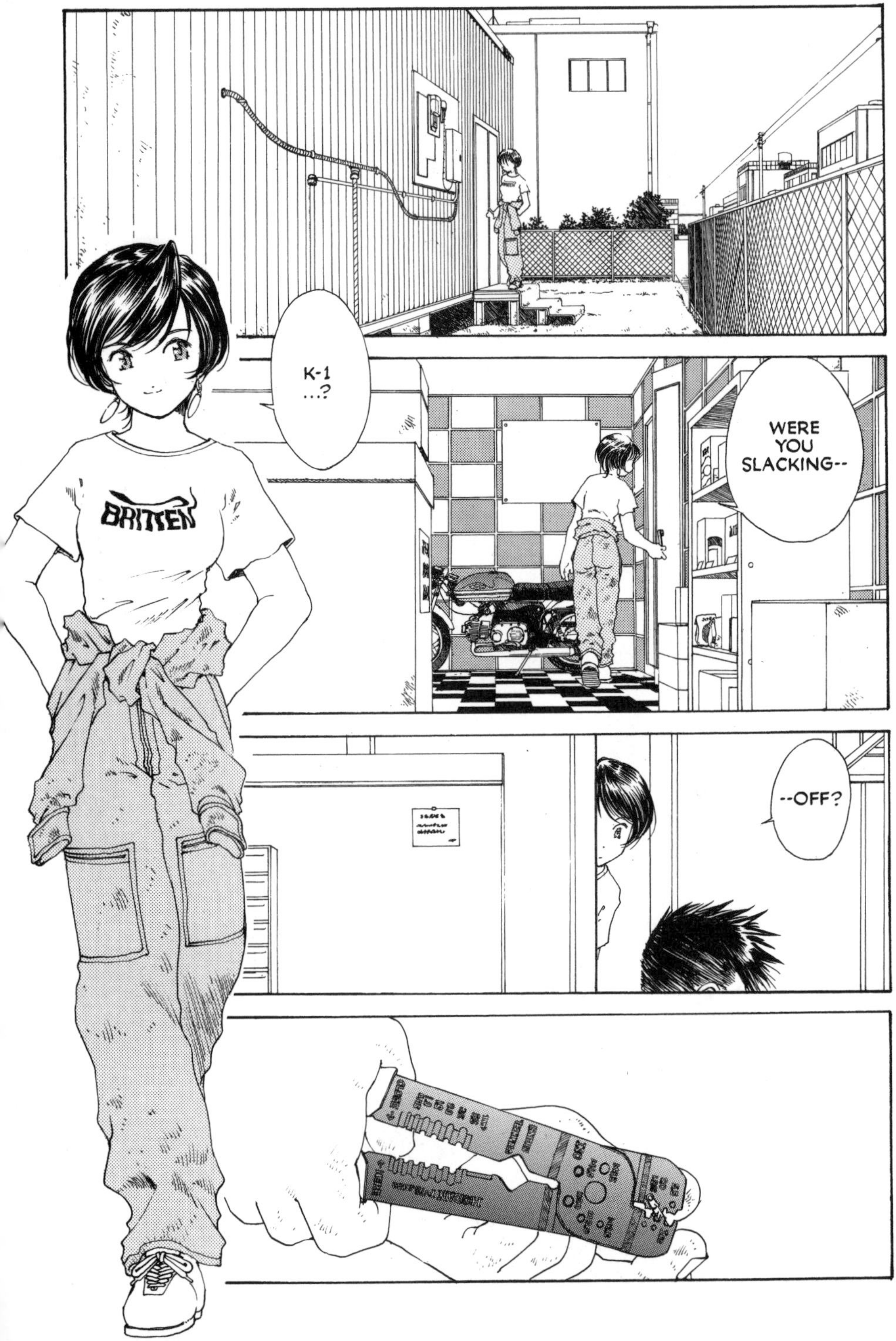
BRITTEN
K-1
...?
WERE YOU SLACKING--
--OFF?

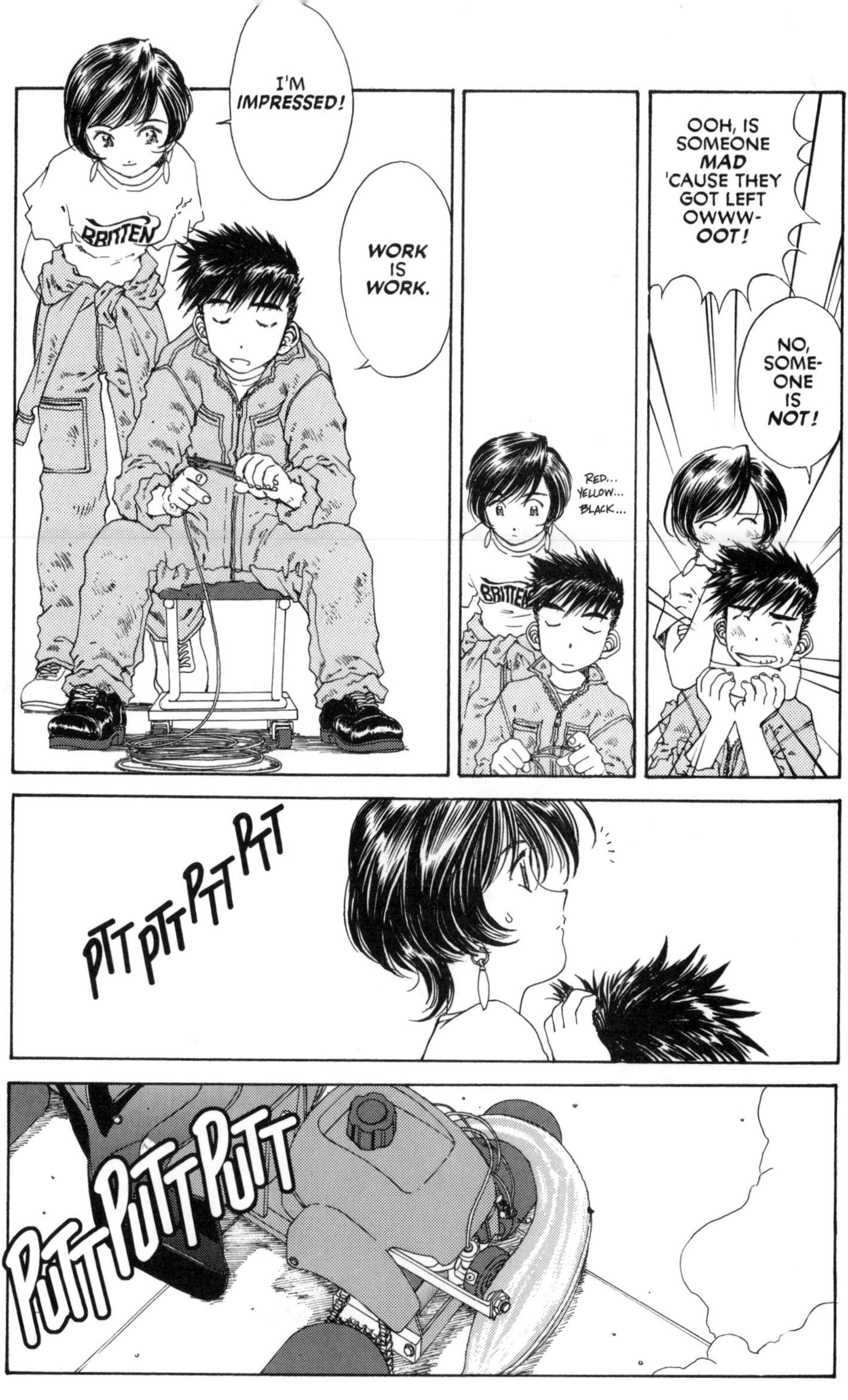

I'M IMPRESSED!
WORK IS WORK.
RED... YELLOW... BLACK...
OOH, IS SOMEONE MAD 'CAUSE THEY GOT LEFT OWWW-OOT!
NO, SOMEONE IS NOT!
PTT PTT PTT PTT
PUTT PUTT PUTT

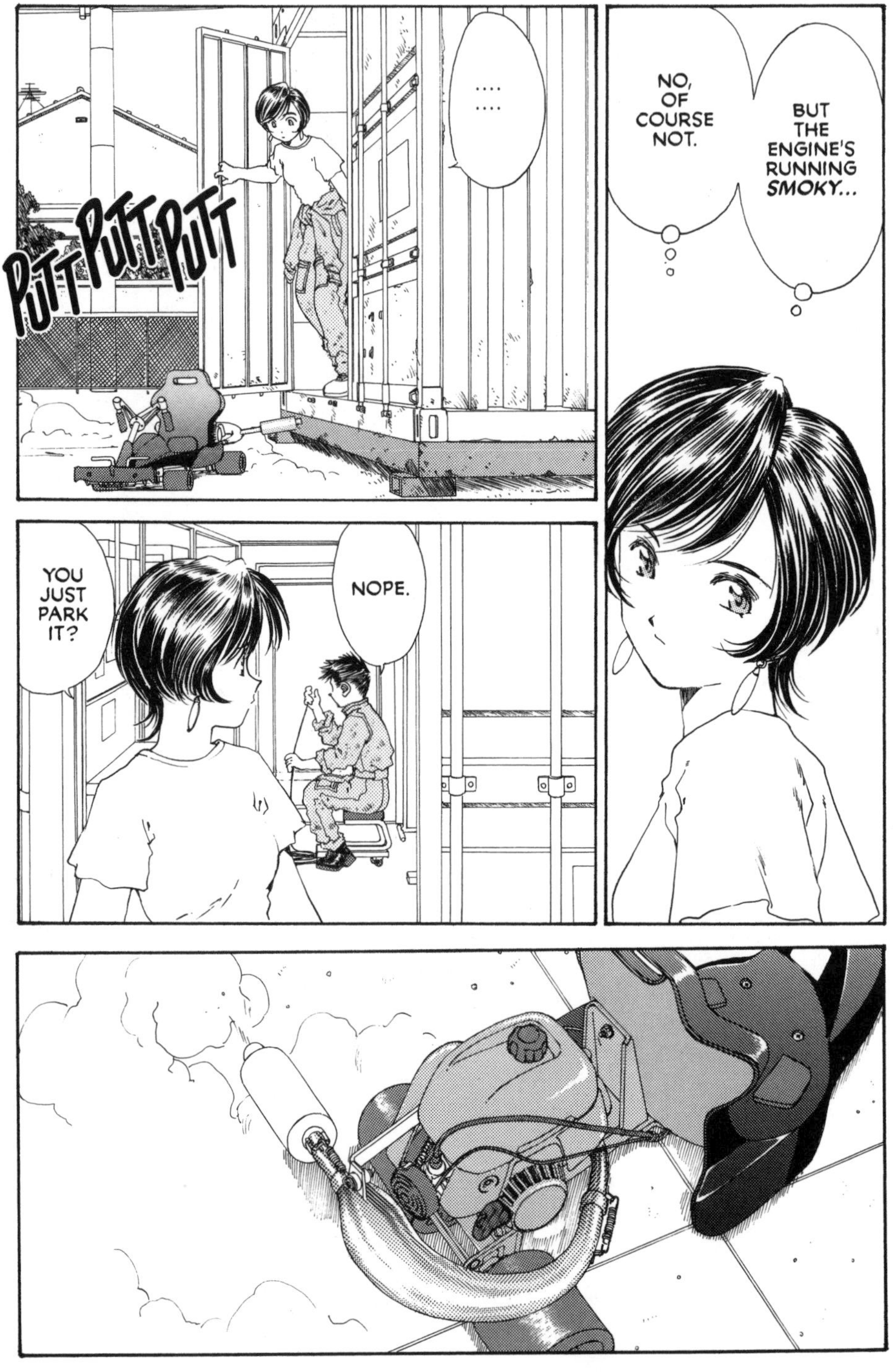
PUTT PUTT PUTT
....
....
YOU JUST PARK IT?
NOPE.
NO, OF COURSE NOT.
BUT THE ENGINE'S RUNNING *SMOKY*...

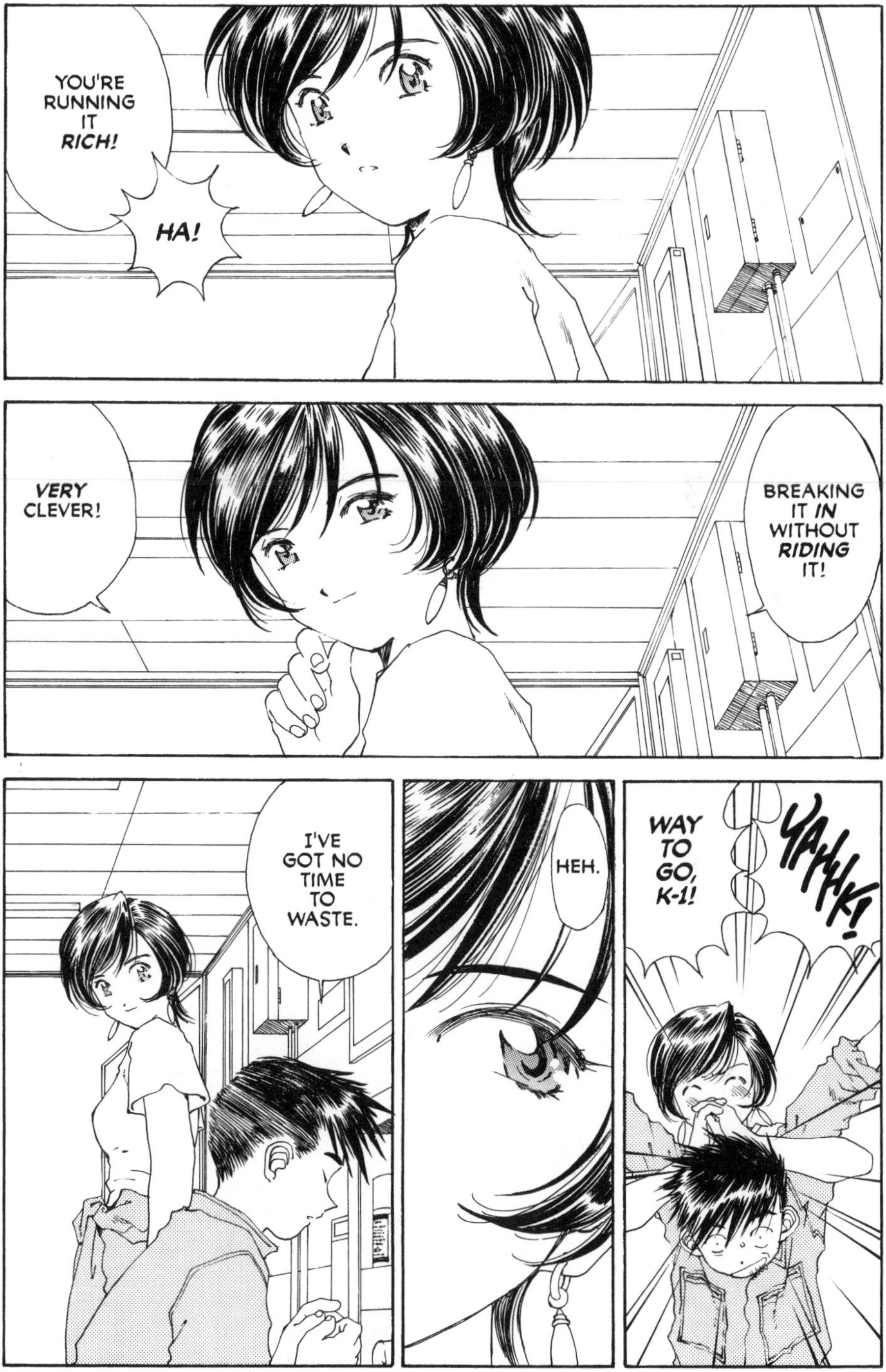
YOU'RE RUNNING IT *RICH!*
HA!
VERY CLEVER!
BREAKING IT *IN* WITHOUT *RIDING* IT!
I'VE GOT NO TIME TO WASTE.
HEH.
WAY TO GO, K-1!
YAHHK!

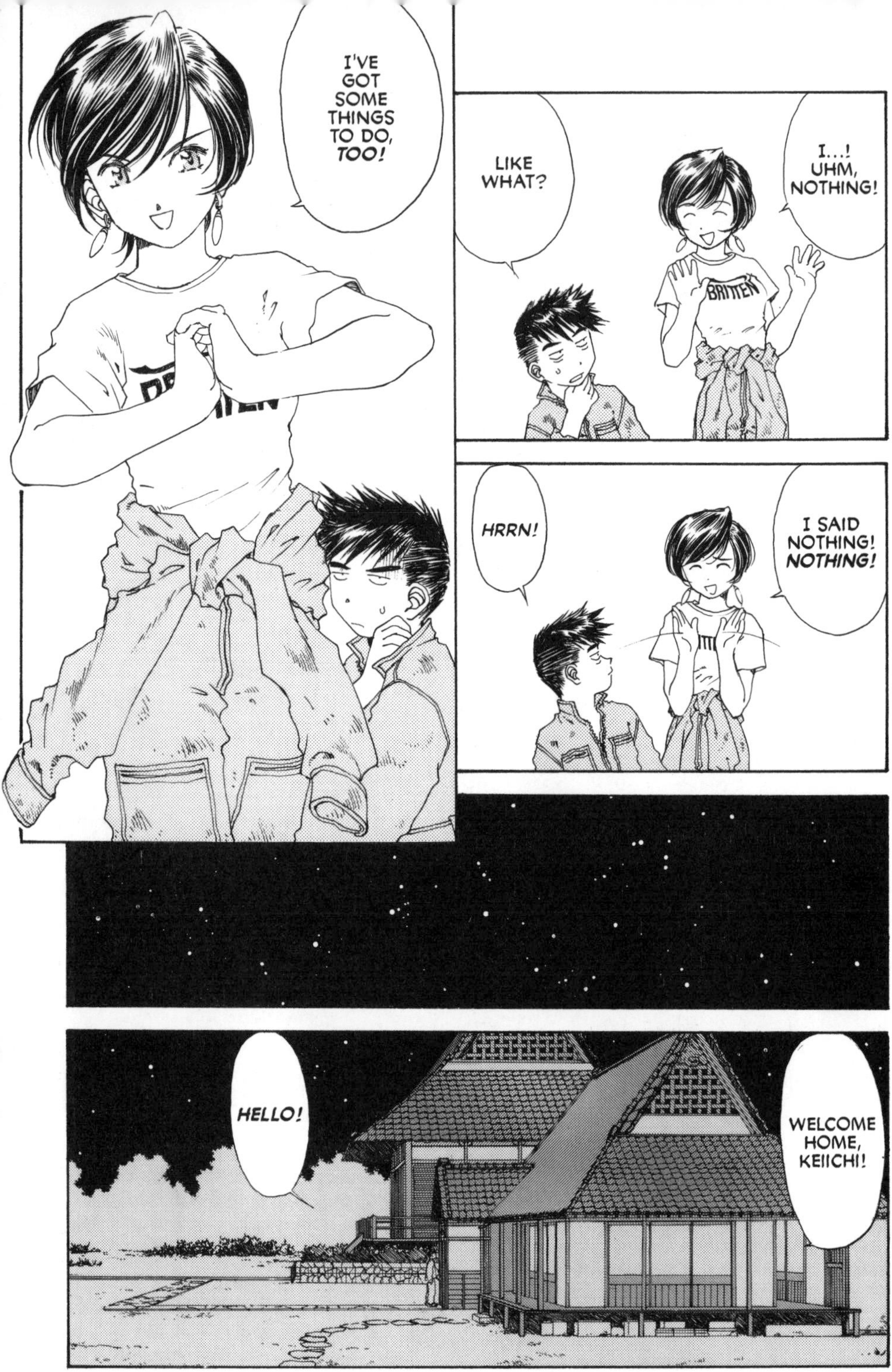
I'VE GOT SOME THINGS TO DO, *TOO!*
LIKE WHAT?
I...! UHM, NOTHING!
BRITTEN
HRRN!
I SAID NOTHING! ***NOTHING!***
HELLO!
WELCOME HOME, KEIICHI!

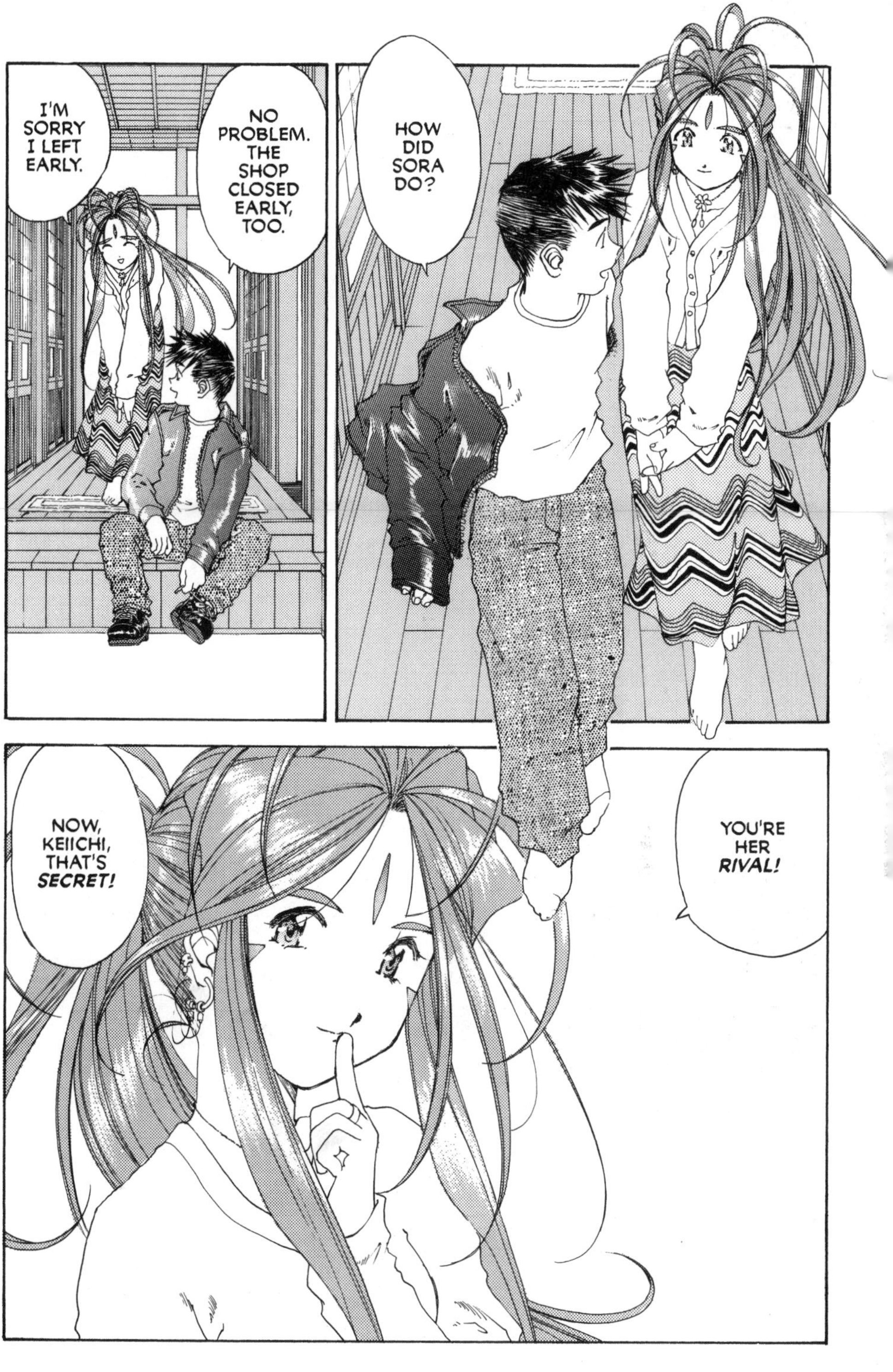
I'M SORRY I LEFT EARLY.
NO PROBLEM. THE SHOP CLOSED EARLY, TOO.
HOW DID SORA DO?
NOW, KEIICHI, THAT'S *SECRET!*
YOU'RE HER *RIVAL!*

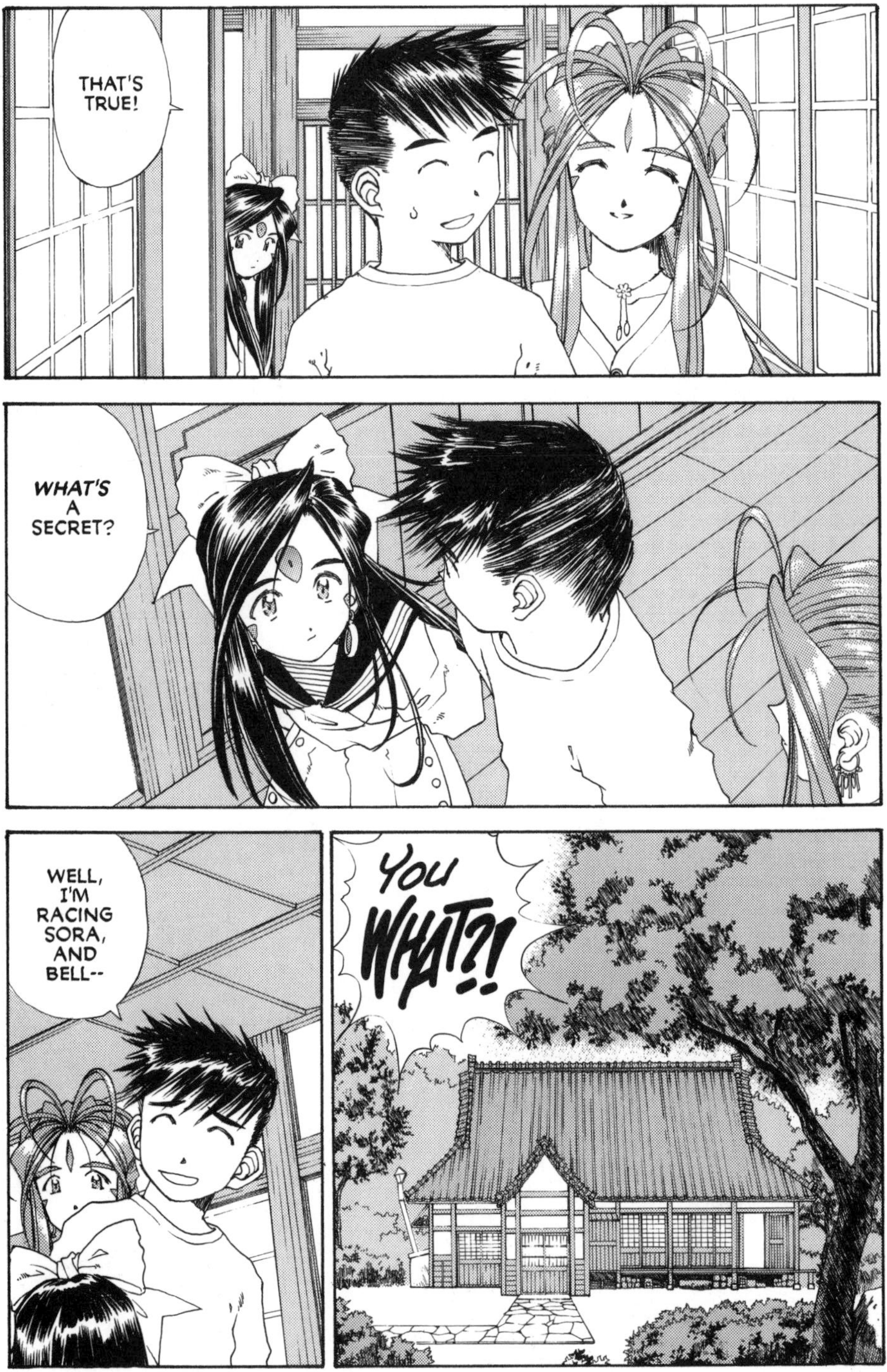
THAT'S TRUE!
WHAT'S A SECRET?
WELL, I'M RACING SORA, AND BELL--
YOU WHAT?!

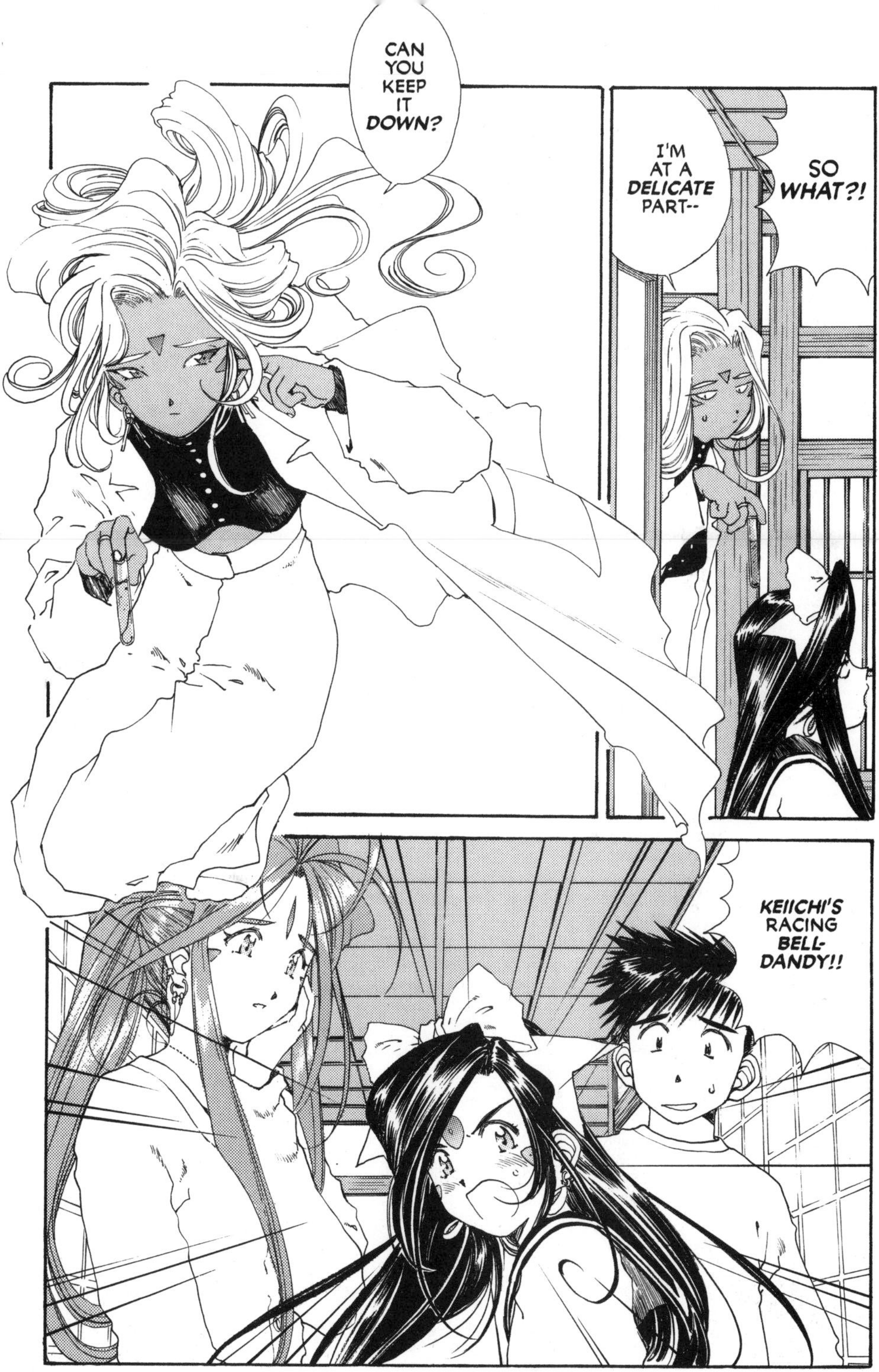
CAN YOU KEEP IT *DOWN?*
I'M AT A *DELICATE* PART--
SO *WHAT?!*
KEIICHI'S RACING BELL-DANDY!!

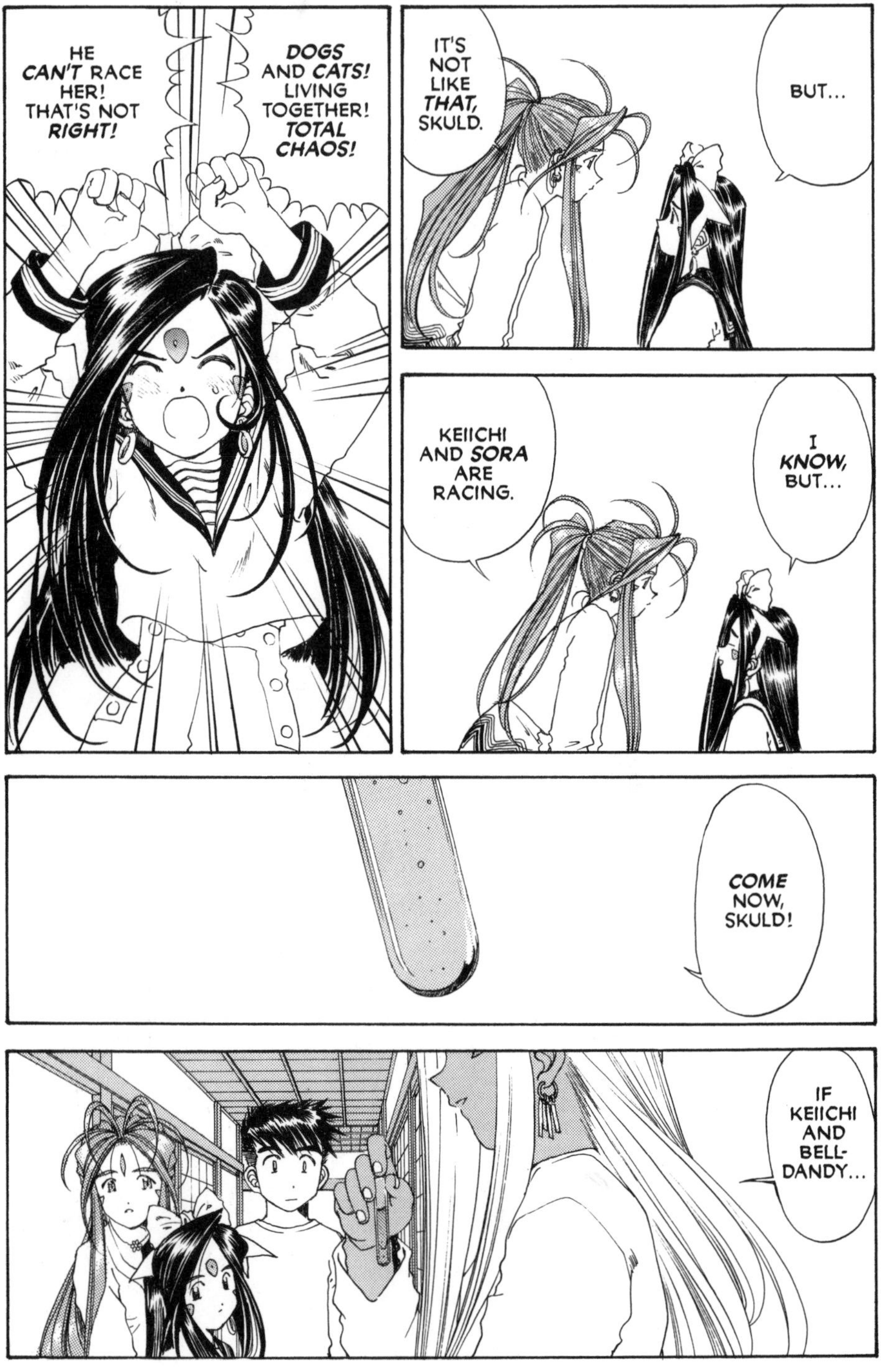
HE CAN'T RACE HER! THAT'S NOT RIGHT!
DOGS AND CATS! LIVING TOGETHER! TOTAL CHAOS!
IT'S NOT LIKE THAT, SKULD.
BUT...
KEIICHI AND SORA ARE RACING.
I KNOW, BUT...
COME NOW, SKULD!
IF KEIICHI AND BELL-DANDY...

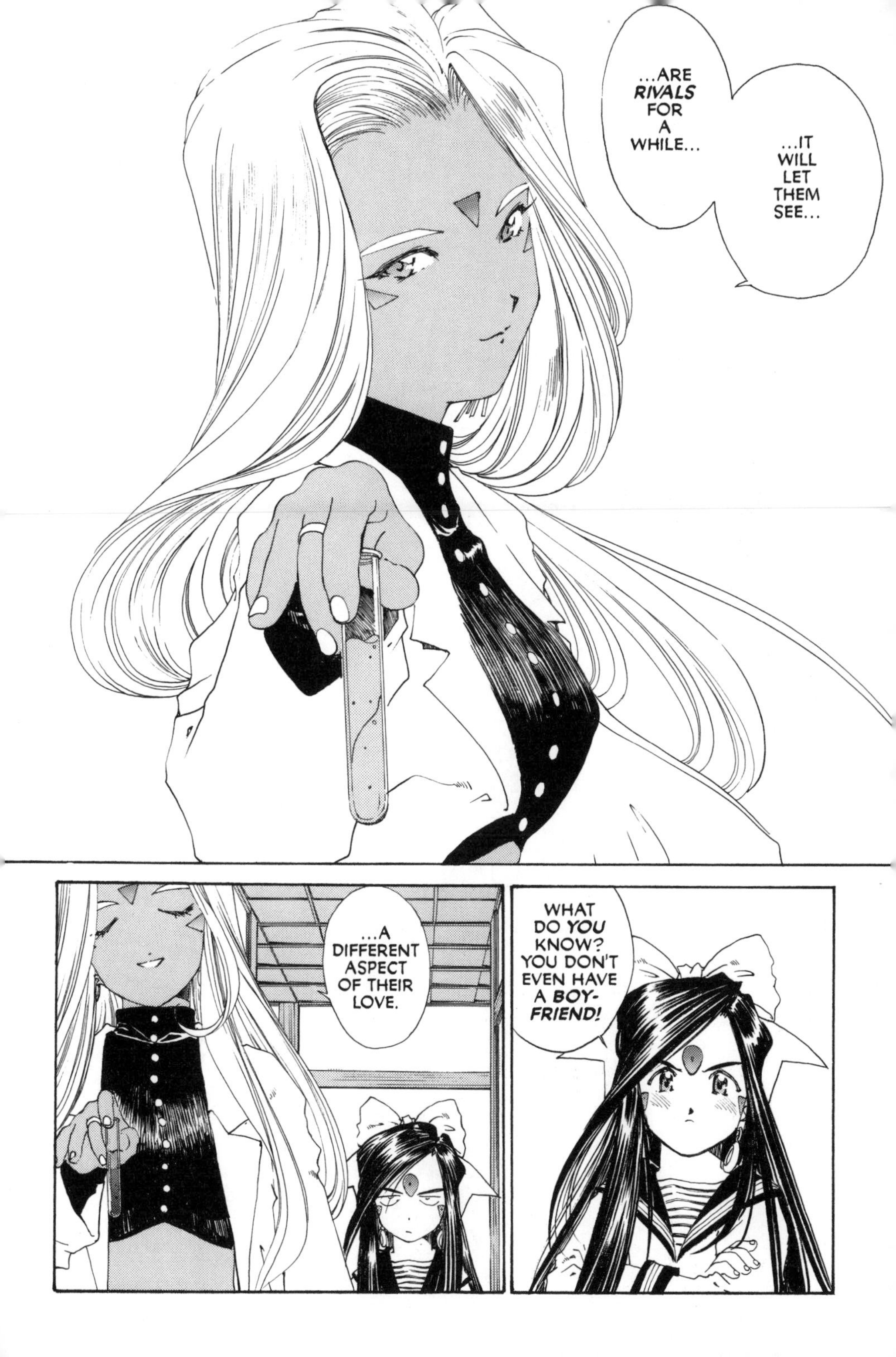
...ARE RIVALS FOR A WHILE...
...IT WILL LET THEM SEE...
...A DIFFERENT ASPECT OF THEIR LOVE.
WHAT DO YOU KNOW? YOU DON'T EVEN HAVE A BOY-FRIEND!

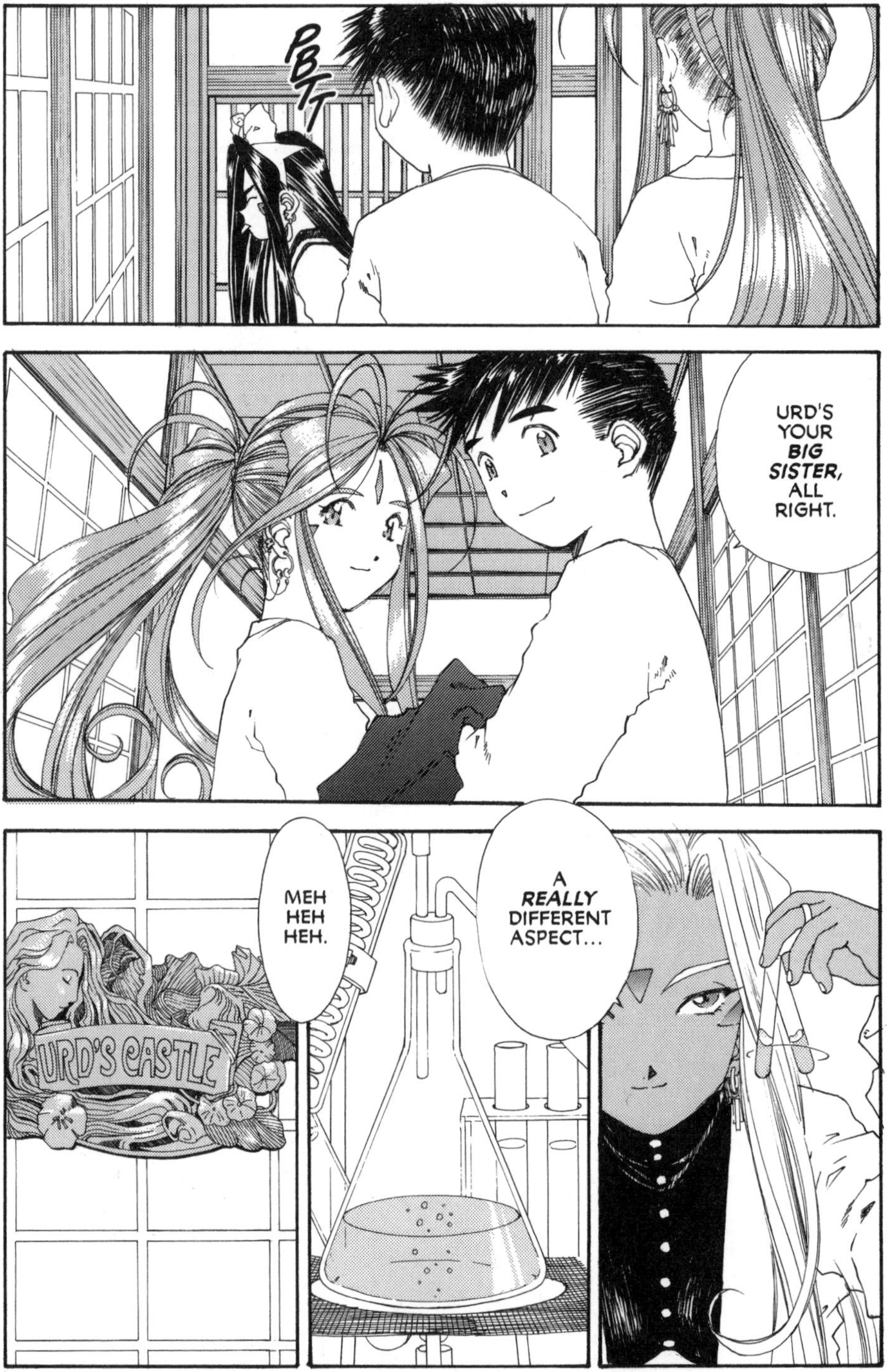
PBTT
URD'S YOUR BIG SISTER, ALL RIGHT.
A REALLY DIFFERENT ASPECT...
MEH HEH HEH.
URD'S CASTLE

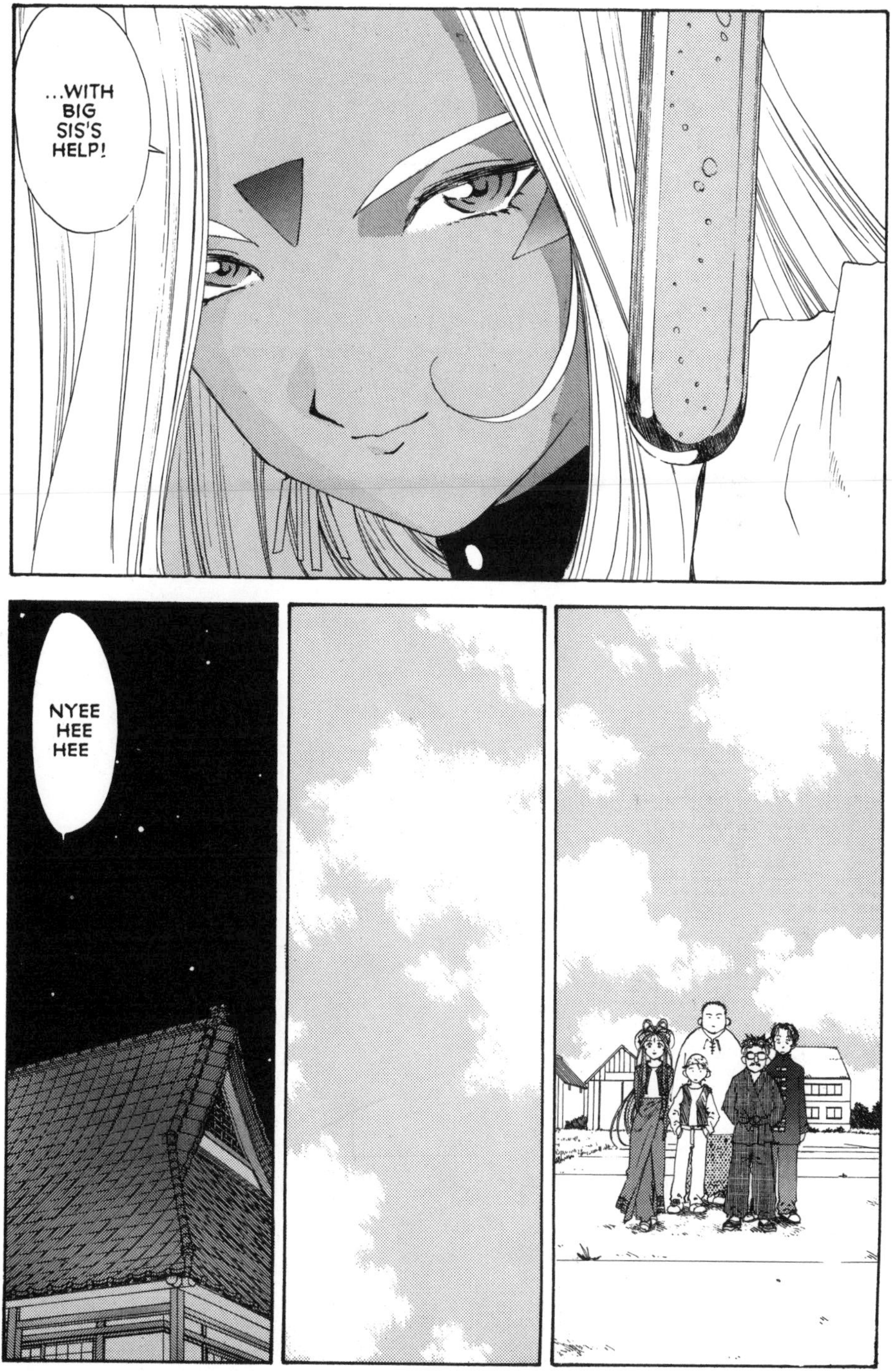
...WITH BIG SIS'S HELP!
NYEE HEE HEE

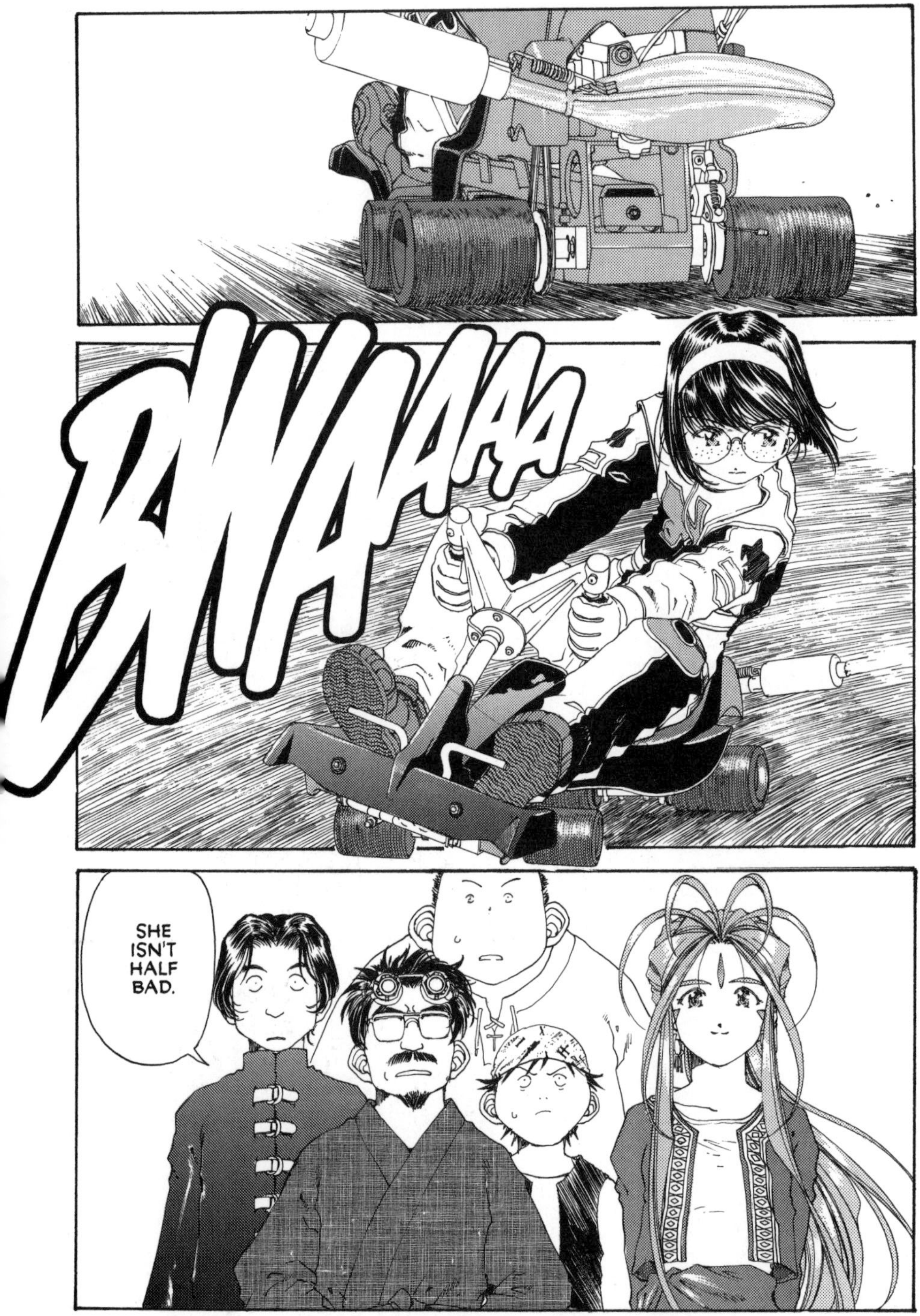
BWAAAAA
SHE ISN'T HALF BAD.

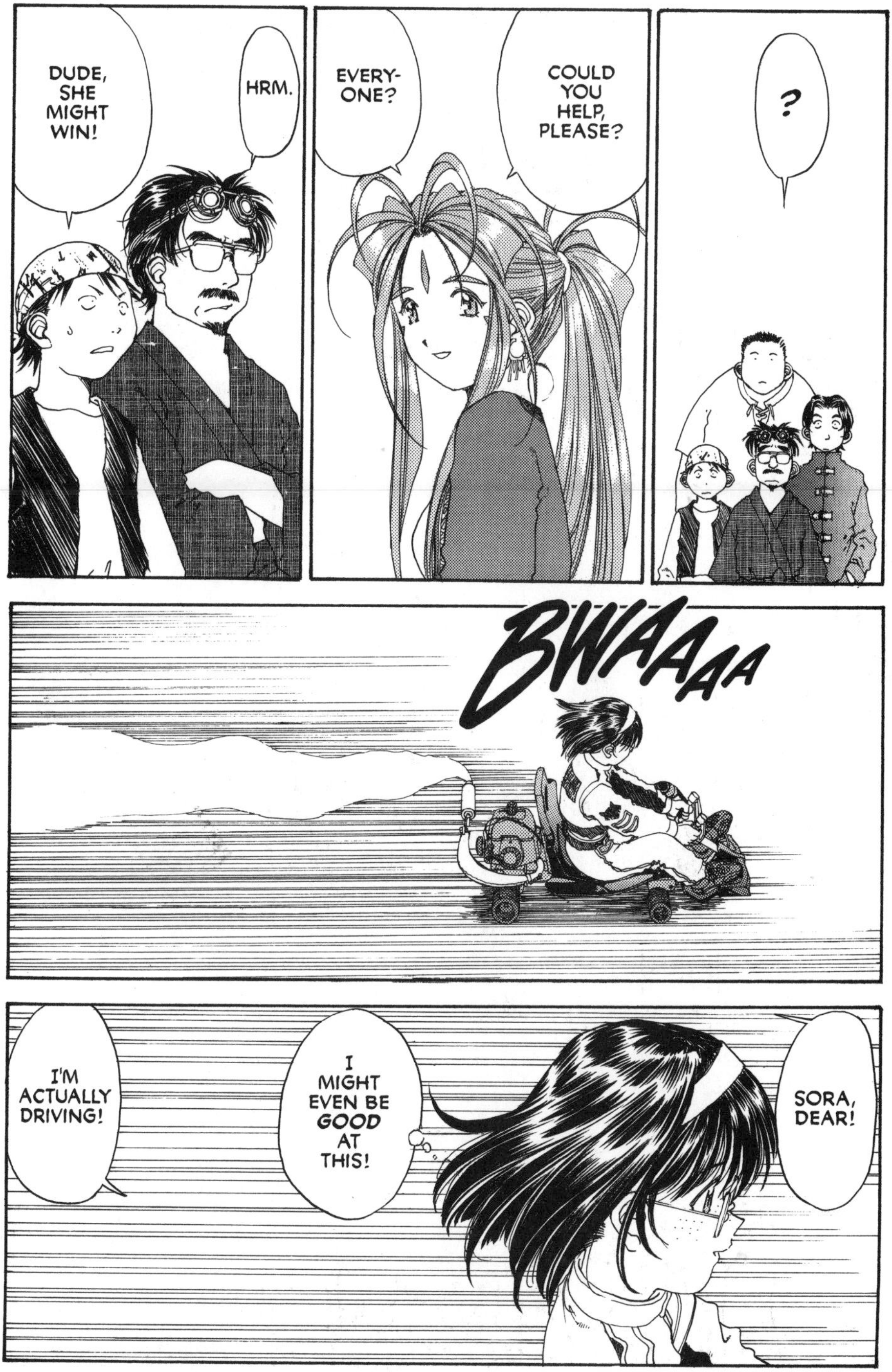

DUDE, SHE MIGHT WIN!
HRM.
EVERY-ONE?
COULD YOU HELP, PLEASE?
?
BWAAAAA
I'M ACTUALLY DRIVING!
I MIGHT EVEN BE *GOOD* AT THIS!
SORA, DEAR!

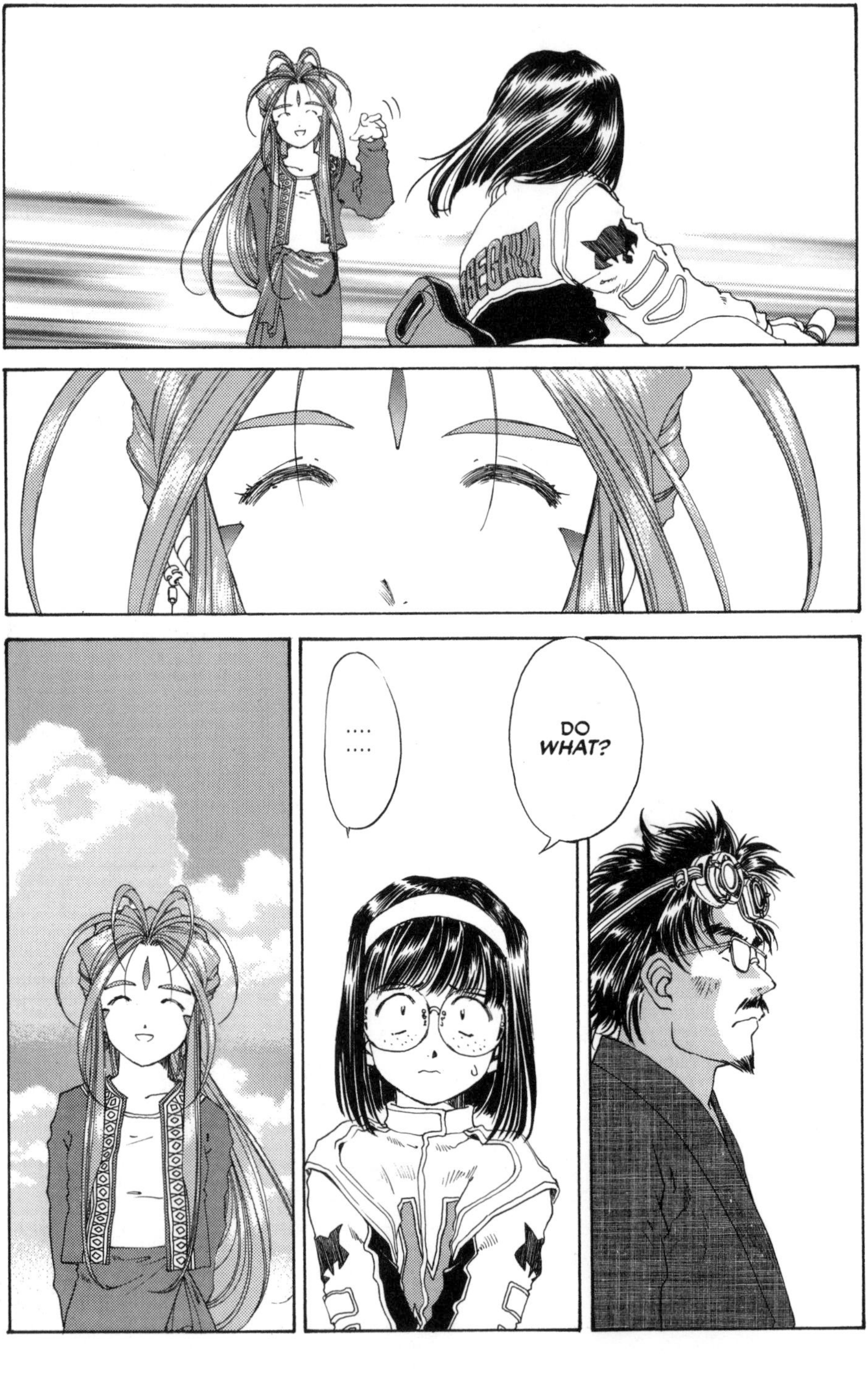
DO WHAT?
....
....

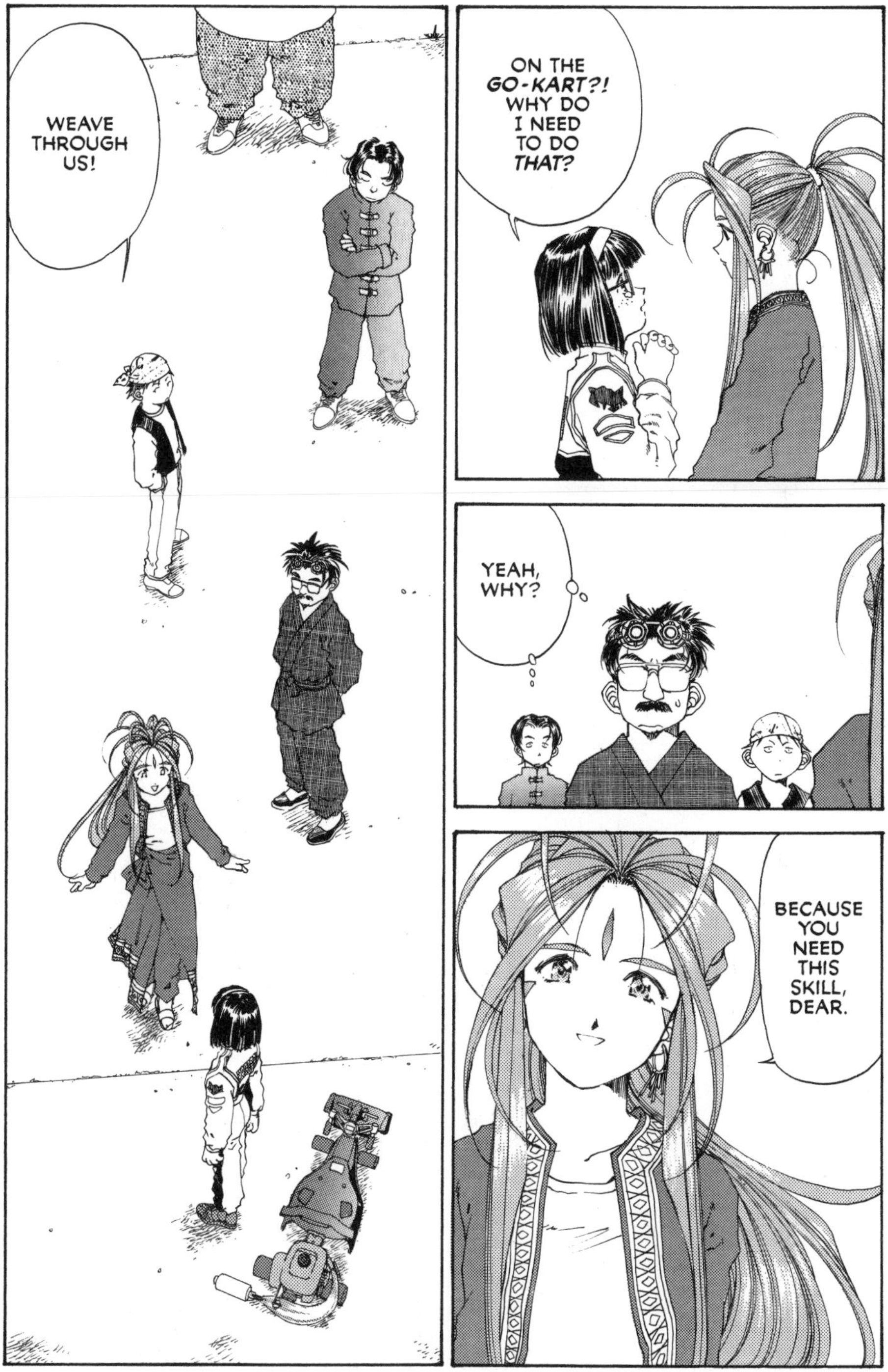
WEAVE THROUGH US!
ON THE GO-KART?! WHY DO I NEED TO DO THAT?
YEAH, WHY?
BECAUSE YOU NEED THIS SKILL, DEAR.

O-OKAY...

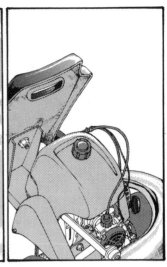

HERE I COME.

BWAAAAA

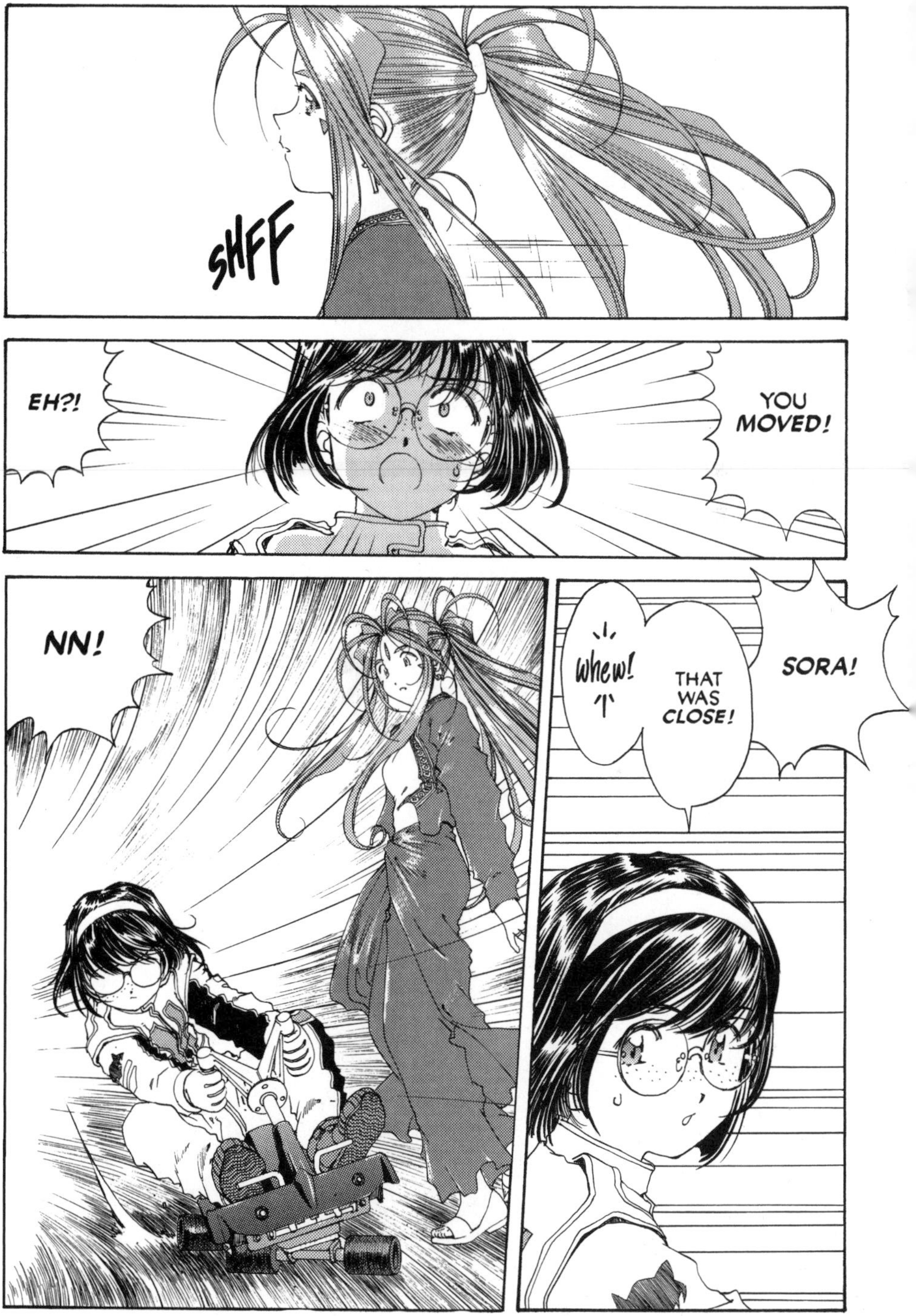
SHFF
YOU MOVED!
EH?!
SORA!
whew!
THAT WAS CLOSE!
NN!

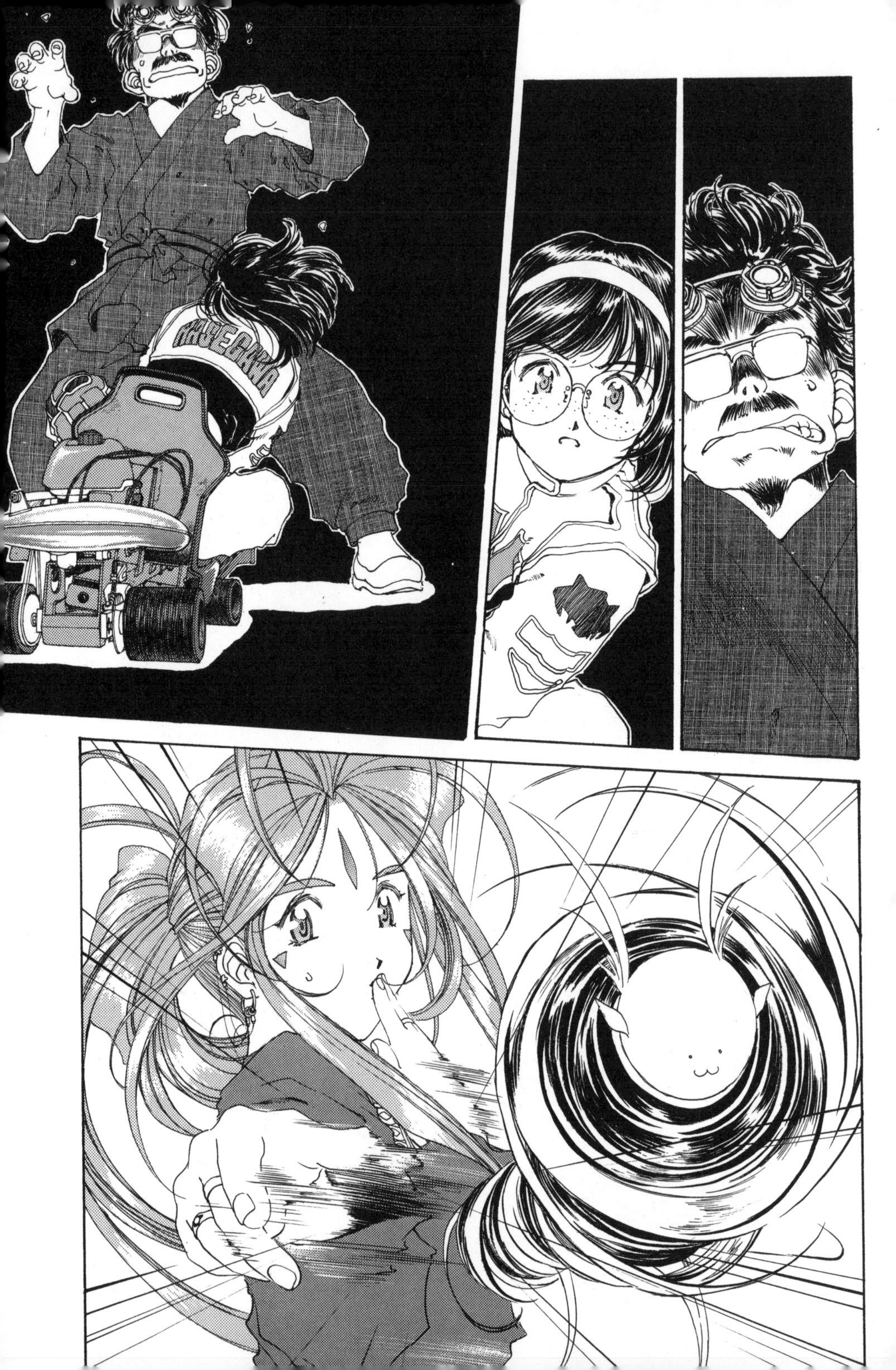
HASEGAWA

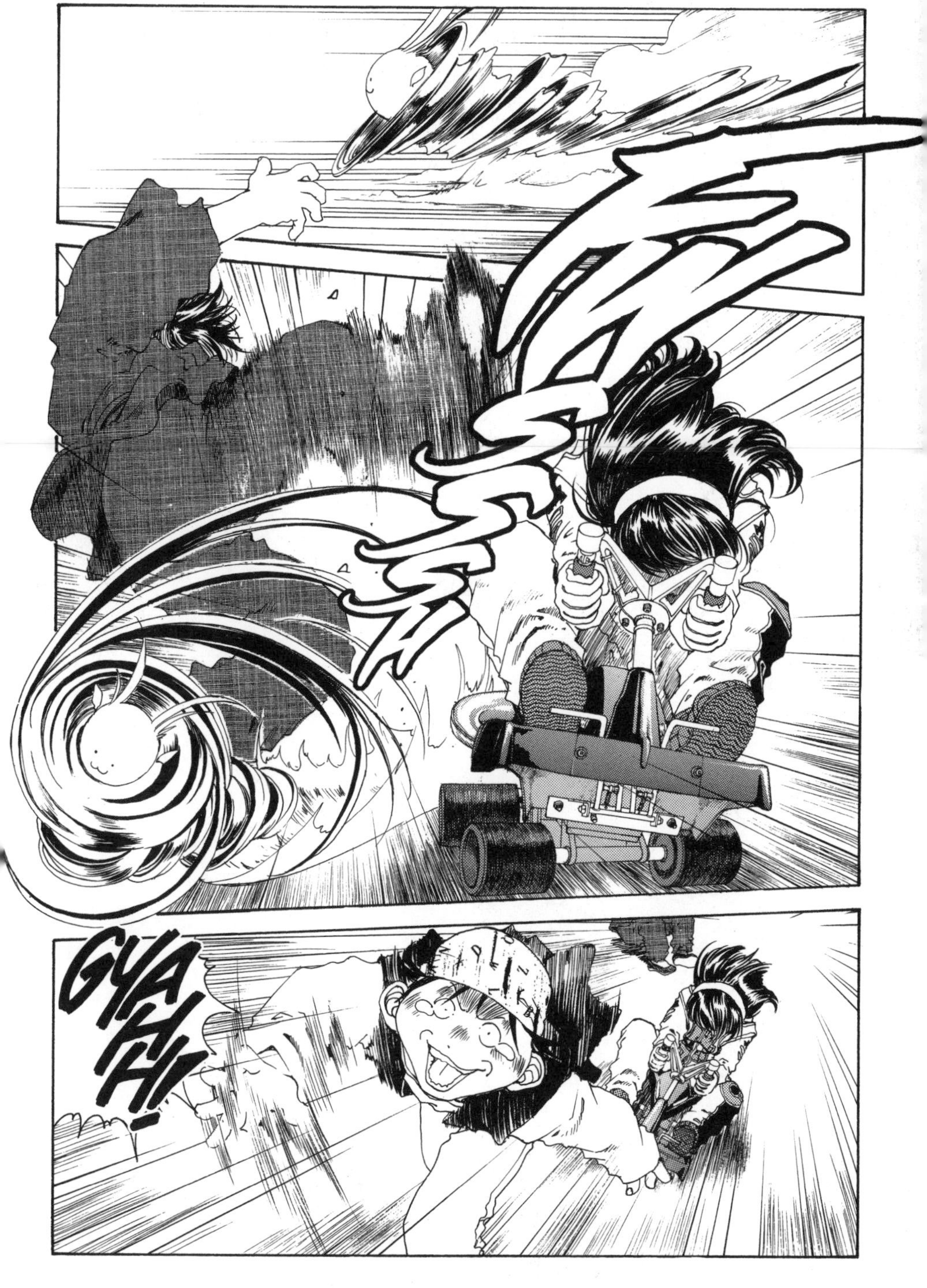
GYAHH!

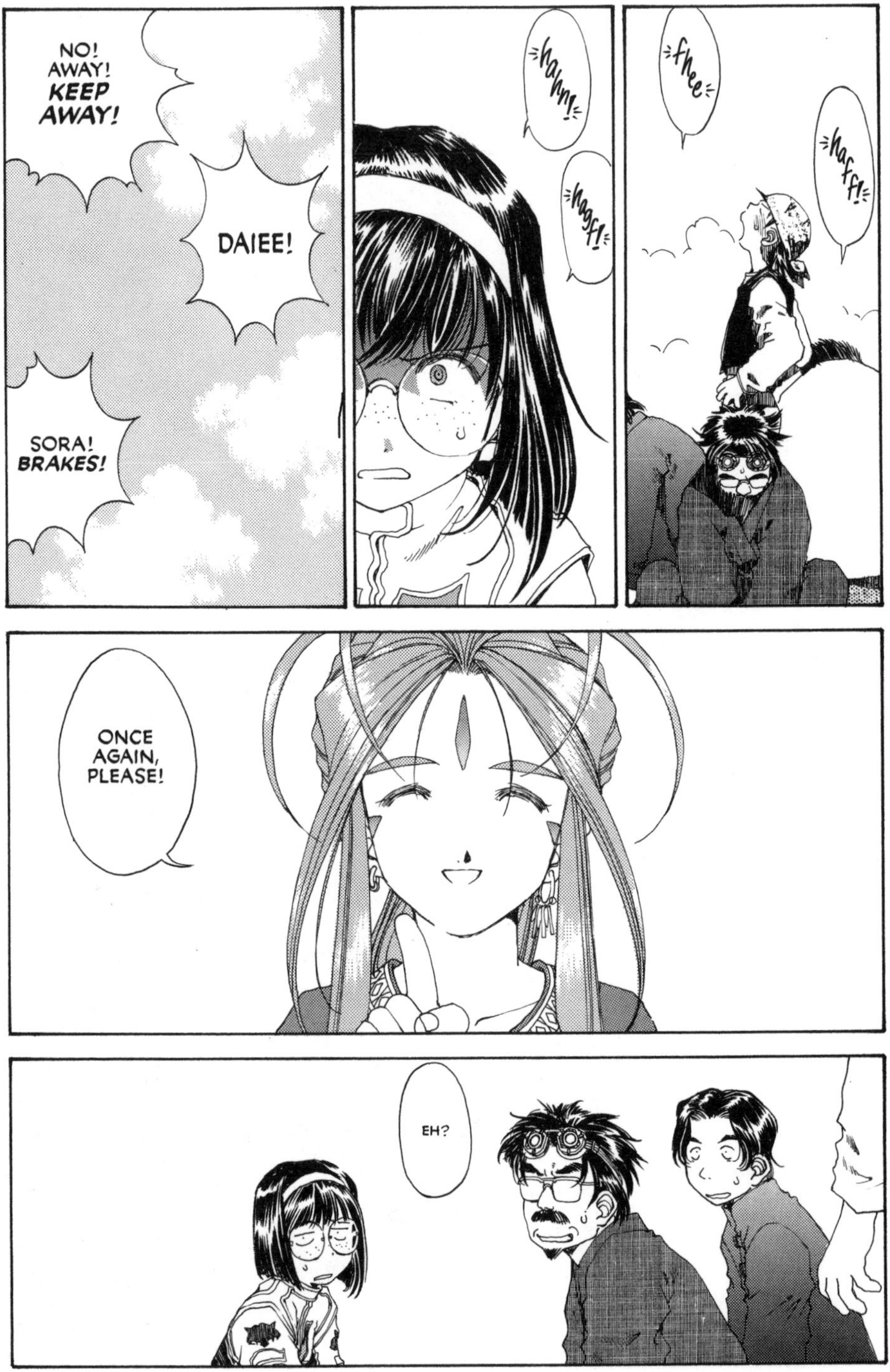

fhee
haff!
hahn!
hagf!
NO! AWAY! **KEEP AWAY!**
DAIEE!
SORA! **BRAKES!**
ONCE AGAIN, PLEASE!
EH?

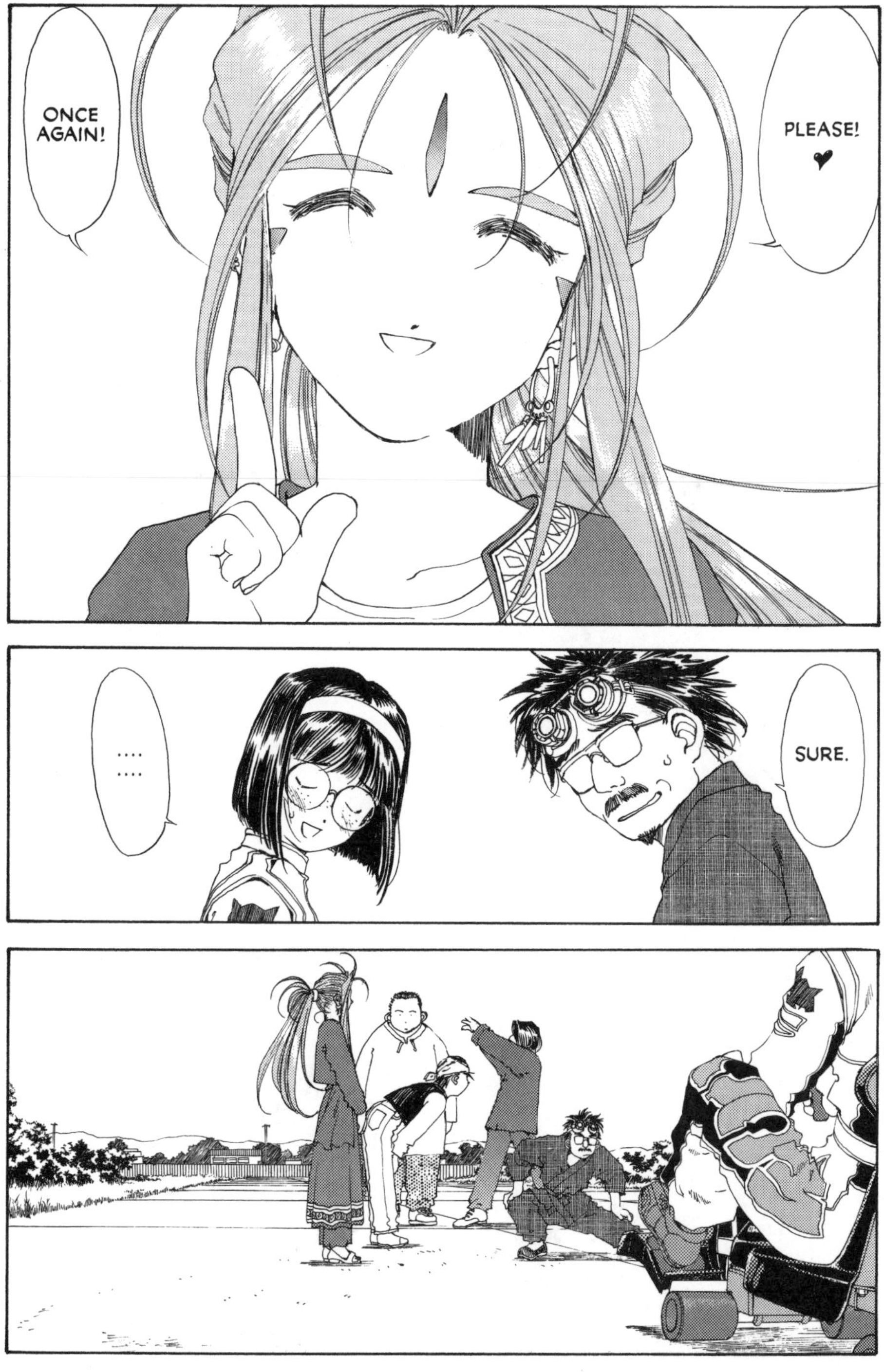
PLEASE! ♥
ONCE AGAIN!
SURE.
....
....

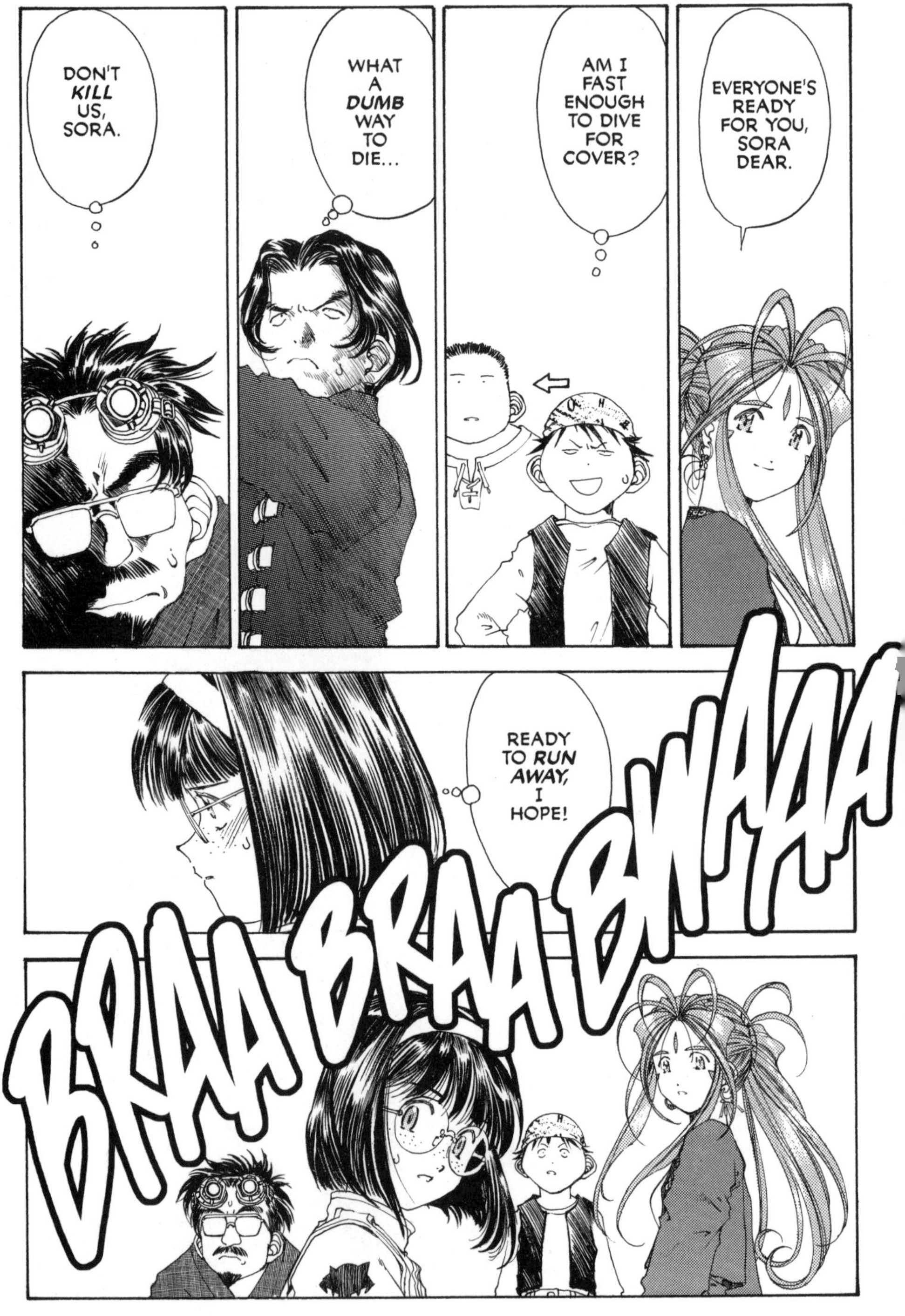
EVERYONE'S READY FOR YOU, SORA DEAR.
AM I FAST ENOUGH TO DIVE FOR COVER?
WHAT A DUMB WAY TO DIE...
DON'T KILL US, SORA.
READY TO RUN AWAY, I HOPE!
BRAA BRAA BWAAAA

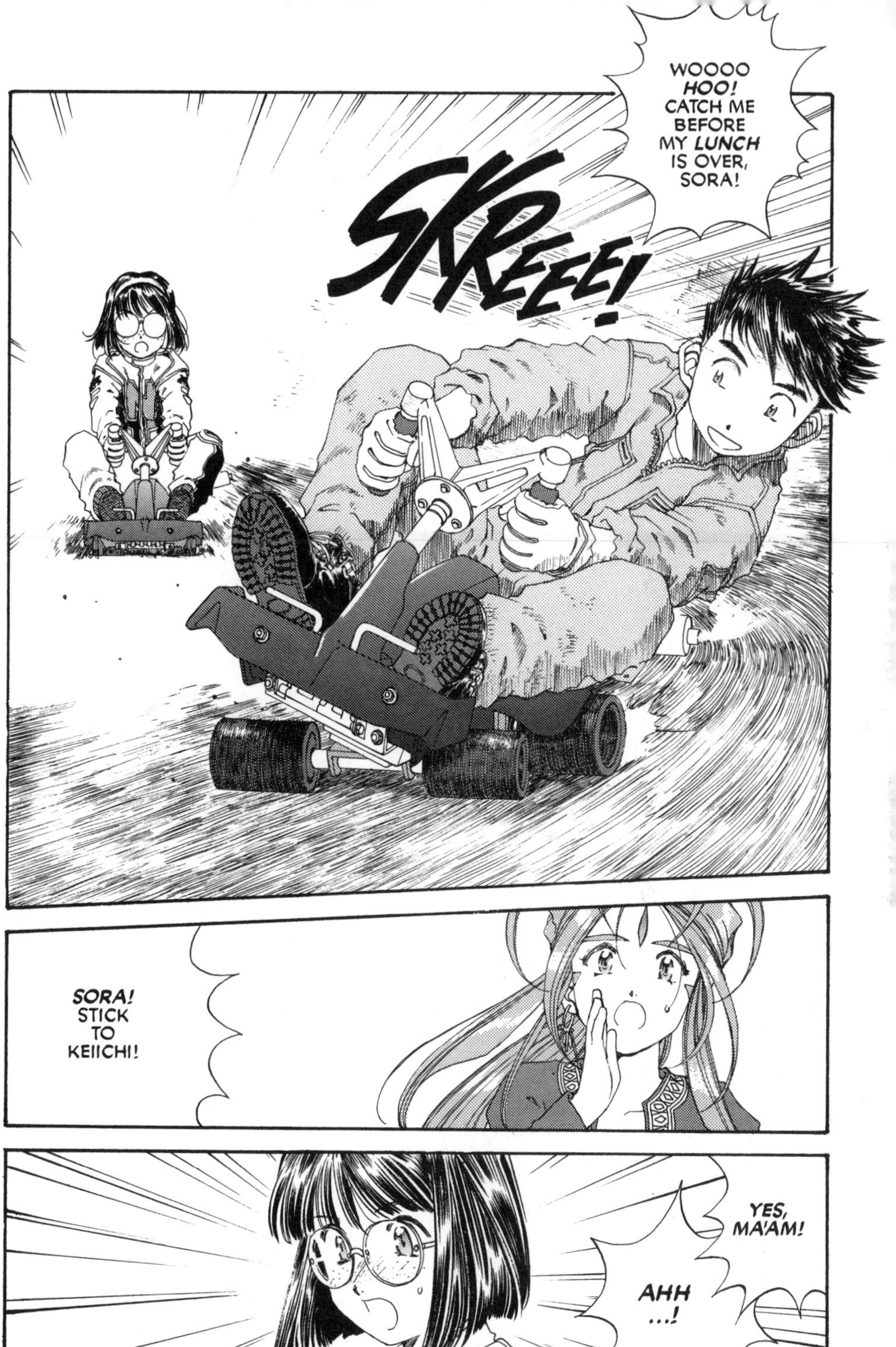
WOOOO HOO! CATCH ME BEFORE MY LUNCH IS OVER, SORA!
SKREEE!
SORA! STICK TO KEIICHI!
YES, MA'AM!
AHH ...!

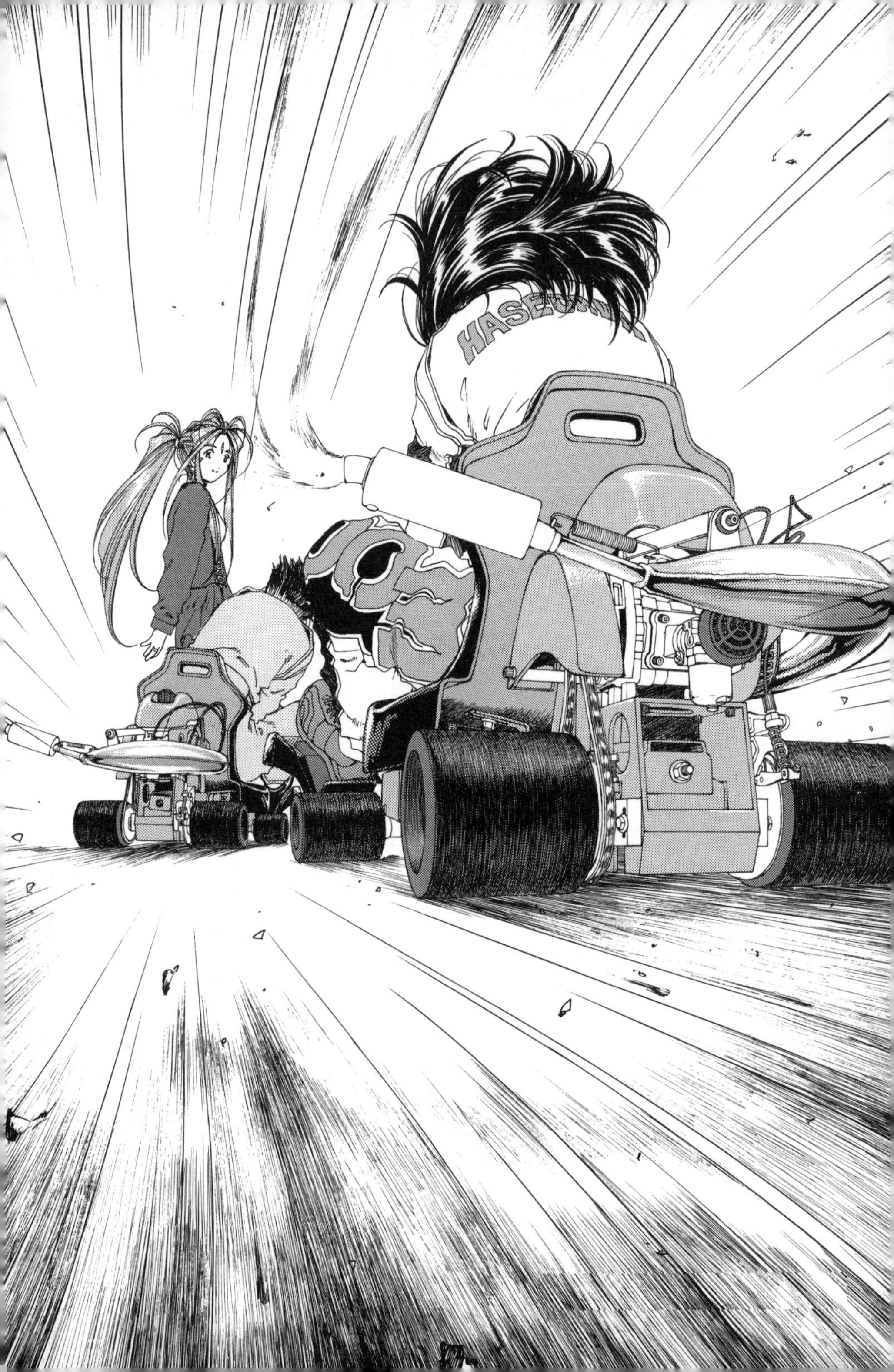

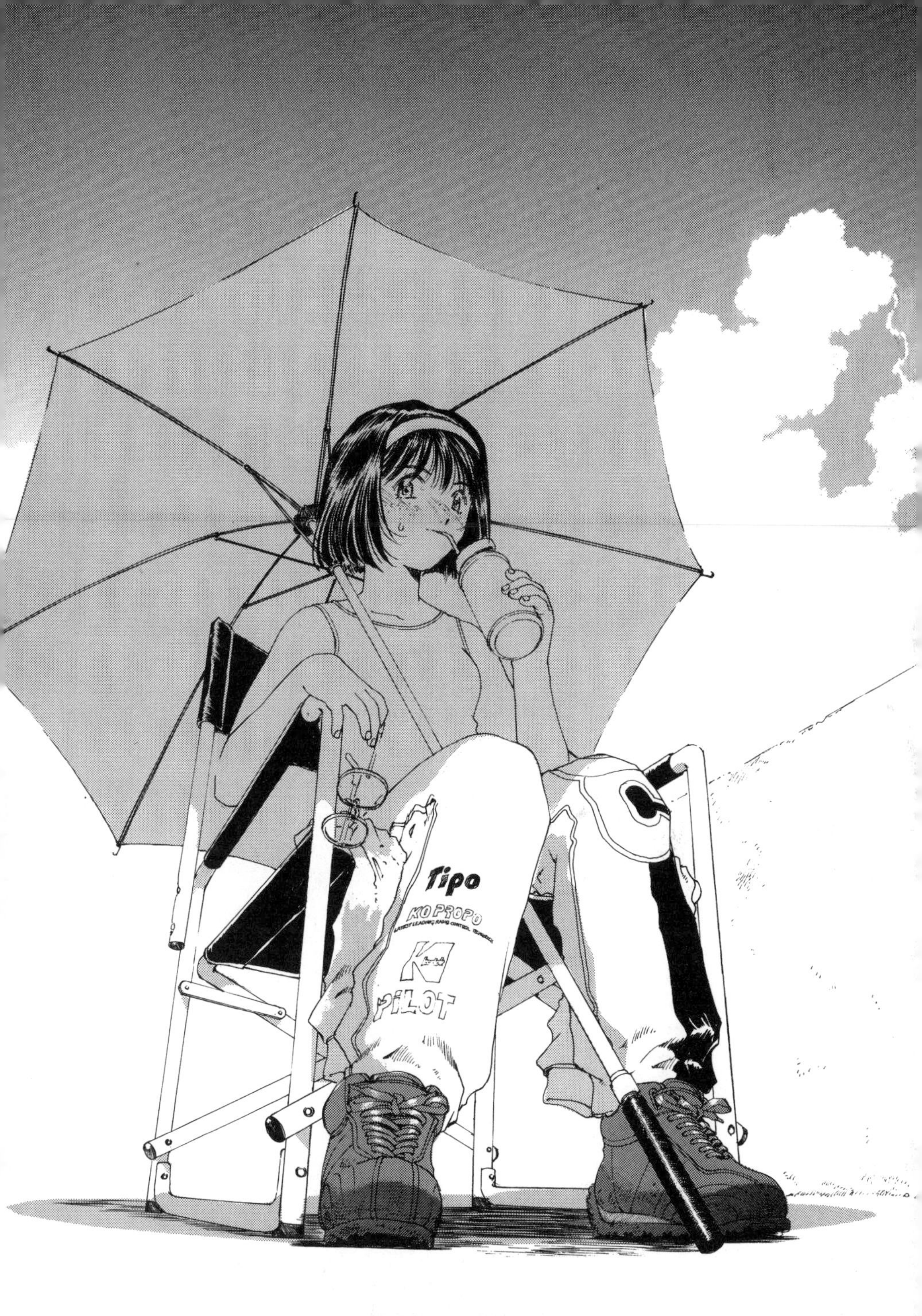
Tipo
KO PROPO
PILOT

DRIVE

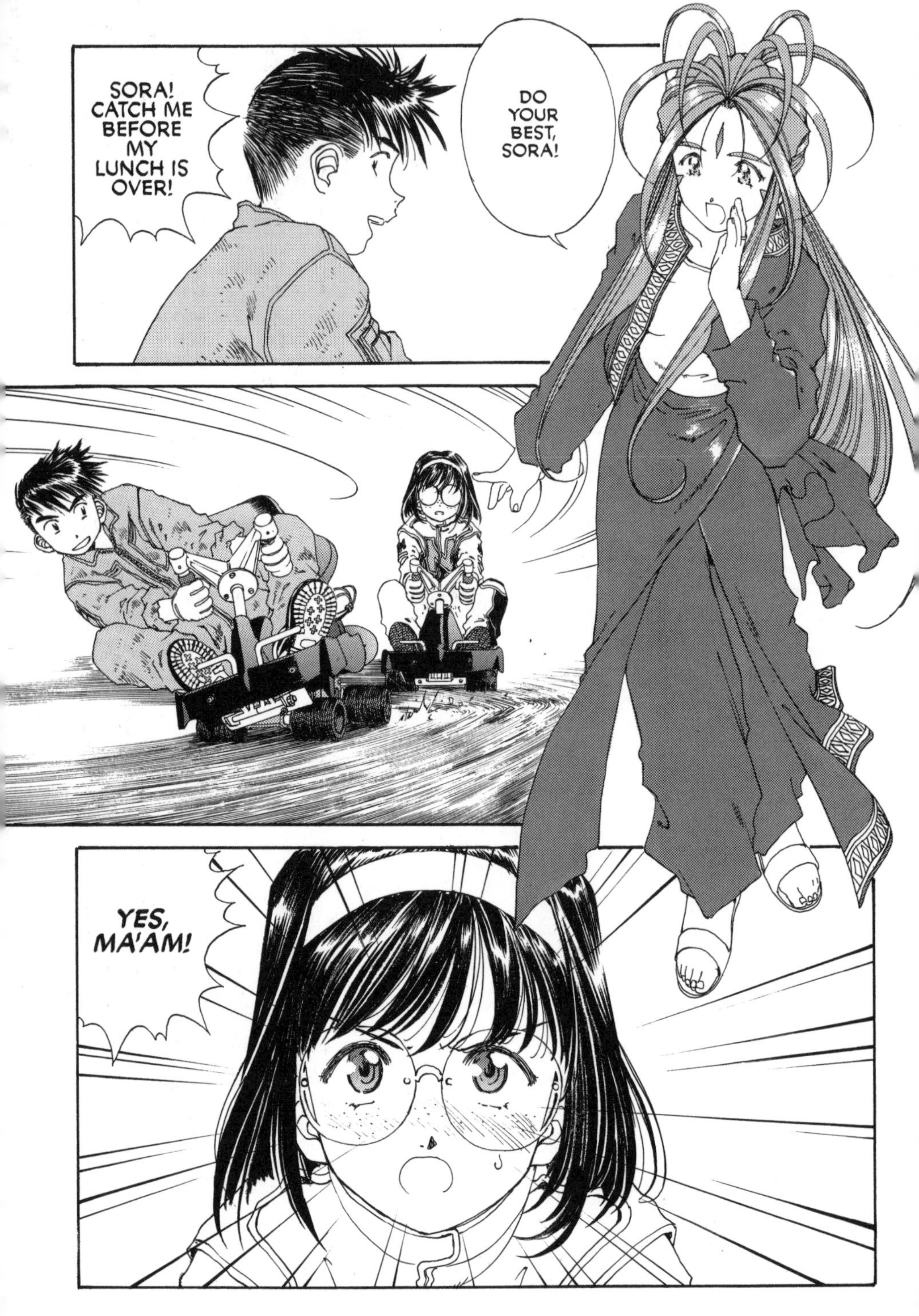
DO YOUR BEST, SORA!
SORA! CATCH ME BEFORE MY LUNCH IS OVER!
YES, MA'AM!

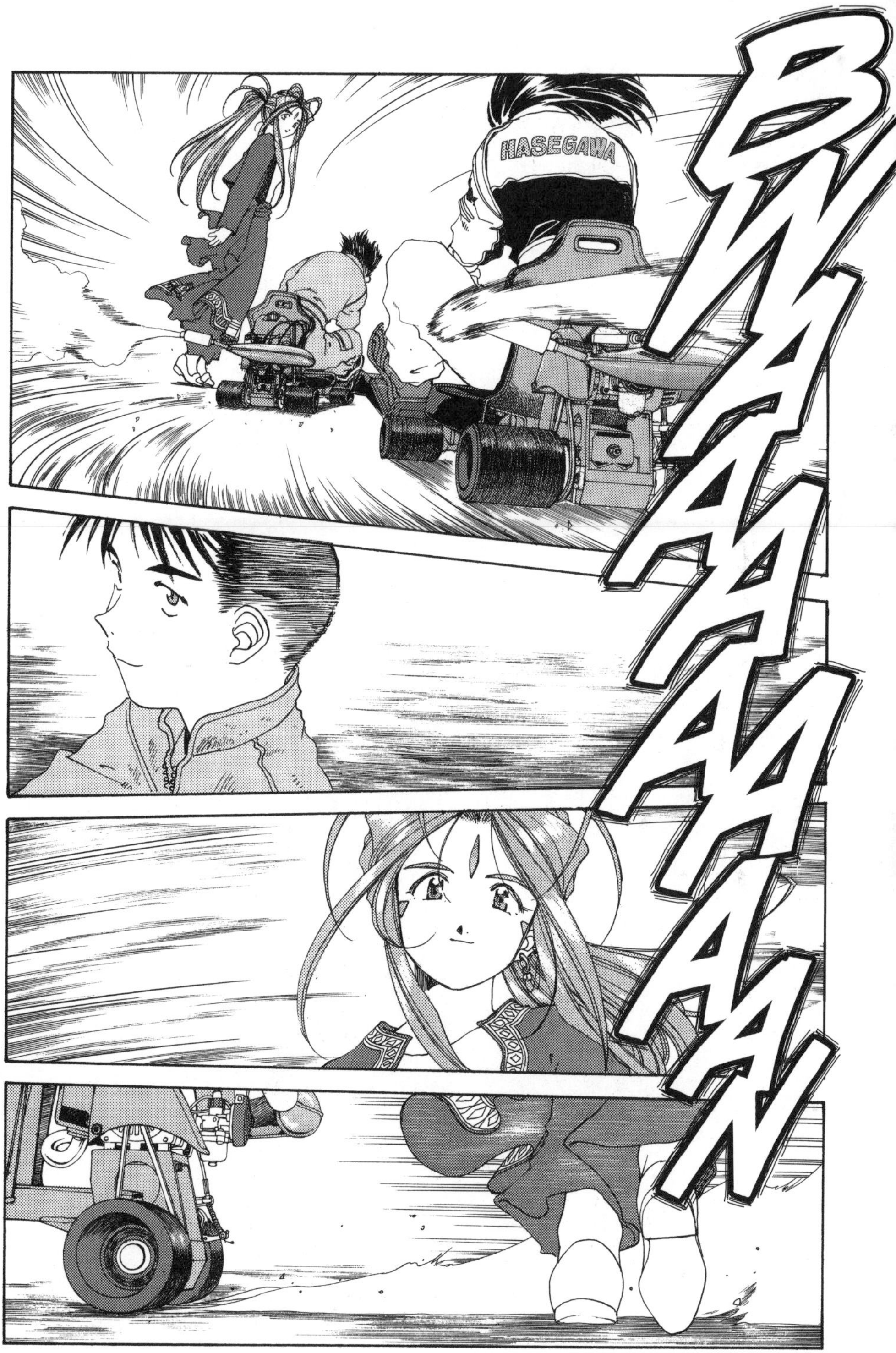
BWAAAAAAN
HASEGAWA

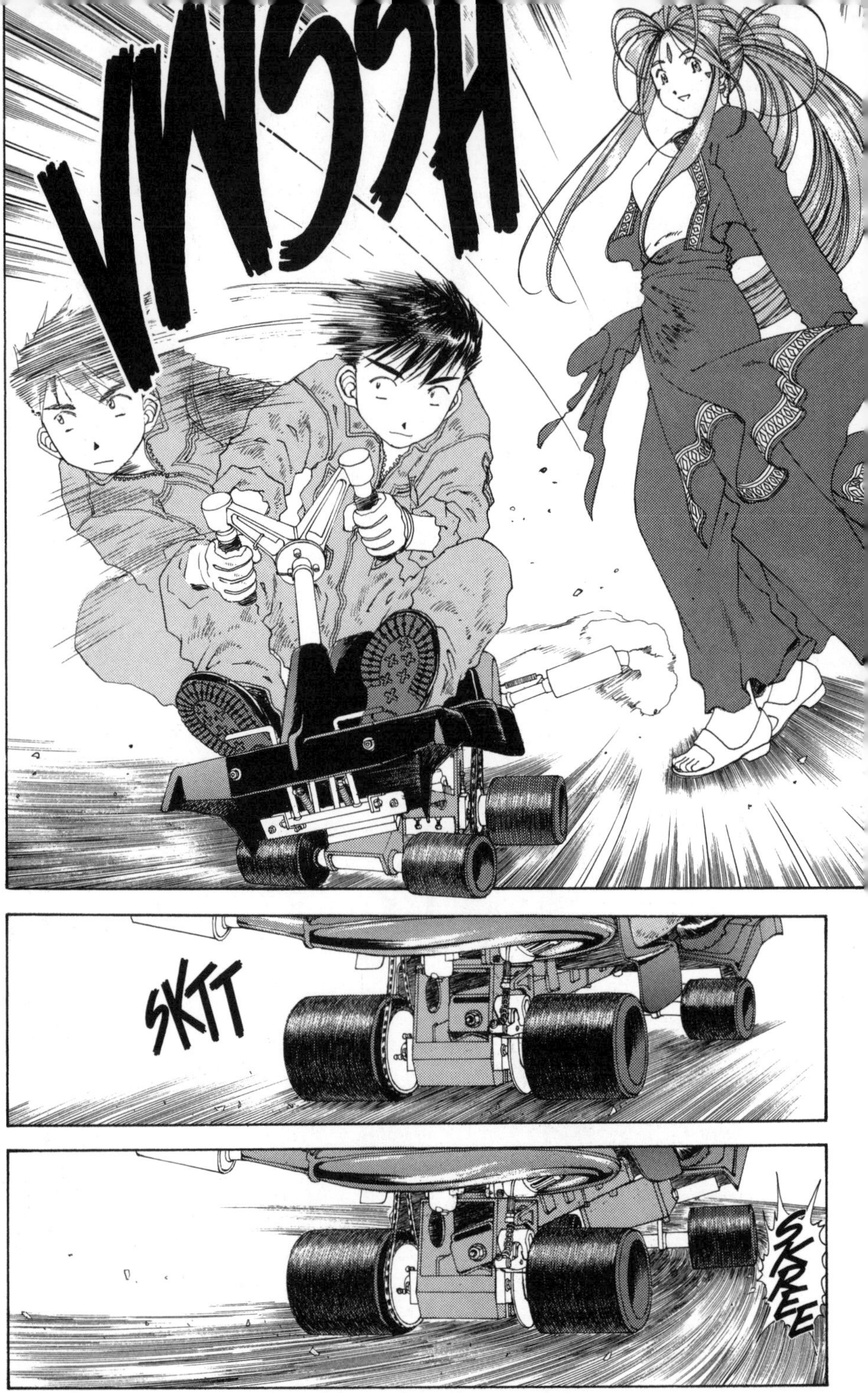
VWSSH
SKTT
SKREE

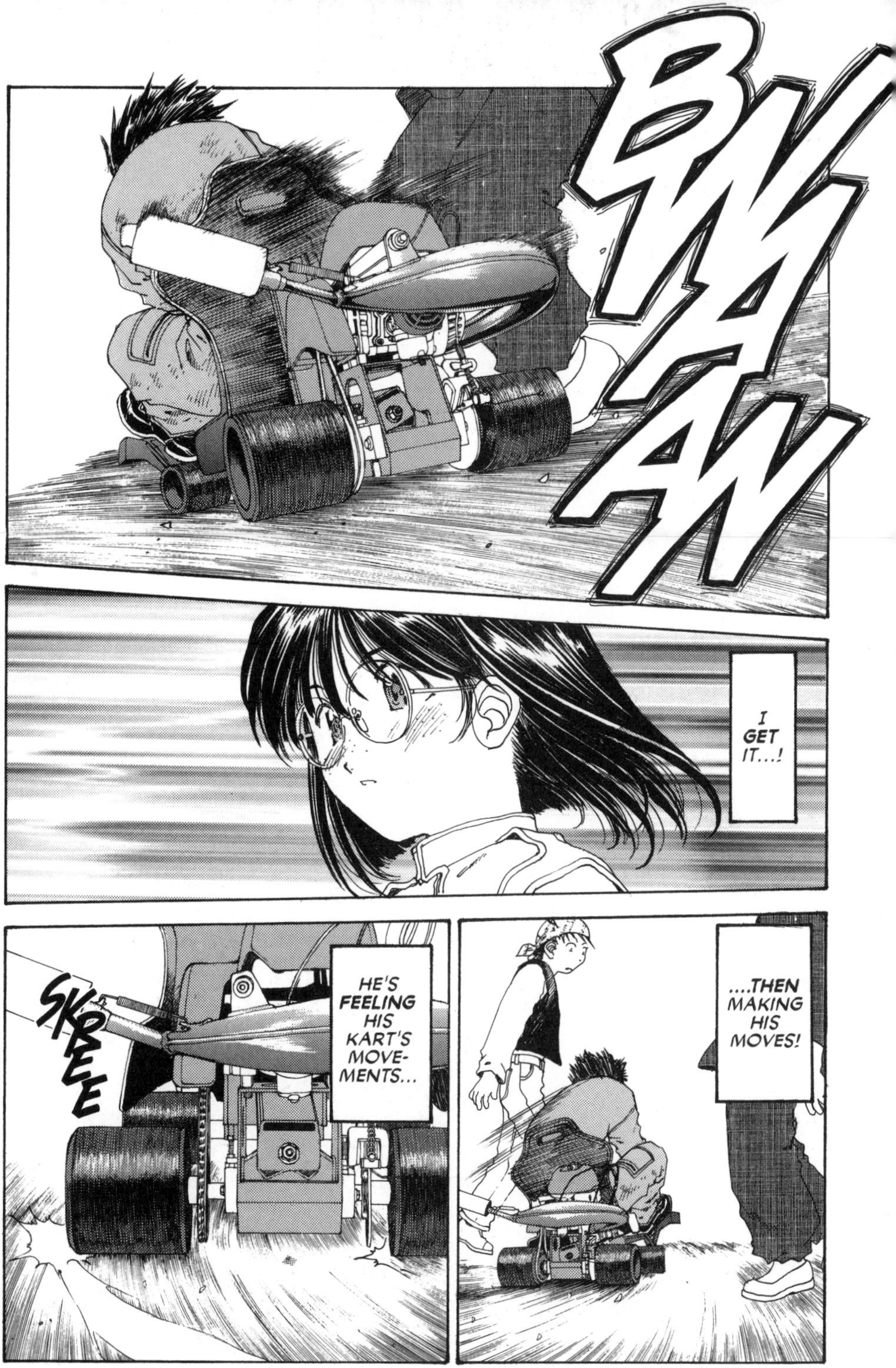
BWAAAN
I GET IT...!
HE'S FEELING HIS KART'S MOVEMENTS...
SKREEE
....THEN MAKING HIS MOVES!

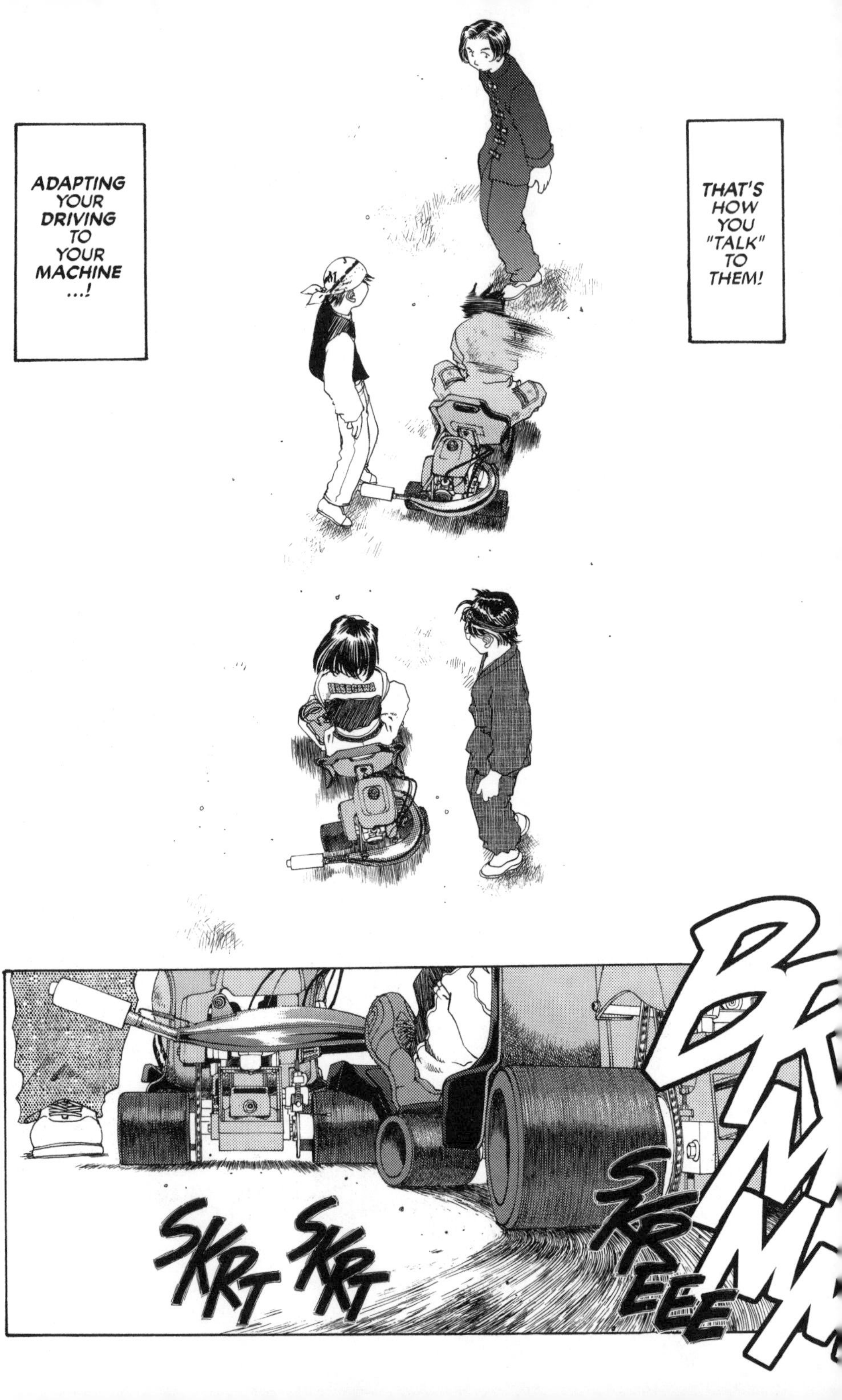
THAT'S HOW YOU "TALK" TO THEM!
ADAPTING YOUR DRIVING TO YOUR MACHINE ...!
HASEGAWA
BAMM
SKREEEE
SKRT SKRT

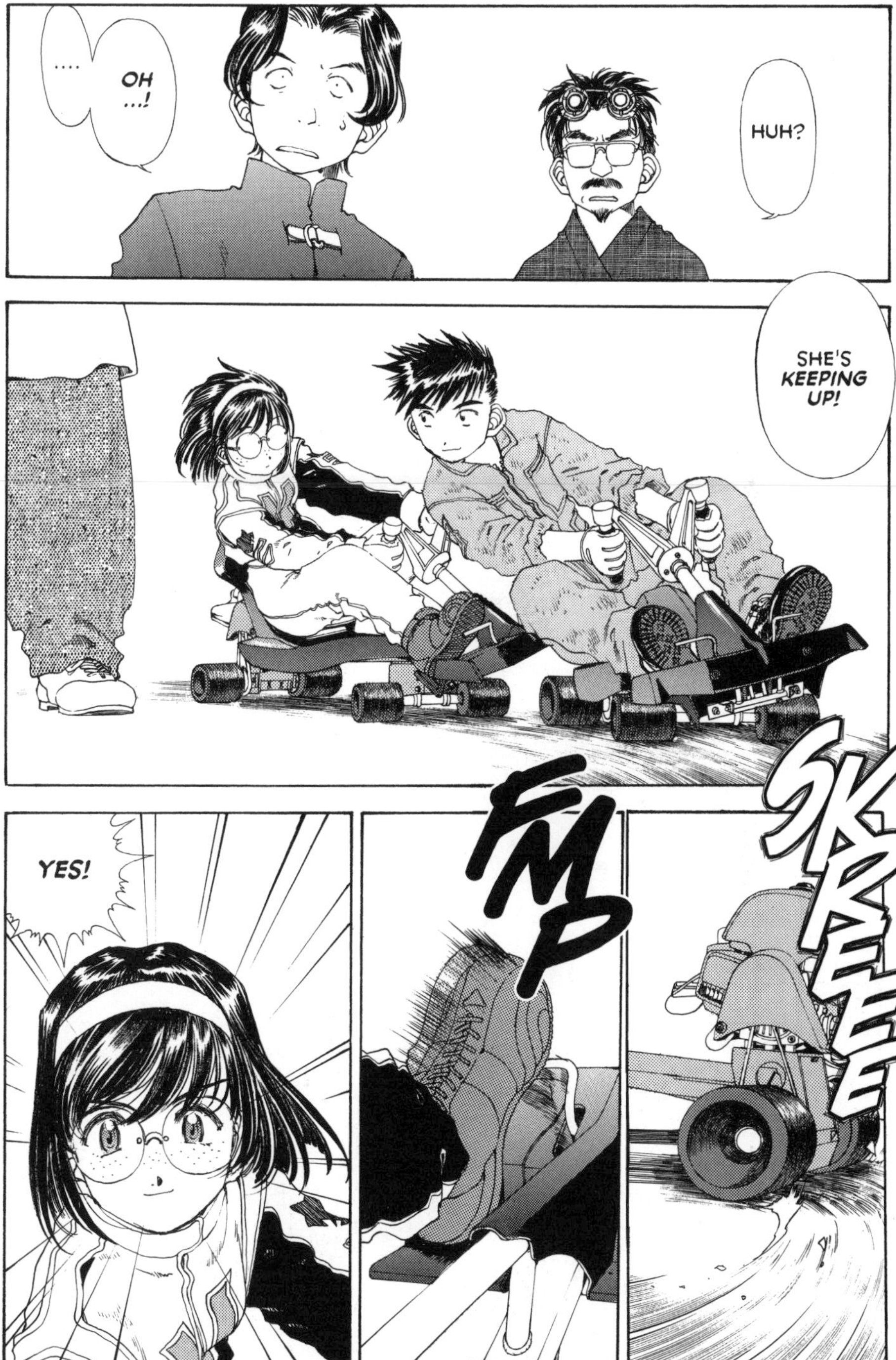
....
OH ...!
HUH?
SHE'S KEEPING UP!
YES!
FMP
SKREEE

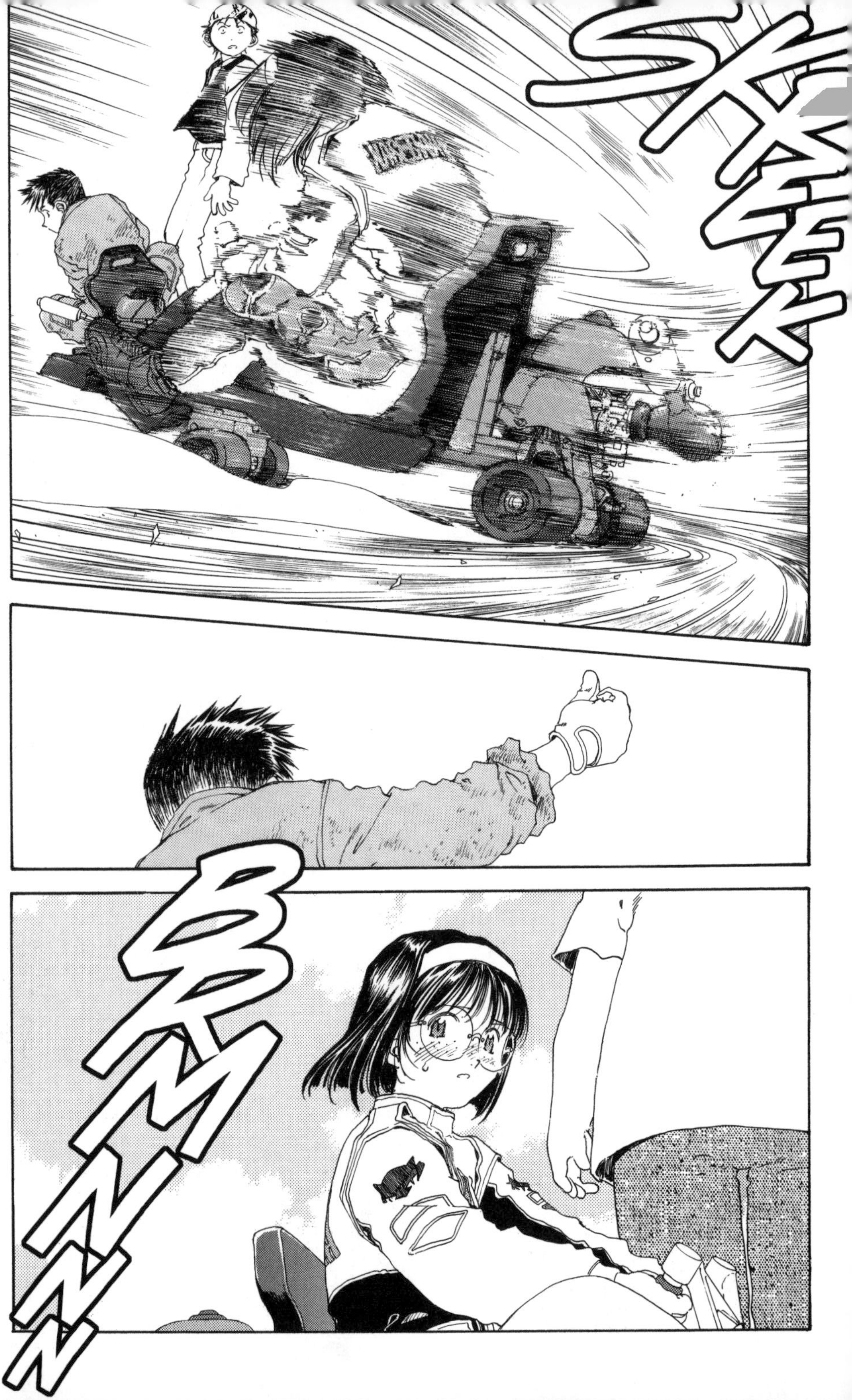
SKEEEK
BMNNN

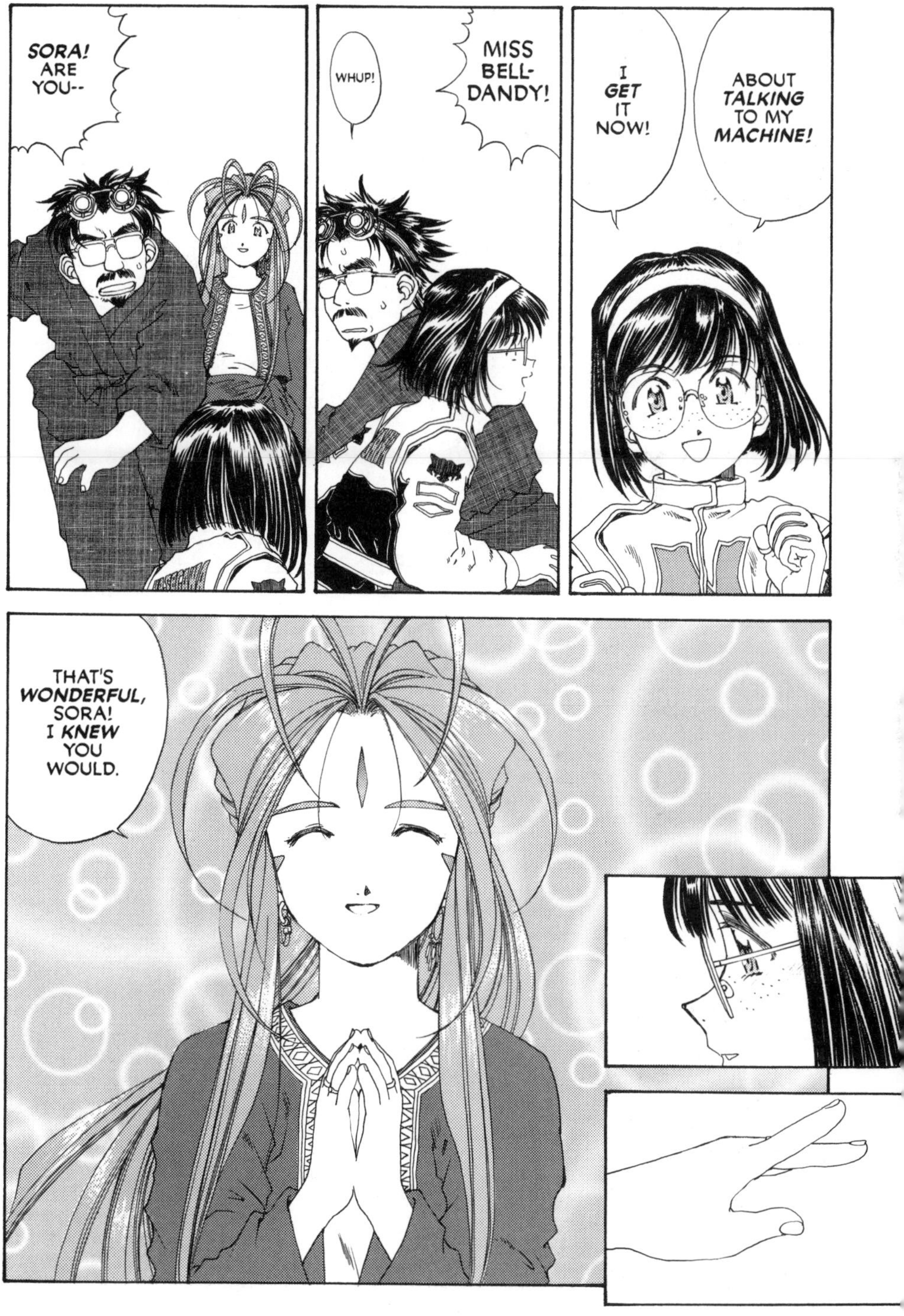
SORA! ARE YOU--
WHUP!
MISS BELL-DANDY!
I GET IT NOW!
ABOUT TALKING TO MY MACHINE!
THAT'S WONDERFUL, SORA! I KNEW YOU WOULD.

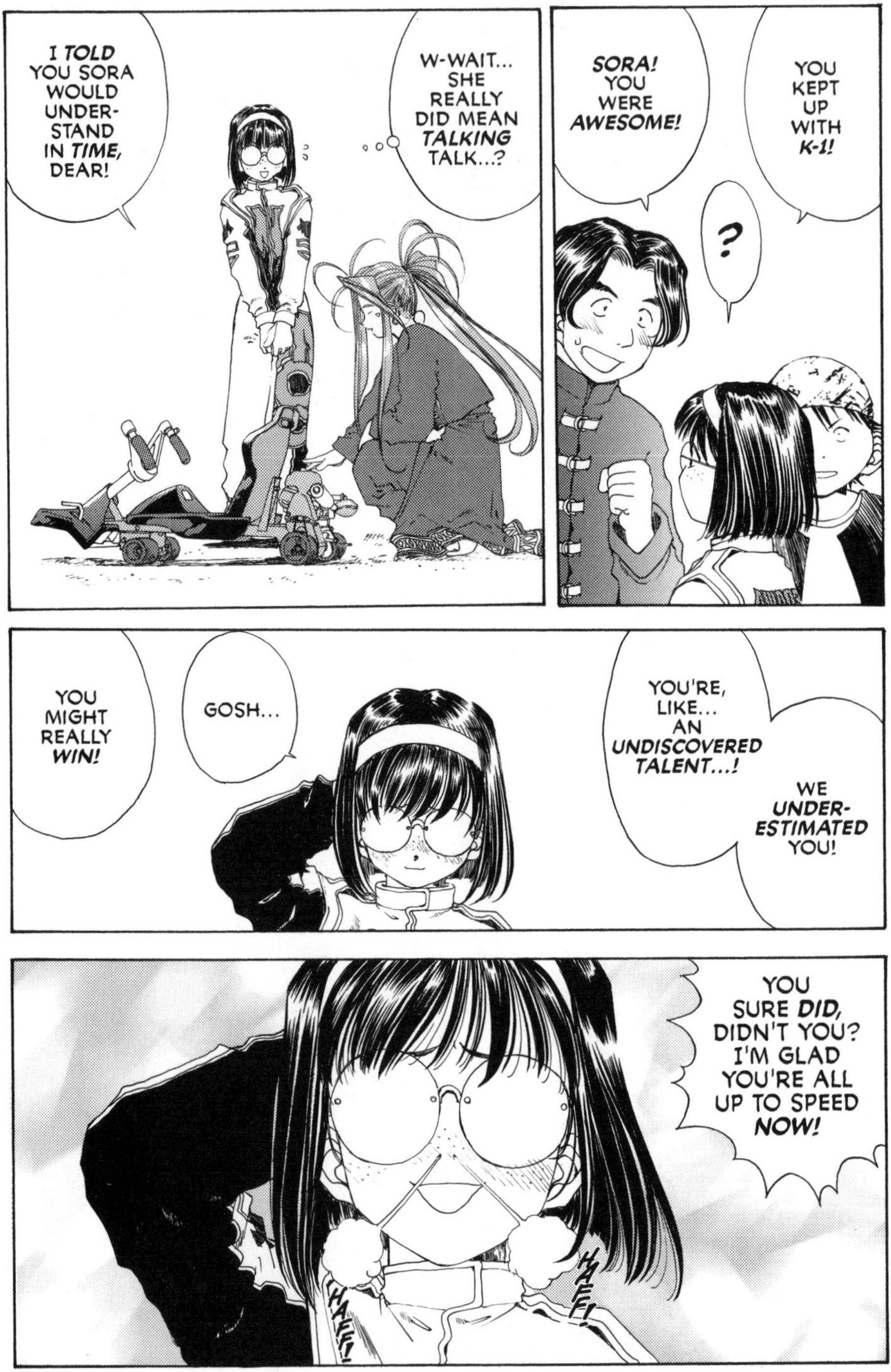
YOU KEPT UP WITH K-1!
SORA! YOU WERE AWESOME!
?
W-WAIT... SHE REALLY DID MEAN TALKING TALK...?
I TOLD YOU SORA WOULD UNDER-STAND IN TIME, DEAR!
YOU'RE, LIKE... AN UNDISCOVERED TALENT...!
WE UNDER-ESTIMATED YOU!
GOSH...
YOU MIGHT REALLY WIN!
YOU SURE DID, DIDN'T YOU? I'M GLAD YOU'RE ALL UP TO SPEED NOW!
HAFF!
HAFF!

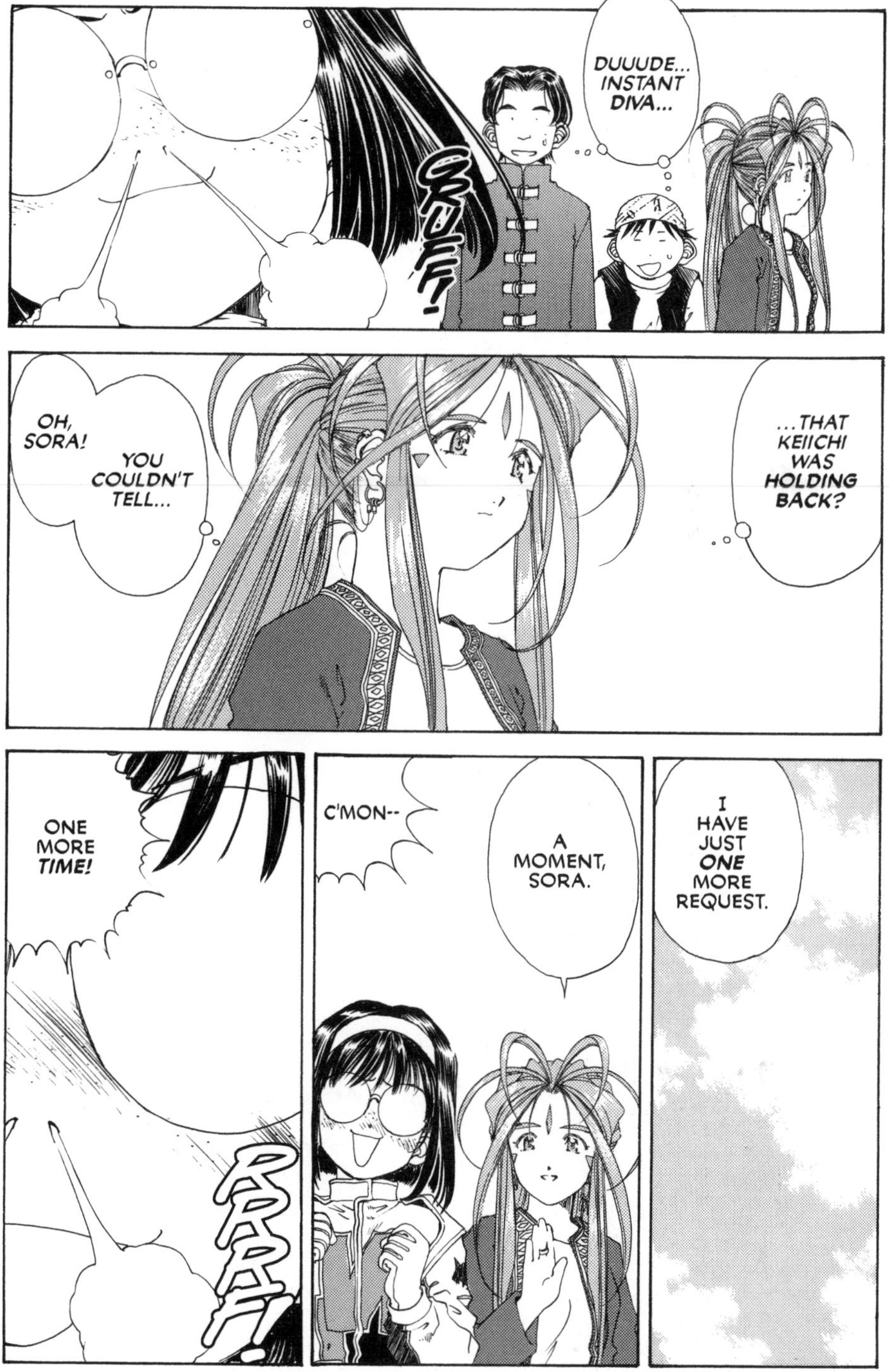
GRUFF!
DUUUDE... INSTANT DIVA...
OH, SORA! YOU COULDN'T TELL...
...THAT KEIICHI WAS HOLDING BACK?
ONE MORE TIME!
C'MON--
A MOMENT, SORA.
I HAVE JUST ONE MORE REQUEST.

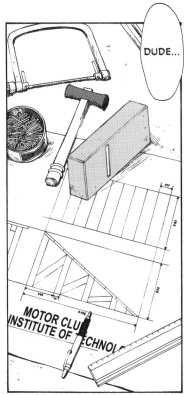

DUDE...

...LIKE, WHY *CARPENTRY?*

MOTOR CLU[B]
INSTITUTE OF TECHNOL[OGY]

HNN.

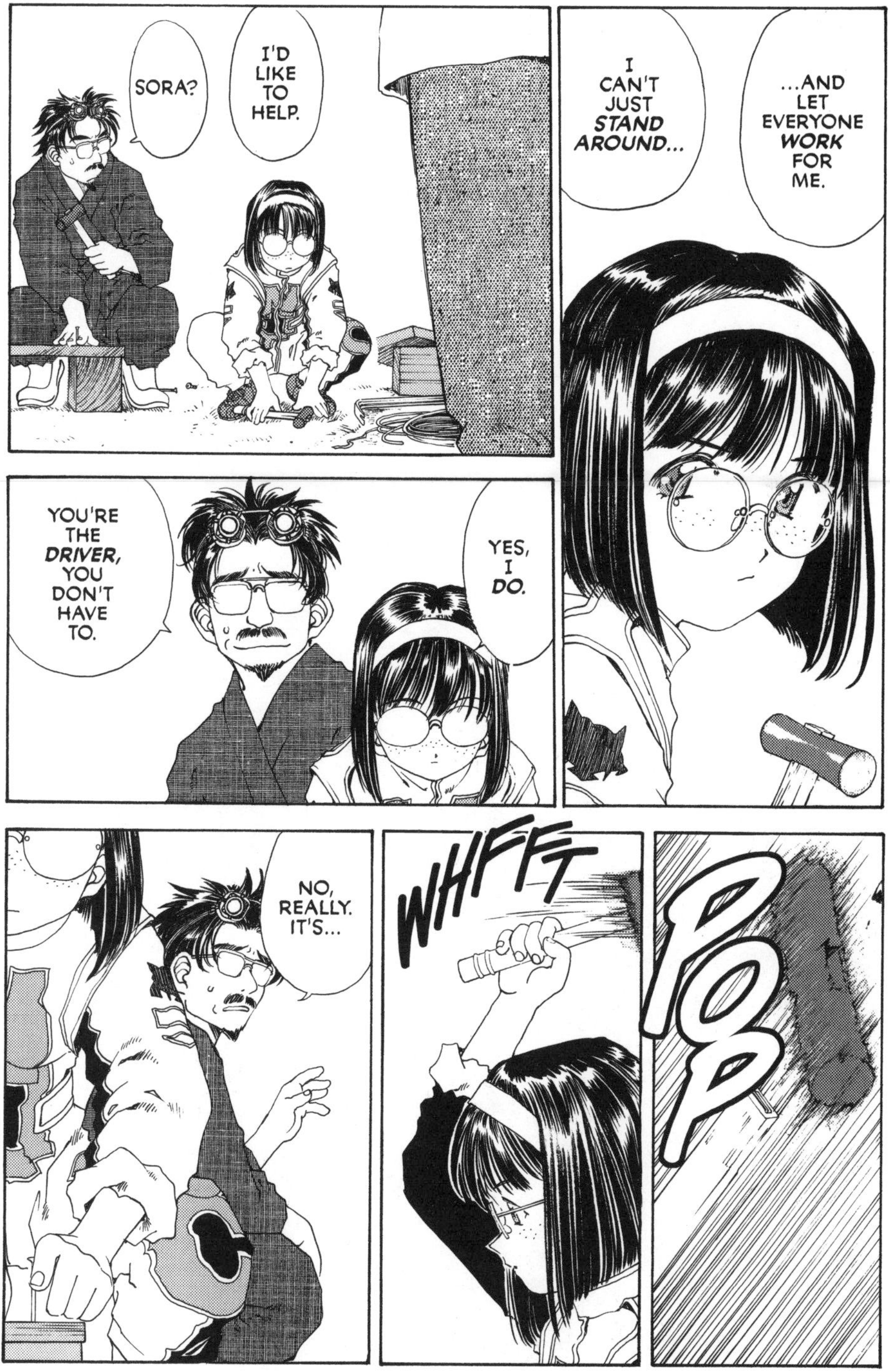
SORA?
I'D LIKE TO HELP.
YOU'RE THE *DRIVER*, YOU DON'T HAVE TO.
YES, I *DO*.
I CAN'T JUST *STAND AROUND*...
...AND LET EVERYONE *WORK* FOR ME.
NO, REALLY. IT'S...
WHFFT
POP

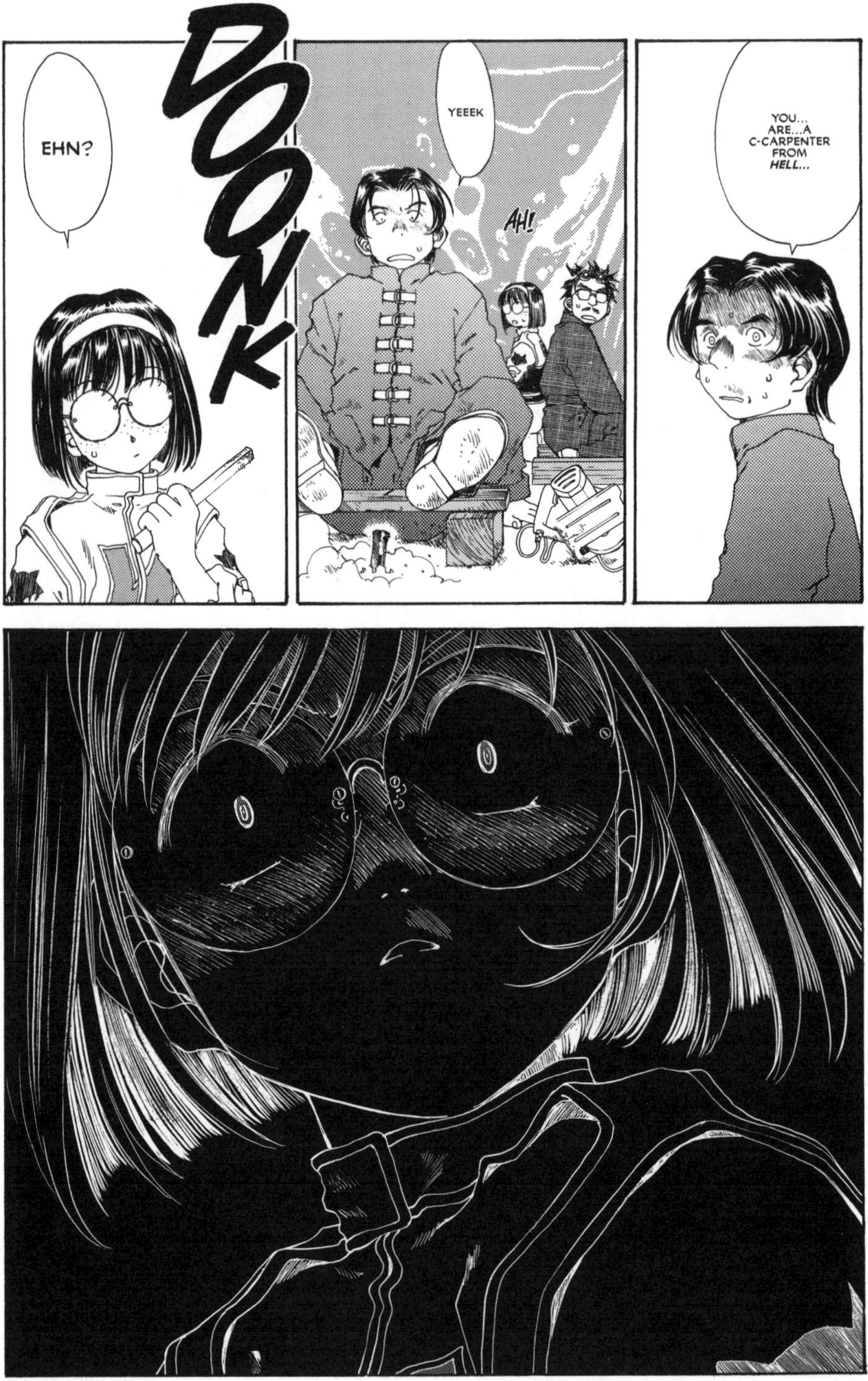
YOU... ARE...A C-CARPENTER FROM HELL...
YEEEK
AH!
DOONK
EHN?

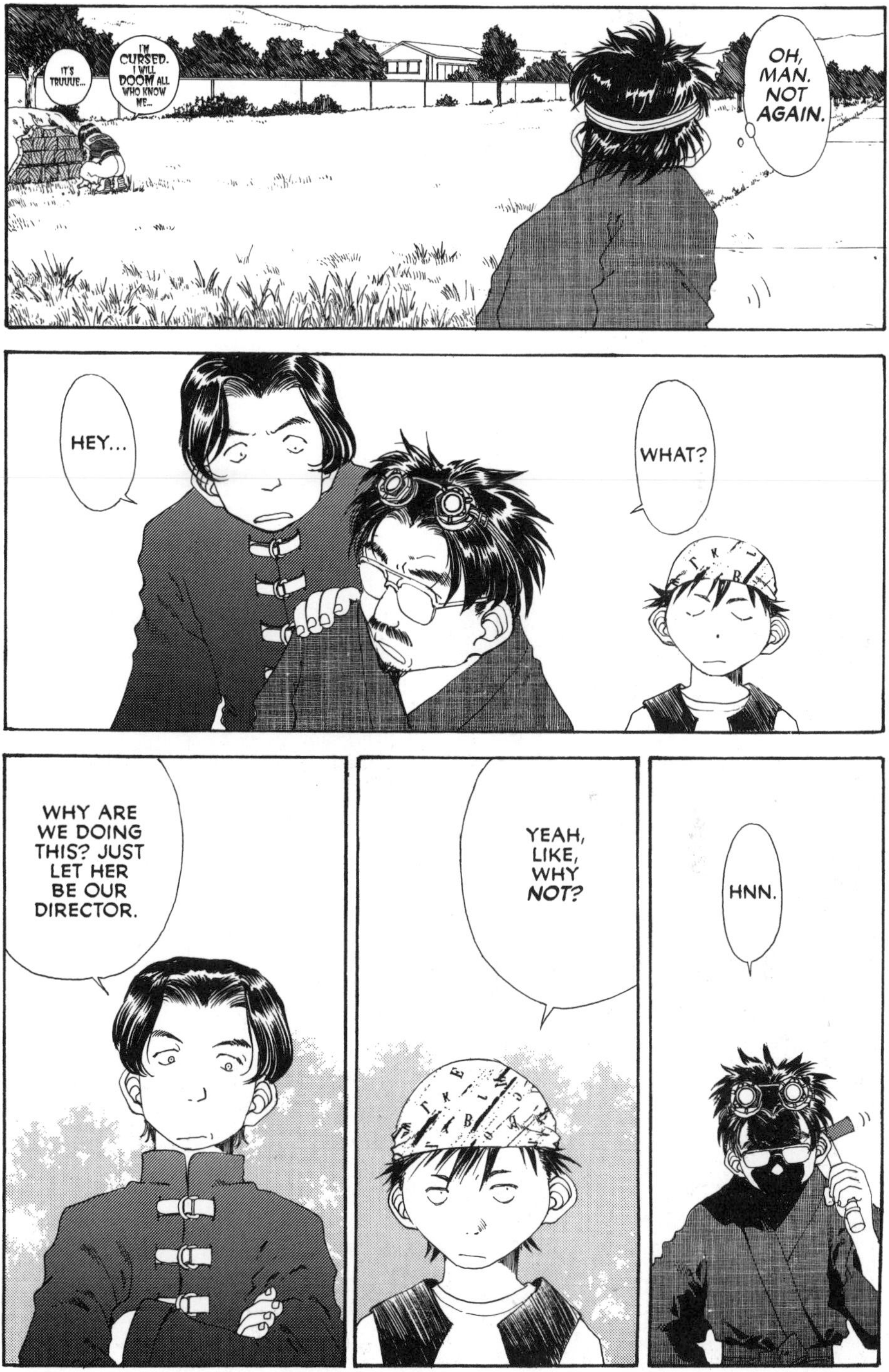
IT'S TRUUUE...
I'M CURSED. I WILL DOOM ALL WHO KNOW ME...
OH, MAN. NOT AGAIN.
HEY...
WHAT?
WHY ARE WE DOING THIS? JUST LET HER BE OUR DIRECTOR.
YEAH, LIKE, WHY *NOT?*
HNN.

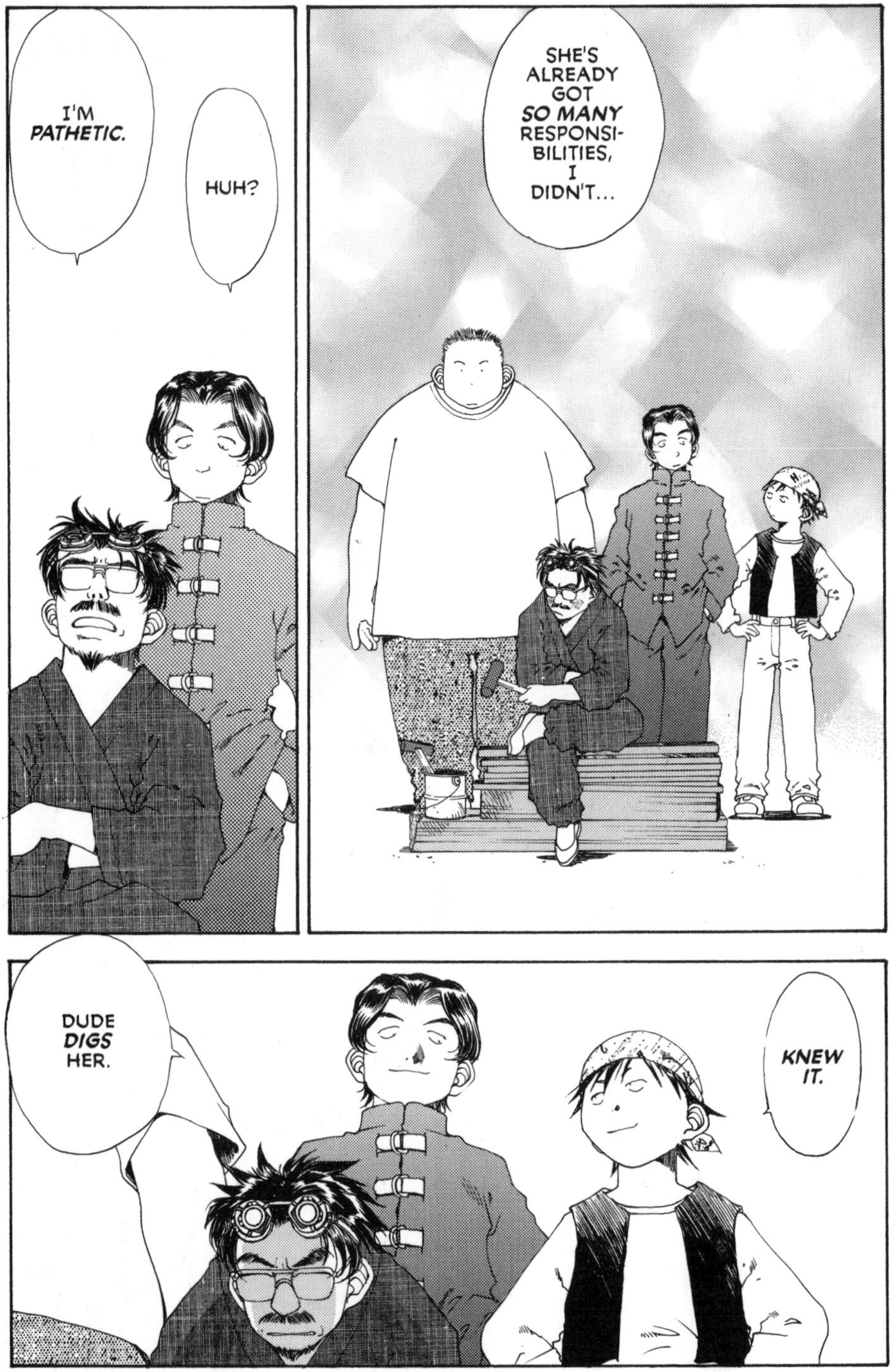
SHE'S ALREADY GOT *SO MANY* RESPONSI-BILITIES, I DIDN'T...
I'M *PATHETIC.*
HUH?
KNEW IT.
DUDE *DIGS* HER.

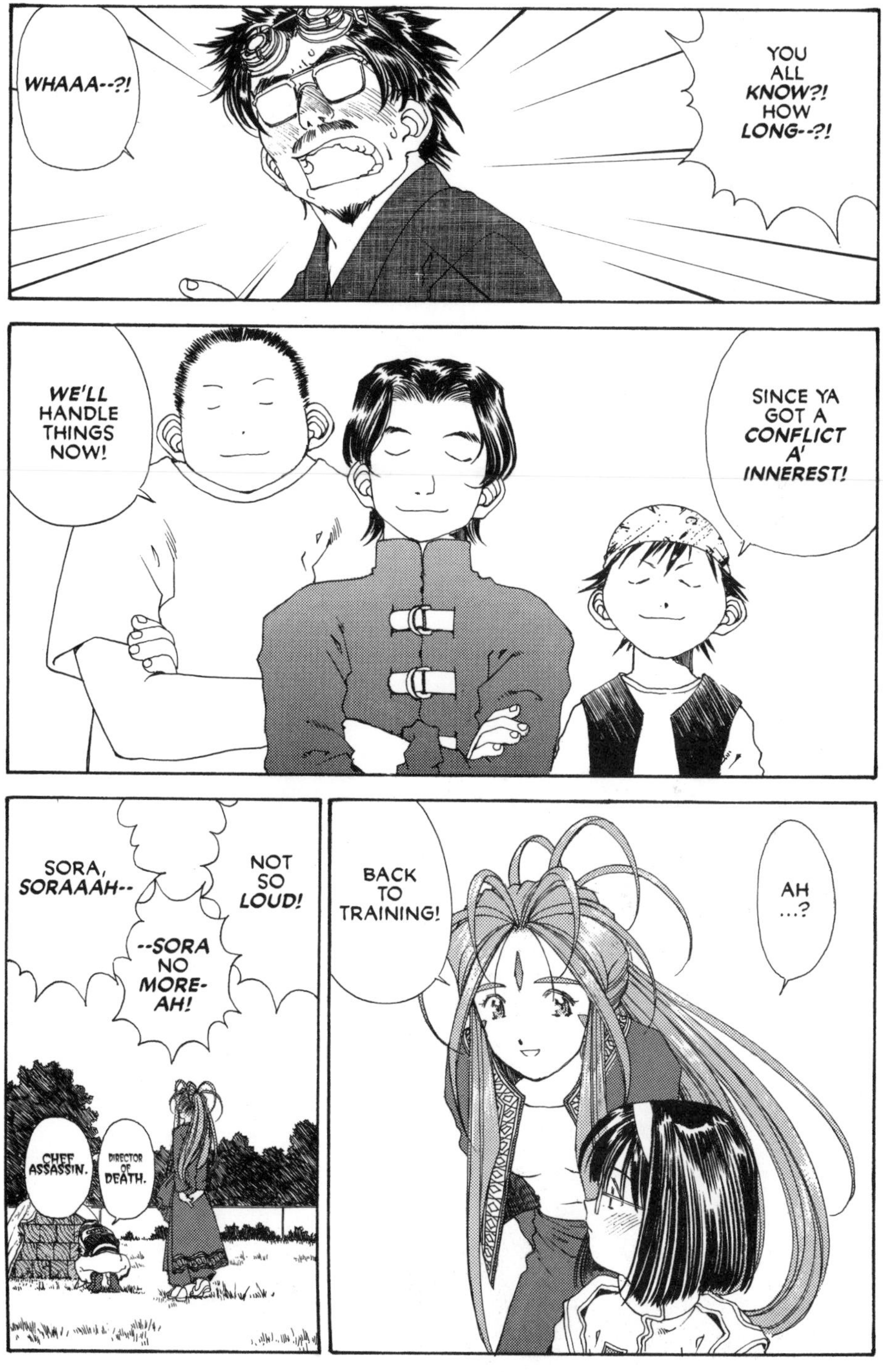
WHAAA--?!
YOU ALL KNOW?! HOW LONG--?!
WE'LL HANDLE THINGS NOW!
SINCE YA GOT A CONFLICT A' INNEREST!
SORA, SORAAAH--
NOT SO LOUD!
--SORA NO MORE-AH!
CHEF ASSASSIN.
DIRECTOR OF DEATH.
BACK TO TRAINING!
AH ...?

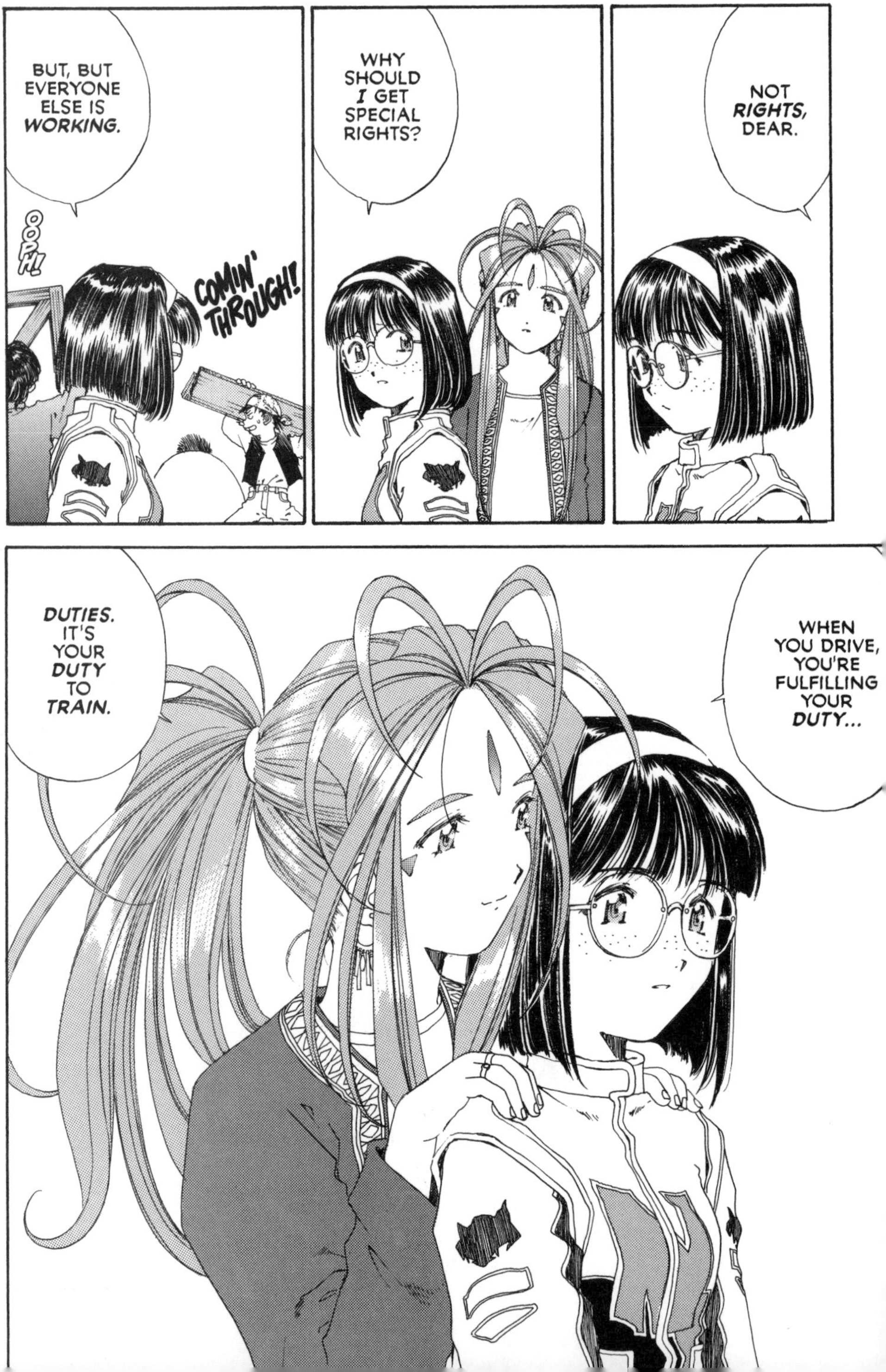

BUT, BUT EVERYONE ELSE IS *WORKING.*
OOPH!
COMIN' THROUGH!
WHY SHOULD *I* GET SPECIAL RIGHTS?
NOT *RIGHTS,* DEAR.
DUTIES. IT'S YOUR *DUTY* TO *TRAIN.*
WHEN YOU DRIVE, YOU'RE FULFILLING YOUR *DUTY...*

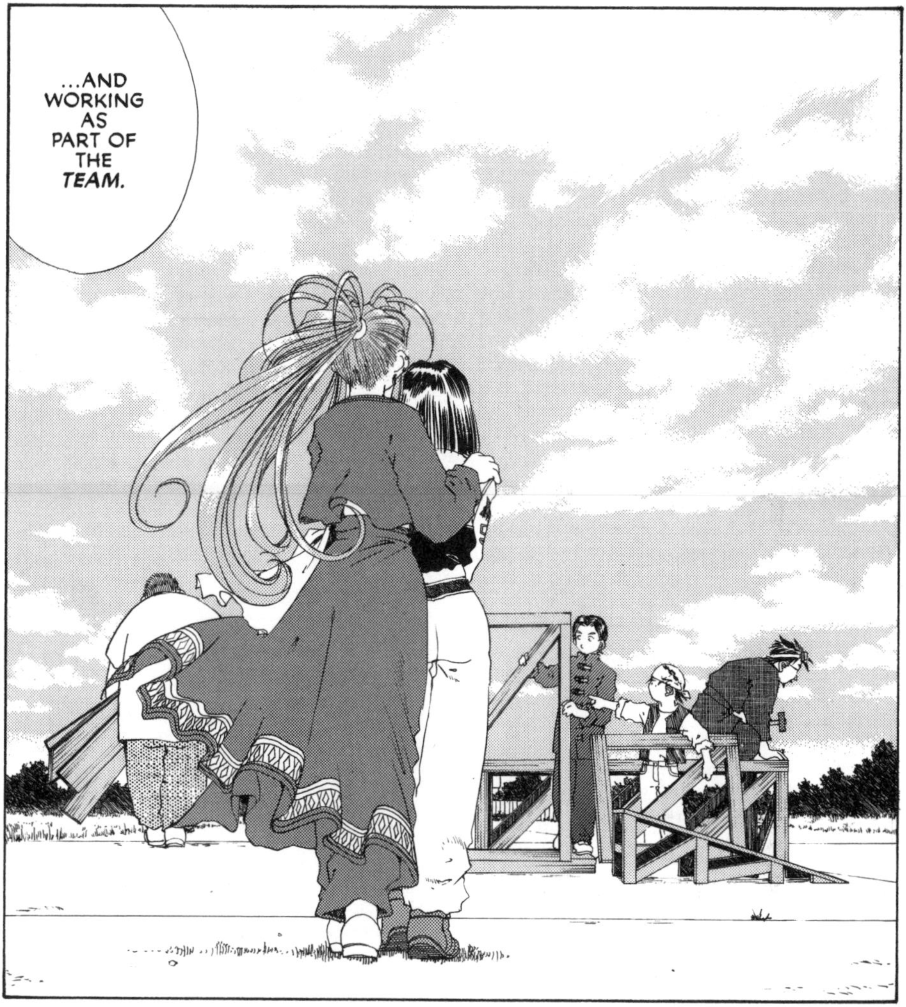
...AND WORKING AS PART OF THE *TEAM.*

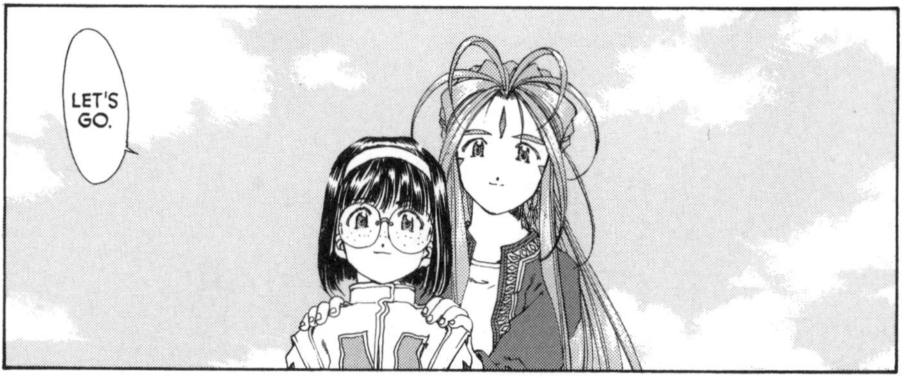
LET'S GO.

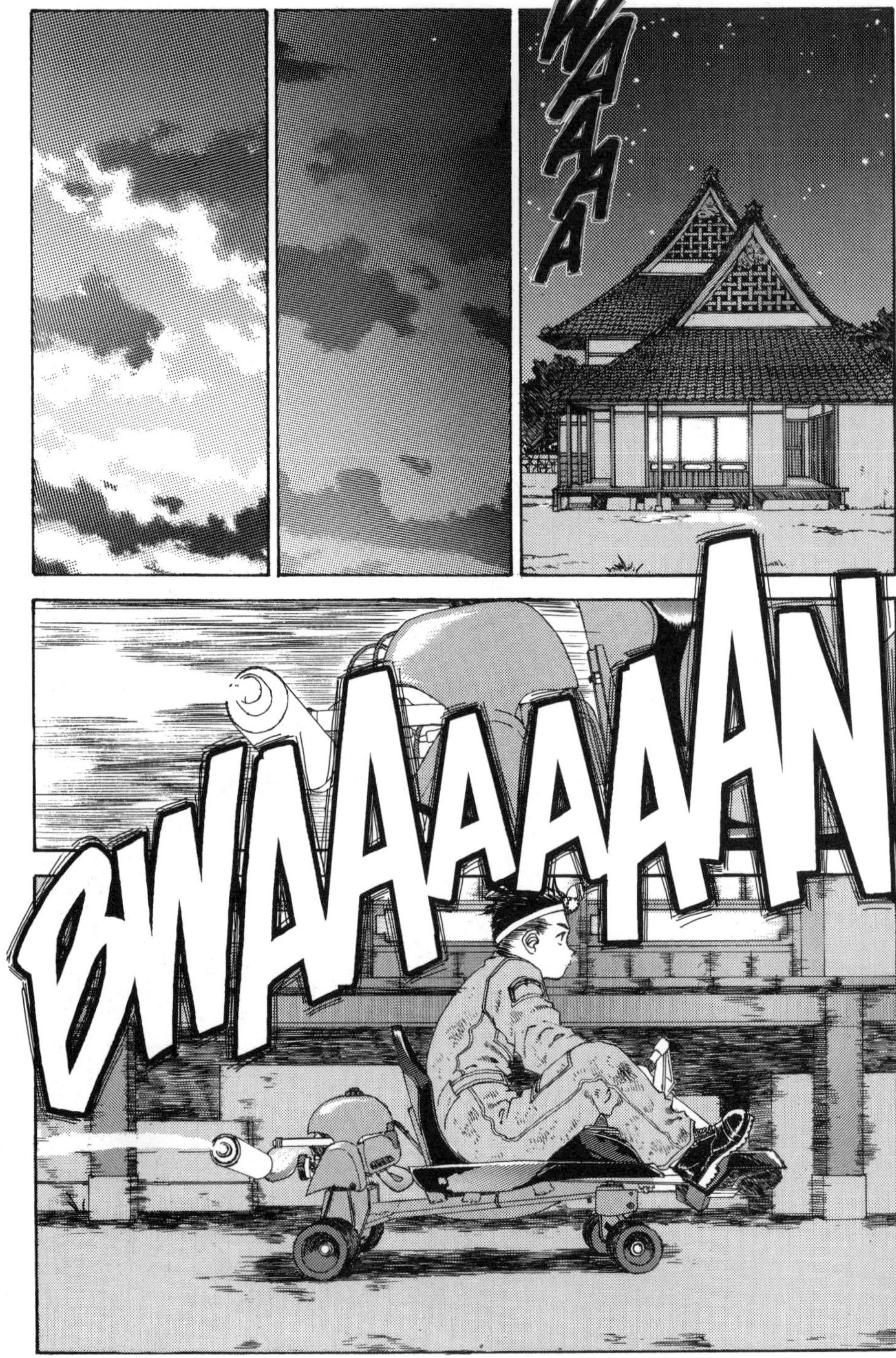
WAAAAA
BWAAAAAAN

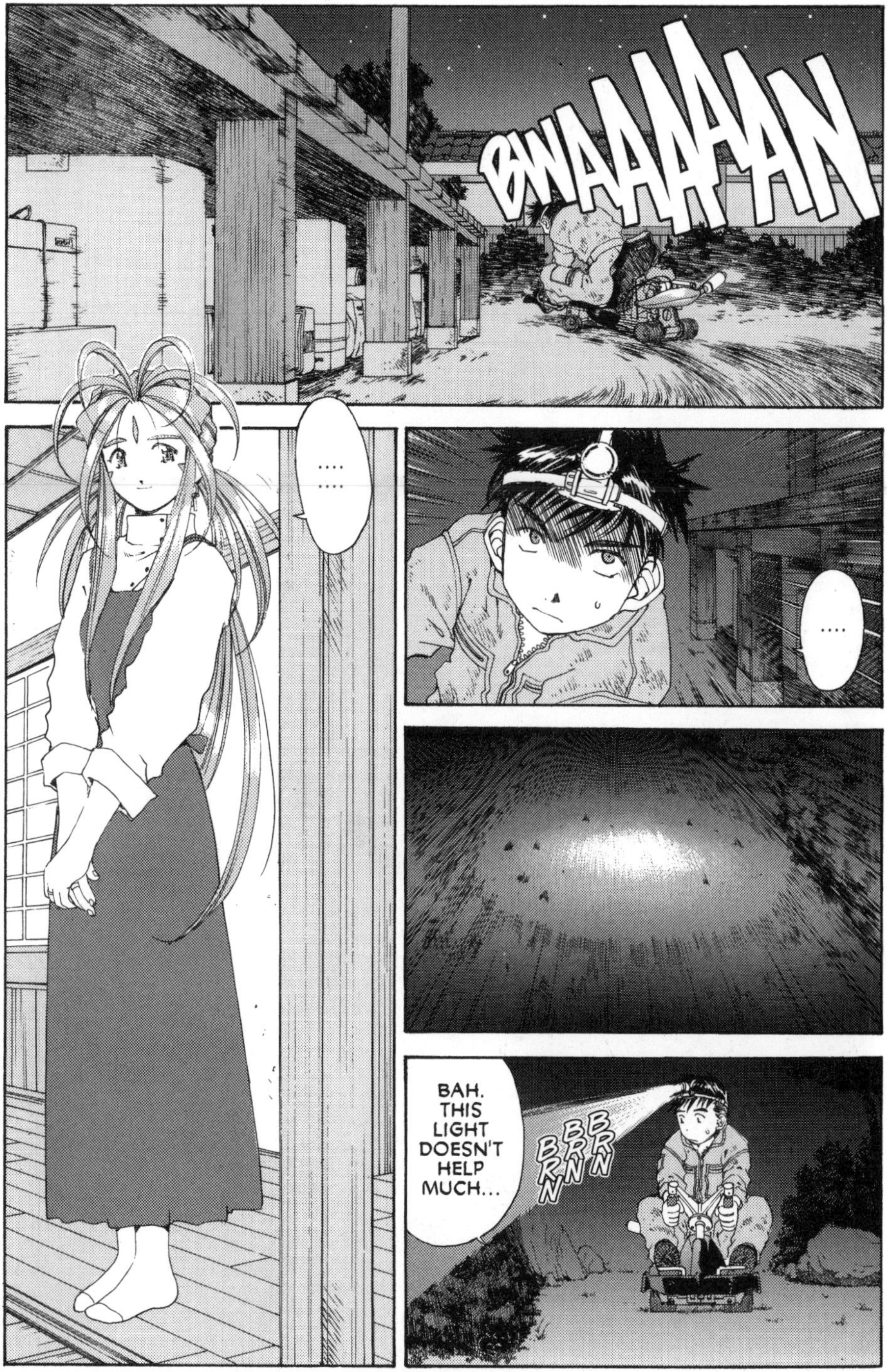
BWAAAAAAN
....
BAH. THIS LIGHT DOESN'T HELP MUCH...
BRRN BRRN BRRN
....
....

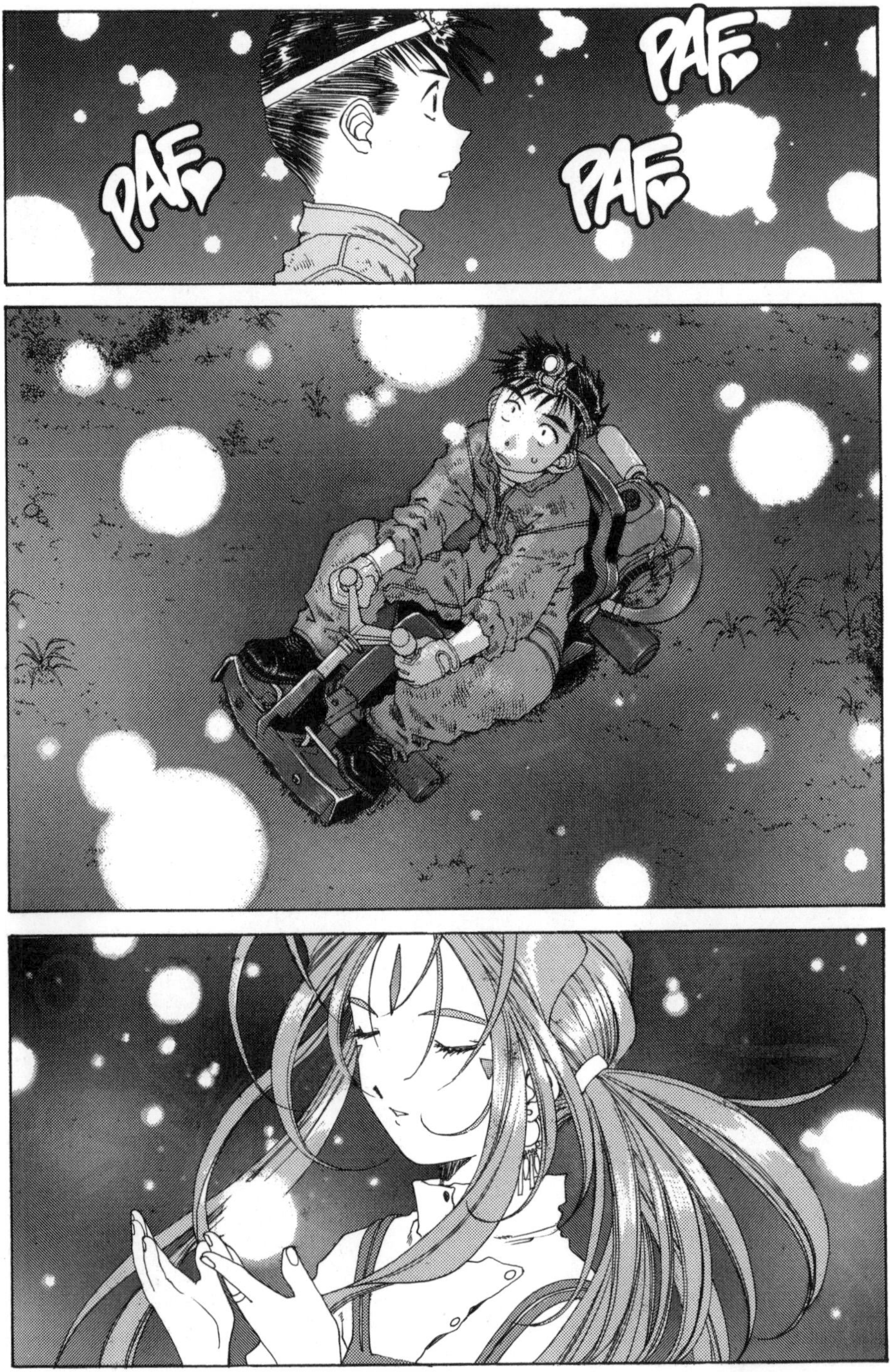
PAF♥
PAF♥
PAF♥

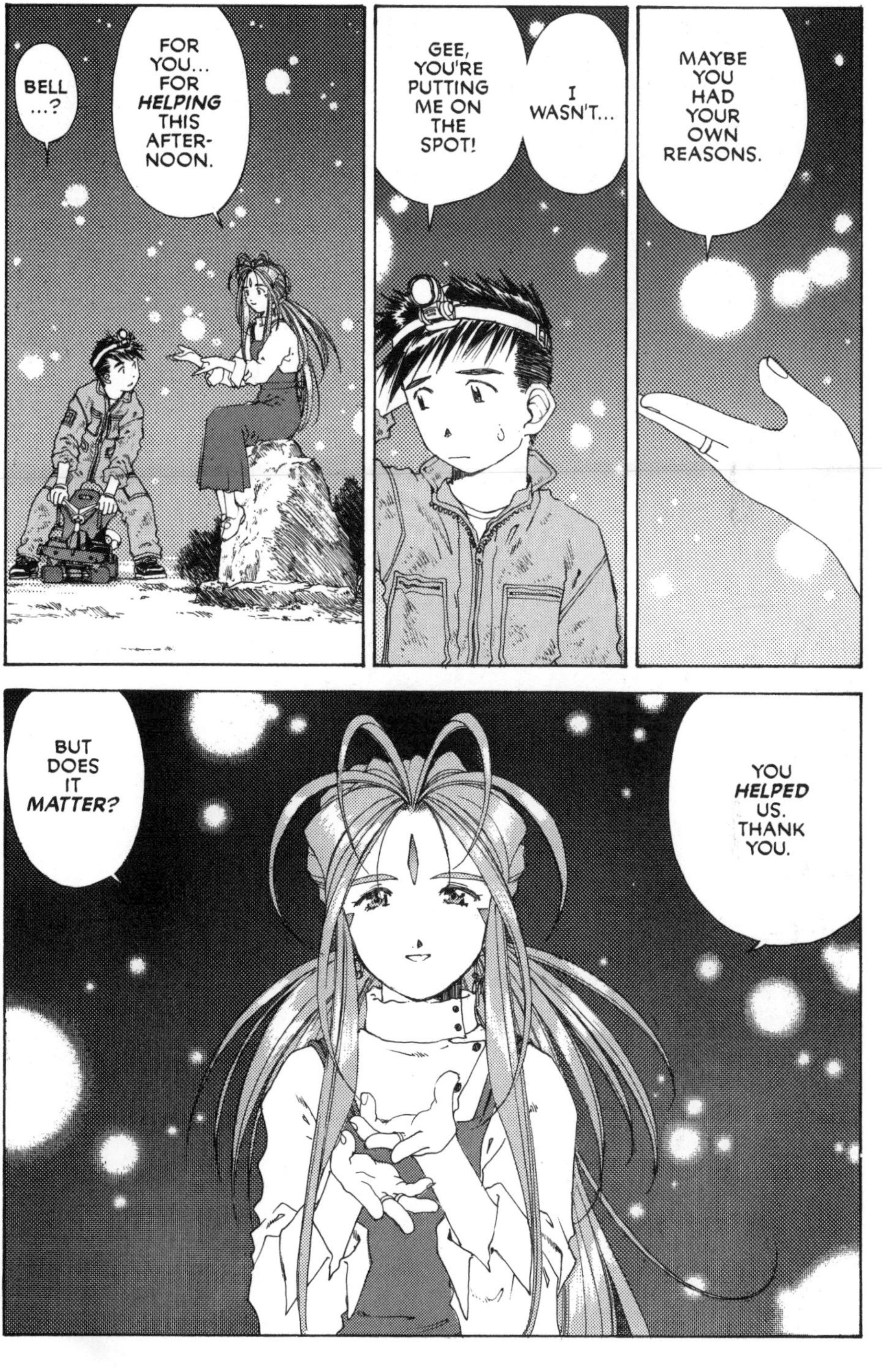
BELL ...?
FOR YOU... FOR *HELPING* THIS AFTER-NOON.
GEE, YOU'RE PUTTING ME ON THE SPOT!
I WASN'T...
MAYBE YOU HAD YOUR OWN REASONS.
BUT DOES IT *MATTER?*
YOU *HELPED* US. THANK YOU.

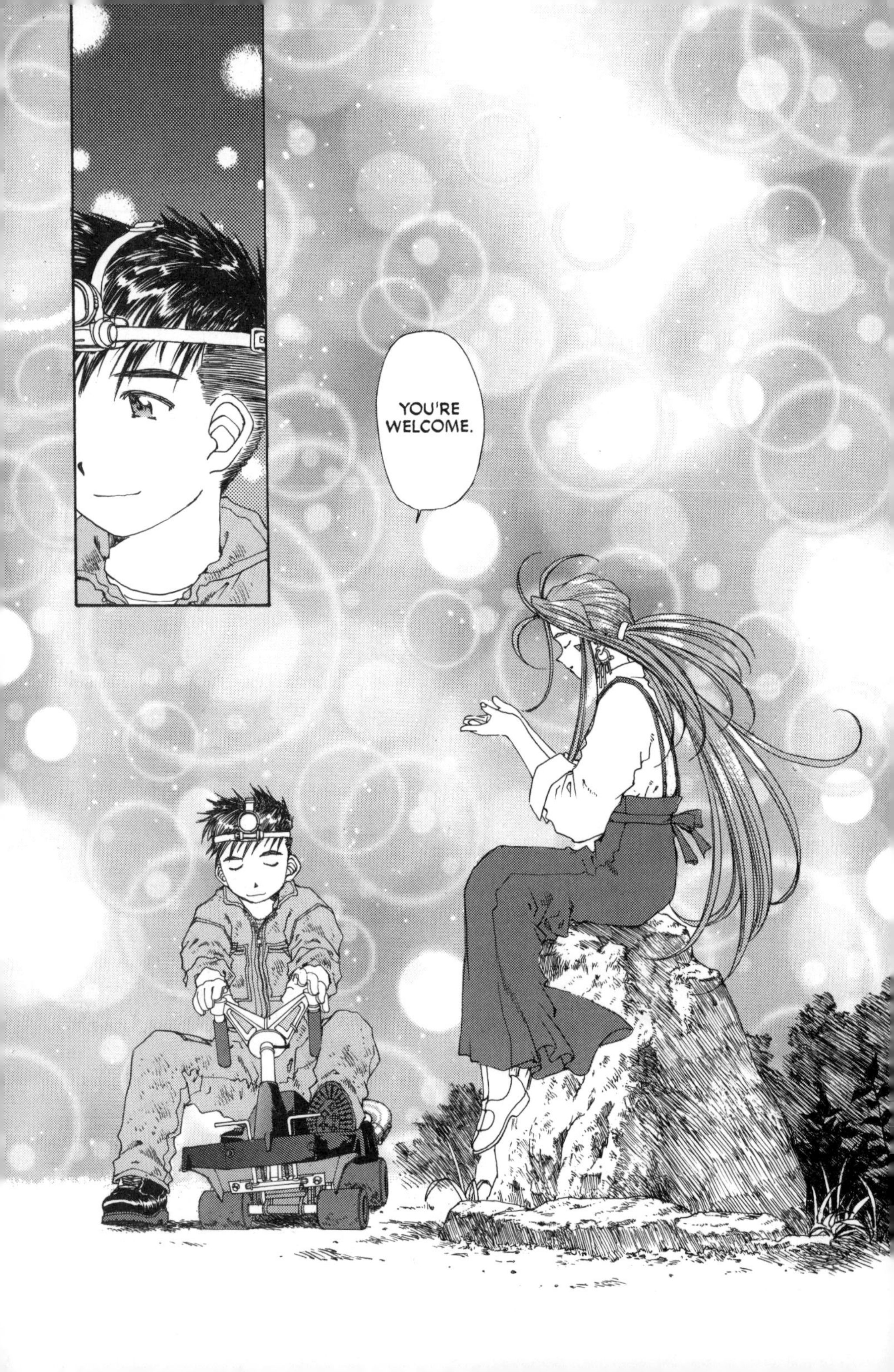
YOU'RE WELCOME.

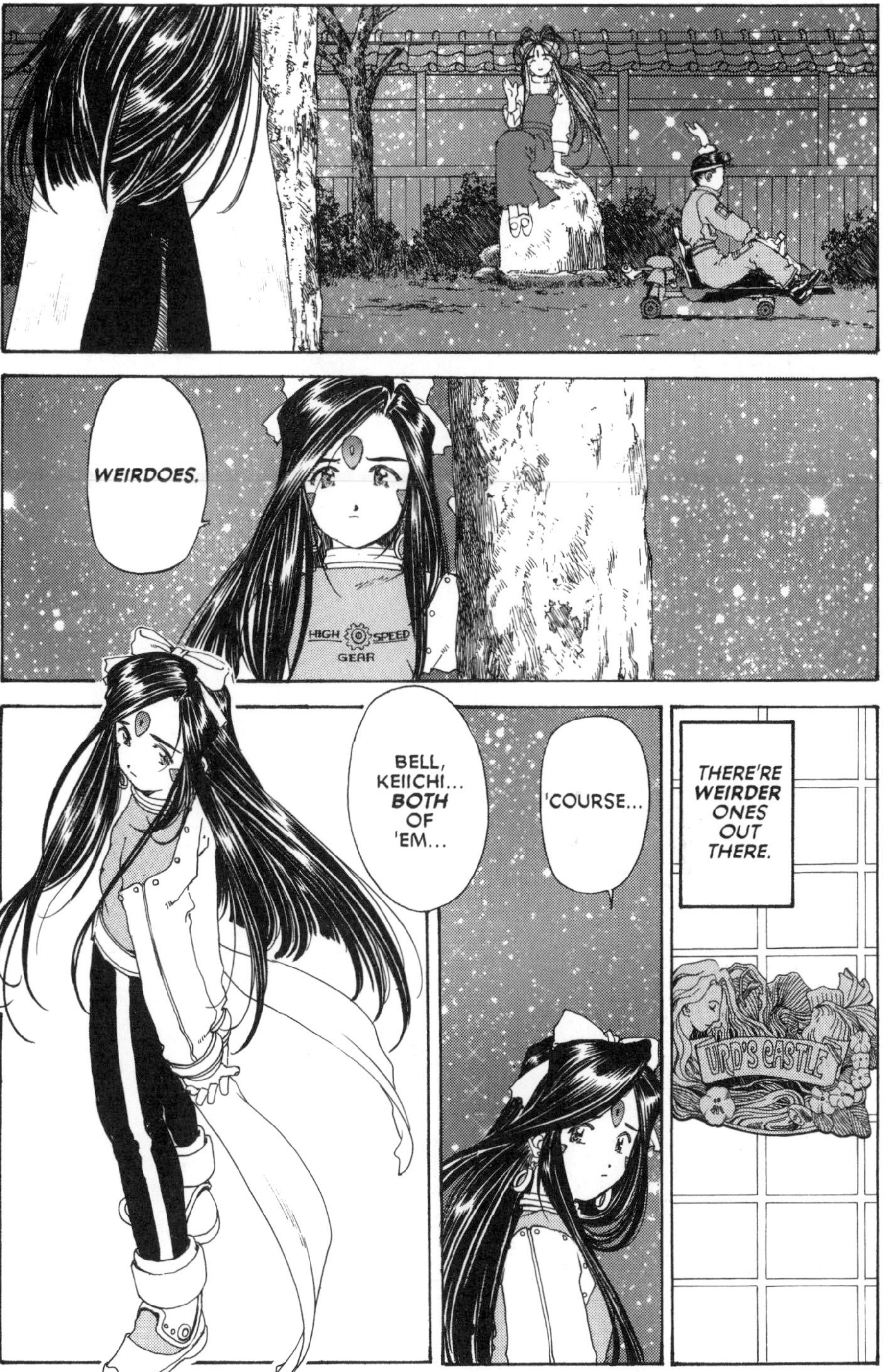
WEIRDOES.
BELL, KEIICHI... BOTH OF 'EM...
'COURSE...
THERE'RE WEIRDER ONES OUT THERE.
URD'S CASTLE

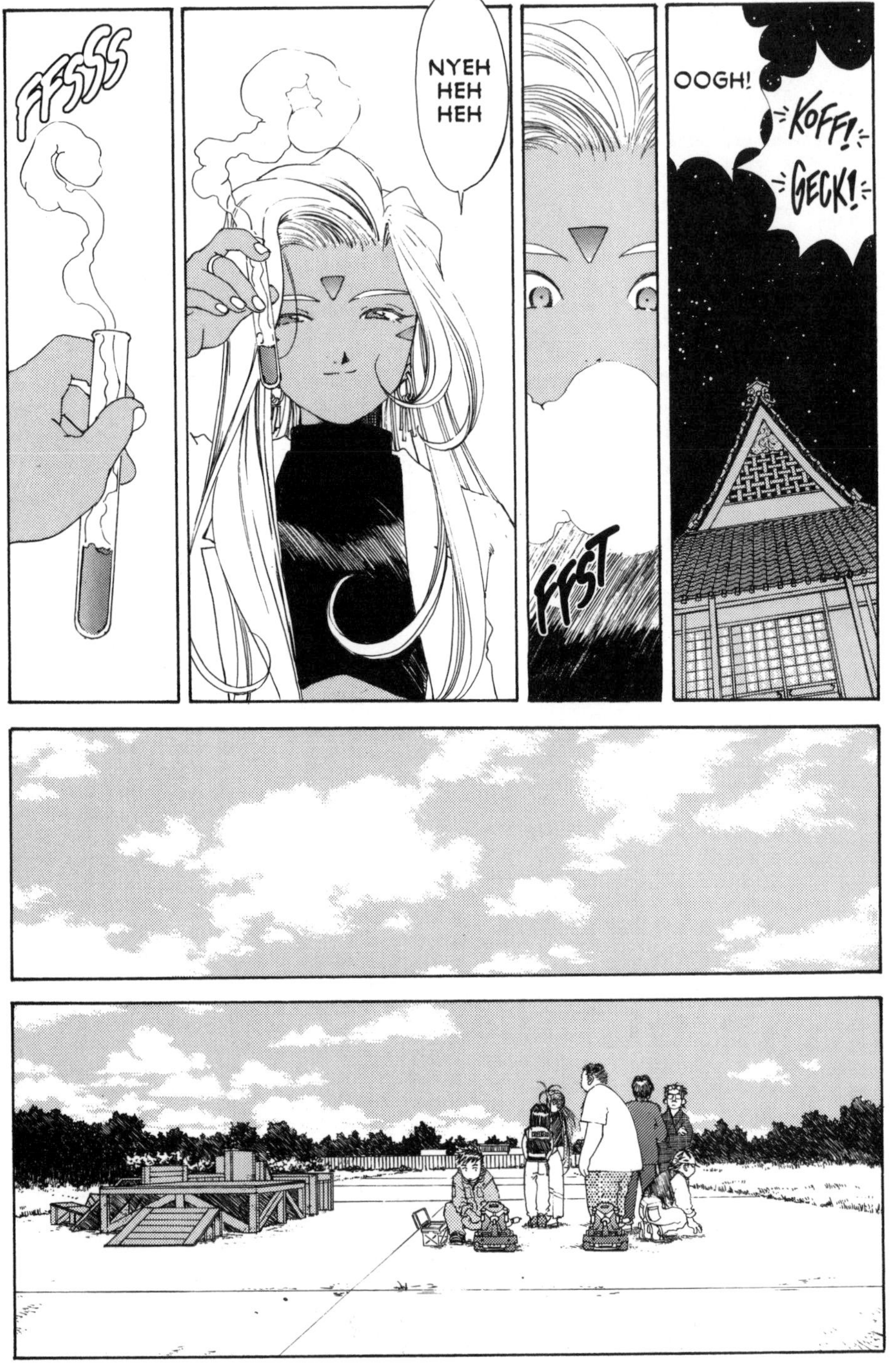
FFSSS
NYEH HEH HEH
FFST
OOGH!
KOFF!
GECK!

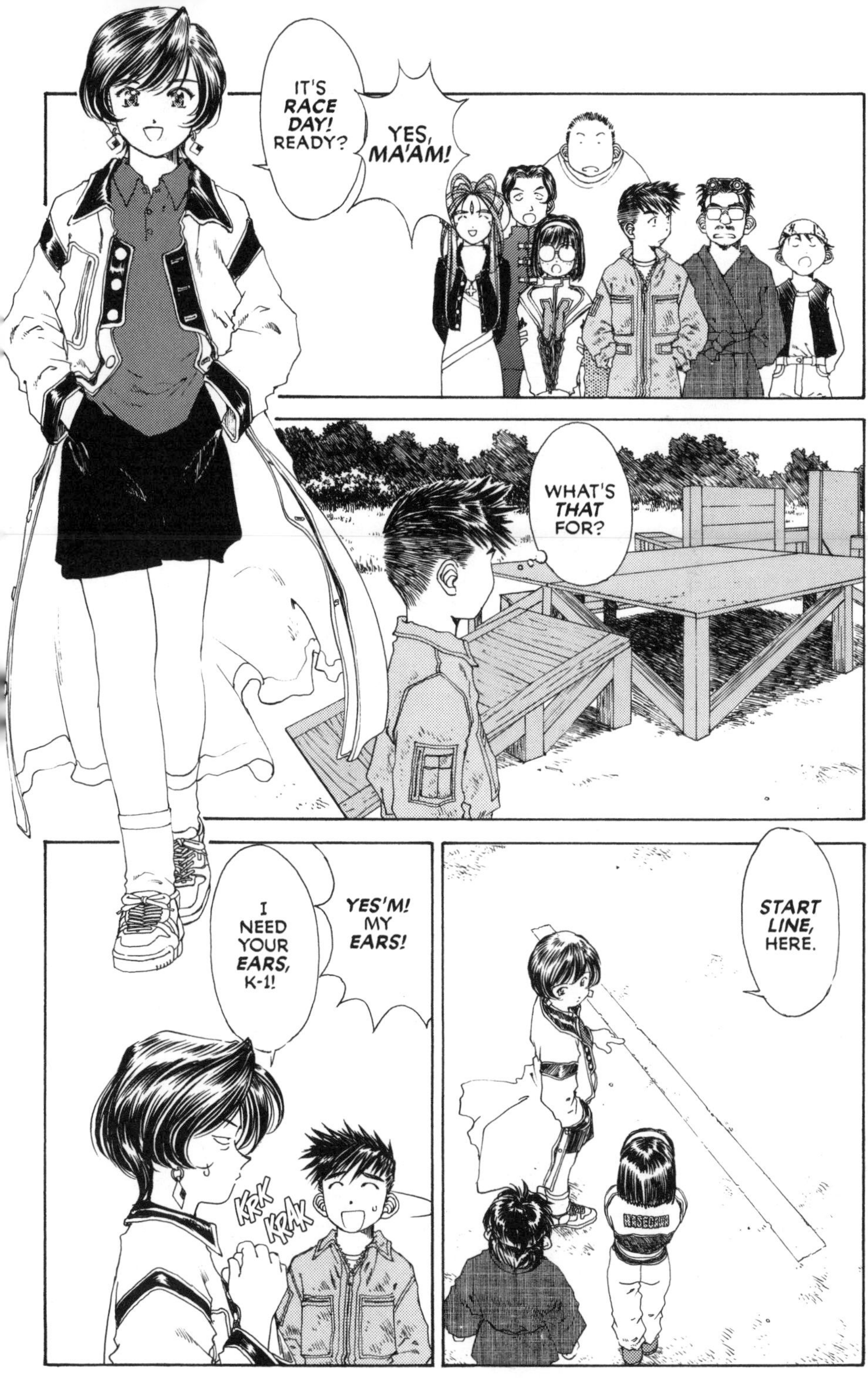
IT'S RACE DAY! READY?
YES, MA'AM!
WHAT'S THAT FOR?
I NEED YOUR EARS, K-1!
YES'M! MY EARS!
KRK KRAK
START LINE, HERE.

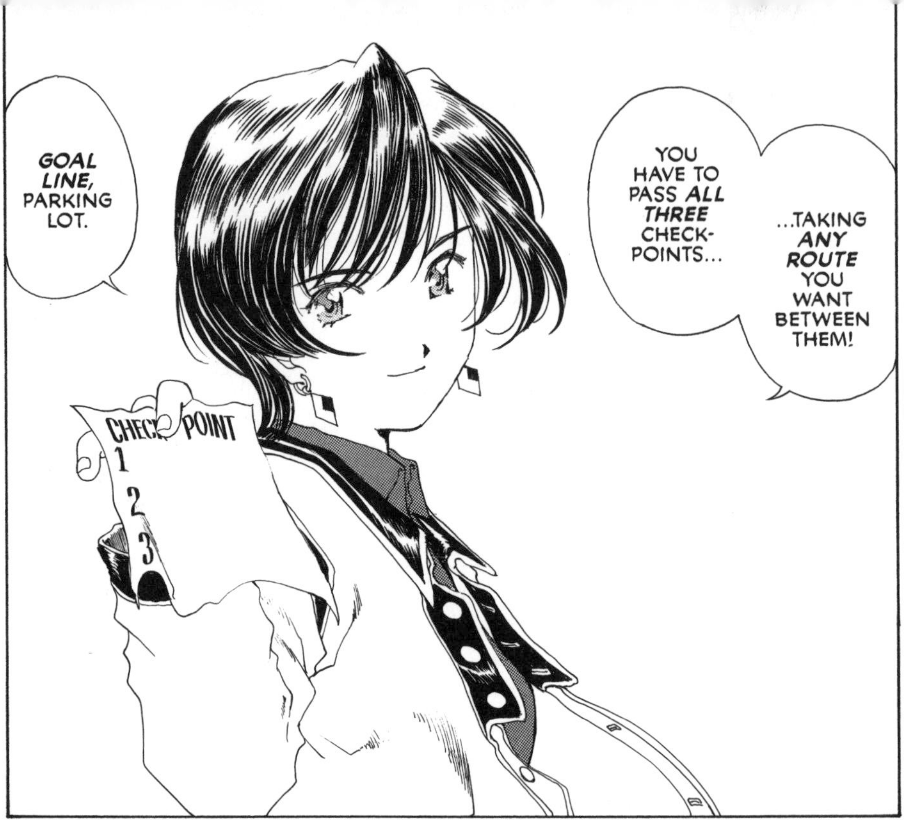
GOAL LINE, PARKING LOT.
CHECK POINT 1 2 3
YOU HAVE TO PASS ALL THREE CHECK-POINTS...
...TAKING ANY ROUTE YOU WANT BETWEEN THEM!
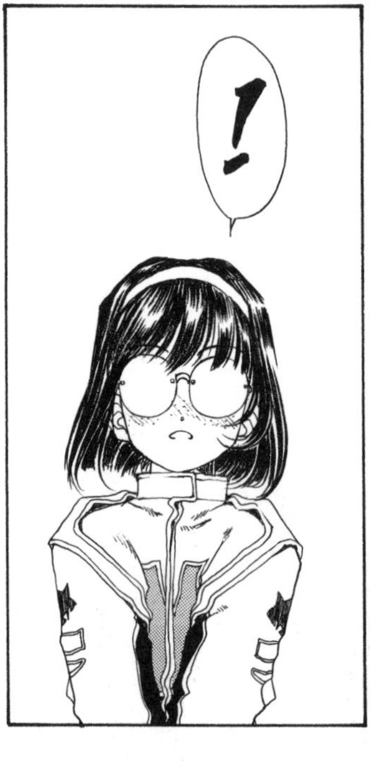
!
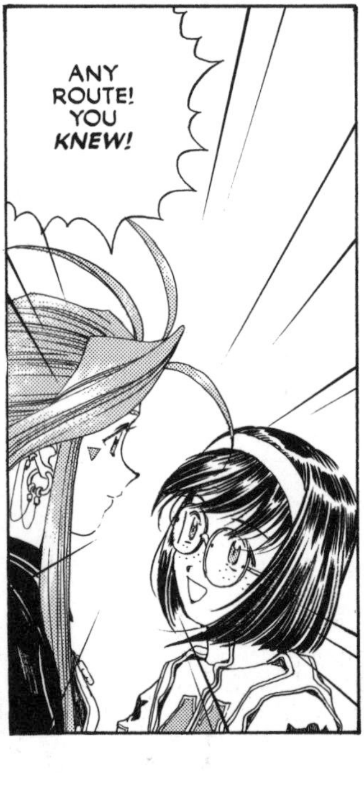
ANY ROUTE! YOU KNEW!
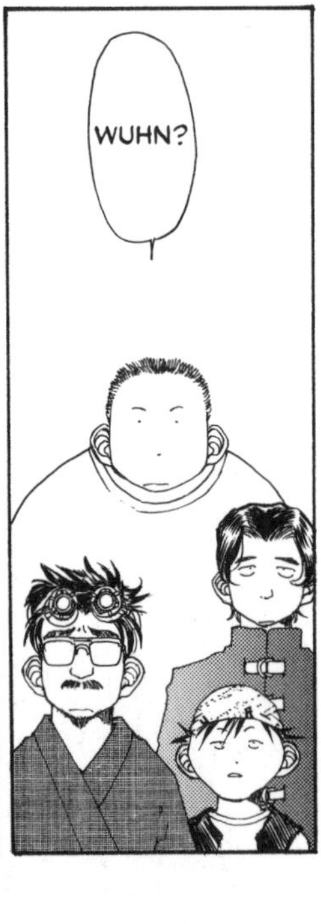
WUHN?

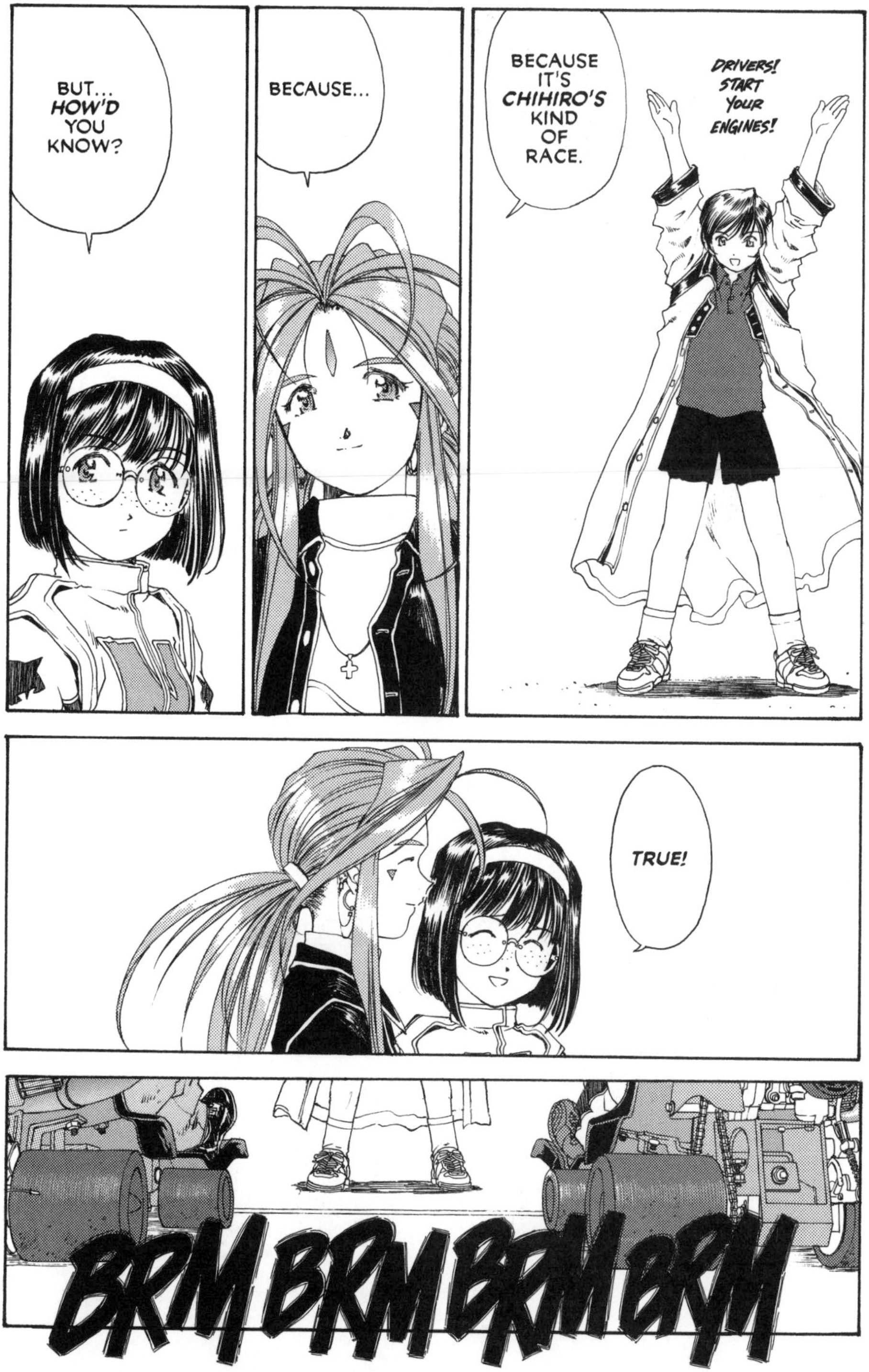
BUT... HOW'D YOU KNOW?
BECAUSE...
BECAUSE IT'S CHIHIRO'S KIND OF RACE.
DRIVERS! START YOUR ENGINES!
TRUE!
BRM BRM BRM BRM

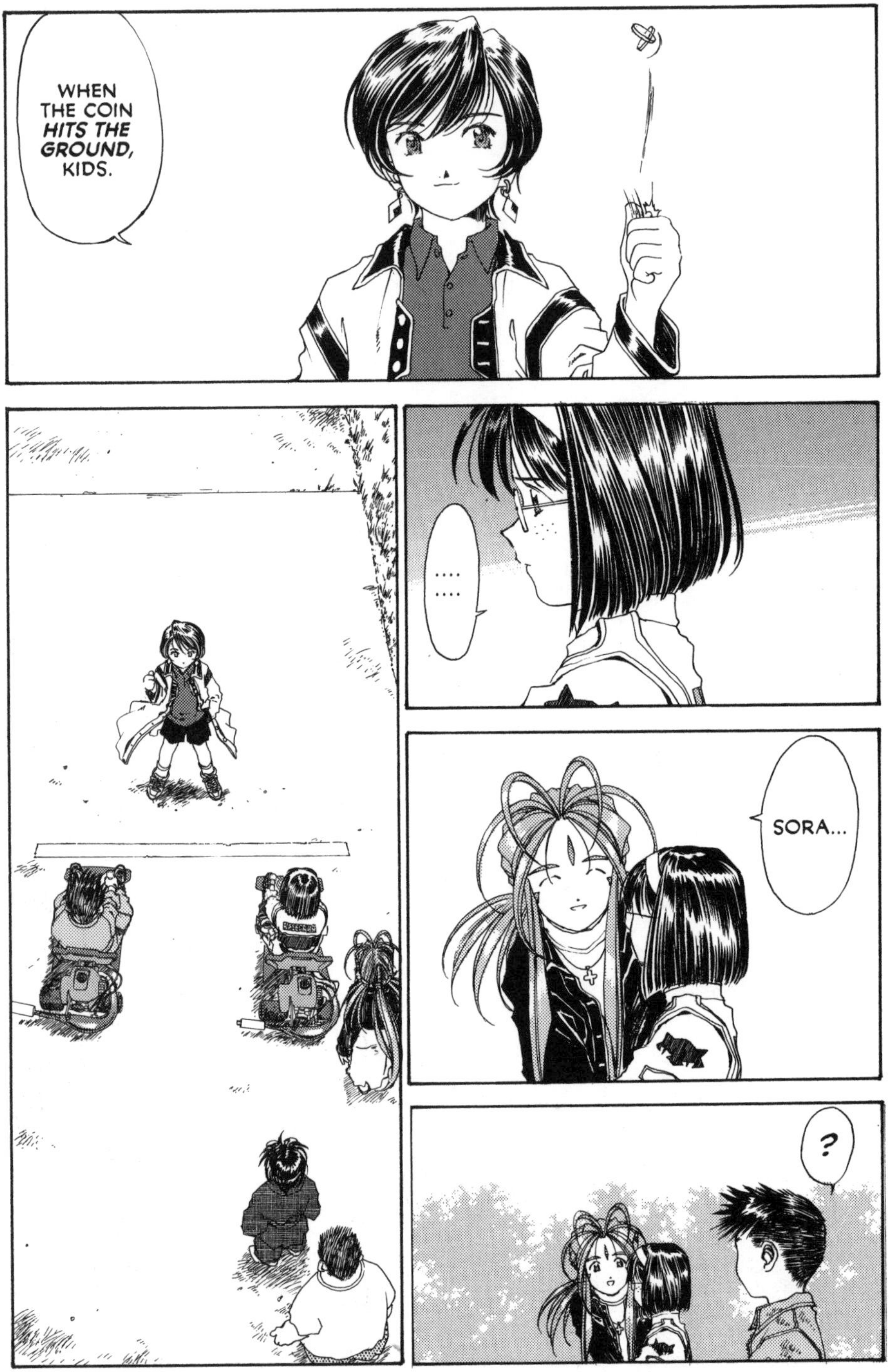
WHEN THE COIN HITS THE GROUND, KIDS.
....
SORA...
?

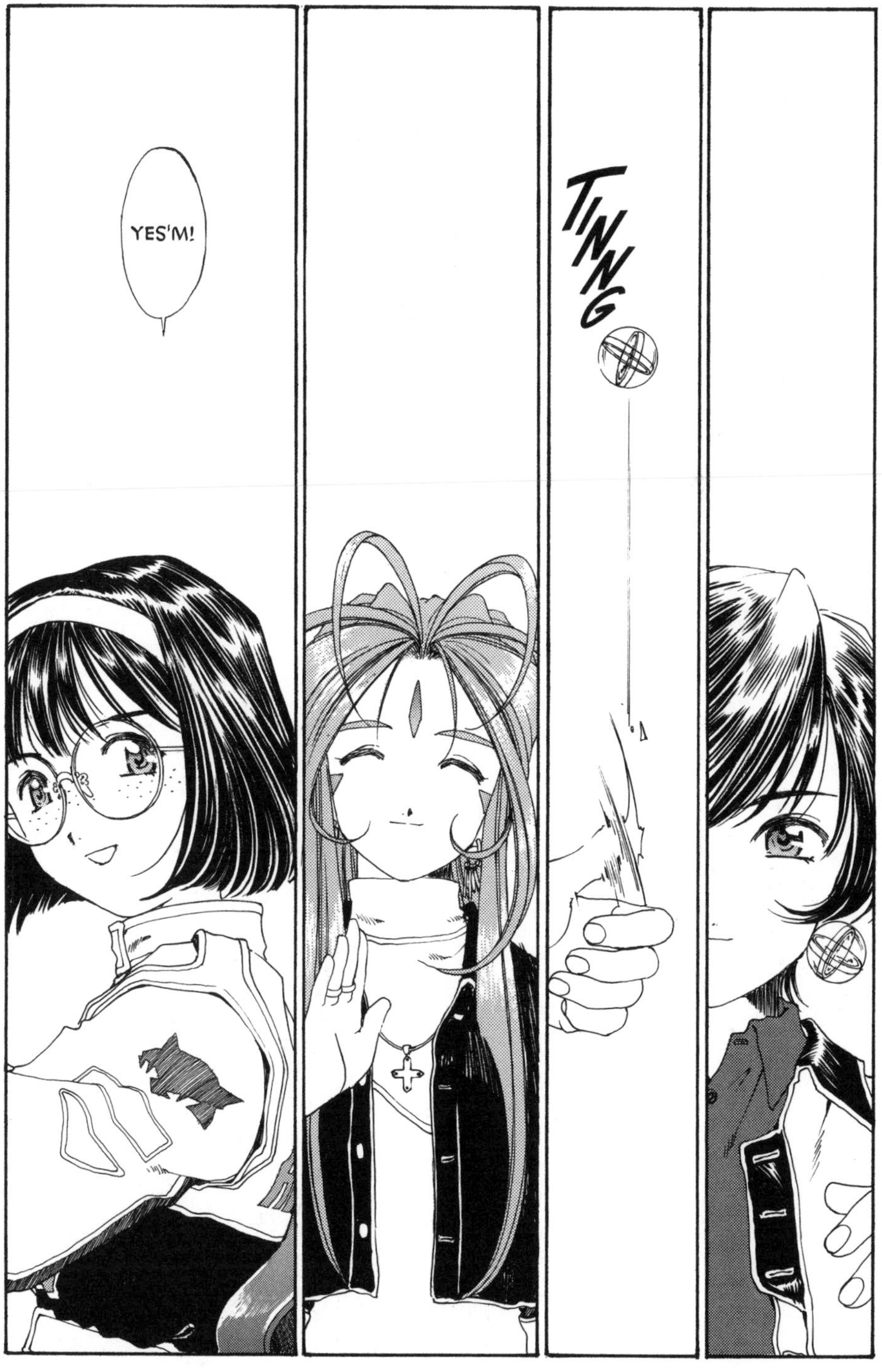
TINNG
YES'M!

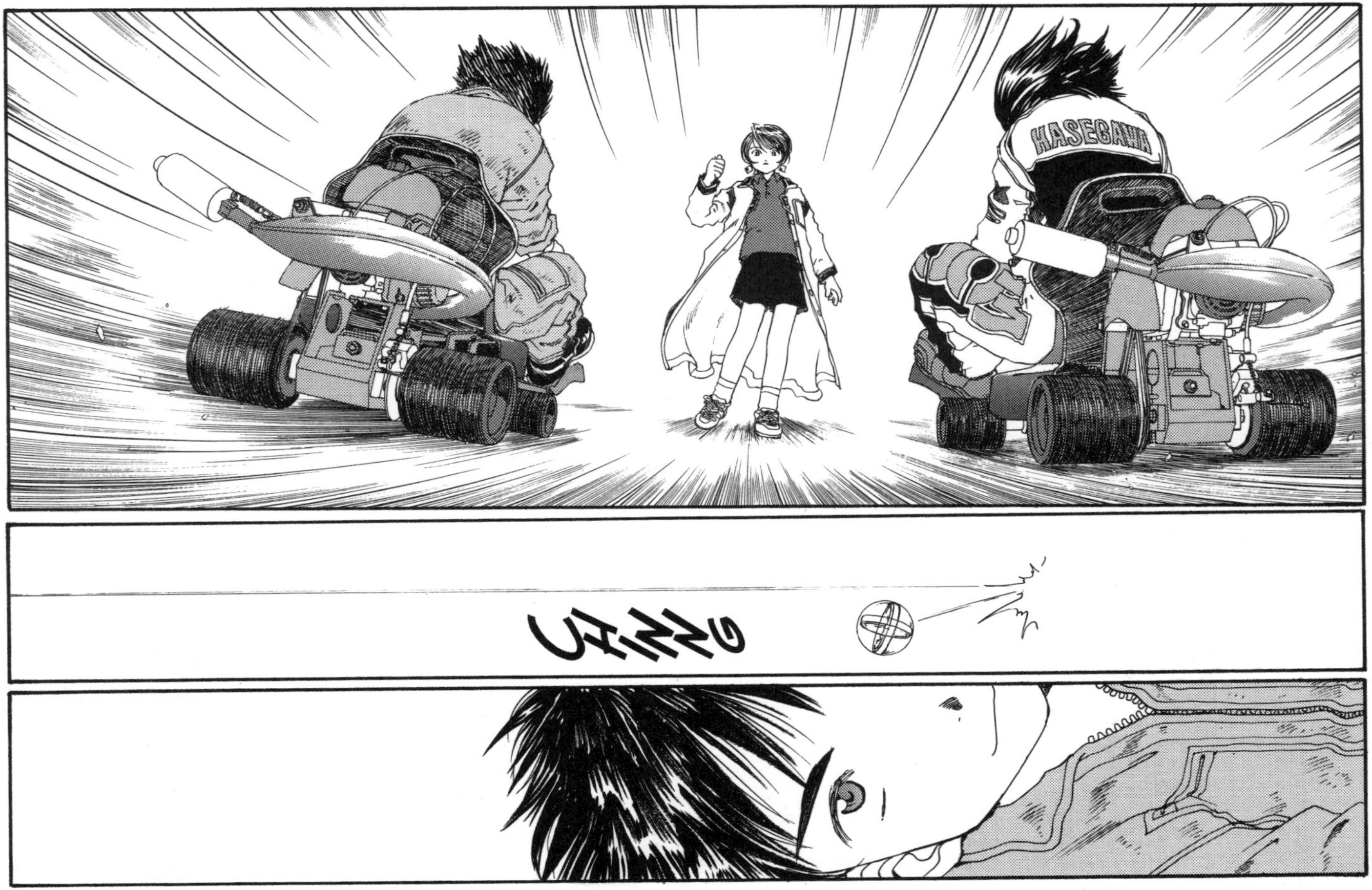
HASEGAWA
CHINNG

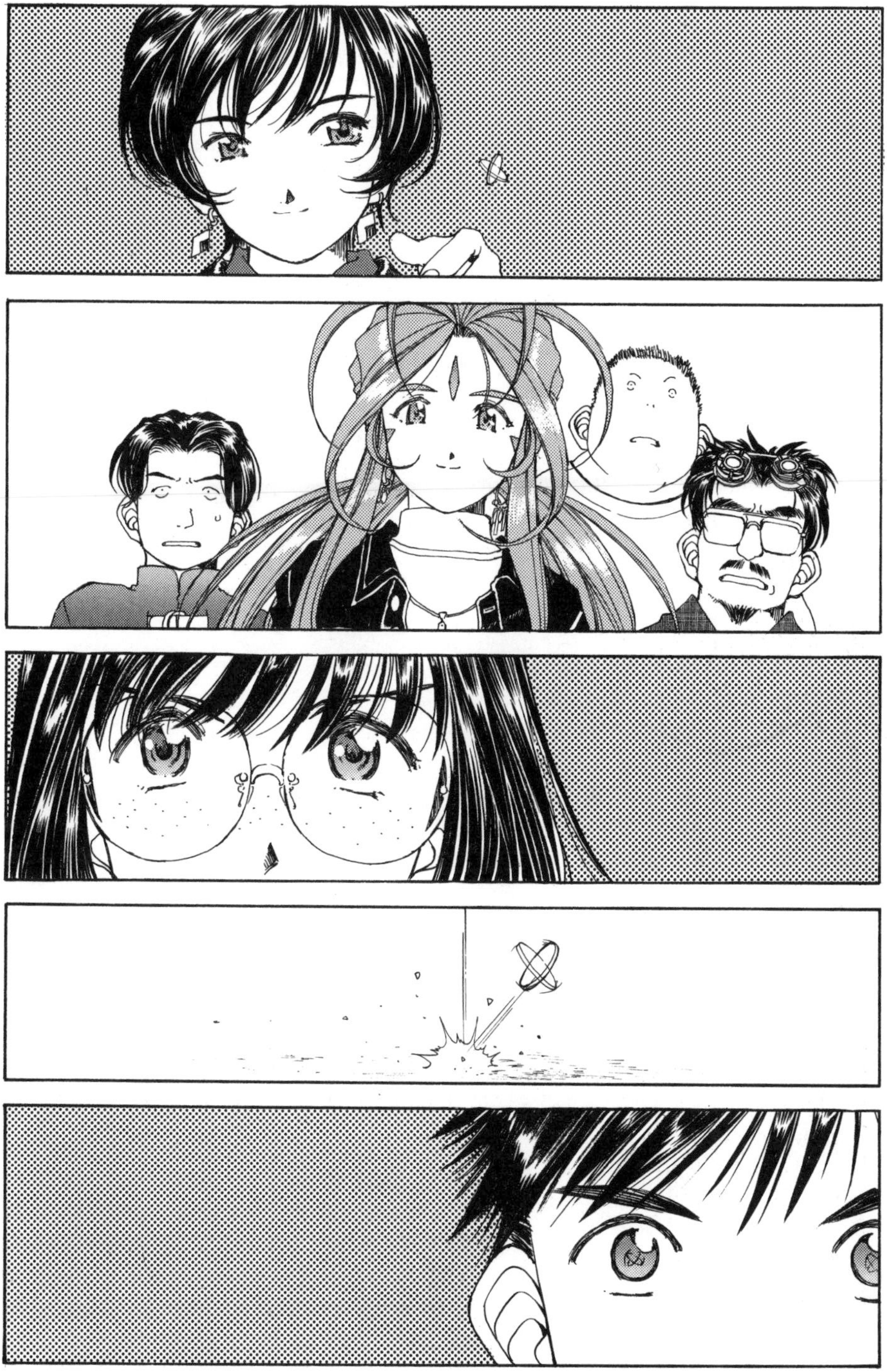

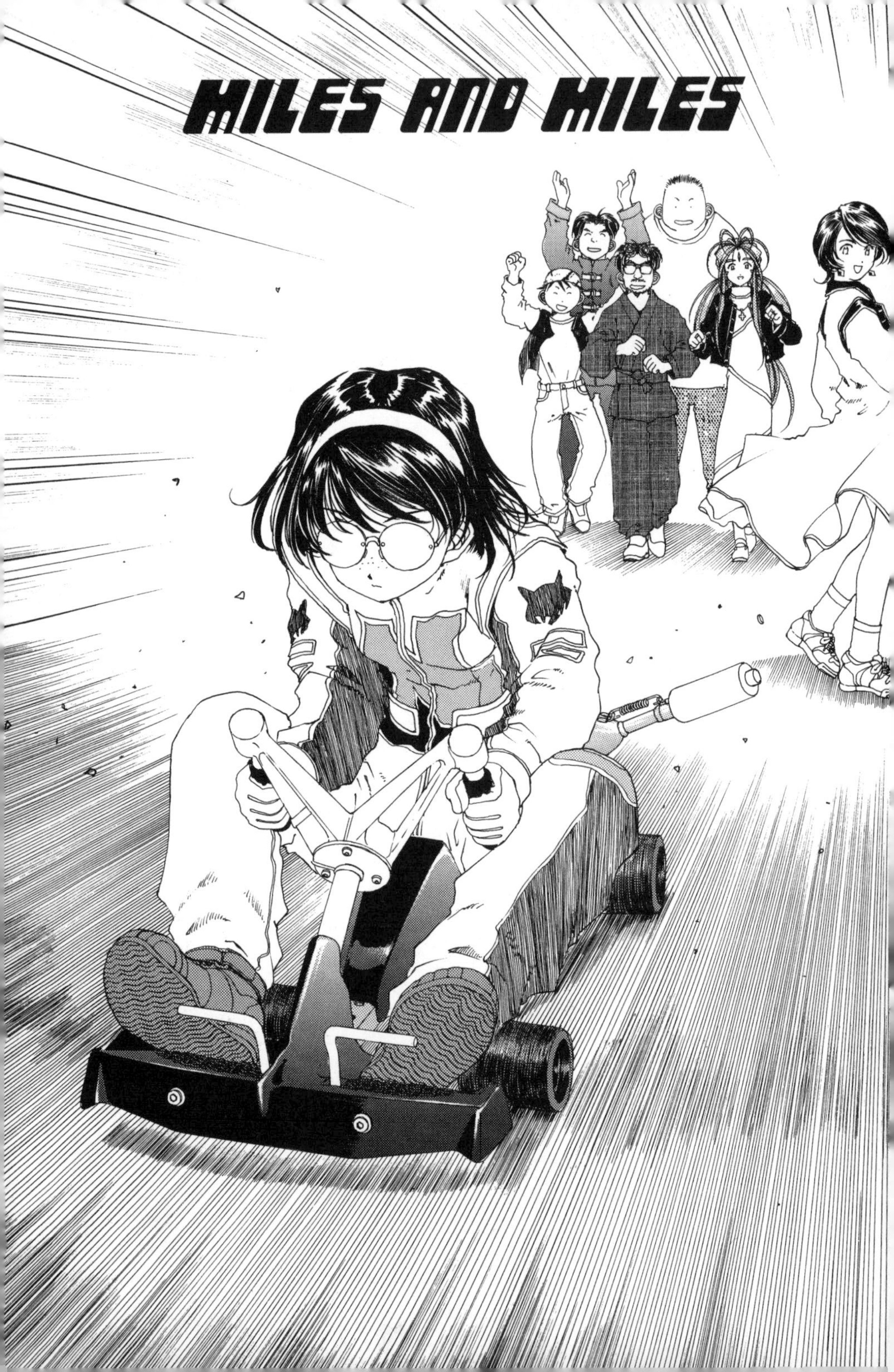
MILES AND MILES

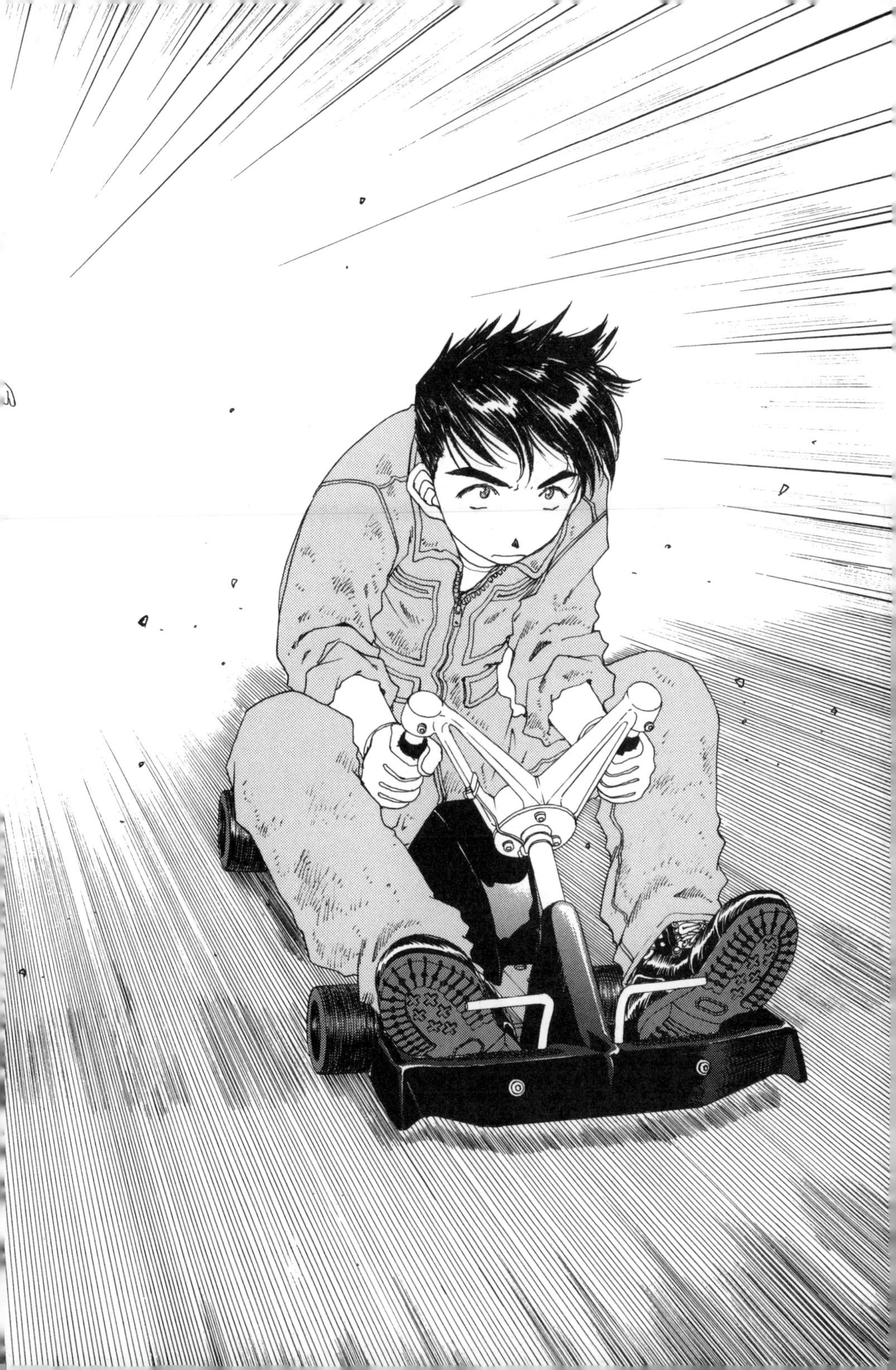

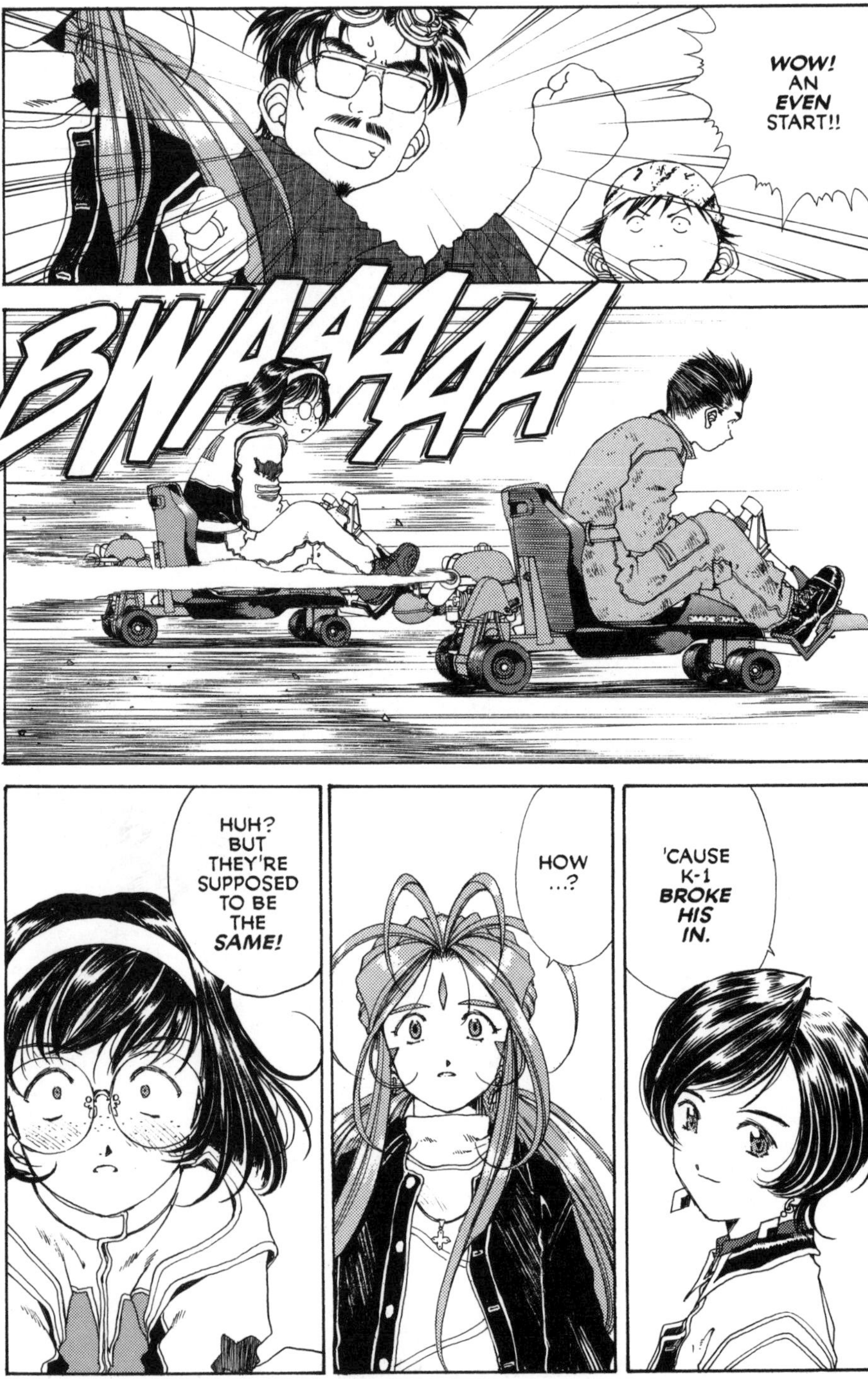
WOW! AN EVEN START!!
BWAAAAAA
'CAUSE K-1 BROKE HIS IN.
HOW ...?
HUH? BUT THEY'RE SUPPOSED TO BE THE SAME!

BROKE IT... IN?

ENGINE BREAK-IN, BELL.

NEW ENGINES ARE *SLUGGISH.*

SO, AT FIRST YOU KEEP THE RPMS *DOWN* TO WORK OUT *BURRS* AND *LOOSE FITS...*

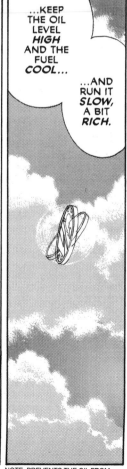

...KEEP THE OIL LEVEL *HIGH* AND THE FUEL *COOL...*

...AND RUN IT *SLOW,* A BIT *RICH.*

NOTE: PREVENTS THE OIL FROM BURNING AND CAKING. UNNECESSARY IN AUTOMOBILES.

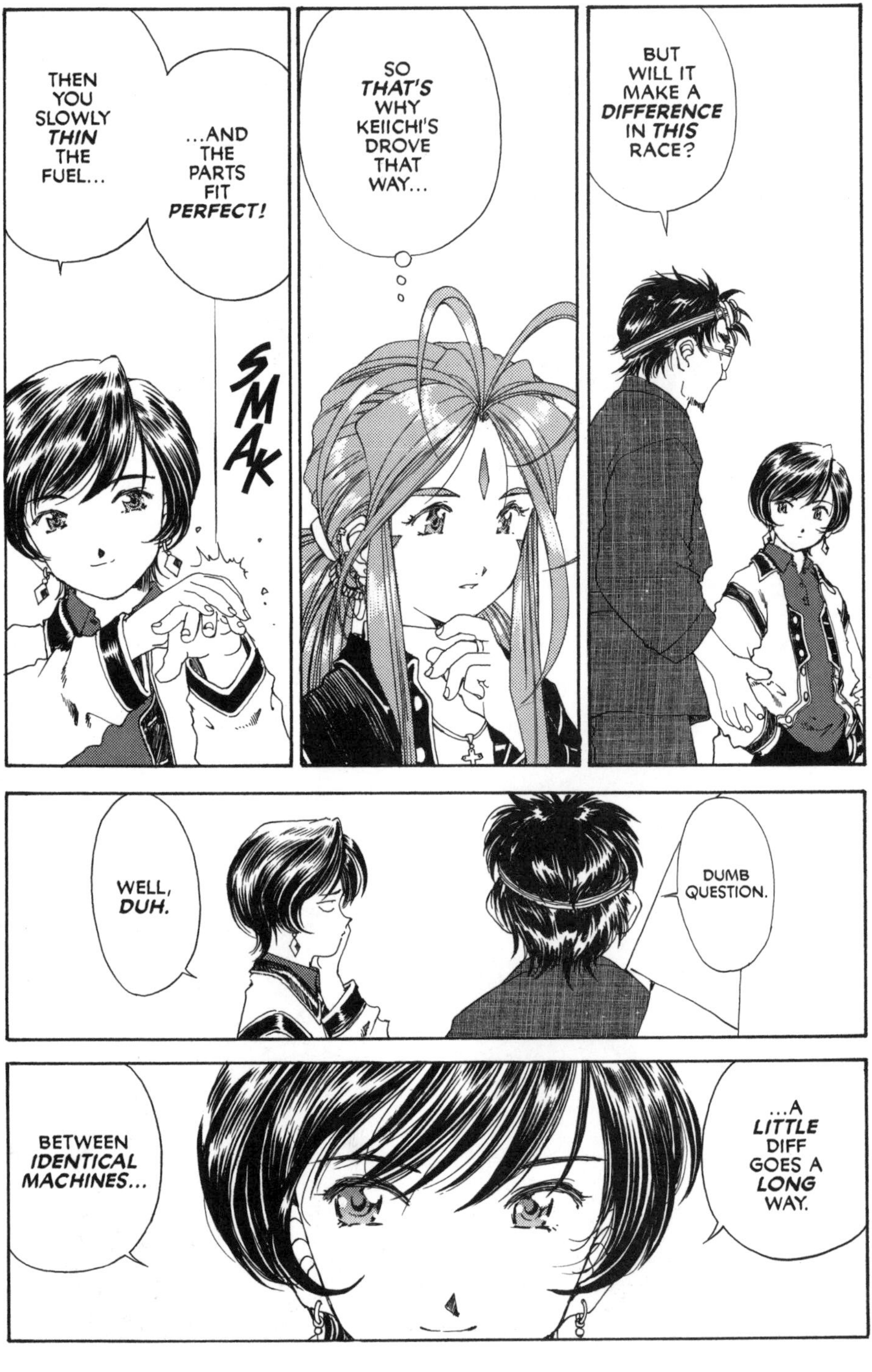
THEN YOU SLOWLY *THIN* THE FUEL...
...AND THE PARTS FIT *PERFECT!*
SMAK
SO *THAT'S* WHY KEIICHI'S DROVE THAT WAY...
BUT WILL IT MAKE A *DIFFERENCE* IN *THIS* RACE?
WELL, *DUH.*
DUMB QUESTION.
BETWEEN *IDENTICAL MACHINES...*
...A *LITTLE* DIFF GOES A *LONG* WAY.

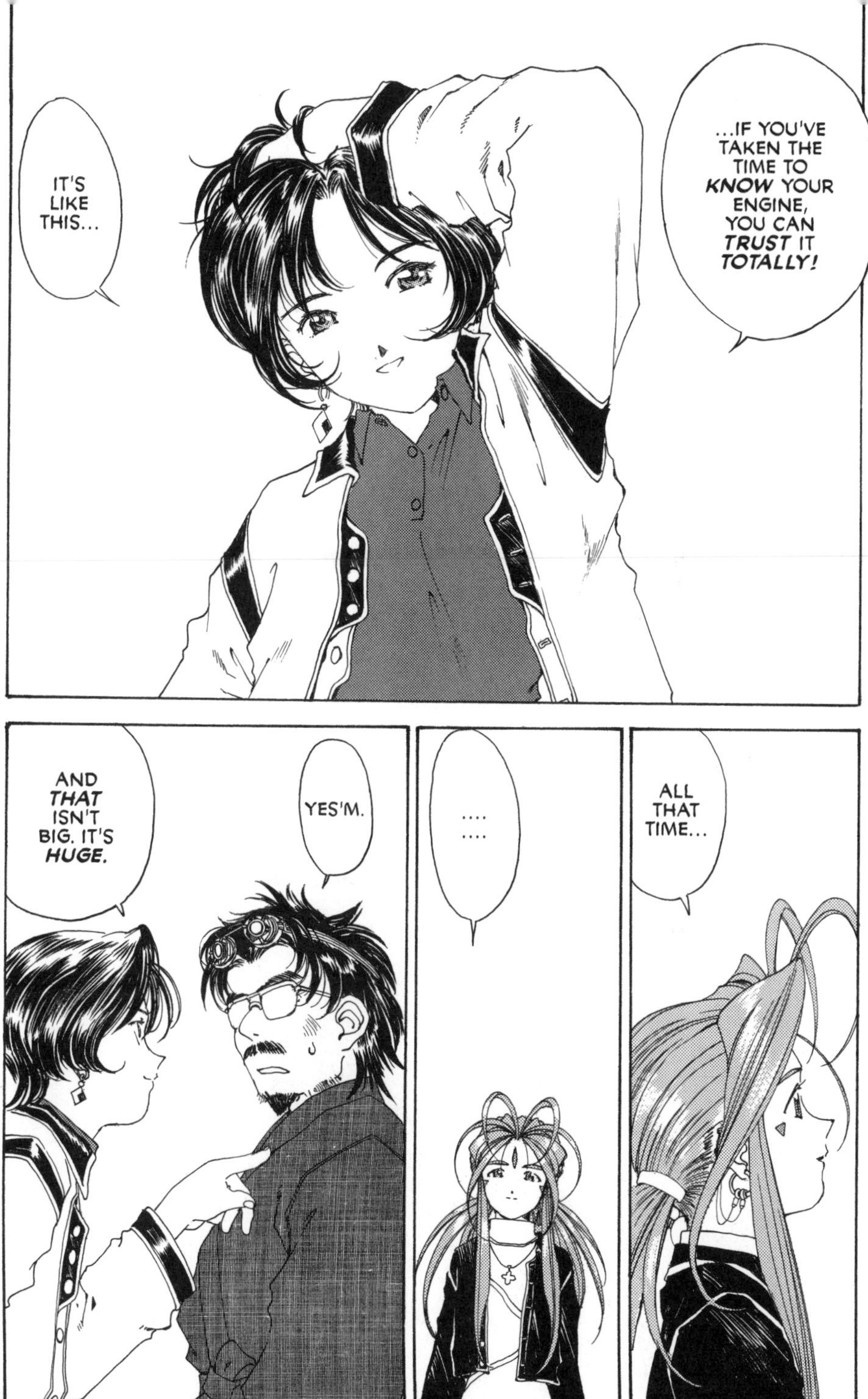
IT'S LIKE THIS...
...IF YOU'VE TAKEN THE TIME TO ***KNOW*** YOUR ENGINE, YOU CAN ***TRUST*** IT ***TOTALLY!***
AND ***THAT*** ISN'T BIG. IT'S ***HUGE.***
YES'M.
....
ALL THAT TIME...

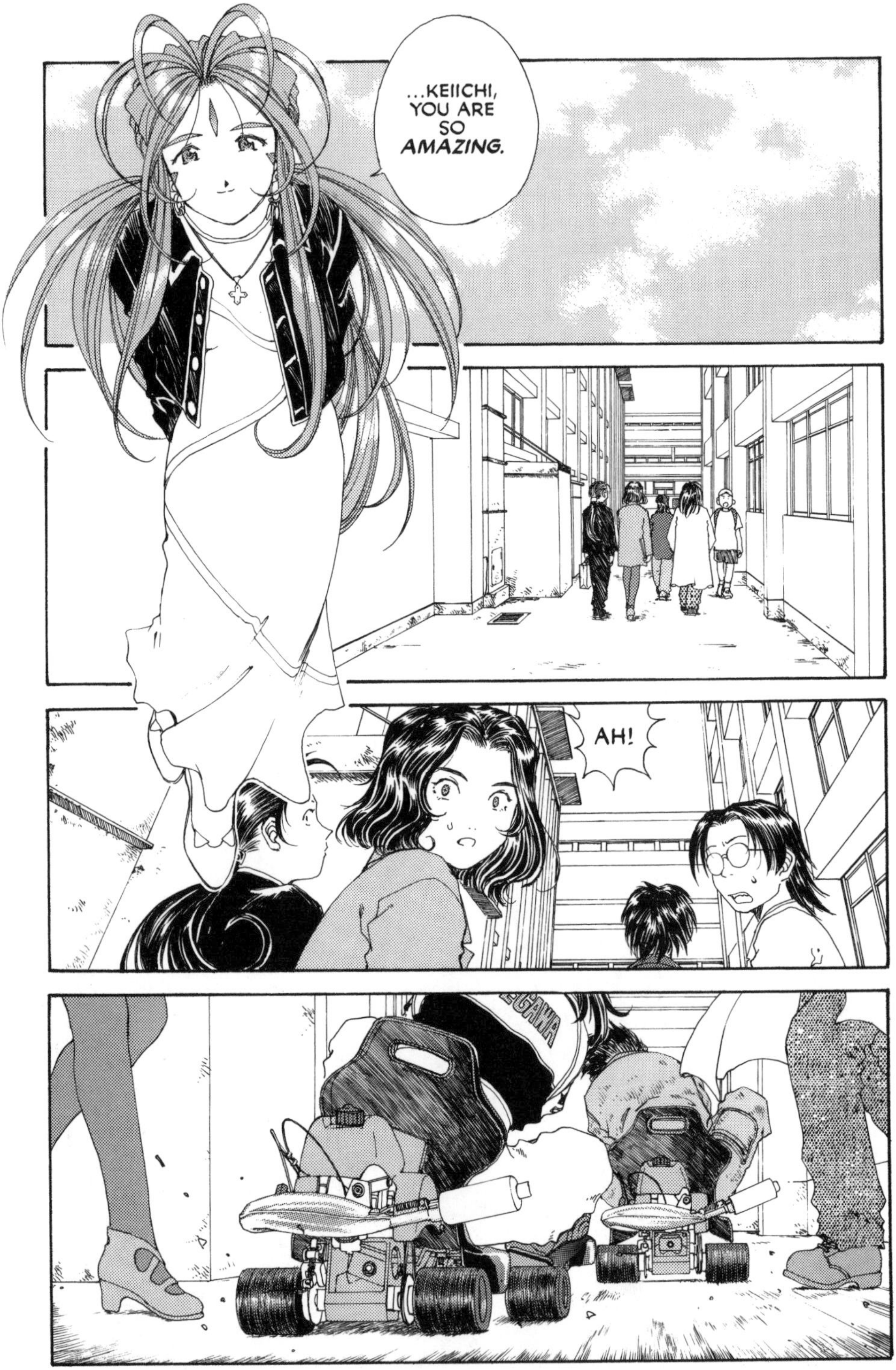
...KEIICHI, YOU ARE SO *AMAZING.*
AH!

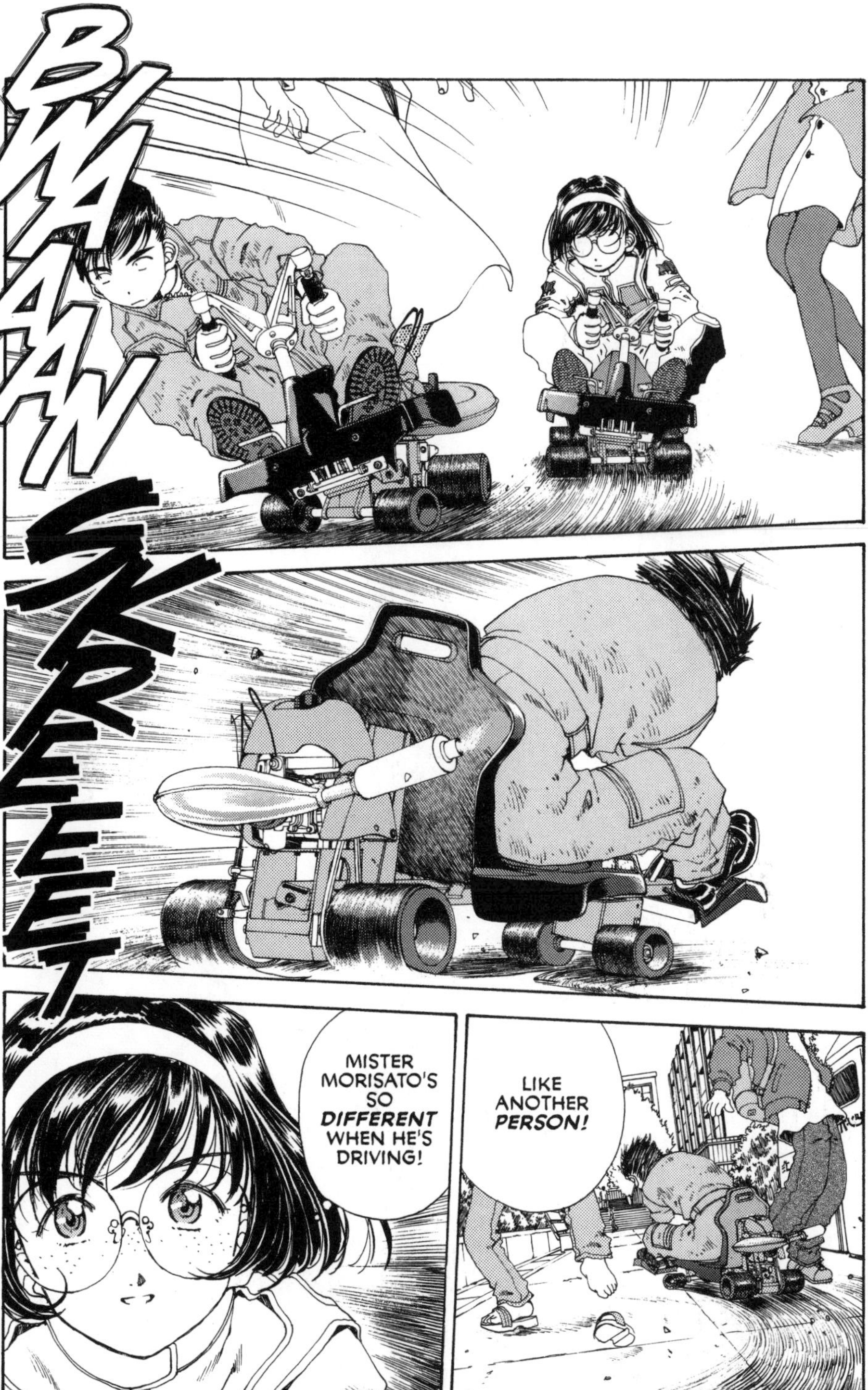
BWAAAN
SKREEET
MISTER MORISATO'S SO DIFFERENT WHEN HE'S DRIVING!
LIKE ANOTHER PERSON!

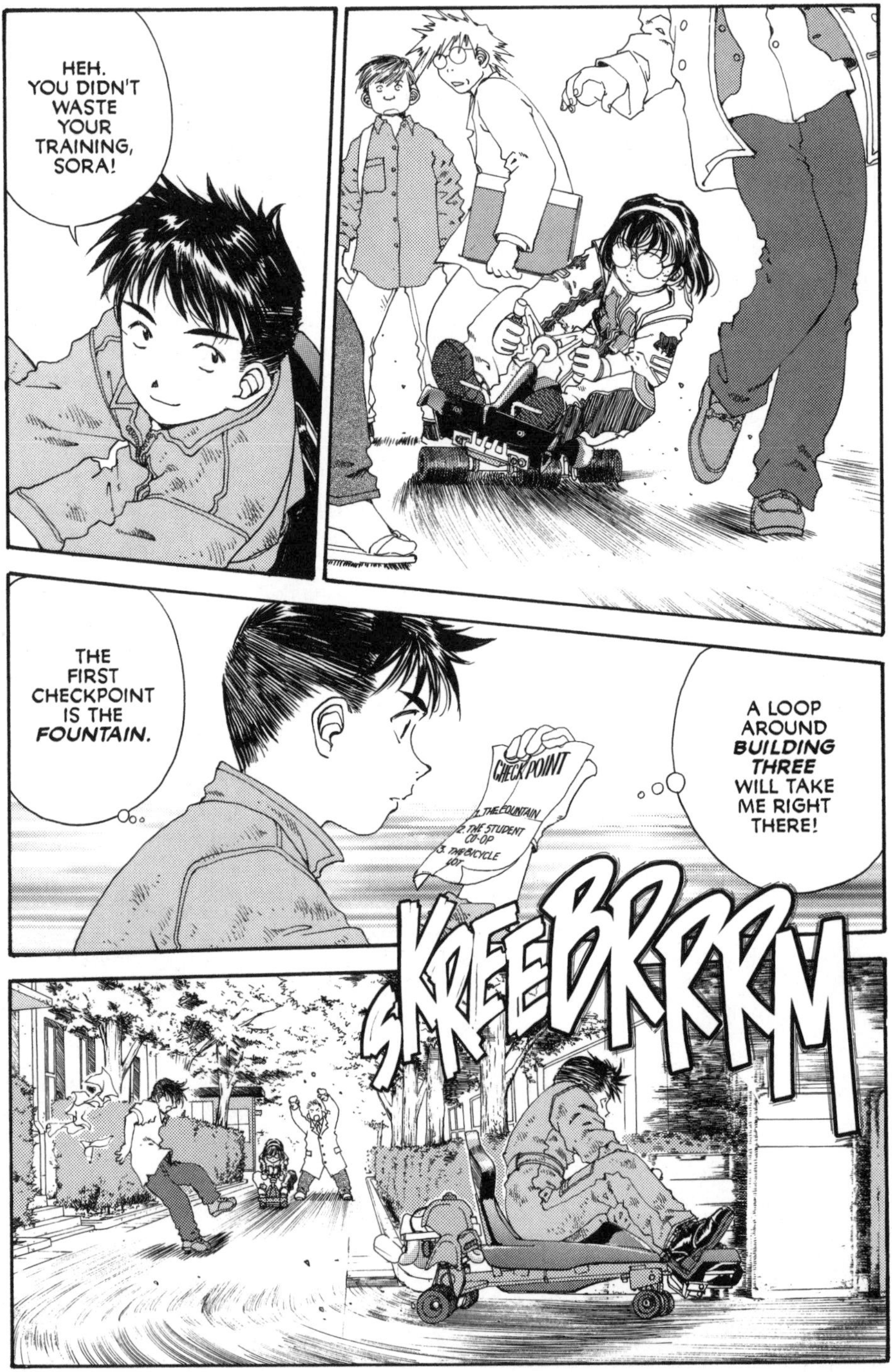
HEH. YOU DIDN'T WASTE YOUR TRAINING, SORA!
THE FIRST CHECKPOINT IS THE *FOUNTAIN.*
CHECKPOINT
1. THE FOUNTAIN
2. THE STUDENT CO-OP
3. THE BICYCLE LOT
A LOOP AROUND ***BUILDING THREE*** WILL TAKE ME RIGHT THERE!
SKREEBRRRRM

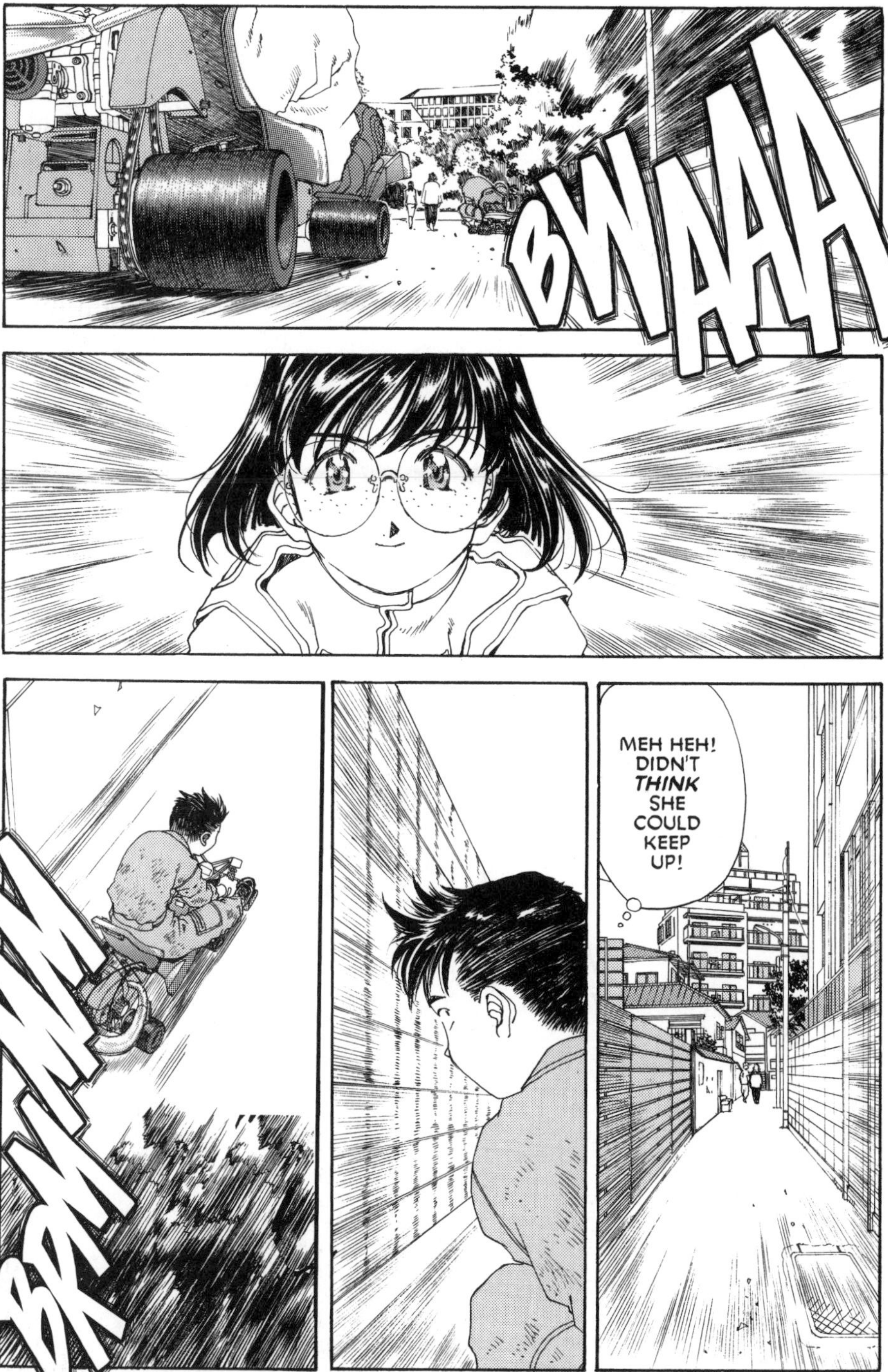
BWAAAA
MEH HEH! DIDN'T *THINK* SHE COULD KEEP UP!
BRMMM

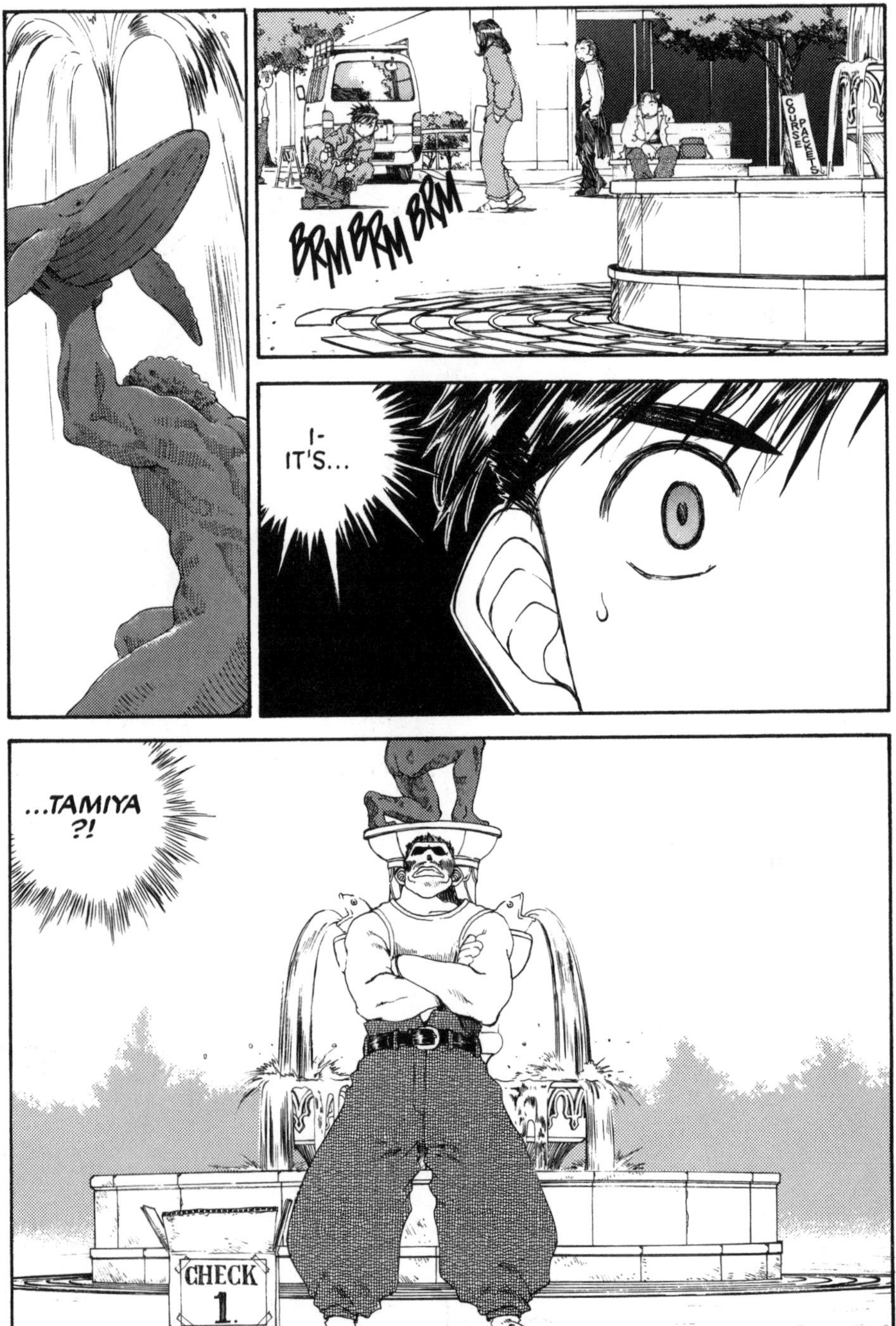
COURSE PACKETS
BRM BRM BRM
I- IT'S...
...TAMIYA?!
CHECK 1.

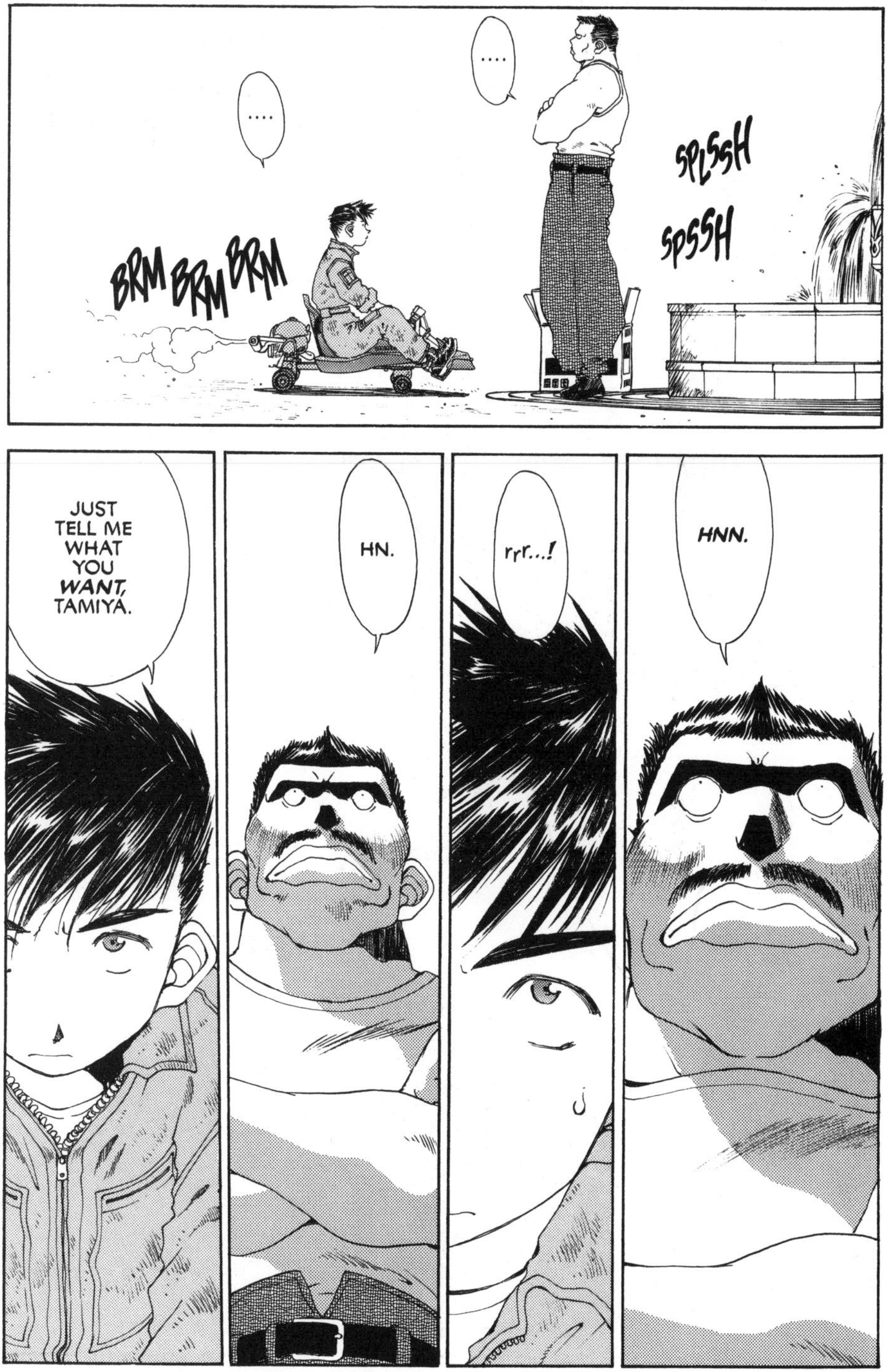
BRM BRM BRM
....
....
SPLSSH
SPSSH
JUST TELL ME WHAT YOU *WANT*, TAMIYA.
HN.
rrr...!
HNN.

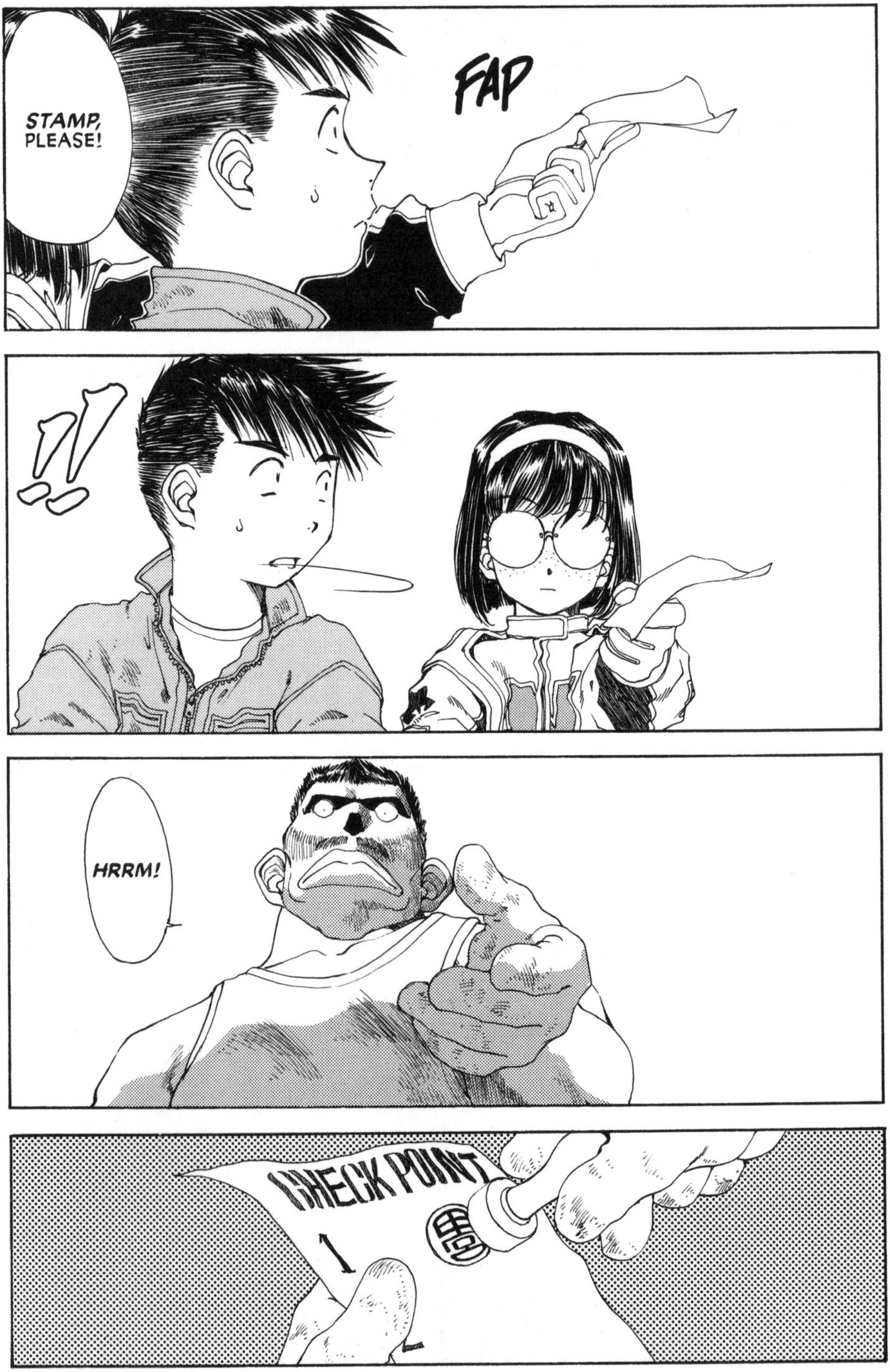
FAP
STAMP, PLEASE!
!!
HRRM!
CHECK POINT
1

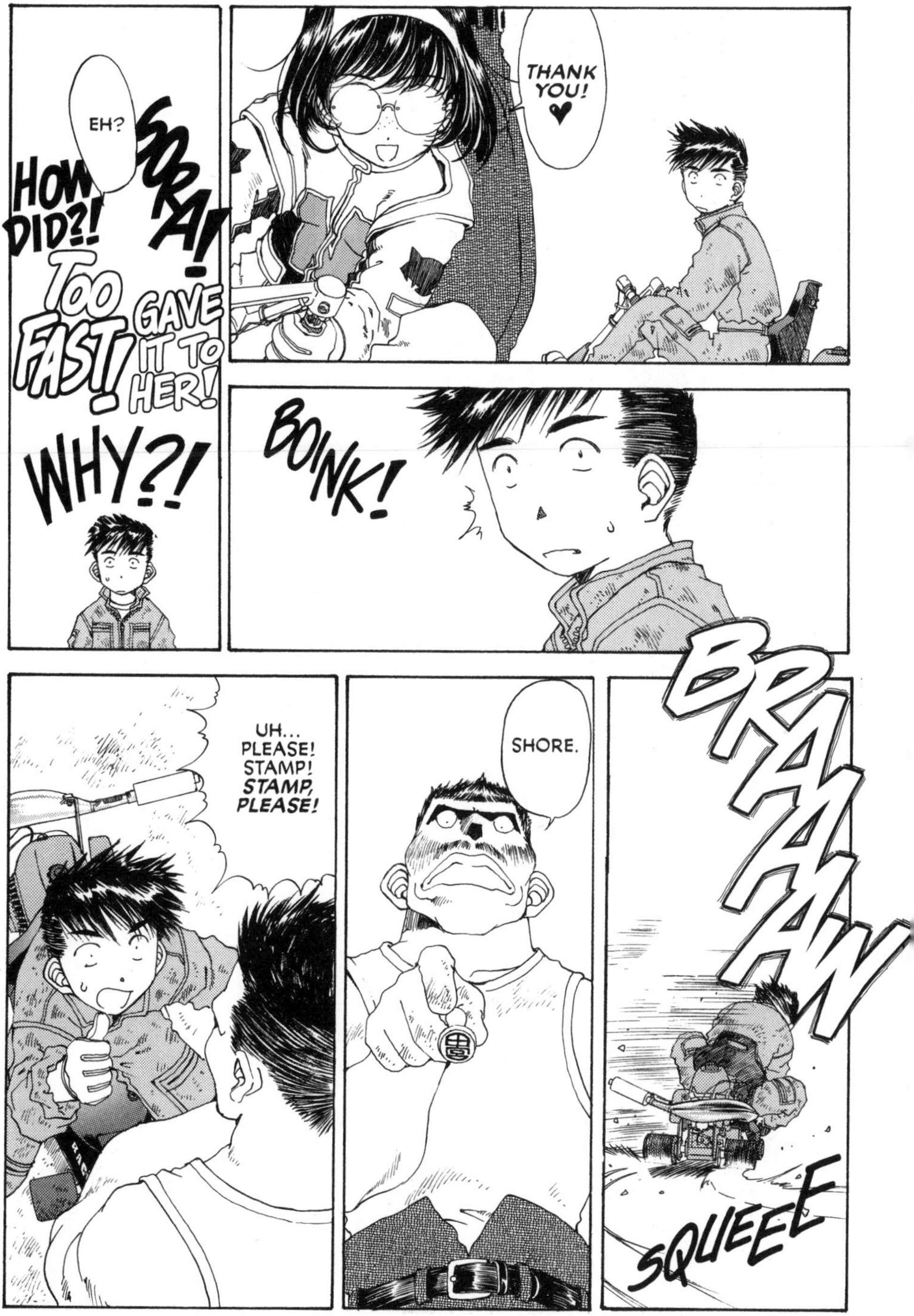
THANK YOU! ♥
BOINK!
EH?
SORA!
HOW DID?!
TOO FAST!
GAVE IT TO HER!
WHY?!
BRAAAAN
SQUEEEE
SHORE.
UH... PLEASE! STAMP! STAMP, PLEASE!

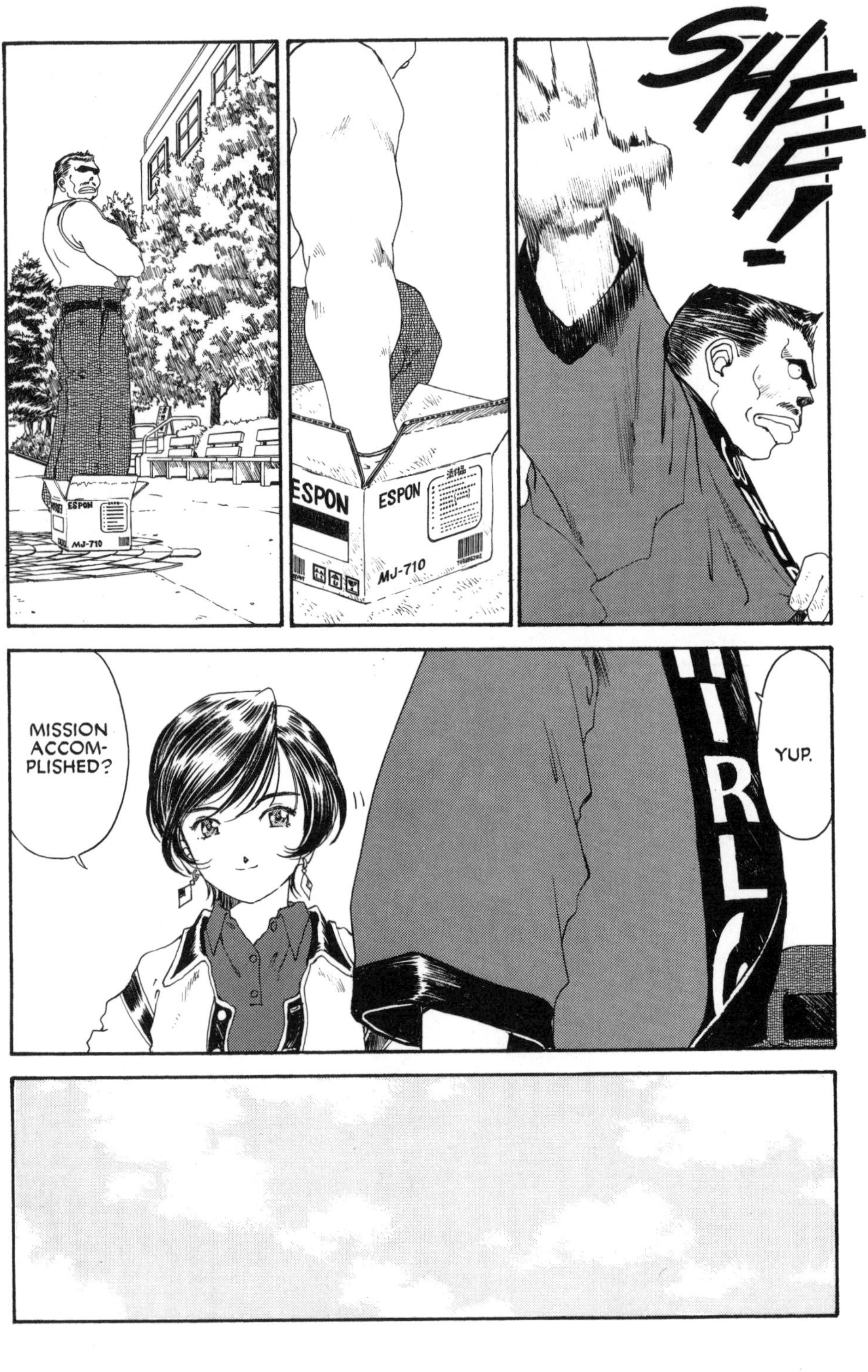
ESPON
MJ-710
ESPON
ESPON
MJ-710
SHFF!
MISSION ACCOMPLISHED?
YUP.

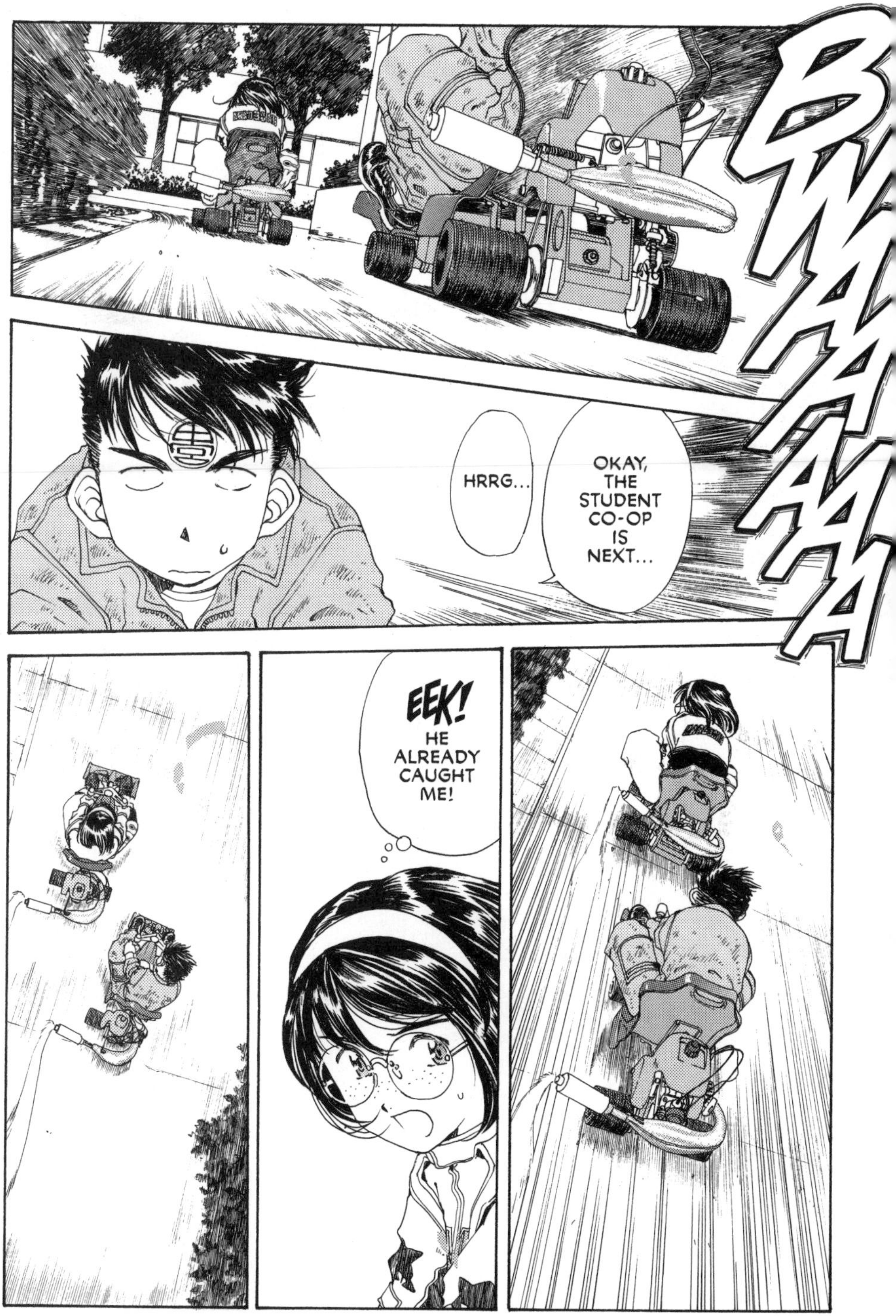
BWAAAAA
OKAY, THE STUDENT CO-OP IS NEXT...
HRRG...
EEK! HE ALREADY CAUGHT ME!

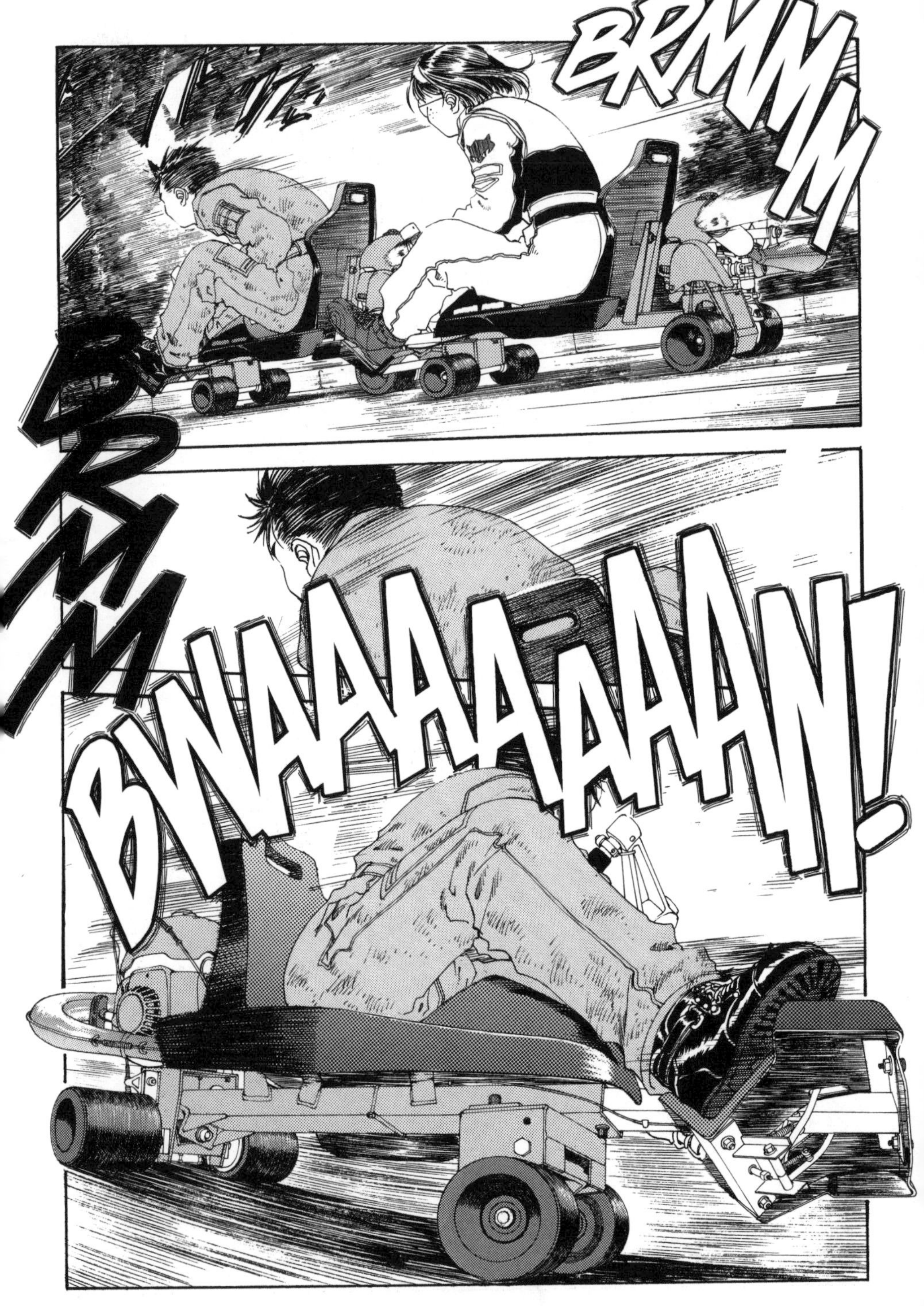
BRMMMM
BRMM
BWAAAAAAAN!

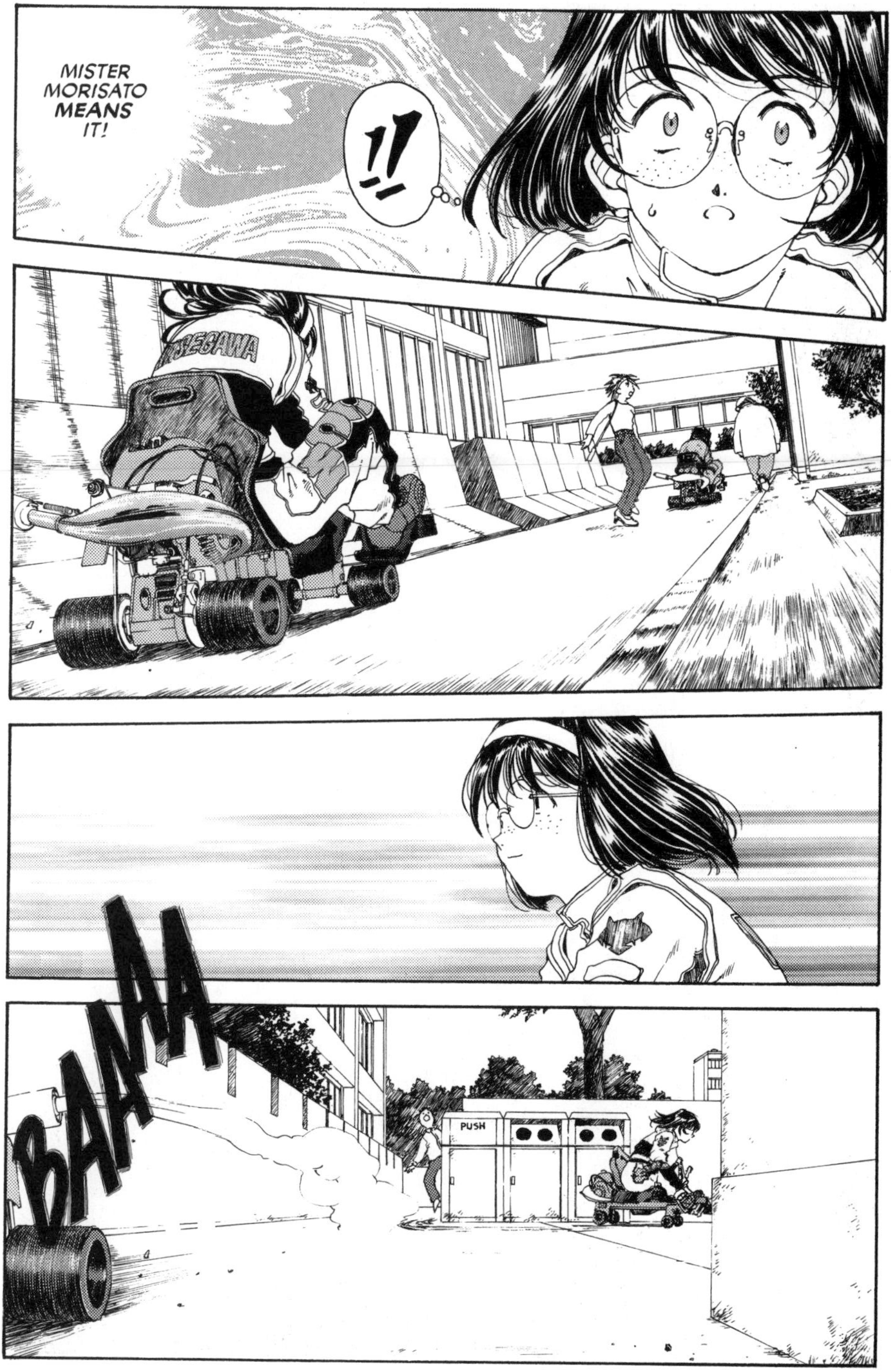
MISTER MORISATO MEANS IT!
!!
HASEGAWA
PUSH
BAAAA

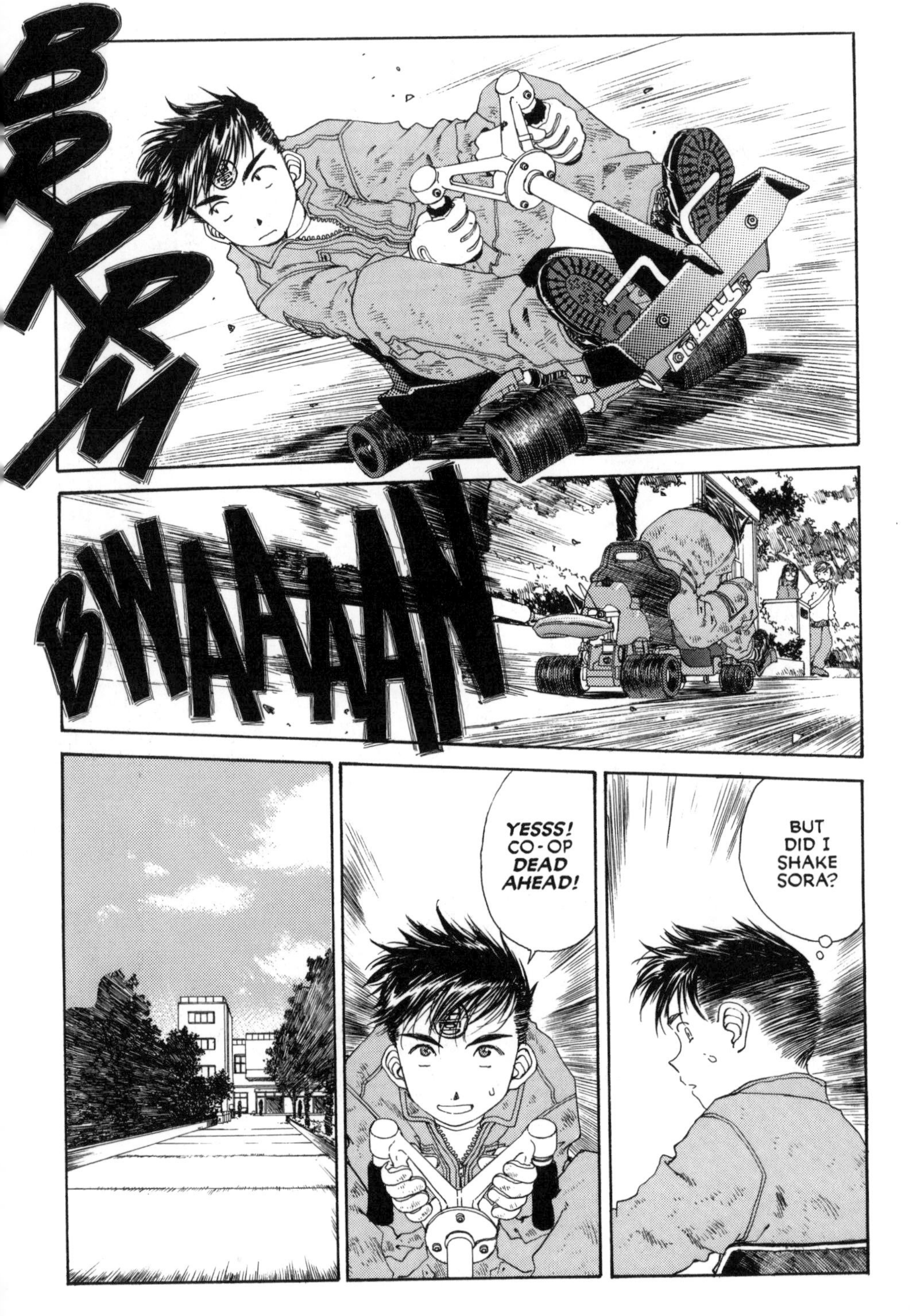
BRRRM
BWAAAAAN
YESSS! CO-OP DEAD AHEAD!
BUT DID I SHAKE SORA?

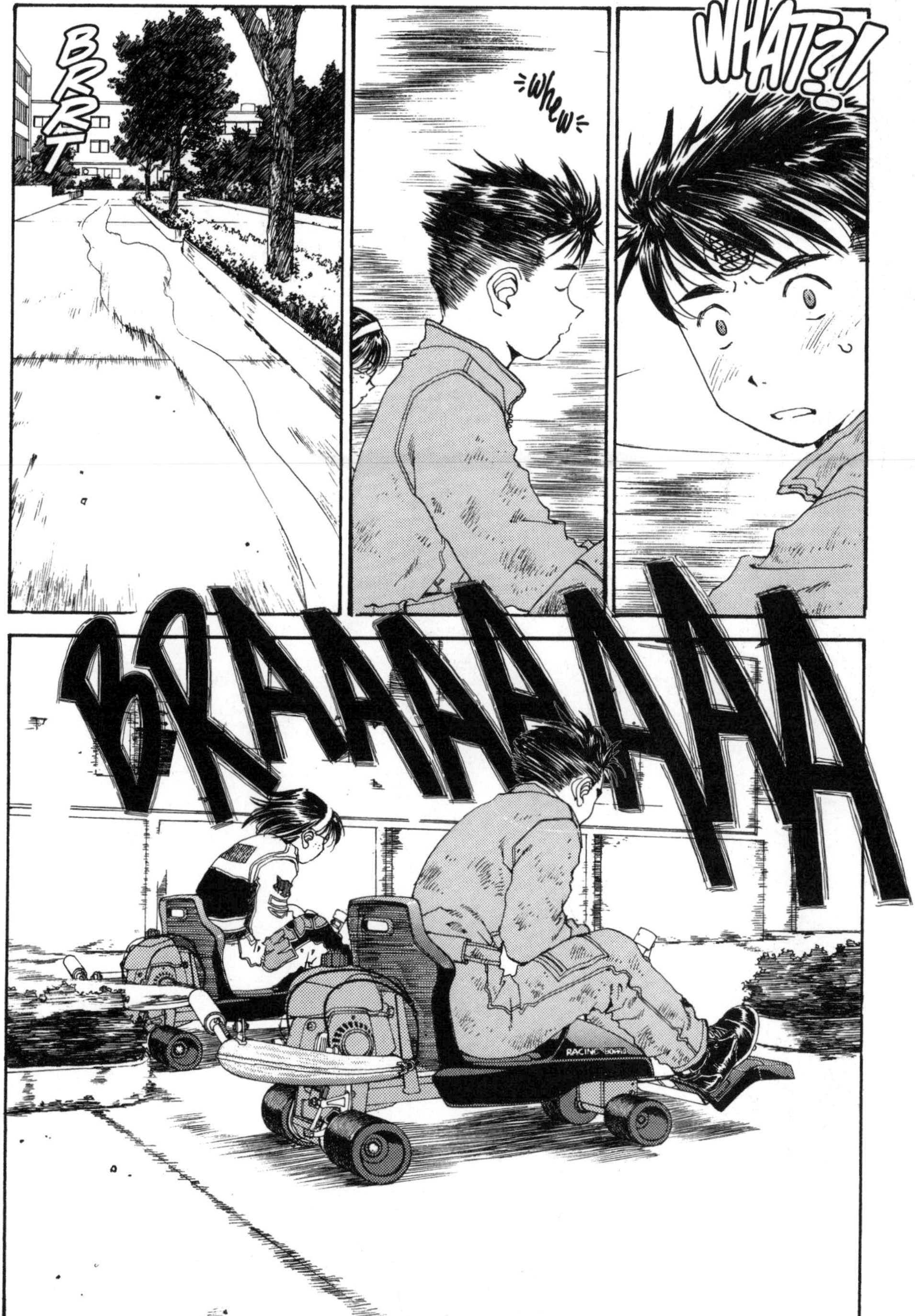
WHAT?!
whew
BRRRT
BRAAAAAAA

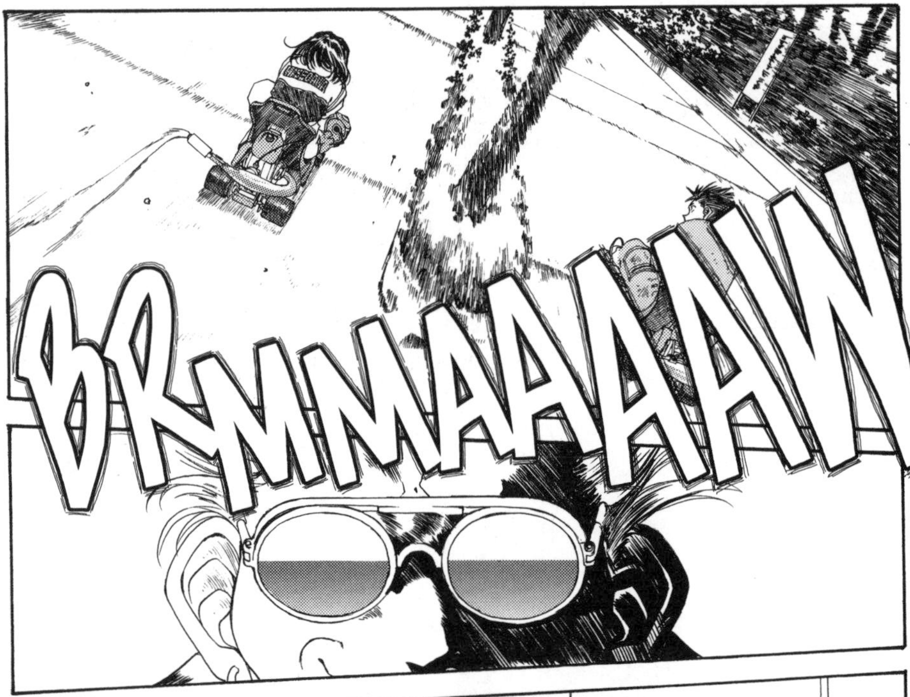
BRMMAAAAAW
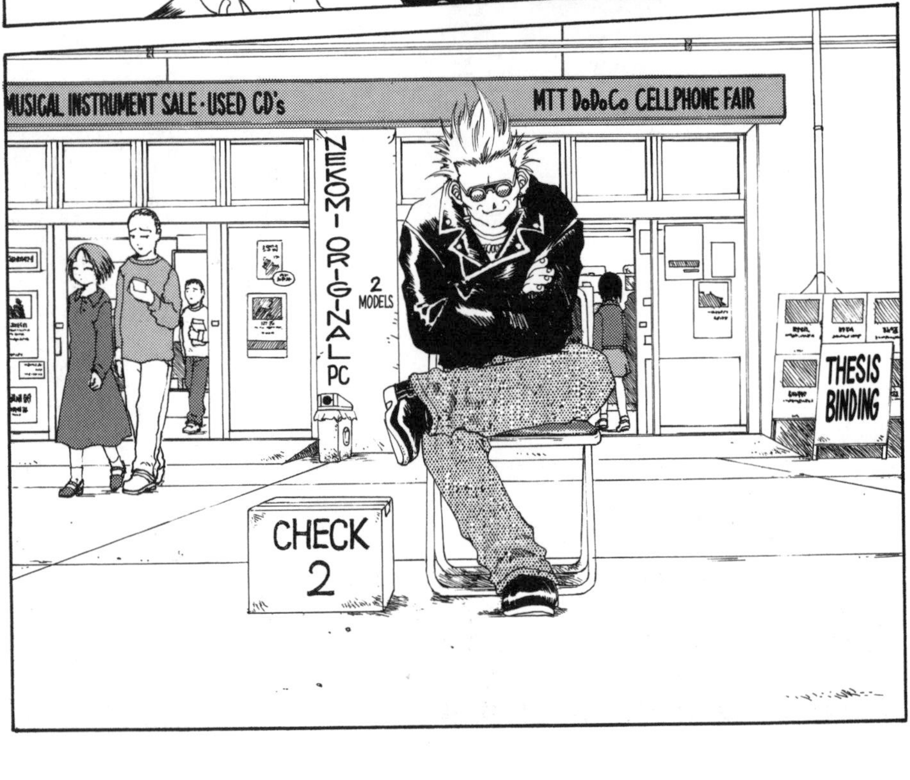
MUSICAL INSTRUMENT SALE · USED CD's
MTT DoDoCo CELLPHONE FAIR
NEKOMI ORIGINAL PC
2 MODELS
THESIS BINDING
CHECK 2

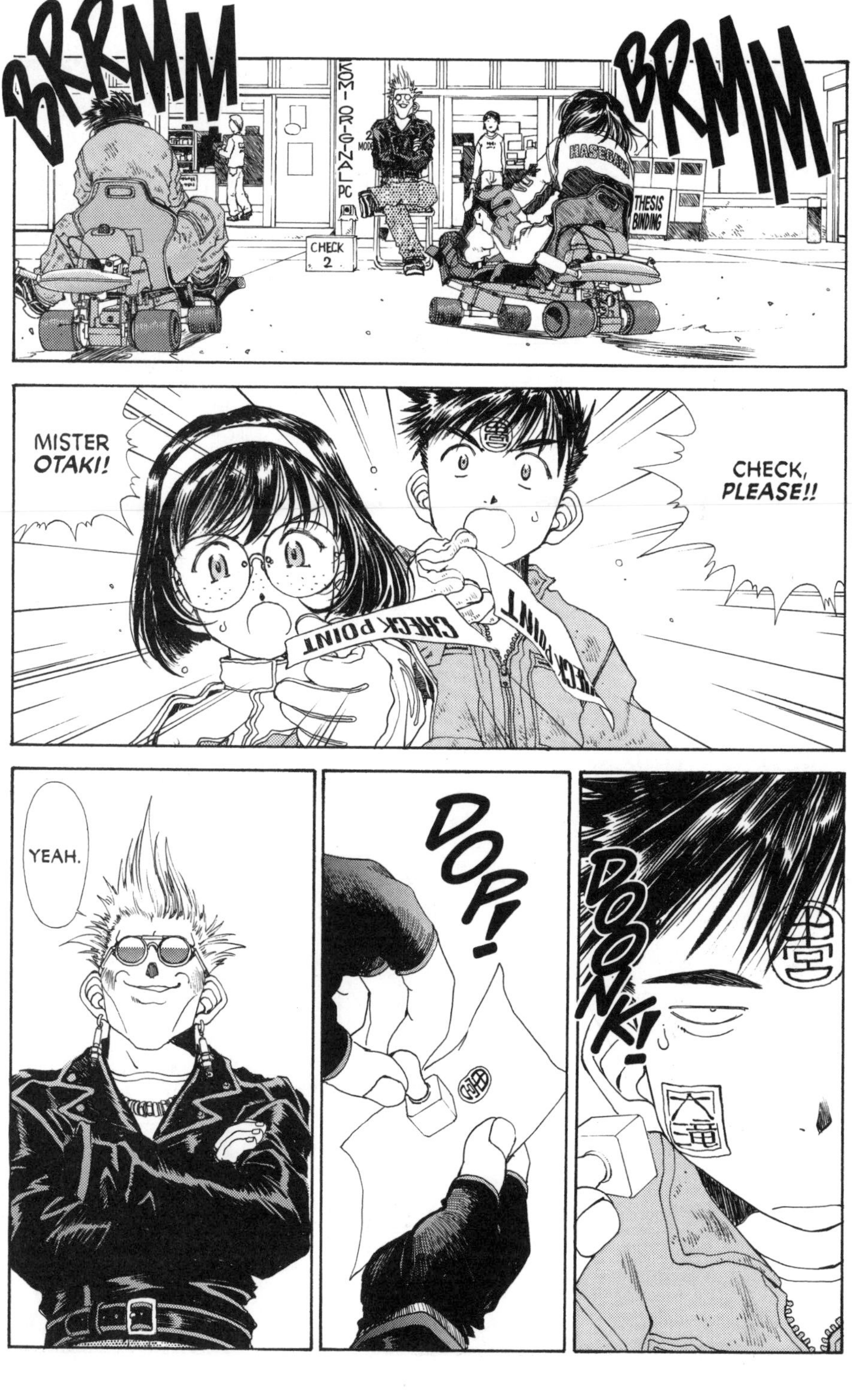
BRMM
BRRMM
KOMI ORIGINAL PC
THESIS BINDING
CHECK 2
CHECK, PLEASE!!
MISTER OTAKI!
CHECK POINT
CHECK POINT
DOOONK!
DOP!
YEAH.

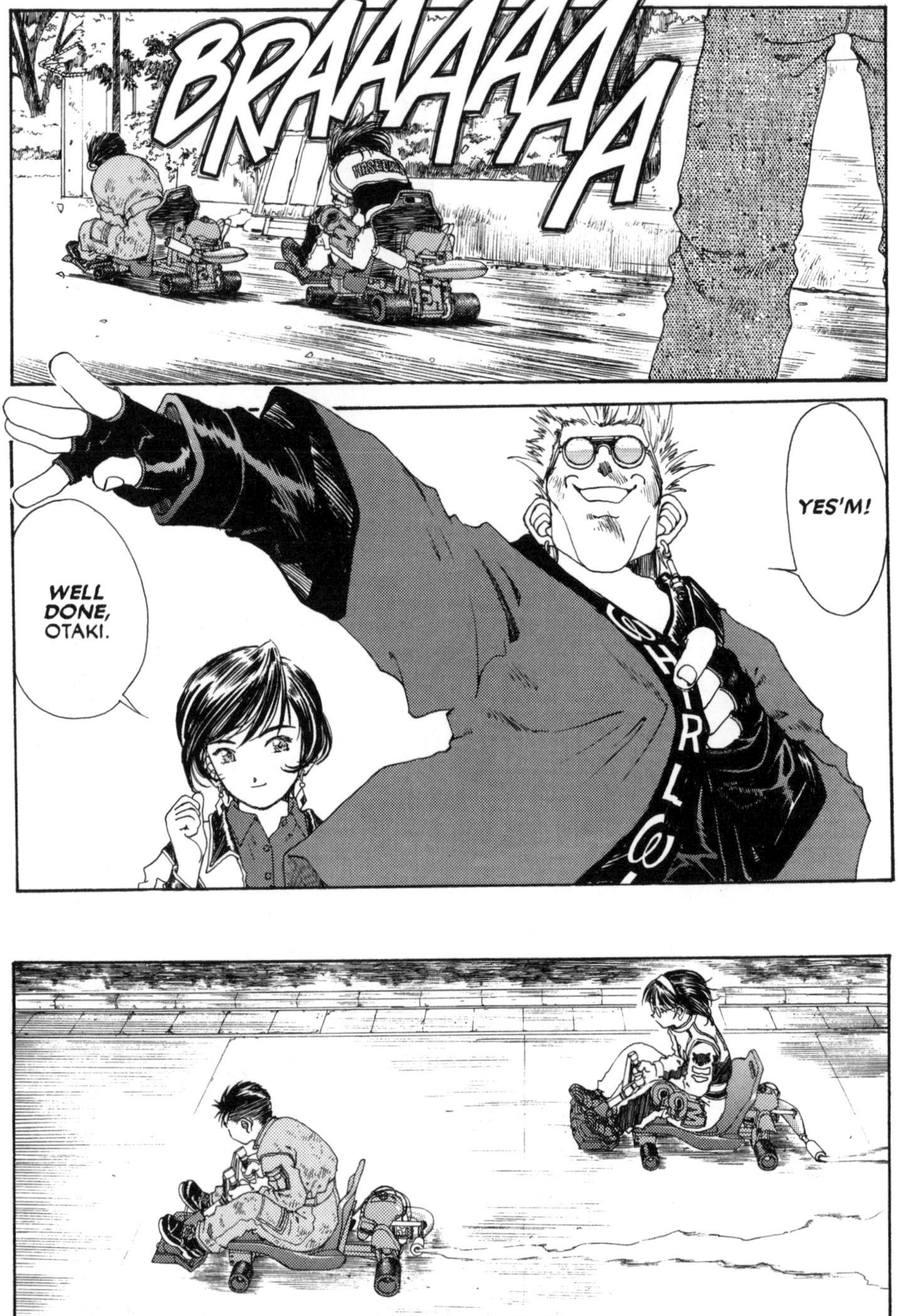
BRAAAAAAA
WELL DONE, OTAKI.
YES'M!

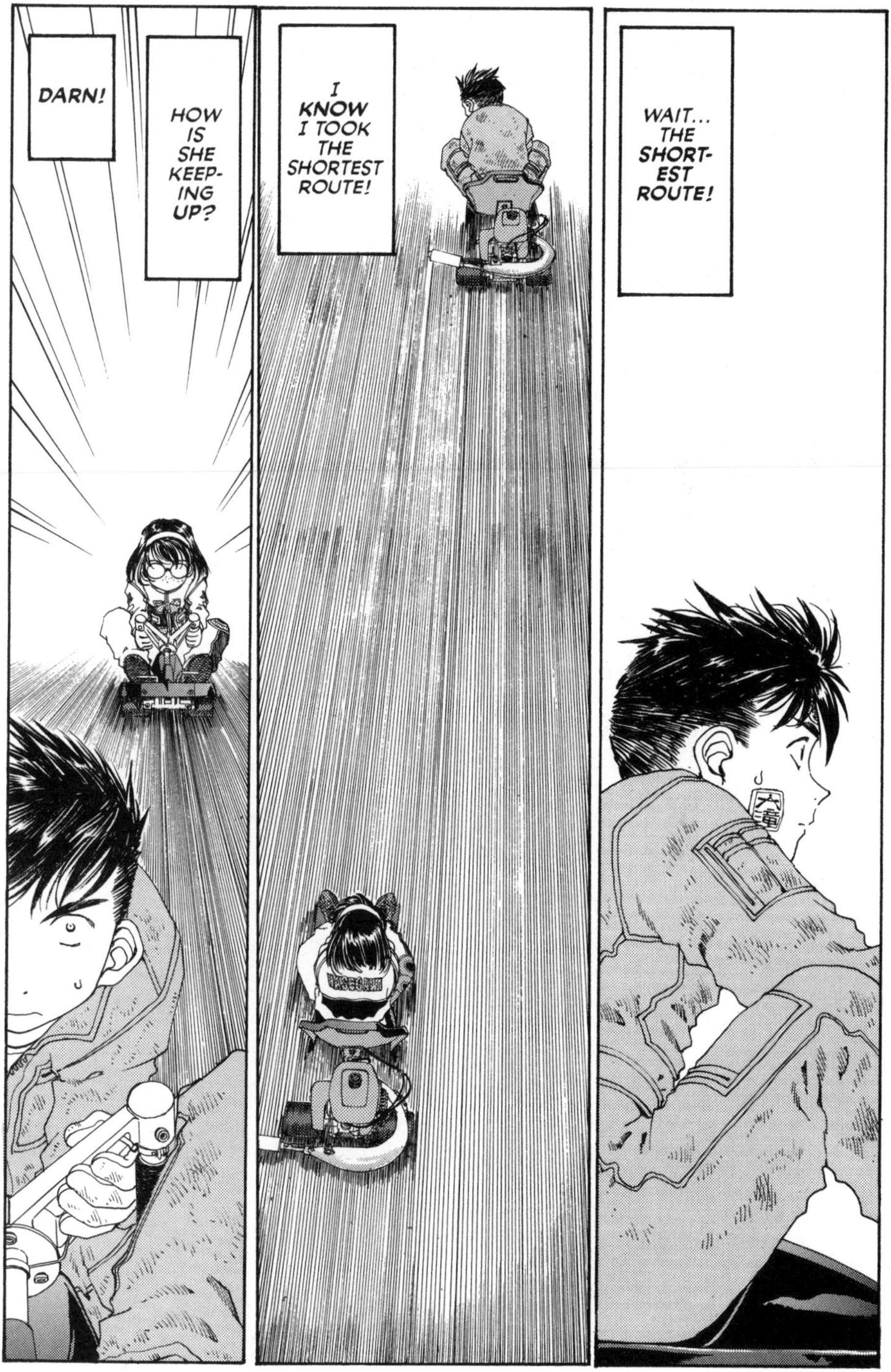
WAIT... THE SHORT-EST ROUTE!
I KNOW I TOOK THE SHORTEST ROUTE!
HOW IS SHE KEEP-ING UP?
DARN!

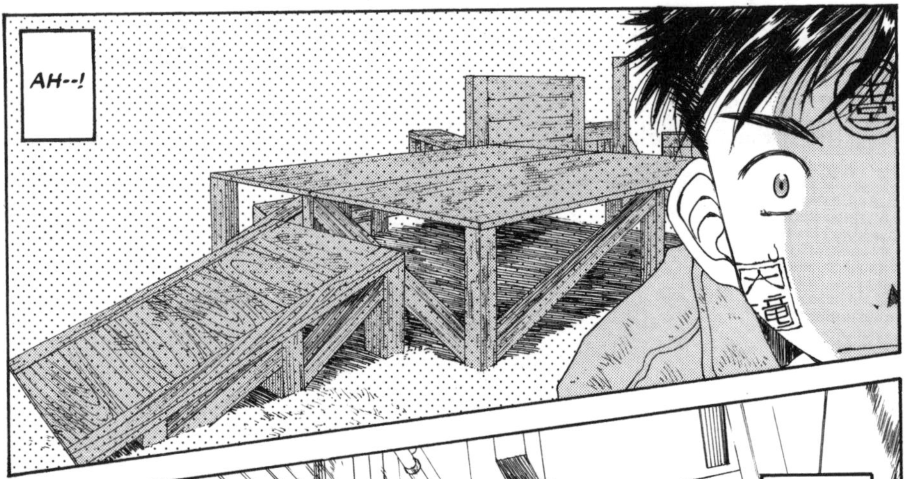
AH--!
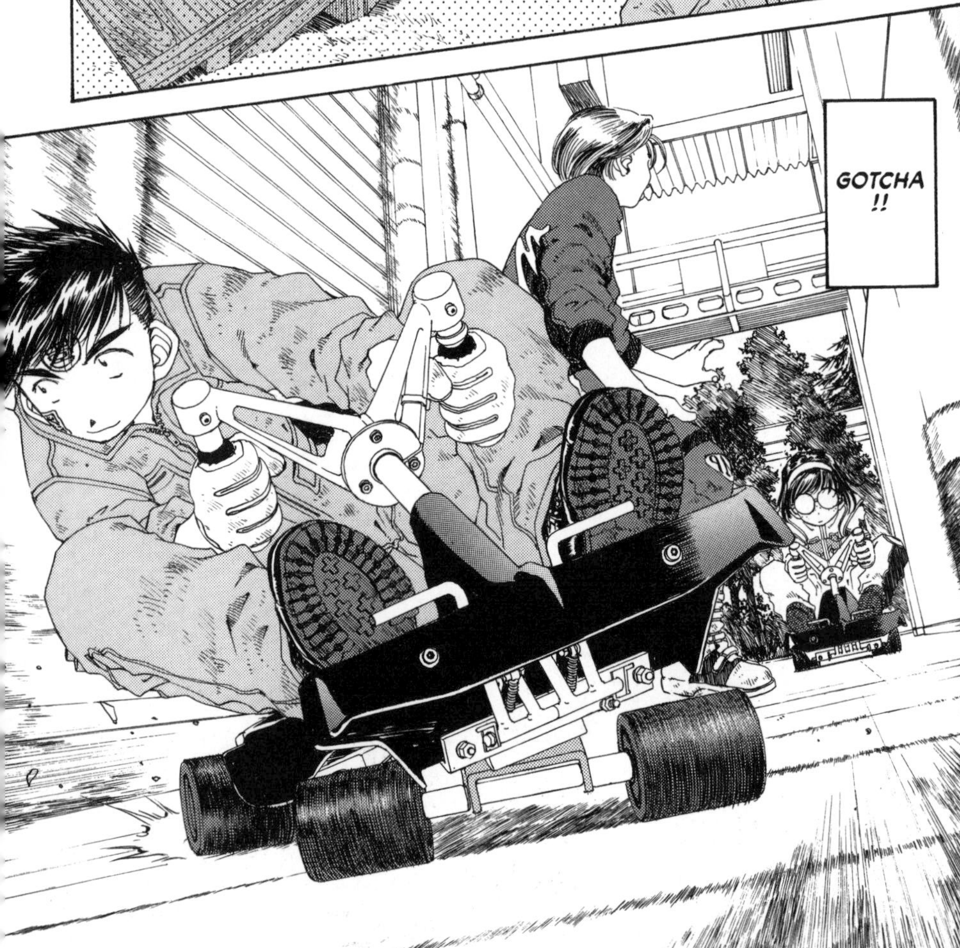
GOTCHA !!

THE RACE GETS HOT, A GODDESS GETS HOTTER!

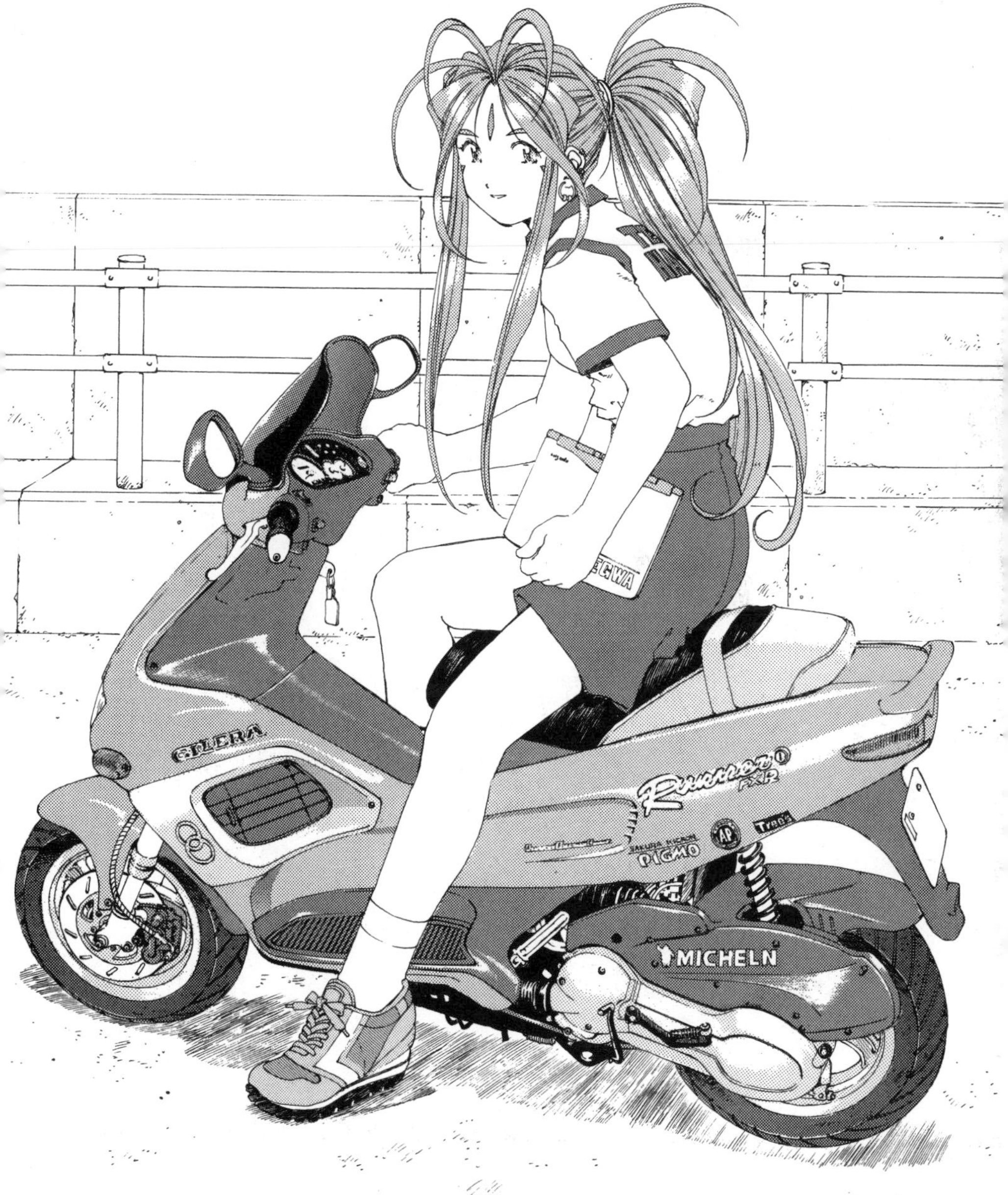
PIGMO
MICHELN

BWAAAAAAH

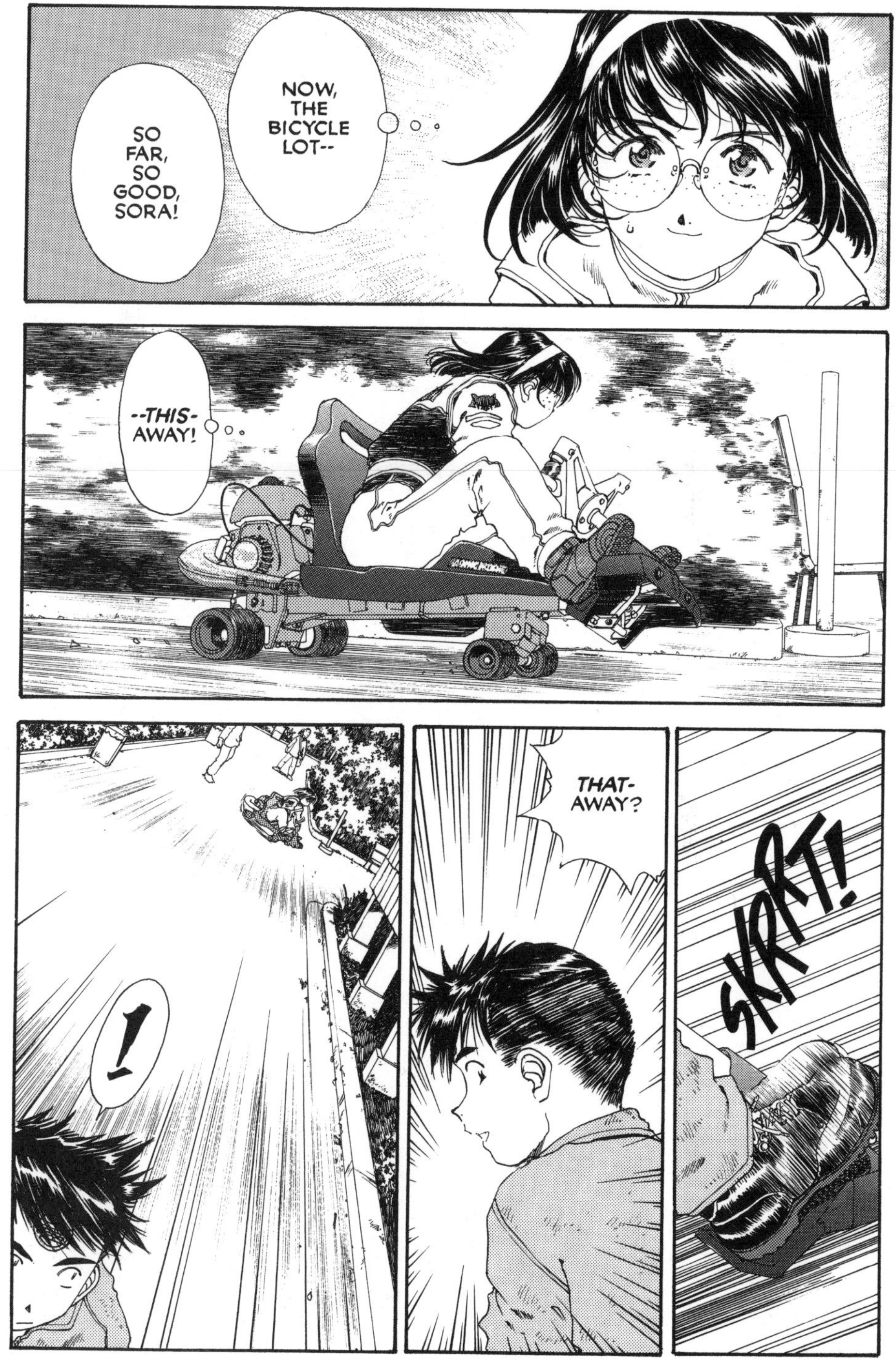
SO FAR, SO GOOD, SORA!
NOW, THE BICYCLE LOT--
--THIS-AWAY!
!
THAT-AWAY?
SKRRT!

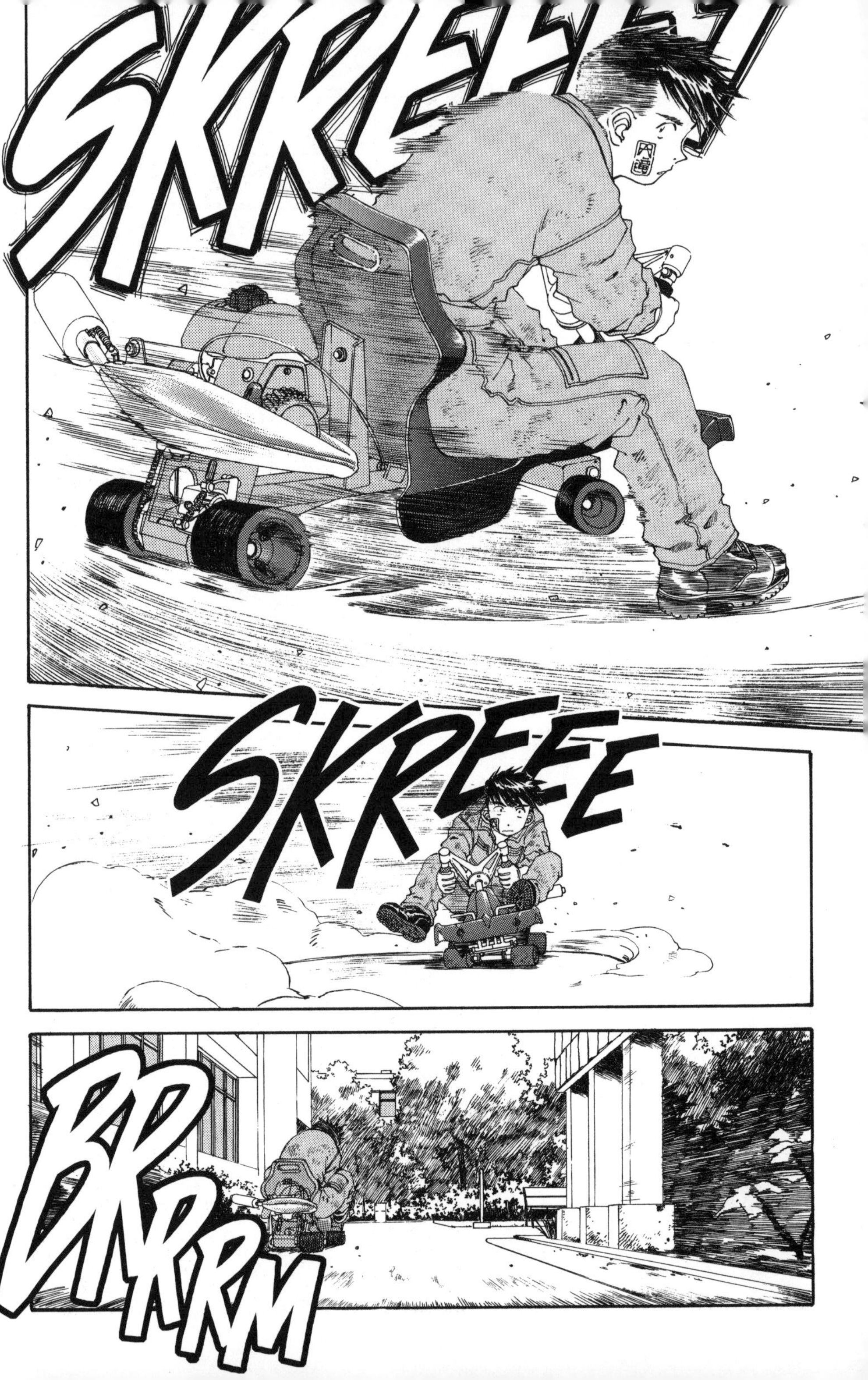
SKREEEE
SKREEE
BRRRRRM

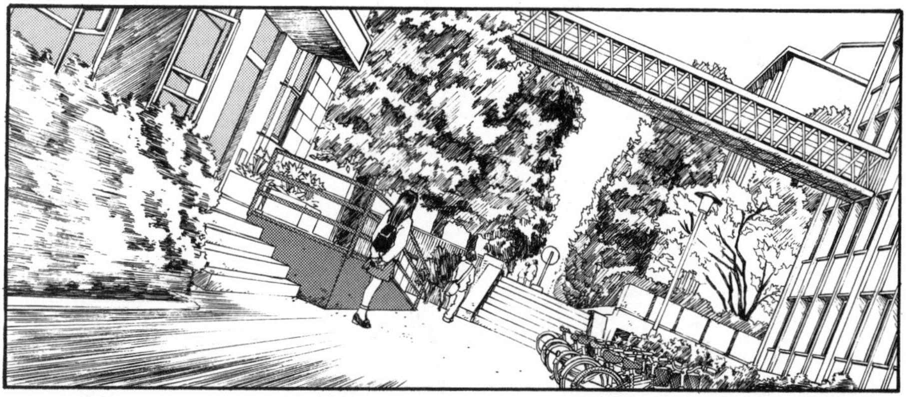

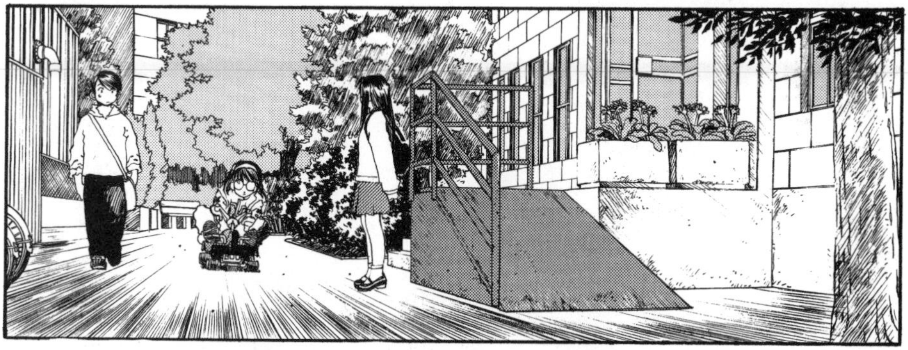

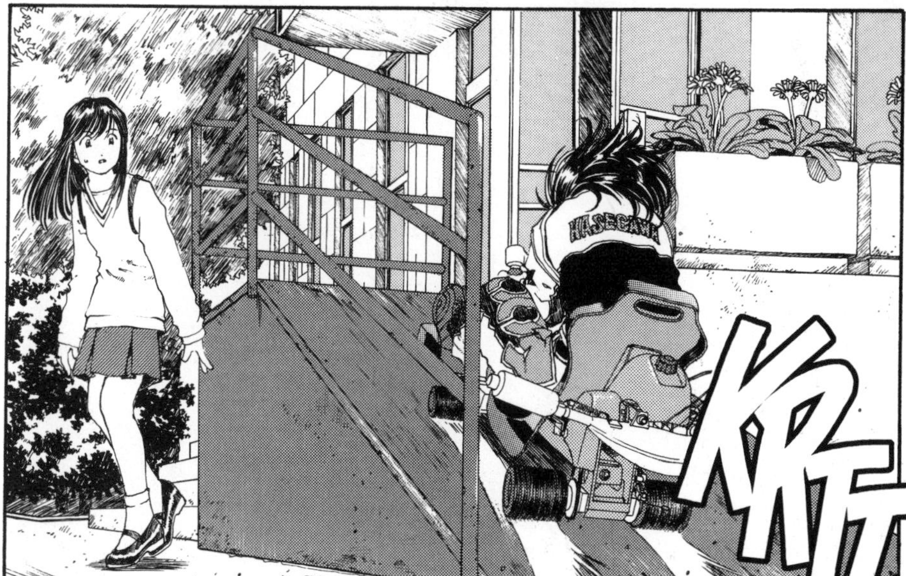
HASEGAWA
KRTT

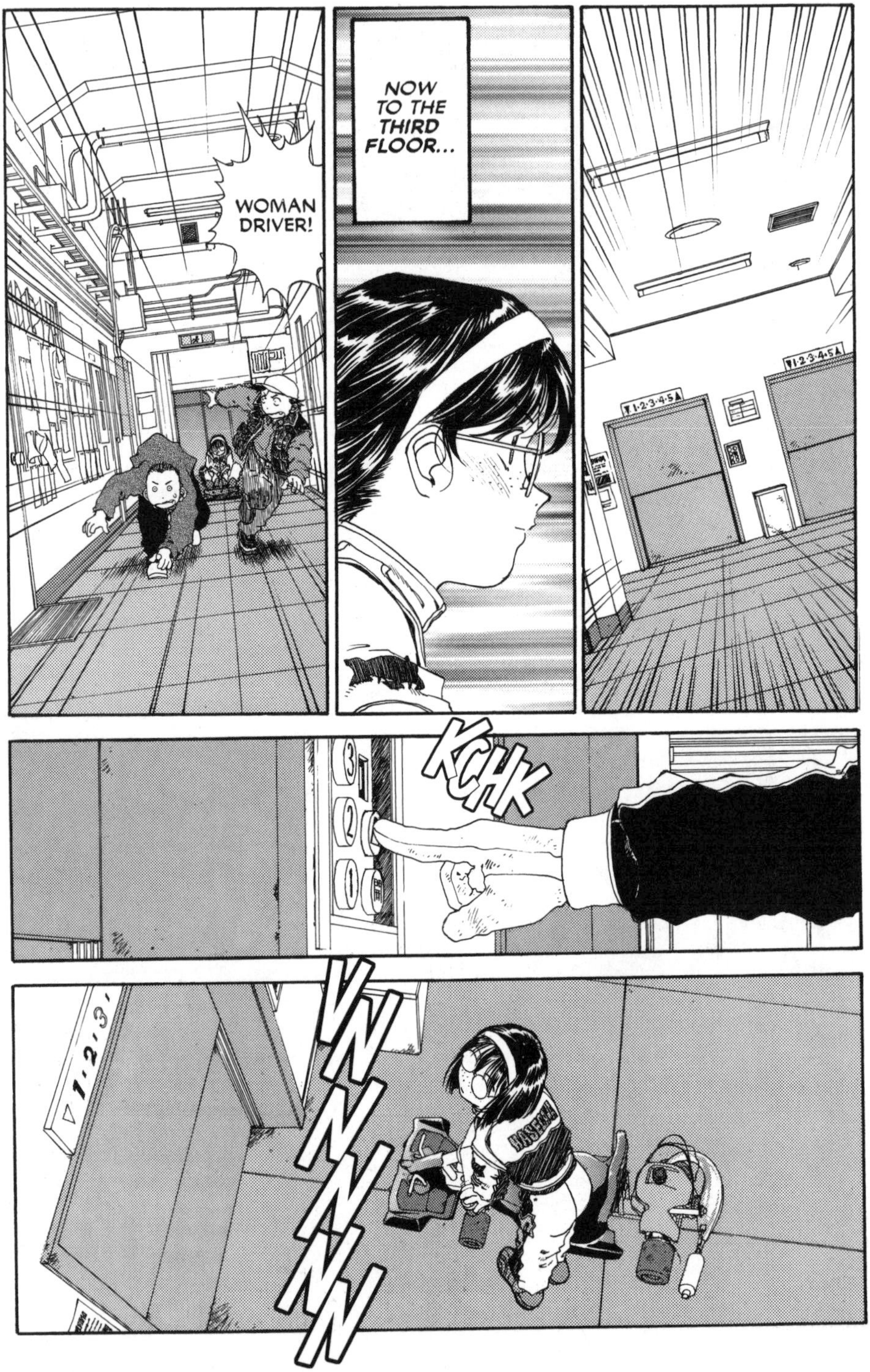
NOW TO THE THIRD FLOOR...
WOMAN DRIVER!
KCHK
VNNNNNN

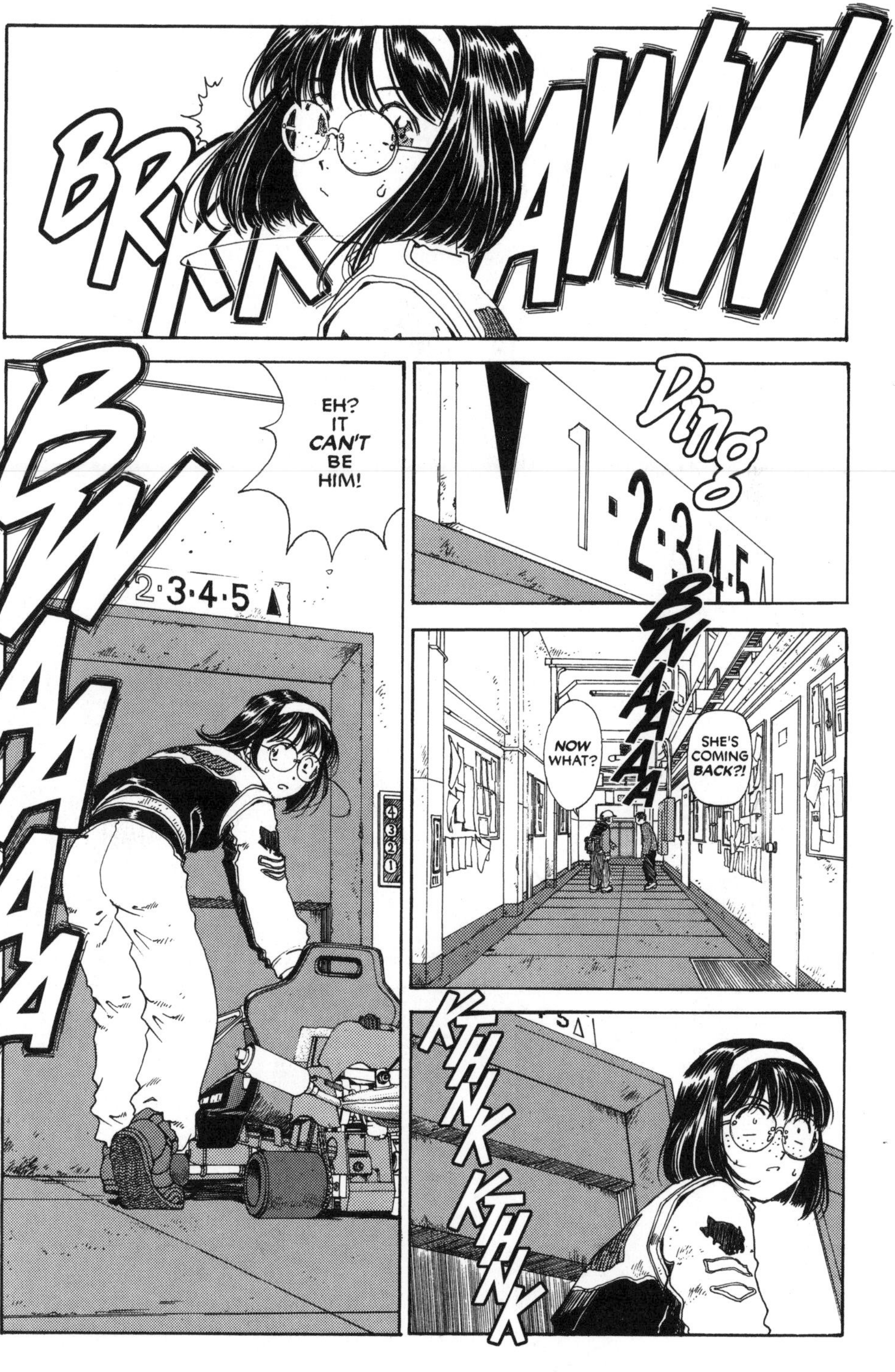
BR AWWW
Ding
1·2·3·4·5
BWAAAA
SHE'S COMING BACK?!
NOW WHAT?
KTHNK KTHNK
EH? IT CAN'T BE HIM!
2·3·4·5
BWAAAAAA

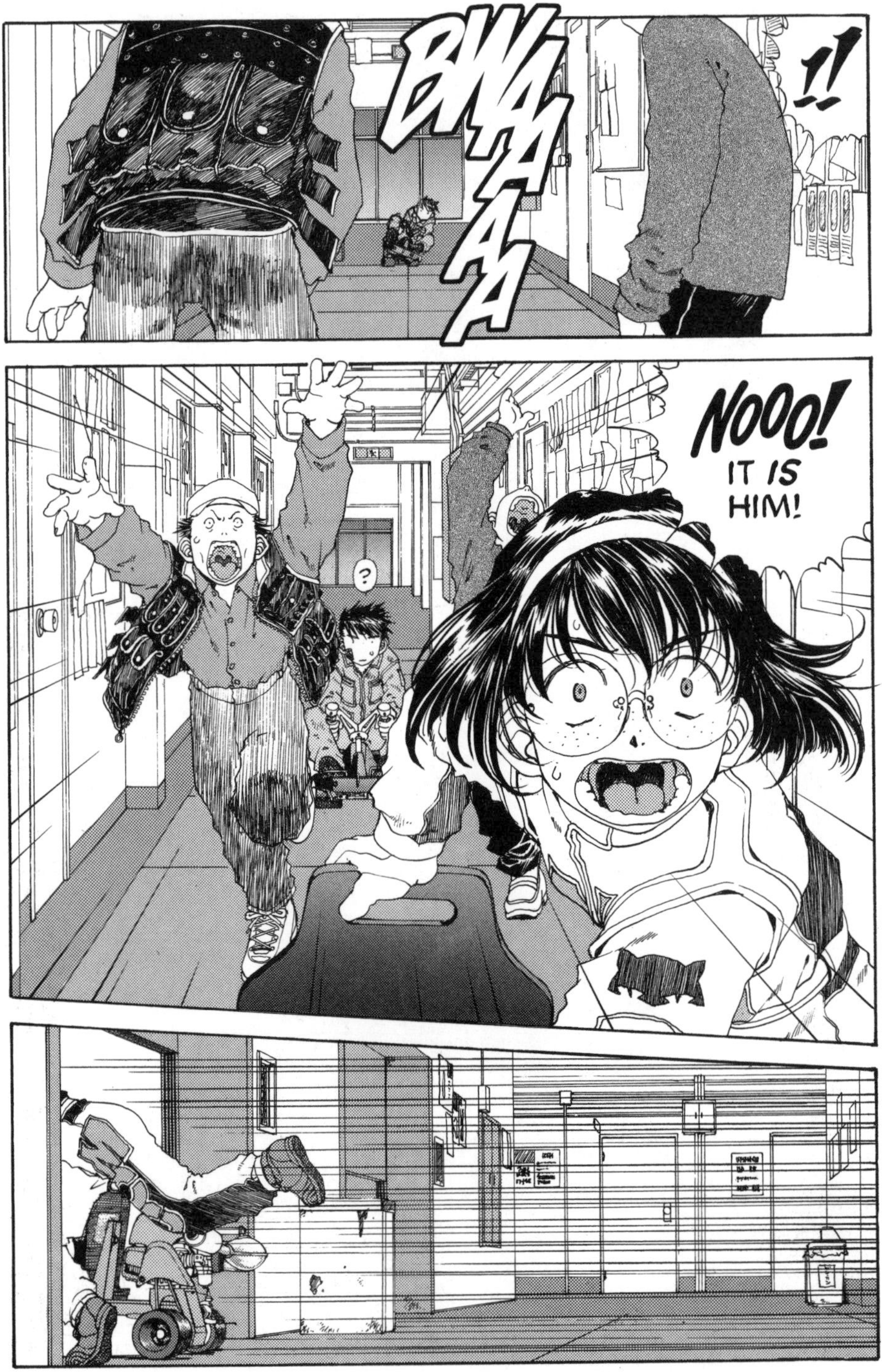
!!
BWAAAAA
NOOO!
IT IS HIM!
?

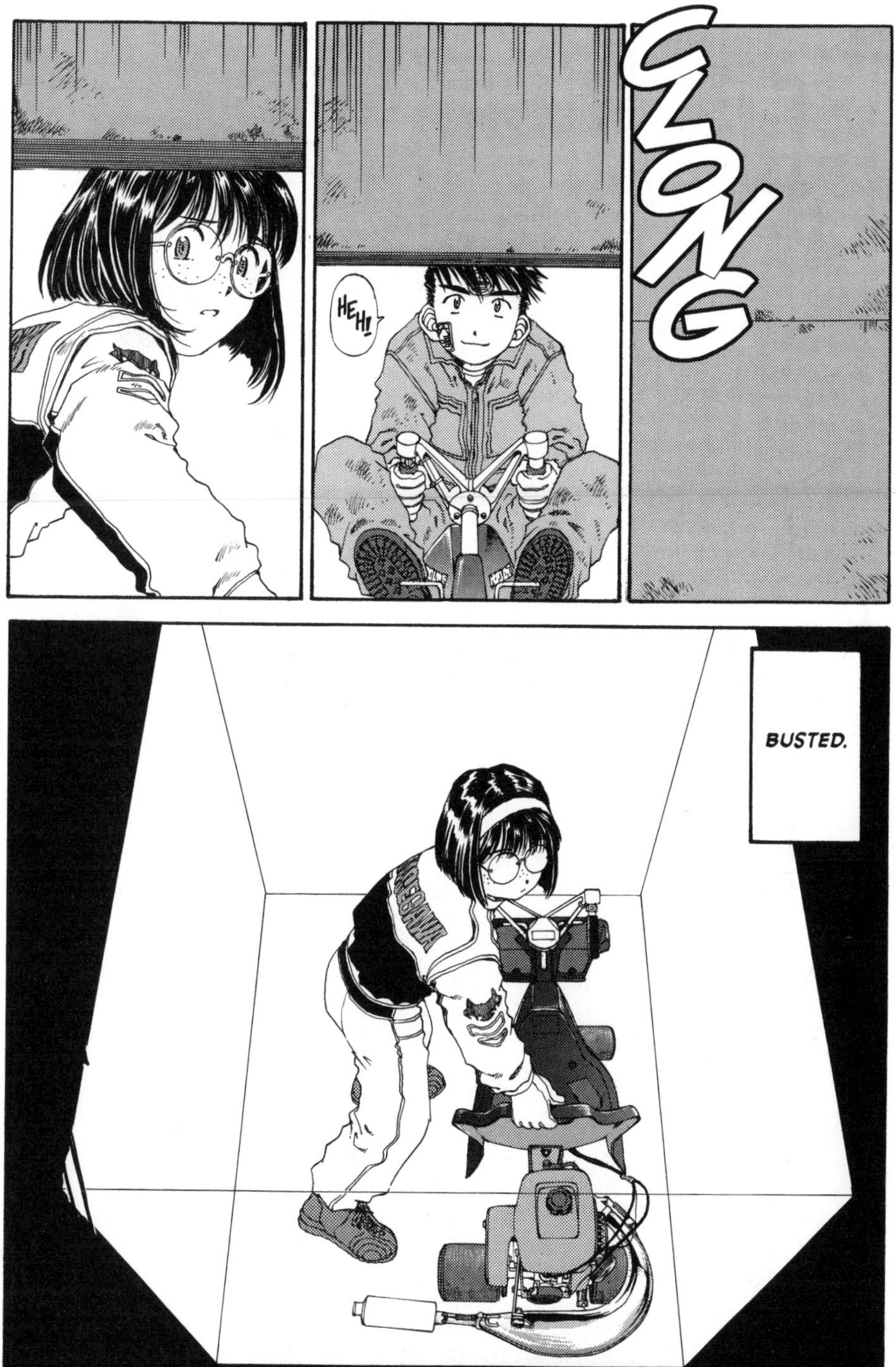
CLONG
HEH!
BUSTED.

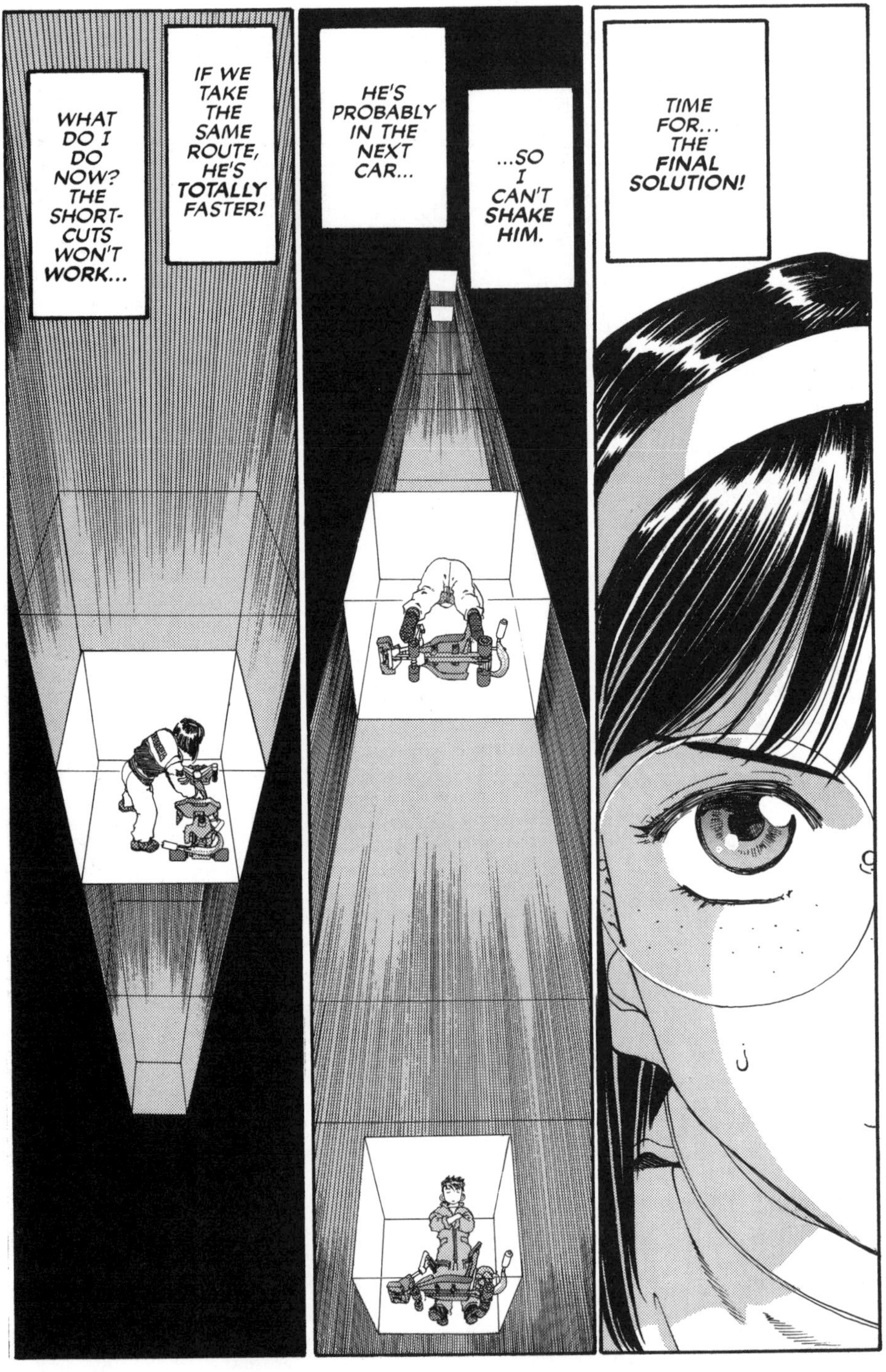
WHAT DO I DO NOW? THE SHORT-CUTS WON'T WORK...
IF WE TAKE THE SAME ROUTE, HE'S TOTALLY FASTER!
HE'S PROBABLY IN THE NEXT CAR...
...SO I CAN'T SHAKE HIM.
TIME FOR... THE FINAL SOLUTION!

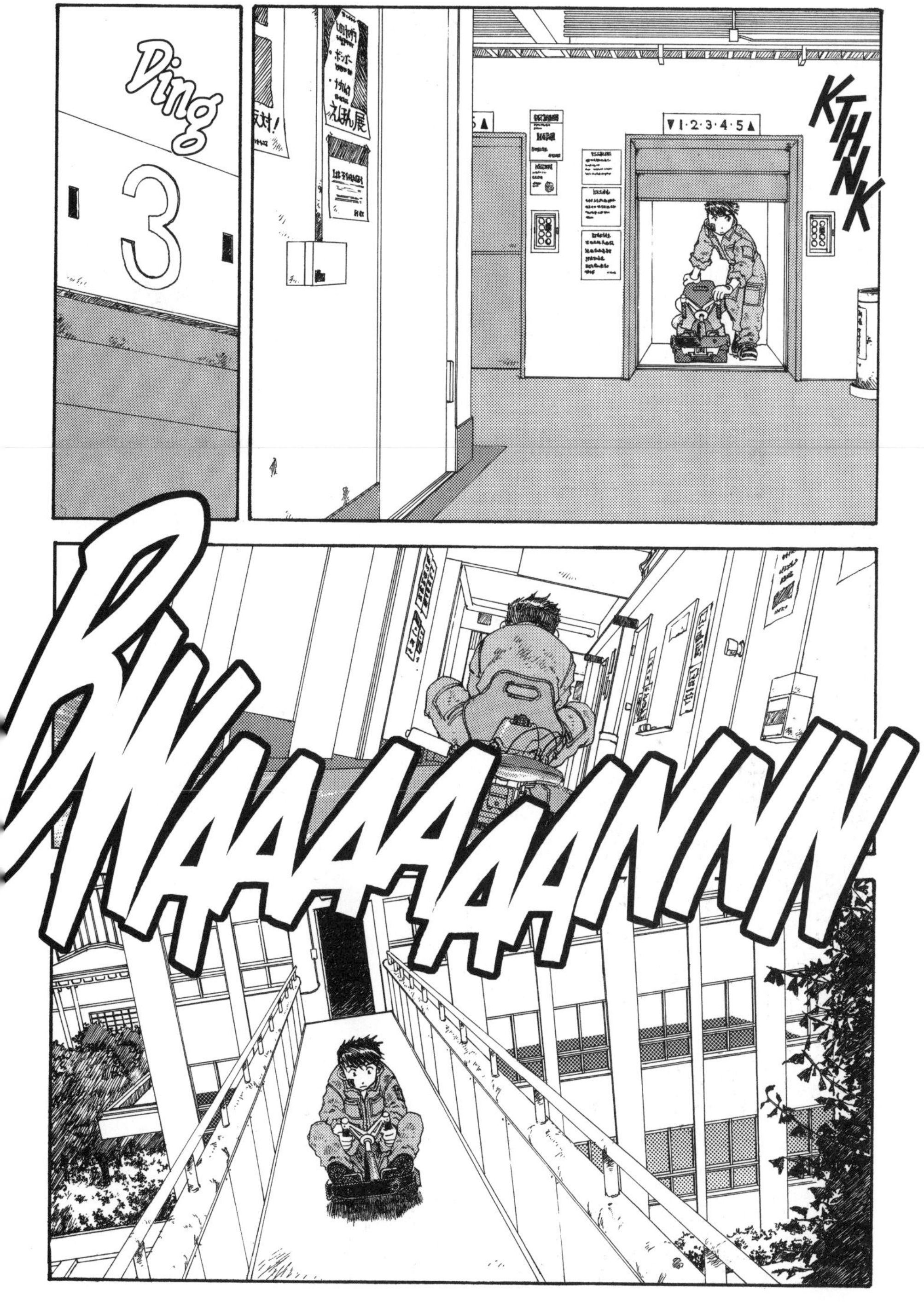
▼1·2·3·4·5▲
KTHNK
えほん展
反対!
Ding
3
BWAAAAAANNN

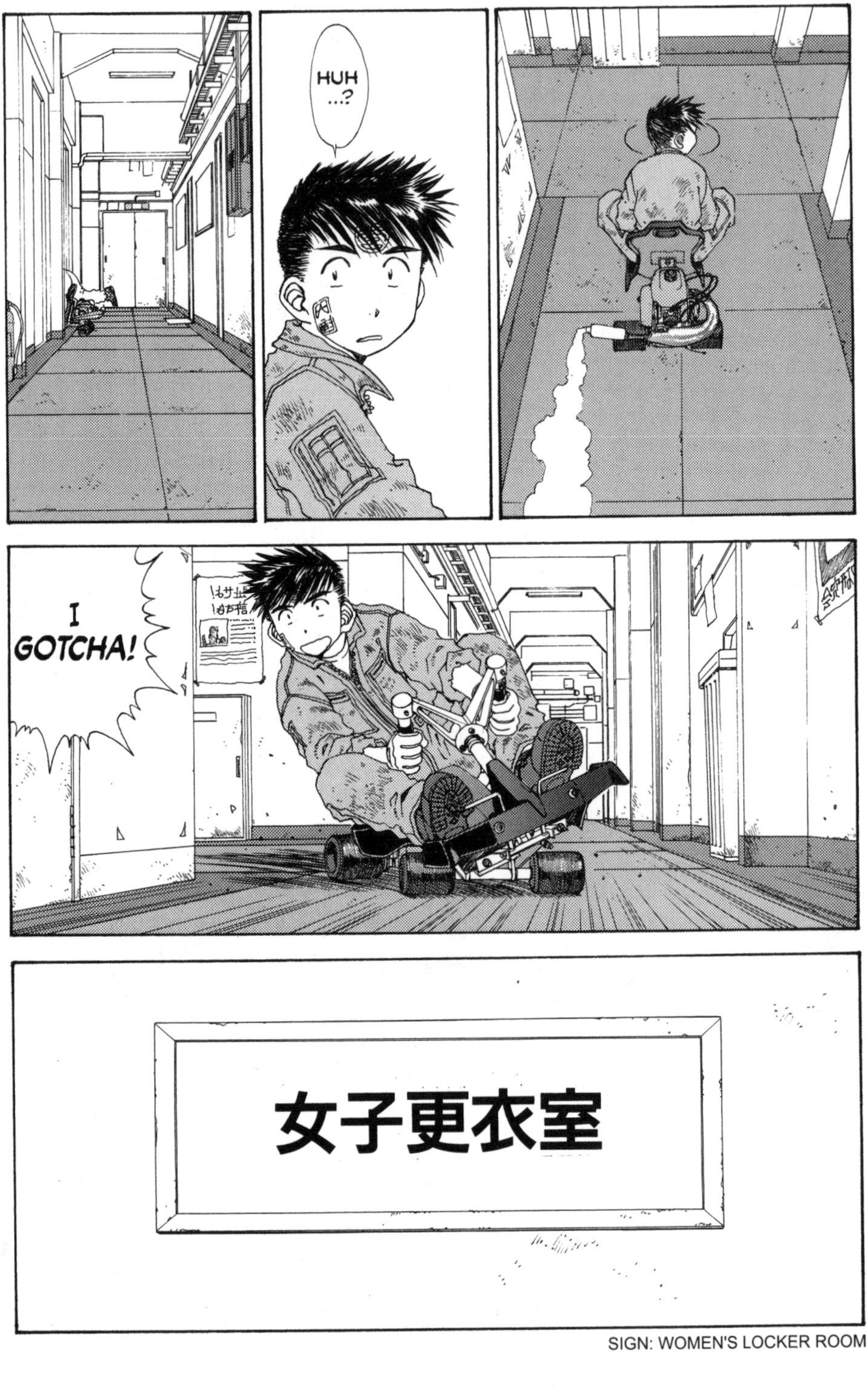
HUH ...?
I GOTCHA!
女子更衣室
SIGN: WOMEN'S LOCKER ROOM

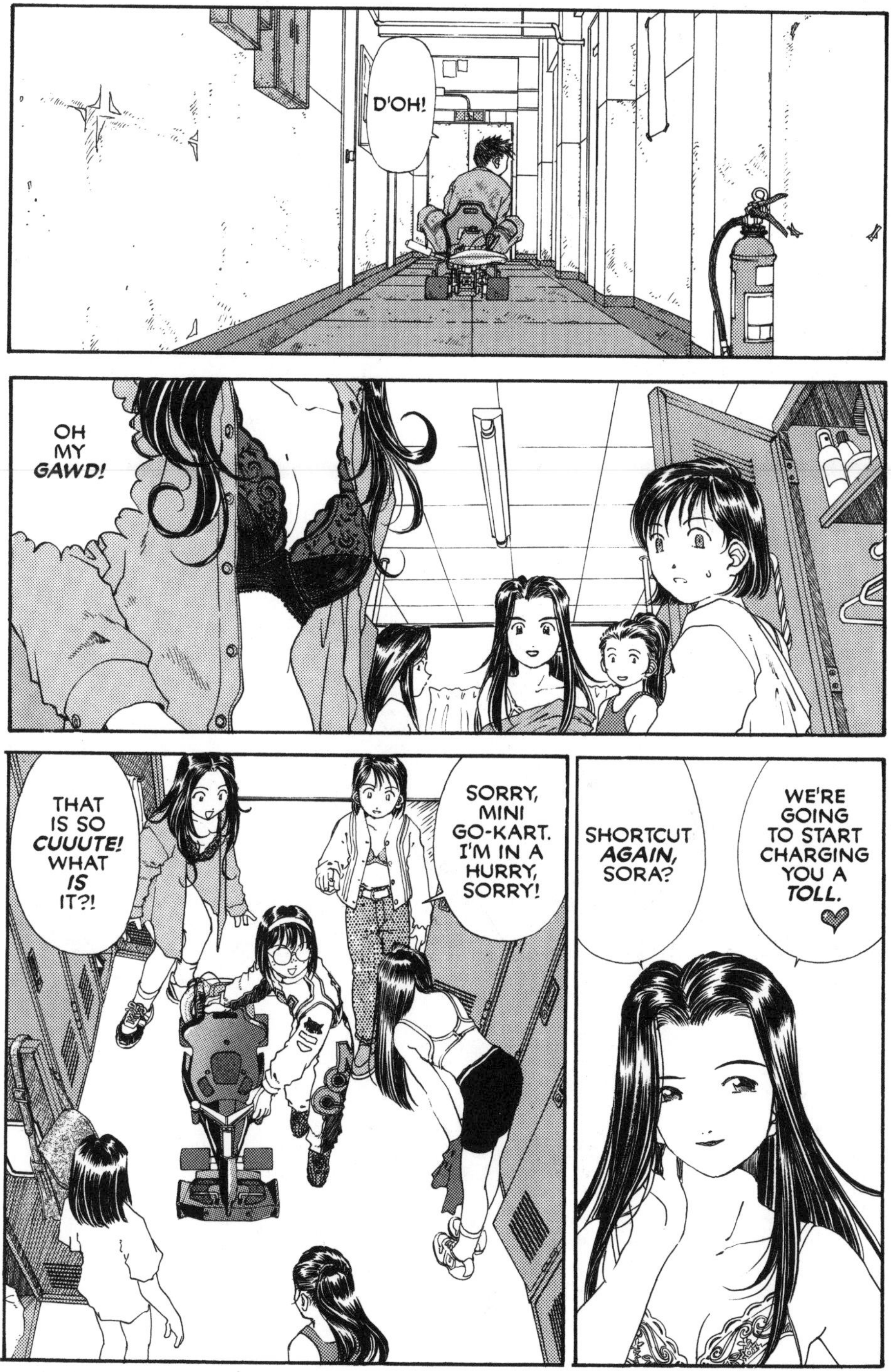
D'OH!
OH MY GAWD!
THAT IS SO CUUUTE! WHAT IS IT?!
SORRY, MINI GO-KART. I'M IN A HURRY, SORRY!
SHORTCUT AGAIN, SORA?
WE'RE GOING TO START CHARGING YOU A TOLL.

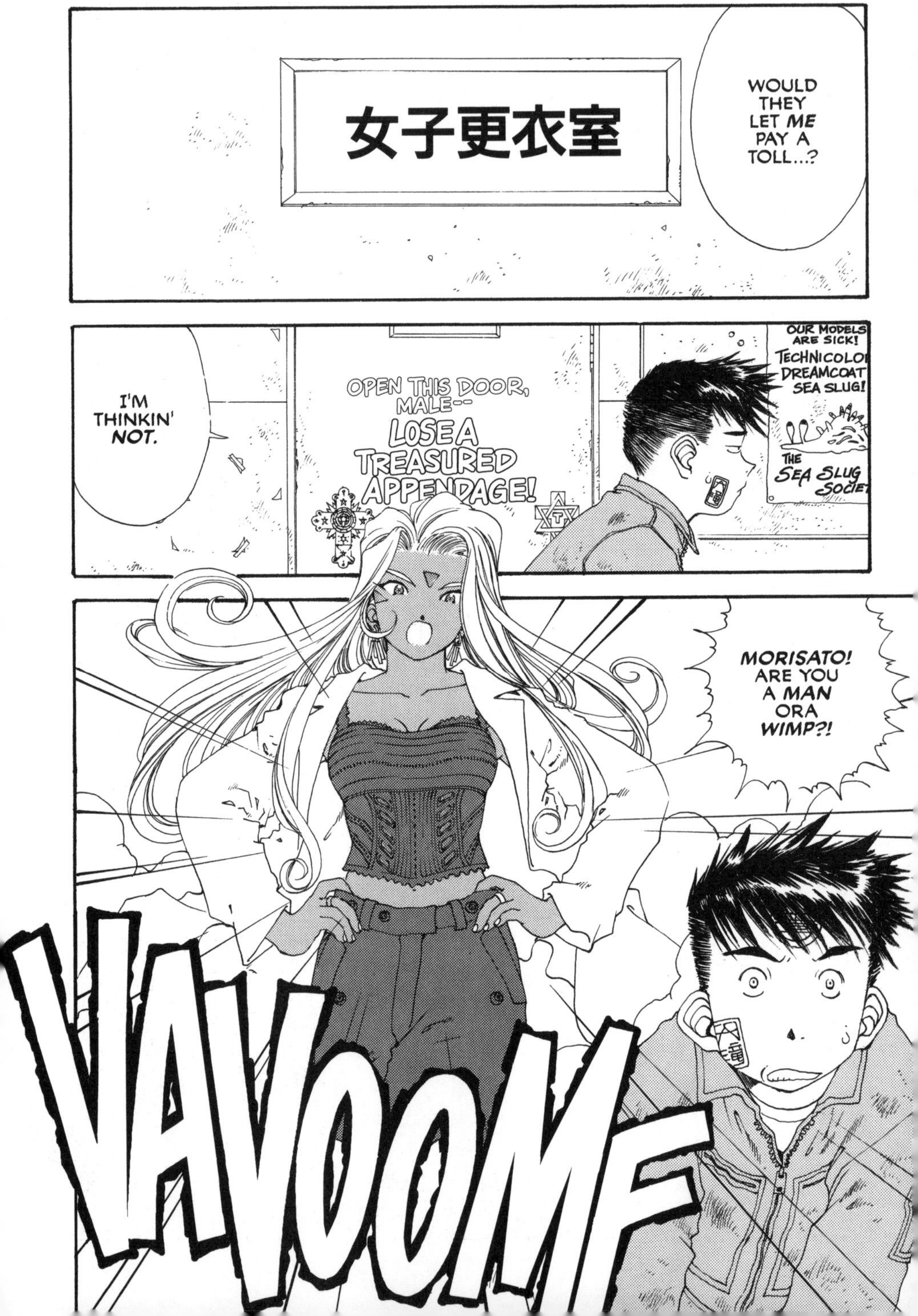
WOULD THEY LET ME PAY A TOLL...?
女子更衣室
OUR MODELS ARE SICK! TECHNICOLOR DREAMCOAT SEA SLUG!
THE SEA SLUG SOCIET
OPEN THIS DOOR, MALE-- LOSE A TREASURED APPENDAGE!
I'M THINKIN' NOT.
MORISATO! ARE YOU A MAN ORA WIMP?!
VAVOOMF

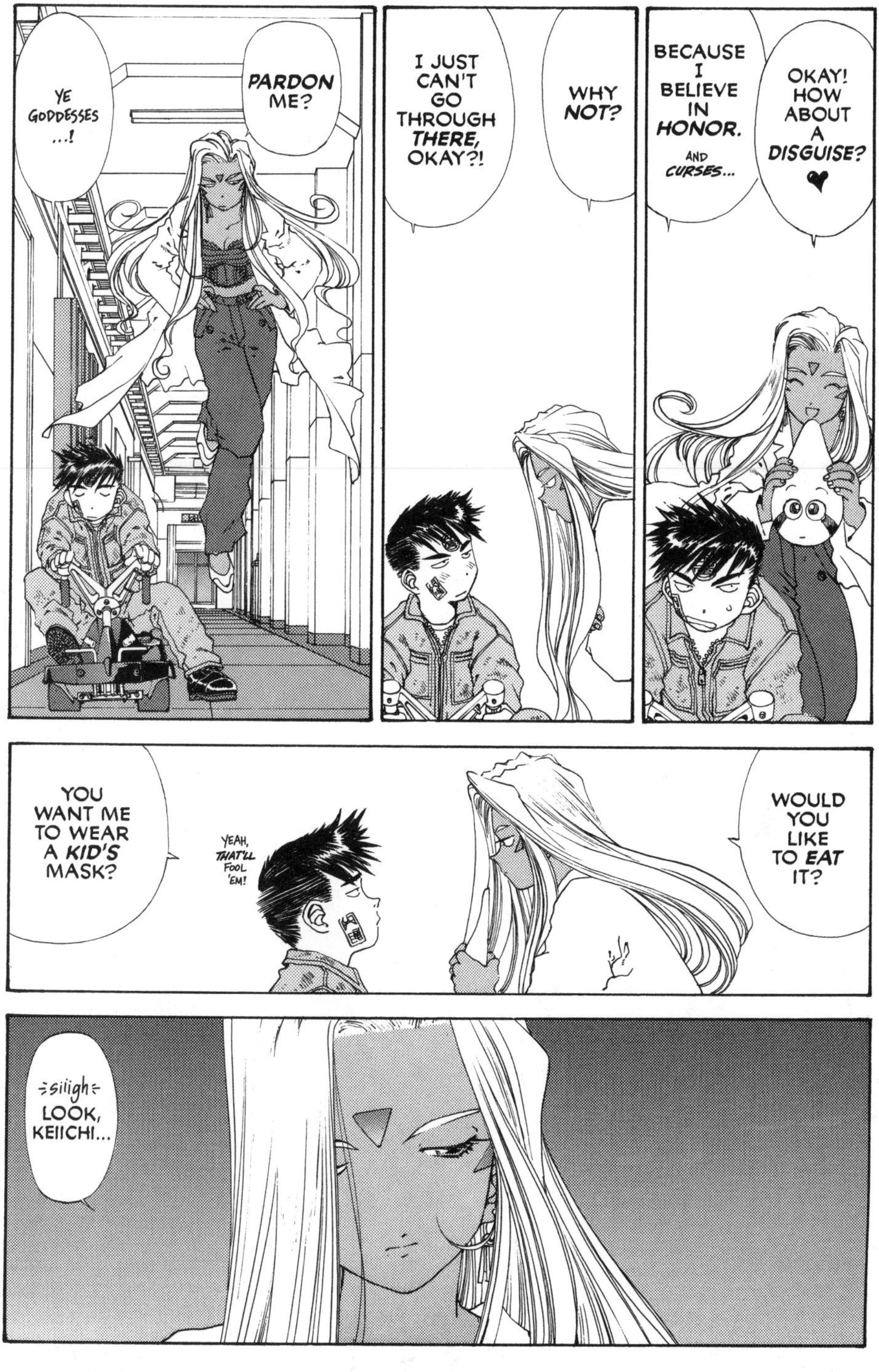
YE GODDESSES ...!
PARDON ME?
I JUST CAN'T GO THROUGH THERE, OKAY?!
WHY NOT?
BECAUSE I BELIEVE IN HONOR.
AND CURSES...
OKAY! HOW ABOUT A DISGUISE? ♥
YOU WANT ME TO WEAR A KID'S MASK?
YEAH, THAT'LL FOOL 'EM!
WOULD YOU LIKE TO EAT IT?
≈siiigh≈ LOOK, KEIICHI...

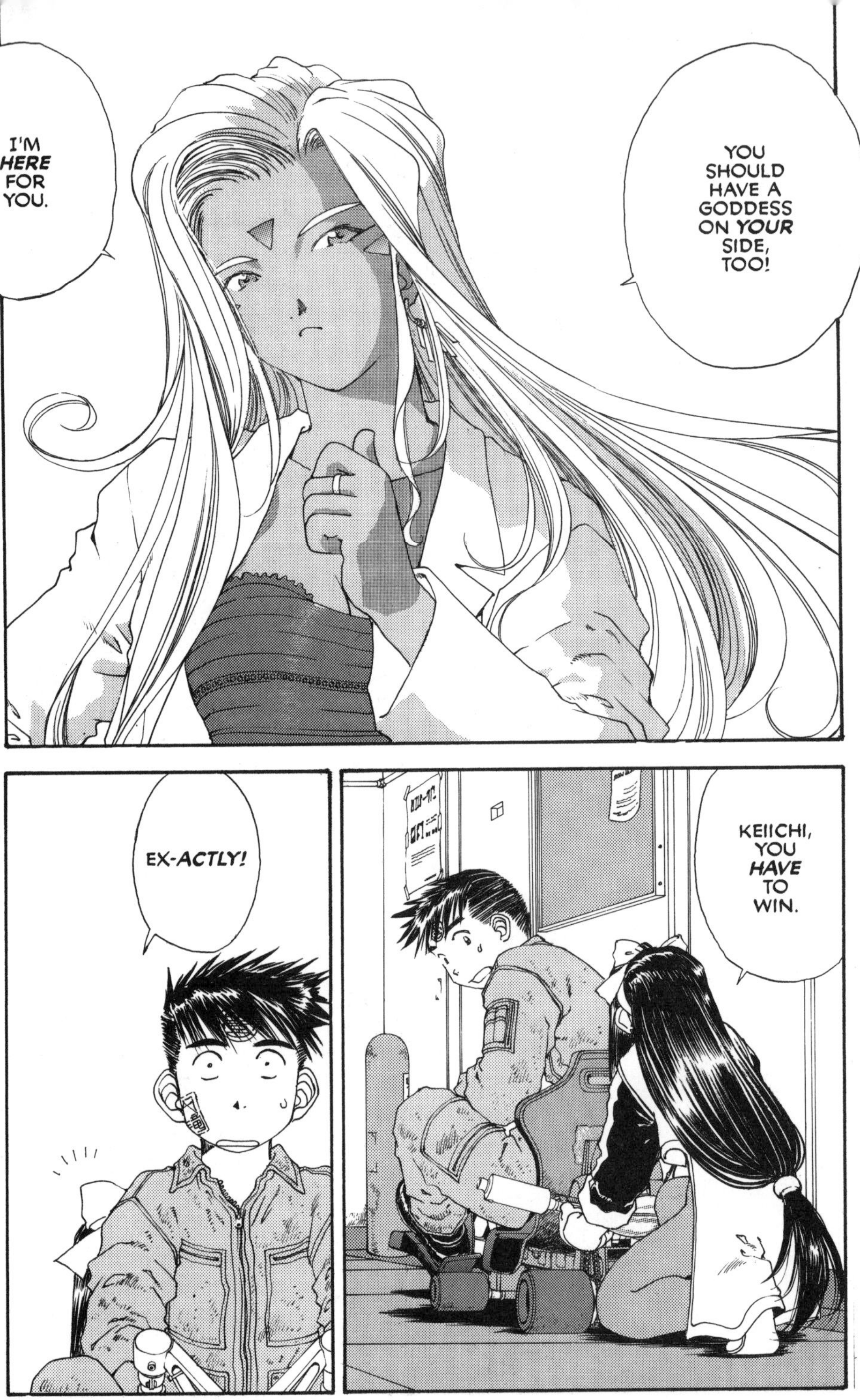
YOU SHOULD HAVE A GODDESS ON *YOUR* SIDE, TOO!
I'M *HERE* FOR YOU.
KEIICHI, YOU *HAVE* TO WIN.
EX-*ACTLY!*

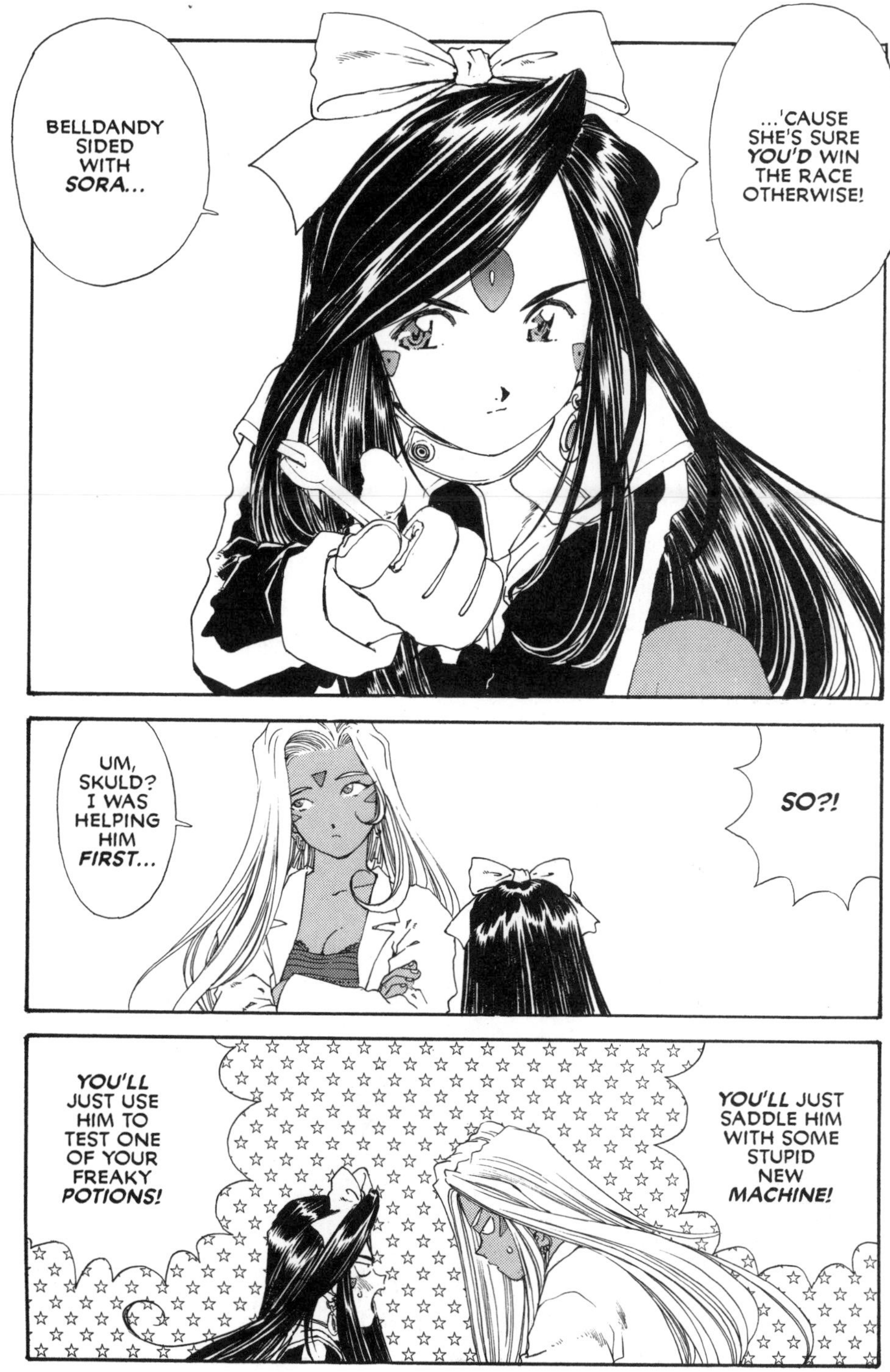

BELLDANDY SIDED WITH SORA...
...'CAUSE SHE'S SURE YOU'D WIN THE RACE OTHERWISE!
UM, SKULD? I WAS HELPING HIM FIRST...
SO?!
YOU'LL JUST USE HIM TO TEST ONE OF YOUR FREAKY POTIONS!
YOU'LL JUST SADDLE HIM WITH SOME STUPID NEW MACHINE!

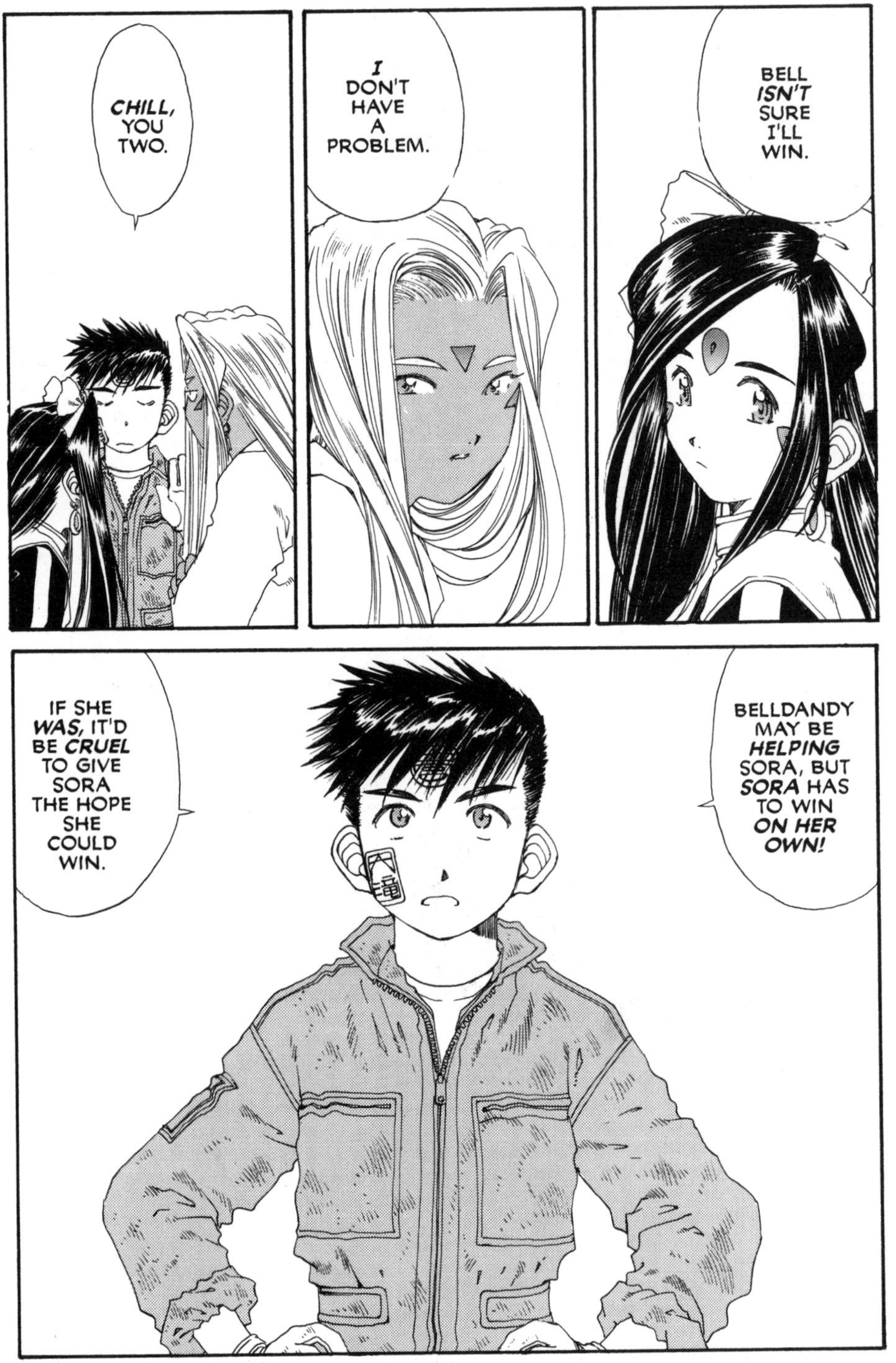
BELL ISN'T SURE I'LL WIN.
I DON'T HAVE A PROBLEM.
CHILL, YOU TWO.
BELLDANDY MAY BE HELPING SORA, BUT SORA HAS TO WIN ON HER OWN!
IF SHE WAS, IT'D BE CRUEL TO GIVE SORA THE HOPE SHE COULD WIN.

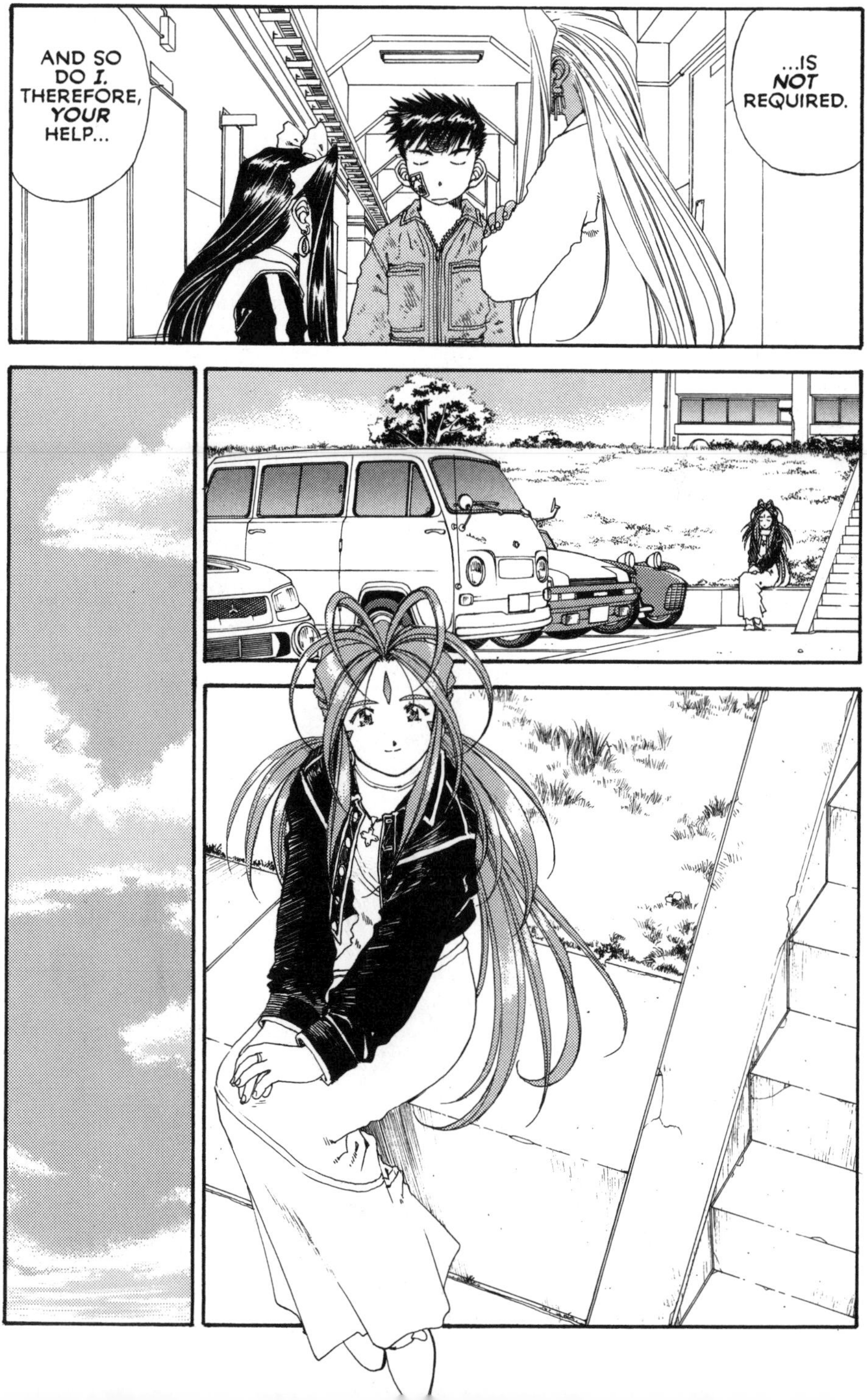
AND SO DO *I.* THEREFORE, ***YOUR*** HELP...
...IS ***NOT*** REQUIRED.

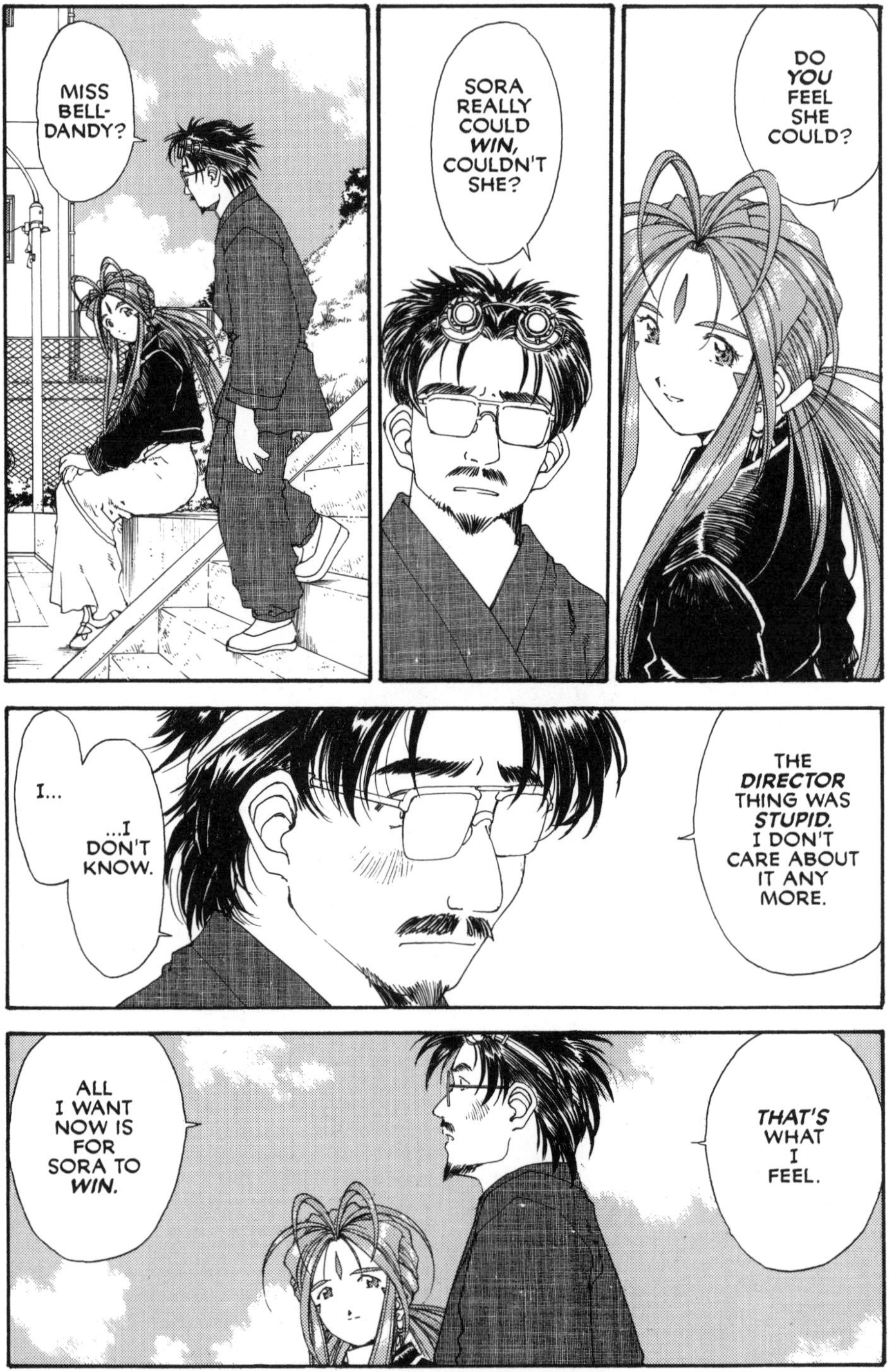
MISS BELL-DANDY?
SORA REALLY COULD *WIN,* COULDN'T SHE?
DO *YOU* FEEL SHE COULD?
I...
...I DON'T KNOW.
THE *DIRECTOR* THING WAS *STUPID.* I DON'T CARE ABOUT IT ANY MORE.
ALL I WANT NOW IS FOR SORA TO *WIN.*
THAT'S WHAT I FEEL.

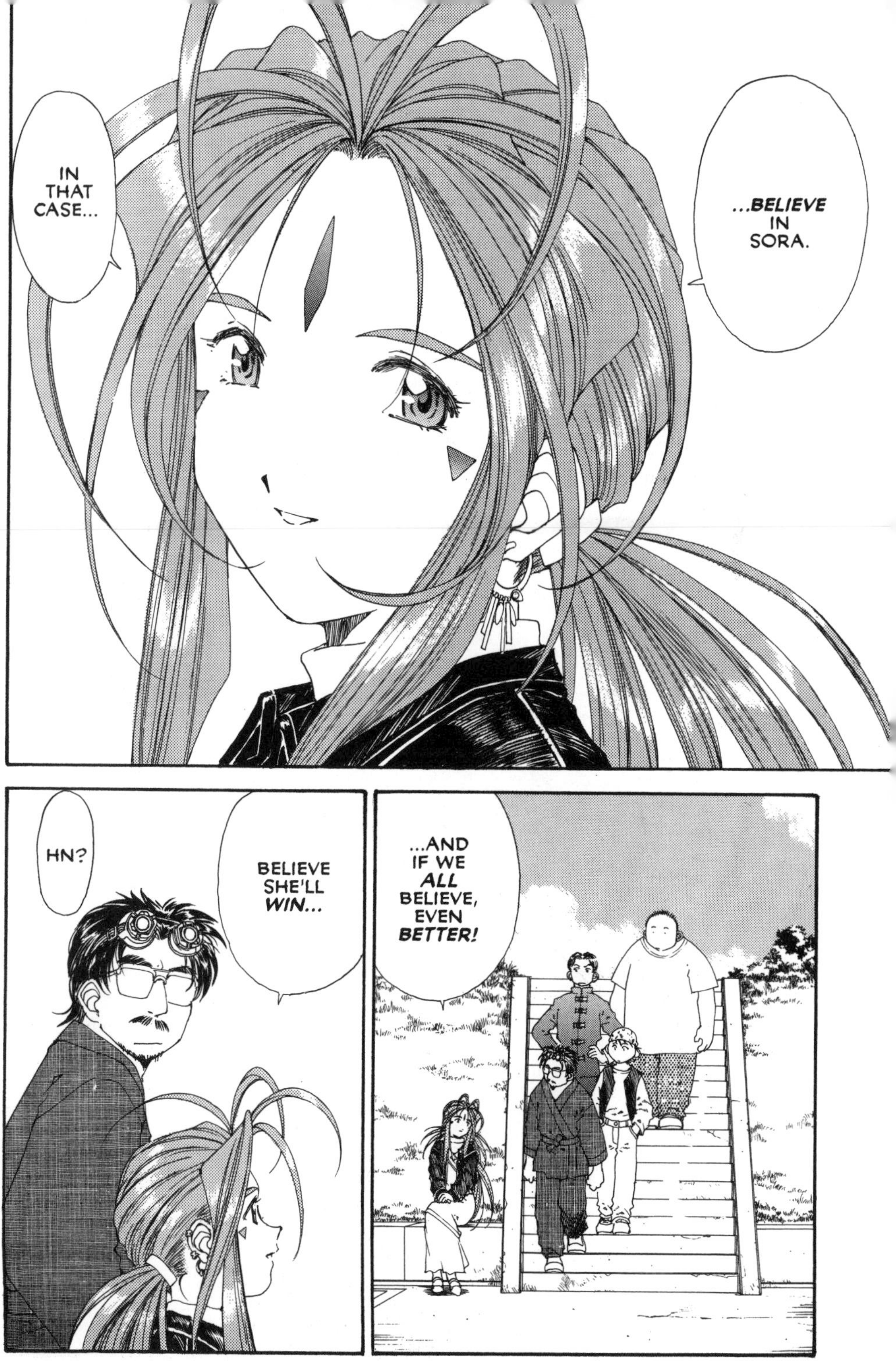
IN THAT CASE...
...**BELIEVE** IN SORA.
HN?
BELIEVE SHE'LL ***WIN...***
...AND IF WE ***ALL*** BELIEVE, EVEN ***BETTER!***

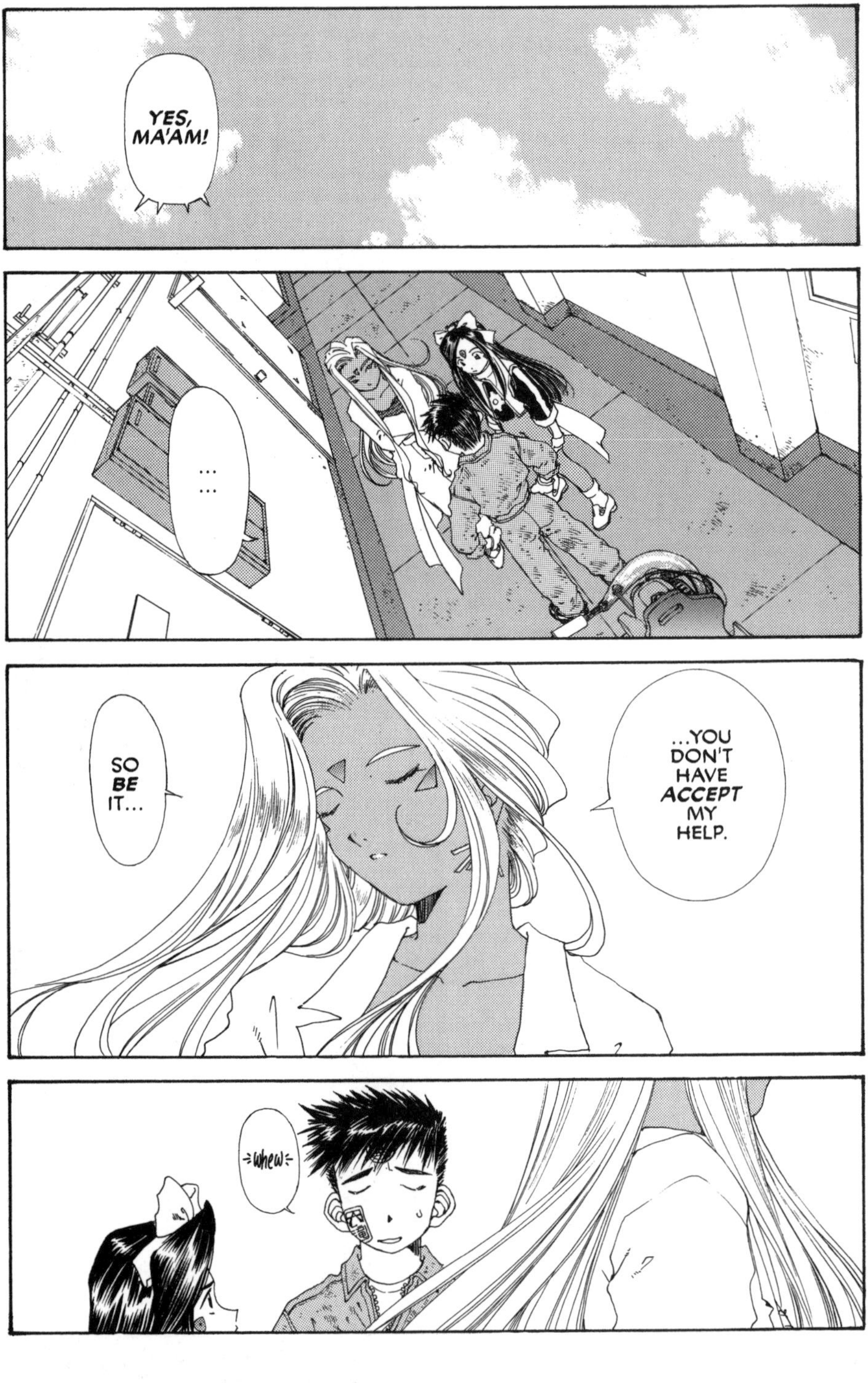
YES, MA'AM!
... ...
...YOU DON'T HAVE ACCEPT MY HELP.
SO BE IT...
whew

BUT
YOU'RE
GONNA
GET IT!
♥

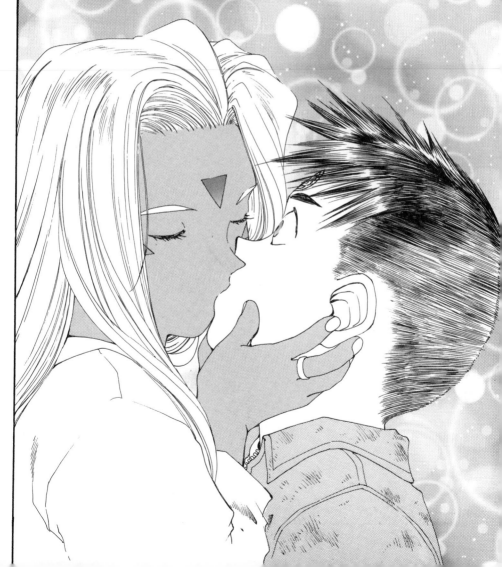

WRECKED BY A KISS

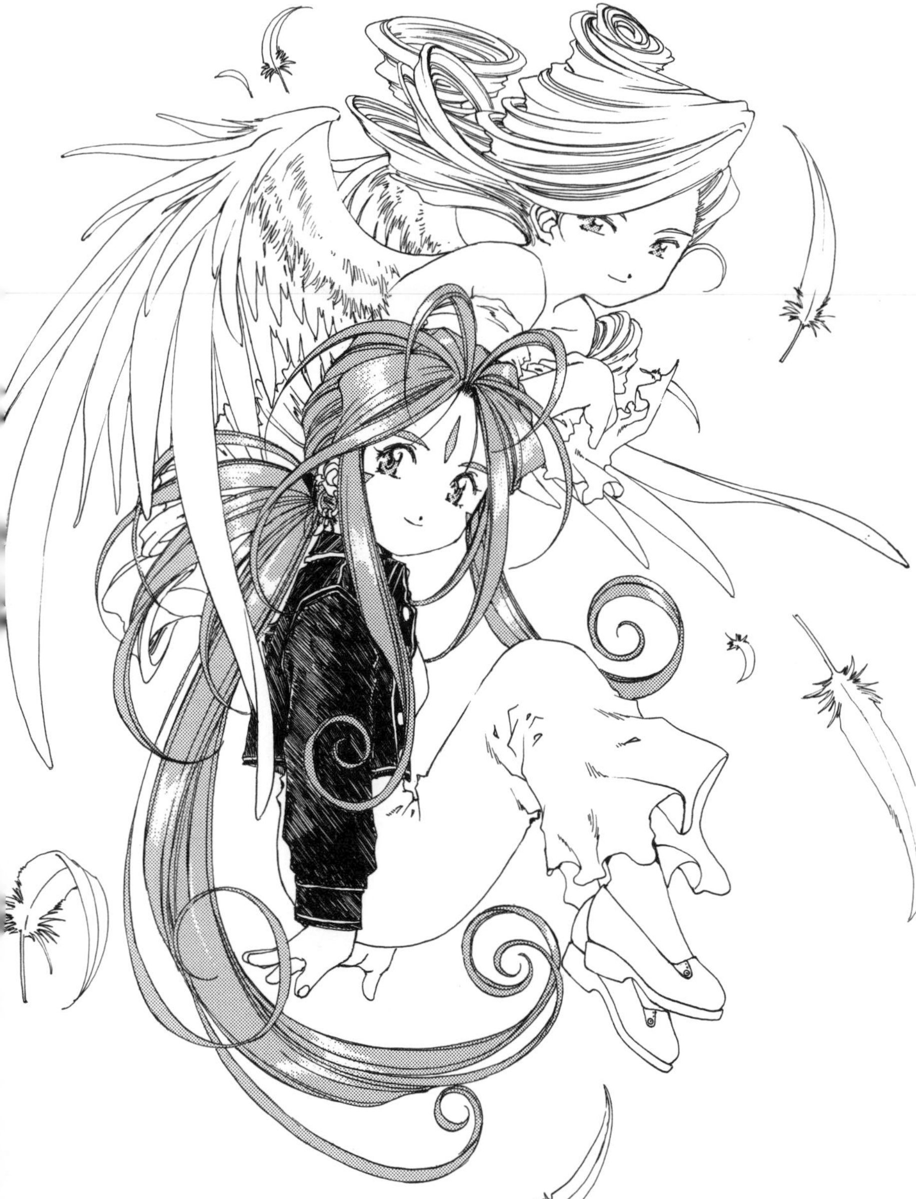

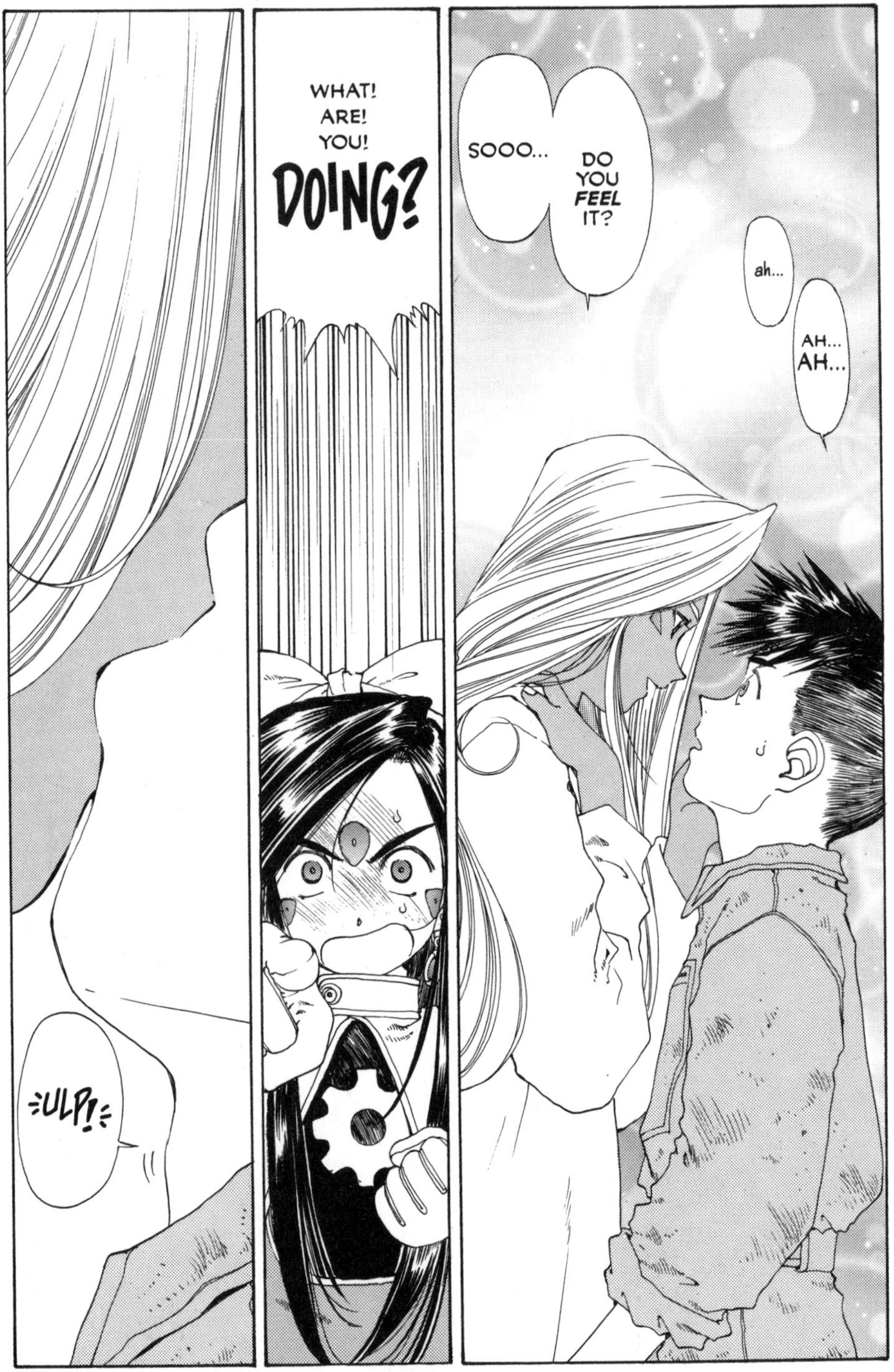
SOOO...
DO YOU *FEEL* IT?
ah...
AH... AH...
WHAT! ARE! YOU! DOING?
ULP!

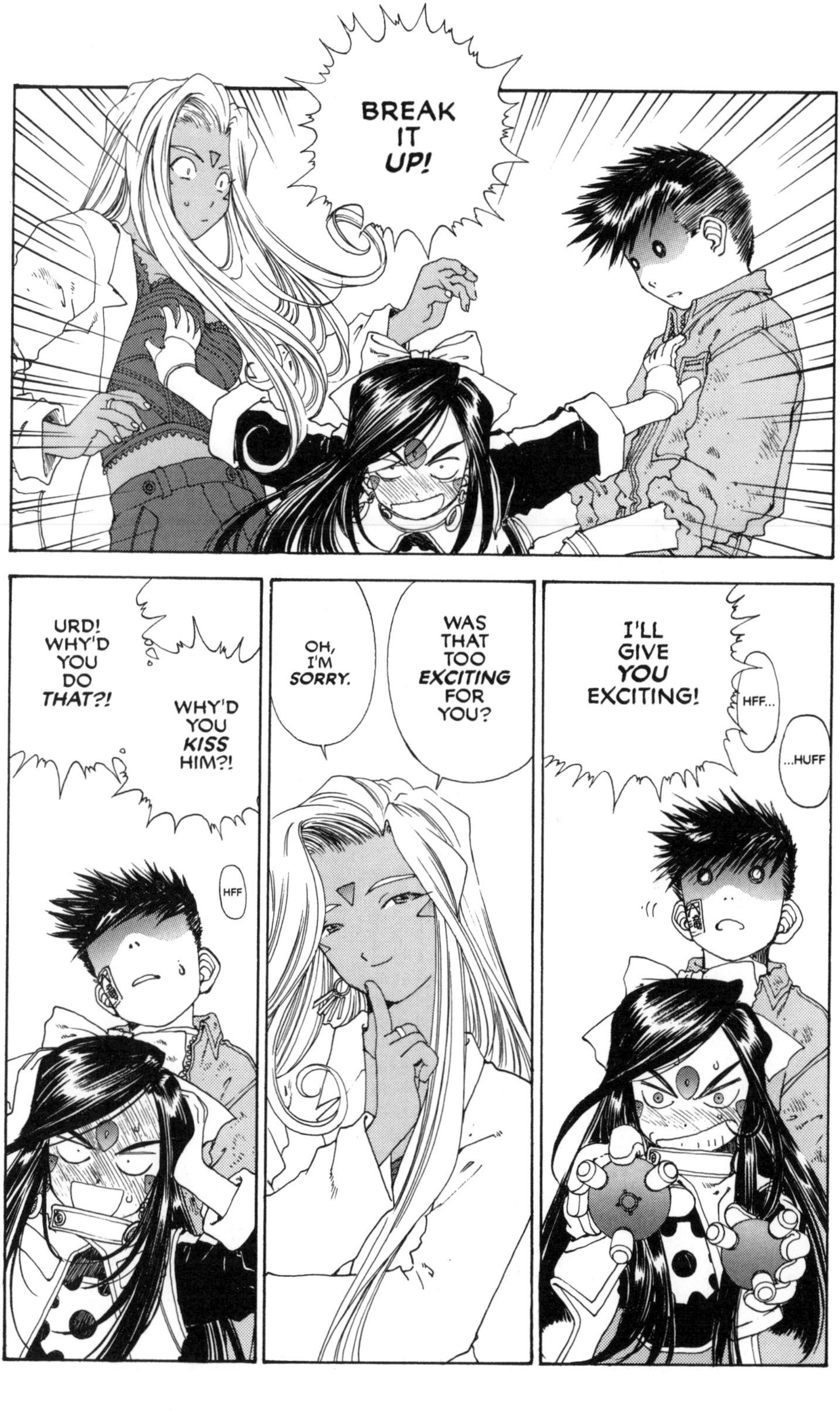
BREAK IT UP!
URD! WHY'D YOU DO THAT?!
WHY'D YOU KISS HIM?!
HFF
OH, I'M SORRY.
WAS THAT TOO EXCITING FOR YOU?
I'LL GIVE YOU EXCITING!
HFF...
...HUFF

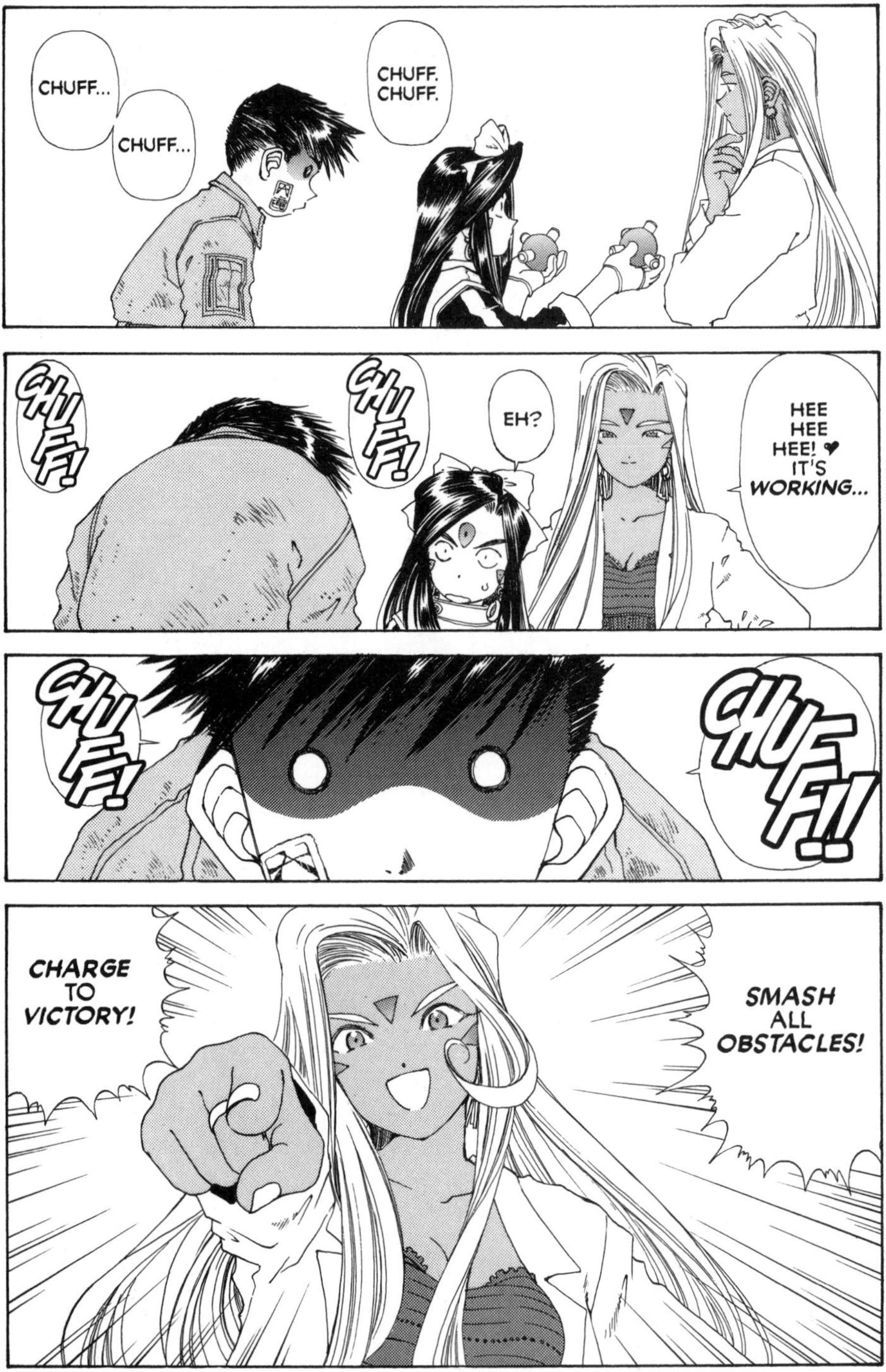
CHUFF. CHUFF.
CHUFF...
CHUFF...
HEE HEE HEE! ♥ IT'S *WORKING...*
EH?
CHUFF!
CHUFF!
CHUFF!!
CHUFF!
SMASH ALL OBSTACLES!
CHARGE TO VICTORY!

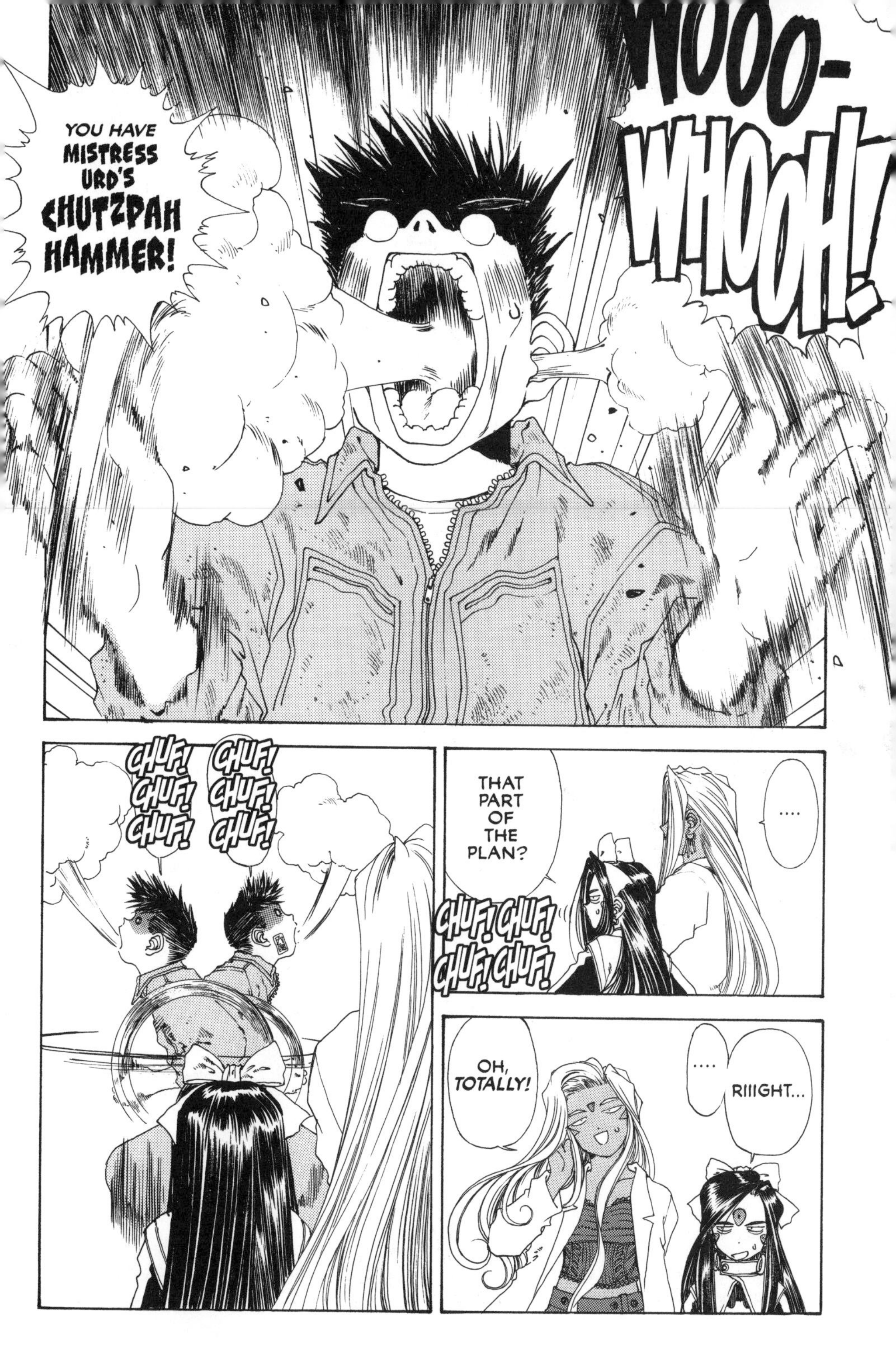
YOU HAVE MISTRESS URD'S CHUTZPAH HAMMER!
WOOO-WHOOH!
CHUF! CHUF! CHUF!
CHUF! CHUF! CHUF!
THAT PART OF THE PLAN?
....
CHUF! CHUF! CHUF! CHUF!
OH, *TOTALLY!*
....
RIIIGHT...

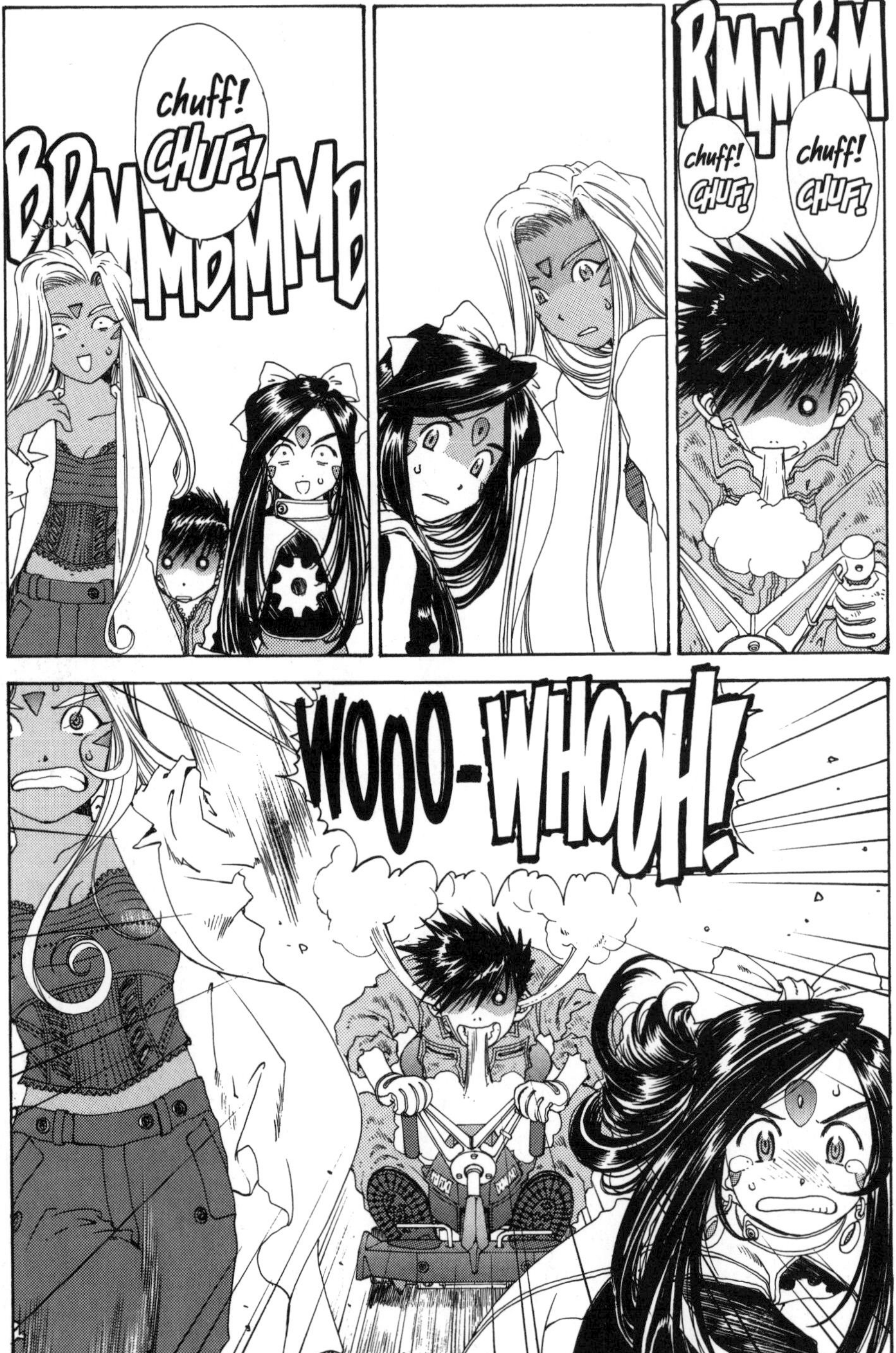
RMMBM
chuff! CHUF!
chuff! CHUF!
chuff! CHUF!
BRMMMDMMB
WOOO-WHOOH!

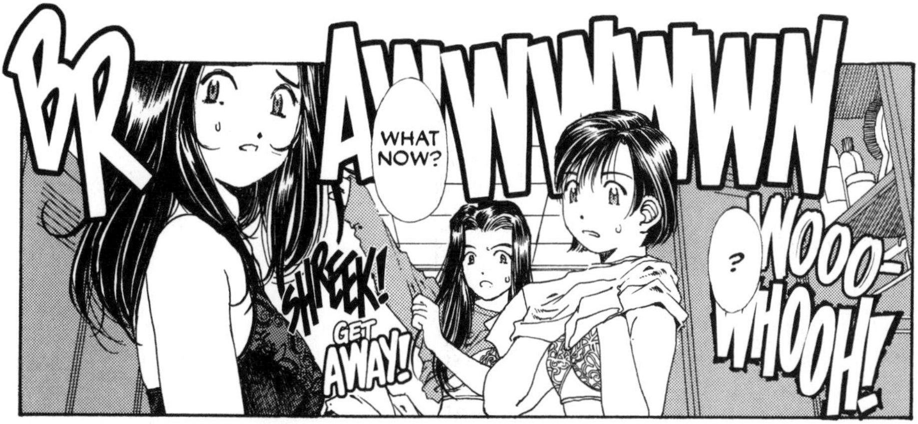
BRAWWWWWWN
?
WOOO-WHOOH!
WHAT NOW?
SHREEK!
GET AWAY!
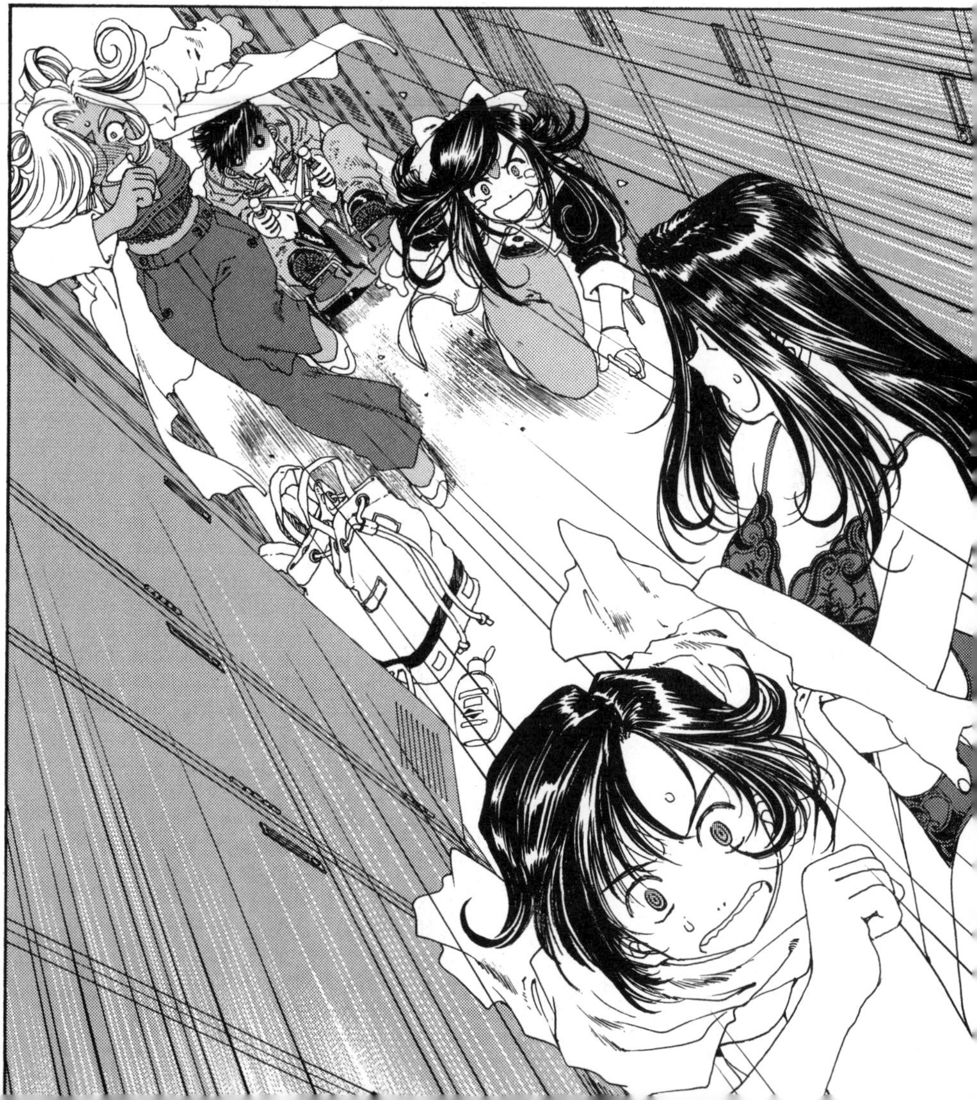

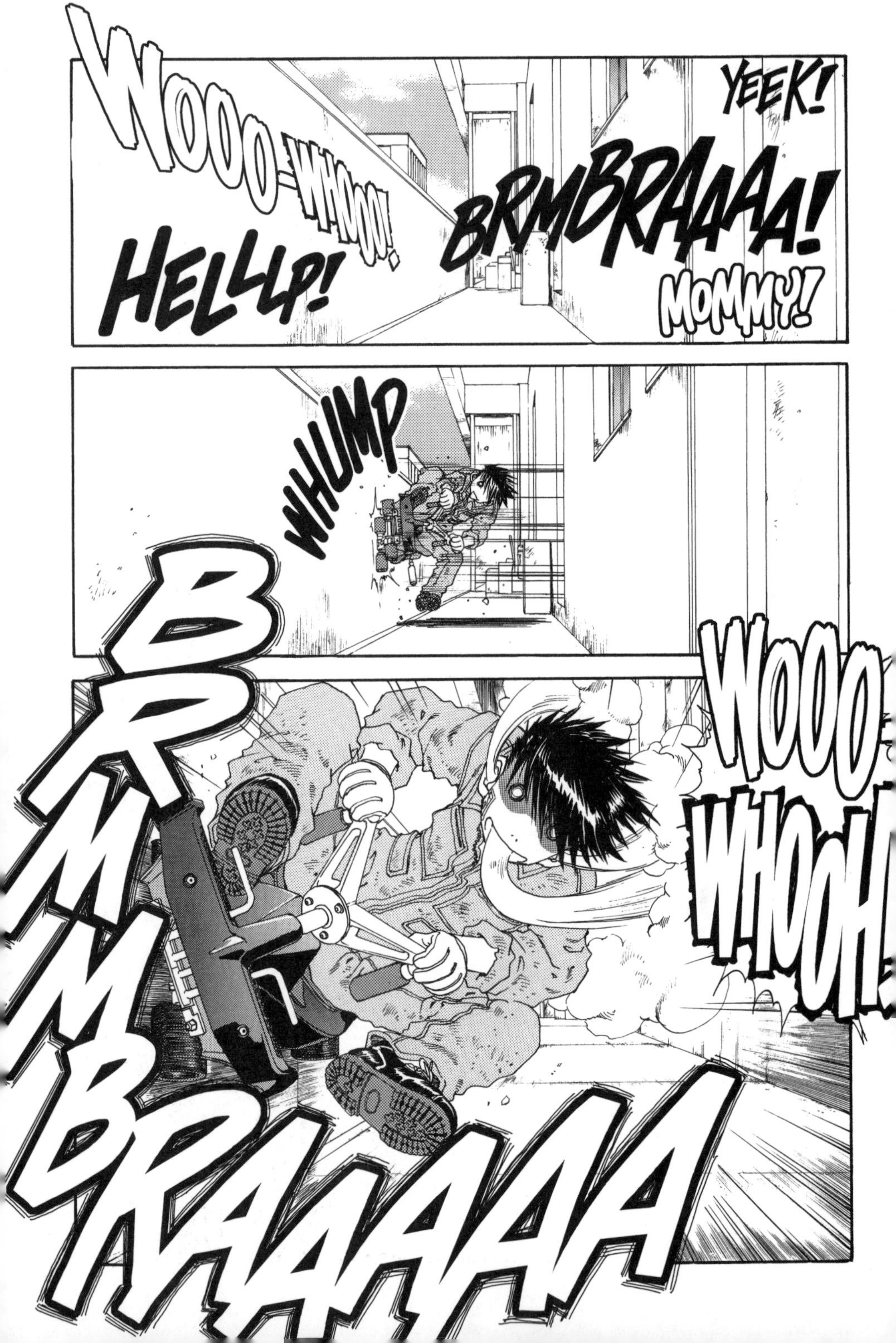
YEEK!
BRMBRAAAAA!
MOMMY!
WOOO-WHOOO!
HELLLP!
WHUMP
WOOO-
WHOOH
BRMMBRAAAAAA

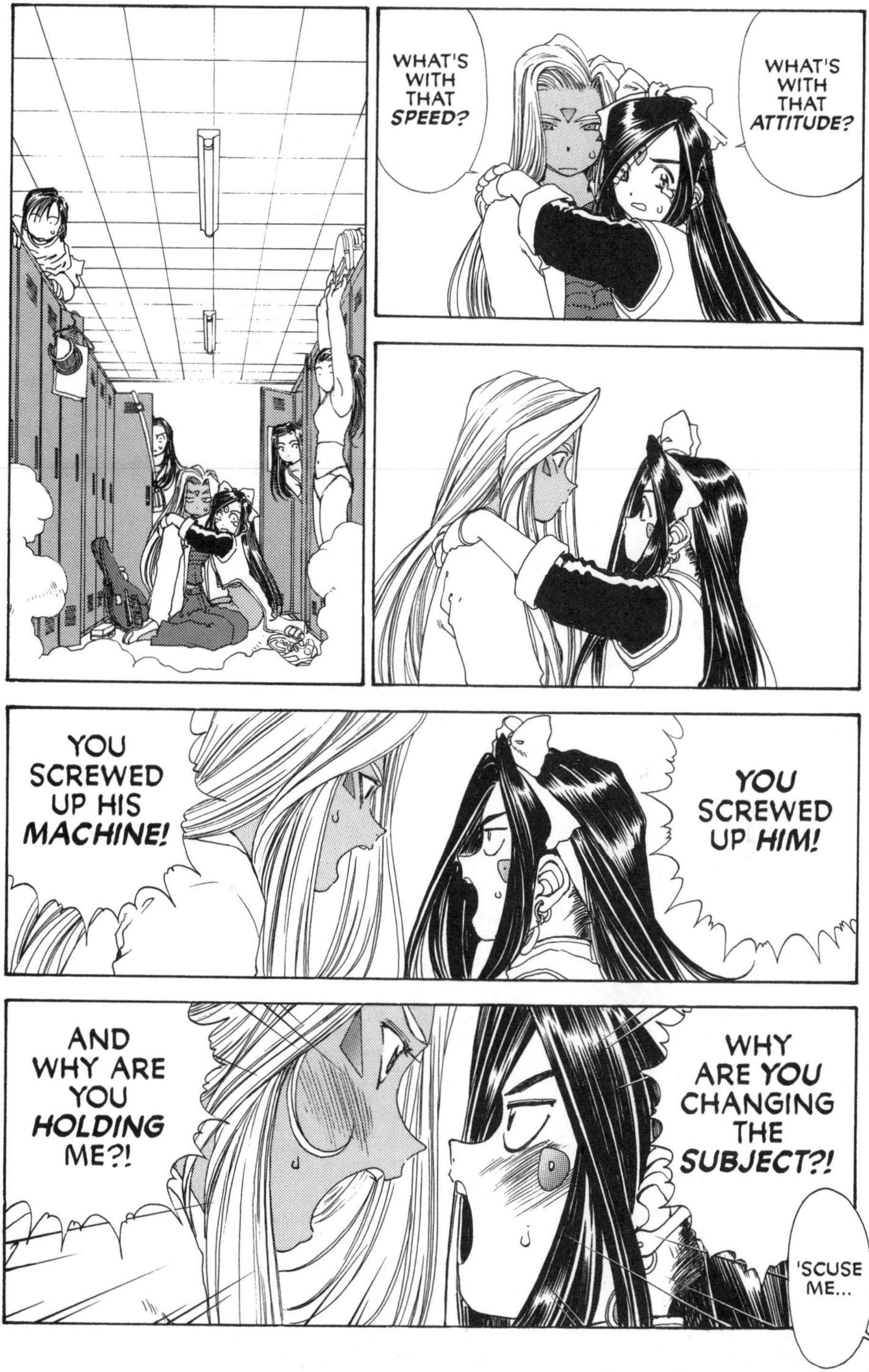
WHAT'S WITH THAT *ATTITUDE?*
WHAT'S WITH THAT *SPEED?*
YOU SCREWED UP *HIM!*
YOU SCREWED UP HIS *MACHINE!*
WHY ARE *YOU* CHANGING THE *SUBJECT?!*
AND WHY ARE YOU *HOLDING* ME?!
'SCUSE ME...

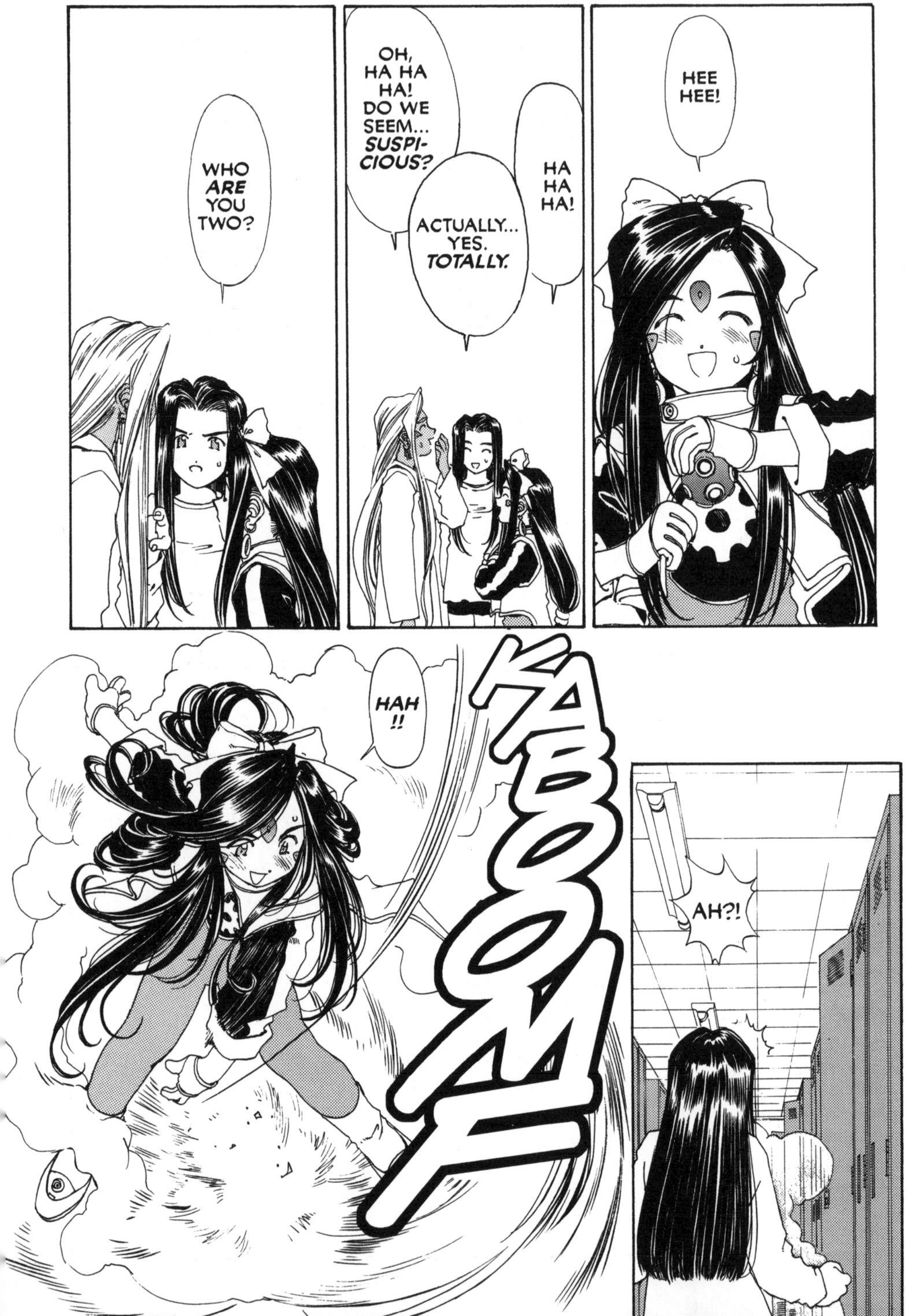
WHO ARE YOU TWO?
OH, HA HA HA! DO WE SEEM... SUSPICIOUS?
ACTUALLY... YES. TOTALLY.
HA HA HA!
HEE HEE!
HAH !!
KABOOM!
AH?!

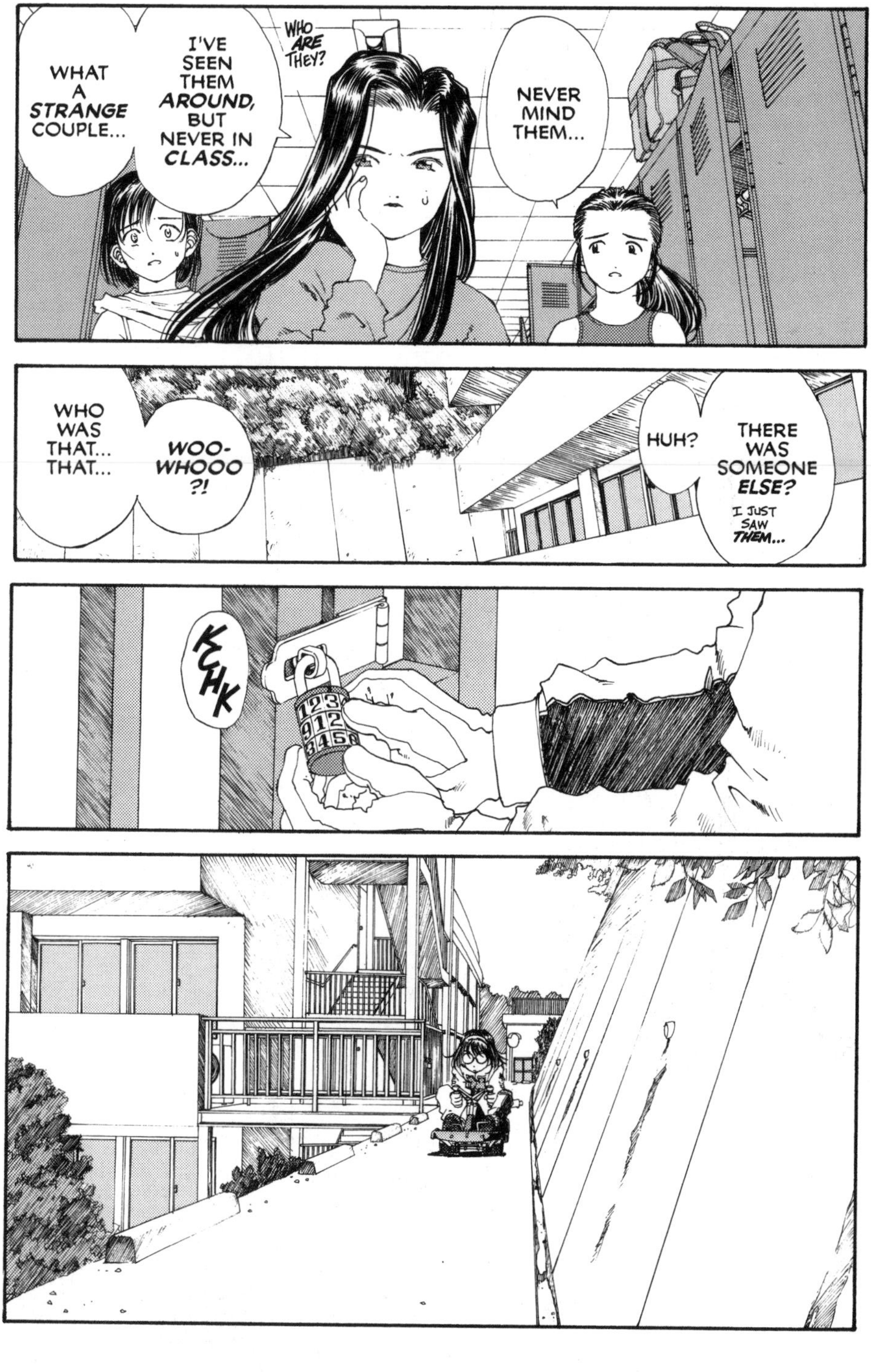
NEVER MIND THEM...
WHO ARE THEY?
I'VE SEEN THEM AROUND, BUT NEVER IN CLASS...
WHAT A STRANGE COUPLE...
THERE WAS SOMEONE ELSE?
I JUST SAW THEM...
HUH?
WOO-WHOOO?!
WHO WAS THAT... THAT...
KCHK

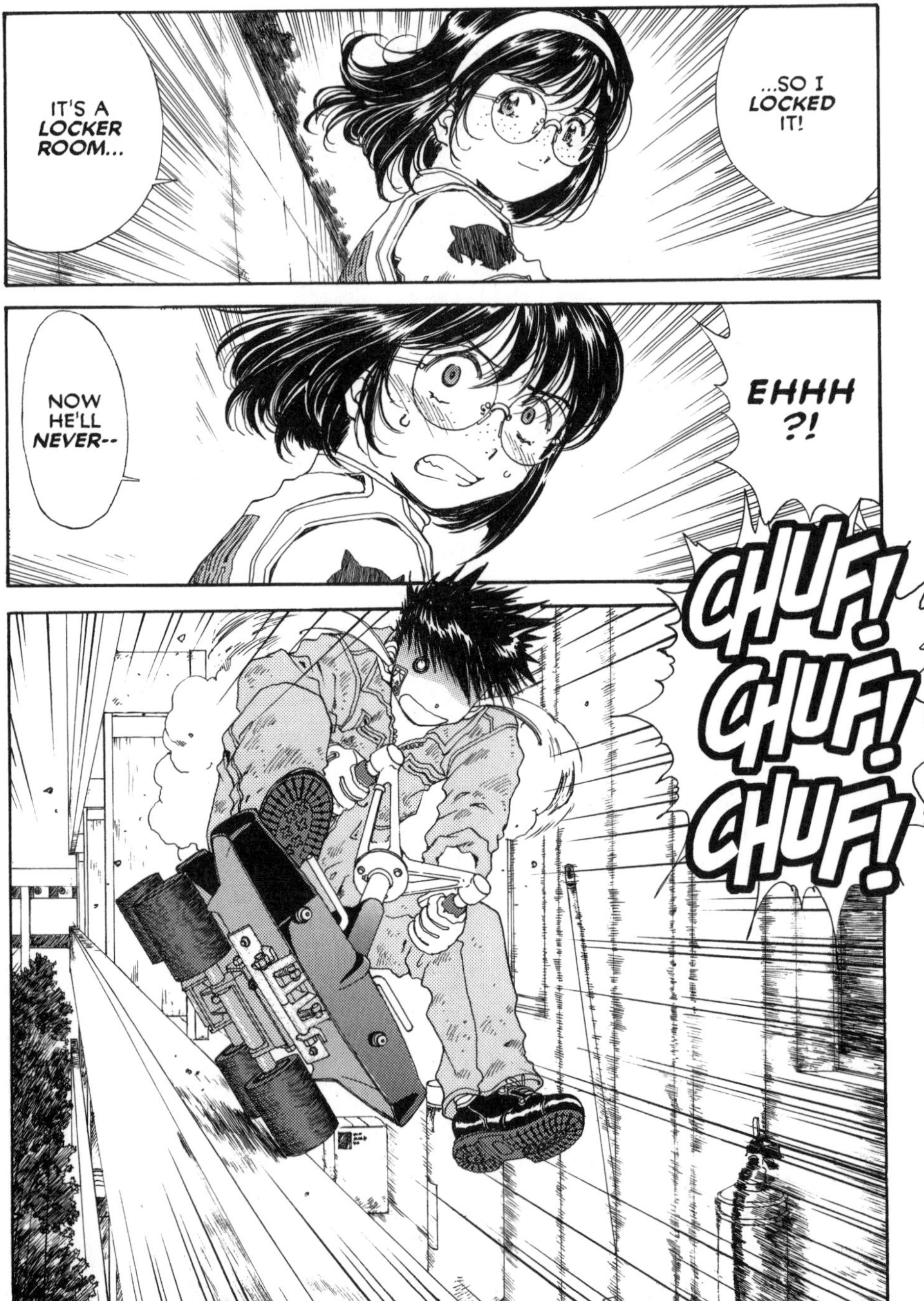
IT'S A LOCKER ROOM...
...SO I LOCKED IT!
NOW HE'LL NEVER--
EHHH ?!
CHUF! CHUF! CHUF!

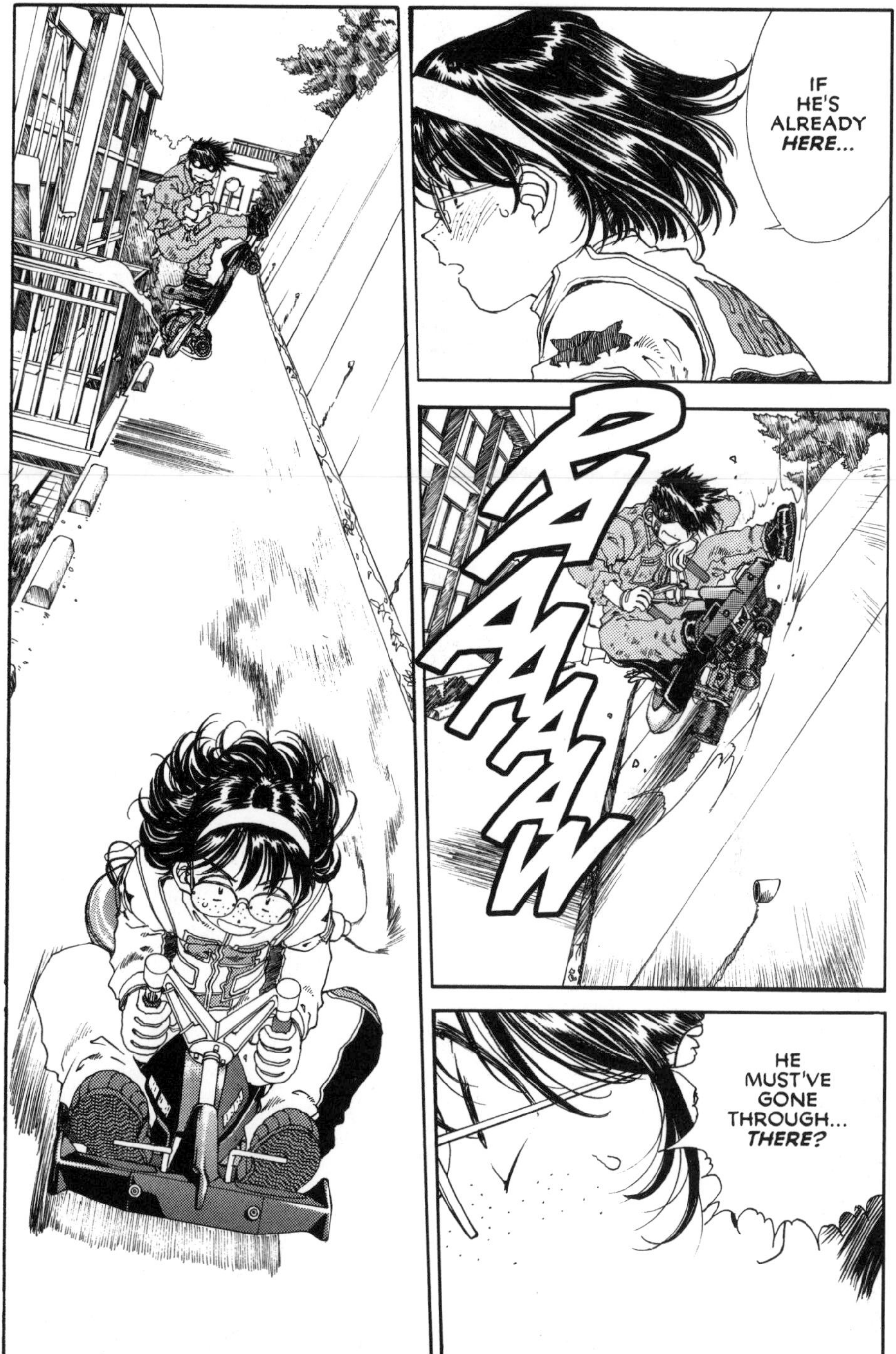
IF HE'S ALREADY *HERE...*
HE MUST'VE GONE THROUGH... *THERE?*

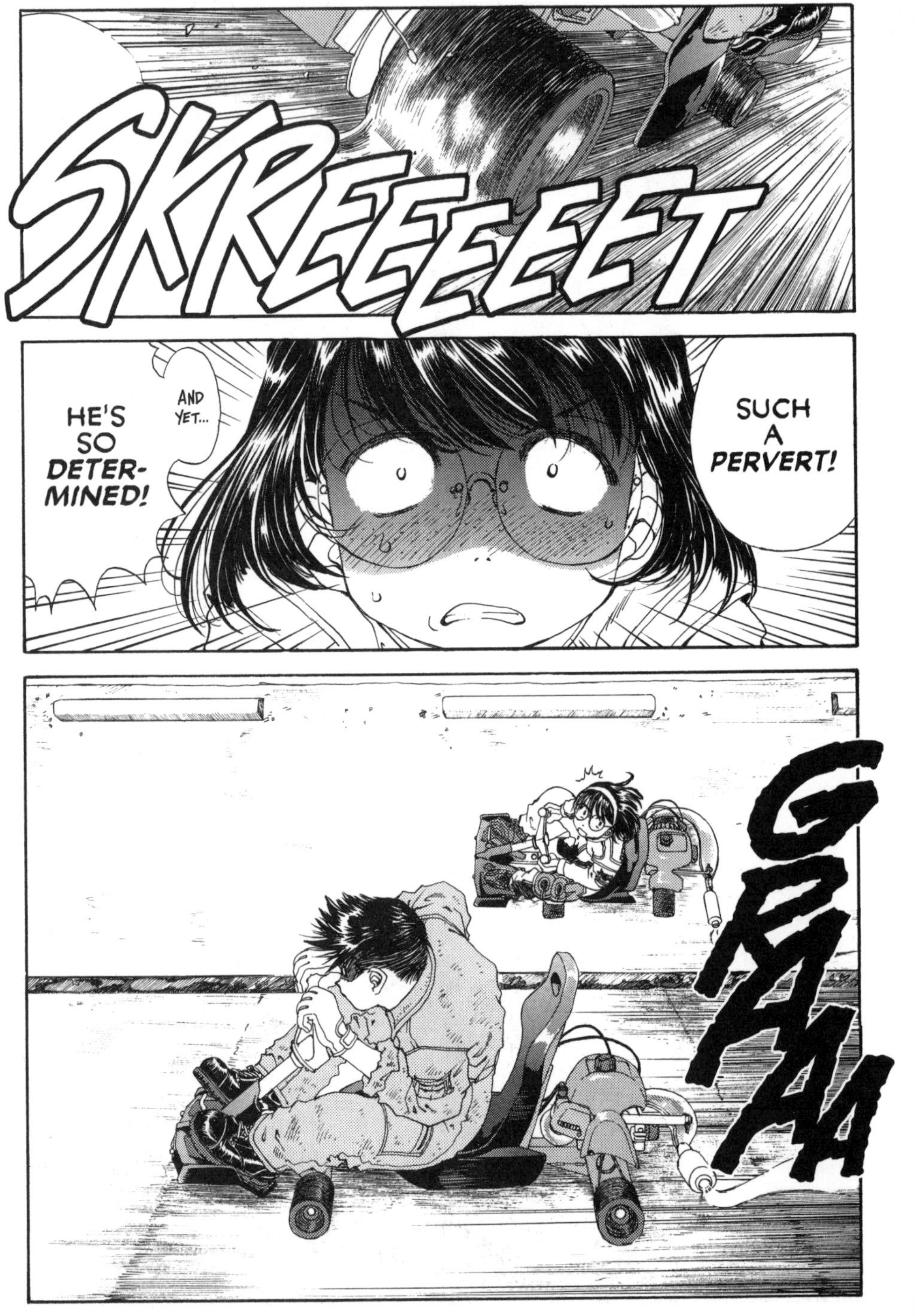
SKREEEEEET
SUCH A PERVERT!
AND YET...
HE'S SO DETERMINED!
GRAAAA

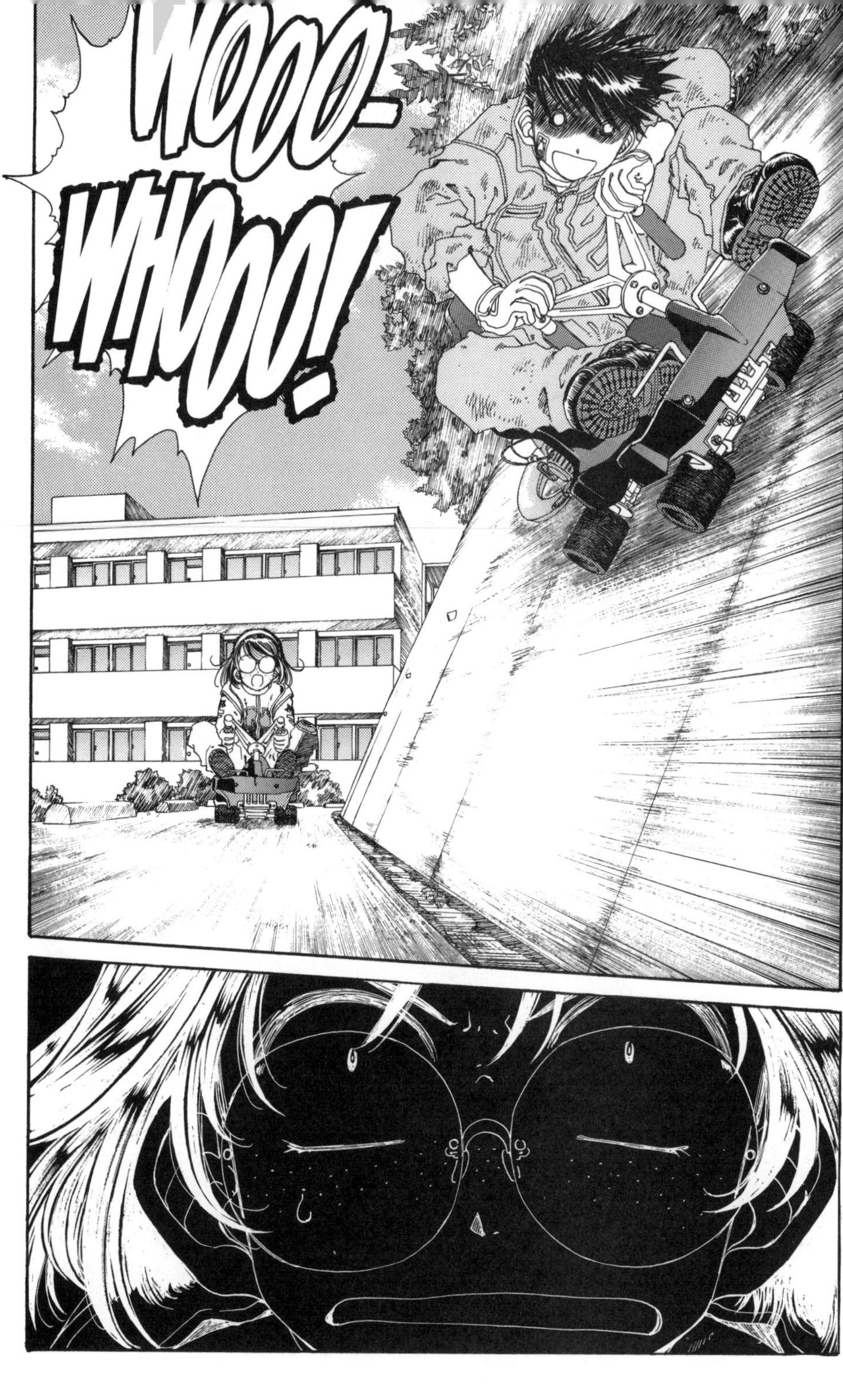
WOOO-WHOOO!

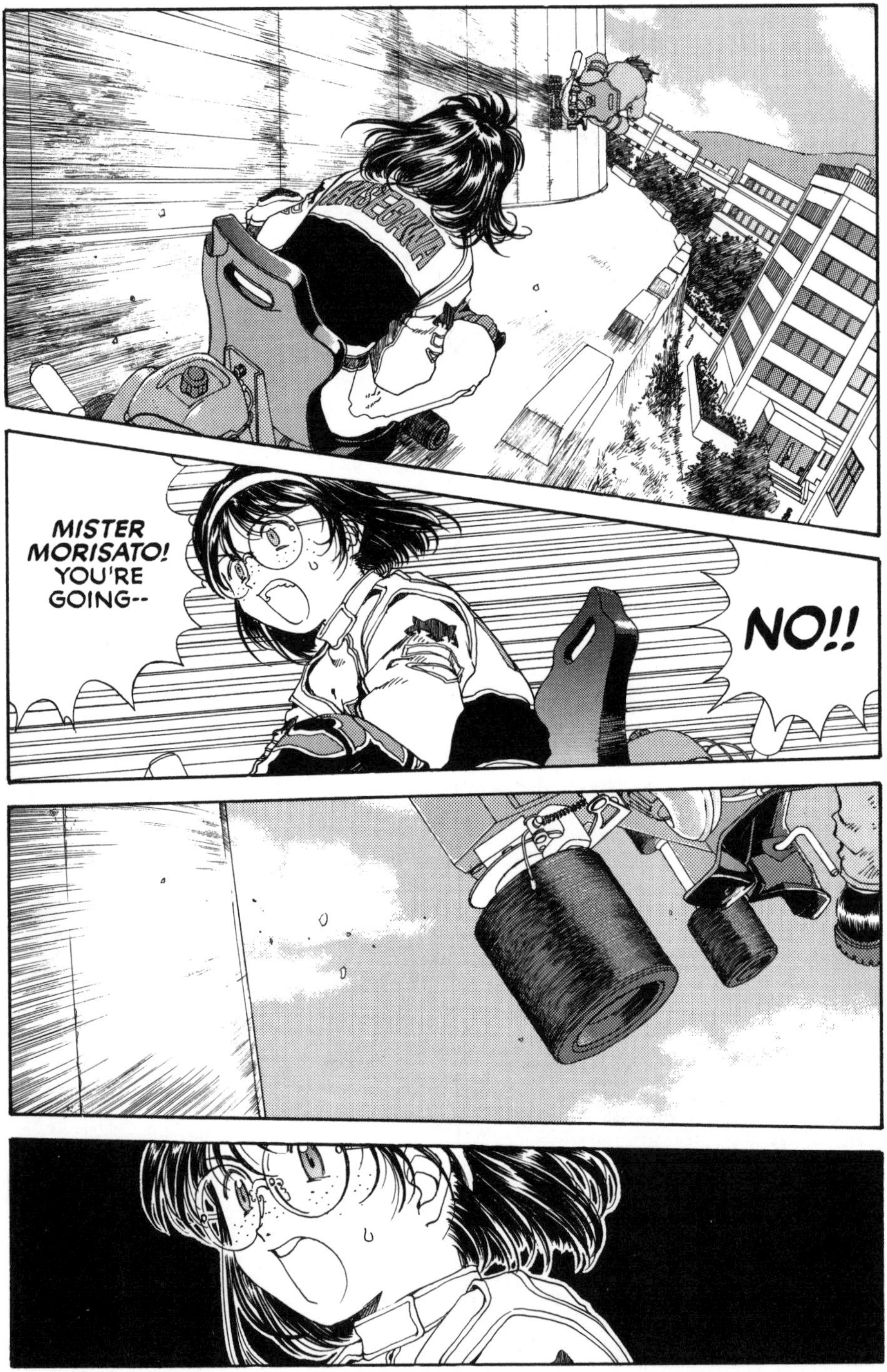
MISTER MORISATO! YOU'RE GOING--
NO!!

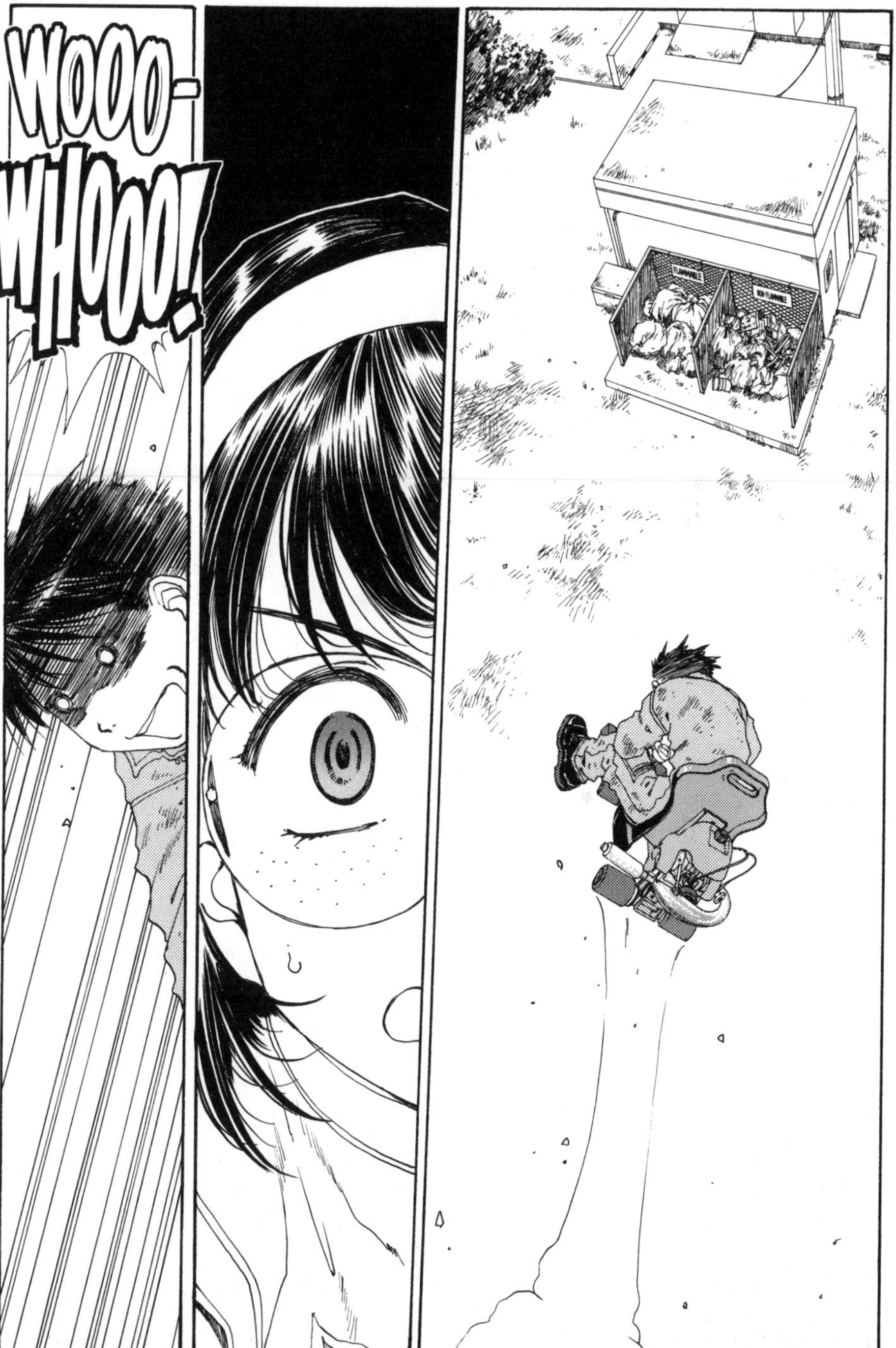
FLAMMABLE
NON-FLAMMABLE
WOOO-WHOOO!

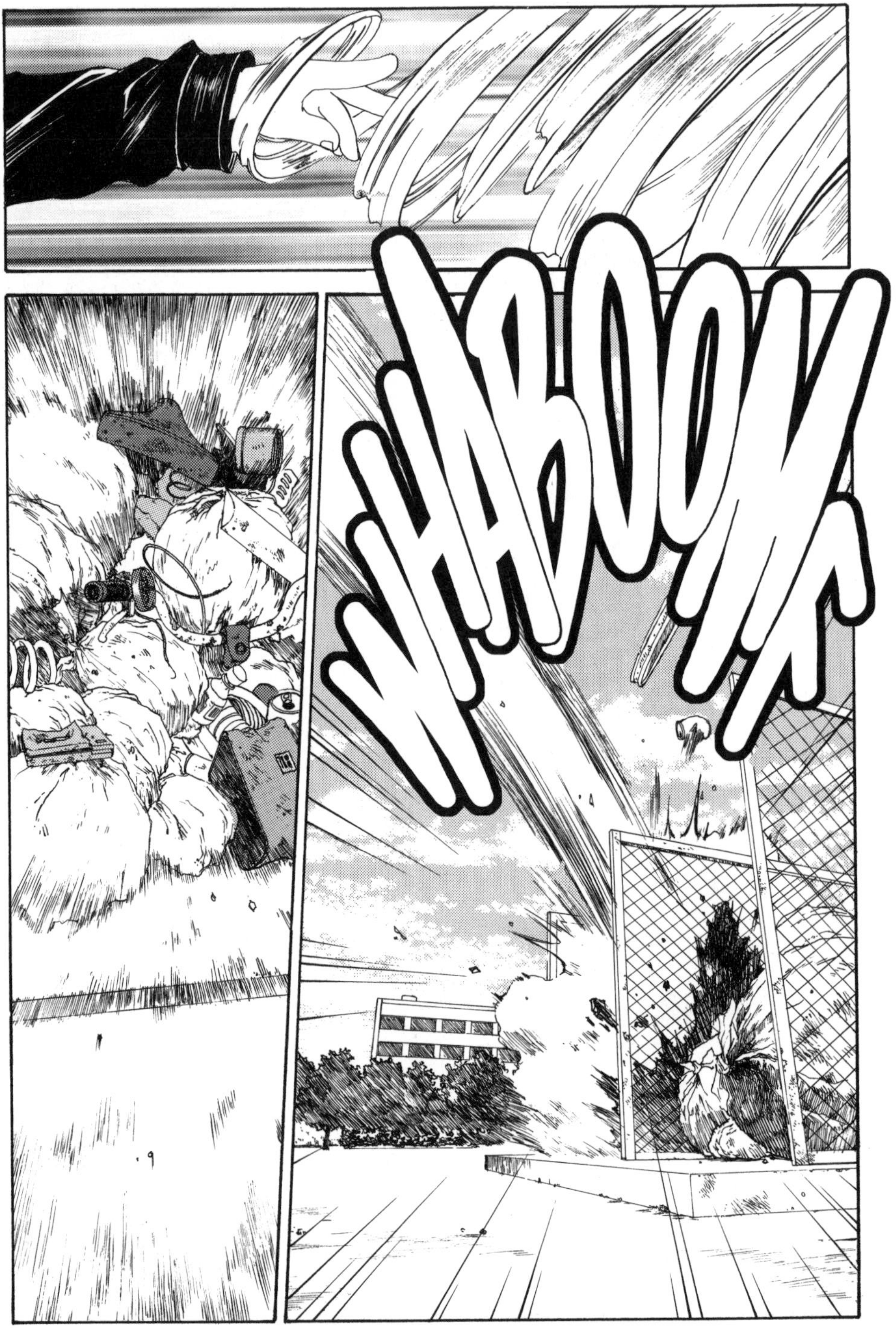
WHABOOM

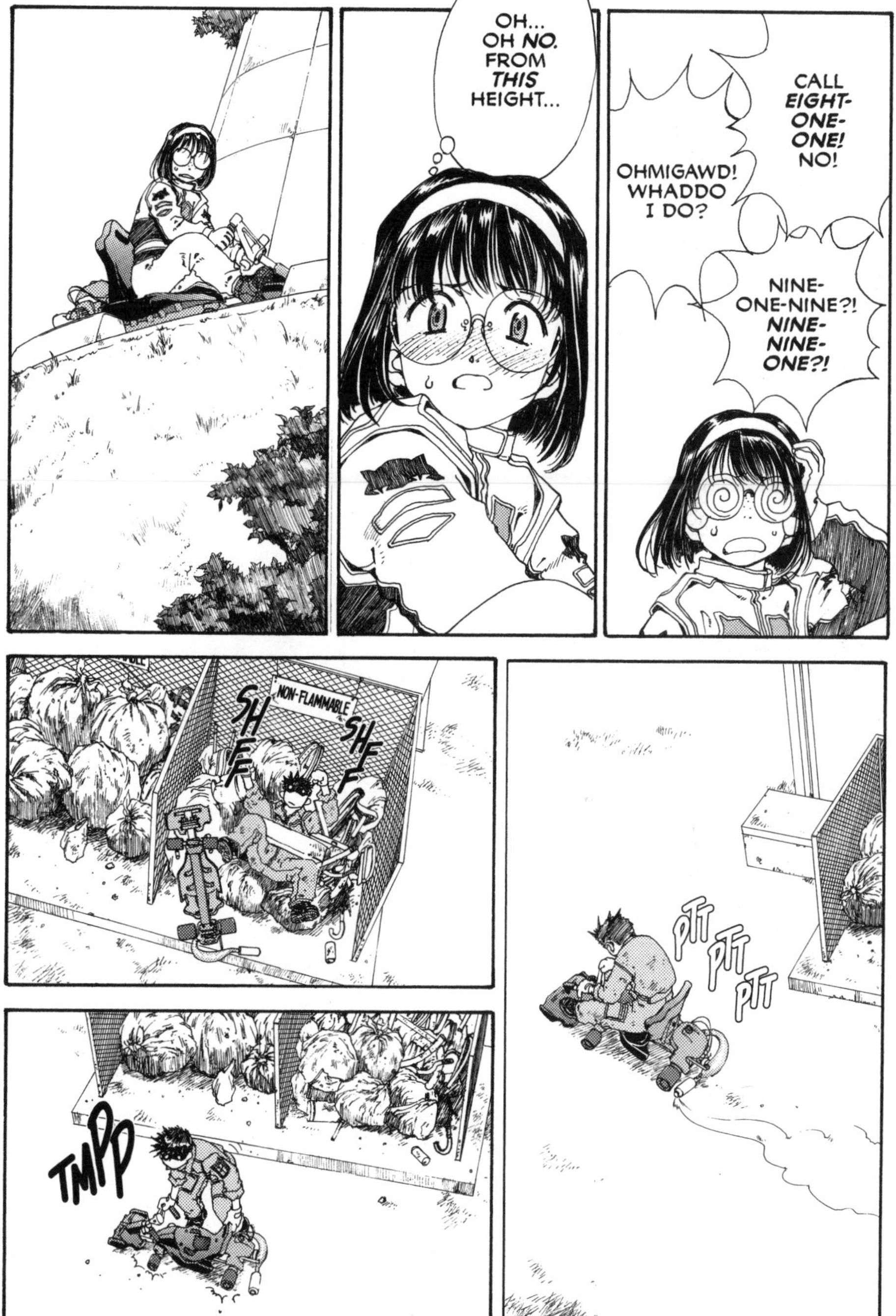
OH... OH NO. FROM THIS HEIGHT...
OHMIGAWD! WHADDO I DO?
CALL EIGHT-ONE-ONE! NO!
NINE-ONE-NINE?! NINE-NINE-ONE?!
NON-FLAMMABLE
SHEFF
SHEFF
TMPP
PTT PTT PTT

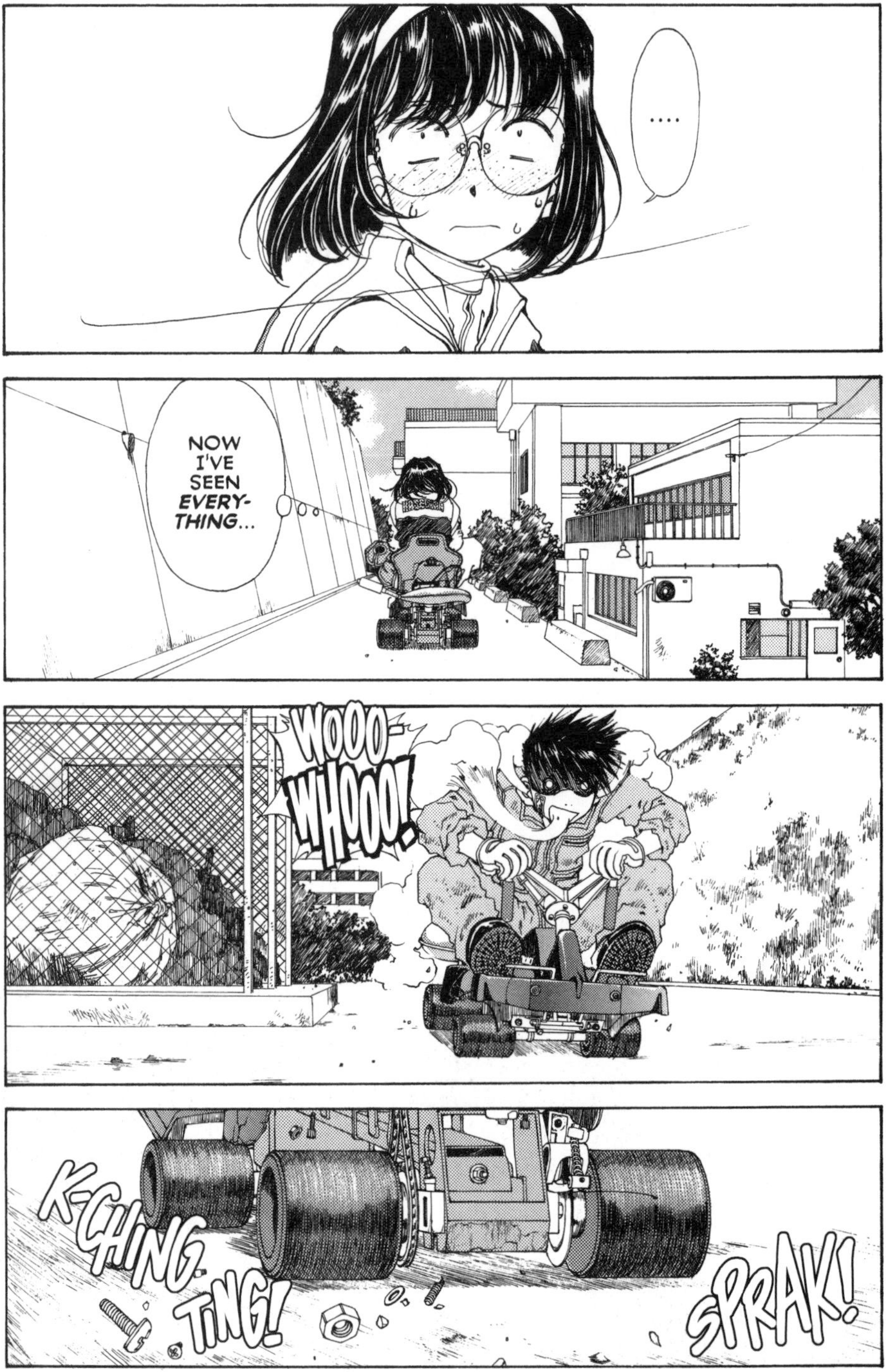
....
NOW I'VE SEEN EVERY-THING...
WOOO-WHOOO!
SPRAK!
K-CHING
TING!

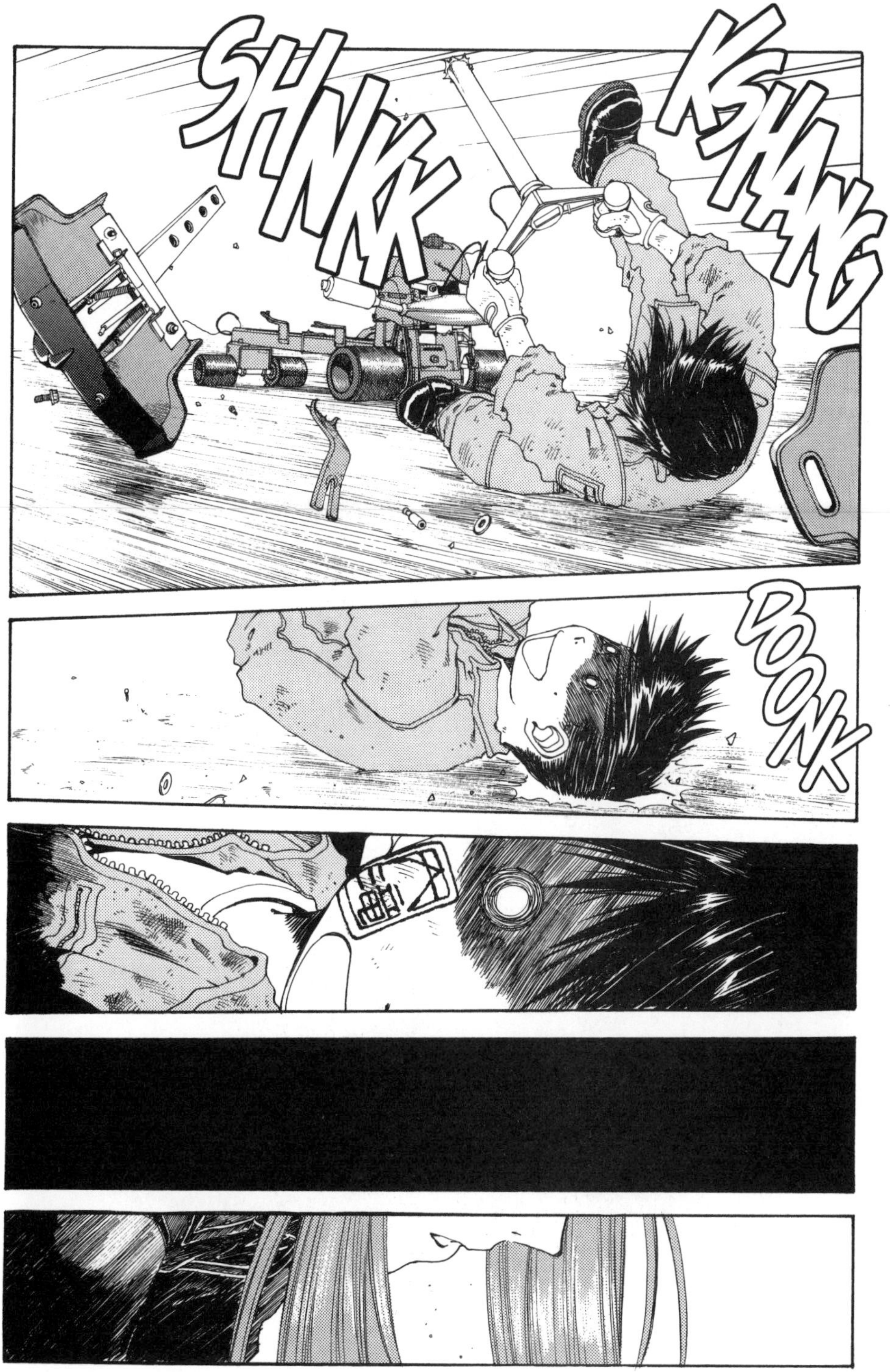
KSHANG
SHNKK
DOOONK

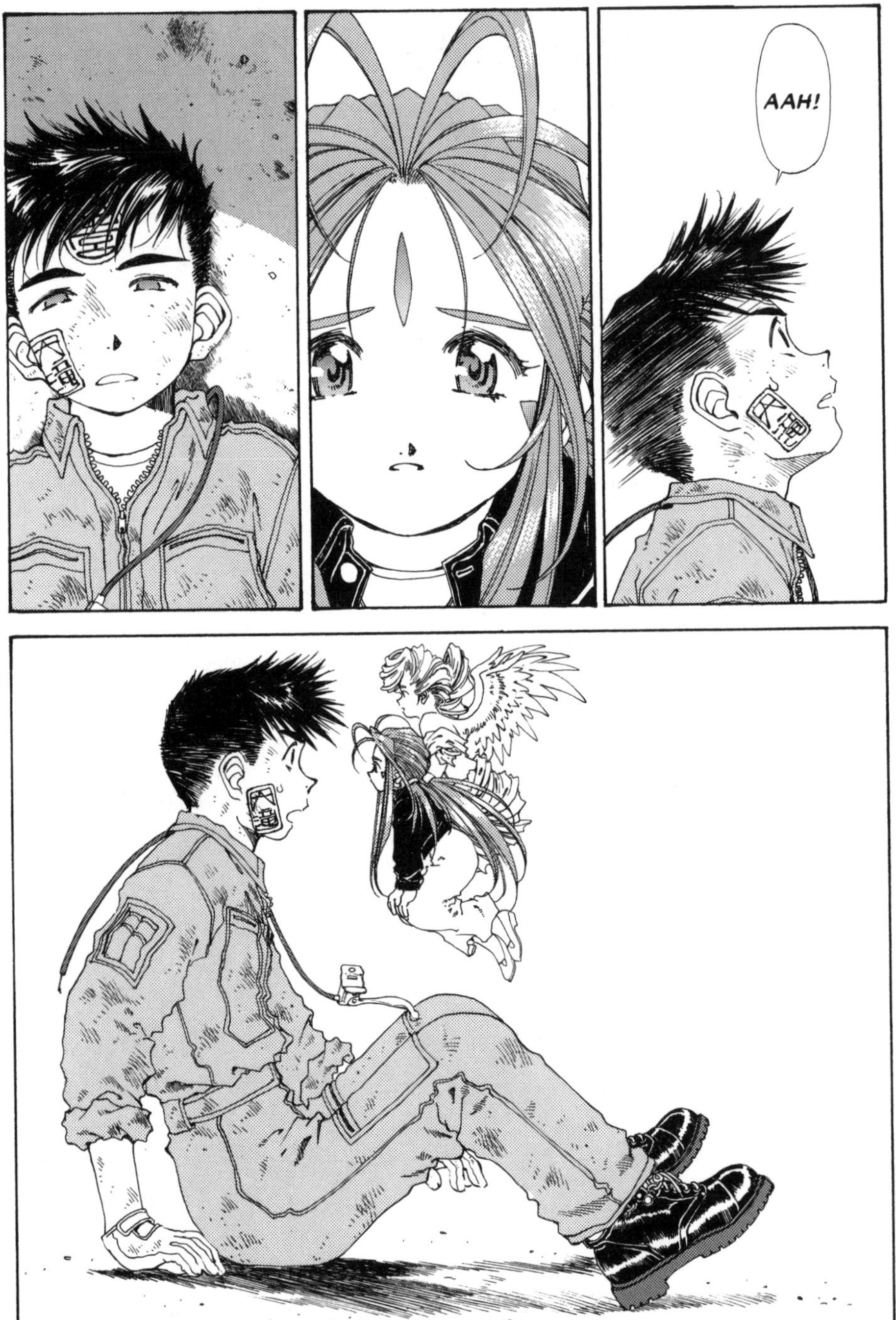
AAH!

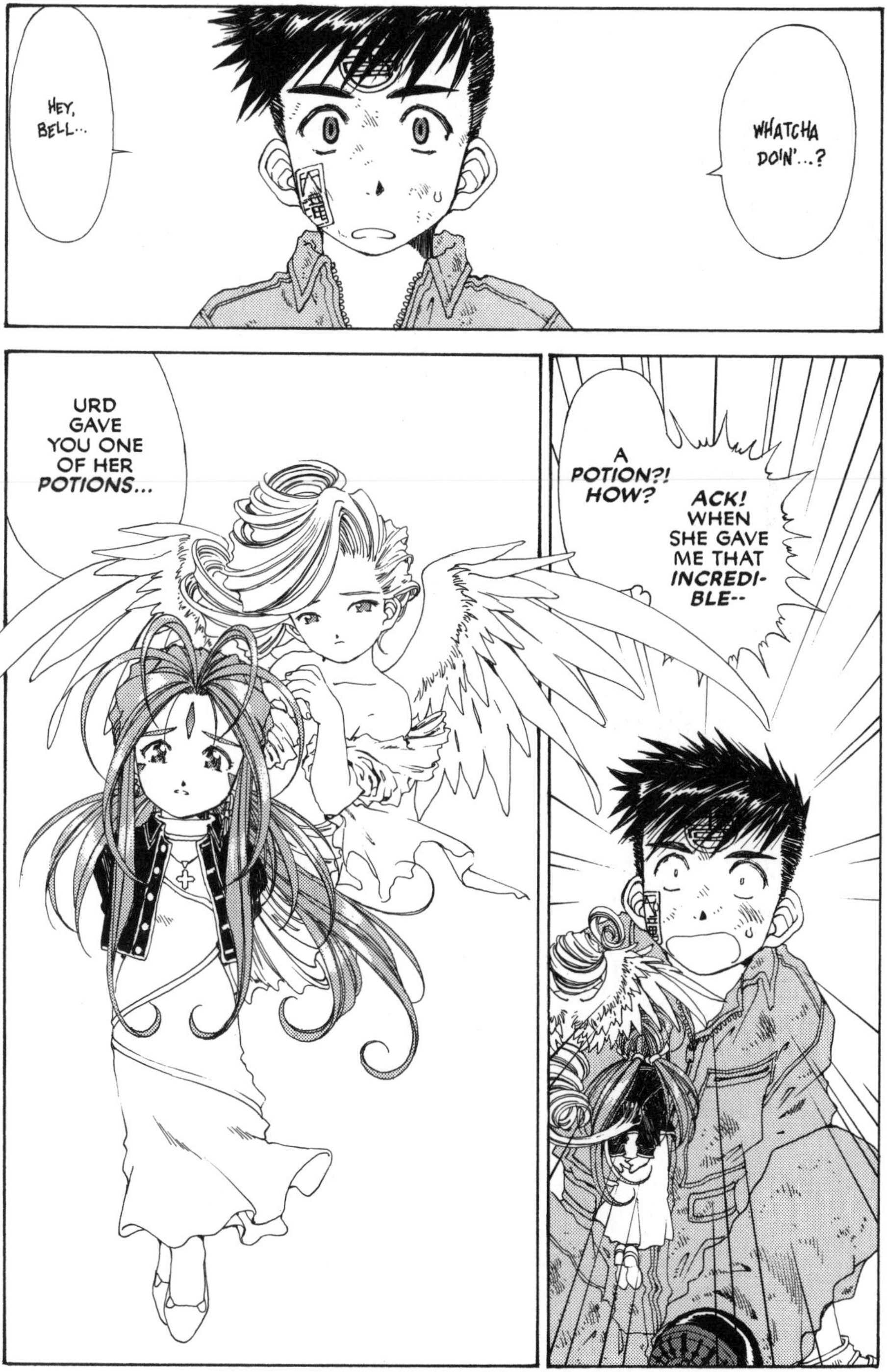
HEY, BELL...
WHATCHA DOIN'...?
URD GAVE YOU ONE OF HER POTIONS...
A POTION?! HOW?
ACK! WHEN SHE GAVE ME THAT INCREDI-BLE--

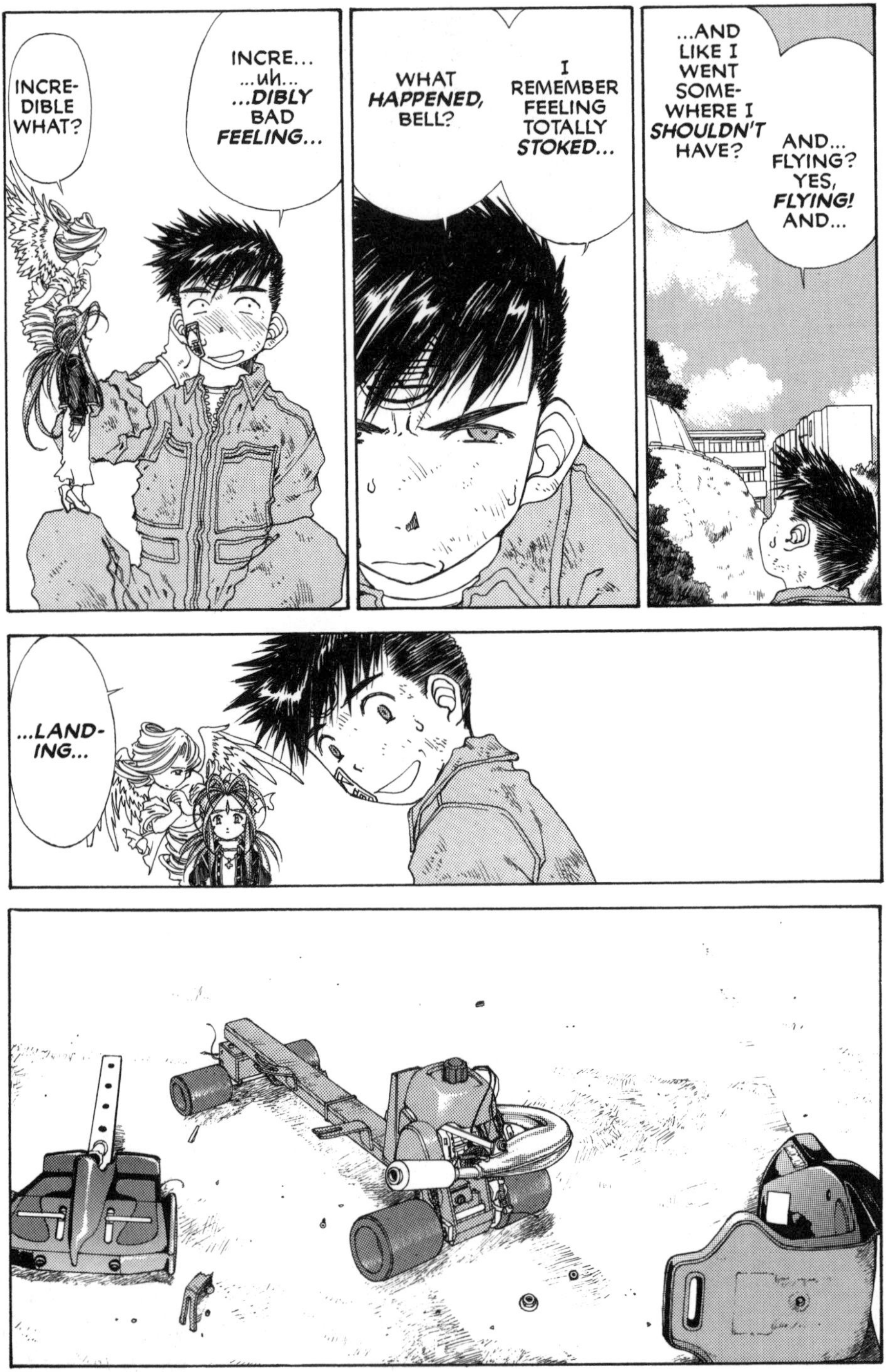
INCRE-DIBLE WHAT?
INCRE... ...uh... ...DIBLY BAD FEELING...
WHAT HAPPENED, BELL?
I REMEMBER FEELING TOTALLY STOKED...
...AND LIKE I WENT SOME-WHERE I SHOULDN'T HAVE?
AND... FLYING? YES, FLYING! AND...
...LAND-ING...

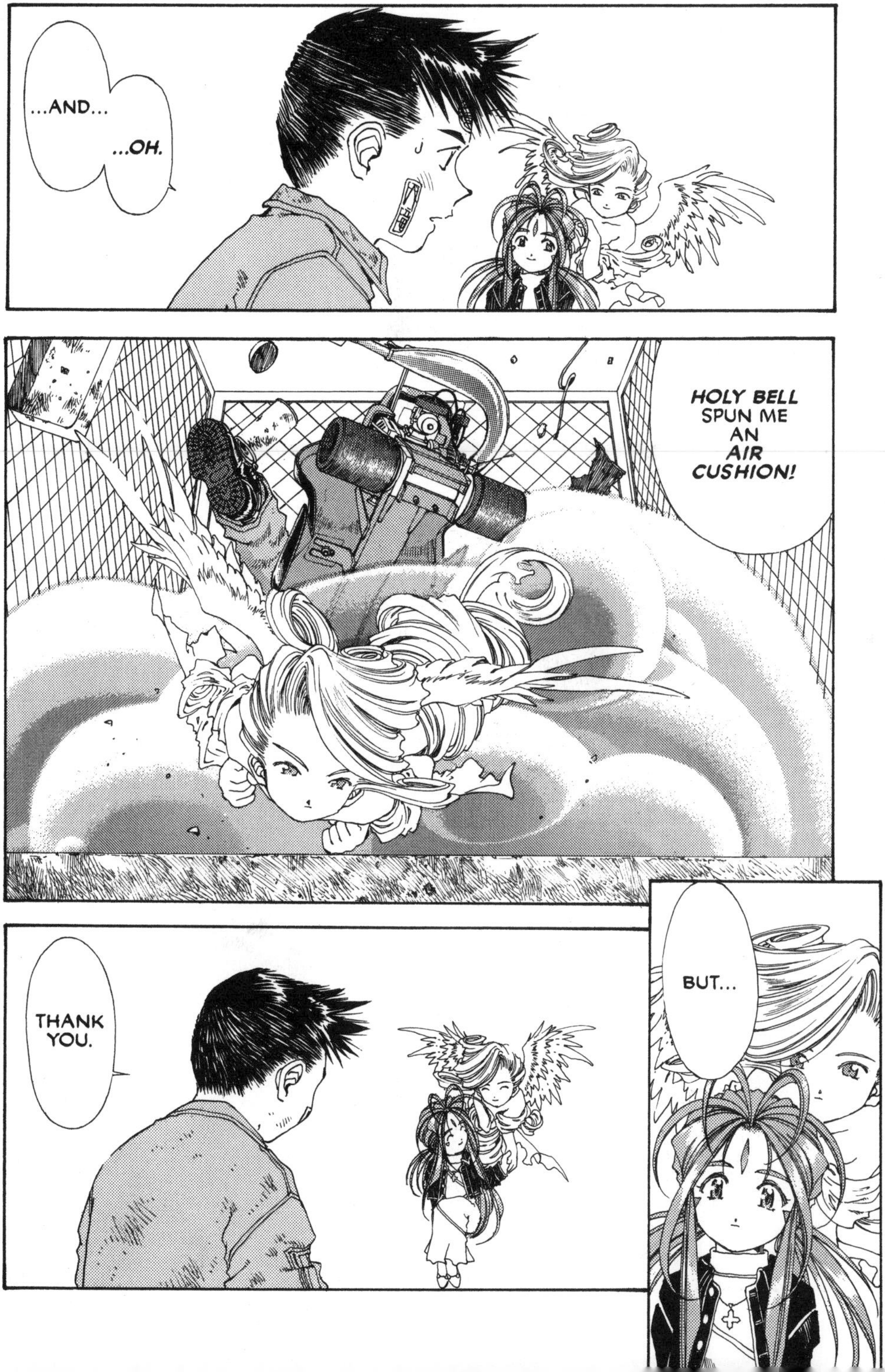

...AND... ...OH.
HOLY BELL SPUN ME AN AIR CUSHION!
THANK YOU.
BUT...

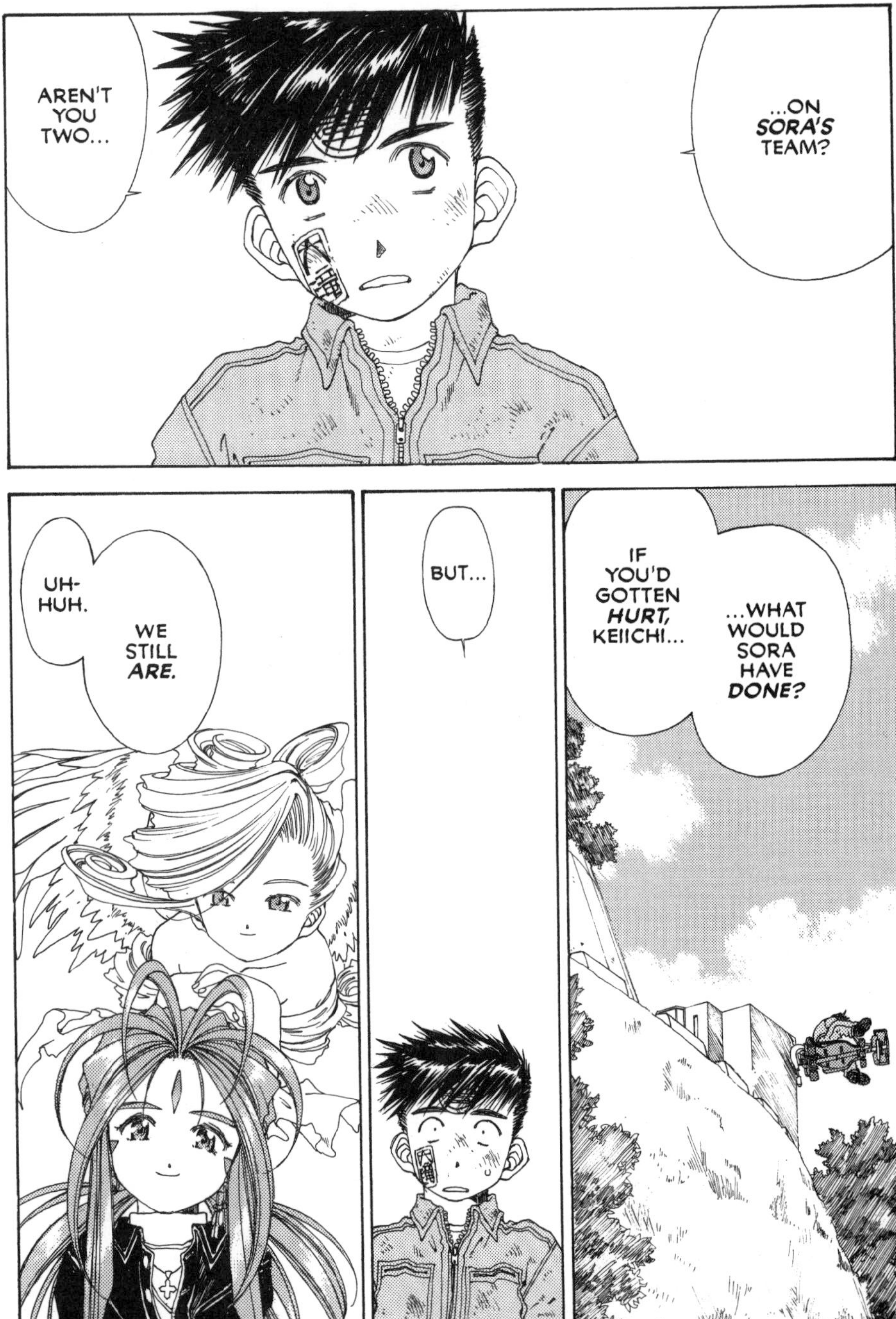
AREN'T YOU TWO...
...ON SORA'S TEAM?
UH-HUH.
WE STILL ARE.
BUT...
IF YOU'D GOTTEN HURT, KEIICHI...
...WHAT WOULD SORA HAVE DONE?

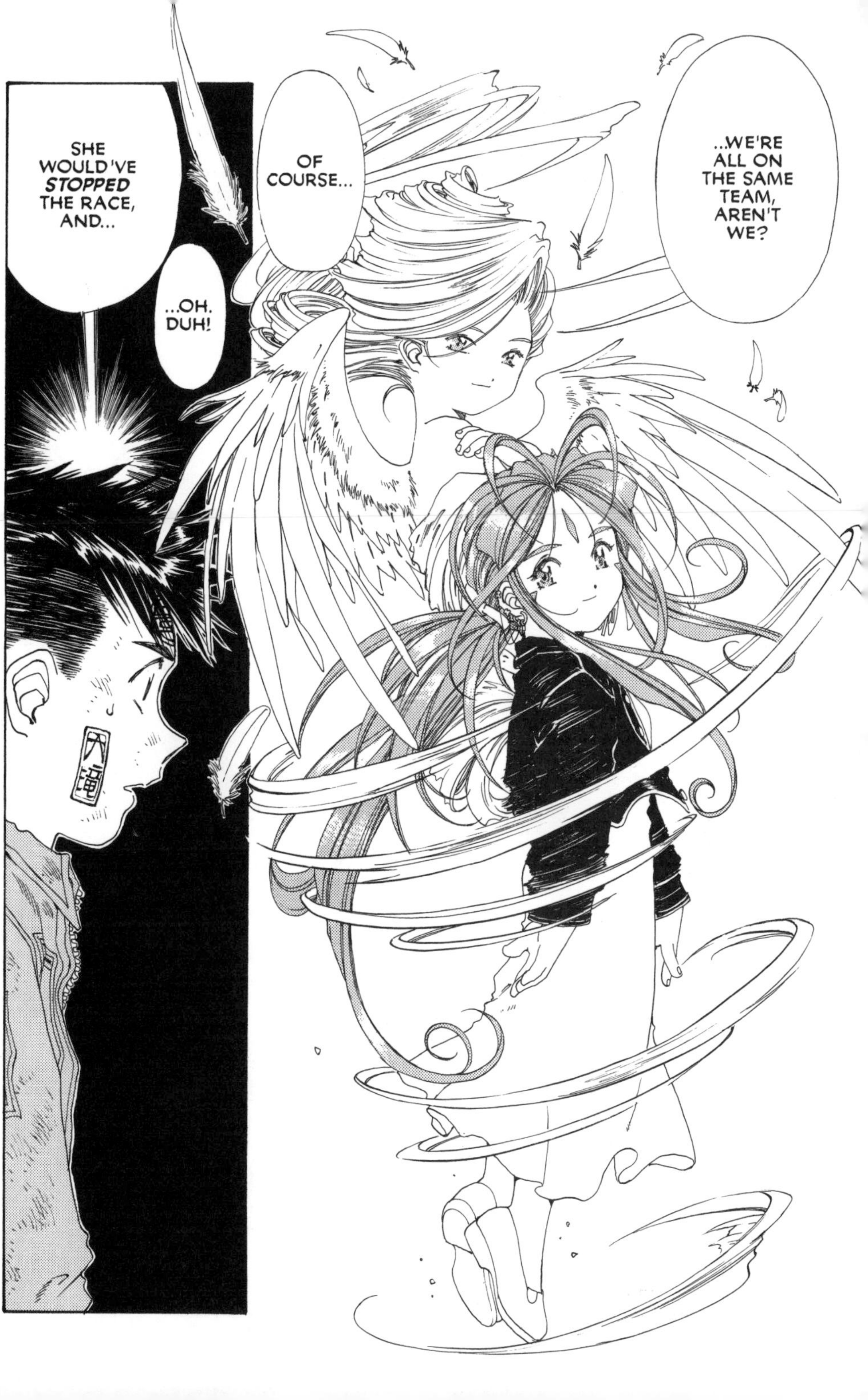
...WE'RE ALL ON THE SAME TEAM, AREN'T WE?
OF COURSE...
SHE WOULD'VE *STOPPED* THE RACE, AND...
...OH. DUH!

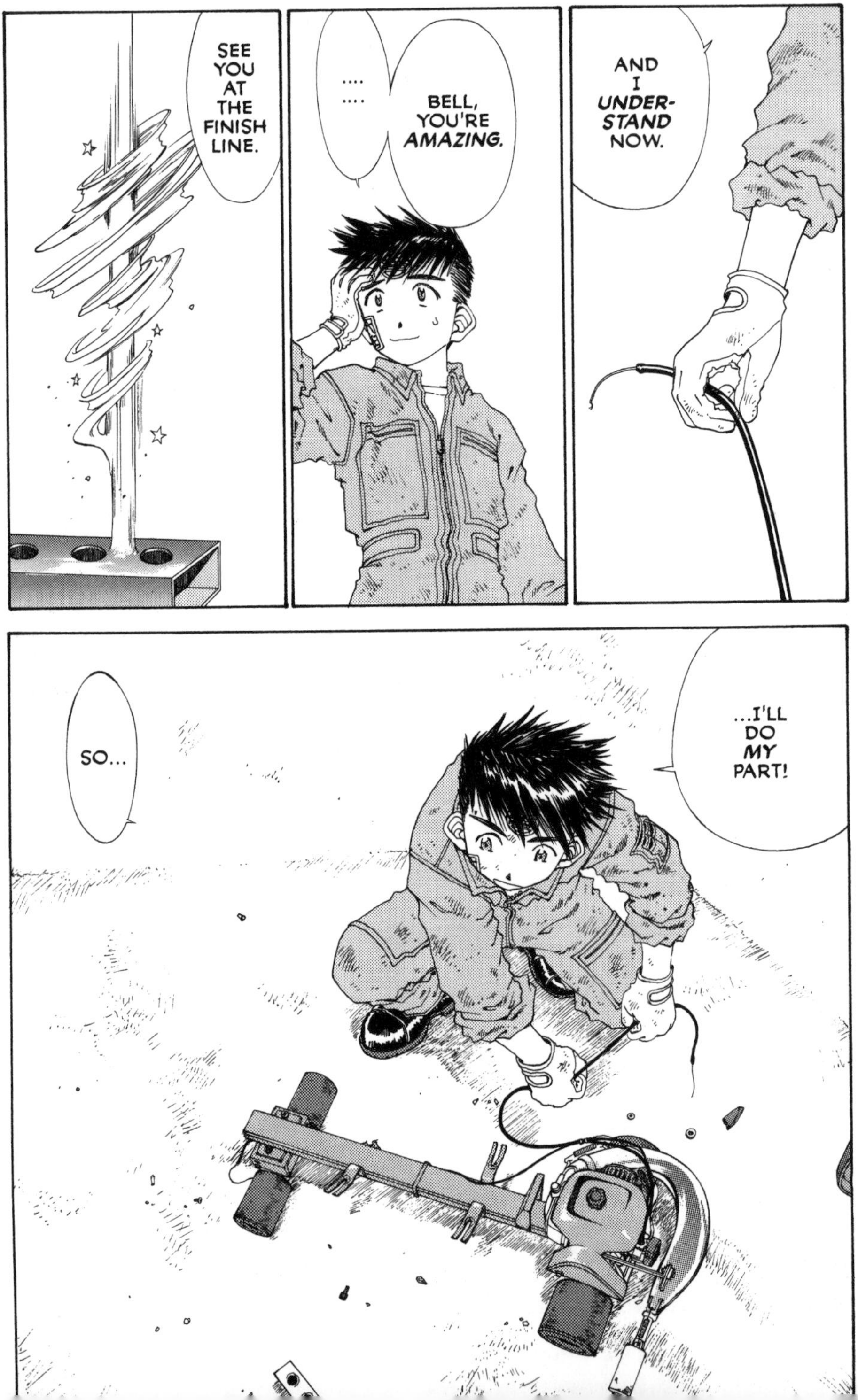
AND I *UNDER-STAND* NOW.
BELL, YOU'RE *AMAZING.*
....
SEE YOU AT THE FINISH LINE.
SO...
...I'LL DO *MY* PART!

SKRIPP
SKRIPP
SKRIPP

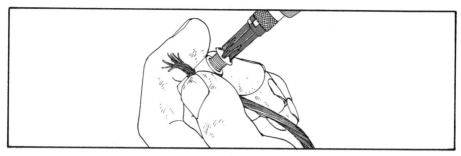

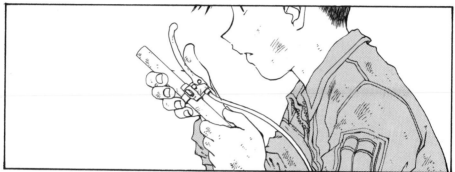

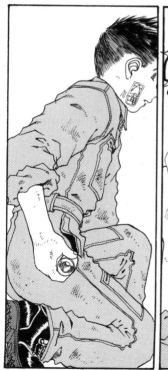

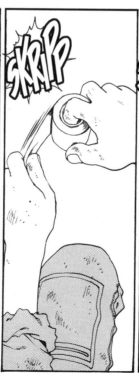

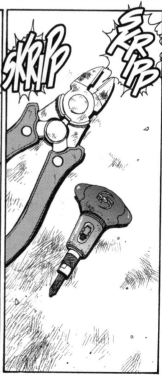

THE BEST MAGIC

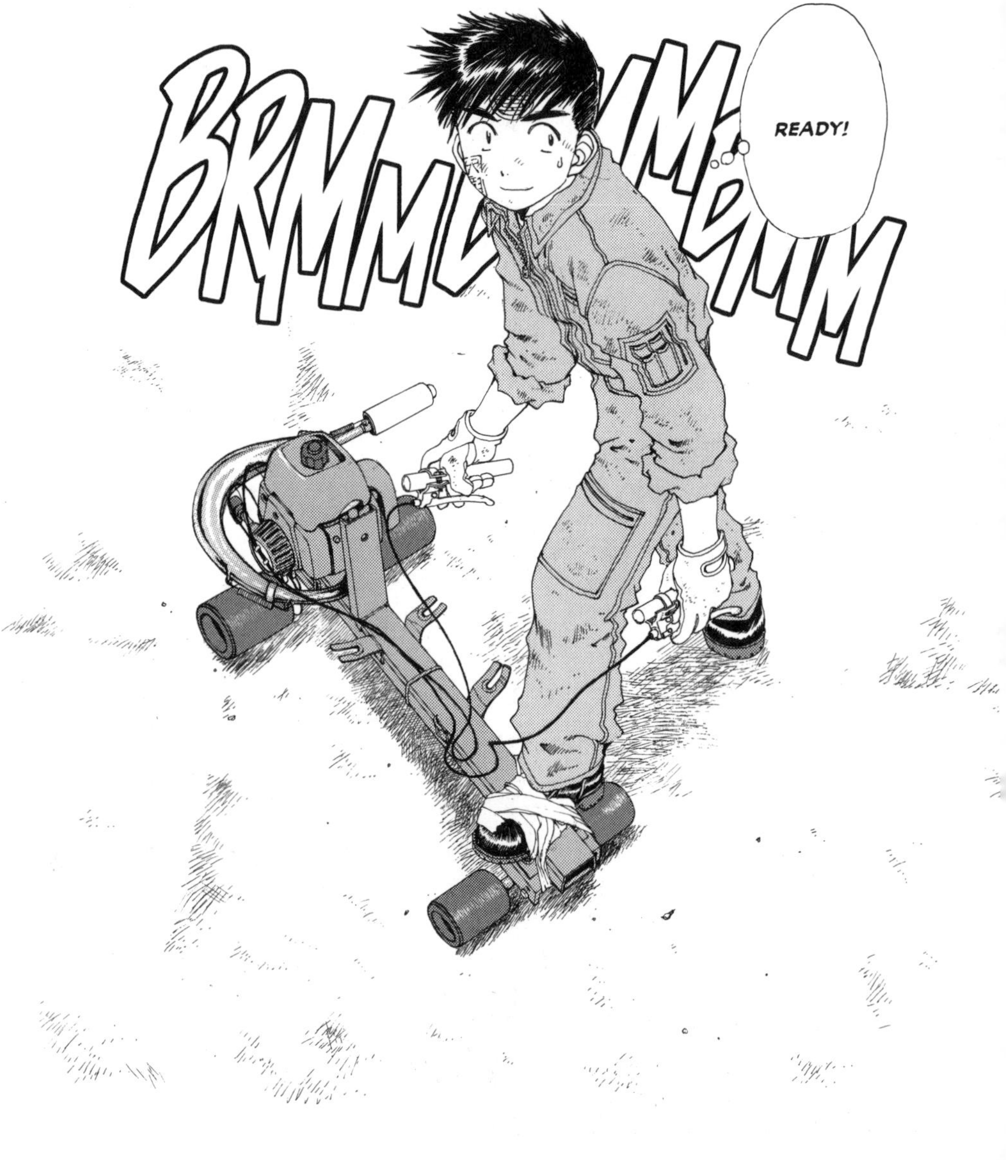
BRMMMMMMMMM
READY!

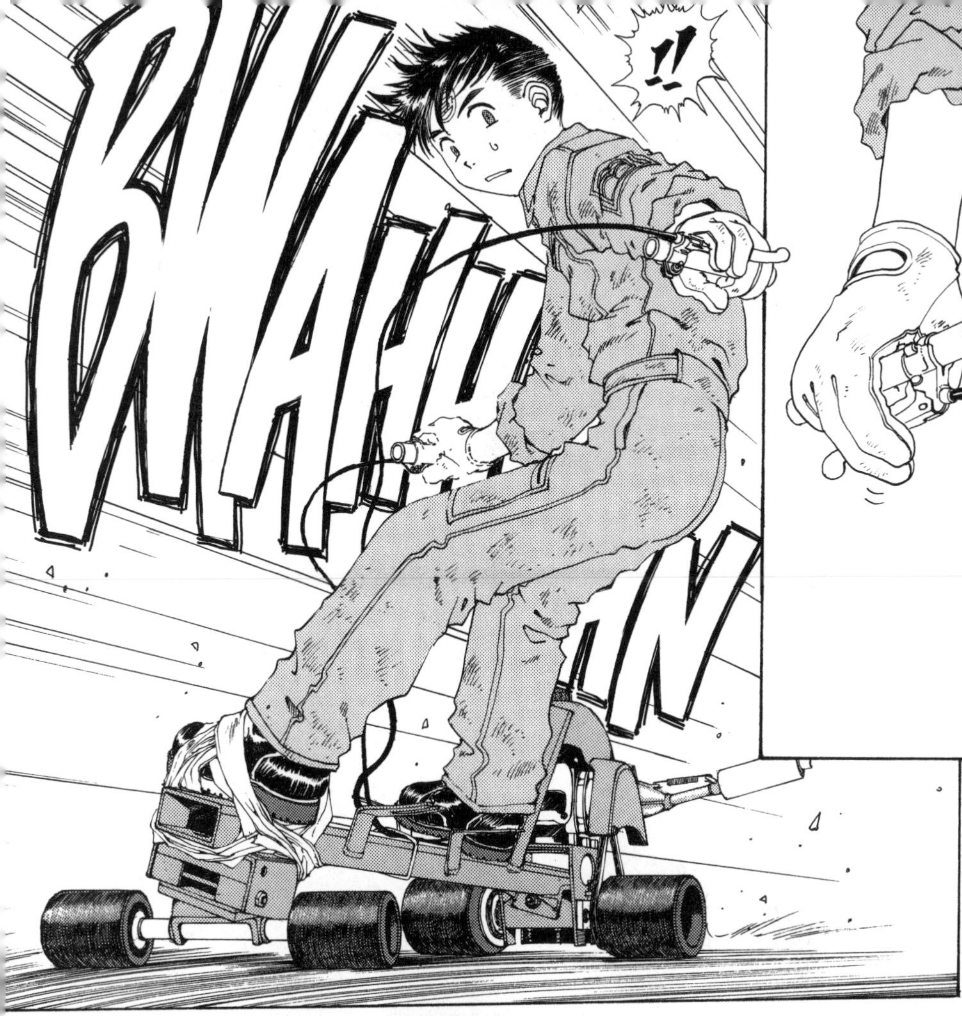
!!
BWAHHN
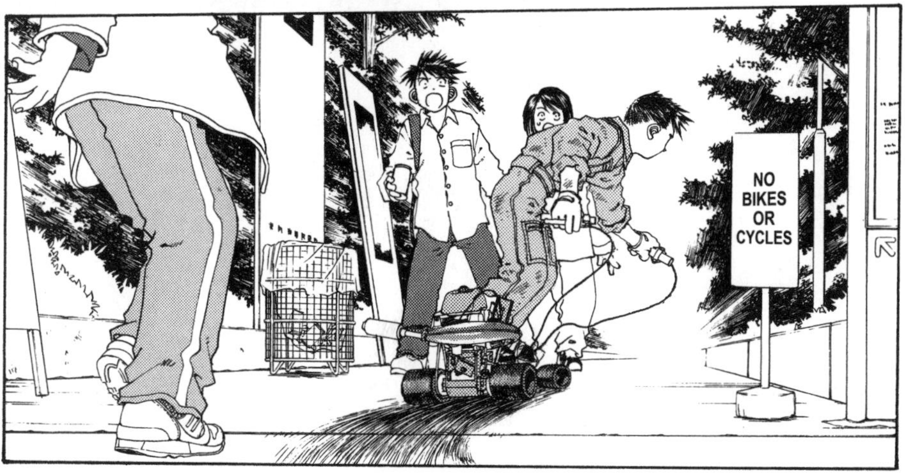
NO BIKES OR CYCLES

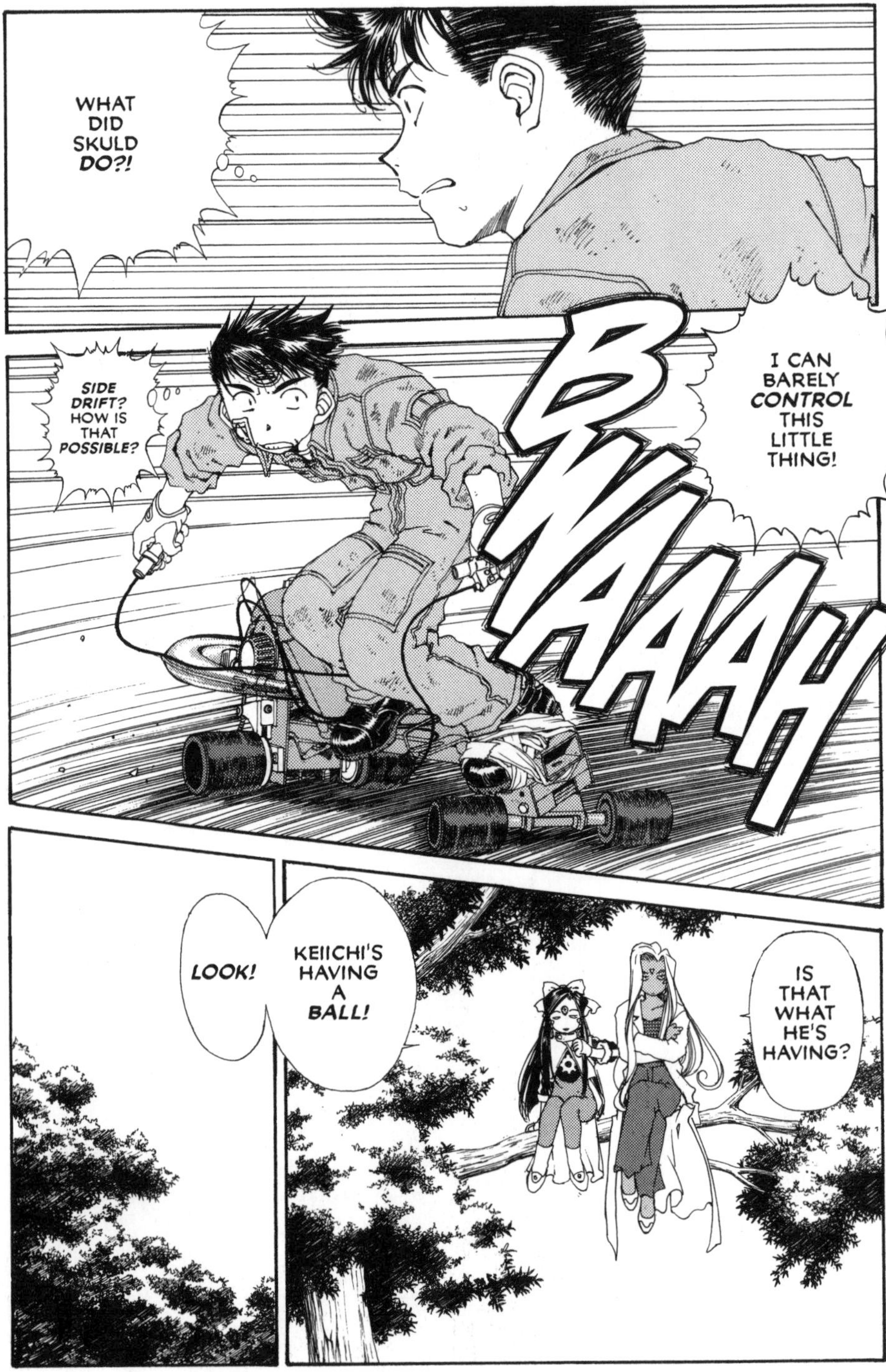
WHAT DID SKULD *DO?!*
SIDE DRIFT? HOW IS THAT *POSSIBLE?*
BWAAAAH
I CAN BARELY *CONTROL* THIS LITTLE THING!
LOOK!
KEIICHI'S HAVING A *BALL!*
IS THAT WHAT HE'S HAVING?

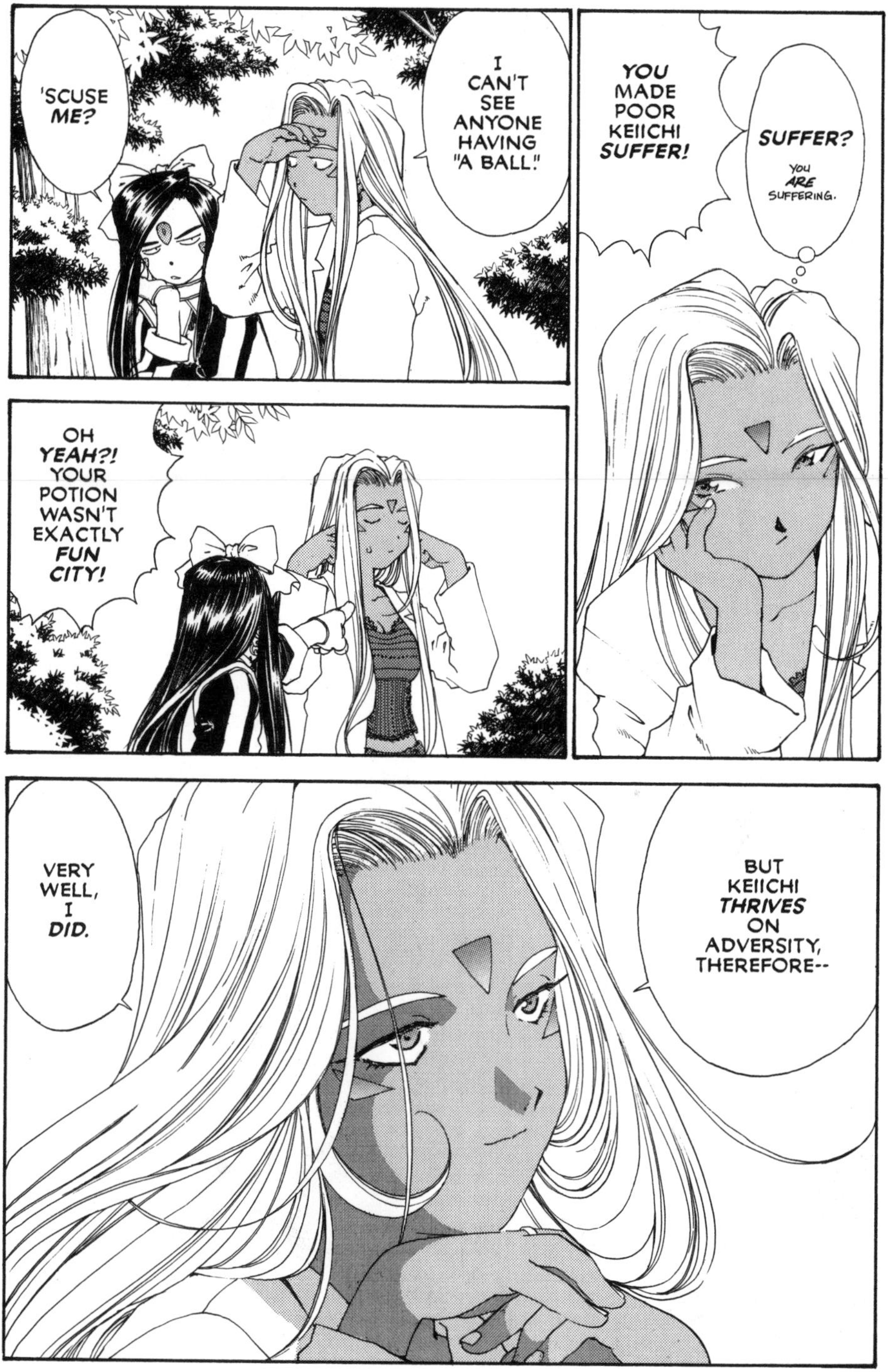
'SCUSE ME?
I CAN'T SEE ANYONE HAVING "A BALL."
OH YEAH?! YOUR POTION WASN'T EXACTLY FUN CITY!
YOU MADE POOR KEIICHI SUFFER!
SUFFER? YOU ARE SUFFERING.
VERY WELL, I DID.
BUT KEIICHI THRIVES ON ADVERSITY, THEREFORE--

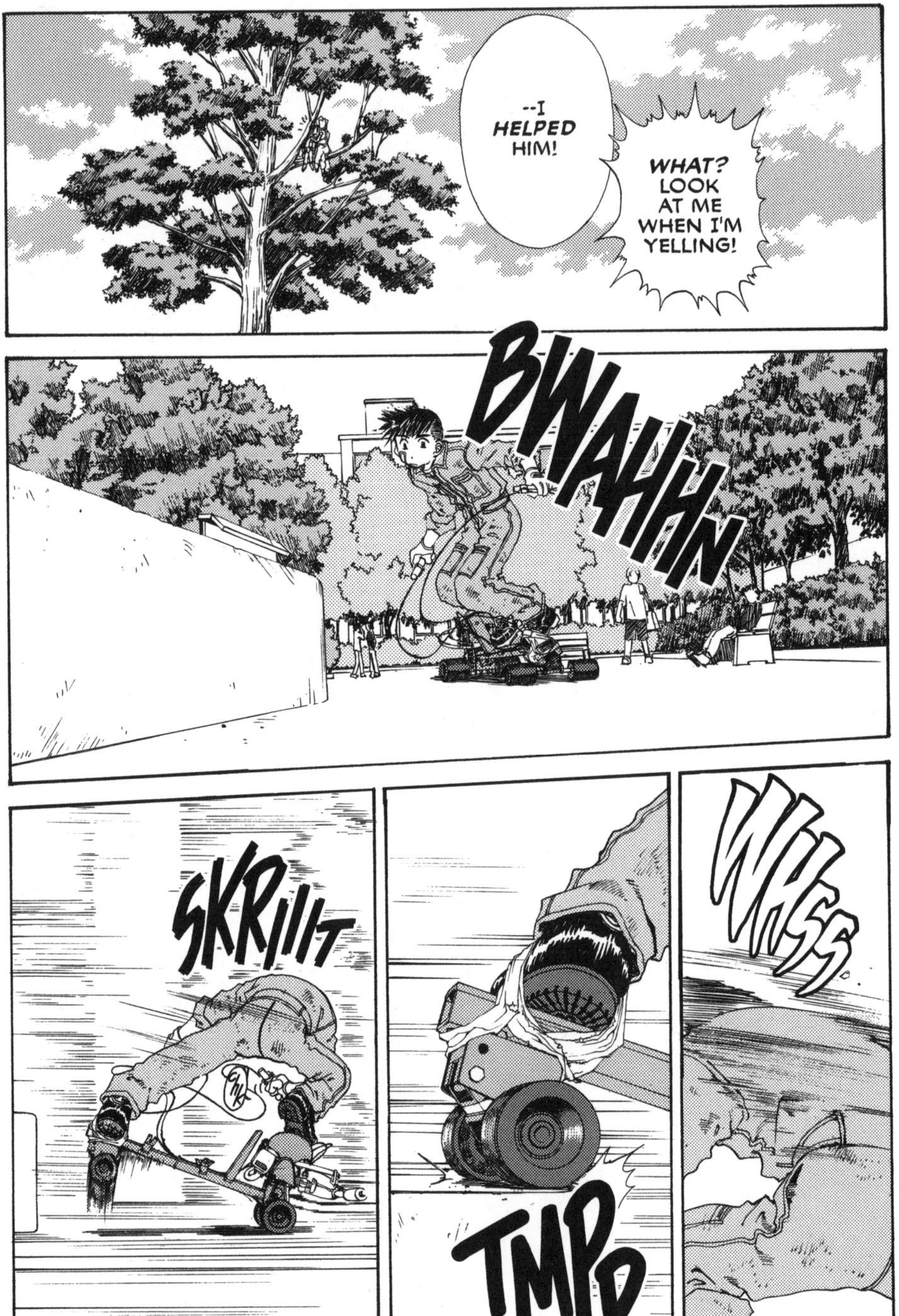
WHAT? LOOK AT ME WHEN I'M YELLING!
--I HELPED HIM!
BWAHHN
WHSSS
TMPP
SKRIIIT

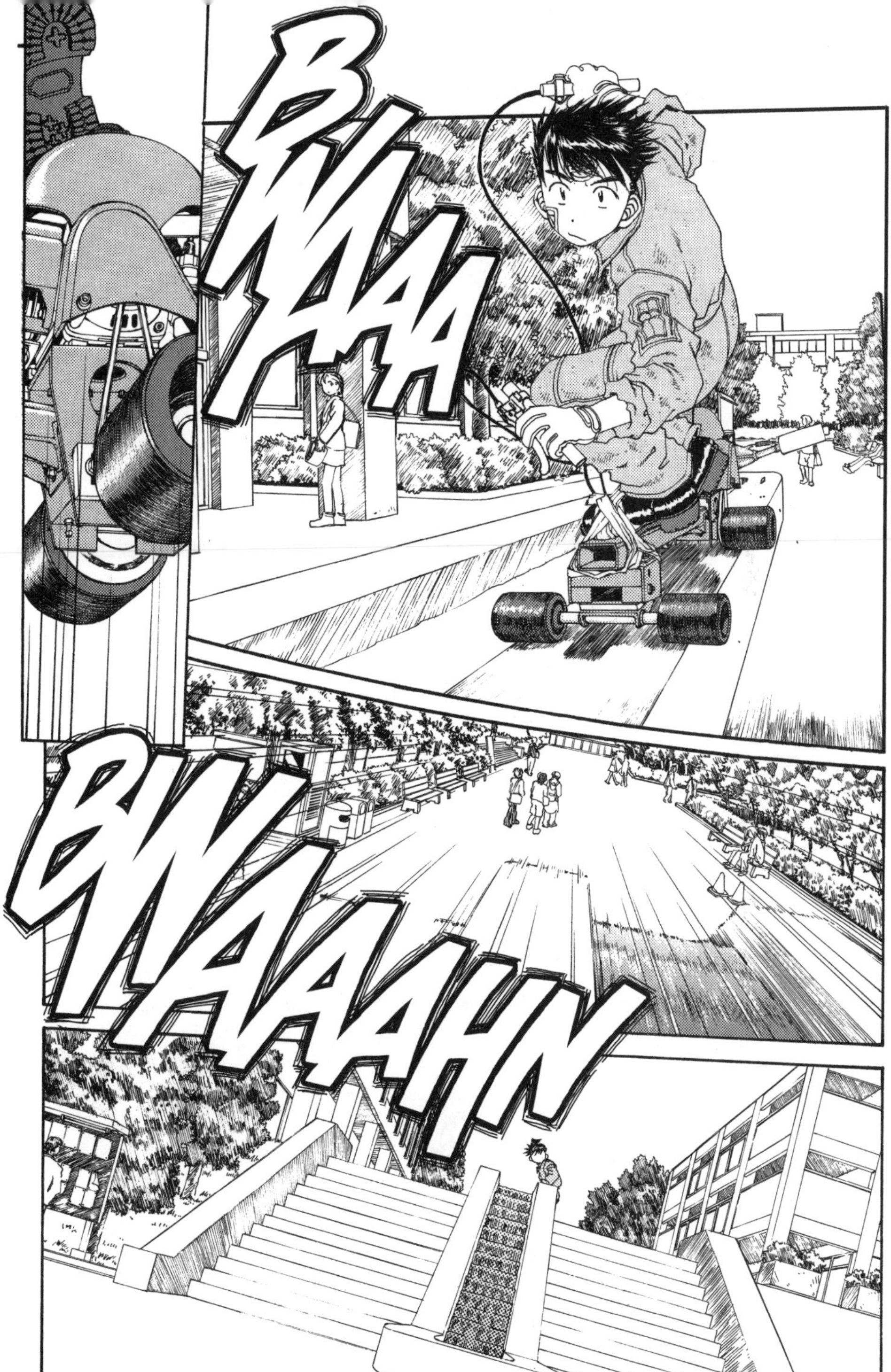
BWAAA
BWAAAAHN

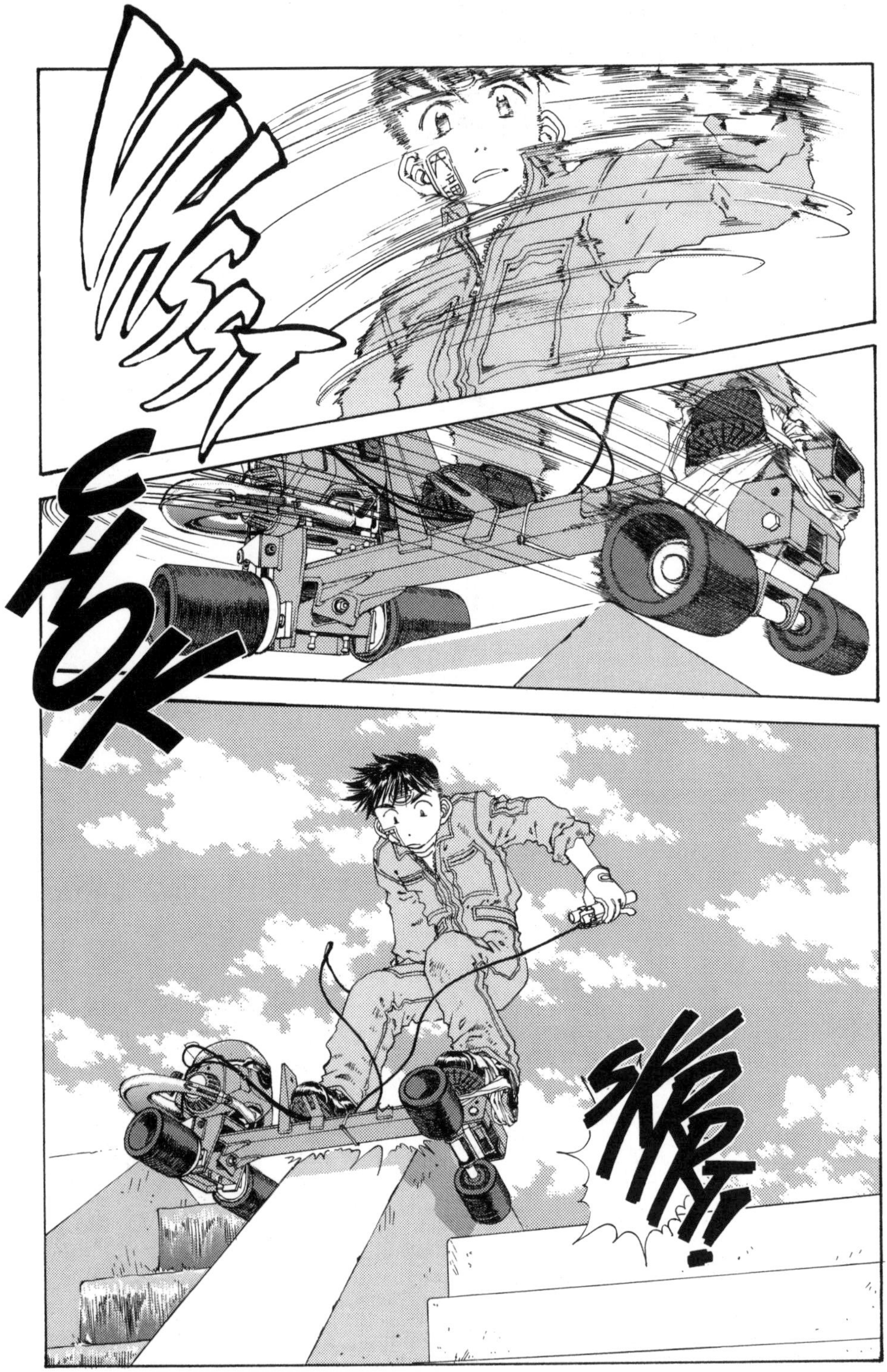
CHOK
SKRT!

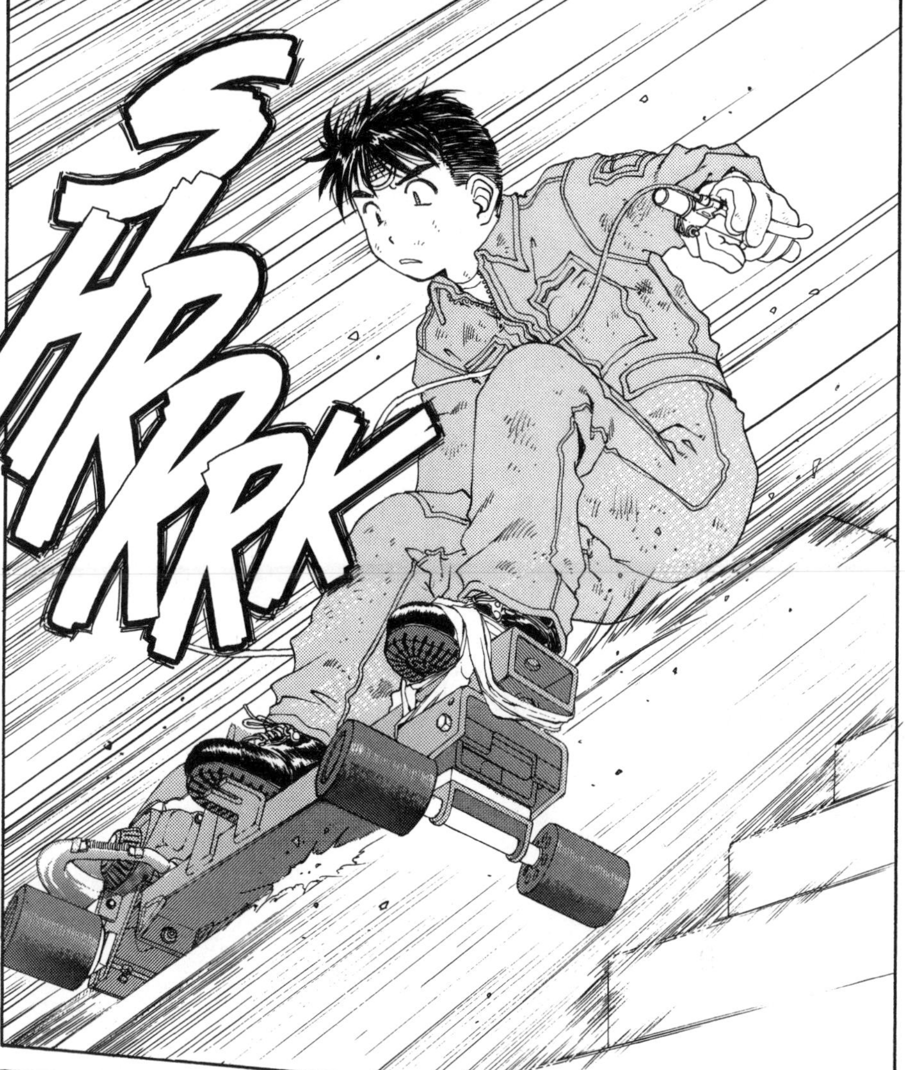
SHRRRK
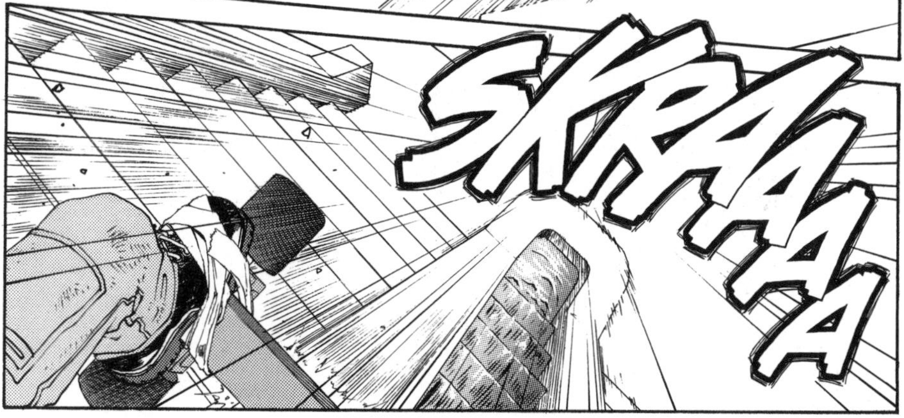
SKRAAAA

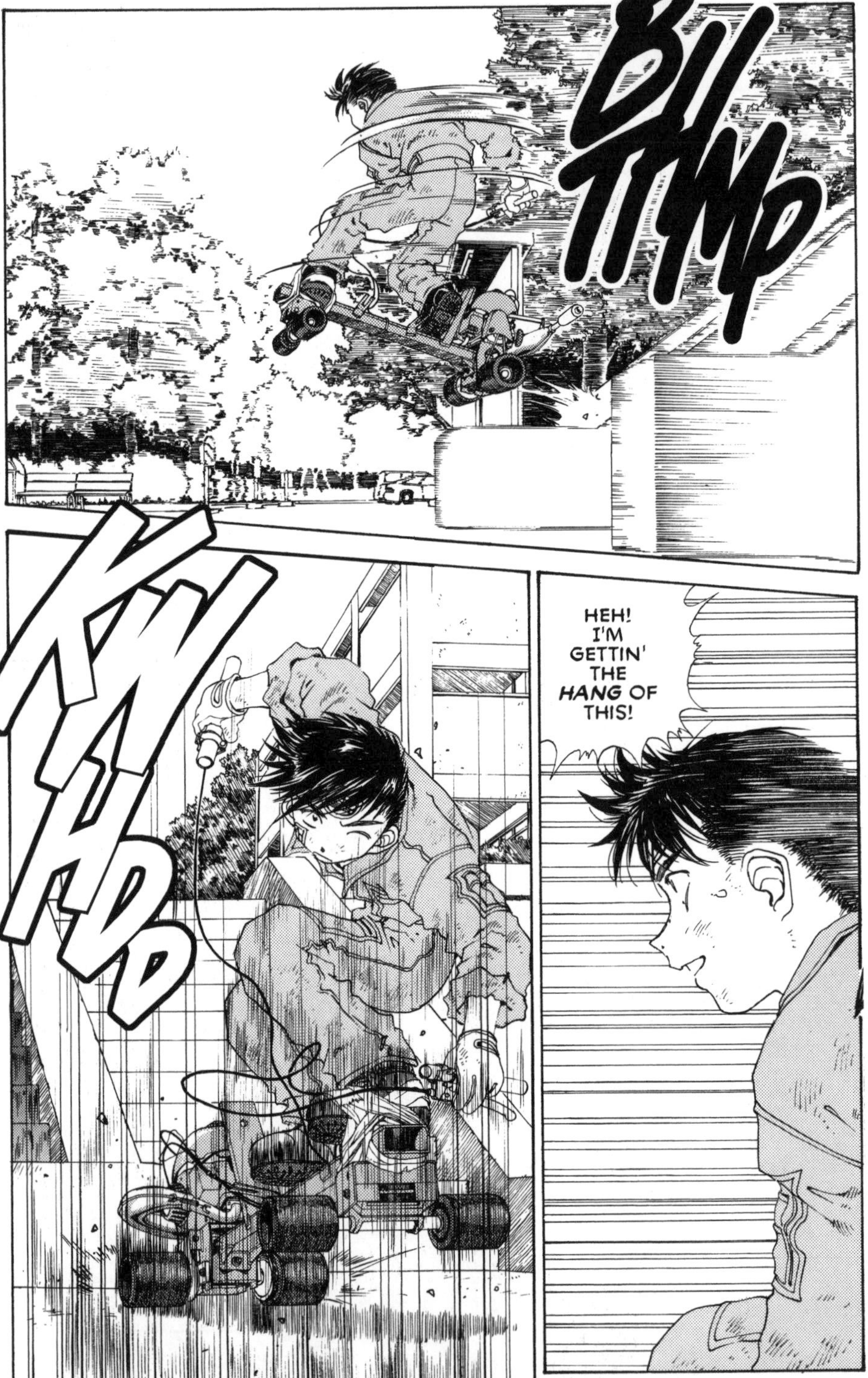
HEH! I'M GETTIN' THE *HANG* OF THIS!

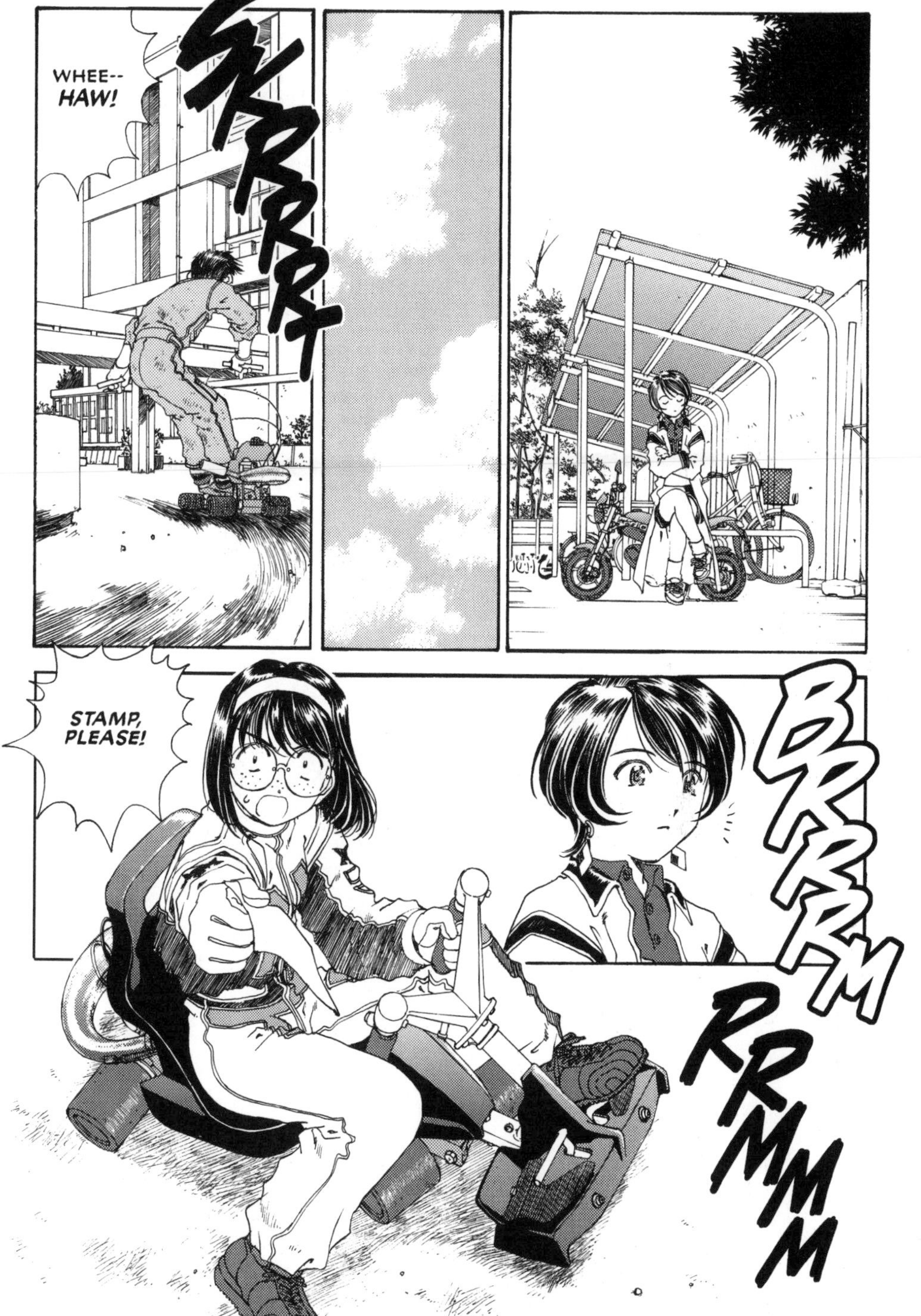
WHEE--
HAW!
SKRRRT
STAMP, PLEASE!
BRRRM
RRMMMM

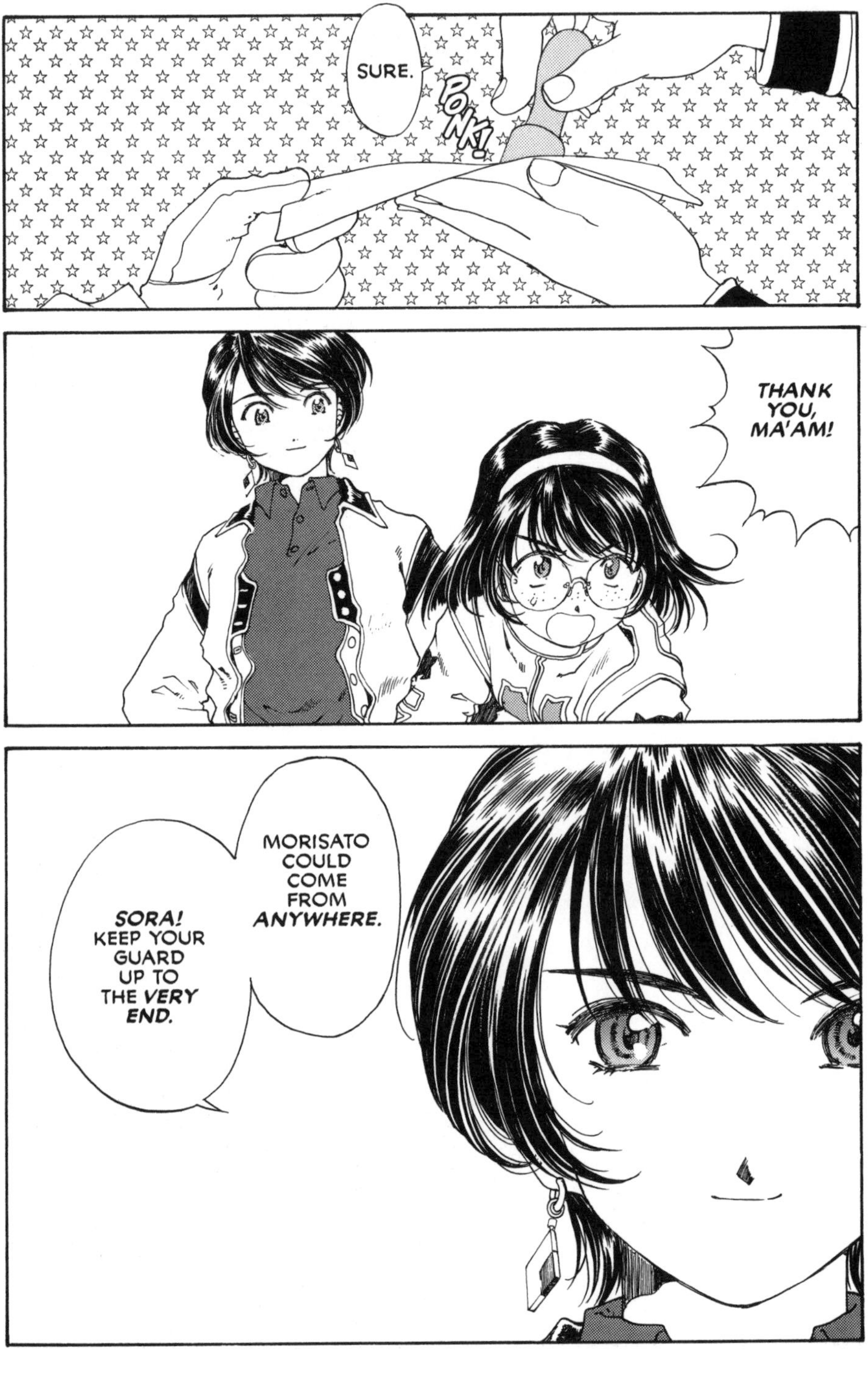
SURE.
PONK!
THANK YOU, MA'AM!
SORA! KEEP YOUR GUARD UP TO THE VERY END.
MORISATO COULD COME FROM ANYWHERE.

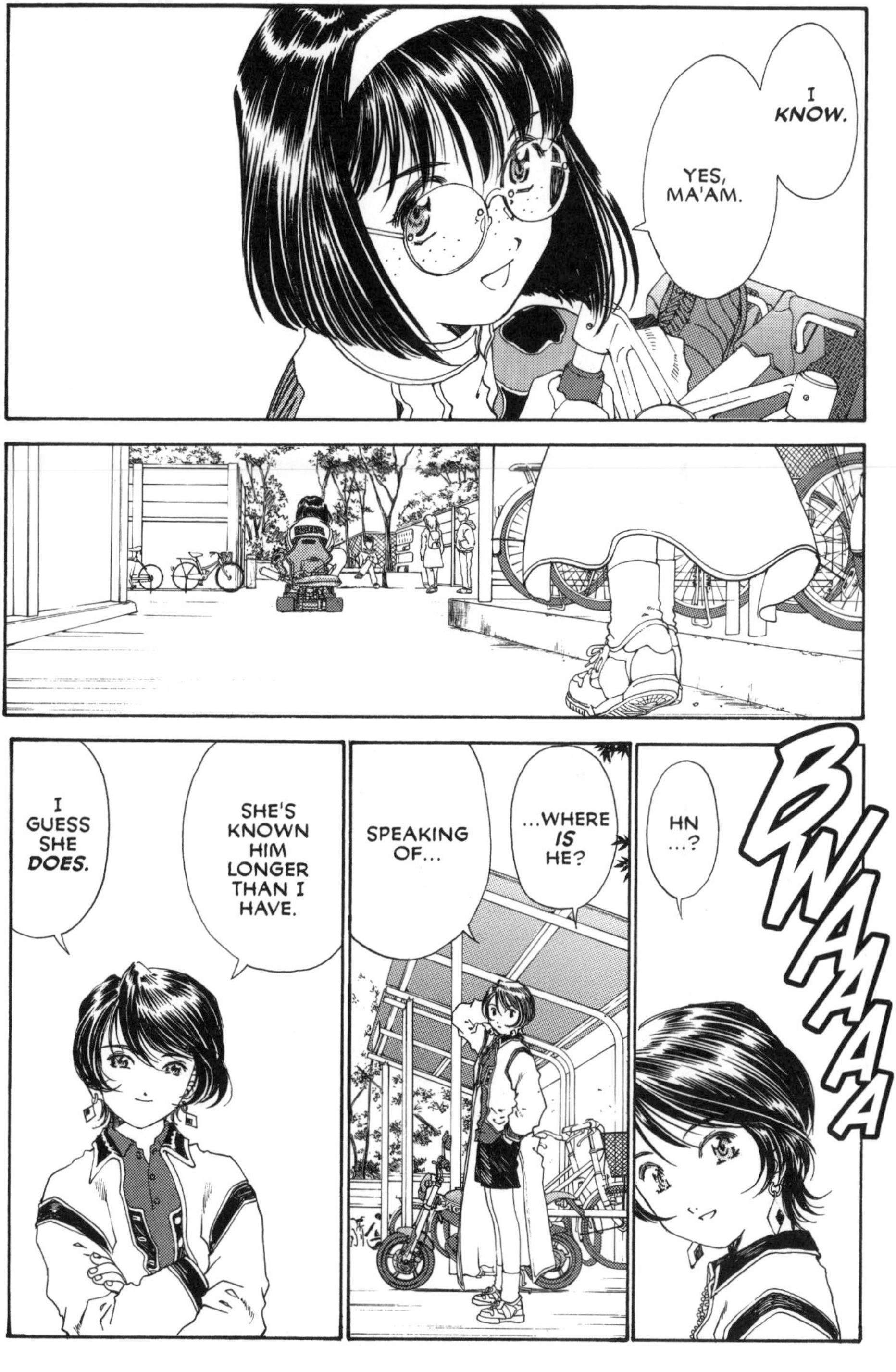
I KNOW.
YES, MA'AM.
I GUESS SHE DOES.
SHE'S KNOWN HIM LONGER THAN I HAVE.
SPEAKING OF...
...WHERE IS HE?
HN ...?
BWAAAAA

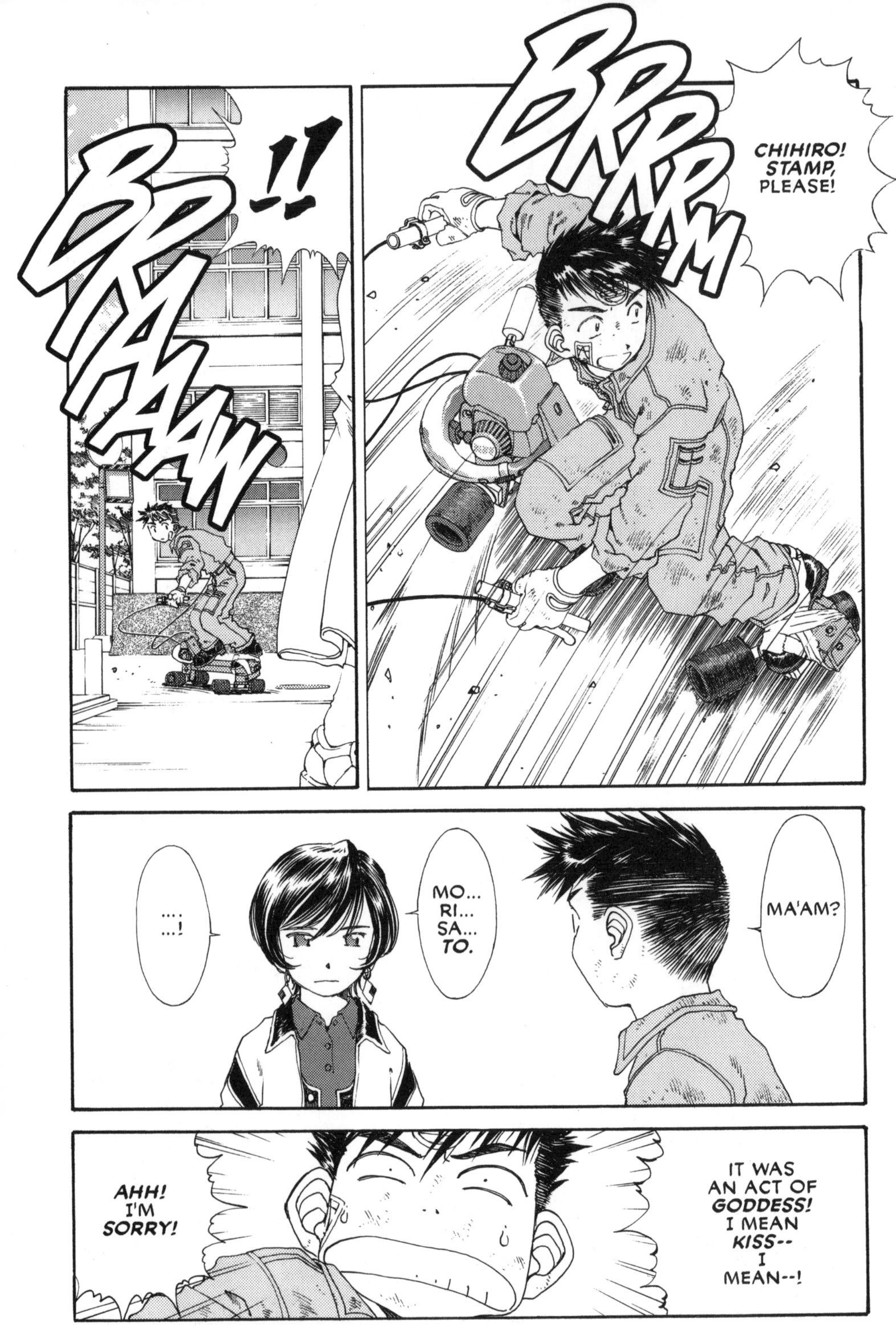
BRRRM
CHIHIRO! STAMP, PLEASE!
BRRAAAW
!!
MA'AM?
MO... RI... SA... TO.
....!
IT WAS AN ACT OF GODDESS! I MEAN KISS-- I MEAN--!
AHH! I'M SORRY!

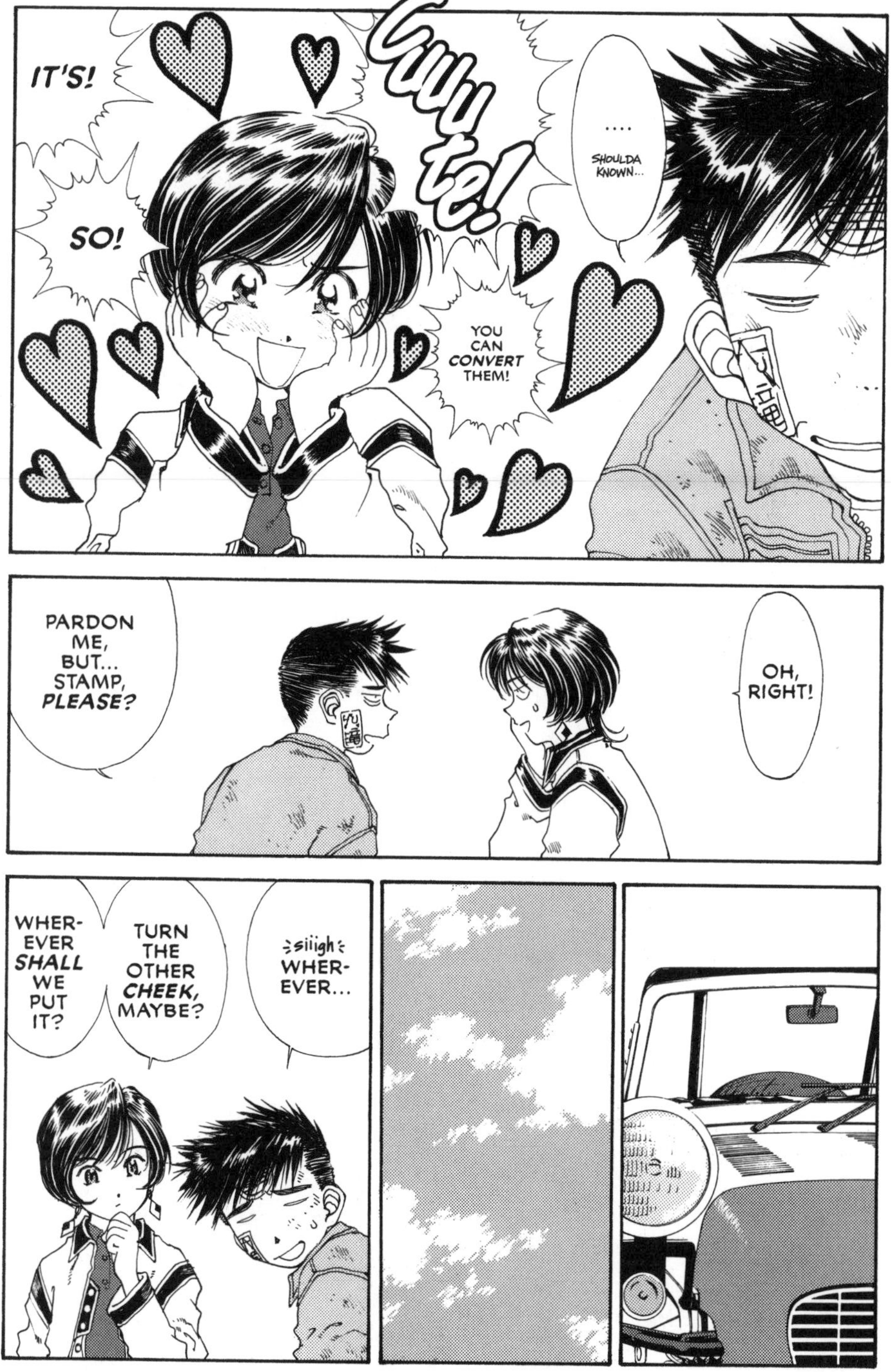
IT'S!
SO!
Cuuute!
YOU CAN CONVERT THEM!
.... SHOULDA KNOWN...
PARDON ME, BUT... STAMP, PLEASE?
OH, RIGHT!
siiigh WHEREVER...
TURN THE OTHER CHEEK, MAYBE?
WHEREVER SHALL WE PUT IT?

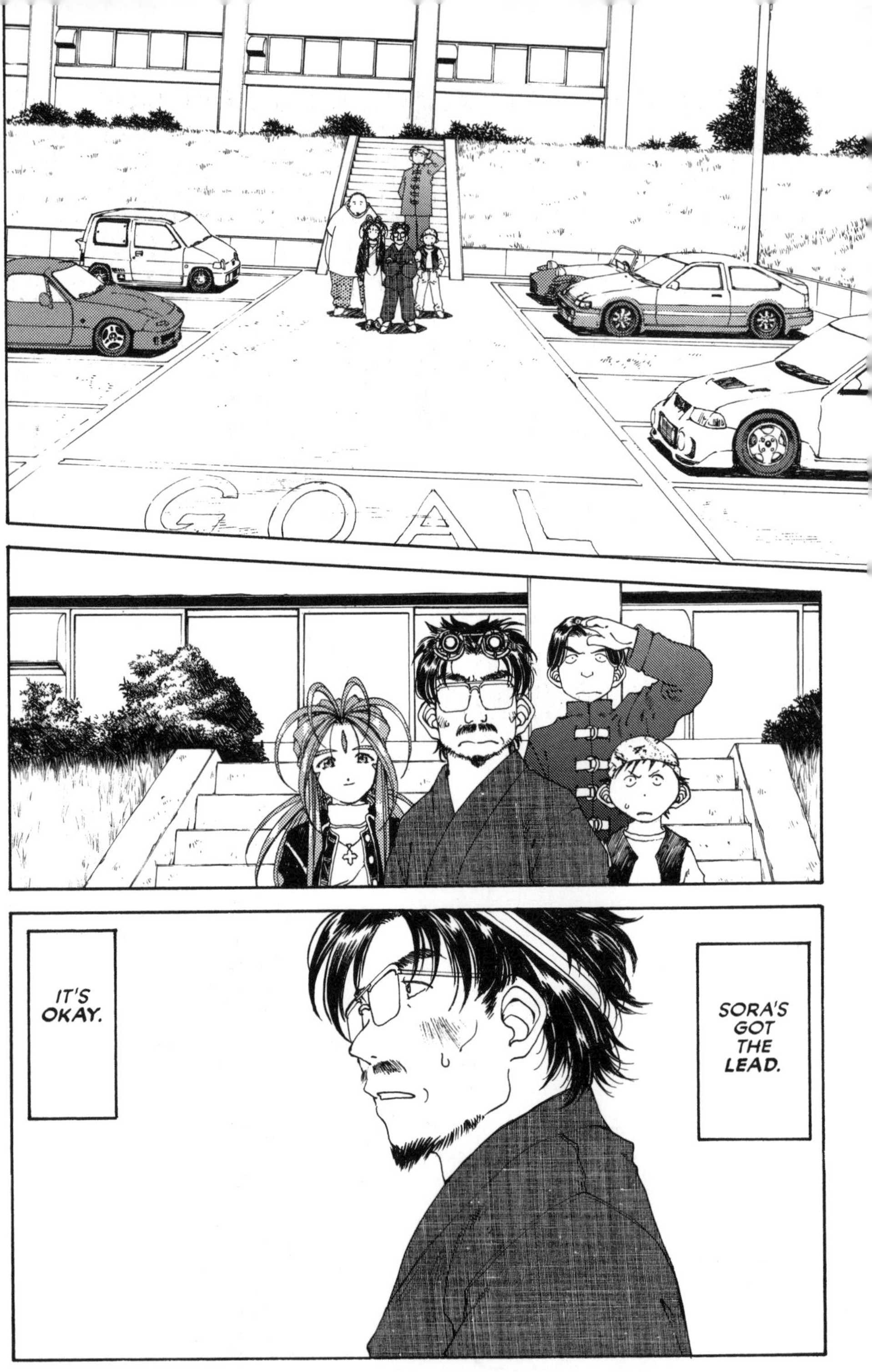
GOAL
SORA'S GOT THE LEAD.
IT'S OKAY.

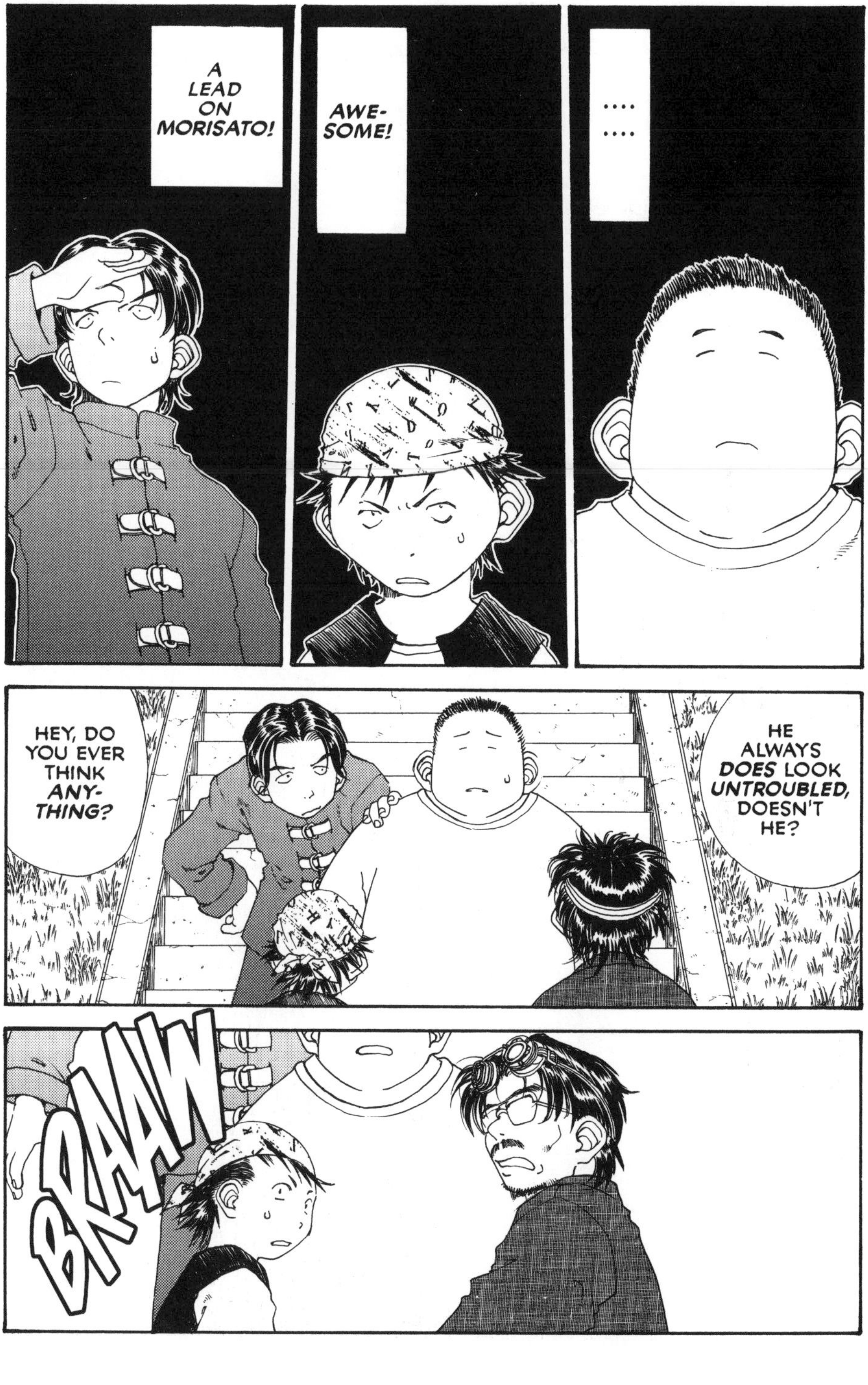
A LEAD ON MORISATO!
AWE-SOME!
....
....
HEY, DO YOU EVER THINK ANY-THING?
HE ALWAYS *DOES* LOOK *UNTROUBLED,* DOESN'T HE?
BRAAAW

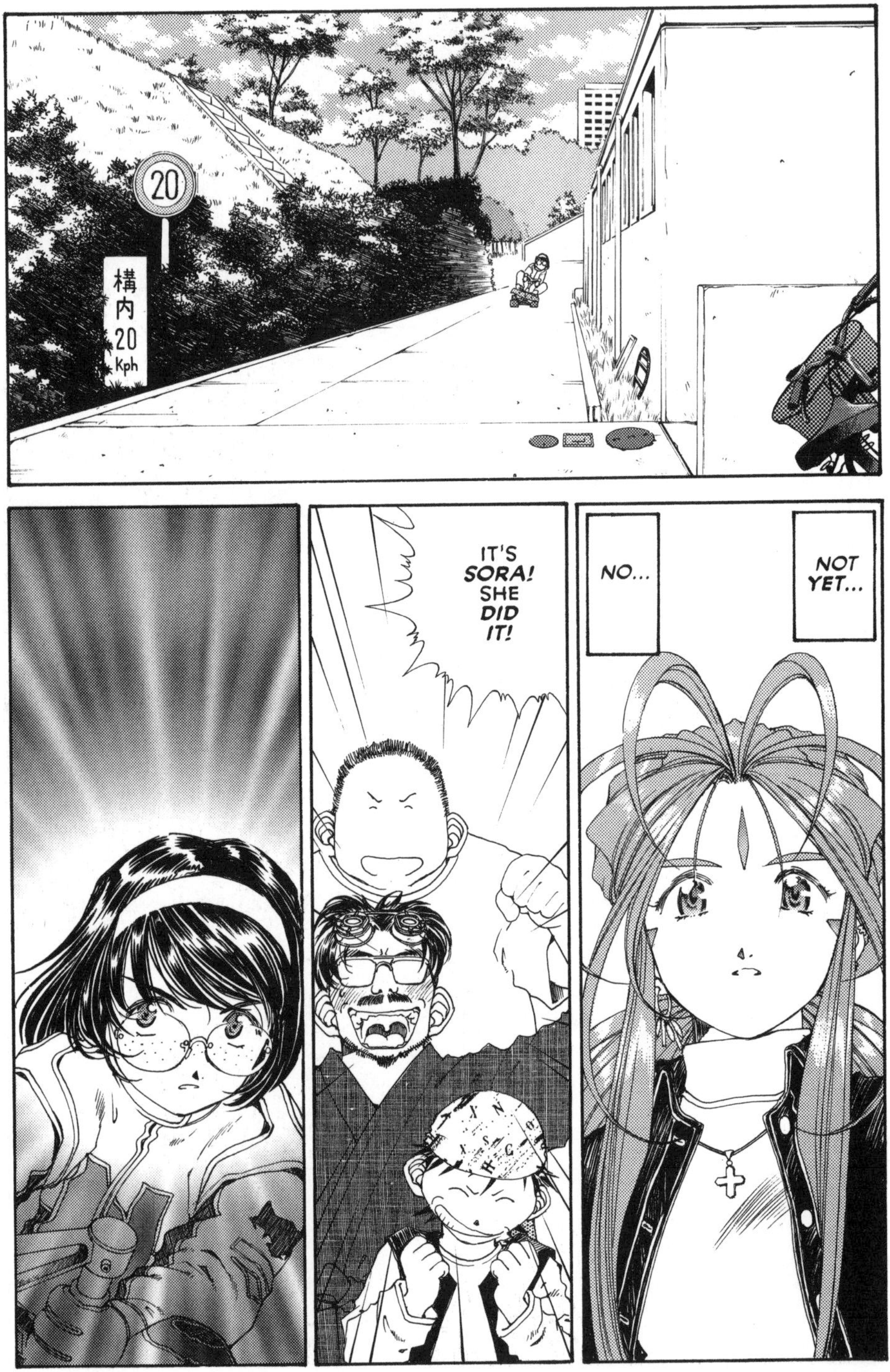
20
構内 20 Kph
NOT YET...
NO...
IT'S SORA! SHE DID IT!

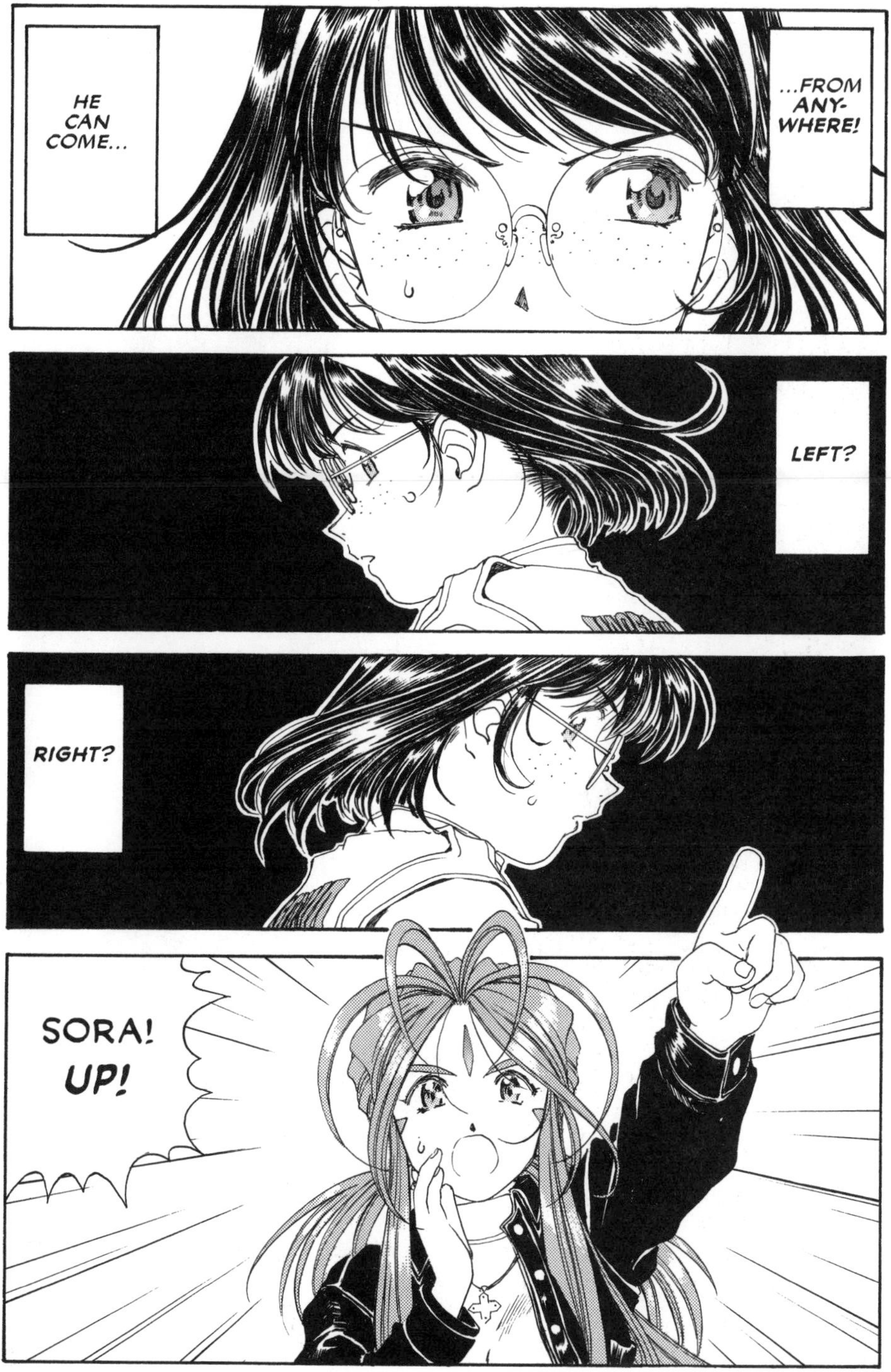
HE CAN COME...
...FROM ANY-WHERE!
LEFT?
RIGHT?
SORA! UP!

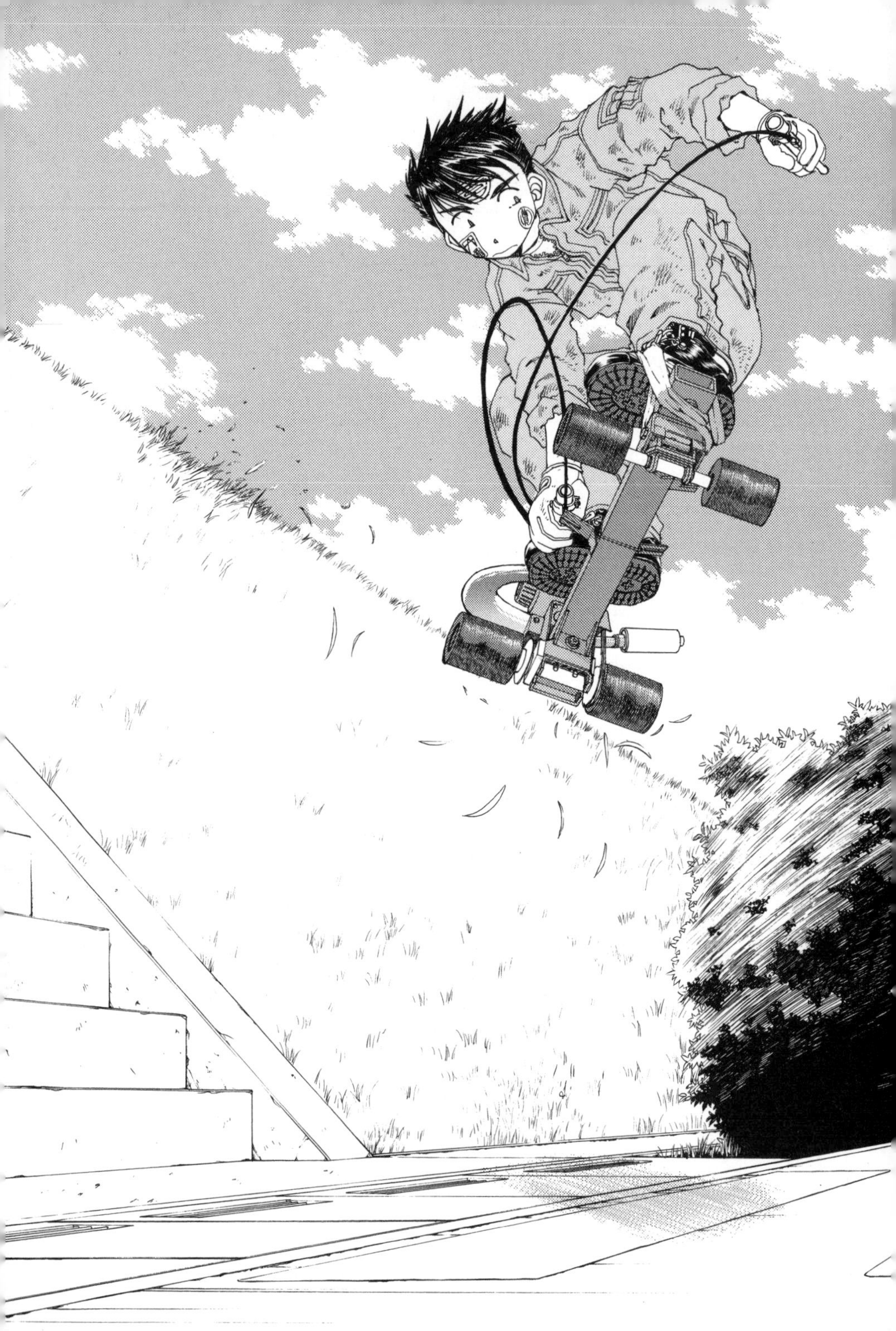

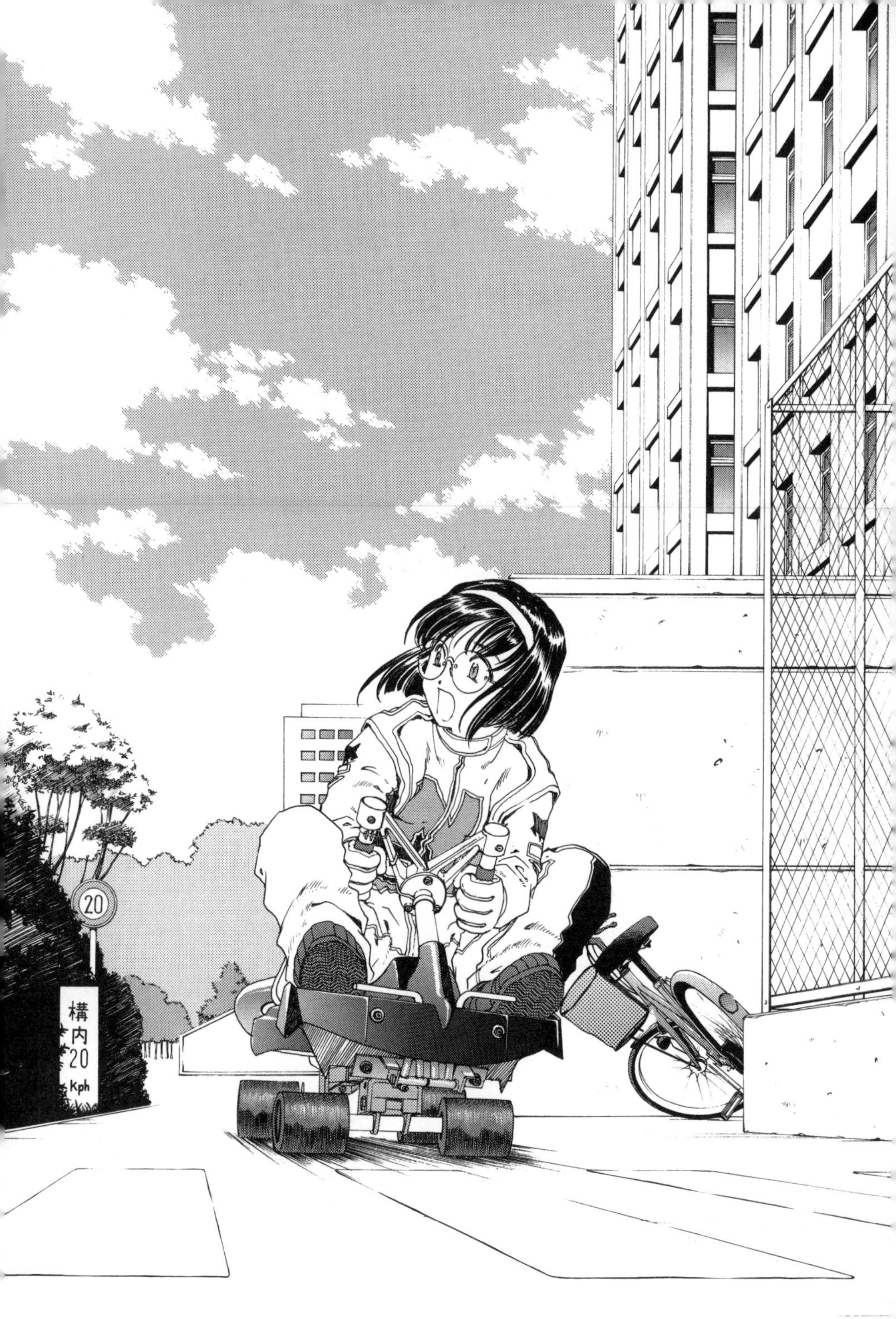
20
構内
20
Kph

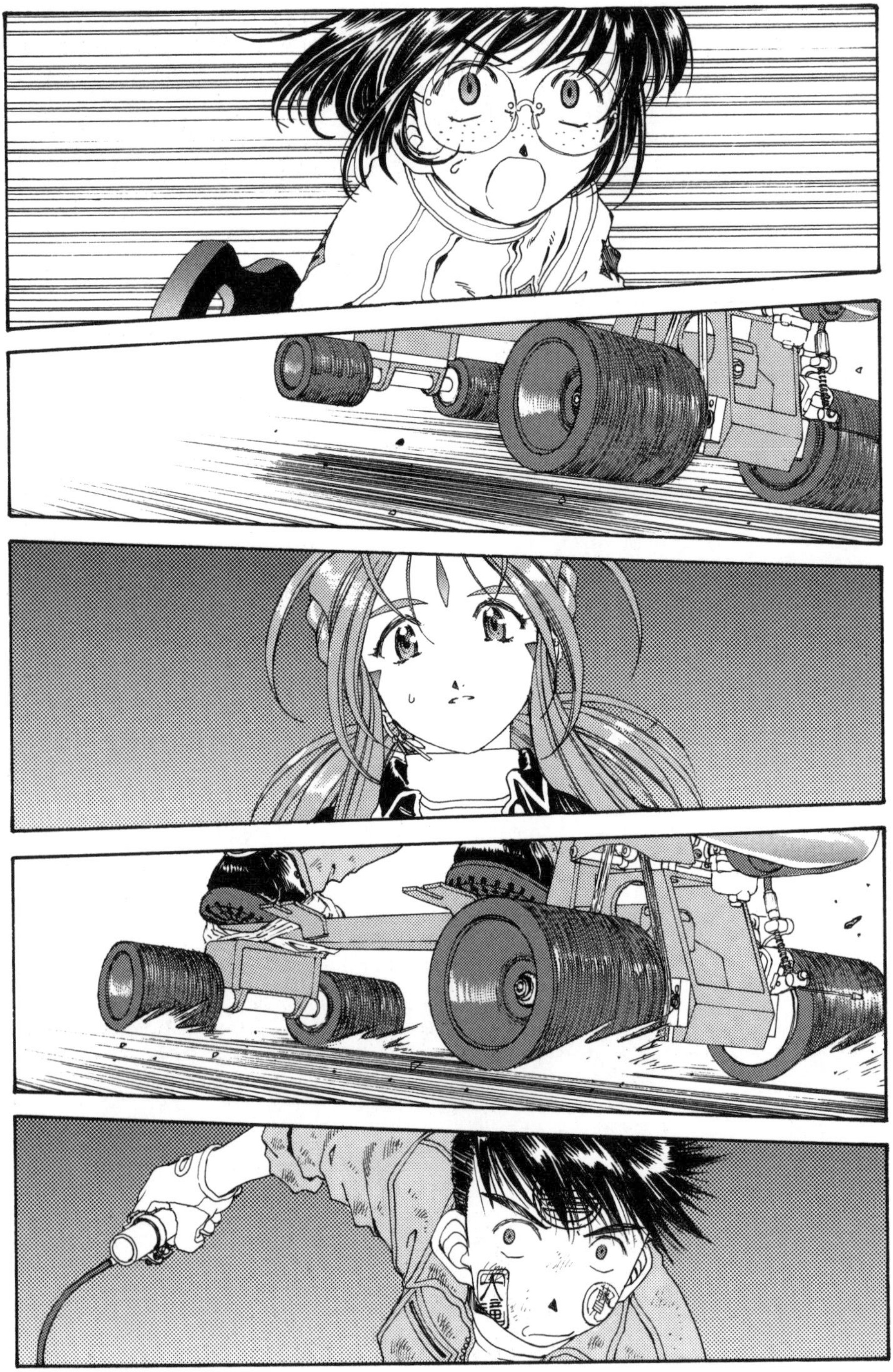

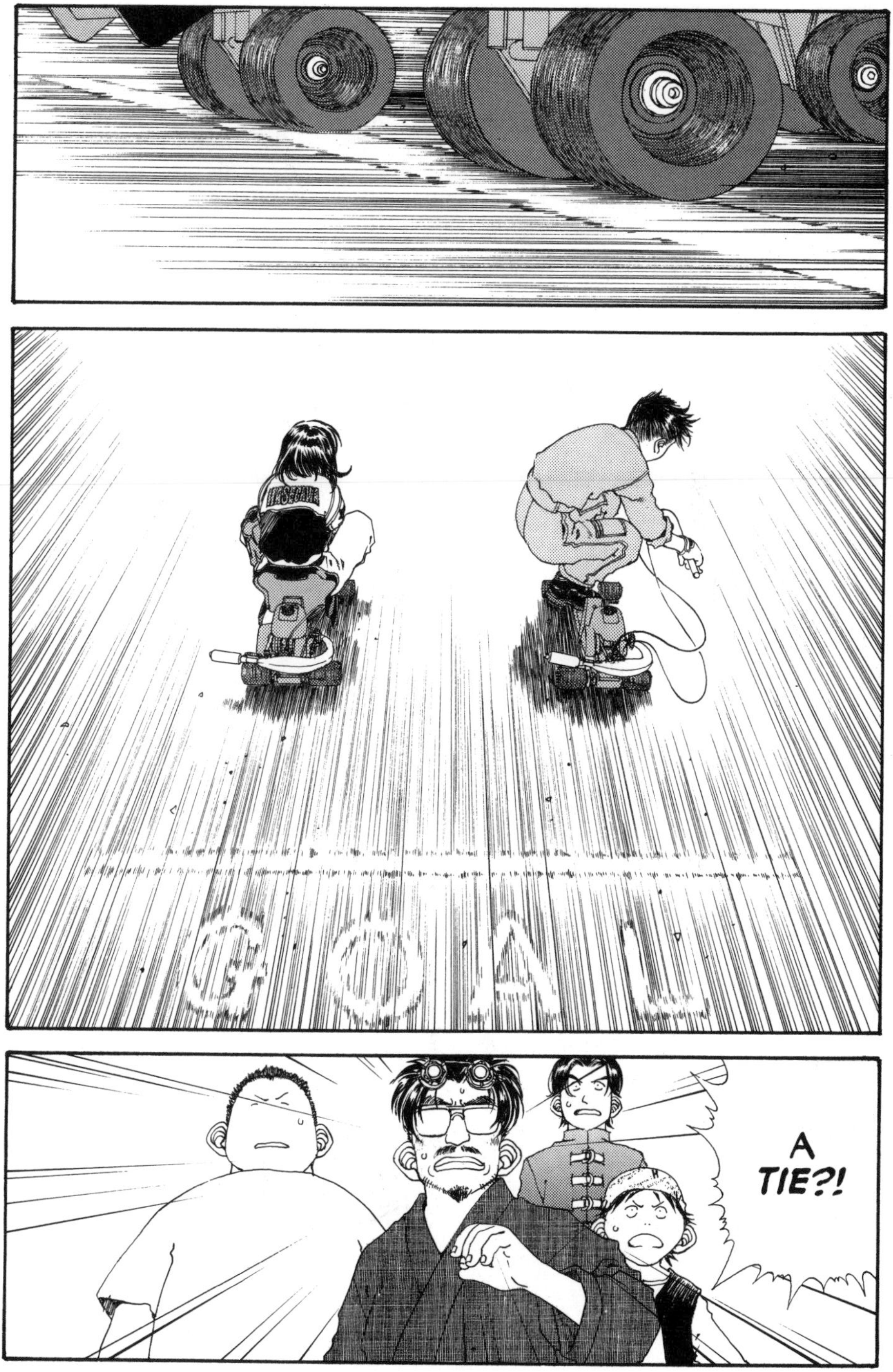
GOAL
A TIE?!

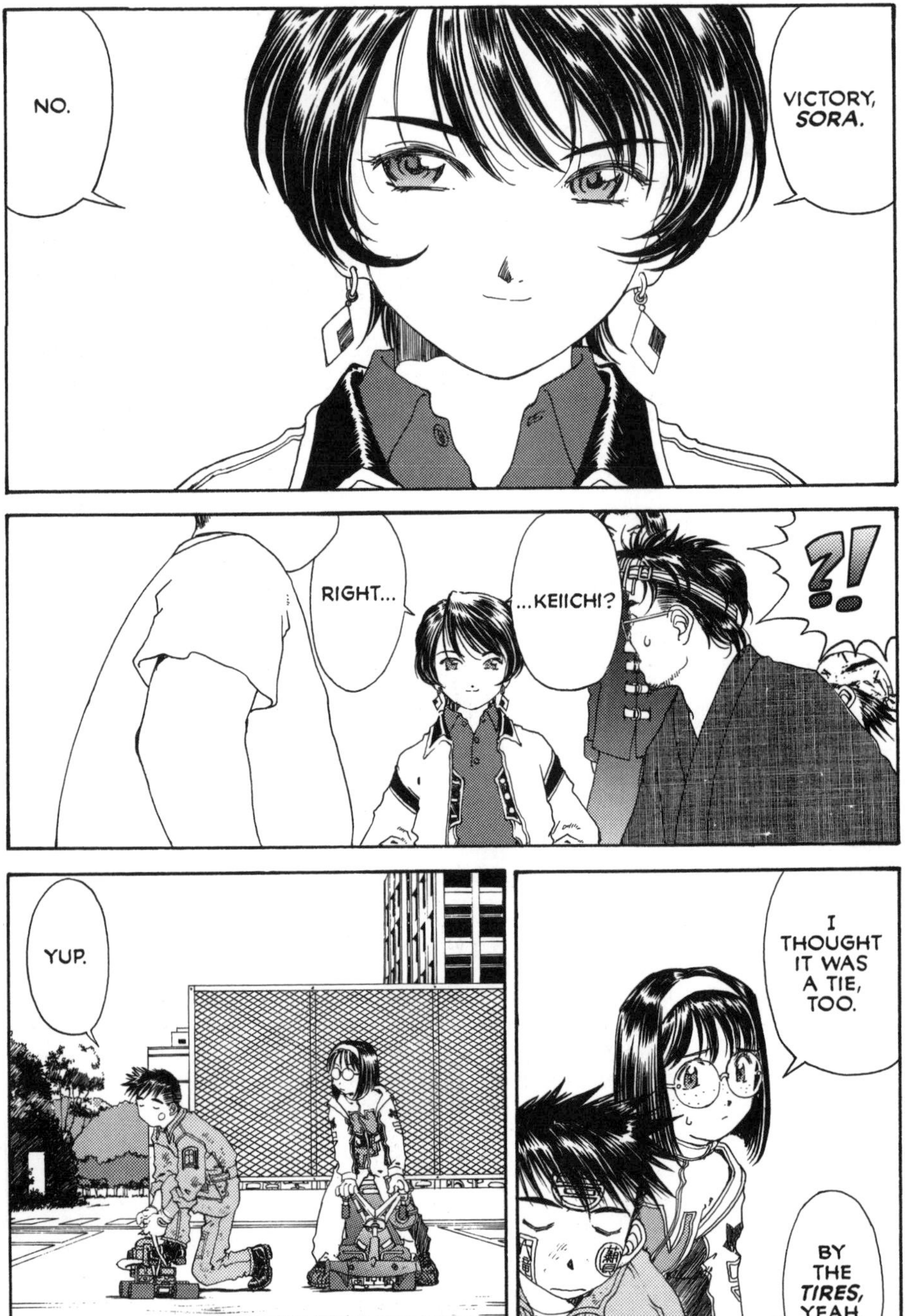
VICTORY, *SORA.*
NO.
?!
...KEIICHI?
RIGHT...
I THOUGHT IT WAS A TIE, TOO.
BY THE *TIRES,* YEAH.
YUP.

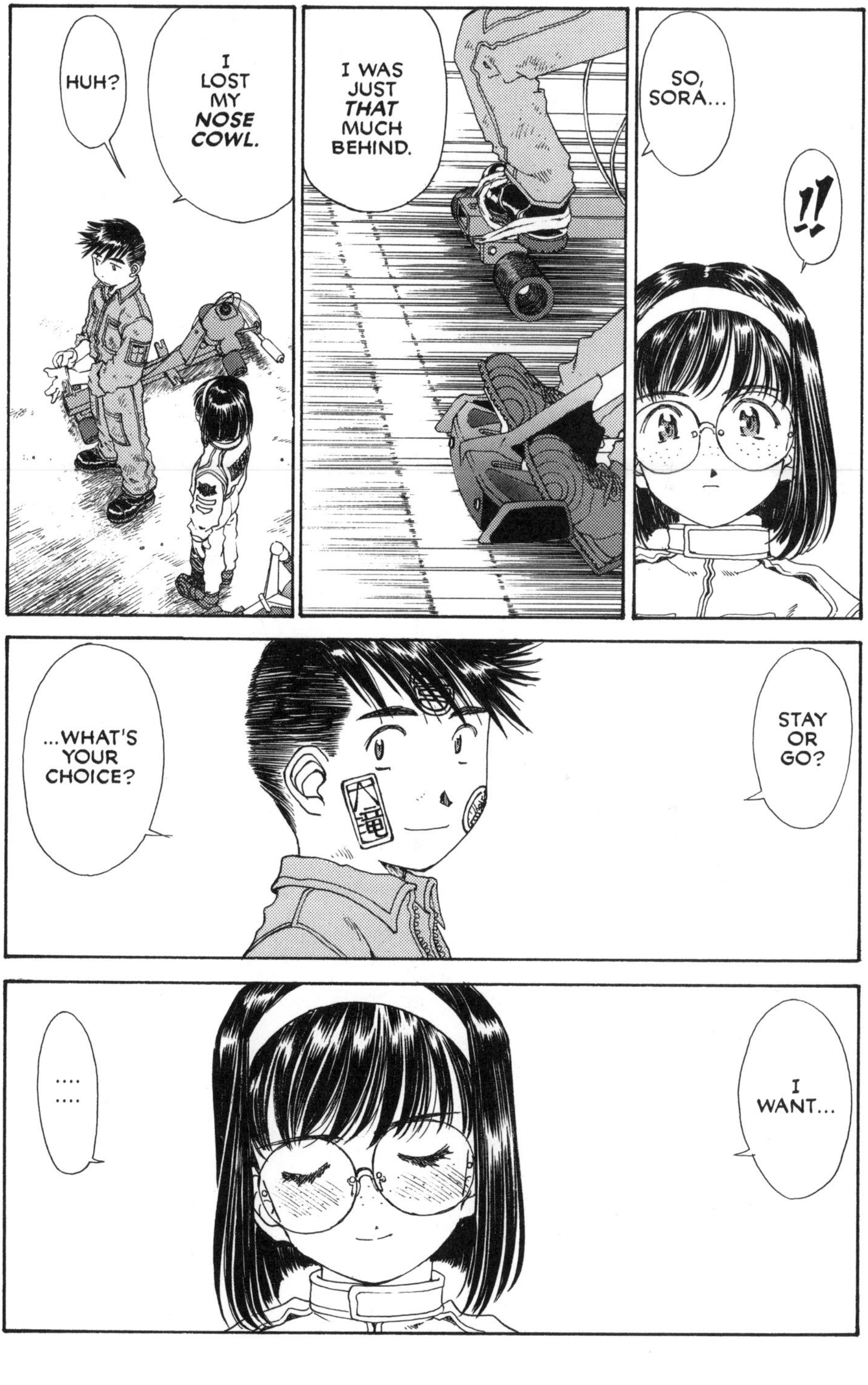
SO, SORA...
!!
I WAS JUST THAT MUCH BEHIND.
I LOST MY NOSE COWL.
HUH?
STAY OR GO?
...WHAT'S YOUR CHOICE?
I WANT...
....

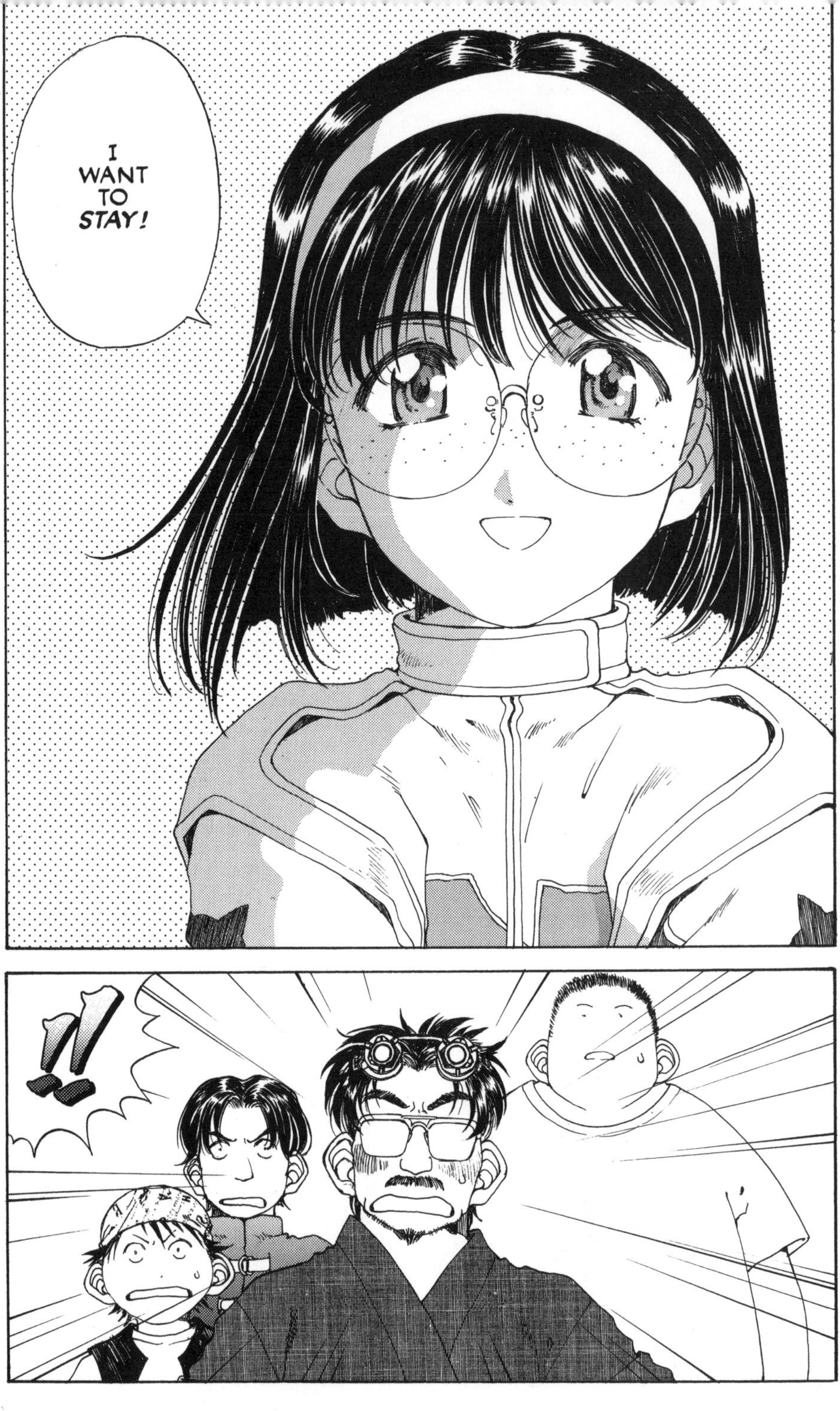
I WANT TO STAY!
!!

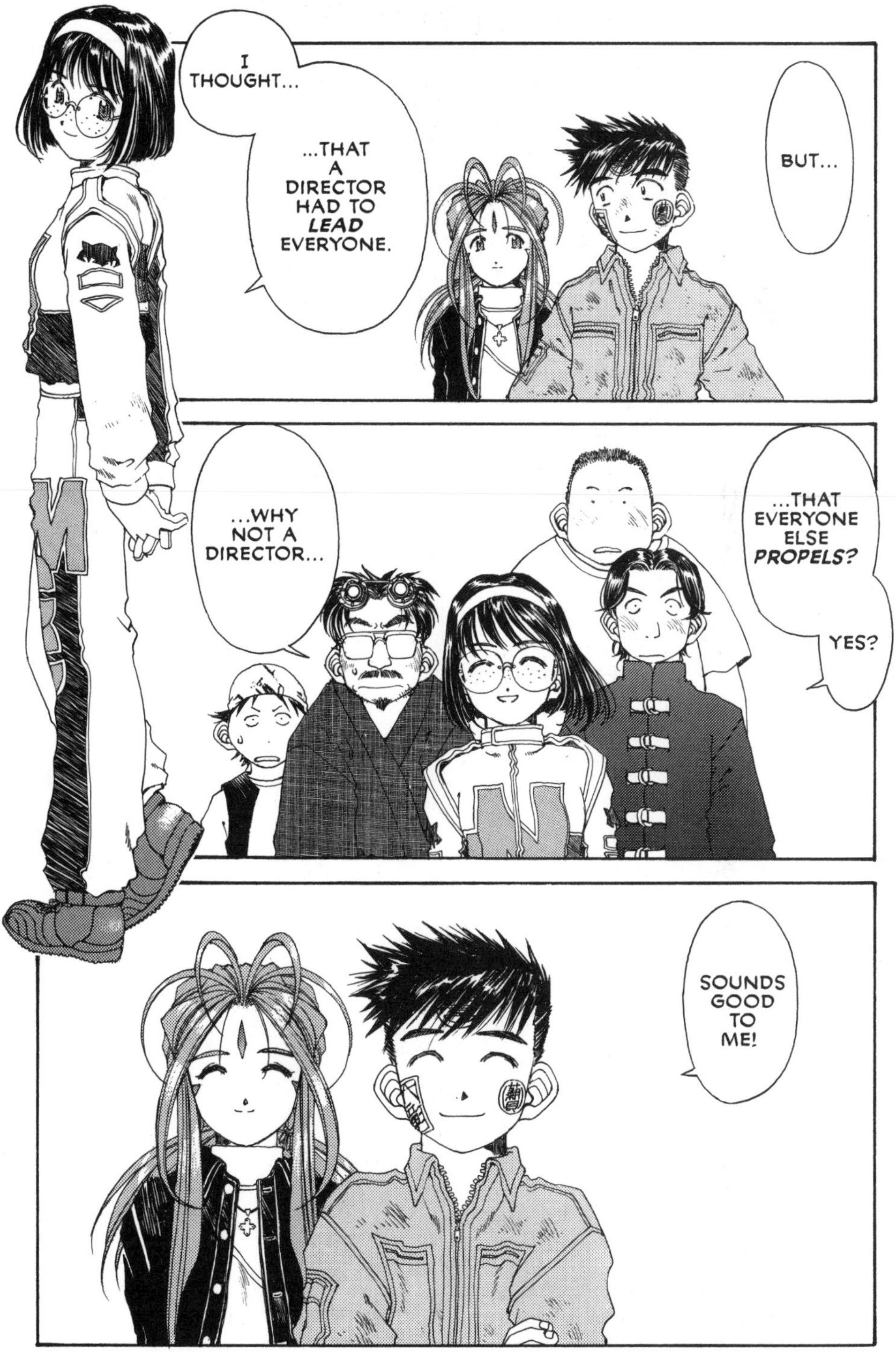
I THOUGHT...
...THAT A DIRECTOR HAD TO *LEAD* EVERYONE.
BUT...
...WHY NOT A DIRECTOR...
...THAT EVERYONE ELSE ***PROPELS?***
YES?
SOUNDS GOOD TO ME!

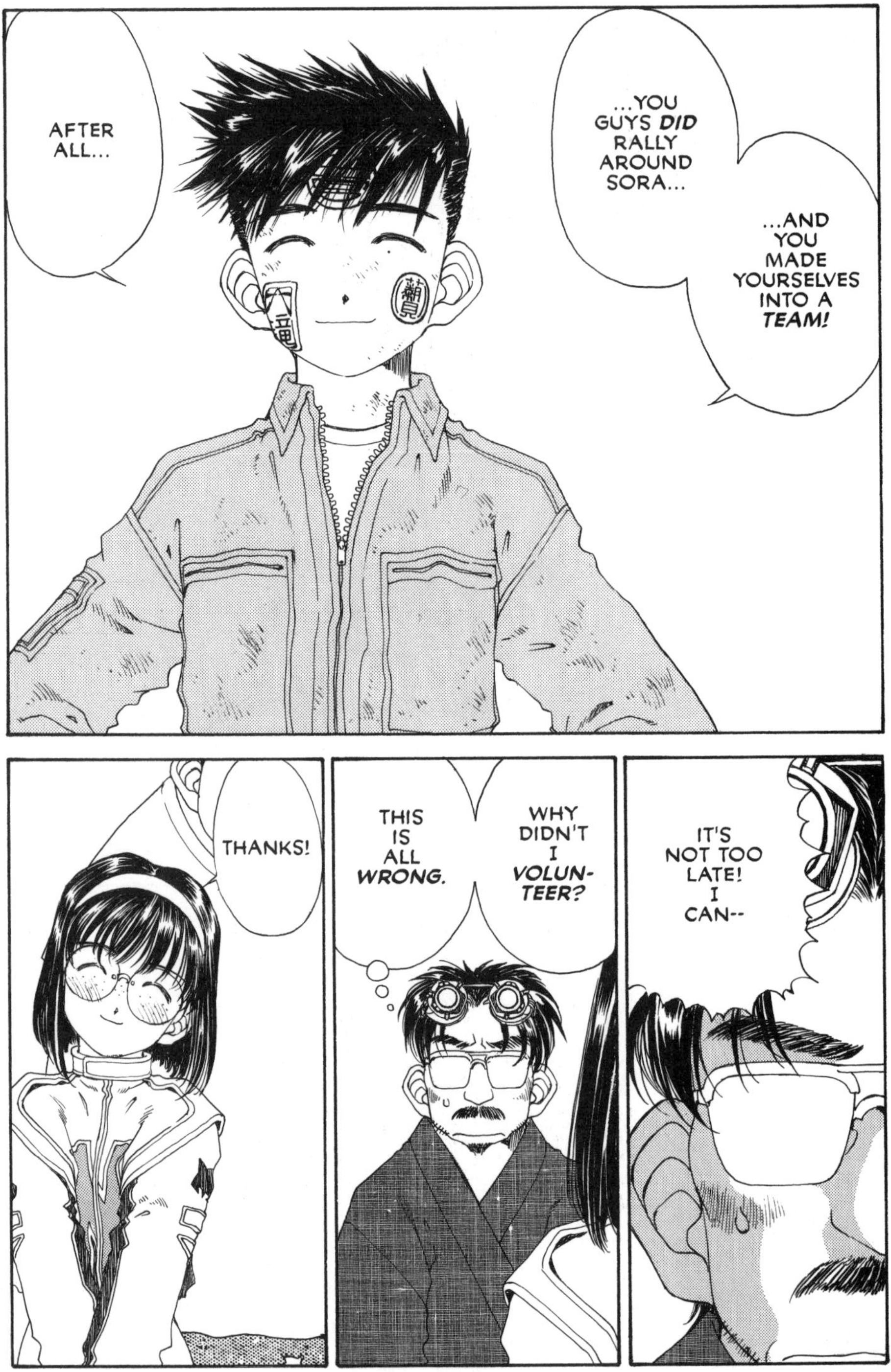
...YOU GUYS *DID* RALLY AROUND SORA...
...AND YOU MADE YOURSELVES INTO A *TEAM!*
AFTER ALL...
IT'S NOT TOO LATE! I CAN--
WHY DIDN'T I *VOLUNTEER?*
THIS IS ALL *WRONG.*
THANKS!

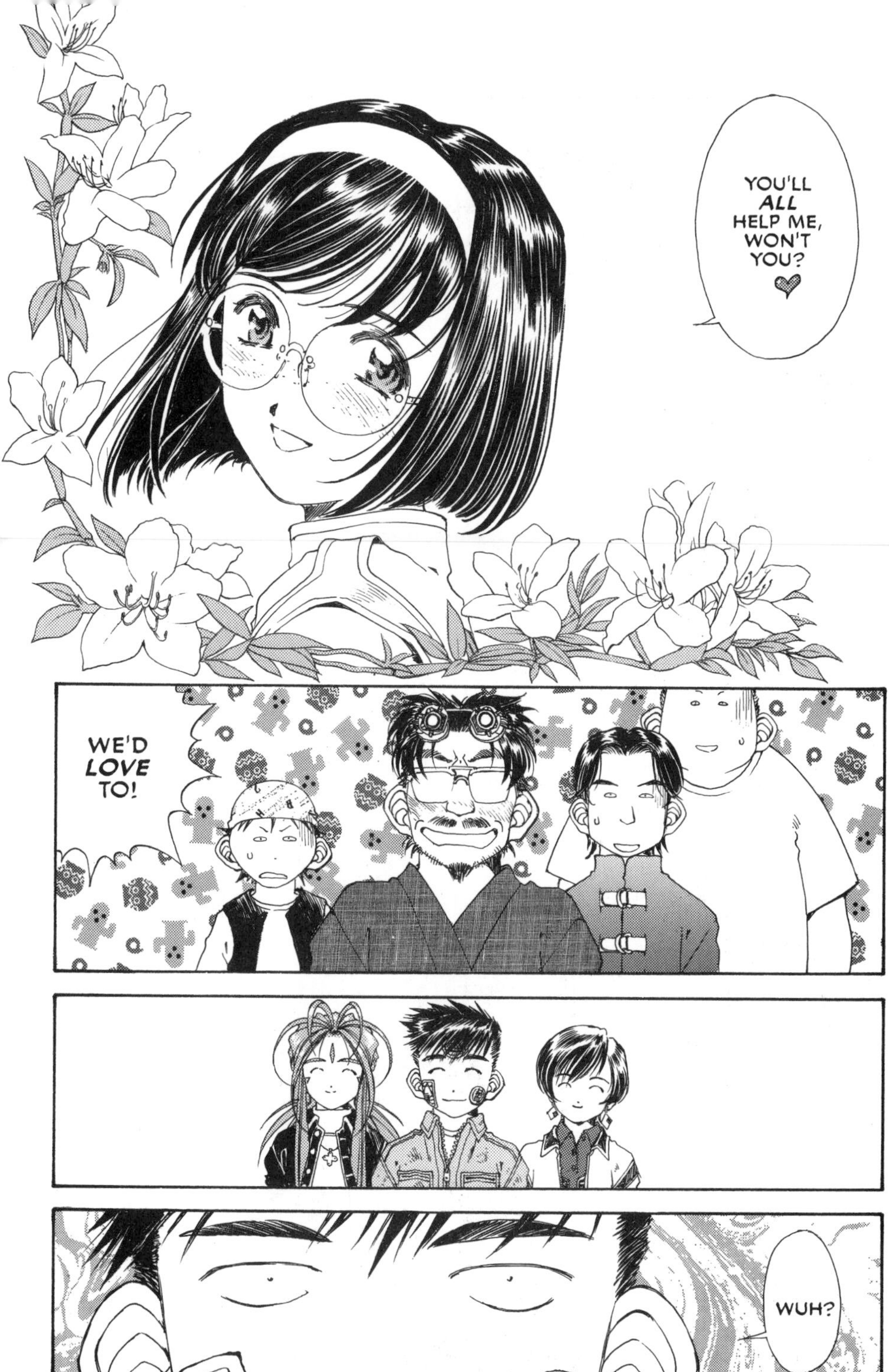
YOU'LL ALL HELP ME, WON'T YOU? ♥
WE'D LOVE TO!
WUH?

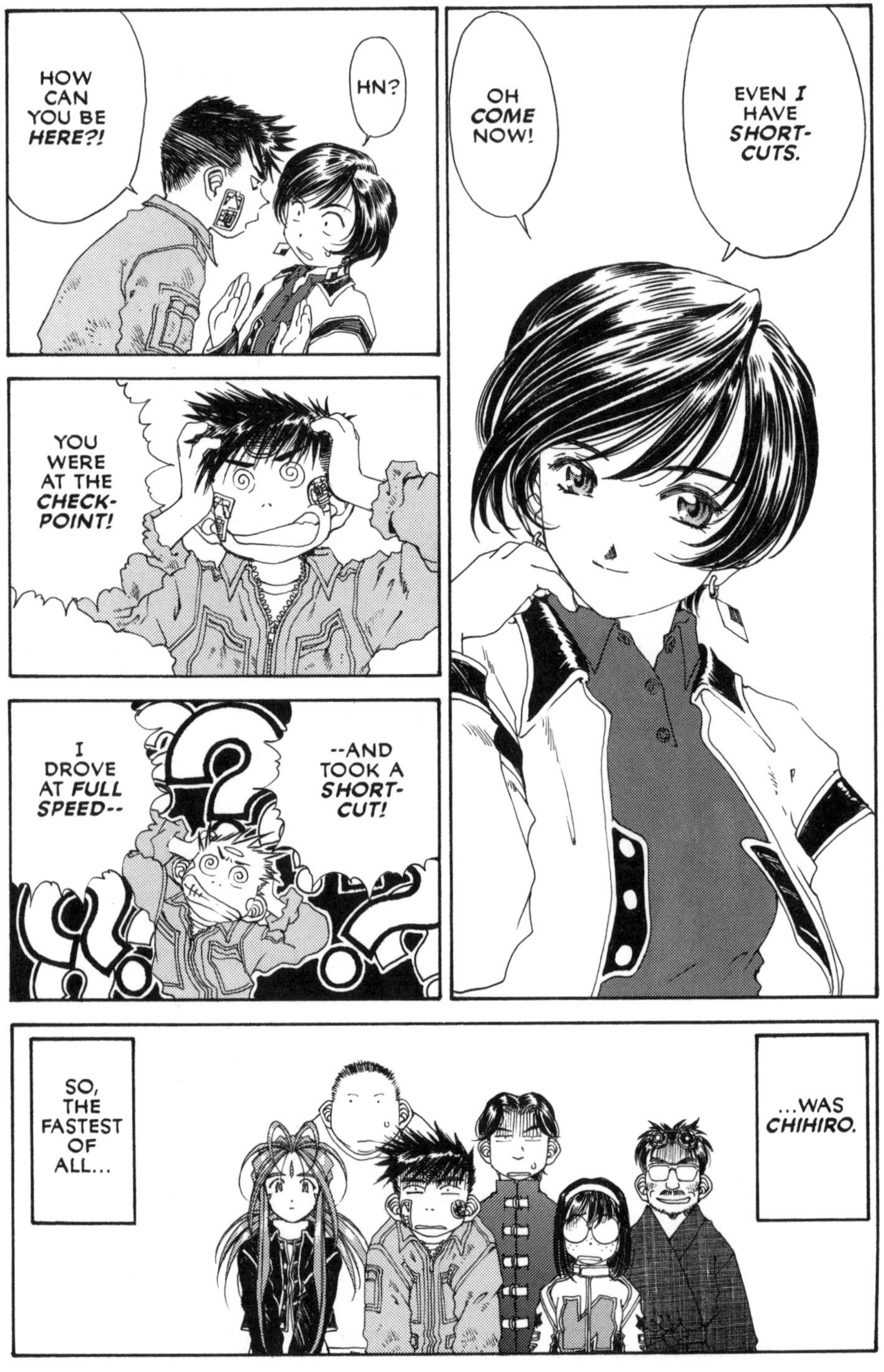
HOW CAN YOU BE *HERE?!*
HN?
YOU WERE AT THE *CHECK-POINT!*
I DROVE AT *FULL SPEED--*
--AND TOOK A *SHORT-CUT!*
OH *COME* NOW!
EVEN *I* HAVE *SHORT-CUTS.*
SO, THE FASTEST OF ALL...
...WAS *CHIHIRO.*

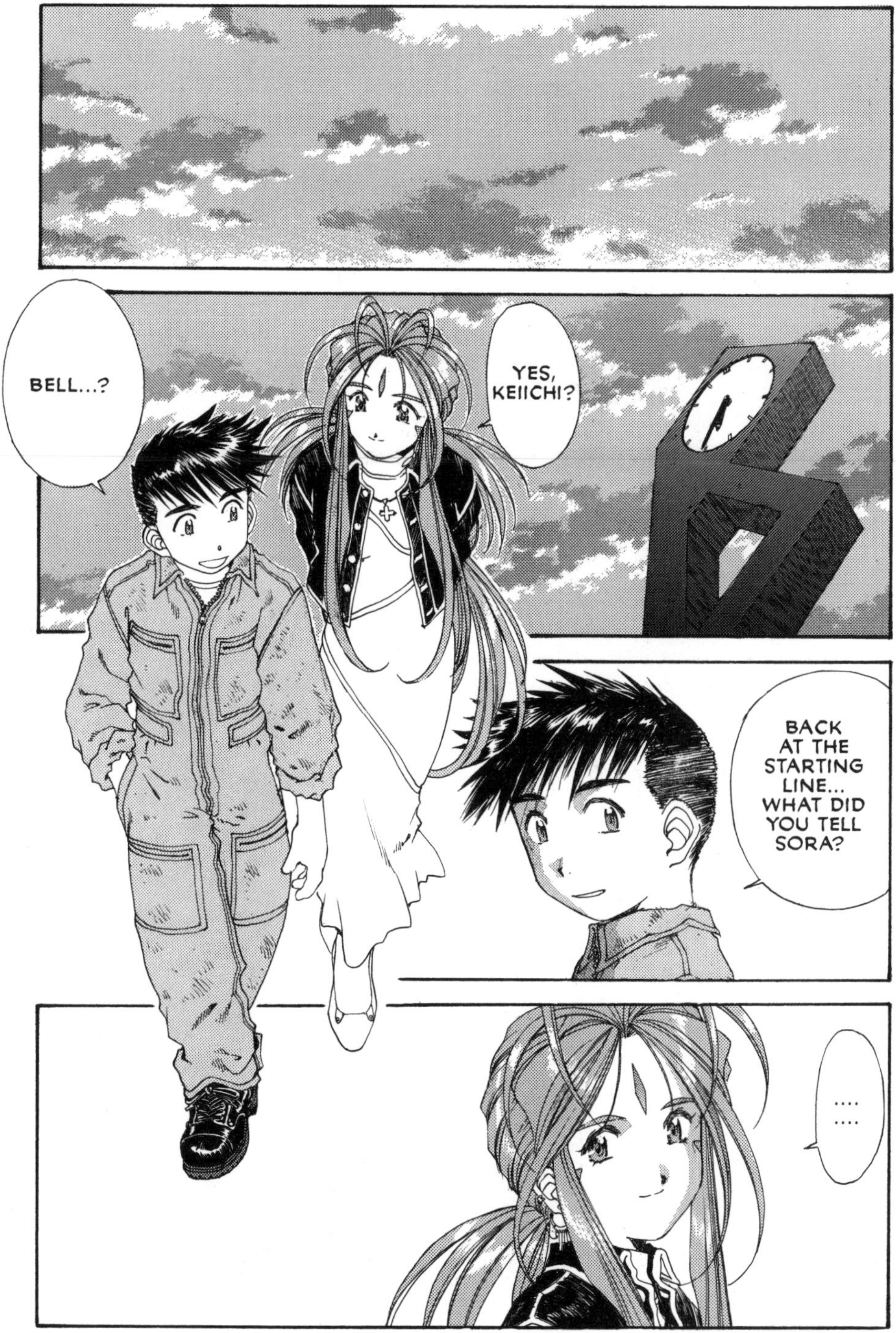
BELL...?
YES, KEIICHI?
BACK AT THE STARTING LINE... WHAT DID YOU TELL SORA?
....
....

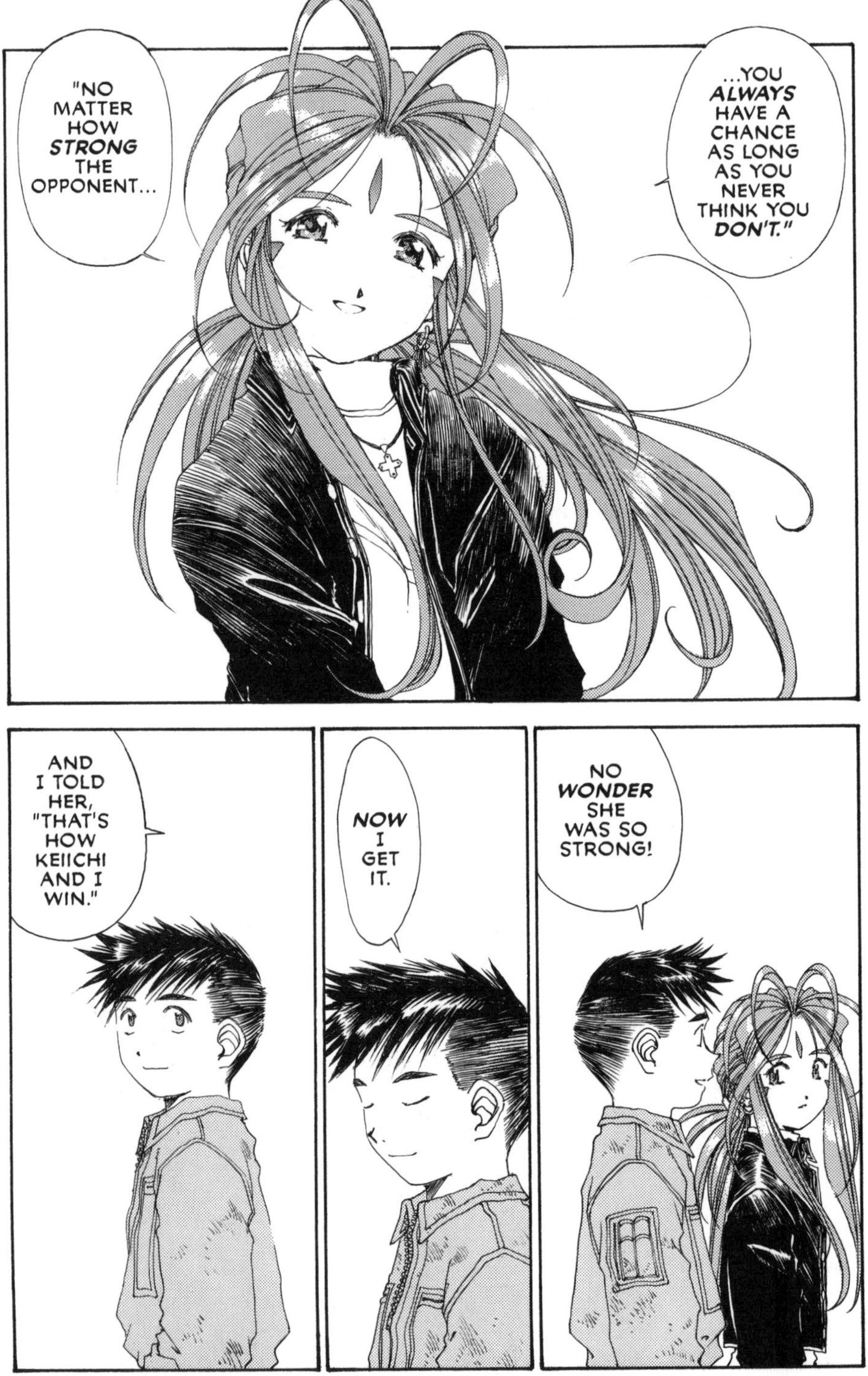
"NO MATTER HOW STRONG THE OPPONENT...
...YOU ALWAYS HAVE A CHANCE AS LONG AS YOU NEVER THINK YOU DON'T."
AND I TOLD HER, "THAT'S HOW KEIICHI AND I WIN."
NOW I GET IT.
NO WONDER SHE WAS SO STRONG!

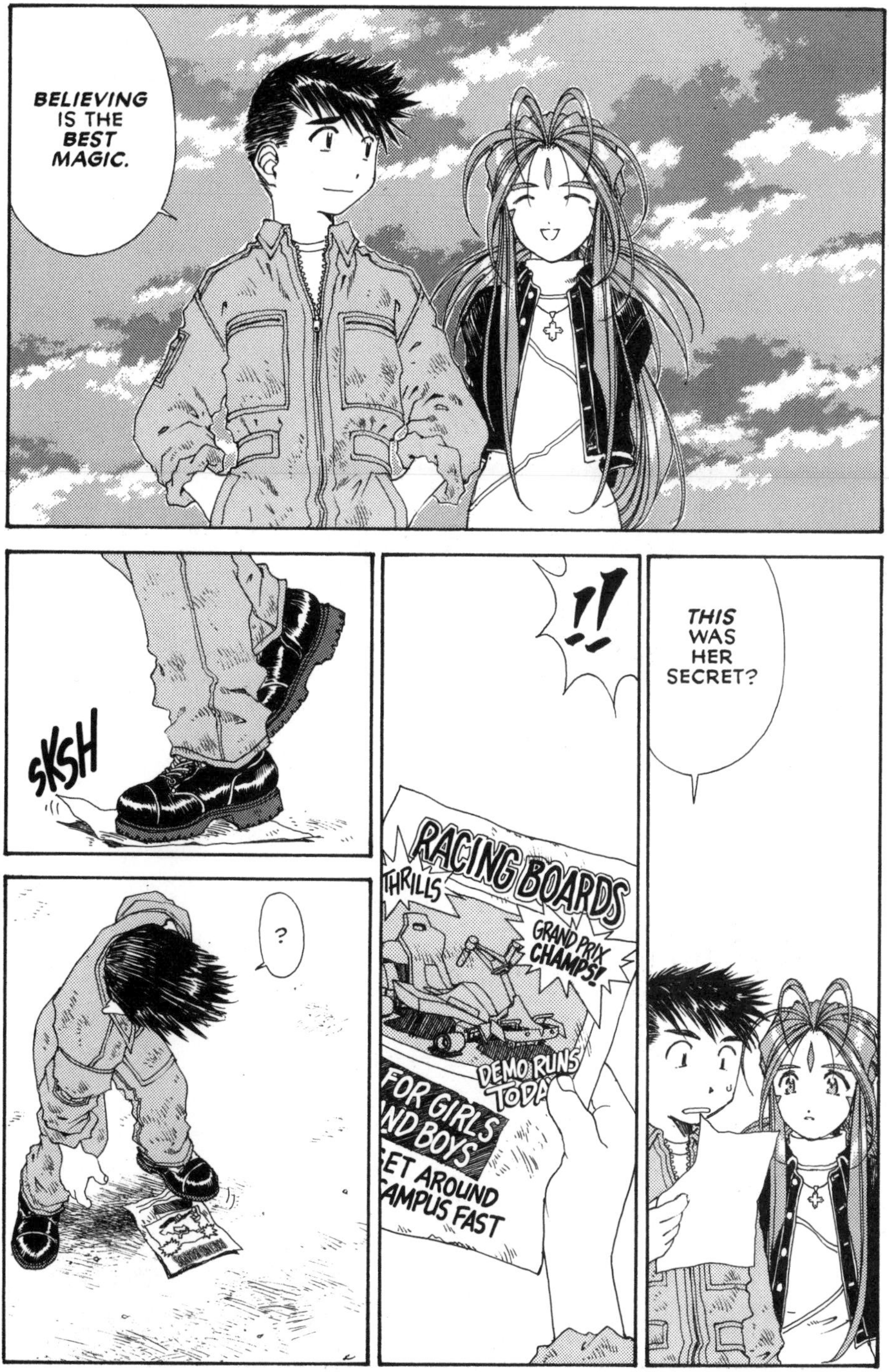
BELIEVING IS THE BEST MAGIC.
SKSH
?
!!
RACING BOARDS
THRILLS
GRAND PRIX CHAMPS!
DEMO RUNS TODA
FOR GIRLS
ND BOYS
ET AROUND
AMPUS FAST
THIS WAS HER SECRET?

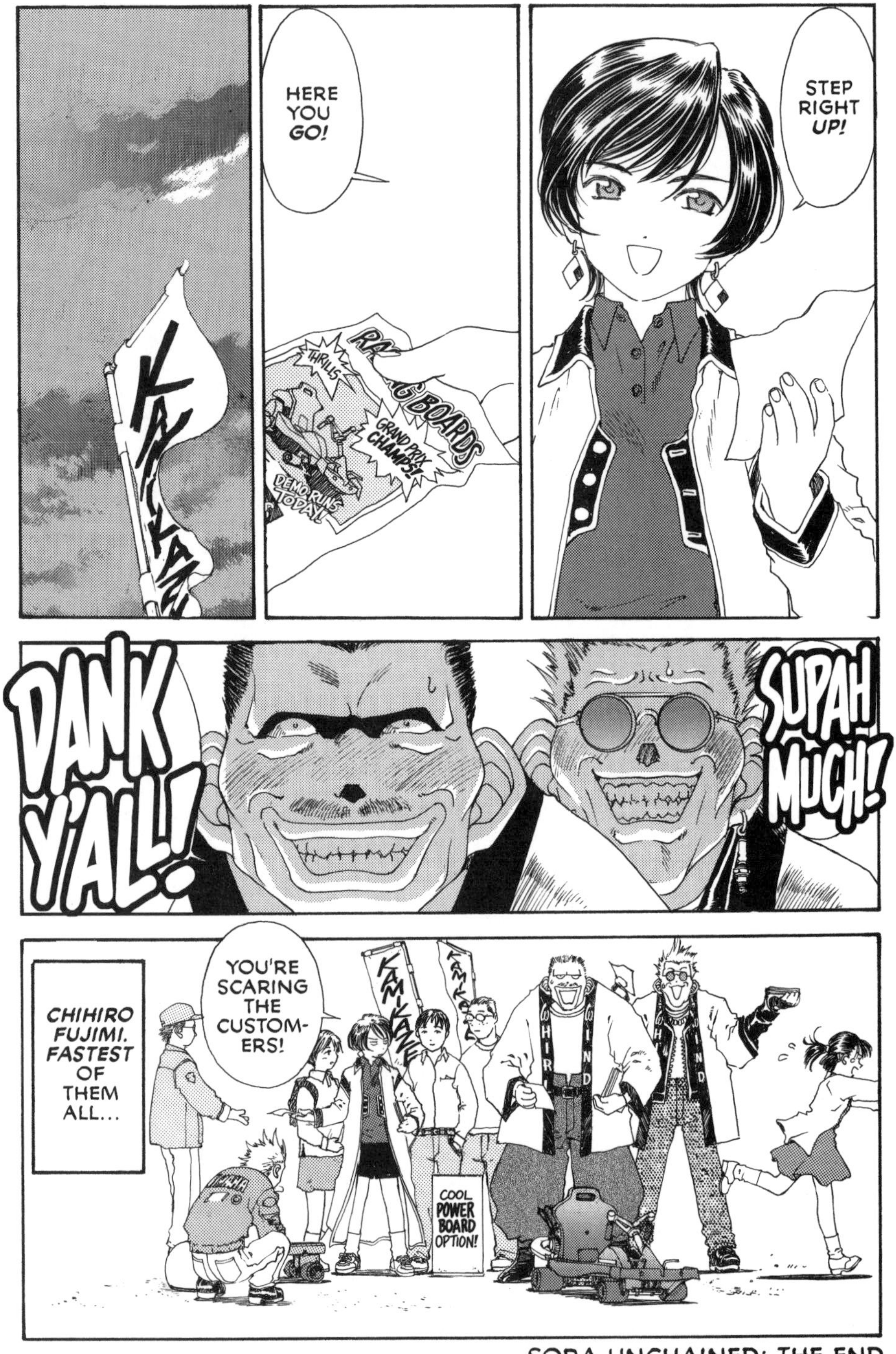
STEP RIGHT UP!
HERE YOU GO!
THRILLS
GRAND PRIX CHAMPS!
DEMO RUNS TODAY!
SUPAH MUCH!
DANK Y'ALL!
YOU'RE SCARING THE CUSTOMERS!
CHIHIRO FUJIMI. FASTEST OF THEM ALL...
COOL POWER BOARD OPTION!

SORA UNCHAINED: THE END

THE ENDLESS BATTLE, PART ONE

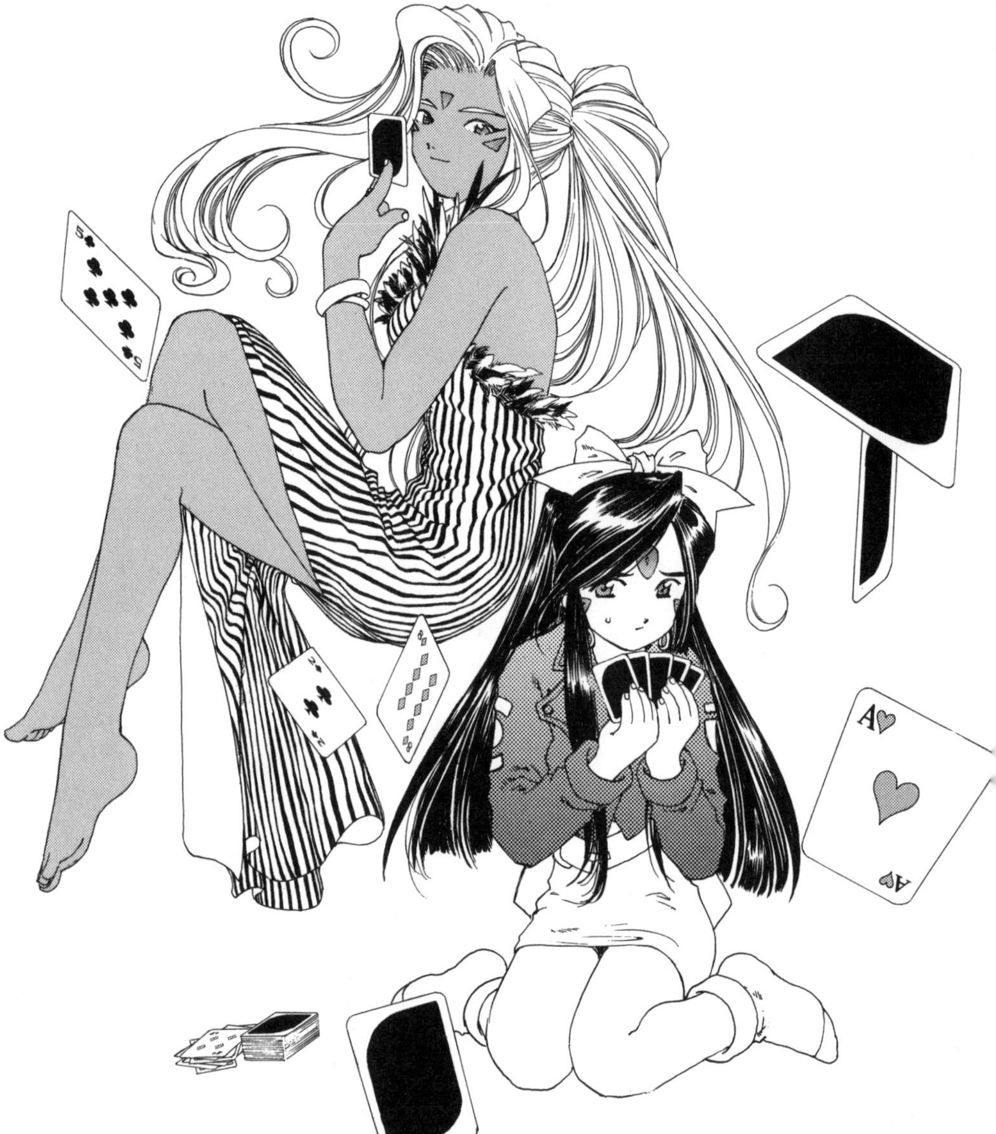

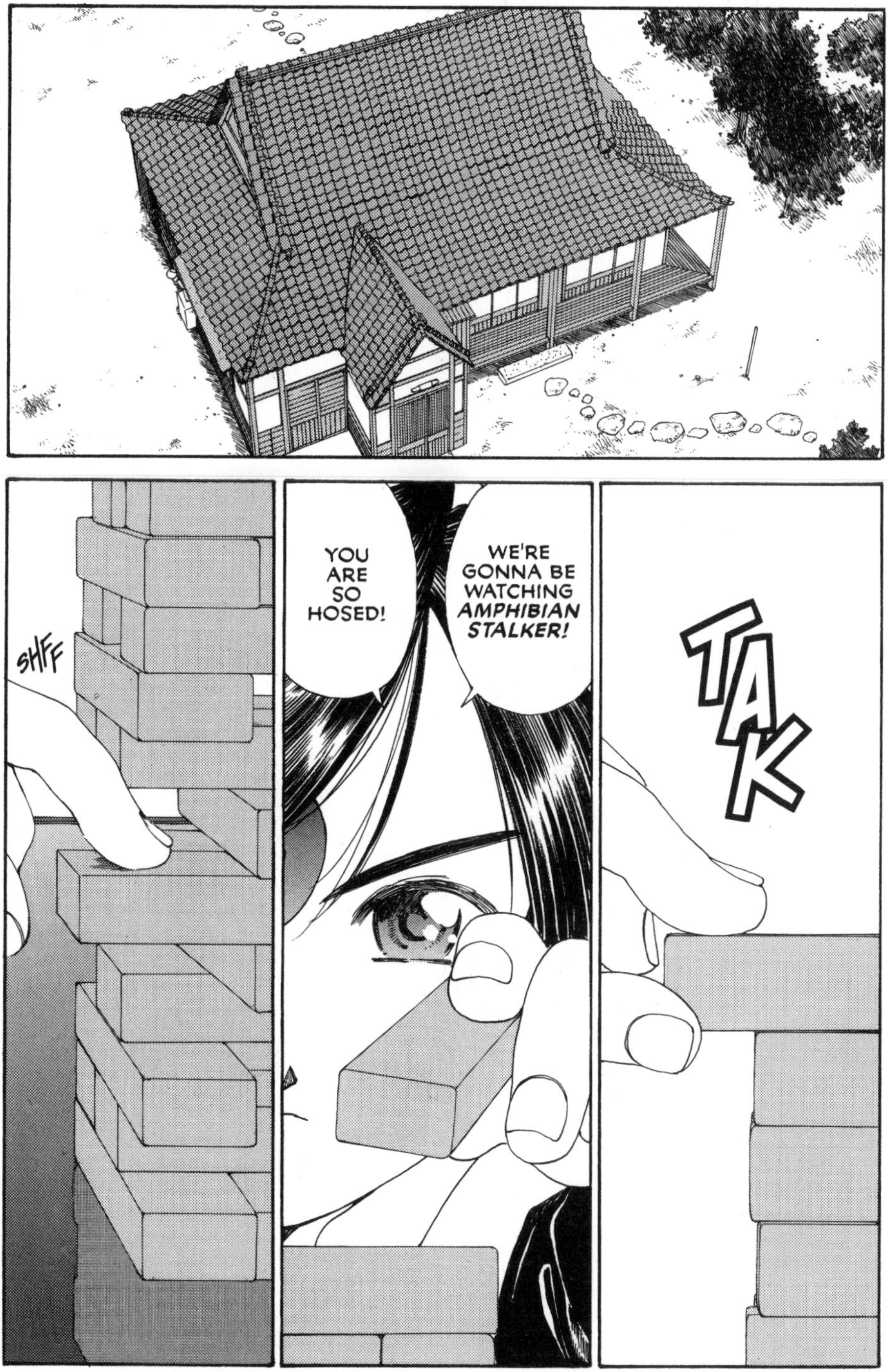
TAK
WE'RE GONNA BE WATCHING AMPHIBIAN STALKER!
YOU ARE SO HOSED!
SHFF

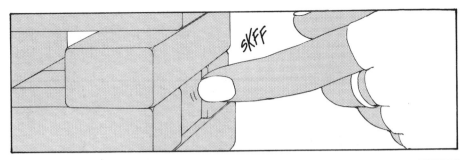

SKFF
...GO CRY TO NBS FOR RUNNING WHEN PLANTS ATTACK!
WHEN YOU LOSE...
TOK
TOPPLE! TOPPLE!
YOU'RE AT THIS AGAIN?

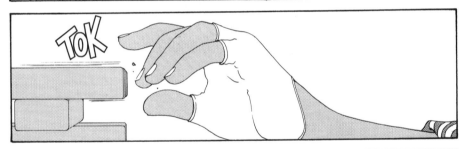

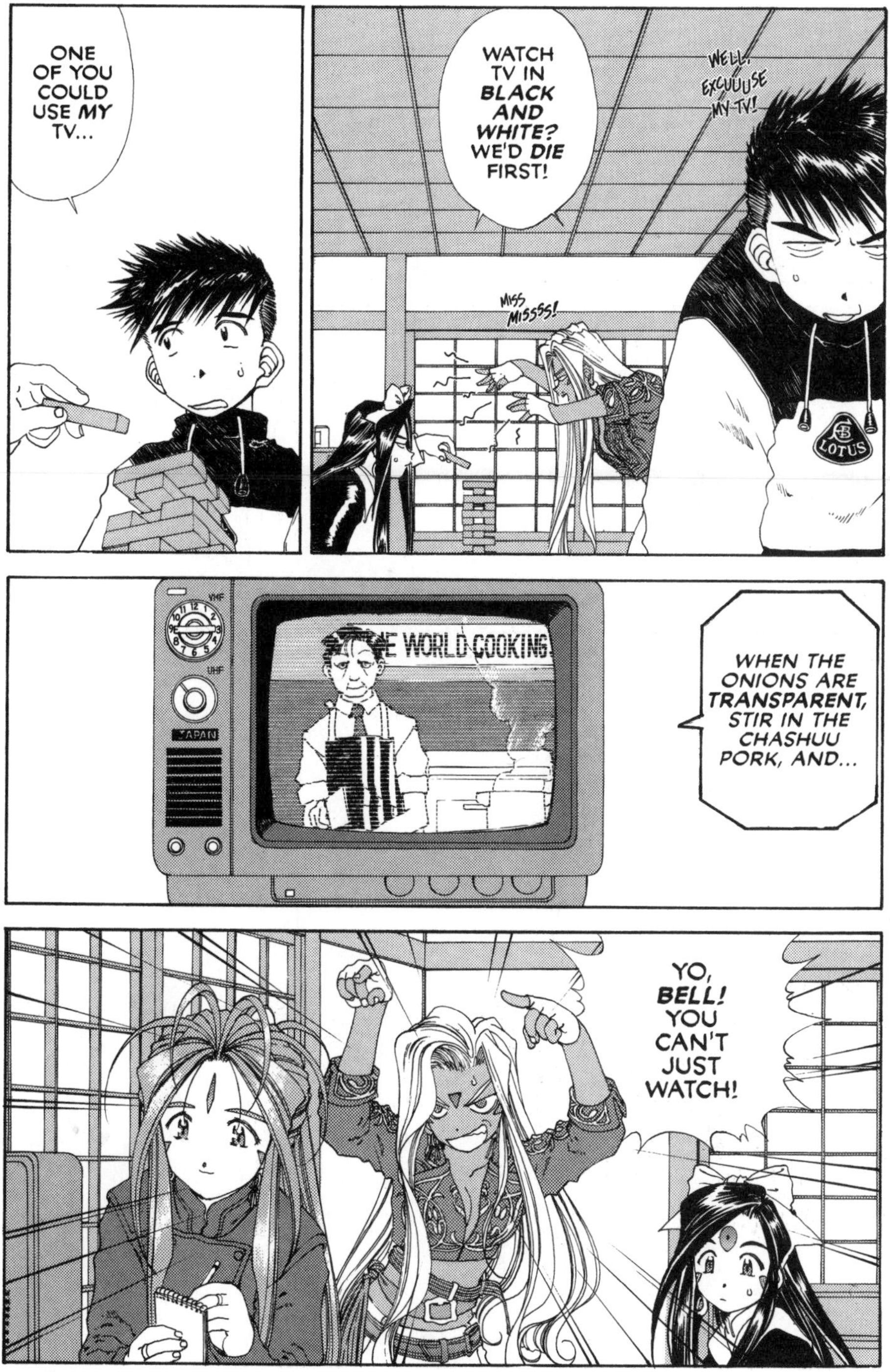
ONE OF YOU COULD USE MY TV...
WATCH TV IN BLACK AND WHITE? WE'D DIE FIRST!
WELL, EXCUUUSE MY TV!
MISS MISSSS!
THE WORLD COOKING
JAPAN
WHEN THE ONIONS ARE TRANSPARENT, STIR IN THE CHASHUU PORK, AND...
YO, BELL! YOU CAN'T JUST WATCH!

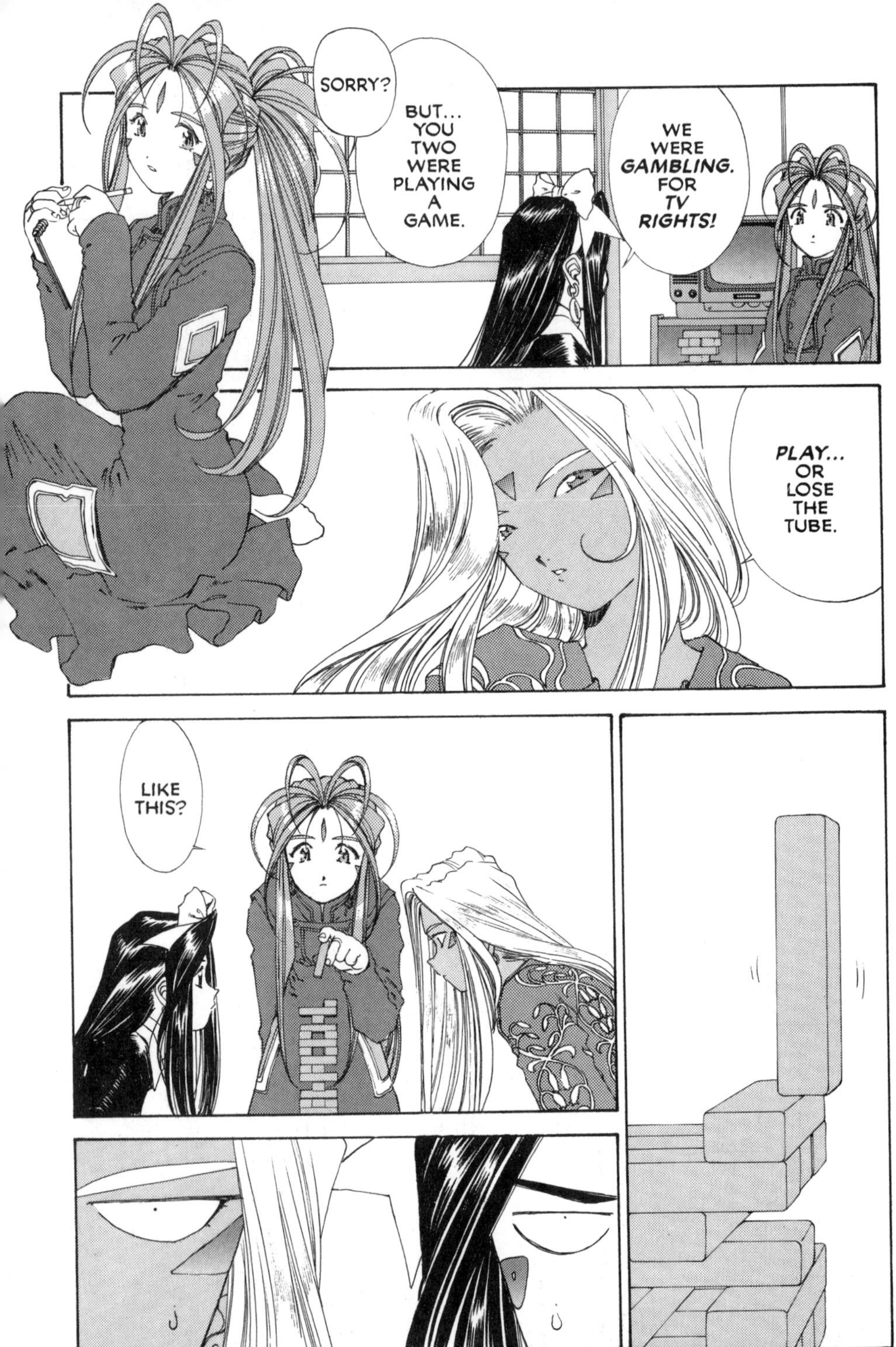
SORRY?
BUT... YOU TWO WERE PLAYING A GAME.
WE WERE *GAMBLING.* FOR *TV RIGHTS!*
PLAY... OR LOSE THE TUBE.
LIKE THIS?

NOTE: THIS IS A SPECIAL GODDESS-ONLY MOVE!

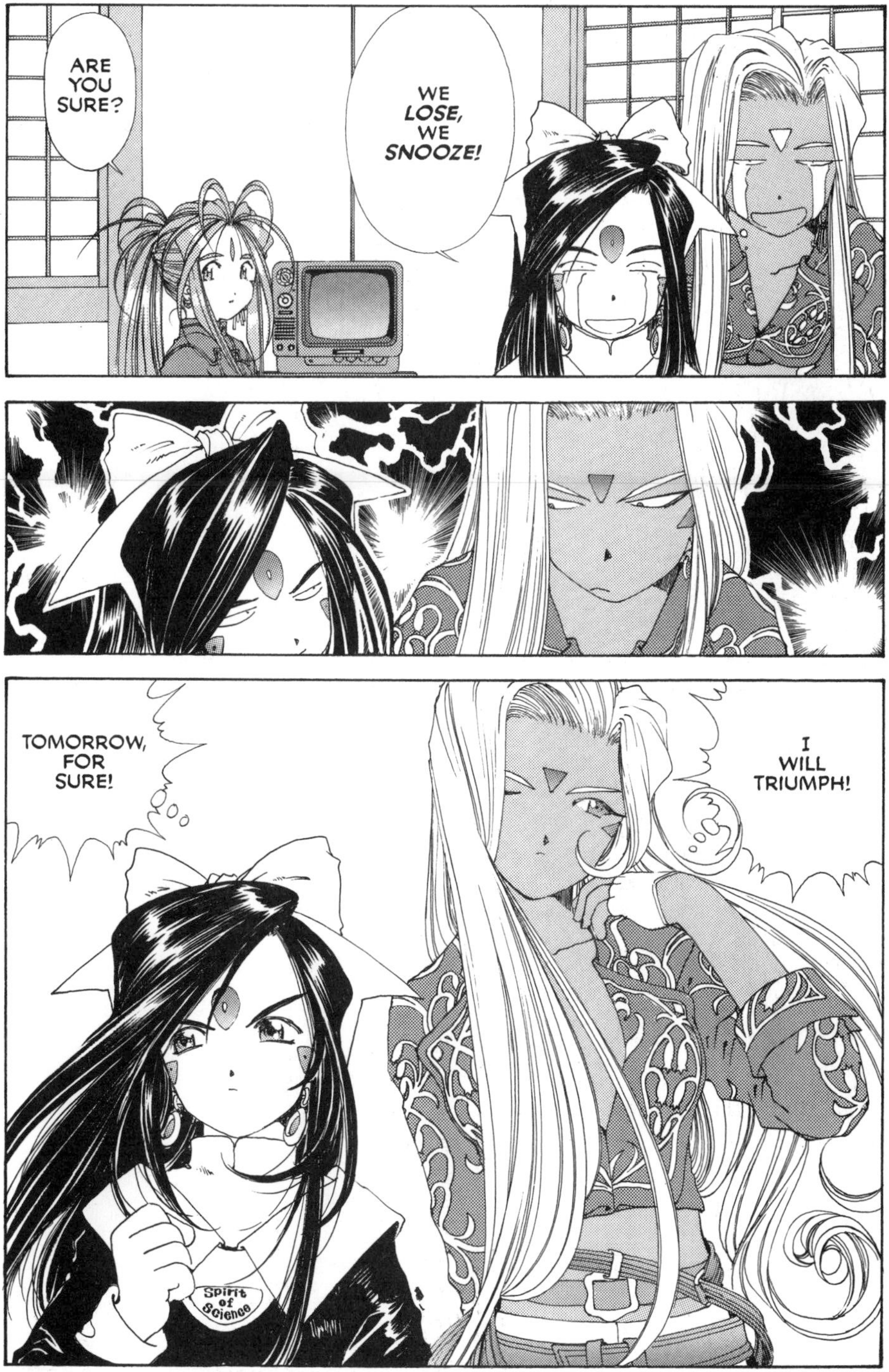
WE *LOSE,* WE *SNOOZE!*
ARE YOU SURE?
I WILL TRIUMPH!
TOMORROW, FOR SURE!
Spirit of Science

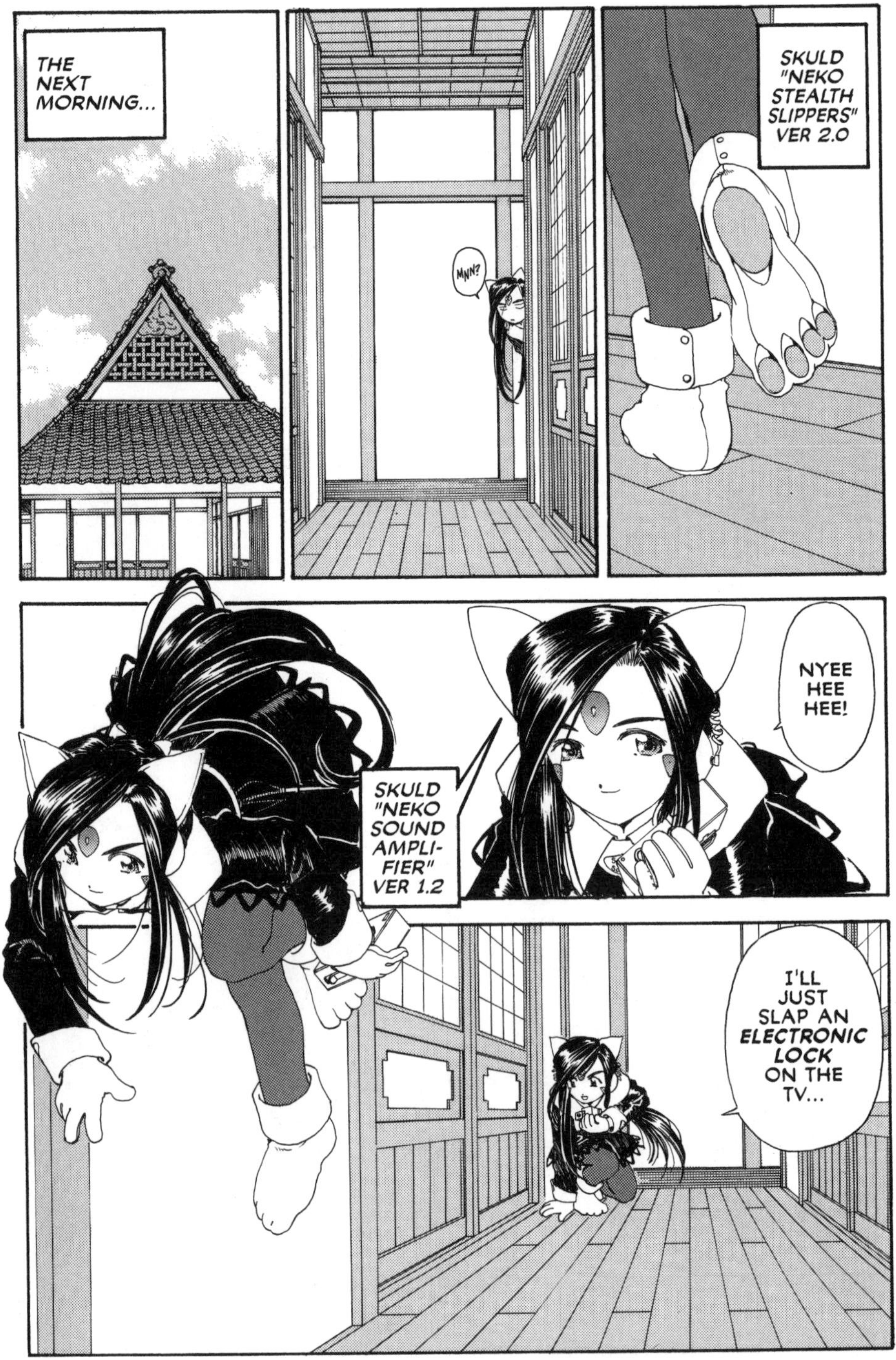
THE NEXT MORNING...
MNN?
SKULD "NEKO STEALTH SLIPPERS" VER 2.0
SKULD "NEKO SOUND AMPLIFIER" VER 1.2
NYEE HEE HEE!
I'LL JUST SLAP AN ELECTRONIC LOCK ON THE TV...

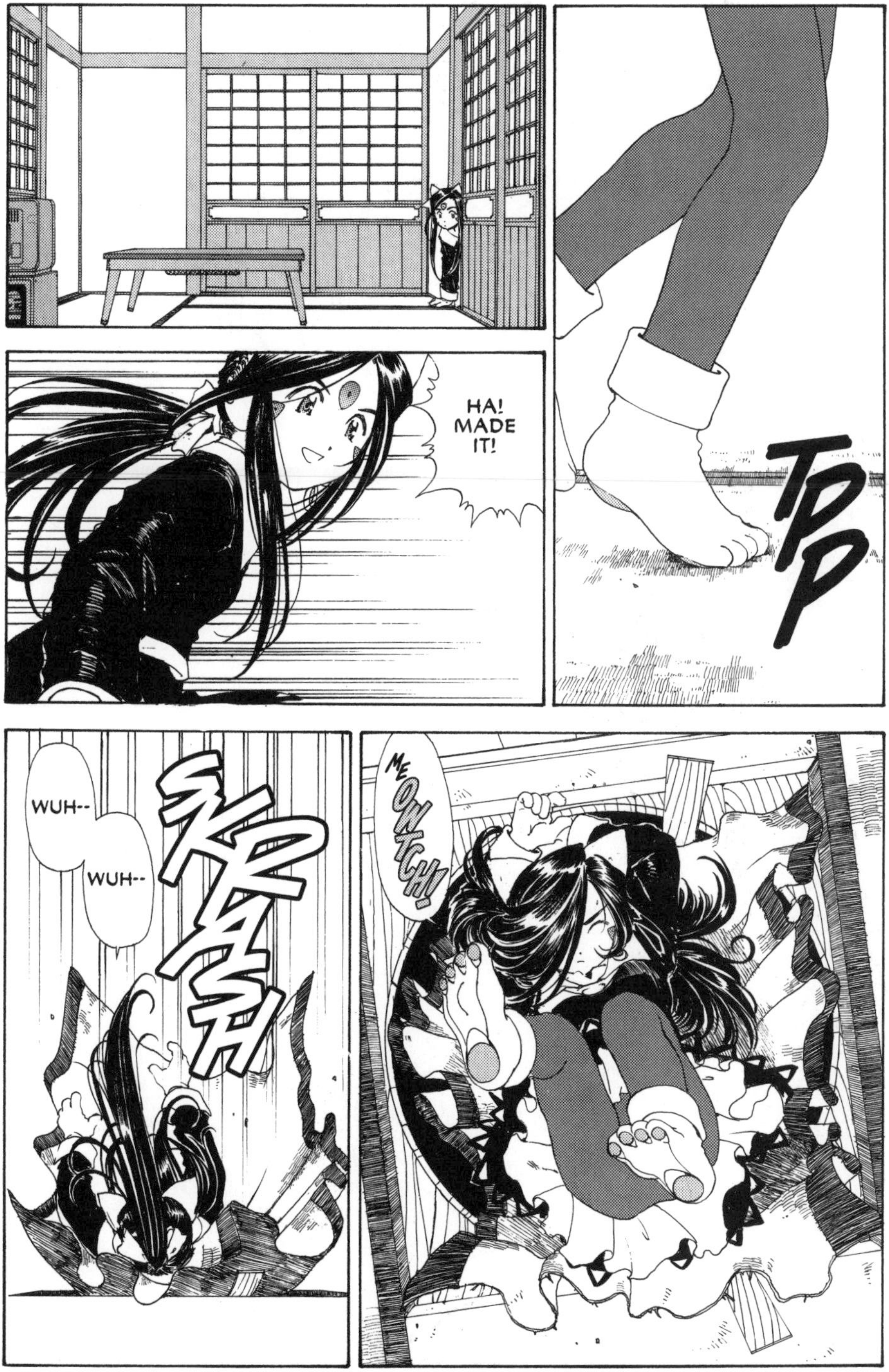
TPP
HA! MADE IT!
MEOWTCH!
WUH--
WUH--
SKRASH

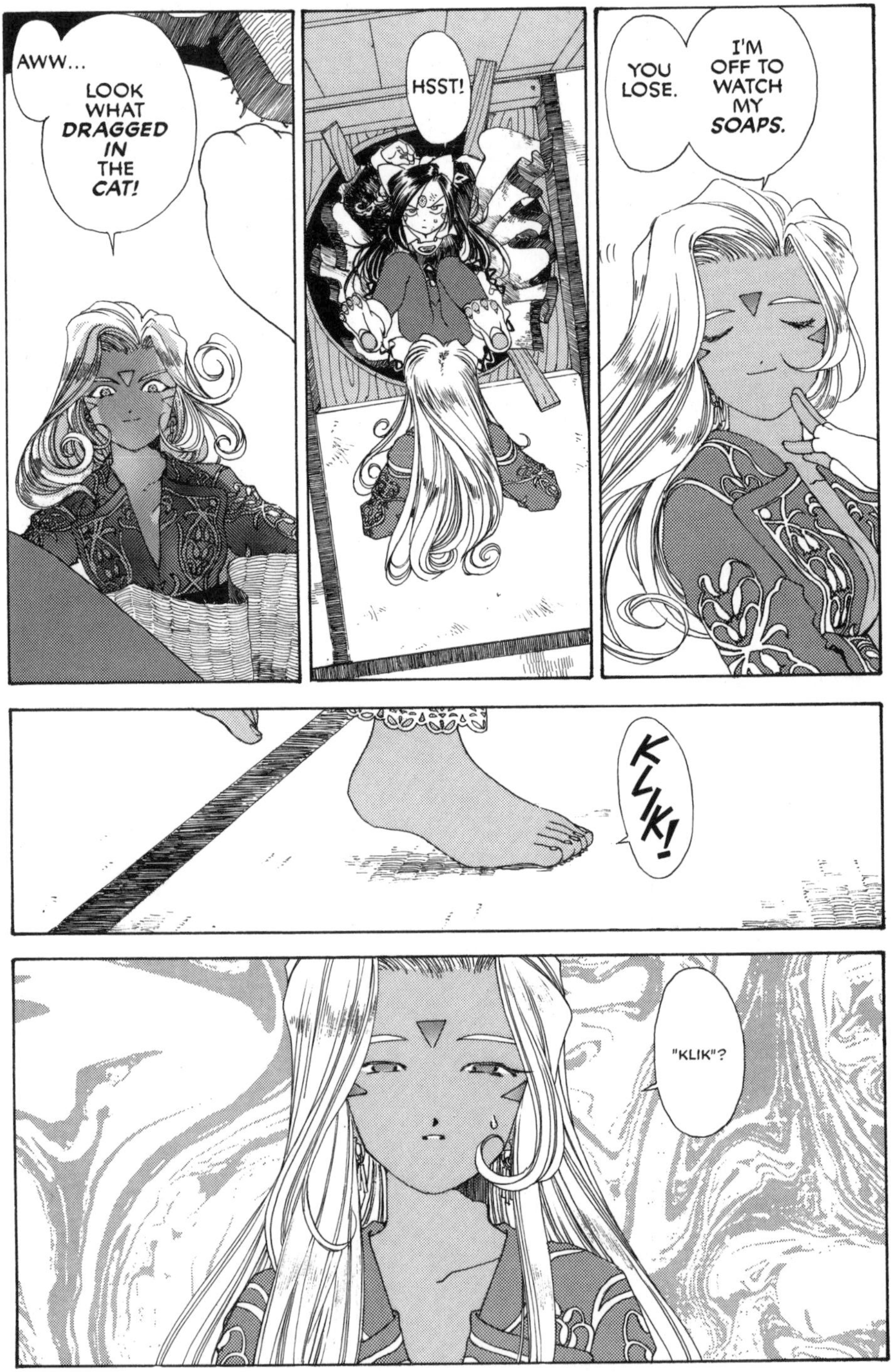
AWW... LOOK WHAT DRAGGED IN THE CAT!
HSST!
YOU LOSE.
I'M OFF TO WATCH MY SOAPS.
KLIK!
"KLIK"?

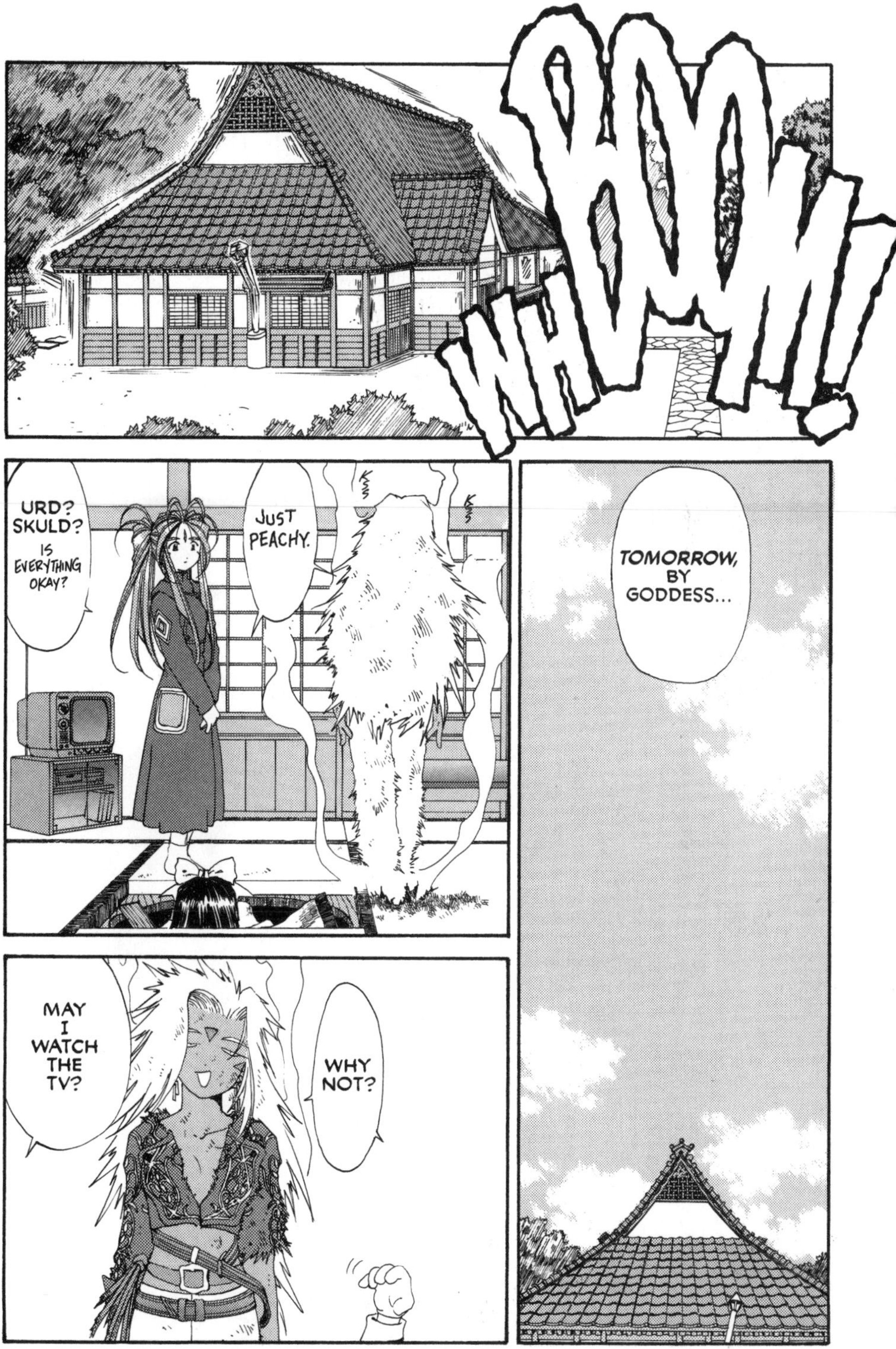
WHABOOM!!
URD? SKULD? IS EVERYTHING OKAY?
JUST PEACHY.
MAY I WATCH THE TV?
WHY NOT?
TOMORROW, BY GODDESS...

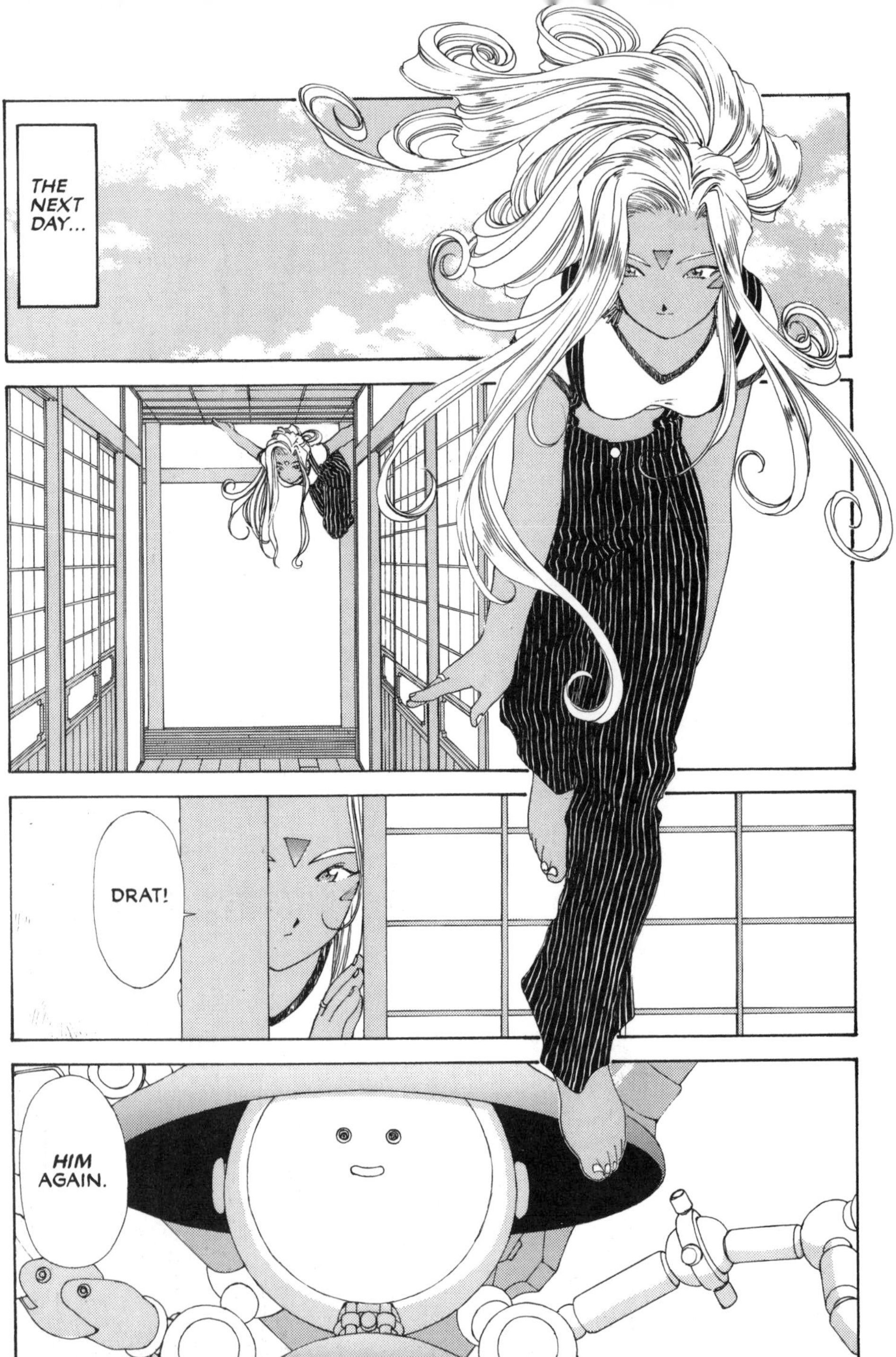
THE NEXT DAY...
DRAT!
HIM AGAIN.

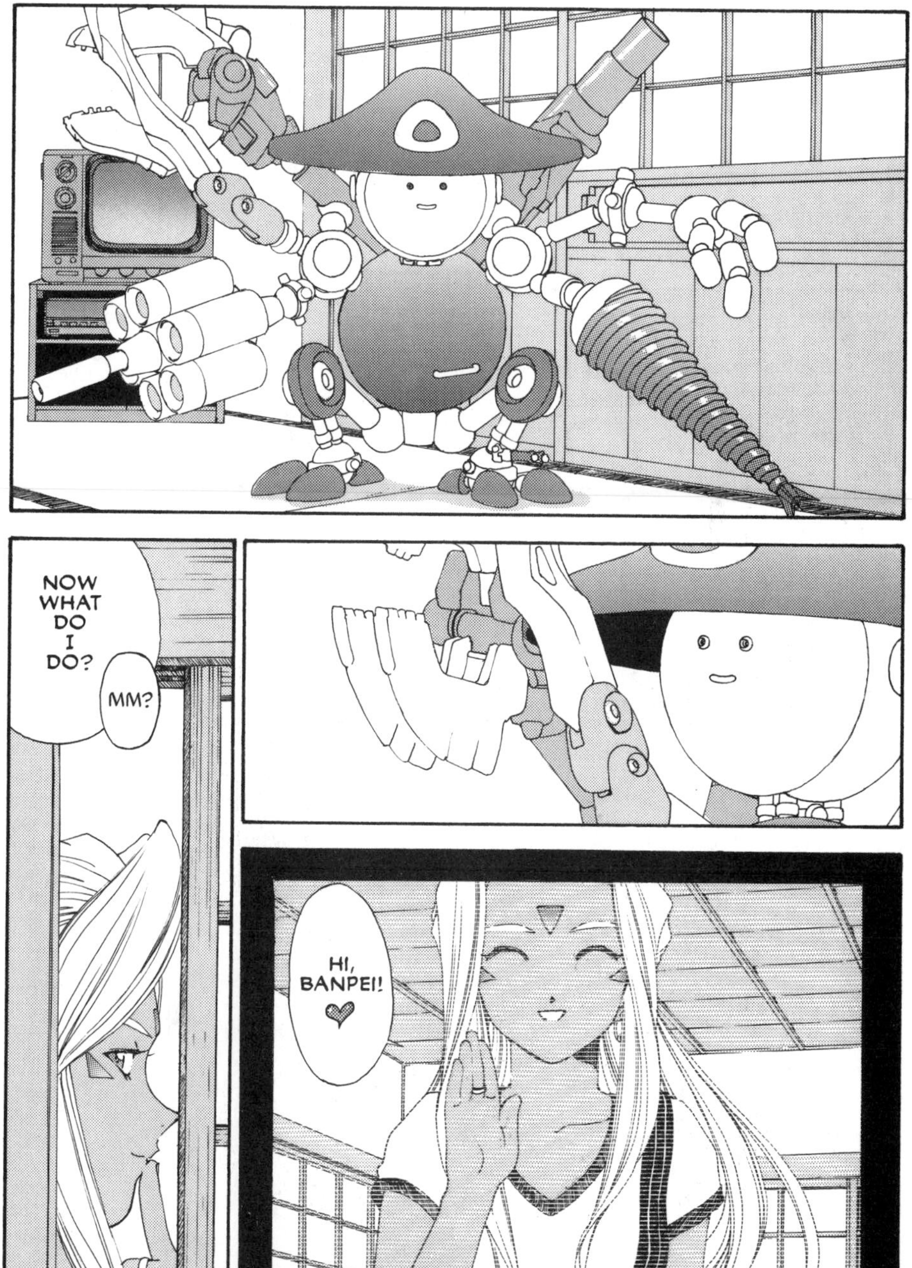
NOW WHAT DO I DO?
MM?
HI, BANPEI! ♥

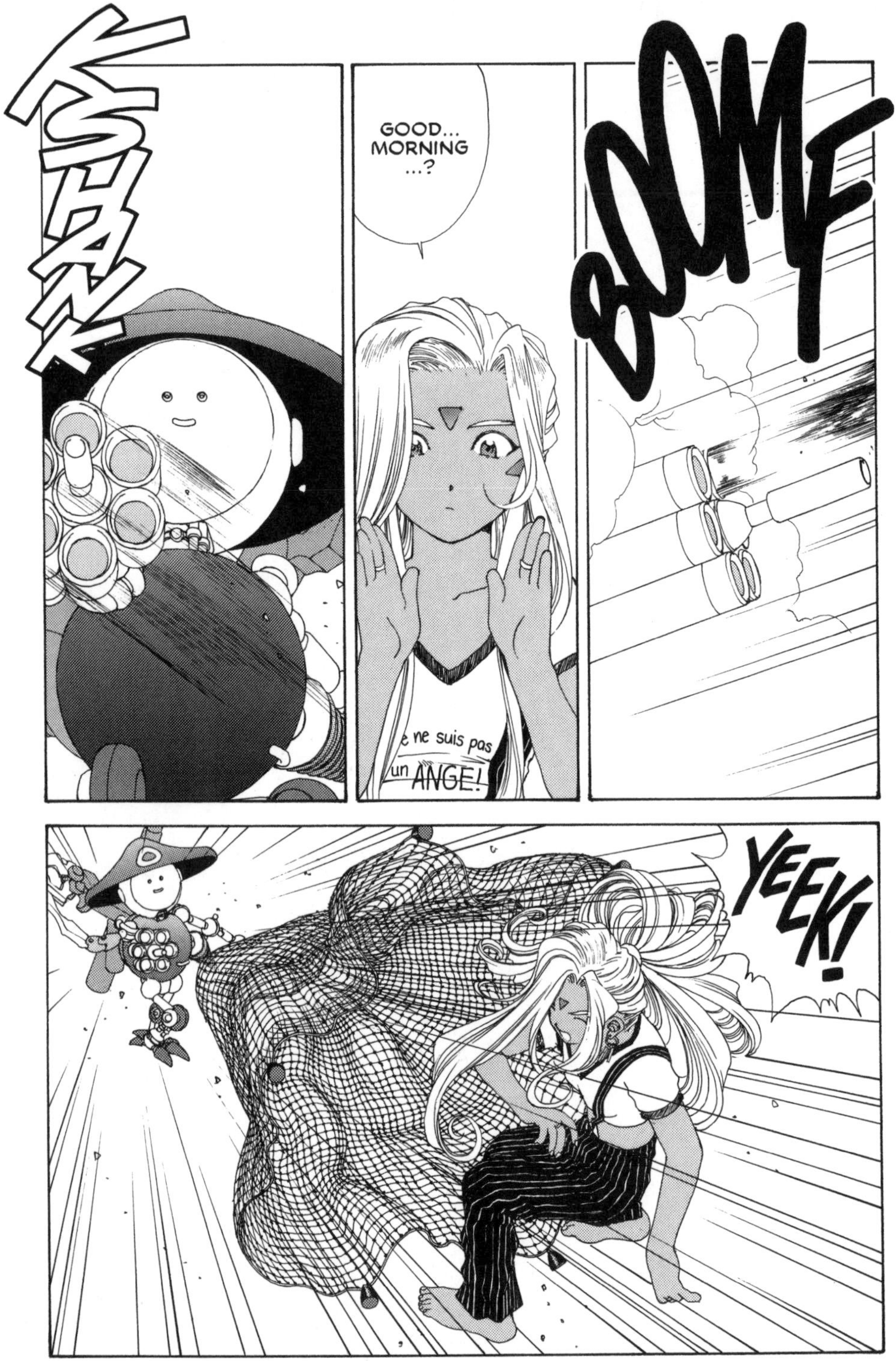
KSHANK
GOOD... MORNING ...?
BOOMF
ne suis pas
un ANGE!
YEEK!

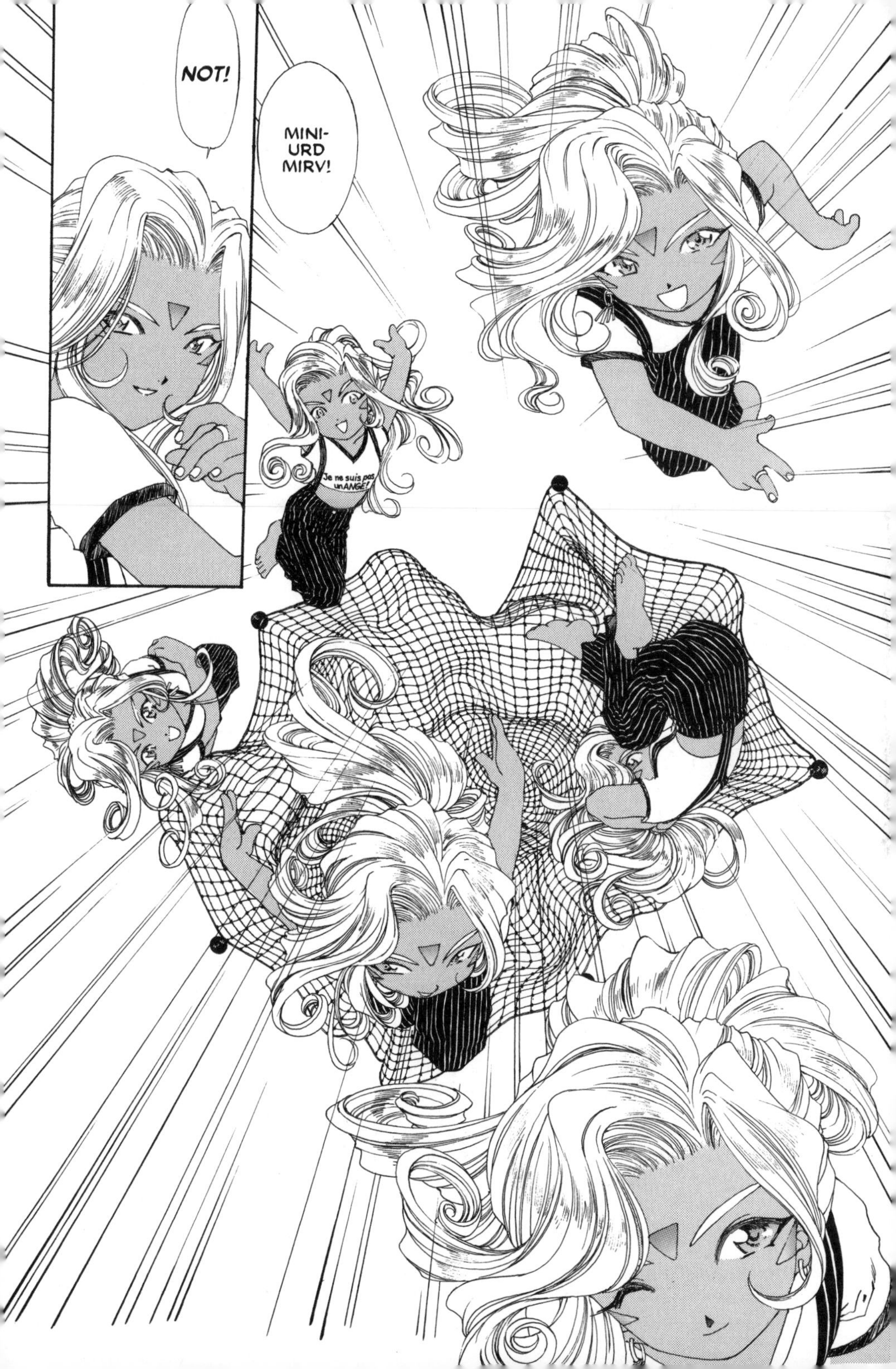
MINI-URD MIRV!
NOT!
Je ne suis pas un ANGE!

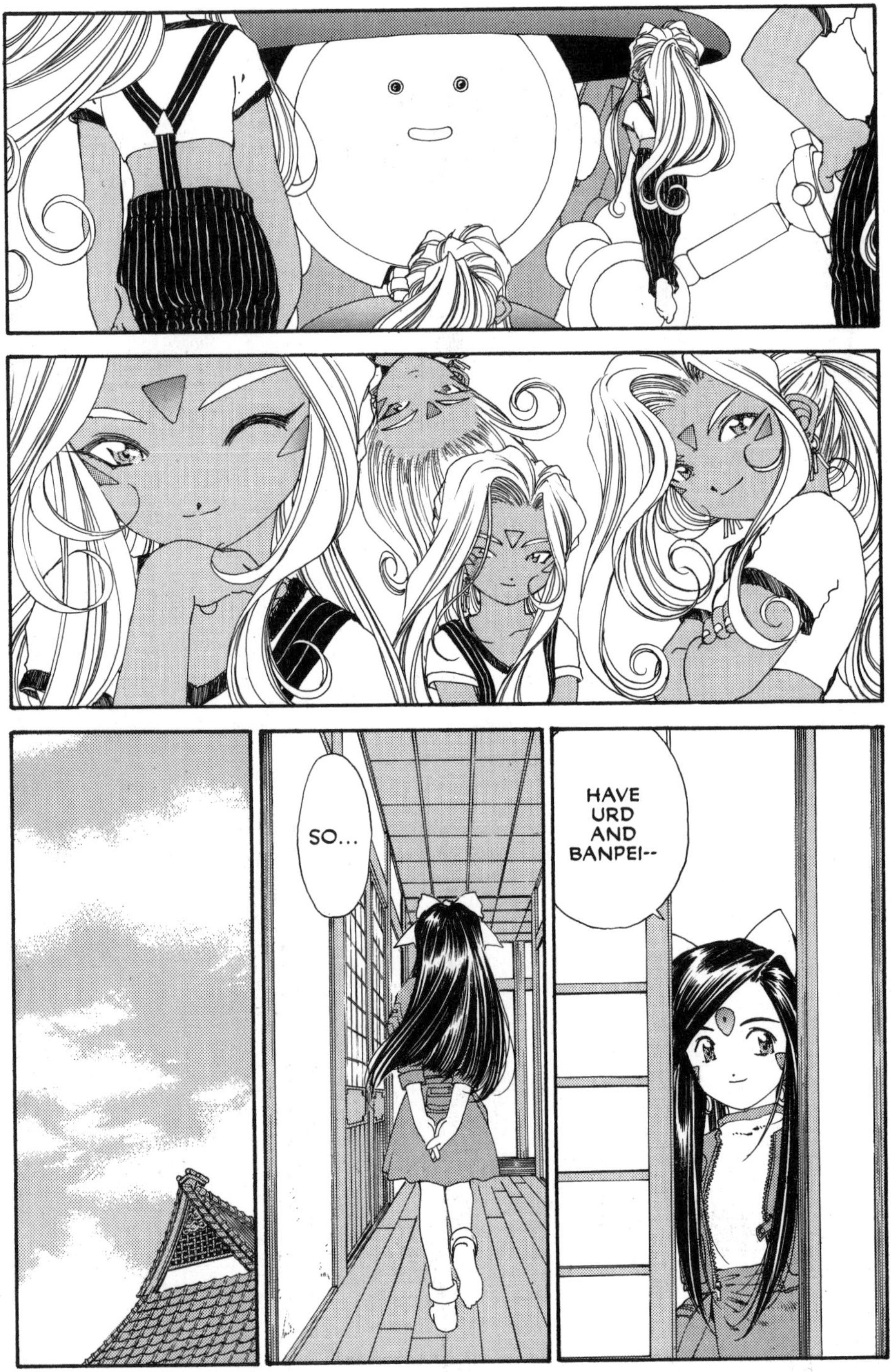
HAVE URD AND BANPEI--
SO...

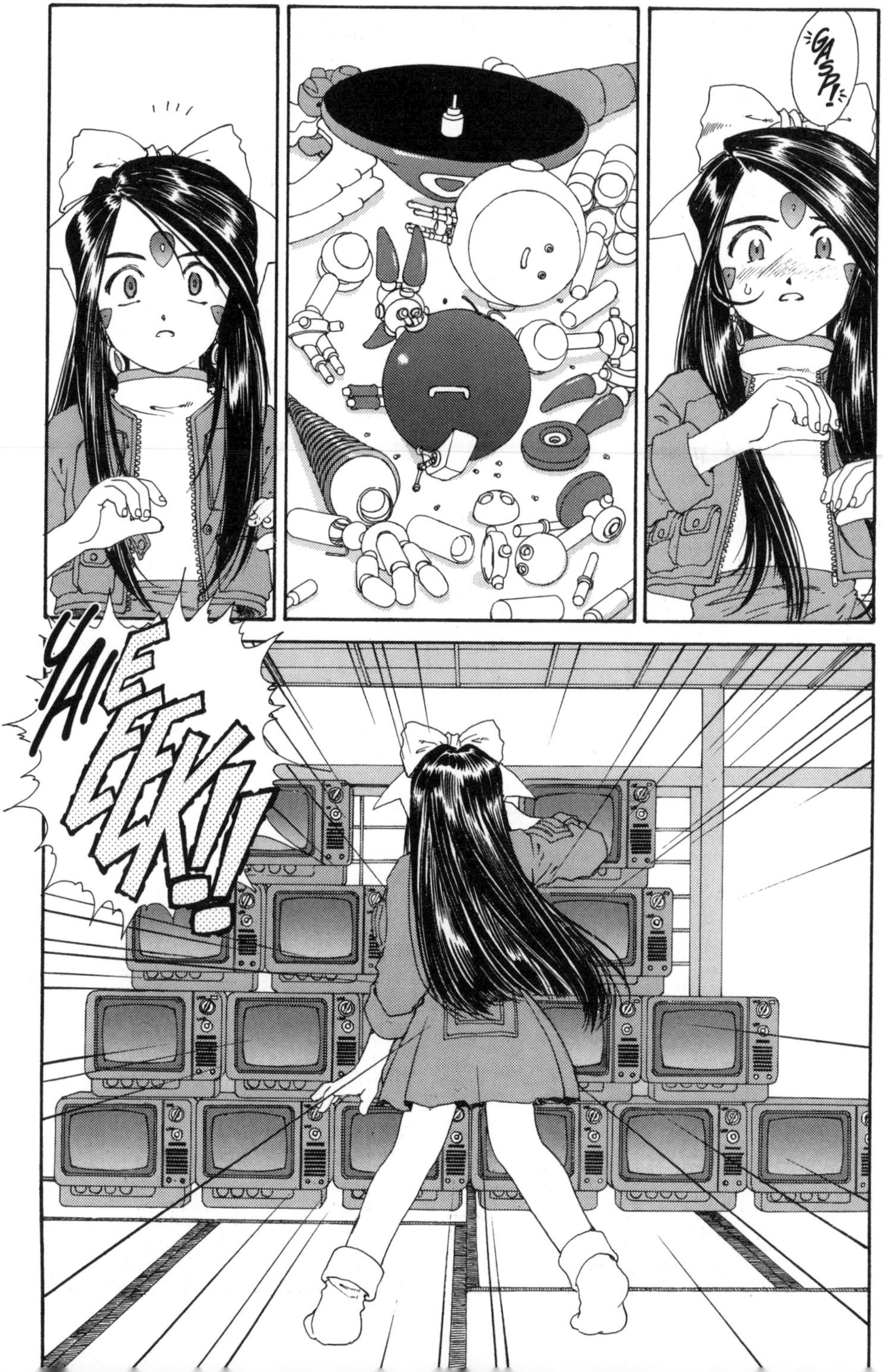
GASP!
YAIEEEEK!!

THE ENDLESS BATTLE, PART TWO

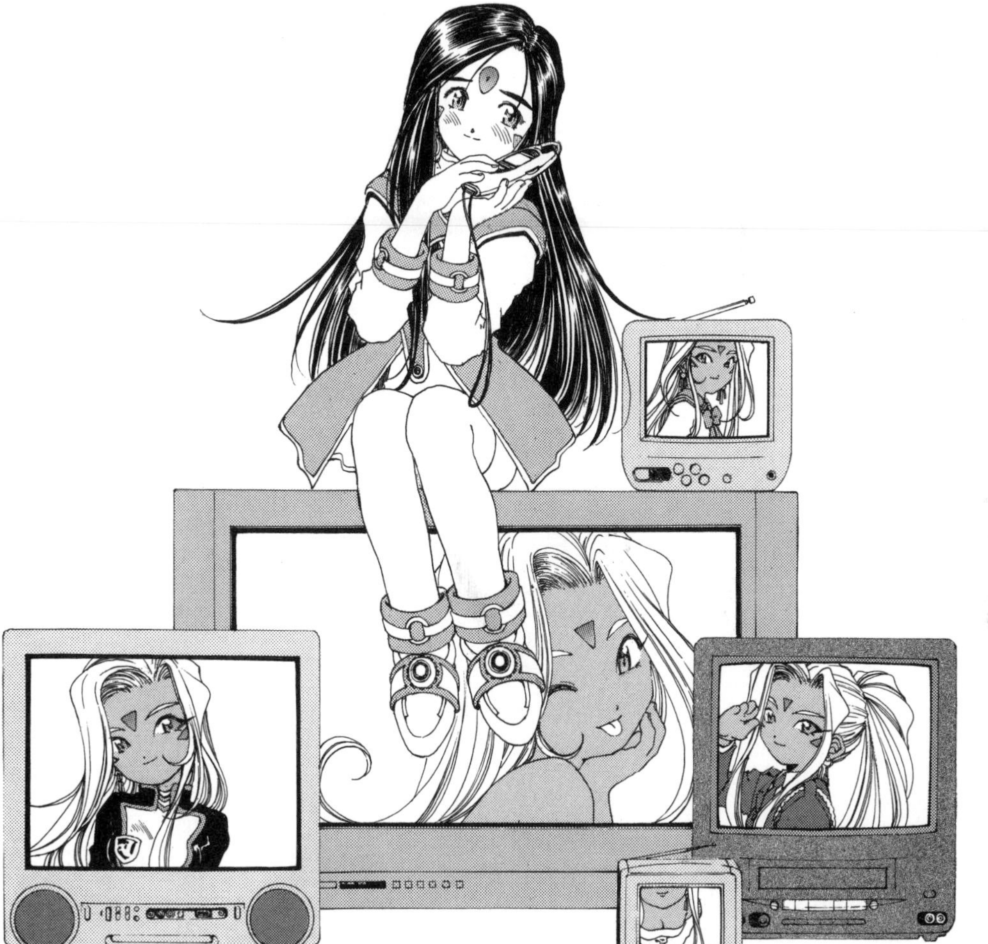

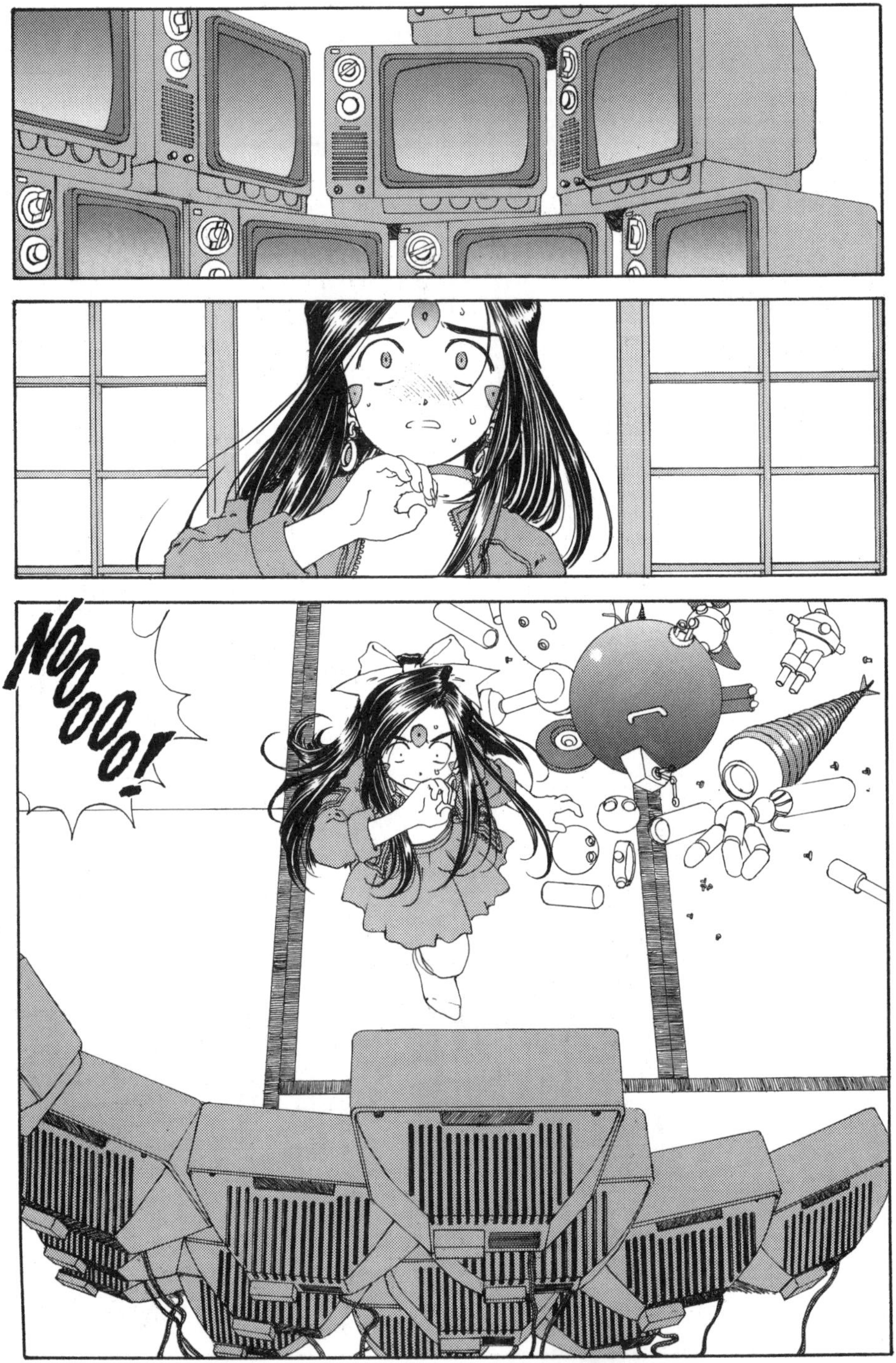
NOOOOO!

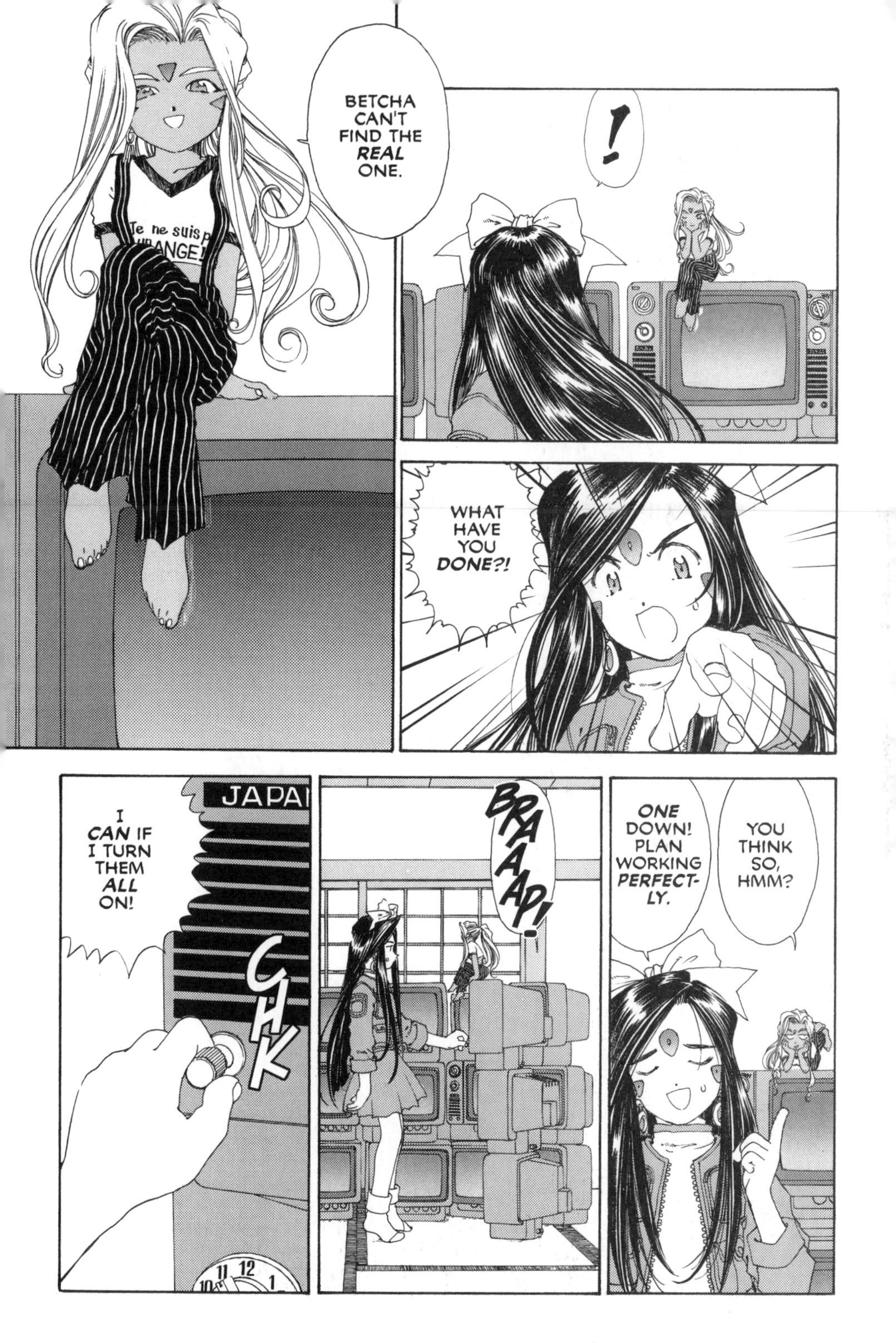
Je ne suis pas UN ANGE!
BETCHA CAN'T FIND THE REAL ONE.
!
WHAT HAVE YOU DONE?!
JAPAN
I CAN IF I TURN THEM ALL ON!
CHK
BRAAAAP!
ONE DOWN! PLAN WORKING PERFECT-LY.
YOU THINK SO, HMM?

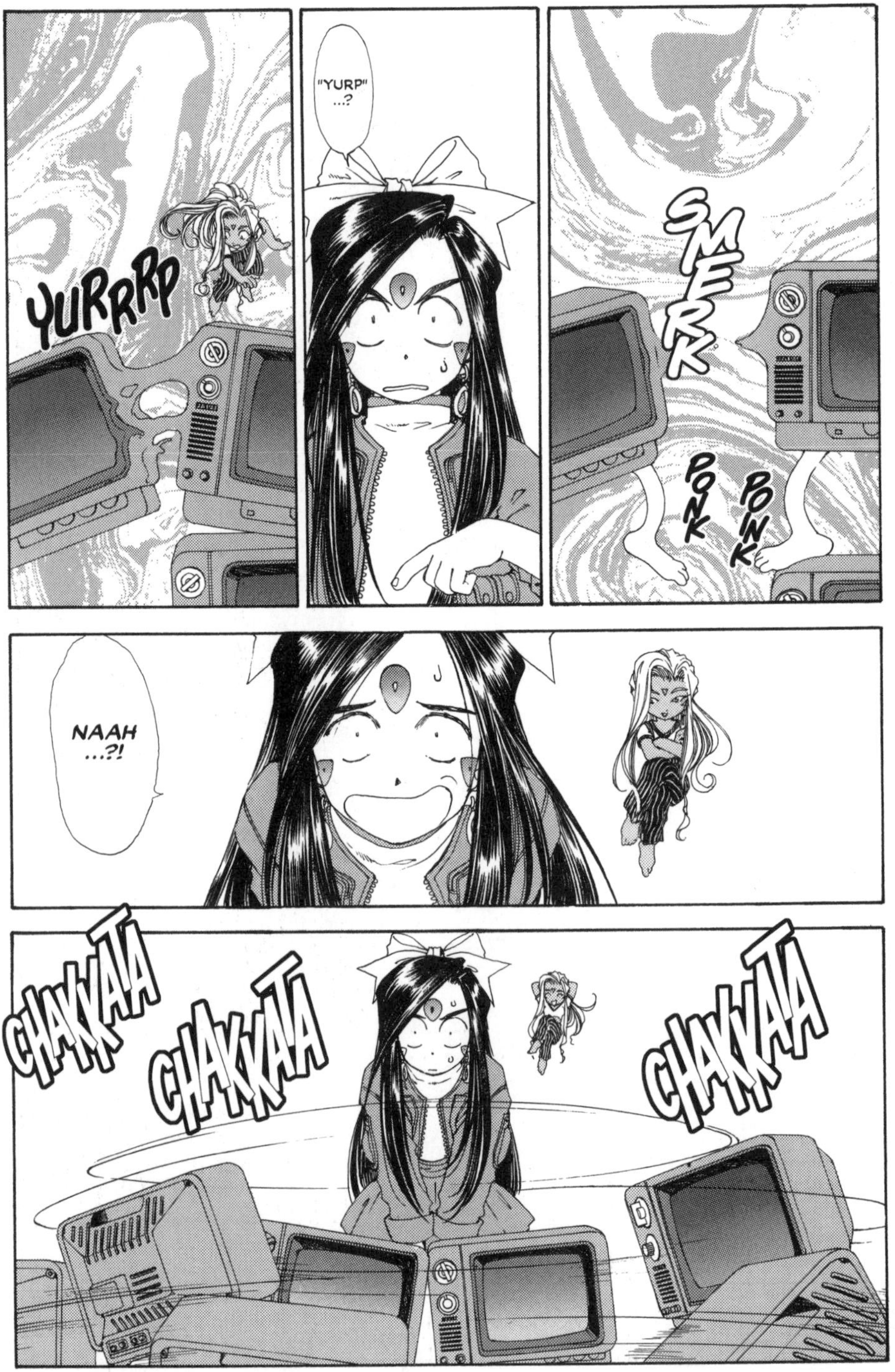
YURRRP
"YURP" ...?
SMERK
PONK
PONK
NAAH ...?!
CHAKKATA
CHAKKATA
CHAKKATA

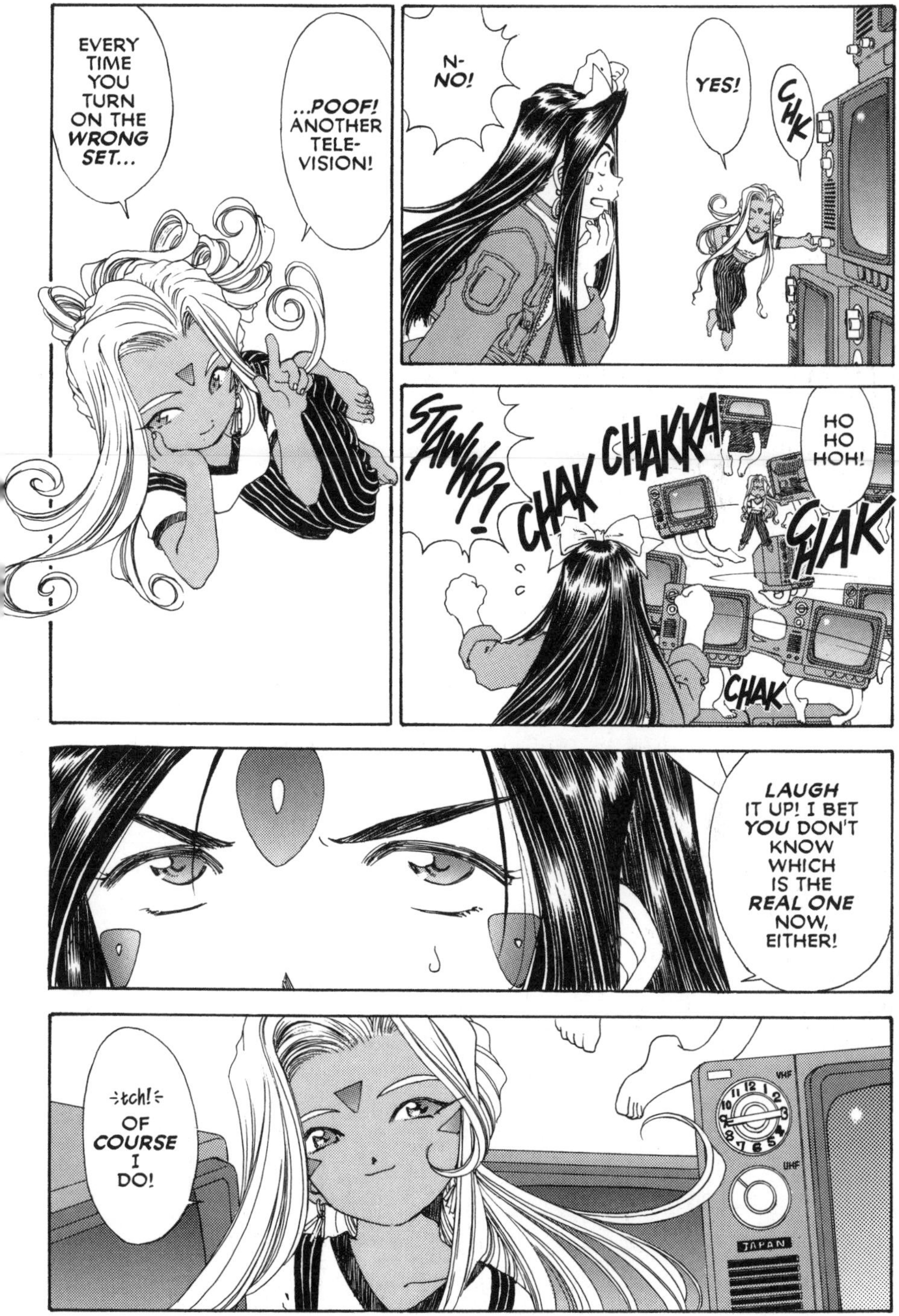
EVERY TIME YOU TURN ON THE WRONG SET...
...POOF! ANOTHER TELE-VISION!
N-NO!
YES!
CHK
STAWWP!
CHAK
CHAKKA
HO HO HOH!
CHAK
CHAK
LAUGH IT UP! I BET YOU DON'T KNOW WHICH IS THE REAL ONE NOW, EITHER!
tch! OF COURSE I DO!
JAPAN

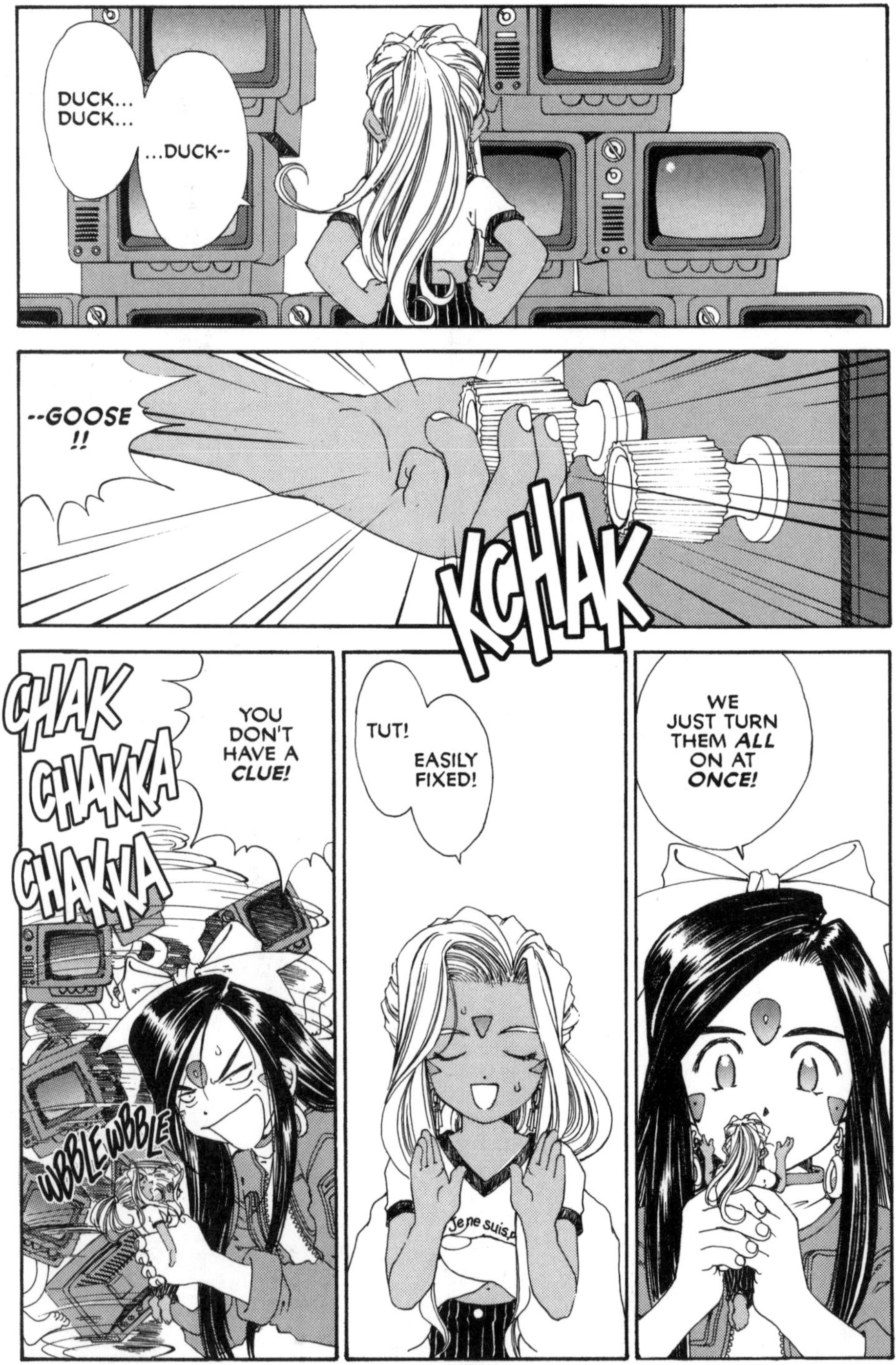
DUCK... DUCK...
...DUCK--
--GOOSE !!
KCHAK
CHAK CHAKKA CHAKKA
WBBLEWBBLE
YOU DON'T HAVE A *CLUE!*
TUT! EASILY FIXED!
Je ne suis p
WE JUST TURN THEM *ALL* ON AT *ONCE!*

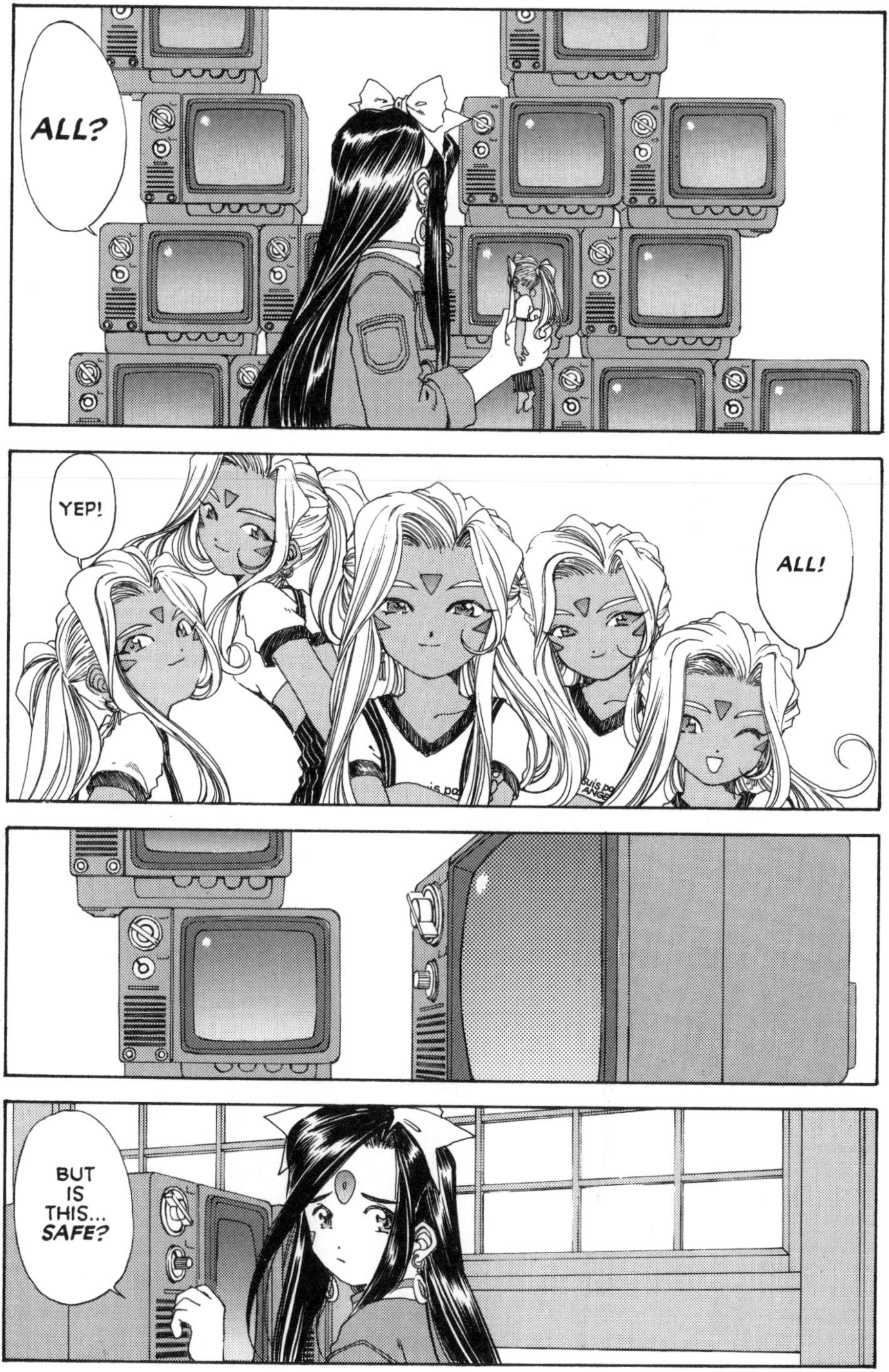
ALL?
ALL!
YEP!
BUT IS THIS... SAFE?

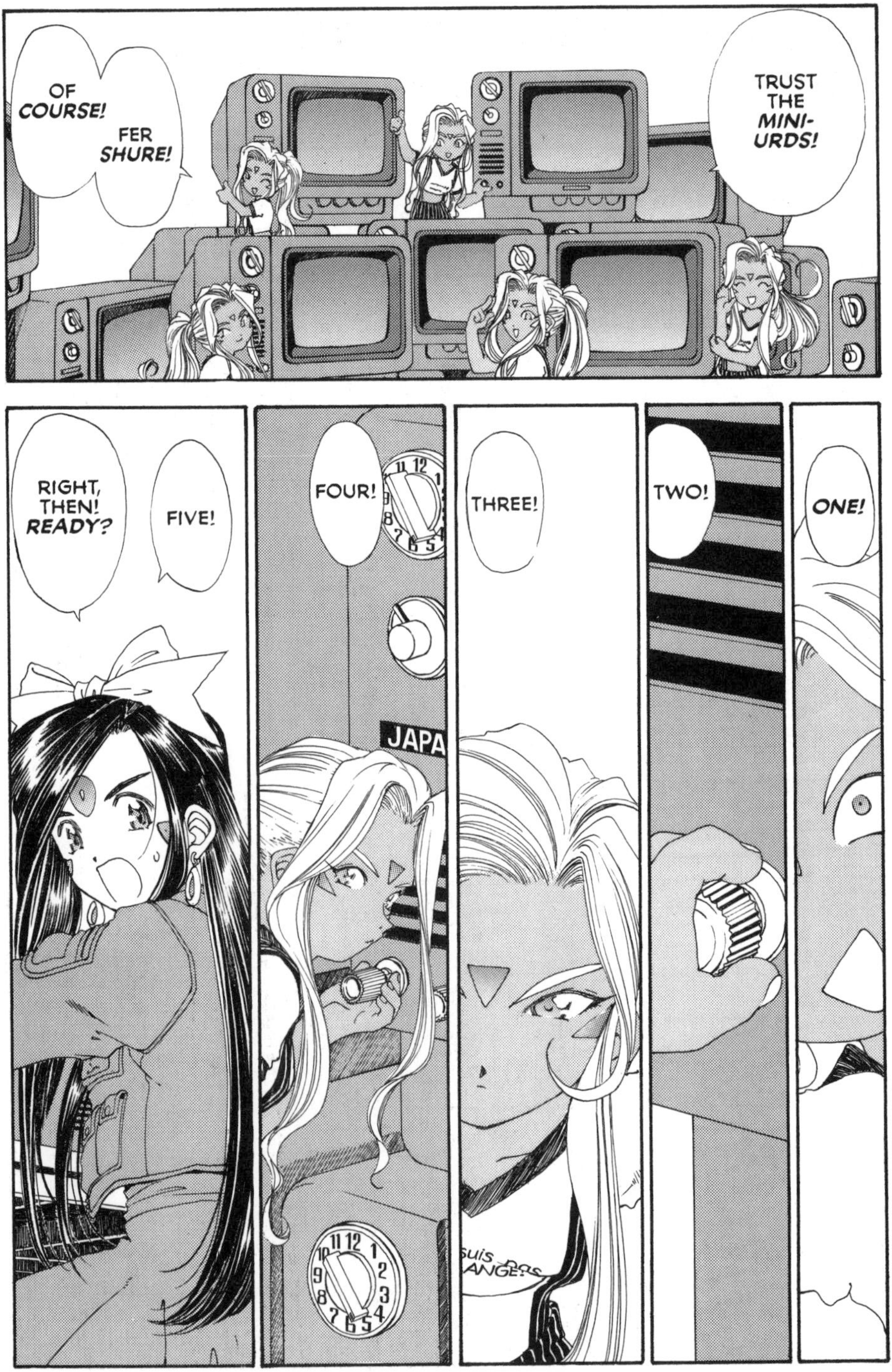
OF COURSE!
FER SHURE!
TRUST THE MINI-URDS!
RIGHT, THEN! READY?
FIVE!
FOUR!
THREE!
TWO!
ONE!

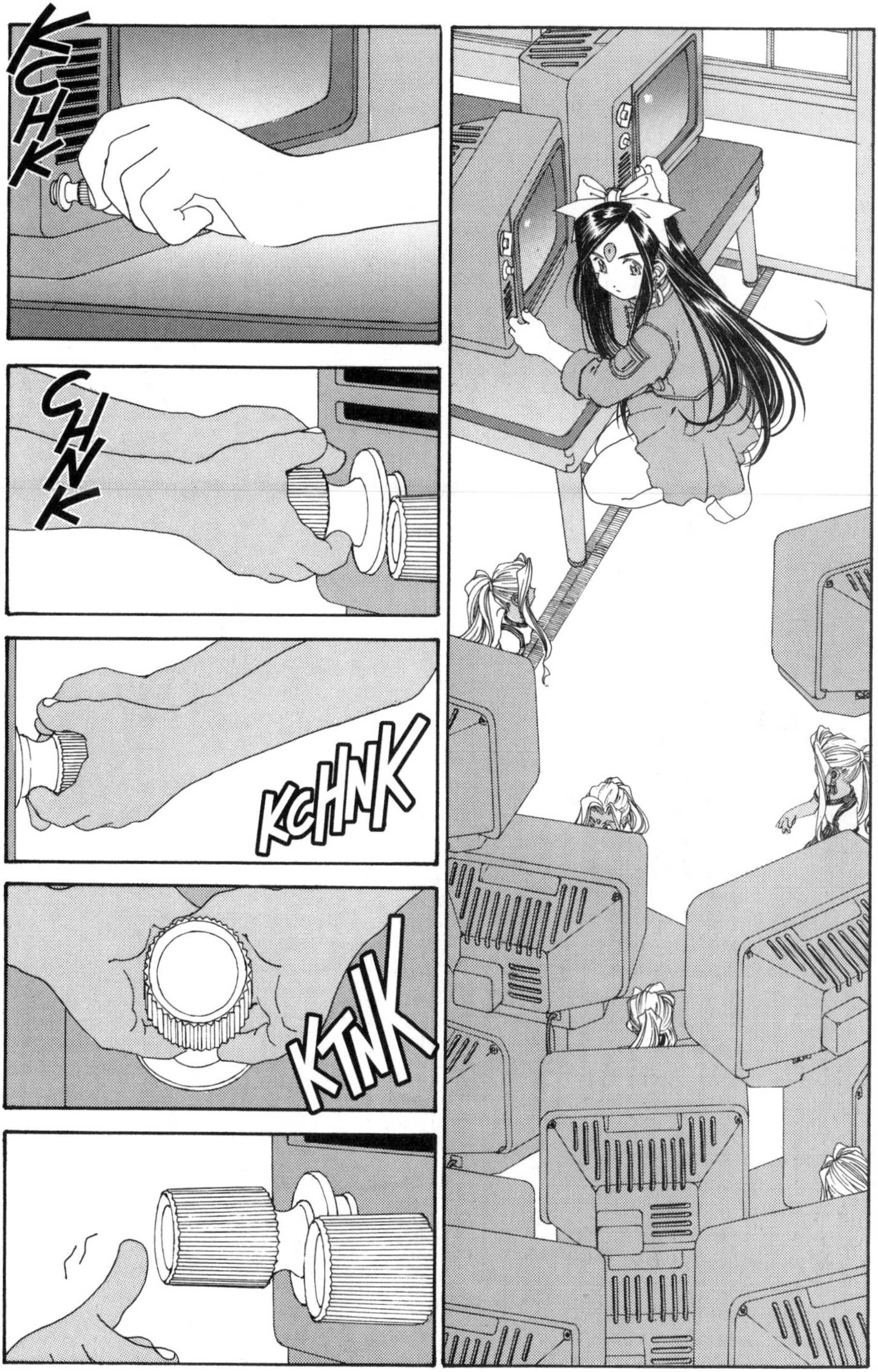
KCHNK
CHNK
KCHNK
KTNK

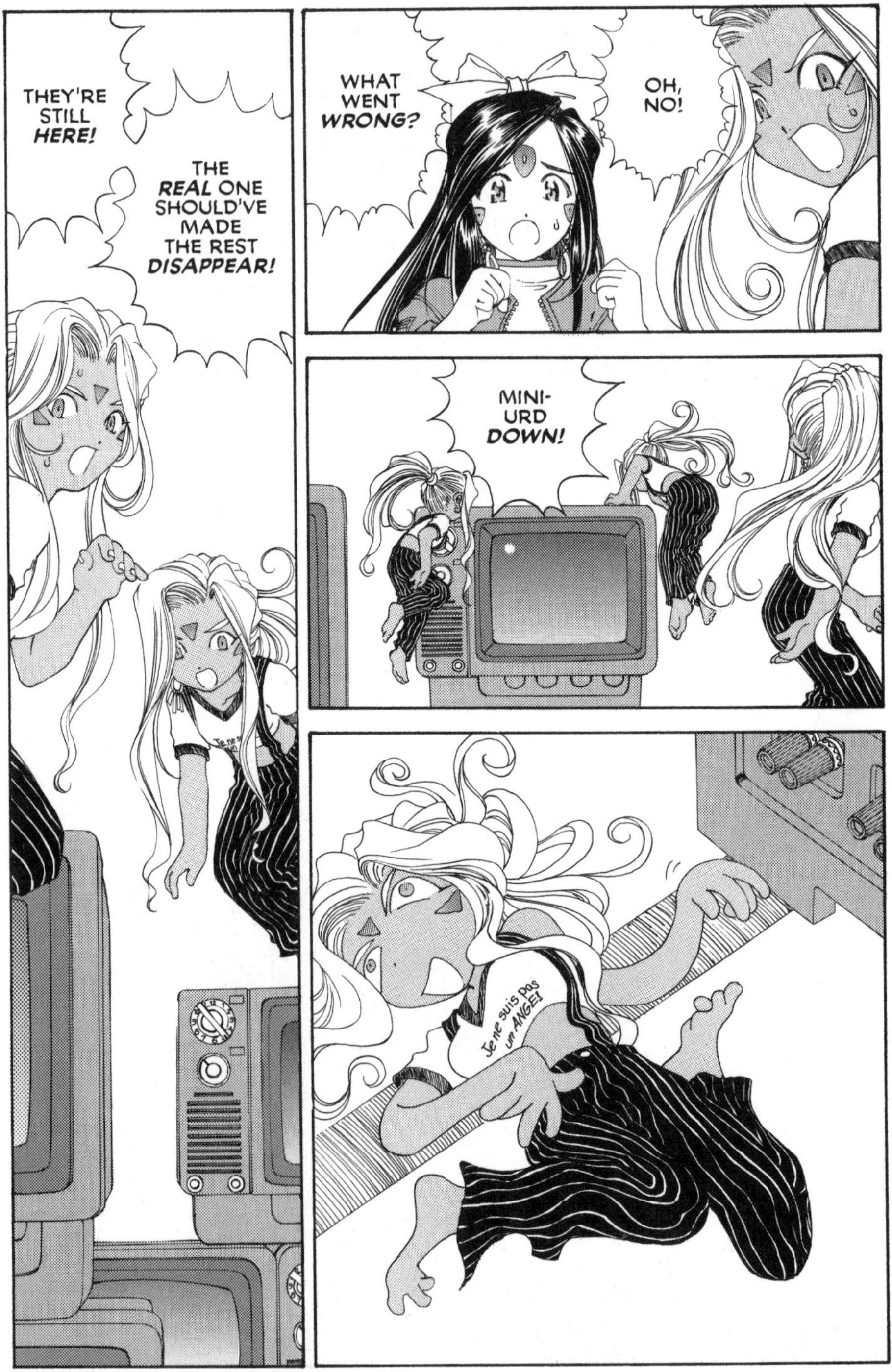
OH, NO!
WHAT WENT WRONG?
MINI-URD DOWN!
Je ne suis pas un ANGE!
THEY'RE STILL HERE!
THE REAL ONE SHOULD'VE MADE THE REST DISAPPEAR!

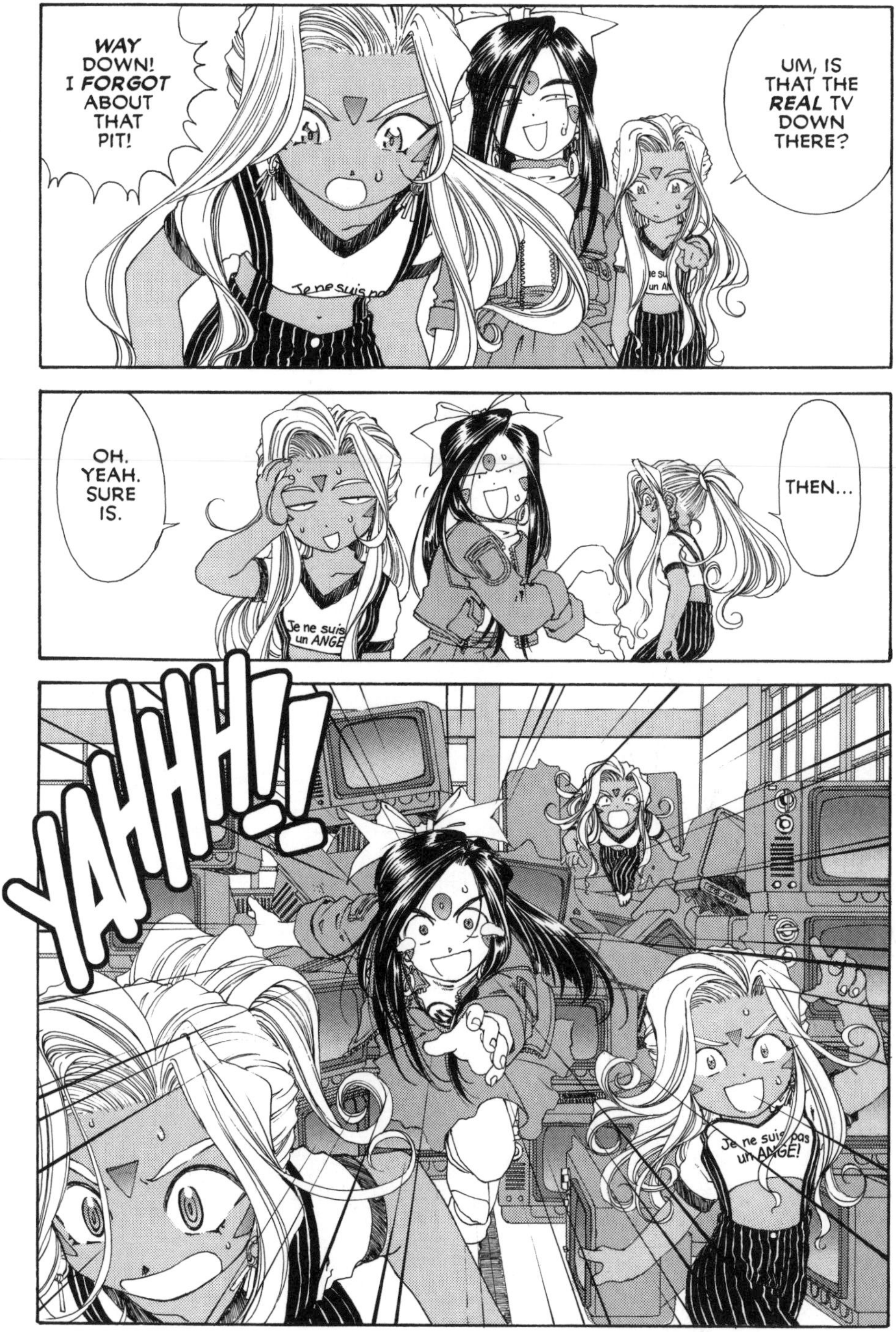
WAY DOWN! I FORGOT ABOUT THAT PIT!
UM, IS THAT THE REAL TV DOWN THERE?
OH. YEAH. SURE IS.
THEN...
YAHHH!!!
Je ne suis pas un ANGE!

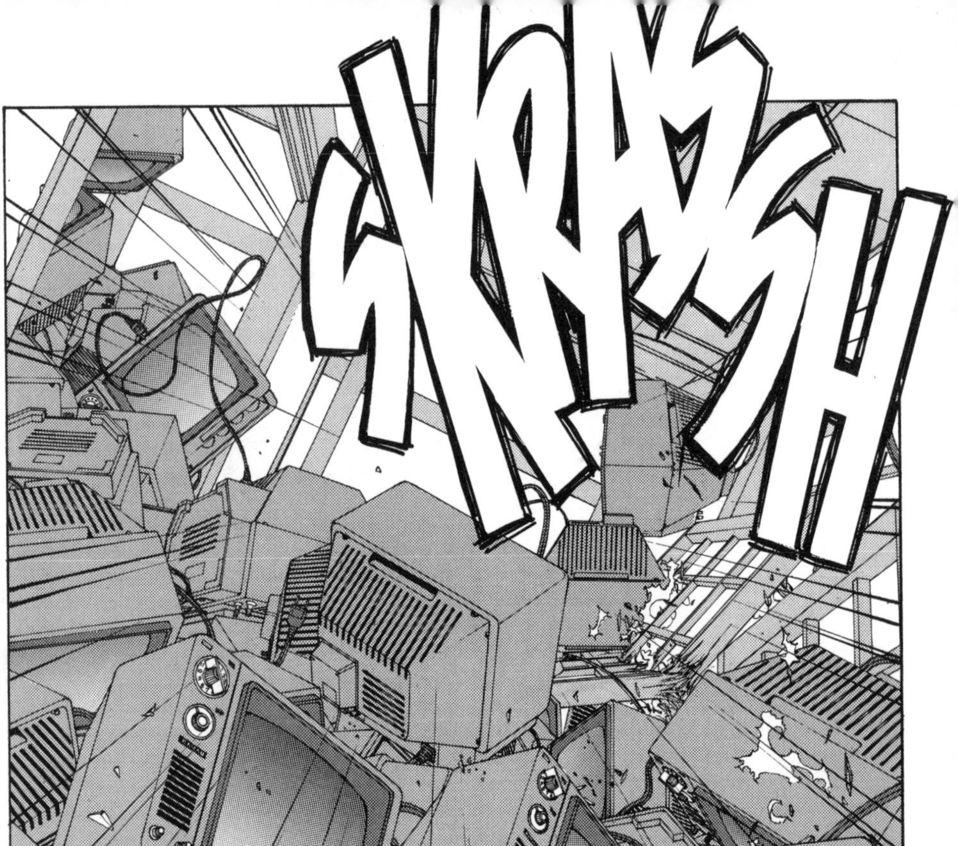
SKRASSH
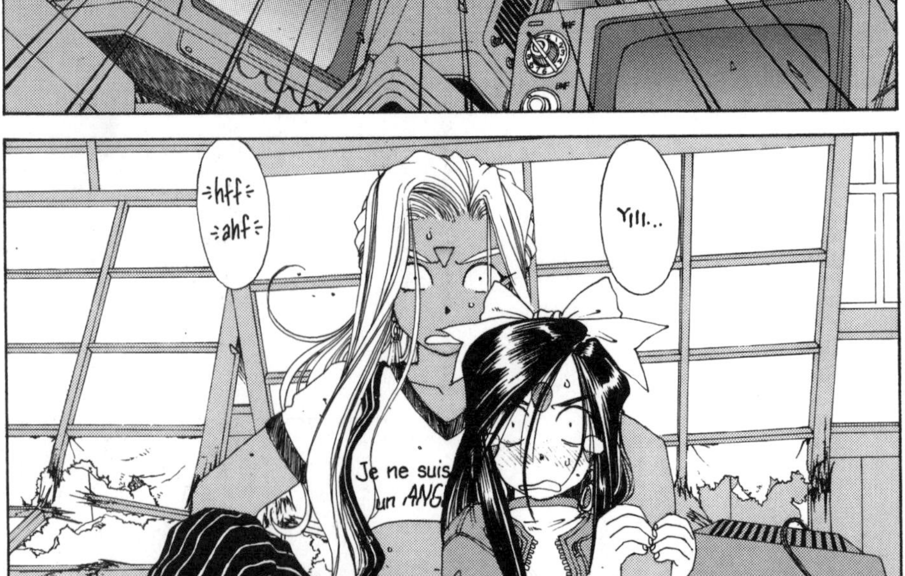
Yiii...
hff ahf
Je ne suis un ANG

OH! WE HAVE *SO* MANY TVS NOW!

MAY I WATCH ONE?

!!

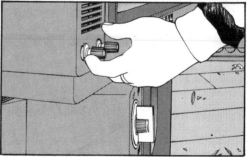

NOOO! DON'T!

YOU'LL MAKE MORE!

CHK

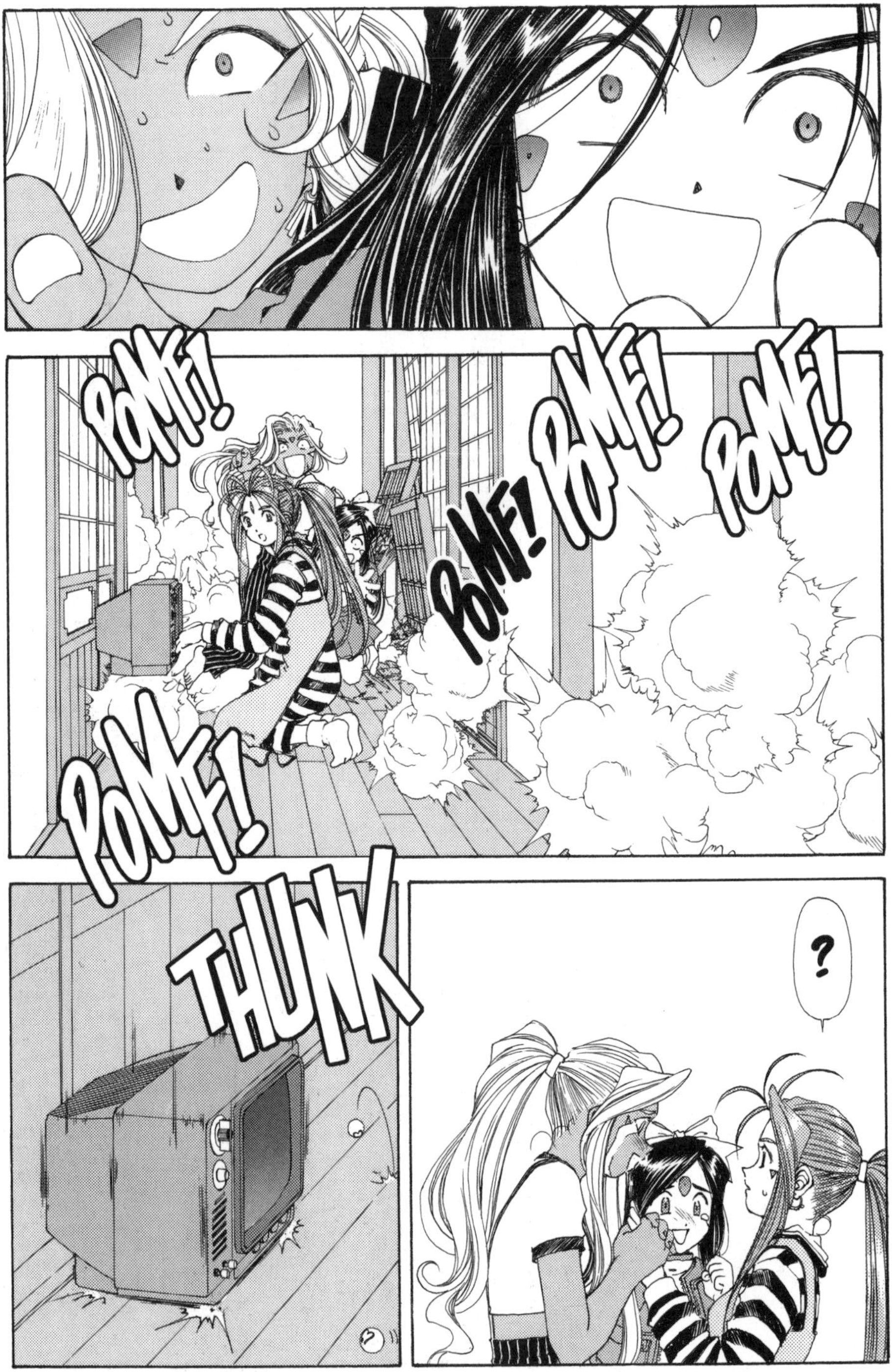

POMF!
POMF!
POMF!
POMF!
POMF!
THUNK
?

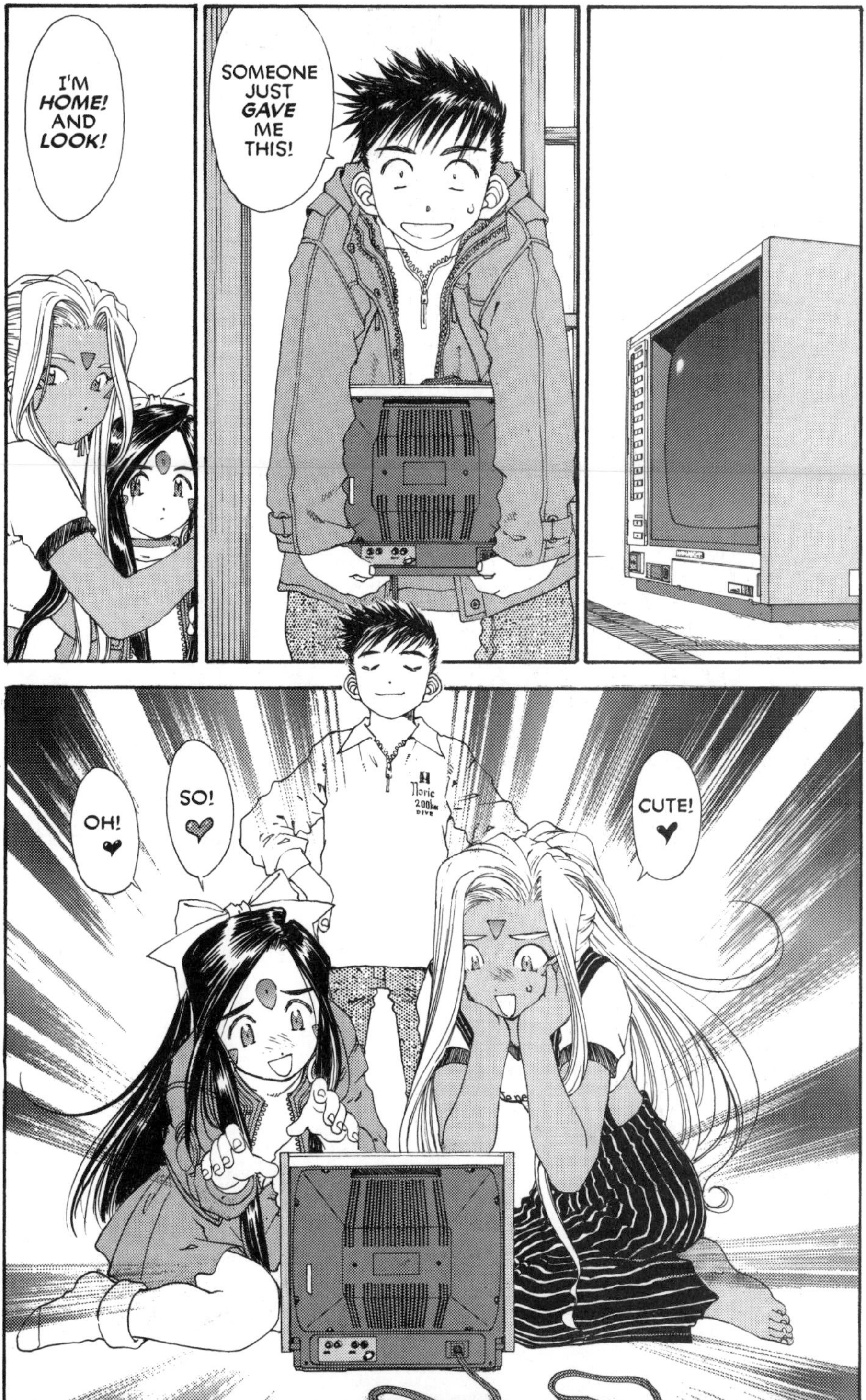
I'M *HOME!* AND *LOOK!*
SOMEONE JUST *GAVE* ME THIS!
OH! ♥
SO! ♥
CUTE! ♥

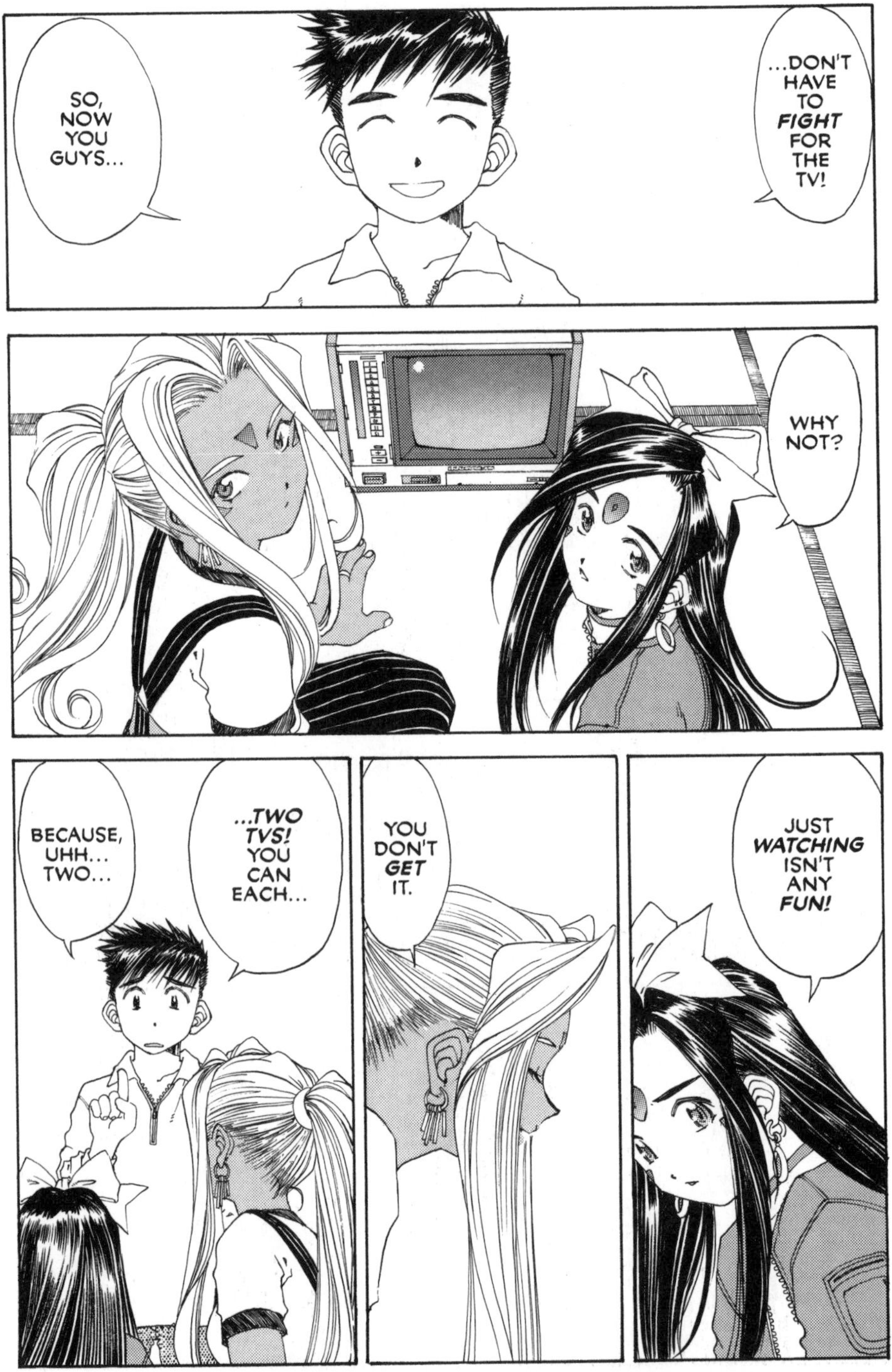
SO, NOW YOU GUYS...
...DON'T HAVE TO *FIGHT* FOR THE TV!
WHY NOT?
BECAUSE, UHH... TWO...
...TWO TVS! YOU CAN EACH...
YOU DON'T *GET* IT.
JUST *WATCHING* ISN'T ANY *FUN!*

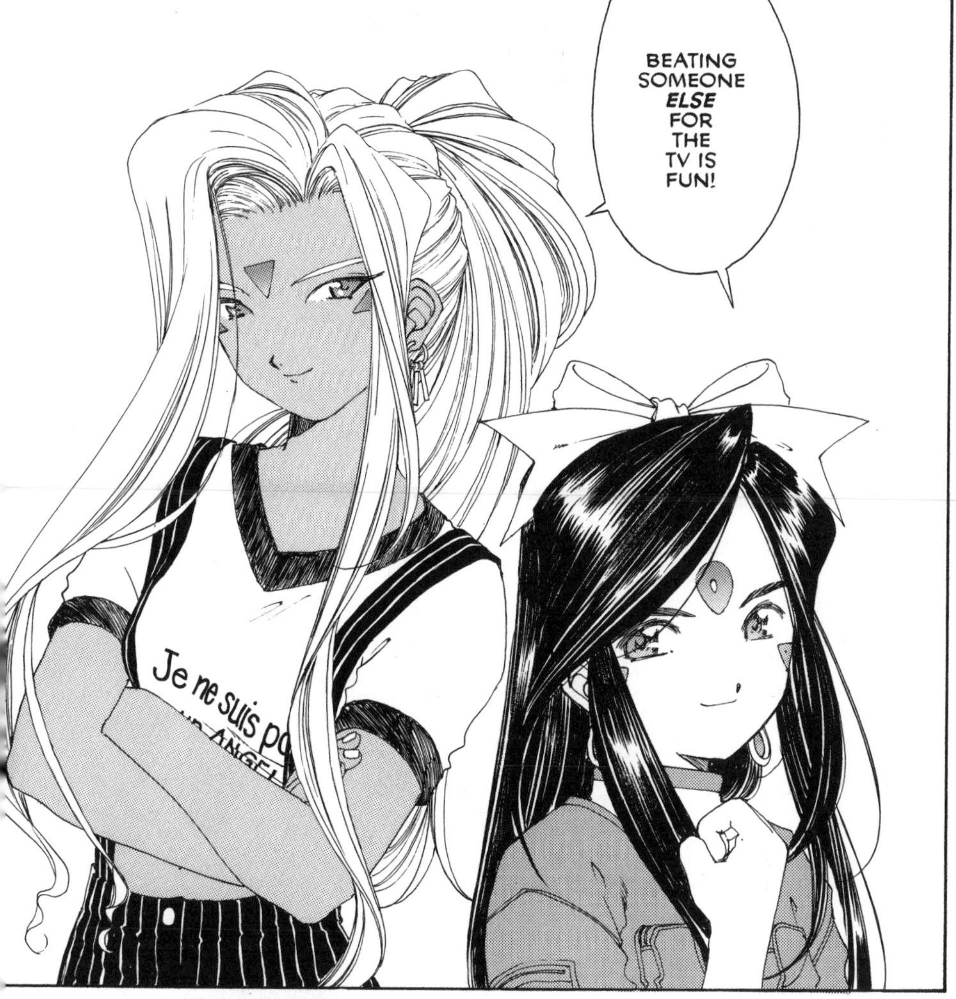
BEATING SOMEONE *ELSE* FOR THE TV IS FUN!
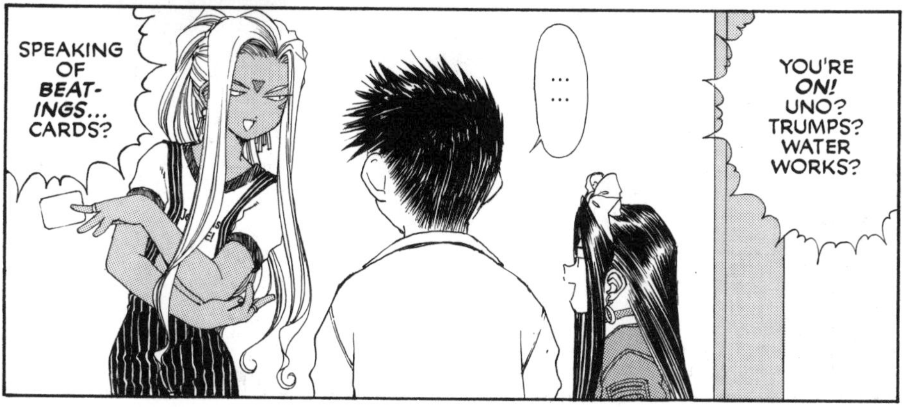
SPEAKING OF *BEAT-INGS...* CARDS?
... ...
YOU'RE *ON!* UNO? TRUMPS? WATER WORKS?

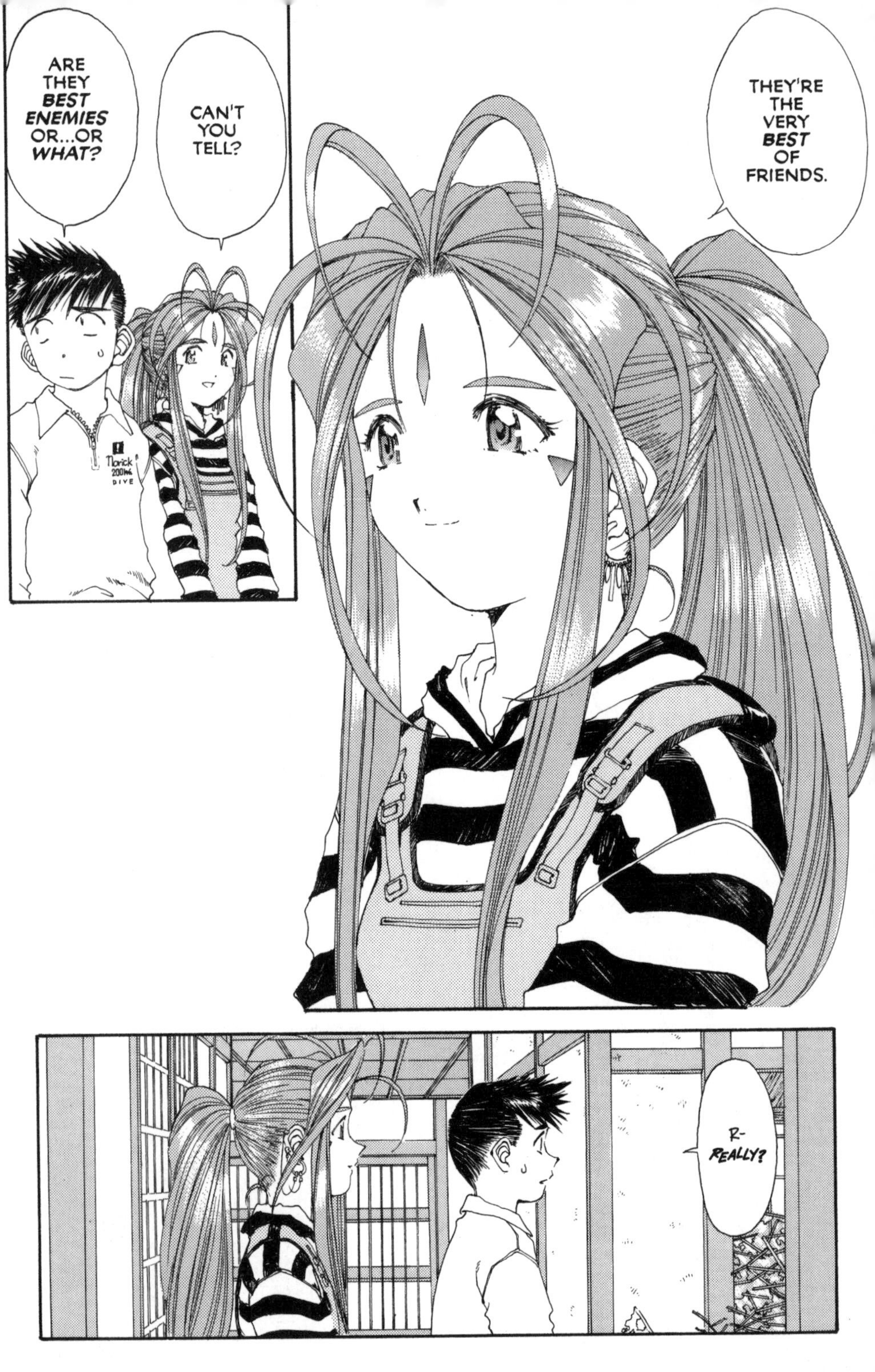
ARE THEY BEST ENEMIES OR...OR WHAT?
CAN'T YOU TELL?
THEY'RE THE VERY BEST OF FRIENDS.
R-REALLY?

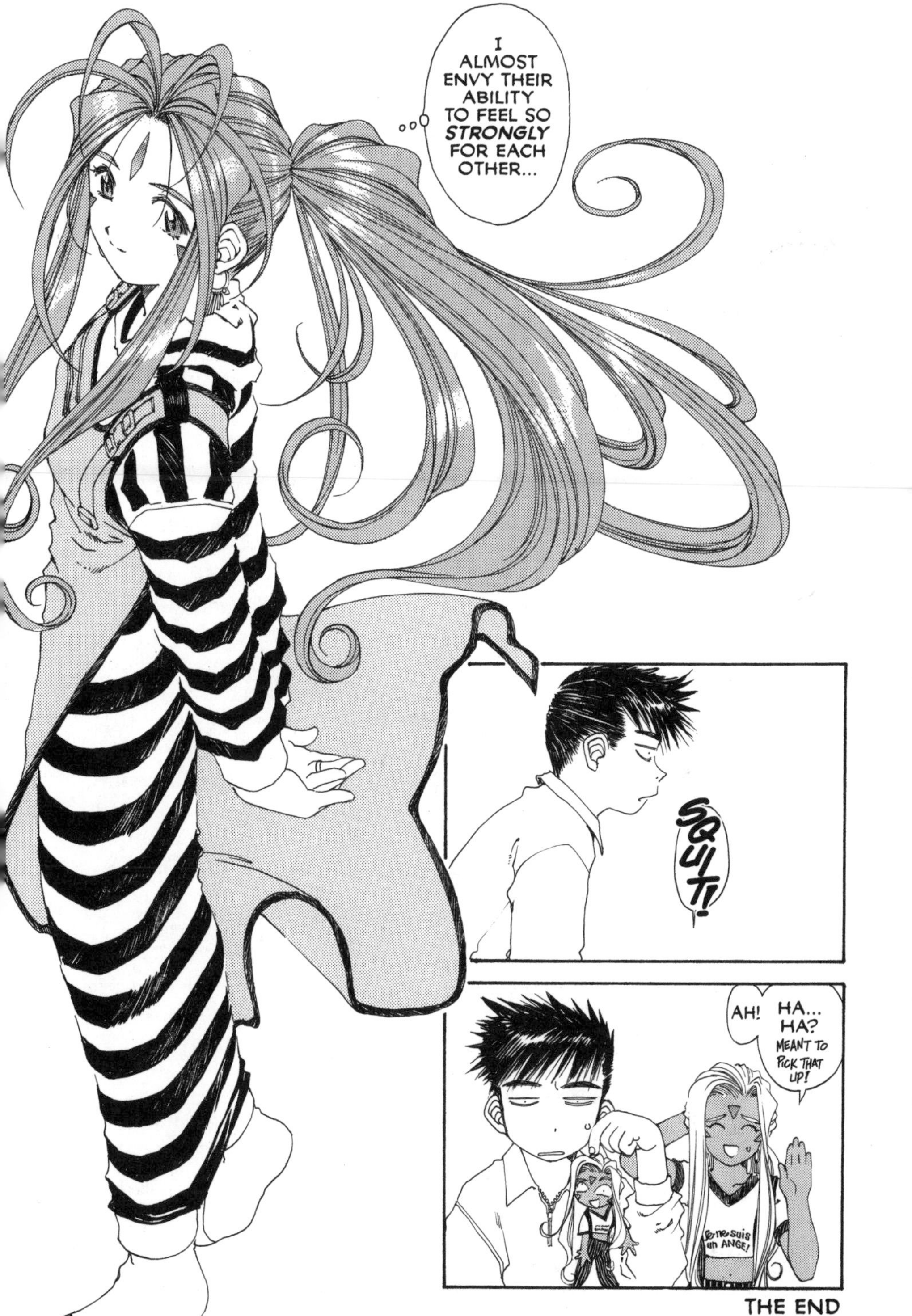
I ALMOST ENVY THEIR ABILITY TO FEEL SO *STRONGLY* FOR EACH OTHER...
SQUIT!
AH!
HA... HA? MEANT TO PICK THAT UP!
Je ne suis un ANGE!

THE END

A NOTE TO *OH MY GODDESS!* READERS

This will be the last collected volume of *Oh My Goddess!* in a Westernized format. Published in America since 1994, the foundation for the Dark Horse program of *Oh My Goddess!* has been the monthly comic-book series, mirror-imaged from the original right-to-left reading layouts and translated into English for a conventional Western reading experience, and then collected into graphic novels organized around complete storylines (which explains why Dark Horse *OMG* collections have varied widely in page count and price). Collected in this manner, the Dark Horse volumes have differed from the original Kodansha collections, which (like most Japanese collections) are of a more uniform page count and price.

With a growing and changing audience for manga in America, and in light of the incredibly successful sales of *Oh My Goddess!* in book form, Dark Horse made the decision to cease publication of the monthly comic-book series and begin a straight-to-collection program for *Oh My Goddess!* in non-Westernized (left-to-right reading layouts) translated editions collecting identical material to the Japanese editions in a similar format and at a new lower price. To this end, the next Dark Horse volume of *Oh My Goddess!* will be numbered as volume 21, identical in content to the Kodansha volume 21. To prevent confusion this final Westernized *OMG* edition has been numbered as Volume 19/20 to help show that the story continuity of *Oh My Goddess!* continues uninterrupted from this final Westernized volume into volume 21. As Dark Horse continues on this new program, the first twenty *OMG* volumes will be released over time in the non-Westernized translated format, identical in content to their corresponding Kodansha editions, and the Westernized volumes will be taken out of print. In time, the Dark Horse *Oh My Goddess!* line will be a translated match to the Kodansha editions.

We hope this changing of approaches won't confuse readers, and we apologize for any inconvenience this may cause. For those readers who haven't yet experienced non-Westernized translated manga, reading in this fashion will take a little getting used to, but once you become adjusted, you'll hardly notice the difference and might well find it more fun. And *Oh My Goddess!* is still one of the most entertaining and beautifully illustrated works of graphic fiction on the planet, whether read left-to-right or right-to-left!

—Dark Horse Manga